Rechts
geschichte
Rg

Zeitschrift des
Max-Planck-Instituts
für Rechtsgeschichte
und Rechtstheorie

Journal of the
Max Planck Institute
for Legal History
and Legal Theory

Herausgeber
Marietta Auer
Thomas Duve
Stefan Vogenauer

Redaktion
Otto Danwerth
Nadine Gurris

Rechtsgeschichte
Legal History

Rg **30** 2022

Impressum:

Rechtsgeschichte – Legal History
Zeitschrift des Max-Planck-Instituts
für Rechtsgeschichte und Rechtstheorie
Journal of the Max Planck Institute
for Legal History and Legal Theory

Herausgeber:
Marietta Auer
Thomas Duve
Stefan Vogenauer
Redaktion:
Otto Danwerth
Nadine Gurris

Anschrift der Redaktion:
Max-Planck-Institut für Rechtsgeschichte
und Rechtstheorie
Redaktion Rechtsgeschichte
Hansaallee 41
60323 Frankfurt am Main
Tel. +49-69-78978-200
Fax +49-69-78978-210
www.rg-rechtsgeschichte.de
www.lhlt.mpg.de

Anregungen und Manuskripte an:
rg@lhlt.mpg.de

Verlag und Anzeigen:
Vittorio Klostermann GmbH
Westerbachstraße 47
60489 Frankfurt am Main
www.klostermann.de
Preis pro Band 49 Euro

Graphische Gestaltung:
Elmar Lixenfeld, Frankfurt am Main

Druck und Bindung:
Hubert & Co., Göttingen

Zitiervorschlag: Rechtsgeschichte – Legal History Rg 30 (2022)
ISSN 1619-4993
ISBN 978-3-465-04584-7

Thomas Duve

Editorial

Woher nehmen wir unsere Vorstellung davon, was richtig oder falsch, gut oder böse, erlaubt oder verboten ist? – Die für jeden Juristen und jede Juristin naheliegende Antwort lautet: Aus dem Wortlaut des Gesetzes. Doch wer die Bedeutung der Wörter bestimmt, ist damit keineswegs geklärt. Jan Schröder geht in der *Recherche* in seinem Aufsatz zur Bedeutung der Wörter in der Rechts- und Sprachtheorie der frühen Neuzeit dieser Frage nach. Die mittelalterliche Lehre von der Imposition, also der Bestimmung der Bedeutung durch eine Autorität, so zeigt er, weicht im 17. Jahrhundert der Ansicht, dass der gewöhnliche Sprachgebrauch maßgeblich – und zugleich historisch relativ sei.

Vorstellungen von richtig und falsch, erlaubt und verboten, wurden in der europäischen Geschichte aber nicht allein von Juristen, sondern auch von der Religion bestimmt. Das stellt Elizabeth Papp Kamalis Beitrag zur rechtlichen Bedeutung von *intoxication* im mittelalterlichen englischen Recht heraus. In diesem greift sie auch auf Beichthandbücher zurück, die sich aus naheliegenden Gründen ausführlicher mit übermäßigem Alkoholkonsum und seinen Folgen auseinandersetzten. Besonders anschaulich wird die Bedeutung der Religion für das Recht in der *Marginalie* von Erk Volkmar Heyen, in der er sich mit der Gerechtigkeitsfiguration im Lichte politischer Marienfrömmigkeit im frühen 16. Jahrhundert beschäftigt. Auch in der zweiten *Marginalie* geht es um die Visualisierung von Recht, allerdings im Medium des Films und der Architektur: Daniel Damler analysiert, wie der permanente Ausnahmezustand in der Heimatstadt von Batman in Szene gesetzt wurde. Gotham City ist nirgendwo und überall, dunkel, gewaltig und schroff – auch das ist eine Botschaft der Batman-Filme, die weltweit von mehr als einer Milliarde Menschen gesehen wurden und mehr als vieles andere unsere Vorstellungen von Recht und Unrecht spiegeln mögen. Die Bildstrecke mit Fotografien aus New York, in den Jahren 1992, 2017 und 2019 von Otto Danwerth aufgenommen und zum Teil in Galerien ausgestellt, nimmt die oft dunkle Bildsprache von Gotham City auf.

Wir widmen uns am Max-Planck-Institut aber nicht allein den Wechselwirkungen von Architektur und Recht – nämlich in einem im Rahmen der sog. LOEWE-Initiative geförderten Vorhaben »Architekturen der Ordnung« –, sondern auch den ganz klassischen Themen der Rechtsgeschichte. Das zeigt der Bericht der Herausgeber und Herausgeberinnen des vierbändigen »Handbuch zur Geschichte der Konfliktlösung in Europa«, das David von Mayenburg als Gesamtherausgeber koordiniert hat. Es dürfte das sichtbarste Ergebnis eines ebenfalls im Rahmen der LOEWE-Initiative geförderten Schwerpunkts »Außergerichtliche und gerichtliche Konfliktlösung« sein, der von der Goethe-Universität und dem Max-Planck-Institut initiiert wurde und 2014 seine Arbeit aufgenommen hatte.

Auch die beiden *Foci* entstammen der Forschung am Institut. Karl Härter und Valeria Vegh Weis haben Beiträge zu transnationaler Strafrechtsgeschichte mit einem Schwerpunkt auf Lateinamerika versammelt. Diese machen nicht zuletzt die aktive Rolle lateinamerikanischer Akteure bei der Herausbildung transnationaler Diskurse, Institutionalisierungsprozesse und völkerrechtlicher Verträge deutlich. Im zweiten *Focus* geht es um Arbeitsrechtsgeschichte, die am Institut bereits seit einigen Jahren im Rahmen der vor allem von Gerd Bender, Peter Collin und Thorsten Keiser getragenen »Initiative Arbeitsrechtsgeschichte« betrieben wird. Ein Beitrag in diesem *Focus* gibt Auskunft über ein digitales Quelleneditionsprojekt, das unter Peter Collins Leitung von Johanna Wolf und zwei Doktoranden, Tim-Niklas Vesper und Matthias Ebbertz, durchgeführt wird. Es ist Teil des Projekts »Nichtstaatliches Recht der Wirtschaft«, bei dem die Arbeitsbeziehungen in der Metallindustrie vom Kaiserreich bis in die frühe Bundesrepublik im Mittelpunkt stehen.

Digitale Quelleneditionen werden immer zahlreicher und wichtiger, so dass sie inzwischen auch einen größeren Raum in unserem Rezensionsteil einnehmen, der *Kritik*. Eine ausführliche Rezension gilt einer Quellensammlung zur portugiesischen Rechtsgeschichte, eine andere der Webseite *Slavery, Law & Power in the British Empire and Early America* (SLP). Im Übrigen spiegelt die *Kritik* mit ihren insgesamt 45 Rezensionen die thematische und sprachliche Vielfalt der rechtshistorischen Forschung wider: Sie reicht eben mindestens vom Codex Hammurapi bis zur europäischen Bankenunion und deren Geschichte.

■

Thomas Duve

Editorial

Where do we get our idea of what is right or wrong, good or evil, what is permitted or prohibited? – The jurists' response is clear: it's the wording of the law. Yet this does not clarify who determines the meaning of the words. Jan Schröder's article in the *Research* section pursues the question of the meaning of the words in the legal and linguistic theory of the early modern period. He shows how the medieval doctrine of imposition, that is, the determination of meaning by means of authority, gives way in the 17th century to the view that the everyday use of language is authoritative and at the same time historically relative.

Not only jurists but also religion played a decisive role in determining notions of right and wrong, permissible and impermissible in European history, a point highlighted by Elizabeth Papp Kamali in her contribution on the legal meaning of *intoxication* in medieval English law. In this context, she also examines confession handbooks, which, for obvious reasons, dealt at length with excessive alcohol consumption and its consequences. The significance of religion for the law is particularly evident in Erk Volkmar Heyen's contribution in the *Marginalia* section in which he takes up the configuration of justice in light of the political Marian piety in the early 16th century. The second of the *Marginalia* also deals with the visualisation of law, this time in the medium of film and architecture. Daniel Damler analyses how the permanent state of emergency in Batman's hometown is portrayed. Gotham City is nowhere and everywhere, dark, towering and harsh – a message also conveyed in the Batman films, which have been seen by over a billion people worldwide and reflect more than other sources our conceptions of just and unjust. The accompanying images of New York taken in 1992, 2017 and 2019 by Otto Danwerth – some of which have been displayed in galleries – take up the often dark visual imagery of Gotham City.

While the Max Planck Institute is directly involved in the LOEWE-funded project »Architectures of Order«, our research interests consist of much more than just the interplay of architecture and law. We also work on the classic topics of legal history. This fact is demonstrated by the report of the editors of the four-volume »Handbuch zur Geschichte der Konfliktlösung in Europa« (Handbook on the history of conflict resolution in Europe), coordinated by the series editor, David von Mayenburg. It is probably the most visible result of the likewise LOEWE-funded research focus »Extrajudicial and Judicial Conflict Resolution«, launched in 2014 and initiated by both the Goethe University and the Max Planck Institute.

Both *Foci* as well stem from research carried out at the Institute. Karl Härter and Valeria Vegh Weis have collected contributions on the transnational history of criminal law, with an emphasis on Latin America. This collection highlights, among other things, the role played by Latin American actors in the development of transnational discourses, processes of institutionalisation and international treaties. The second *Focus* contribution deals with the history of labour law, which has been a subject of research here at the Institute for a number of years in the context of the History of Labour Law initiative carried out by Gerd Bender, Peter Collin and Thorsten Keiser. One contribution in this *Focus* provides information about a digital source edition project – under the direction of Peter Collin – carried out by Johanna Wolf and two doctoral students, Tim-Niklas Vesper and Matthias Ebbertz. It is part of the project »Non-state law of the economy«, which examines the industrial relationships in the metal industry from the German Empire to the early years of the Federal Republic of Germany.

The number and importance of digital source editions continue to grow year by year, so much so that they now make up a larger portion of our *Critique* section. One review offers a detailed assessment of a source collection devoted to Portuguese legal history, and another treats the website *Slavery, Law & Power in the British Empire and Early America* (SLP). And once again, the *Critique* section, consisting of 45 reviews, reflects the thematic and linguistic diversity of legal historical research: from the Code of Hammurabi to the European Banking Union and its history.

■

Fokus focus

Transnational Criminal Law

Fokus focus

Arbeitsrechtsgeschichte

Kritik critique

Kritik critique

Kritik critique

Kritik critique

Kritik critique

Recherche research

Elizabeth Papp Kamali

The Horrible Sepulture of Mannes Resoun: Intoxication and Medieval English Felony Law*

This synne hath manye speces. The firste is dronkenesse, that is the horrible sepulture of mannes resoun; and therfore whan a man is dronken he hath lost his resoun, and this is deedly synne.

– Chaucer, *The Parson's Tale*[1]

On a late February night in 1272 in the Bedfordshire village of Bromham, four men departed Robert Malin's tavern. Making their way down the road, they met the local vicar, Ralph son of Ralph, as he entered the road opposite the Bromham church. Under a waning crescent moon, the encounter may have been shrouded in darkness.[2] An inquest narrative, surviving in the rolls of a local coroner, fails to explain why Ralph was outside the churchyard late at night, but it does record a brief exchange: one of the men, Robert Bernard, asked Ralph who he was, to which the vicar answered, »a man, who are you?«[3] Robert was not amused by Ralph's cheeky response. The inquest narrative recounts that Robert, »because he was drunk (*eo quod ebrius fuit*), sprang forward and struck Ralph across the crown of the head with a ›spart‹ axe«, issuing a fatal wound.[4] Ralph immediately lost his capacity to speak and died by the following midday.

An inquest was held by the coroner with jurors from four local villages. Those representing Bromham blamed Robert Bernard alone for the death but said that the other three men had been with Robert at the tavern that evening. The representatives of three other villages took matters a step further: while conceding that Robert was the only one to strike Ralph, they also indicated that the other men »consented to do any other misdeed and were waiting to do injury to someone else there.«[5] An order was issued to arrest all four men. The tavern host, Robert Malin, found pledges, presumably to secure his appearance later, as did a companion of the ill-fated Ralph, who fled in fear after the event. The incident, to which we will return later, raises several questions. Was this a chance encounter, or had Robert Bernard and his companions deliberately ambushed the vicar? Was Robert Malin's tavern the site of conspiratorial plotting to attack Ralph or perhaps another individual?

* Special thanks to Thomas Green, who provided feedback on several iterations of this article. Thanks are also due to Monica Bell, Rabia Belt, Molly Brady, Paul Brand, Daniel Coquillette, Andrew Crespo, Charles Donahue, John Goldberg, Tamar Herzog, Genevieve Lakier, Anna Lvovsky, John Manning, Ruth Okediji, Robert Palmer, John Rappaport, Daphna Renan, Jocelyn Simonson, Kathryn Spier, Kristen Stilt, and Ian Williams; the participants in the Harvard Law School Legal History Workshop, the Oxford Legal History Forum, and the Harvard Law School Faculty Workshop; my intrepid research assistants, namely, Jonathan Baddley, Ama Doyal, Emma Keteltas, and Urjita Sudula; and the three anonymous readers whose feedback greatly improved this article. As ever, I owe a debt of gratitude to the staff of the Harvard Law Library. Unless otherwise indicated, translations and modernizations are my own. This article is dedicated to the memory of Dr. F. Donald Logan (1930–2022), master of friendship and conviviality.

1 Benson (ed.) (1987) 316 (Canterbury Tales, The Parson's Tale, X(I).821).

2 The incident occurred on a Thursday in the feast of St. Mathias the Apostle, i. e., 24 February. In 1272, the moon was in its last quarter on 23 February, and there was a new moon on 1 March. See https://moon.nasa.gov/moon-in-motion/moon-phases/ and http://astropixels.com/ephemeris/phasescat/phases1201.html (last accessed 4 May 2022). My thanks to Gerald Neuman.

3 The details of the case are recorded in Hunnisett (ed. and trans.) (1961) 55, no. 123. The original entry in the coroner's roll may be viewed at TNA JUST2/1, m. 7, AALT no. 0019, (1272), http://aalt.law.uh.edu/AALT7/JUST2/JUST2no1/aJUST2no1fronts/IMG_0019.htm (incipit »Contigit in villa de Bromham …«, last accessed 3 March 2022).

4 Hunnisett (ed. and trans.) (1961) 55.

5 Hunnisett (ed. and trans.) (1961) 55.

Robert Bernard, after all, was carrying an axe that evening, which could be indicative of premeditation. Would the fact of Robert Bernard's drunkenness, which was specifically highlighted in the narrative produced by the coroner's inquest, have aggravated or mitigated his culpability in striking Ralph? At the heart of all these questions is a fundamental mystery about the treatment of intoxication in the early English common law of felony: did intoxication matter in adjudicating felony cases? Did it inculpate, exculpate, or both (or, for that matter, neither)? While not definitively solving that mystery, this article attempts to shine light on a topic nearly as dark as the road on which Ralph met a violent end at the hands of an intoxicated aggressor. It is intended to lay the groundwork for further exploration of the role of intoxication in the adjudication of felony cases in thirteenth- and fourteenth-century England by myself and others.

Modern American criminal law, which I teach to first-year law students, exhibits great ambivalence toward the issue of intoxication. The U.S. Supreme Court has declared that there is no constitutional right to introduce evidence of voluntary intoxication to negate the mens rea necessary to commit a crime.[6] Some U.S. jurisdictions permit the introduction of evidence of intoxication in order to negate specific intent, such as the heightened mens rea required for first-degree murder.[7] In that sense, intoxication can be partially exculpatory. It can also be an aggravator: in some jurisdictions, when a criminal statute requires a mental state of recklessness, an intoxicated actor will be presumed to have acted recklessly even if evidence suggests the individual was not actually aware of the risks involved due to their inebriation.[8] Perhaps because it can push in opposite directions, intoxication is seldom listed explicitly in sentencing guidelines but may fall within the bounds of »catch-all« provisions that permit the consideration of various mitigating factors.[9] Remarkably, while courts routinely grapple with the admissibility of intoxication evidence, there tends to be little explicit case law on the issue.[10] This ambivalent treatment of intoxication in modern U.S. law may be attributable to a variety of factors, including the challenges of measuring the level of impairment experienced by a defendant – particularly when the intoxicating substance is one for which there is no simple breath test or the like – and a desire to deter excessive substance use, particularly with regard to impaired driving. The matter is further complicated by the fact that some individuals *do* lose their capacity to reason effectively once intoxicated, suggesting that they might not be able to fully exercise their volitional and rational capacities in the moment, and by the problem of addiction, which might gravely impair a person's capacity to choose freely whether to ingest the substance in question in the first place.

Such ambivalence may also be found in medieval English texts, although the manifestation is contextually quite different. On the one hand, legal records exhibit reliance on intoxication in some instances to explain the circumstances behind a homicide and occasionally to condemn the behavior of an intoxicated actor. The coroner's inquest investigating Ralph's death, for example, attributed Robert Bernard's homicidal attack to his drunkenness, although admittedly there remains ambiguity in the inquest's statement that Robert struck Ralph »because he was drunk« – was this inculpatory or exculpatory? In other instances, men killed by self-defenders were described as having attacked the self-defender while in a state of drunkenness; the deceased's condemnable intoxicated behavior could help justify the self-defender's lethal response. On the other hand, accidental deaths precipitated by drunkenness – a fall from a horse while riding home more than tipsy from a tavern, a fire started by a bedside candle left unattended by a drunken person – were treated like any other misadventure, with no property forfeitures or other negative consequences for the deceased or their families. What conclusions might be drawn from such scattershot and sometimes contradictory evidence?

The most glaring evidence concerning drunkenness, however, is the fact that it is so often ab-

6 *Montana v. Egelhoff*, 518 U.S. 37 (1996).
7 Marlowe et al. (1999) 199.
8 Marlowe et al. (1999) 199.
9 Marlowe et al. (1999) 203.
10 Marlowe et al. (1999) 203.

sent from the plea rolls documenting medieval English felony trials. In fact, the relative paucity of head-on discussions of intoxication in the legal record is *itself* worthy of exploration. As in the case of Robert and Ralph, drunkenness was sometimes highlighted in the narratives recorded in the wake of a coroner's inquest. In cases of homicide, such inquests were geared toward setting out the circumstantial facts that might help rule out felony or assist a later trial jury in reaching a reasoned verdict, and drunkenness was a probative circumstance.[11] They typically covered the *quis, quid, ubi* – the who, what, where – and other circumstances surrounding an unnatural death, such as the fact that a fatal altercation transpired outside a tavern shortly after curfew, as men, and occasionally women, were wending their ways home. Trial records, on the other hand, seldom reveal precisely how intoxication factored into a jury's ultimate decision-making process. This, I argue, is due to the fact that the common law largely remained silent on the issue of intoxication, leaving the »rules« of how to treat the issue up to jury discretion; by comparison, while juries also exercised discretion in determining whether a defendant had acted in self-defense or in a state of insanity, the common law defined the bounds of these issues crisply and categorically. In these areas of law, we can discern the rules by examining the rationale provided in the jury's verdict: the self-defender could run no further and was in fear of his life, or the insane person had been ill for a lengthy period and was in an acute phase of her illness at the time she committed an alleged felony. Because they served as explicit grounds for seeking a pardon *de cursu*, as a matter of right, from the crown, insanity and self-defense appear comparatively frequently in coroners' rolls and trial records alike. To the extent that intoxication entered into the circumstantial calculations of jurors tasked with determining a defendant's guilt or innocence, it often did so without leaving a significant trace – sometimes only a faint smell of alcohol through reference to a tavern setting or an evening spent drinking with companions – on the historical record.

If the trial records are largely silent on the matter, is there a history to be told about the treatment of intoxication in medieval English felony cases? Must historians be resigned to picking up the story of intoxication's place in felony law only in the sixteenth century, when common-law commentators begin to expound on the subject, and when *Reniger v. Fogossa*, a case about an ill-fated shipment of woad, gives us a dictum that will live on in *Plowden's Reports* and then in case law for centuries to come?[12] The answer to this second question, from my perspective, is emphatically no, or else I would not be writing this article as a précis to a lengthier treatment of the topic. There *is* a history to be told about the treatment of intoxication in felony cases in the first two centuries of the medieval English trial jury. It is a complicated story and an important one, insofar as it contributes to our picture of medieval English conceptions of intentionality, capacity, and responsibility in the common-law tradition of jury trial for felony, as well as our own understanding of the discretion wielded by medieval English juries in defining the bounds of criminal responsibility through fact-intensive prudential decision-making. It is a story that cannot be told through an entirely internalist exploration of plea rolls, law reports, and statutes. Rather, it is a history that requires an expanded legal-historical toolkit, a toolkit as equipped with hortatory texts as with legal records, with literary tales as with law reports. And it is a history that

11 This was true beyond England, too. See, e. g., the instructions for a coroner's inquest in Waterford, Ireland, circa 1300, which included the following guidance for investigating a suspicious death: »And if the inquest says that such a one is guilty and that they know none other guilty but him only, the bailiffs must inquire, as of their office, how and in what way he is guilty, as in defending himself, or in play, or in hate or rage or drunkenness, or through ill-will between them, or by the incitement of another, whereby the dead man was further from life and nearer to death, and whether he who is dead might have escaped if he had chosen.« Bateson (ed. and trans.) (1904) 14–15.

12 The 1551 case of *Reniger v. Fogossa*, which dealt with the matter of woad lost at sea, observed in dictum: »a Person that is drunk kills another, this shall be Felony, and he shall be hanged for it, and yet he did it through Ignorance, for when he was drunk, he had no Understanding nor Memory; but inasmuch as that Ignorance was occasioned by his own Act and Folly, and he might have avoided it, he shall not be priviledged thereby«. *Reniger v. Fogossa* (1551), in Plowden (1816) 19. My thanks to Ama Doyal.

draws upon concrete but scattered textual evidence in the service of informed speculation about the legal-historical past.

While the method may yield results that at times evoke the drunkard's walk more than the straight shot of a sober archer, even such unsatisfactory findings relay some insight into the treatment of intoxication in the first two centuries of the English criminal trial jury. The findings also stand in stark contrast to the clear pronouncements made by sixteenth- and seventeenth-century common-law authors, from Coke to Hale and beyond, who explicitly condemned the vice of drunkenness as an exacerbator of criminal culpability. What emerges is a shift from a medieval English world in which such condemnations of intoxication were the purview of theologians and pastoral authors, to an early modern world in which legal treatise authors railed against drunken misbehavior, too. Just as we might doubt that religious scruples always guided the judgments of medieval English jurors, we might ask whether there was some disparity between the treatment of intoxication in early modern legal treatises and law reports and the handling of the issue by judges and jurors staring defendants in the face.[13] These are questions, however, beyond the scope of this article.

1 Methodology

While there have been earlier treatments of the history of intoxication in criminal law, none have focused squarely on the early centuries of the criminal trial jury in England.[14] Studying the treatment of intoxication in medieval English felony law has many barriers: there are no statutes addressing the issue, like the Jacobean statute of 1606, which outlined a crime of drunkenness and prescribed punishments and processes for dealing with alleged offenders; there are neither lengthy treatments of the topic of intoxication in the surviving trial records nor instructions from judges to jurors telling them how to weigh the issue of intoxication when reaching a verdict; and there is evidence of great ambivalence in the legal record and in literary and theological treatments of intoxication, making it difficult to intuit from such sources the attitudes jurors would have brought with them to the task of judging their neighbors.

Despite these obstacles, this paper takes a modest first step toward understanding thirteenth- and fourteenth-century English approaches to dealing with drunkenness in felony cases, relying on coroners' rolls and plea rolls – records of trials at eyres and gaol delivery sessions – as well as other evidence of cultural attitudes toward intoxication during these crucial first two centuries of the criminal trial jury.[15] This choice of methodology – reading widely in legal records and literary and religious texts – is driven by the fact that the terse records of the king's courts, taken on their own, do not offer sufficient insight into the motivations of the medieval English jury in deciding upon the guilt or innocence of those haled before them. To understand what ideas jurors brought with them to the task of reaching a verdict, one has to seek out broader evidence of cultural mores.

This article will begin with the excavation of legal texts, including the mention of intoxication in coroners' rolls, which often leave us in the dark about the eventual outcome of a case, and in trial records, which only rarely treat the issue directly.

13 See, e. g., Rabin (2004) 78–85 (illuminating the disparities between legal treatises' zero-tolerance discussions of intoxication and the openness of judges and juries to claims of »simple drunkenness« made by sympathetic defendants).

14 See, e. g., Mittermaier (1840); Singh (1933); Hall (1944); Keiter (1997); McAuley (1997). I limit my inquiry here to felony cases, but there remains further work to be done in other areas of law as well. For an impressive contribution focused on contracts, see Swain (2020).

15 In my 2019 book on mens rea in medieval England, I touched briefly on the issue of drunkenness but did not devote any lengthy discussion to the issue given the relative paucity of evidence I encountered on the topic while reading broadly and deeply in the records of the royal courts. See Kamali (2019) 108, 123, 139, n. 75; 160–161, 307. In the years since, I have continued to gather evidence of discussions of intoxication – often fleeting, frequently ambiguous – in felony records. Any given run of records might have a few, or one, or no references to the topic, impeding any attempt at a numerical analysis of the frequency with which intoxication factored into jury decision-making. Some attempts at statistical analysis have been undertaken in the past, and surely more work of that kind remains to be done. See, e. g., Hanawalt (1976b) 312.

Next, the article will examine other kinds of textual evidence, including religious texts and other literary sources that illuminate the extent to which religious ideas informed perspectives on the ground. This task is admittedly complicated by an issue like intoxication, where there is always the possibility of a disconnect between expectations conveyed by judges and by the common law itself, with its failure to address intoxication head-on, and the lived experience of jurors. After all, alcohol consumption was quotidian and also, when engaged in to greater excess, sometimes intimately connected with major life events and celebrations. Furthermore, there is the possibility of tension between that same lived experience and the religious condemnation of excess alcohol consumption as a form of gluttony, a cardinal sin known to lead down an inexorable path toward further sin and crime, death and destruction. There was also a kernel of truth to priestly preaching against overindulgence, as jurors who had witnessed a tavern brawl or seen a neighbor squander his earnings on ale and gambling could attest.

To say there may be disconnects is not to suggest that the enterprise is hopeless. As I have argued elsewhere, ideas about mens rea were in wide circulation in medieval England, both in religious texts, such as sermons and guides for confessors, and in literary works in Latin and the English and French vernaculars.[16] This is true for ideas about intoxication, too. While many jurors were no doubt illiterate, medieval England's largely oral culture facilitated the dissemination of ideas, some of which appear in a diverse range of registers, from elite to more popular literary forms.[17] What emerges from an interdisciplinary analysis of legal and extralegal texts is a complicated picture of medieval English understandings of the interplay between intoxication and criminal responsibility, suggesting that the present conflicted state of the law has deep roots in as well as sharp discontinuities with the common-law past.[18] Particular attention will be paid to the conceptual intersection between intoxication and two other mental or emotional states that appear in medieval English sources: insanity, which was presumptively exculpatory, and anger, which could push in inculpatory or exculpatory directions depending upon the circumstances.

2 Intoxication in Medieval English Legal Records

Alcohol intoxication would appear to be referenced both everywhere and almost nowhere in the medieval English plea rolls. Scribes were tasked with compressing the vernacular testimony of witnesses and the conclusions of coroners and jurors at an inquest or during a trial into formulaic, abbreviated Latin. In doing so, they often alluded to occasions of drinking – typically in taverns at night – but only sporadically used the words and phrases – *ebrius*, *per ebrietatem*, etc. – that signal clearly to the historian that inebriation and not simply benign social drinking was at play.[19] In her study of violent death in fourteenth- and early fifteenth-century Northamptonshire, London, and Oxford, Barbara Hanawalt made the following observations: »In both rural and urban society the traceable influence of drink is very low. The drunken brawl figured in only 4.3 percent of the rural homicides and in 6 percent of the urban ones. The tavern was the scene of a murder in only 7 percent of the cases in both.«[20] Hanawalt acknowledges that these figures might fail to capture the full extent of alcohol's influence on homicide fact patterns. »Probably many more of the arguments involved people who had been drinking,« Hanawalt speculates, »but the evidence from which to make an estimate on the role of alcohol in homicide is not available.«[21] It was not unusual

16 See, e. g., Kamali (2019) 11.

17 See Kamali (2019) 12–13.

18 On the present state of the law, see, e. g., Keiter (1997); Ingle (2002).

19 Some words may have offered a stronger signal than we are aware of today. While *potus*, the base of the verb *poto, potare*, can simply refer to a drink or an act of drinking, in classical Latin to say one was »*bene potus*« meant that they were drunk. *Dictionary of Medieval Latin from British Sources* (hereafter »*DMLBS*«), *s. u.* »potus«; *Basiswoordenlijst Latijn (BWL), s. u.* »potus«. While »*crapula*« could mean drunk, it also signified the after-effects of overeating. See *DMLBS*, *s. u.* »crapula«. Interpreting words like these is complicated by the tendency, even today, to employ euphemism when describing someone as drunk.

20 Hanawalt (1976b) 312.

21 Hanawalt (1976b) 312.

for homicides to occur inside or outside taverns shortly after locally mandated curfews, giving rise to the natural suspicion that intoxication might have been a factor in some of these lethal brawls.[22] The fact that the plea rolls only rarely mention drunkenness explicitly does not necessarily mean that inebriation was not involved, but might point to a reluctance to rely on it as either inculpatory or exculpatory evidence, perhaps especially when both parties to a felony – victim and perpetrator – were intoxicated. In some instances, local communities might have felt conflicted about how to respond to a death or homicide involving some measure of intoxication. Sympathy could have been in order under some circumstances, less so in others. In the paragraphs to follow, I trace a few examples of alcohol intoxication in cases of accidental death and homicides committed in self-defense, two of the contexts in which references to drinking and drunkenness most often appear. I then address the combination of alcohol consumption and group misbehavior before turning, in the next section, to a discussion of the cultural underpinnings of this issue.

2.1 *Alcohol and Accidental Death*

In thinking about deaths classified as accident or misadventure, it is crucial to distinguish between pure *infortunium*, an accidental death with no human agent other than the deceased (e. g. a fall from a height, drowning), and accidental homicide, when a person killed another in circumstances we might describe as negligent or even reckless today. Drunkenness is explicitly mentioned in some cases resulting in a finding of misadventure based on pure *infortunium*, and the evidence points to an unwillingness to impugn the deceased's memory even when the antecedent drinking was freely undertaken. Where another human actor was involved, such as a death resulting from a fall onto an outstretched knife during a tavern brawl, jurors will still sometimes classify such a death as misadventure, avoiding the possibility of a felony conviction, with all its serious consequences, for the knife wielder. We might, of course, wonder whether there was some creative narrative construction at work in such cases.[23] Whether truth or fiction or something in between, in coroners' rolls and trial records alike, drunken accidents tend to be presented matter-of-factly, without any explicit moral judgment, and they result in a verdict of misadventure, as opposed to a finding of either felonious homicide (when someone else was involved) or suicide (when no other individuals were involved). I turn now to a few illustrative examples.

When Simon of Coughton, through drunkenness (*per ebrietatem*), fell dead from his horse in the village of Alcester, a local jury classified the death as misadventure at the 1221 Warwickshire eyre, treating the incident no differently than a sober fall from a horse.[24] The villages of Alcester and Coughton were fined, however, for failing to present the death to the coroner and for burying the body without a coroner's viewing, respectively, suggesting a fear of further inquiry into the facts of the death. The community might have been attempting to safeguard the reputation of the deceased, a man of some local prominence.[25]

22 Localities often regulated tavern hours, imposing a mandatory curfew. In late medieval London, 90 percent of homicidal attacks occurred after nightfall, »with a peak … at the hour of curfew«. Hanawalt (1976b) 305. On the commonality of homicides following an evening in the tavern, see Bolland et al. (eds.) (1912) lxxxvii–lxxxviii. Examples abound in the coroners' and plea rolls, and I provide here a small sampling. For a fight arising at a tavern and resulting in an allegedly felonious homicide, see, e. g., TNA JUST2/17, m. 4, AALT no. 0012, (1336), http://aalt.law.uh.edu/AALT7/JUST2/JUST2no17/aJUST2no17fronts/IMG_0012.htm (*incipit* »Accidit in villa de Lyntone Magna …«, last accessed 3 March 2022); TNA JUST2/18, m. 4, AALT no. 0146 (1351/2), http://aalt.law.uh.edu/AALT7/JUST2/JUST2no18/aJUST2no18fronts/IMG_0146.htm (*incipit* »Accidit apud Crippelowe die dominica …«, last accessed 3 March 2022). See also, e. g., Clanchy (ed. and trans.) (1973) 324, no. 808; Harding (ed. and trans.) (1981) 225–226, no. 600; Sharpe (ed.) (1913) 203–204 (Roll G, no. 3).

23 See, generally, Green (1985); Davis (1987).

24 Stenton (ed. and trans.) (1940) 344–345, no. 762. For another example of a drunk man falling to his death, which was later classified as misadventure, see TNA JUST2/4, m. 4 (of continuous roll), AALT no. 0098 (1276), http://aalt.law.uh.edu/AALT7/JUST2/JUST2no4/IMG_0098.htm (*incipit* »Contigit in villa de Helnestone …«, last accessed 3 March 2022). And for the case of a woman who died after breaking her tibia in a drunken fall outside St. Martin le Grand in London, see Sharpe (ed.) (1900) 265.

25 Simon appears to have inherited the manor of Coughton. See Styles (ed.) (1945) 80.

Significantly, Simon had been accompanied by his son, also named Simon, and it could be that the village was trying to protect the younger Simon against a possible accusation of felony, particularly given the fact that he does not appear to have raised the hue and cry.[26] The horse was treated as deodand, valued at one mark.[27] This suggests that the horse was nominally marked as the instrument of death, rather than placing blame directly upon the elder Simon for causing his own demise. This was similarly the case with two deaths treated at the 1275 Worcester eyre: both the vessel of hot water into which the drunken (*ebrietate*) William Dewy fell and the beam at the Pershore watermill from which the intoxicated Adam of Defford tumbled were valued as deodands when the deaths were classified as misadventure.[28]

A late thirteenth-century case, similarly treated as misadventure, involved the death of Margery, wife of Adam Golde.[29] A coroner's inquest determined that Margery and Adam had, on the preceding Friday, gotten drunk at a tavern and then returned home to bed. Margery lit a candle and left it burning as she drifted off to sleep, with disastrous consequences: her straw bedding caught fire. She died a day later after having received last rites, and Adam barely managed to survive, having been burned to the bone on his hands and feet. The jury was asked whether Adam could have liberated Margery from the fire so that she might have survived, and they answered in the negative. Margery's death was determined to be a case of *infortunium*, an accident, despite the couple's voluntary intoxication. In the interrogation of Adam, we see a need for further inquiry when another person was involved in or proximate to an accidental death. This was all the more true when death resulted from a stab wound. A larger-than-usual inquest of twenty-six men was assembled to inquire into the death of John de Markeby in London in 1339.[30] The inquest determined that John, while drunk, accidentally wounded himself by jumping about with his knife hanging at his girdle, self-inflicting a mortal wound above his knee. The inquest's narrative thereby removed any possible suspicion from John's daughter and a servant who were both in the house at the time.

Even when circumstantial evidence pointed toward violence fueled by drink, a jury might, in some instances, be inclined to classify a death as accidental. In a Yorkshire homicide case circa 1309, the plea roll describes a nocturnal gathering of guildsmen in a home in the village of Nortone.[31] The guildsmen specifically came to the house »to drink together« (*ad simul potandum*). The accused and the deceased, William Calf and John son of Thomas of Nortone, respectively, arrived at the house and were drinking when »contumelia arose« (*mota fuit contumelia*) between William and a man identified as Henry son of Agnes. Notably, the plea roll relates that William took out his knife to defend himself against Henry, who was attacking William and John. Others tried to intervene, »hoping to pacify that contumelia« (*illam contumeliam pacificare volentes*). William eventually fell to the ground, and John, pressed by the crowd of men, fell on top of William and his extended knife, thus receiving a fatal wound.[32] The narrative portrays William and John as companions, facing an attack from Henry, thereby suggesting the implausibility of William having intentionally taken John's life. Queuing up a narrative fit for a pardon, the plea roll specifies »that the aforesaid John son of Thomas was killed by misadventure and not by any

26 On the practice of raising the hue and cry, see Duggan (2017).

27 Stenton (ed. and trans.) (1940) 345.

28 Röhrkasten (ed.) (2008) 396, no. 838 (William Dewy). The vessel was valued at three shillings as deodand. Röhrkasten (ed.) (2008) 409, no. 875 (Adam of Defford). The jurors were fined for concealing the deodand (i. e., the beam, valued at four pence) in their verdict.

29 TNA JUST2/128, m. 1, AALT no. 0004 (1297), http://aalt.law.uh.edu/AALT7/JUST2/JUST2no128/IMG_0004.htm (*incipit* »Contigit die Sabati proxima ante festum Nativitatis sancti Johanni Baptisti …«, last accessed 3 March 2022). For a similar case of a drunken woman burning to death after leaving a candle lit by her bedside, see TNA JUST2/128, m. 1v, AALT no. 0006 (1298), http://aalt.law.uh.edu/aalt7/just2/just2no128/img_0006.htm (second entry on folium, last accessed 3 March 2022). And for an intoxicated man meeting a like fate in London circa 1275–1276, see Sharpe (ed.) (1900) 261.

30 Sharpe (ed.) (1913) 231 (Roll G, no. 40).

31 TNA JUST3/74/3, m. 14, AALT no. 0103 (1309/10), http://aalt.law.uh.edu/AALT7/JUST3/JUST3no74_3/IMG_0103.htm (*incipit* »Willelmus Calf de Waletone indictatus …«, last accessed 3 March 2022). For an outbreak of violence at another large gathering within a home in London in 1276, see Sharpe (ed.) (1900) 263–164. In this instance, the record does not describe the killing as accidental.

32 On cases of self-defense being transformed into accidental deaths due to fact patterns like this one, see Green (1985) 90.

felony or malice aforethought of the aforesaid William«.[33] As a result, William was remanded to gaol to await the king's pardon, which would have been granted as a matter of course (*de cursu*), insofar as pardons were issued routinely by the early thirteenth century in cases of self-defense, accident, and insanity.[34] Although all the men involved appear to have been drinking, the intervening force of the crowd pressing in, the absence of antagonism between William and John, plus the victim's allegedly accidental fall onto the defendant's outstretched knife, combined to create a fact pattern that could be treated by a jury as misadventure rather than felonious homicide.

To take one final, to my mind puzzling, example, an inquest was summoned in 1254 to inquire into the death of William of Yerdelegh (likely Yardley, Northants.), a carter. The inquest determined that Robert son of Robert de Olneye and others had been drunkenly singing (*ebrii cantantes*) when William de Yerdelegh came along in his cart, similarly drunk, and collided with the singers.[35] Robert ran after William and struck him on the head with a hatchet; William died at his father's home more than two weeks later. Remarkably, the jury concluded that Robert had not struck William feloniously or out of malice prepense given the fact that the men were strangers to each other, and the death – though precipitated by a hatchet blow to the head – was determined to have been a misadventure. Drunken street revelers, a drunken carter, a drunk-driving collision, and a hot-headed hatchet blow, all added up to an accidental death in the eyes of this particular inquest.

In short, whether an untended candle or a fall onto an outstretched knife provided the proximate cause for a drunken death, the factor of inebriation appears to have been set aside by jurors who were willing to classify such deaths as accidental rather than holding the deceased or their companions accountable for deliberately imbibing to excess.[36] In some instances, the absence of an interceding act of aggression could have made all the difference. In others, the contributory negligence of the victim, such as John's alleged stumbling onto William's outstretched knife or (the other) William's drunk cart-driving, might have inclined a jury to classify a death as accidental.

Admittedly, it is difficult to imagine an alternative to treating the pure *infortunium* variety of drunken accidents – e. g. Simon's fall from his horse – as excusable misadventures: perhaps the common law could have categorized some such incidents akin to *felonia de se*, deliberate suicide, transferring the sinful intent to drink excessively to the later accidental act or omission resulting in the intoxicated individual's death. This would have required comfort with a highly attenuated chain of causation, looking for mens rea in a preceding act – the decision to drink – and pairing it with a later actus reus – the physical cause of death.[37] Rather than collapsing the causal and temporal chain of events, the common law leaned toward leniency in cases of accidents resulting from drunkenness. This might be done to remove the taint of suspicion from a companion who had the misfortune of being with the deceased at the time of an accidental death, thereby avoiding a possible felony prosecution. It might also reflect an unwillingness to punish the deceased's kin through the property forfeitures that would follow from a felony conviction, as was the case for individuals found guilty of feloniously taking their own lives by suicide. Notably, drunkenness was not raised as an excusing

33 TNA JUST3/74/3, m. 14, AALT no. 0103 (1309/10), stating »quod predictus Johannes filius Thome per infortunium interfectus fuit et non per aliquam feloniam aut maliciam predicti Willelmi excogitatam.«

34 See Green (1985) 30–31. For a summary of pardon procedure and changes to it over the thirteenth century, see Hurnard (1969) 31–67.

35 Lyte (ed.) (1916), 520, no. 2087. On the place name, see Ekwall (1960) 542.

36 This marks a point of tremendous difference between the treatment of intoxication and anger in medieval English law. While the former could provide the basis for a finding of misadventure, the latter was sometimes given as an example of the *opposite* of misadventure. See, e. g., Kamali (2019) 110, n. 83 (citing Hurnard (1969) 76).

37 There would have been some precedent for this in Christian moral theology, which found no contradiction in treating acts committed unknowingly while a person was drunk as grave sins. See, e. g., Aquinas' borrowing from Ambrose: »›We learn that we should shun drunkenness, which prevents us from avoiding grievous sins. For the things we avoid when sober, we unknowingly commit through drunkenness.‹ Therefore drunkenness, properly speaking is a mortal sin.« Aquinas (1948) vol. 4, Pt. II–II, Q. 150, Art. 2.

factor in cases of suicide, although other impediments to the exercise of reason, most notably insanity, were relied upon to classify some suicides as non-felonious.[38] This suggests that intoxication was not available as an excuse when a person exercised some apparent agency in taking their own life, despite the fact that it served as the basis for classifying accidental deaths as non-felonious misadventures.

2.2 *Self-defense Against an Intoxicated Aggressor*

Unlike those who died in drunken accidents, victims of self-defense homicide were not viewed with the same measure of sympathy when they had, due to intoxication, initiated an altercation. In self-defense cases generally speaking, the narrative told by the self-defender in pursuit of a pardon frequently portrayed the homicide victim in an exceedingly negative light. In some instances, the victim was described as an anger-driven, bloodthirsty first attacker, to whom the self-defender had responded only reluctantly with lethal violence.[39] Like anger, drunkenness might be highlighted as a decisive factor in maligning a homicide victim as a vicious first aggressor in a self-defense narrative. By contrast, self-defenders tended to present themselves as sober, able to calculate precisely their likelihood of survival before employing deadly force. Naomi Hurnard speculates that a self-defender would have weakened his case for a pardon if he admitted being drunk, which would have called into doubt the absence of provocation and the idea that he had only struck the deceased to save his own life.[40] That said, there are exceptions to this pattern, suggesting that jurors grappled with these cases in all their circumstantial complexity, with no hard-and-fast rules to guide them.

To take an example of the kind of drunk-sober contrast as described by Hurnard, a 1310 gaol delivery case tells a tale of two sailors (*garcones de mari*), Geoffrey son of Odo and Robert Bathe, both of Kyngeburgh.[41] Robert fought with Geoffrey due to intoxication (*per ebrietatem contendebat*), striking him with a sword. Wishing to take refuge (*refugio habendo*) in a nearby village, Geoffrey fled from the boat, only to be pursued by his attacker. Eventually cornered by Robert, Geoffrey took out his staff and struck Robert in self-defense, killing him only to avoid his own death, and »not out of any felony or malice aforethought« (*non per aliquam feloniam aut maliciam excogitatam*). Geoffrey was remanded to gaol to await the king's pardon.[42] It is noteworthy that the plea roll explicitly attributed drunkenness only to the initial aggressor, not to the self-defender, who appears to have been able to calculate, with great sobriety, his chance of survival before counter-attacking in self-defense.

In a 1218–1219 York case, Malger the smith of Burton was accused of mortally wounding Robert son of Agnes in the head with an axe.[43] Malger was imprisoned, but the jurors at trial reported that the deceased, Robert, had been drunk (*ebrius*) and had attempted to enter Malger's house by force at night. In fact, it was only after Robert succeeded in forcefully entering the home that Malger struck him in the head. Rather than being convicted of felonious homicide, the self-defender was returned to prison to await a pardon.[44] Admittedly, sympathy for Malger's plight could have been enhanced not only by Robert's drunkenness but also by his

38 See Seabourne / Seabourne (2000) 8, 28. In Roman law, drunkenness might be regarded as a mitigating circumstance with regard to the suicide of soldiers. See Mittermaier (1840) 293.

39 See Kamali (2017) 17–19, 29–30.

40 Hurnard (1969) 98. On the frequent appearance of tavern brawls in self-defense fact patterns, see Hanawalt (ed. and trans.) (1976a) 13–14.

41 TNA JUST3/74/3, m. 8, AALT no. 0078 (1310), http://aalt.law.uh.edu/AALT7/JUST3/JUST3no74_3/IMG_0078.htm (*incipit* »Galfridus filius Odonis …«, last accessed 3 March 2022). This may be modern Conisbrough, derived from Cyningesburh, in Yorkshire's West Riding.

42 A quick search of the calendar of patent rolls for this portion of Edward II's reign did not turn up confirmation of Geoffrey's pardon.

43 Stenton (ed. and trans.) (1937) 354, no. 977.

44 I did not manage to find a record of pardon for Malger in the Calendar of Patent Rolls for this stretch of Henry III's reign.

attempt at a nocturnal housebreaking.[45] Such a combination of housebreaking and drunkenness similarly appears in a 1283 inquest into the death of John Bonde.[46] There, it appears that John Bonde and his killer, John de Tikehill, had been engaged in a drunken quarrel after leaving a tavern, and that Bonde had struck Tikehill thrice across the shoulders with a stick. Tikehill had fled home and taken refuge indoors. Bonde, however, came to the house, broke down the door, and dragged Tikehill's wife outside by the hair, beating her. When Tikehill came outside to protect his wife, Bonde pursued him with a drawn knife. Tikehill ultimately struck Bonde on the head with a stick, from which blow Bonde died. Although it sounds as though both men had been drinking, the inquest determined that Tikehill had killed Bonde in self-defense, and not of malice aforethought. In cases like this, drunkenness was just one of the factors held against the first aggressor, and in this instance the self-defender's case for a pardon was bolstered by the deceased's brutal assault on Tikehill's wife and by Tikehill's use of a stick, as opposed to a disproportionately lethal weapon, in response to a knife attack.

As should be clear from the examples above, it is exceedingly difficult to discern clear patterns in the treatment of intoxication by juries. Just as one begins to see a pattern, another case surfaces to throw it into doubt. For example, the 1248 death of Terry de Estland would appear, at first glance, to be a likely candidate for a pardon based on self-defense. Conrad de Bruneseye, in his own home, had argued with Terry, who proceeded to knock Conrad down and lie on top of him. Unable to escape with his life otherwise, according to the narrative that survives in a Chancery record, Conrad wounded Terry's shoulder with a knife. Terry succumbed to death ten days later, but this was after consuming half a gallon of wine after dinner. A writ was issued to the sheriff of Northampton to inquire into the death and specifically to ascertain whether Conrad killed Terry feloniously or by misfortune. The writ did not raise the possibility that Terry might have been responsible for his own death, having overindulged in wine while recovering from a shoulder wound. Neither did the writ suggest that Conrad might have killed Terry in self-defense, possibly due to the fact that it was unclear whether Terry had wielded a weapon against Conrad in the initial altercation, and also due to the intervening cause of Terry's excessive drinking on the evening of his death. While attributing the death to Conrad, the inquest concluded that Conrad had killed Terry by misfortune. A record of his pardon appears on Henry III's patent rolls.[47]

In a 1298 homicide case, to take one final example, a coroner's inquest was held into the death of John Burel in a case in which all involved appear to have been drinking.[48] Burel had died in the Oxford gaol, exhibiting severe head wounds, reaching to his brain (*usque ad cerebrum*). An inquest was summoned to inquire further into the death. The inquest explained that Burel, an Irish cleric, had been at Thomas de Graunton's tavern with other Irish clerics, including Nicholas Vilers and John de Suthfolk.[49] An argument arose (*mota fuit contentione verborum*), and the men stepped outside, still fighting (*contendentes*). Burel immediately wielded his sword and threatened (*insultabat*) Vilers, who raised the hue while attempting to flee the attack. Suthfolk similarly fled. Burel pursued, and he did so *viriliter*, with his sword outstretched and with a desire to kill his two fellow clerics. Vilers, feeling he had no alternative but to repel force with force (*vim vi repellendo*) in order to preserve his own life, struck Burel, but not mortally. Burel responded with a further attack on Vilers, an assault described as »*virilius, velocius, et acerbius*«. At this, Suthfolk swung into action, striking Burel at the base of his head (*cervice capitis*)

45 By the late thirteenth century, treatise evidence suggests that slaying a housebreaker could result in an outright acquittal. See Green (1985) 77–78, n. 34.

46 Lyte (ed.) (1916) 604, no. 2258.

47 Lyte (ed.) (1916) 553, no. 2059; Lyte (ed.) (1908) 35.

48 TNA JUST2/128, m. 1v, AALT no. 0007 (1298), http://aalt.law.uh.edu/AALT7/JUST2/JUST2no128/IMG_0007.htm (*incipit* »Contigit die Jovis proxima post festum Exaltationis sancte Crucis …«, last accessed 3 March 2022).

49 Clerics visiting taverns was a constant concern for the thirteenth-century English church, which repeatedly cautioned against the practice. See, e. g., Powicke / Cheney (eds.) (1964) 425 (no. 11).

with an axe (*hachia*), inflicting a wound from which Burel would later die in the Oxford gaol. Both Vilers and Suthfolk were imprisoned. Burel was acquitted of the homicide in a jury trial before the justices of gaol delivery. Suthfolk, on the other hand, was convicted by a jury but handed over to the bishop of Lincoln due to his clerical status, thereby avoiding a trip to the gallows. While the record provides an explanation for Vilers' acquittal, insofar as the blow he struck while facing down a vicious attack by the sword-wielding Burel was not mortal, the record is a bit more ambiguous as to why Suthfolk merited a felony conviction under the circumstances. It could be that Suthfolk's own alcohol consumption that evening, behavior unbefitting a cleric, made him an unworthy candidate for more lenient treatment once it was determined that he, and not Vilers, had struck the fatal blow. Other considerations could have swayed the jury toward a conviction, too, including the fact that the altercation involved two men against one; the circumstance that Suthfolk had used an axe, as opposed to a knife or sword that he might reasonably have carried on his person; and the jury's awareness that Suthfolk's clerical status would preserve him from the gallows, making a conviction less consequential. The role of alcohol, in other words, remains fundamentally ambiguous, and one could imagine a similar set of facts resulting in a finding of self-defense in other circumstances.[50]

All in all, in contrast to the apparent sympathy afforded those who died accidentally due to drunkenness, medieval juries appeared ready to judge as culpable those who attacked others while in a drunken state, with the possibility of a royal pardon for the sober self-defender who responded in kind with lethal violence. Individual cases resist categorization, however, particularly when all parties to a confrontation had been drinking, sometimes requiring further inquiry into whether a killing had been felonious, in self-defense, or even accidental.

2.3 *Taverns as a Locus for Alcohol-Fueled Misbehavior*

The case of the Irish clerics above highlights an oft-repeated refrain in the coroners' and plea rolls of medieval England: homicides occurring in, near, and on the way home from taverns. Taverns served as legitimate sites for people to gather and drink together, but they could also be sites of competitive play, gambling, quarreling, and even conspiring to commit crimes. In thinking about taverns as potential dens of criminal conspiracy, we might return briefly to the incident that opened this article: the 1272 slaying of Ralph the Bromham vicar by Robert Bernard and his group of fellow tavern-goers. At the coroner's inquest in late February, representatives from one village blamed Robert alone for the death, while three other villages also ascribed blame to Robert's three companions, who had consented to Robert's ill deed and were prepared to act if needed. Less than a month later, as the vernal equinox arrived, Ralph's widow brought a private accusation of felony against the four tavern-goers. In contrast to the coroner's inquest, which only attributed physical violence to Robert Bernard, Agnes described in gruesome detail the direct involvement of all four men in the fatal assault on her husband:

> There Robert Bernard struck Ralph with a ›spart‹ axe on the right side of the head, giving him a wound 15 inches long, 4 inches deep and 1 inch wide, from which he died. At the same time and place Robert of Shefford struck him with the back of a ›denesch‹ axe on his loins, breaking them, of which blow he would have died if he had not died of the first wound. Richard Norman struck him with a staff of apple-wood called ›clobbe‹ on the left side, breaking 2 ribs, of which he would have died if he had had no other blow. At the same time and place Roger Brien struck him on the back between the shoulders with an oak staff called

50 As was true in the case of the killing of Michael son of Rocsia by Arnald le Knyth in 1265. According to an inquest into whether Arnald had killed Michael in self-defense, the two men had been drinking together at a tavern and fell into argument on their way home. Michael ran into his house and retrieved a scythe. Then, telling Arnald to wait so that he might drink to him, Michael struck Arnald between the shoulders. Seeing that Michael intended to kill him, Arnald struck him on the head with an axe (*hachia*), killing him immediately. The inquest determined that this had been self-defense, and Arnald received a pardon. Lyte (ed.) (1916) 568, no. 2123; Lyte (ed.) (1910) 617.

›clobbe‹, of which he would have died if he had had no other blow.[51]

Robert appears, in Agnes' formulation, to have been *primus inter pares*, the first in time to act but otherwise matched in the use of lethal violence by his companions. The widow went even further, launching accusations against the tavern host, Robert Malin of Bromham, and his wife Malina, whom she accused of »sending, ordering and harbouring [the others] in committing the felony«.[52] This aspect of Agnes' private appeal suggests that the brutal attack on Ralph, though possibly fueled by the men's drinking, might have been plotted in advance. Agnes stood ready to prove her accusation, and had backup as well in case she died before avenging her husband's death: Ralph's sister was ready to take responsibility for the private prosecution if needed. Ralph's death in late February would occupy his widow's time through spring and summer, as she asserted her intent to prosecute at county court sessions in April, May, June, and July, finally securing Robert Bernard's outlawry.[53] The other accused individuals produced sureties, and when Agnes asserted her prosecution again in August, Richard Norman, Robert Malin, and Malina his wife were handed over to the sheriff for safekeeping; later bailed, the three would be recommitted to gaol at the time of the Bedfordshire eyre, where they were ultimately acquitted by a jury.[54] Failing to appear, Robert of Shefford and Roger Brien were outlawed. It is unclear whether any man, Robert Bernard included, paid the ultimate price for Ralph's death, but the flight of some of them suggests a fear of this distinct possibility. In other words, Robert's attack on Ralph was not a simple instance of a single, extremely agitated drunk person lashing out at a victim; it was potentially a coordinated attack conceived within the walls of a local tavern, although a jury would acquit several who were allegedly involved.

Taverns could be sites of great danger, a locale for plotting vengeance and gathering an armed retinue in advance of a planned attack. In London in 1325, Walter de Benygtone came with seventeen companions to the brewhouse hosted by Gilbert de Mordone; their ill intent was manifested by the stones, swords, and knives they carried with them.[55] They proceeded to consume four gallons of beer while »lying in wait to seize and carry off Emma«, a young woman under the care of Gilbert the host. Asked to leave, the men responded that they would stay and spend their money, insofar as the house was a *mercatoria*, a public market. When Gilbert's wife then tried to take Emma to safety, Walter and his companions, »moved with anger«, assaulted Gilbert's brewer, Geoffrey, and others present, one of whom, Robert de Mordone, raised the hue and cry and fled into the high street. The coroner's inquest records that Walter de Benygtone pursued Robert outside with a knife in one hand and a misericorde (a type of dagger) in the other. Neighbors, including a man named Benedict de Warde, approached to try to pacify the men, and Walter responded with violence toward Benedict. Benedict seized a staff from a stranger, striking Walter on the head. Walter was carried to a nearby fountain and left outside overnight, perhaps indicative of how deep were the loyalties of his companions; he died shortly after being moved into a house the following day. The coroner's roll indicates that Benedict fled the locality, and I have not located a corresponding trial record. The narrative produced by the coro-

51 Hunnisett (ed. and trans.) (1961) 55–56. Agnes is described as the widow of Ralph the clerk of Bromham. Following a homicide in London in 1325, a coroner's inquest similarly described both aggressors as having inflicted mortal wounds on the deceased. See Sharpe (ed.) (1913) 112–113 (Roll D, no. 20).

52 Hunnisett (ed. and trans.) (1961) 56. Robert's name is spelled Malyn in Agnes' appeal of felony but he is likely the same Robert Malin identified in the coroner's report as the tavernkeeper.

53 When a person was repeatedly contumacious in responding to a private accusation of felony in the county court, they could be outlawed. The treatise *Bracton* indicates that the person could be outlawed at the fifth non-appearance. Thorne (ed. and trans.) (1968) 354.

54 Hunnisett (ed. and trans.) (1961) 56–57.

55 Sharpe (ed.) (1913) 114–115 (Roll D, no. 24).

ner's inquest paints Benedict in a sympathetic light, a neighbor stepping in to quell conflict within his local tavern and struck down by a man who had come to the tavern that evening armed with weapons and a large retinue, intent on engaging in criminal behavior.[56]

Violent deaths committed by groups of men inside and after leaving taverns appear with some frequency in the plea rolls. According to a 1280 case, Hugh son of Simon and Richard Freeman left a tavern and »fought together while drunk« (*ebrietate litigaverunt adinvicem*).[57] Hugh wounded Richard, who died three days later; he then fled and was outlawed as a result. Another man, William son of Adam, was attached for the same homicide but acquitted by a jury, and yet another individual connected to Richard's death managed to claim benefit of clergy. Hugh does not appear to have returned for trial, as his frankpledge group was ordered to pay a fine. His flight suggests that drunkenness would not have realistically excused his attack on his drinking companion. This was similarly the case with regard to a homicide that took place circa 1279 after an evening of drinking at an inn in Deneby (possibly Danby in North Yorkshire). Paulinus de Weteleye (likely Whitley, also in North Yorkshire) had been drinking with his brother, Thomas, and struck him fatally in the chest with a knife after they left the inn.[58] The truth only came to light when a second jury, composed of knights, rejected the story presented by an earlier trial jury that had pinned blame on one »Hugh la Ley«, who had reportedly been drinking with the two brothers and had argued with Thomas over the quality of some arrows he had sold to him. It appears that Paulinus or his supporters had invented the tale of Hugh's involvement in order to save Paulinus from the noose. The plot failed, and Paulinus ultimately faced the gallows.

Cases like these reinforced the view of taverns as a source of felonious activity, with alcohol easing the path toward individual and collective criminal behavior. A statute issued by Edward I in 1285 for the governance of London prescribed:

> And Whereas such Offenders as aforesaid going about by Night, do commonly resort and have their Meetings and hold their evil talk in Taverns more than elsewhere, and there do seek for shelter, lying in wait, and watching their time to do Mischief; It is enjoined that none do keep a Tavern open for Wine or Ale, after the tolling of the aforesaid Curfew; but they shall keep their Tavern shut after that hour, and none therein drinking or resorting; Neither shall any Man admit others in his House except in common Taverns, for whom he will not be answerable unto the King's Peace.[59]

Monetary penalties were threatened, with a fifth offense resulting in the taverner's loss of the trade forever. London's *Liber Albus* records an ordinance regulating taverners and brewsters, prescribing imprisonment for taverners who knowingly house a transgressor, an offense equated with receiving felons.[60] Above all, tavern behavior potentially threatened the king's peace. In Bedfordshire in the 1350s, a jury of presentment alleged that William Tolouse, John Hunte, and their associates were »common disturbers of the peace« (*communes perturbatores pacis*) who haunted taverns by night and day; William secured pledges, promising to respond to the allegations, while John, failing to

56 For a similar death of a person responding to violence within a London tavern in 1325, see Sharpe (ed.) (1913) 134–135 (Roll E, no. 2).

57 TNA JUST1/664, m. 42, AALT no. 3782 (1280), http://aalt.law.uh.edu/AALT4/JUST1/JUST1no664/aJUST1no664fronts/IMG_3782.htm (*incipit* »Hugo filius Syman de Cotum et Ricardus Freman …«, last accessed 3 March 2022).

58 The case is reported in Hurnard (1969) 363, n. 2, and the case record may be viewed at TNA JUST1/1060, m. 5 (1279), http://aalt.law.uh.edu/AALT4/JUST1/JUST1no1060/aJUST1no1060fronts/IMG_4799.htm (*incipit* »Juratores presentaverunt …«, last accessed 3 March 2022). The record describes a dispute arising (*orta contentione*) between the brothers after they exited the tavern after a night of drinking together.

59 Raithby (ed.) (1963) 102. Similar local regulations issued from London's Guildhall, too. See, e. g., Sharpe (ed.) (1901) 85.

60 Riley (ed.) (1862) 95.

appear, was outlawed.[61] In 1371, a jury of presentment reported to the justices of the peace at Winchester that John Hogyn had assaulted and wounded William Maistre, and that John furthermore was a »common disturber of the peace« who slept by day and kept vigil by night in taverns, »playing at checkers« (*ludendo ad scaccarium*) and »penny-prick«, while his neighbors knew not whence he derived his money.[62] Taverns could thus be sites of risky behavior and even criminal conspiracy. As the next section will illustrate, taverns were also ubiquitous, particularly in urban locations, and the center of social life, rivaling only the church as a foundation of local communities. To understand the mixed outcomes of felony cases involving alcohol consumption and intoxication, one necessarily has to grapple with the similarly mixed nature of religious exhortations and popular attitudes, a potent cocktail marrying the sweetness of alcohol's community-building potential with a realistic dash of bitters.

3 The Role of Alcohol in Medieval English Culture

The consumption of alcoholic drink was part of daily life in medieval England, where ale was a staple beverage.[63] Labor contracts might specify a ration of ale for agricultural workers, for example, and throughout the kingdom the production of ale, like bread, was closely regulated to ensure quality and price protections for consumers.[64] In urban centers, taverns were ubiquitous, a site for socializing, conducting business, and even contracting marriage, although the last was discouraged by church authorities.[65] One estimate suggests that London alone in 1309 had 354 taverns and 1,334 alehouses.[66] Ale and wine were widely enjoyed, with the latter increasingly available in the fourteenth century due to the expanding wine trade.[67] Admittedly, it was likely weak ale that accompanied most meals, ale that was frequently brewed by women.[68] That said, evidence from late thirteenth-century London suggests widespread wine consumption, too, with debts frequently recorded by taverners and others for casks of wine purchased from merchants hailing from Bordeaux, Toulouse, and other locales.[69] Londoners took their wine so seriously that a taverner, John Penrose, convicted of selling unwholesome wine in 1364, was sentenced »to drink a draught of his own wine, the remainder to be poured on his head, and he was to foreswear the calling of vintner unless he obtained the King's favour.«[70]

All told, alcohol consumption was widespread and largely non-controversial. Even the most moralizing of medieval theologians would not have

61 Putnam (ed.) (1938) 48 (no. 44).

62 Putnam (ed.) (1938) 207–208 (no. 18). Penny-prick (*penyprik*) was a game involving throwing something toward a penny target. See *Oxford English Dictionary*, 3rd edition (2005), *s. u.* »penny-prick«.

63 Bennett observes that medieval English people rarely drank water, milk, or wine, relying mostly on ale and later beer as well. See Bennett (1996) 8, 16–17. For estimates of ale and wine consumption, see Martin (2001) 29. On the late fourteenth-century introduction of beer, which was cheaper, more clear, and easier to ship due to its resistance to spoilage, see Martin (2009) 62. On the distinction between ale and beer and the timetable for the introduction of hopped beverages from Germany, see the glossary entry for »cerveise« in Riley (ed.) (1860) 707–708; Bennett (1996) 9.

64 For an example of laborers receiving bread, meat, and ale while helping with the harvest in a thirteenth-century manor, see Maitland (ed. and trans.) (1889) 103. On the regulation of ale, see Bennett (1996) 98–106.

65 For an example of an exhortation not to hold wedding in taverns, see Stephen Langton's guidance for Canterbury in the 1220s. Powicke / Cheney (eds.) (1964) 165–167. My thanks to Charles Donahue.

66 Austin (1985) 100. See also Sharpe (ed.) (1902) xix.

67 See Austin (1985) 100–101. On the distinction between alehouses and wine-taverns, and on the strict inspection of ale quality, see Riley (ed.) (1859) lxi–lxiii.

68 See Austin (1985) 88. On the history of women in brewing, see generally Bennett (1996). See also Riley (ed.) (1859) lix–lx (indicating that the best ale in fourteenth-century London was thin and unlikely to intoxicate); Martin (2001) 32–33 (on strength of ale and wine).

69 See, e. g., Sharpe (ed.) (1899) 9 (debt owed by taverner to a burgess of Bordeaux for wine), 21 (casks of wine as security for a final concord between a vintner and two other men), 41 (debt for wine owed to a merchant from Toulouse). Dozens of such debts appear throughout this volume.

70 Sharpe (ed.) (1905) 178. Penrose was readmitted to his trade roughly four years later. See Sharpe (ed.) (1905) 178–179.

suggested that alcohol should be eliminated from one's diet.[71] While scriptures included cautionary tales, like the story of Lot's drunken incest, wine also played an approved starring role in gospel narratives, from the wedding at Cana to the Last Supper.[72] As A. Lynn Martin observes, excessive drinking »could provoke disorder and violence, but recreational drinking also promoted celebration, socialization, and jollification.«[73] Drinking was at the heart of community-building events that might, in fact, disrupt violence.[74] It was also tied to important life and death events and celebrations. When William de Schaftow, aged 50, was interrogated about a birth two decades earlier during an inquisition post mortem, the memory marker on which he relied was an episode of drinking in celebration of the baby's arrival. The festivities were all the more memorable because William had become so drunk that he had fallen and broken his leg.[75] New lives were celebrated with drinking, and deaths were commemorated by drinking, too, both by those gathering to mourn an individual's passing and by the beneficiaries of charitable largesse. When Gilbert Lyndeseye, a tiler, died in London in 1376, his bequest directed the expenditure of money to purchase spices, wine, and ale to entertain his neighbors on the day of his funeral, as well as ale to be consumed at his *dirige*, the service for the dead.[76] Because it was a necessity, ale might also be distributed as a work of charity.[77] At the 1319 funeral of Lady Margaret de Neville, an incredible 1,440 gallons of ale were distributed.[78] Parishes might raise operating funds by holding special festivities, often referred to as »scotales«, although admittedly evidence for this phenomenon tends to be concentrated in the fifteenth and sixteenth centuries.[79]

Drinking was part of daily life. Yet it held its dangers, too, and these were well known from lived experience and from religious sermonizing. In Dan Michel's *Ayenbite of Inwyt*, a mid-fourteenth-century translation of the French *Somme le Roi*, the author suggests that a drunk man imperils his prospects for the afterlife:

> Those who live by the flesh, as says Saint Paul, slay their souls. For they make of their bellies their god. The same neither hold reason nor measure. And therefore they shall have in the other world pain without measure.[80]

Confessors' manuals often harp upon the particular perils of routine excessive drinking. For example, Thomas of Chobham (d. circa 1233–1236) treated »habitual drunkenness« (*ebrietas consuetudinaria*) as a mortal sin in light of the fact that »the habit of drunkenness is a sign and *indicium* that man places before God the pleasure that he has from drinking.«[81] Elsewhere in his *Summa*, Chobham listed »drunkenness, if constantly repeated« (*ebrietas, si assidua sit*) alongside sins such as sacrilege, homicide, adultery, fornication, false testimony, rape, theft, pride, hatred, avarice, and long-held anger.[82] Texts like these distinguished habitual drinking as especially worthy of condemnation, suggesting the possibility of a different, more lenient treatment for the occasional overindulgence on a feast day or other special occasion.

71 Aquinas (1948) vol. 4, Pt. II–II, Q. 149, Art. 3 (relying on Matthew 15:11 for the idea that »No meat or drink, considered in itself, is unlawful«, although he conceded that drinking wine could »become unlawful accidentally« depending upon the circumstances, including a drinker who was bound by a vow not to drink or who voluntarily drank out of measure).

72 Genesis 19:30–38 (Lot and his daughters), John 2:1–11 (wedding at Cana), Matthew 26:20–29 (Last Supper).

73 Martin (2009) 13.

74 Martin (2009) 13.

75 Dawes et al. (eds.) (1988) 123–124. William had been drinking with the baby's father, Roger de Wyderyngton (Widdrington, Northum). Regarding the place name, see Ekwall (1960) 517. His testimony confirmed that of other witnesses who attested to the fact that the baby was now twenty-one years of age.

76 Sharpe (ed.) (1890) 192. On the *dirige*, see Skeel (1926) 301.

77 Martin (2001) 20 (describing a 1265 gift of 147 gallons of ale to the poor from the household of Eleanor de Montfort).

78 Martin (2001) 20.

79 French (1997) 129–131; Rosser (1994); Martin (2001) 2.

80 Gradon (ed.) (1965) 53. »Þo þet libbeþ be þe ulesse ase zayþ zaynte paul hi slaȝeþ hire zaulen. Uor hi makeþ of hare wombe hare god. Þe ilke ne hyealdeþ scele ne mesure. And þeruore hi ssolle habbe ine þe oþre wordle [sic] pine wyþ-oute mesure.«

81 Chobham (1968) 409. »… quia consuetudo ebrietatis est signum et indicium quod homo preponit deo delectationem quam habet ex potu«. It is noteworthy, however, that habitual drunkenness did not begin to appear in the act books of ecclesiastical courts until the early seventeenth century, along with premarital sexual activity and other social ills. See Helmholz (2019) 88.

82 Chobham (1968) 18.

Drunkenness had long been condemned in penitentials and manuals for confessors as a gateway to other sins and was also treated topically in manuals for preachers.[83] In his *Liber Poenitentialis* (circa 1208–1213), Robert of Flamborough, canon-penitentiary of Saint-Victor at Paris, described drunkenness as a great evil »from which all evils spring forth« (*unde omnia mala pululant*).[84] Other texts associated taverns and intoxication not just with sin, a problem of the internal forum, but also with capital crime. Thomas of Chobham, in his *Summa Confessorum*, linked drunkenness with adultery and homicide, as well as argumentativeness and contention generally.[85] The Dominican Jofroi of Waterford's French translation of the *Secretum Secretorum* specifically mentioned the tendency to overconsume wine leading a person to »homicide, larceny, adultery, and other horrible and hideous sins« (*a homecide et a larechin et a avvoltierge et a autres pechiés oribles et hidous*).[86] The *Ayenbite of Inwyt* described the gluttonous overconsumption of food and drink, much like some of the sins listed by Chobham above, as leading stepwise to the gallows:

> For first of all he becomes a frequenter of taverns. Then he plays at dice. Then he sells his own [property]. Then he becomes a ribald, fornicator, and thief. And then he is hanged. This is the price that one often pays.[87]

Not surprisingly, persons frequenting taverns caused anxiety for lawmakers, who prescribed during the reign of Edward II (r. 1307–1327) that the view of frankpledge should include an inquiry into »such as continually haunt Taverns, and no Man knoweth whereon they do live«.[88]

Writing later in the fourteenth century, John Wycliffe (d. 1384) similarly railed against those who overindulged in drinking, particularly on holy days. Wycliffe targeted his critique first toward burgesses, merchants, and other rich commoners, who believed it a great advantage to spend excessively on their household and enjoy lavish feasts.[89] He also attributed the same gluttonous tendency to »many poor laborers« who might suffer »uneven nourishing« due to drunkenness, particularly those who, rather than eating and drinking in good measure throughout the work week, would spend all their earnings on a holy day, thereby being ill-equipped to serve God.[90] While the plea rolls may say little directly about drunkenness, religious and popular literature reveal a world in which excessive drinking was both common and commonly criticized as a rejection of God and a privileging of pleasure over piety.

The legal records explored in the preceding section demonstrate that jurors treated intoxicated actors harshly, except when they treated them leniently. They sometimes excused as misadventure a death resulting from an alcohol-fueled brawl, and other times were comfortable treating a drinking partner as a felon even when the facts could have been framed to support a claim of self-defense. Jurors' reactions to drinking and drunkenness in felony cases resist easy categorization, suggesting that circumstantial, prudential judgments, rather than rigid rules or expectations, guided juries' decisions in individual cases. This apparently contradictory treatment of drinking

83 In this last category, see John Bromyard's treatment of »ebrietas« in his alphabetically organized summa for preachers. Bromyard (1586) 218–220.

84 Flamborough (1971) 264.

85 Chobham (1968) 412, mentioning »… adulteria, homicidia, rixe, contentiones, et omnium mandatorum dei oblivio«.

86 Henry (1986) 16.

87 Gradon (ed.) (1965) 51. »Vor alþeruerst he becomþ tauernyer. Þanne he playþ ate des. Þanne he zel his oȝen. Þanne he becomþ ribaud, holyer, and þyef. And þanne me hine anhongeþ. Þis is þet scot þet me ofte payþ.« A more literal translation of »þanne me hine anhongeþ« would be »then man hangs him«.

88 Raithby (ed.) (1963) 246 (not my translation). On taverns as ambiguous and often disorderly spaces, see Hanawalt (1999).

89 Wycliffe (1871) 160 (»burgeis and marchaundes and oþer riche comynes. Hom þenke it is a grete avaunt to spende myche in household, and make grete festis to lords; and hereof comes myche yvel; ffor by þis ben parties made, and many wrongis mayntened.«). See also Wenzel (ed. and trans.) (1989) 632–633.

90 Wycliffe (1871) 160 (»And not onely riche comyns synnen þus in glotonye, bot mony pore laboreres ben blemyschid by þis synne, and specialy in dronkenesse, for uneven norisching … for soche men schulden warly ete and drinke, and take sum drinke on werk day, and not spende al on holy day; ffor þis þing unables hom to serve God on holy day …«). Similar complaints appear in sixteenth-century regulations. See McIntosh (1998) 112.

and intoxication in felony cases makes greater sense in light of two competing factors visible in medieval English culture: the centrality of drinking to daily life and important celebrations, and the condemnation of excessive drinking in moralizing literature, which aimed at discouraging gluttony and demonstrating how alcohol intoxication tended to lead stepwise towards more serious sinful and criminal behavior. Jurors might have heeded the strict religious messaging to some degree, but done so with a greater inclination toward indulgence when a defendant's drunkenness in a particular case did not fall too far beyond the bounds of acceptable or understandable social behavior.

4 Drunkenness as Metaphor

In modern American criminal law casebooks, intoxication is sometimes paired with insanity to help students recognize the commonalities between the two conditions and the ways in which the law nevertheless treats the two topics distinctly.[91] Intoxication is not pedagogically paired with the doctrine of provocation, through which anger-fueled acts can sometimes give rise to a partial excuse.[92] In medieval England, we find anger and insanity alike fusing with the issue of intoxication both in legal records and in literary sources, with the former concepts sometimes providing a metaphor for intoxication, and vice versa. Nonetheless, in its treatment of drunken actors, the common law of felony ultimately handled intoxication more like anger and less like insanity, the latter being presumptively exculpatory. Like anger, drunkenness was a matter to be weighed circumstantially by jurors, who engaged in complex ethical and moral calculations worthy of inclusion in William of Pagula's *Oculus Sacerdotis*, which guided priests in discerning the nuances in various scenarios involving uncertainty, drunkenness included.[93] In homicide cases, jurors' prudential decision-making was hampered by the absence of doctrinal nuance; a clearly delineated manslaughter category, punished less severely than murder, could have eased the pressure on jurors forced to decide more starkly between capital homicide or not. Nevertheless, the mixed bag of outcomes – convictions, acquittals, and pardons – in cases involving alcohol consumption and intoxication indicate that jurors had latitude in weighing that factor among the many circumstances of an alleged felony.

4.1 *Intoxication and Insanity*

In medieval English felony law, insanity was treated as a presumptively excusing condition, while intoxication was not.[94] This is despite the fact that, in literary texts, we can find the metaphor of insanity used to signify a state of drunkenness, such as in the story of Chaucer's summoner, who was described as behaving »wood«, or mad, after consuming too much wine:

> Wel loved he garleek, onyons, and eek lekes,
> And for to drynken strong wyn, reed as blood;
> Thanne wolde he speke and crie as he were wood.[95]

Chaucer similarly approved of the words of Seneca, whose stoical tendencies led him to condemn the vice of drunkenness:

> Senec seith a good word doutelees;
> He seith he kan no difference fynde
> Bitwix a man that is out of his mynde
> And a man which that is dronkelewe
> [i. e., habitually drunk] …[96]

91 See Kadish et al. (2017) 1004–1071.

92 In the same casebook, provocation appears within the discussion of homicide doctrine rather than under excusing conditions like intoxication and insanity. See Kadish et al. (2017) 462–489. For a discussion of anger and drunkenness in modern law, see Mittermaier (1840) 308–320 (arguing that any equation of the two conditions for legal purposes is inapt, insofar as the angered actor has allowed his passions »dominion over his life« and usually lashes out due to some preexisting circumstance, while a drunken actor lashes out without reference to preceding circumstances). See also Hall (1944) 1052 (observing that courts never count drunkenness as a form of provocation, thereby denying »legal effect to the admitted fact that drunken persons are more easily aroused and lose self-control more readily than do sober ones«).

93 See Corran (2017) 31.

94 See Kamali (2019) 53–56; Butler (2010).

95 Benson (ed.) (1987) 33 (Canterbury Tales, General Prologue, I(A).634–636).

96 Benson (ed.) (1987) 196 (Canterbury Tales, The Pardoner's Tale, VI(C).492–495).

Thus, intoxication's effects might be likened to madness, particularly in the literary context.[97] Only occasionally do we see a hint of this idea making its way into legal records. In a 1286 inquest organized by the sheriff of Cumberland into the self-inflicted death of Ralph Deublet, the question posed to the jurors was whether Ralph had killed himself »in a fit of madness (*furore ductus*) or by misadventure«.[98] The inquest described how Ralph, on the evening of All Saints Day (a feast day, incidentally, on which people might indulge more than usual in intoxicating drink), became so drunk »that he did not know what he was doing (*nichil scivit de seipso*)«. He entered the home of Thomas le Tayllor, walked upstairs, and fell on top of the sleeping Thomas. Thomas awoke with a start; Ralph, fleeing downstairs, fell upon a cartload of wood, receiving a fatal head wound. Rather than ascribing his drunken death to madness, the inquest determined that it had been a misadventure. It is noteworthy that »felonious« was not among the options posed to the inquest by the writ, which was instead geared toward ascertaining whether Ralph's intoxicated behavior – a fall to his death after an illicit housebreaking – was categorically insanity or misadventure. The inquest's conclusion that Ralph did not understand his own actions suggests a level of intoxication that gave rise to severe cognitive impairment. Nevertheless, the jury settled on misadventure and not insanity in determining which category of excuse applied to Ralph's tragic death.

Generally speaking, intoxication does not appear to have been equated with insanity in medieval English legal records. When a jury concluded that a person had committed a felony while in the throes of a severe mental illness, a record was produced detailing the duration and nature of the person's affliction and confirming that they were impaired by that condition at the time of their alleged felony.[99] Robert son of Adam, for example, was found by a Northamptonshire jury in 1329 to have been ill with lunacy for fourteen years and suffering acutely from that illness at the time that he killed his servant.[100] The treatise *Bracton*, comparing an insane person's lack of reason to that of a minor, alludes to the »unkindness of fate« in describing why lunatics are to be treated with leniency, providing some insight into why the common law provided pardons *de cursu*, as a matter of course, for those who committed alleged felonies while in a state of insanity.[101] While a drunk person might appear to behave like a lunatic, the cause of actual lunacy was distinct from the cause of the *appearance* of lunacy brought on by drunkenness. Unlike insanity, which was understood to be an illness of long-standing duration, intoxication – even of the habitual variety – was not yet understood to be indicative of a diagnosable illness. While an illness was an affliction, intoxication was a voluntarily acquired condition, setting aside the comparatively rare instance of involuntary intoxication.

In her study of the royal pardon, Hurnard identified a rare occurrence in which a man, Thomas le Potter, subject to periodic lunacy, became drunk while dining away from home. When his host tried to ensure that he returned home safely, Thomas killed him. The jurors described Thomas as having been led to the killing »by lunatic illness, raving fury, and drunkenness«, and he was remanded to prison to await the king's pardon.[102] Presumably such a pardon would not have been issued had Thomas' only excuse been his drunken state. Intoxication's attendant impairments might resemble or, as in this instance, accompany madness, but the comparison was mere metaphor. Extreme anger, too, might give a person the appearance of madness, yet in the medieval English common law it was never treated as presumptively exculpatory like insanity.

97 Note, however, that Chaucer's emphasis on habitual drunkenness in his choice of the term »dronkelewe« would seem to foreshadow much later legal characterizations. See, e. g., Odgers / Odgers (1920) 1385, which states: »Habitual drunkenness, although not in itself affording excuse for crime, may induce insanity …« This was treated as an exception to the rule regarding voluntary drunkenness, which did not excuse a person from crime. For a similar treatment of *delirium tremens* as the equivalent of insanity and therefore giving rise to an excuse, see Jenks (ed.) (1922) 26.

98 Lyte (1916) 611, no. 2285.

99 Kamali (2019) 53–56. See also Butler (2010).

100 Sutherland (ed. and trans.) (1983) 215–216; Kamali (2019) 53–54.

101 Thorne (ed. and trans.) (1968) 384.

102 Hurnard (1969) 168.

4.2 *Intoxication and Anger*

Like intoxication and insanity, anger and insanity served as metaphoric signifiers for each other. Thinking back to the case that opened this article, Robert acted out violently »because he was drunk«, according to the coroner's inquest, and one senses the presence of anger in his physical reaction – no slight jab, but a vicious axing – to Ralph's literal-minded response to his question, »Who are you?« Anger and alcohol presented a toxic combination, channeling two deadly sins – *ira et gula*, wrath and gluttony – toward a single lethal end. Of course, anger alone could be deadly, giving rise to felonious acts.[103] Anger's affinity with intoxication did not escape medieval English writers, who played with the language of ire and inebriation in cautioning against sin and vice. The confessor-narrator of John Gower's *Confessio Amantis* describes the »mischief« that results from a person failing to control his anger:

My son, for your heart's ease
I shall fulfill this prayer,
So that you might the better learn
What mischief this vice causes,
When one in his anger does not forebear,
Such that he regrets,
When he is sober and thinks
About the folly of his deed.[104]

Unchecked anger, in Gower's treatment, produces a witlessness that can only be looked upon soberly once the passion has passed.

William Langland, in Passus V of *Piers Plowman*, would in turn suggest a causal connection between excessive drink and the generation of wrath, with the character of Repentance cautioning Anger: »Don't drink with too much delight, nor too deeply either, / Lest your will and your wits be overwhelmed by wrath.«[105] Thus, just as anger might function like drunkenness, the state of intoxication might give rise to anger. Seneca, whose writings on anger were widely drawn upon by medieval theologians and authors, observed: »Wine kindles anger because it increases the heat; some boil over when they are drunk, others when they are simply tipsy, each according to his nature.«[106] Aquinas drew upon Aristotle in arguing that those who were extremely drunk do not get angry, while »those who are slightly drunk, do get angry, through being still able, though hampered, to form a judgment of reason«.[107] Aristotle had attributed this to the fact that »those who are only slightly intoxicated can still exercise their judgement because they are not very drunk, but they exercise it badly because they are not sober, and they are ready to despise some of their neighbors and imagine that they are being slighted by others«.[108]

Anger and inebriation were understood as sister sins, or perhaps criminal kin, and so treated similarly in the medieval English common law of felony. Unlike insanity, intoxication offered no grounds for a royal pardon. One will not find in the plea rolls a defendant making the case that they did commit an alleged felony, but did so only because they were drunk and therefore ought to be excused. Similarly, the medieval English common law made no explicit concession to anger, as it would come to do by the sixteenth and seventeenth centuries with the development of the doctrine of provocation.[109] This parallel treatment of anger and drunkenness may be due to the fact that drunkenness, like extreme anger, could manifest a long-standing failure to cultivate commendable life habits. Both the angered and the inebriated individual might be condemned for having voluntarily contracted their condition (by developing a habit toward angered responses, or by choosing to drink excessively, respectively). Just like anger, drunkenness might be highlighted in a self-defense narrative in order to emphasize the out-of-control, murderous actions of the deceased, as contrasted with the calm, sober response of the self-defender, who only killed after perceiving no other way to preserve his own life.

There remain other parallels between anger and intoxication in medieval England. As we saw earlier, quarreling and alcohol consumption were

103 See generally Part II of Kamali (2019).
104 Gower (2003) 154 (Book 3, lines 134–141).
105 Langland (2006) 73 (Passus V, lines 184–185).
106 Seneca (1928) 206–207.
107 Aquinas (1948) vol. 2, Pt. I–II, Q. 46, Art. 4, Reply Obj. 3.
108 Aristotle (1927) Book 3.2. My thanks to Jonathan Baddley.
109 See generally Kamali (2017).

sometimes intertwined in discussions of disorder arising in taverns. Long-held anger and alcohol consumption could grease the wheels of conspiracy when men gathered in taverns to plot vengeance. On the other hand, both anger and drinking had positive valences: anger could be a justified response to an injustice, and above-average levels of alcohol consumption could be socially acceptable in celebration of feast days and major life events. Both conditions were ultimately left to the prudential judgment of jurors to weigh in their circumstantial examination of all the facts in a felony case. Admittedly, anger less often provided grounds for a finding of misadventure, but even here there is the occasional example of an angered individual thrusting himself upon a self-defender's outstretched knife, thereby bringing about his own death accidentally.[110]

4.3 *Intoxication and Loss of Reason*

Intoxication's affinity with both insanity and anger derived from its effects on a person's reason or »wit«, as it is often referenced in medieval English sources. Chaucer, in *The Parson's Tale*, would colorfully describe drunkenness as »the horrible sepulture of mannes resoun« and, therefore, a deadly sin.[111] This was due in part to the tendency of drunkenness to deprive a person of »the discrecioun of his wit«.[112] Providing some insight into this impairment of reason in *The Knight's Tale*, Chaucer's knight observed:

> A drunk man knows well he hath a house,
> But he knows not which the right way is thither,
> And to a drunk man the way is slider [i. e., slippery].[113]

Consider, too, this exhortation toward sobriety in Robert Mannyng's *Handlyng Synne*:

> If at a feast or at a tavern,
> With immoderation you drink so profusely,
> That you your clear speech have lost,
> Your wit is not as it was before.
> And your eyes may not see
> But [one] of a thing seems three,
> And you your steps may not guess,
> All such thing gluttony is.[114]

Despite this emphasis on condemning deliberate overindulgence, legal treatises and religious texts also acknowledged that drunkenness, like anger, might lead to impulsive behavior, which might seem to be less culpable than intentional behavior. The *Bracton* treatise, for example, discusses drunkenness in the context of sorting more from less deliberate offenses, observing: »Robbers commits [sic] offences intentionally, by deliberation; those who are drunk, by impulse (*impetu*), moved by their drunkenness (*per ebrietatem*), when a matter comes to blows or the sword; by accident, when they occur through misadventure, as where in hunting one kills a man by a spear thrown at a beast, or does some similar act.«[115] This would

110 See, e. g. Green (1985) 91 and n. 89. Such cases might end in acquittal or pardon.

111 Benson (ed.) (1987) 316 (Canterbury Tales, The Parson's Tale, X(I).821).

112 Benson (ed.) (1987) 316 (Canterbury Tales, The Parson's Tale, X(I).823).

113 Benson (ed.) (1987) 42 (Canterbury Tales, The Knight's Tale, I(A).1262–1264). »A dronke man woot wel he hath an hous, / But he noot which the righte wey is thider, / And to a dronke man the wey is slider.« The word »slider« meant slippery or uncertain. See *Middle English Dictionary*, *s. v.* »slider«. The distinction loosely parallels the legal notion today that an intoxicated person might be capable of forming general but not specific intent. See, e. g., *Regina v. Stopford* (1870), in Cox (ed.) (1871) 643–645; *Rex v. Beard* (1920), in Cox (ed.) (1921) 573–590; Odgers / Odgers (1920) 1385. See also Jenks (ed.) (1922) 24, citing *R. v. Meade*, 1 K.B. 895 (1909); *Regina v. Doherty* (1887), in Cox (ed.) (1890) 306–310. On the problematic logic, or lack thereof, underpinning the distinction between general and specific intent in the context of intoxication, see Hall (1944) 1061–1066.

114 Mannyng (1983) 163, lines 7–14 of the Osborn MS interpolation. »Yf at feste oþer at tauerne, / Oute o skyll drynkes soȝerne, / Þat þou þi clere spech hase lorne, / Þi wytte es noȝte als was be forne. / No þine eghene may noghte se / Bot of a thynge semes thre, / Na þou þi steppes may noghte gesse, / All swylk thynge glotony es.«

115 Thorne (ed. and trans.) (1968) 299. The Roman jurist Marcian similarly treated *ebrietas* (drunkenness) as a form of *impetus*, which Mittermaier takes to suggest an inclination to ascribe culpability to drunken acts, but to assign lesser punishment than for a calculated, cold-blooded act. See Mittermaier (1840) 293.

seem to place drunken acts of violence somewhere between intentional and accidental acts on a volitional scale, although we find in the plea rolls evidence that some alcohol-fueled deaths were treated as intentional felonious homicides and others as misadventure, depending on the circumstances. This correlation between drunkenness and impulsivity may be found as well in Thomas of Chobham's *Summa Confessorum*, which described an impulsive cause as »that which, suddenly born, compels a man to any evil act, such as drunkenness, anger, love, a feminine figure, hunger, thirst, nudity, and the like«.[116] Thus, alcohol intoxication could at once be condemned as a voluntary choice and yet also be understood to give rise to impulsivity, which could, in turn, make a resulting act appear more compelled than freely willed.

All in all, the common law's mixed approach to cases involving drunkenness – sometimes using it to demonstrate that a death was accidental, other times using it in support of a felony conviction – reflects a cultural understanding of the sinful nature of deliberate intoxication as well as an awareness that extreme inebriation might separate a person from his or her capacity to exercise reason. Because drunkenness, like anger, could push in either inculpatory or exculpatory directions, the common law, rather than prescribing explicit rules for the treatment of inebriation in felony fact patterns, left the matter largely up to the discretion of judge and jury, who would sort cases based upon their evaluation of the circumstances.[117] Jurors might have sometimes found cause to sympathize with a defendant despite their anger or inebriation, although the cause of such sympathy remains largely invisible to the historian who sees only an acquittal or a pardon on the plea rolls.

Conclusion

The medieval English common law treated the factor of drunkenness in felony fact patterns with some ambivalence, leaning in some instances toward condemnation rather than excuse, anticipating the proverb cited in the sixteenth century that one who »kyllyth a man dronk, sobur schalbe hangyd«.[118] Thomas Starkey (circa 1495–1538), in fact, quoted Reginald Pole (1500–1558) for the idea that by making a man the cause of his own ignorance, drunkenness »makyth hym more worthy of punnyschement and blame«.[119] Similarly minded was Sir Edward Coke, who was quick to blame the Danes for having introduced excessive drinking to England.[120] Elsewhere he wrote: »As for a drunkard who is *voluntaries daemon*, he hath, as has been said, no privilege thereby, but what hurt or ill so ever he doth his drunkenness doth aggravate it. *Omne crimen ebrietas et incendit et detegit.*«[121] Also taking a tough stance against intoxicated behavior in the early seventeenth century, Sir Francis Bacon (1561–1626) contended that »if a drunken man commit a felonie, he shall not be excused because his imperfection came by his owne default«.[122] Mathew Hale (1609–1676) argued, in like fashion, that a drunken person »shall have no privilege by this voluntary contracted madness, but shall have the same judgment as if he were in his right senses«.[123] Hale made an exception for persons placed in the condition of drunkenness by an unskilled physician or by enemies, and in the case of a »habitual or fixed phrenzy«, which would be treated like involuntary intoxication even if the person initially began drinking willfully.[124] Michael Hawke, in *The Grounds of the Lawes of England* (1657), would

116 Chobham (1968) 56 (»… que subito nata impellit hominem ad aliquod scelus, ut ebrietas, ira, amor, forma muliebris, fames, sitis, nuditas et similia«).

117 On the interplay between justices and juries in English felony cases, see generally Kamali / Green (2018). And on the likelihood of justices leaning toward granting deference to jury verdicts, see Kamali (2019) 258–262.

118 Herrtage (ed.) (1878) 31, lines 171–172. For a similarly stern stance, see Putnam (ed.) (1924) 378–379. See also Baker (ed. and trans.) (1994) 424, no. 80. Frequently cited in discussions of the intoxication defense is the 1551 case of *Reniger v. Fogossa*; see note 12 above. It is noteworthy that complaints about alehouses and drunkenness became more common during the sixteenth century. See McIntosh (1998) 31, n. 20.

119 Herrtage (ed.) (1878) 31, lines 169–170.

120 Coke (1644) 200.

121 Wharton (1880) 49 (citing Co. Litt. 247a). The Latin maxim translates to »drunkenness inflames and exposes every crime«.

122 Bacon (1630) 34. On changes in English drinking culture in the early seventeenth century, see Withington (2011).

123 Hale (1847) 32.

124 Hale (1847) 32.

describe such a drunken wrongdoer as »worthy of double punishment« because of having doubly offended by setting a bad example of drunkenness and committing the accompanying prohibited act.[125] This would seem to be a modification of the Aristotelian approach to intoxication, one which Aquinas chose not to follow to the letter: »The Philosopher does not say that the drunkard deserves more severe punishment,« observed Aquinas, »but that he deserves double punishment for his twofold sin.«[126]

Yet one must be cautious in interpreting these condemnations of intoxication in early modern treatises. While they appear to demonstrate a new, zero-tolerance approach to intoxication in felony cases, they were articulations of principles that would ultimately be applied – or not – by judges and juries faced with felony defendants, just as religious condemnations of intoxication were applied – or not – by medieval English jurors weighing the circumstances of a particular case centuries earlier. In her work on criminal responsibility in eighteenth-century England, Dana Rabin has illuminated the arguments presented by defendants hoping to excuse their drunken behavior by emphasizing such side effects of excessive drinking as memory loss and susceptibility to persuasion.[127] Such excuses of »simple drunkenness«, often presented by men who might capitalize upon the sympathies of »jurors and judges who drank to drunkenness themselves«, as well as claims of »insanity-drunkenness«, through which defendants tried to argue that their behavior was influenced by mental illness rather than the effects of alcohol intoxication alone, stand in contrast to the stark pronouncements of legal treatise authors.[128] Writing in the mid-eighteenth century, for example, William Blackstone pronounced: »… as to artificial, voluntarily contracted madness, by drunkenness or intoxication, which, depriving men of their reason, puts them in a temporary phrenzy; our law looks upon this as an aggravation of the offence, rather than as an excuse for any criminal misbehaviour«.[129] Blackstone likely borrowed the idea of a temporary »phrenzy« from the writings of Hale.[130] Recognizing, however, as his medieval forebears did, that drunkenness might impair a person's capacity to reason, Blackstone also listed intoxication alongside infancy, idiocy, and lunacy as an example of a case involving »a defect of understanding« such that will and act might not coincide.[131] All told, Blackstone's approach emphasized several insights: the voluntariness of intoxication for those who chose to drink to excess, the metaphor that might nevertheless be drawn between drunkenness and insanity, and the fact that the common law would generally treat intoxication as an aggravating rather than an excusing factor. We can find similar tendencies in the medieval English approach to dealing with drunkenness, particularly the condemnation of voluntary drunkenness and the tendency to treat inebriation as a damning factor rather than an excuse under some circumstances. Rabin's work suggests that there may also be some continuity in the tendency of jurors and judges – in medieval as well as early modern England – to treat some defendants' behavior as partially or wholly excusable despite the more severe tendencies of religious, moral, and legal treatises.

In short, the medieval English common law did not have a simple answer to the question of how drunkenness, like anger and other strong emotions, should affect the outcome of felony cases. Drunkenness might help a jury make the case for calling a death a misadventure, might assist a self-defender in arguing that he had no alternative but to kill the drunken person assaulting him, and might also incline a jury toward a felony conviction when a post-curfew brawl outside a tavern ended in homicide. In this last instance, the presumption appears to have been toward treating

125 Hawke (1657) 233–234. See also Hicks (trans.) (1659) 20, arguing that if a drunk man kills another, even though he acted out of ignorance, »this ignorance cometh by his own act and folly, which he might have resisted; therefore he shall not be priviledged, because he himself was the cause of such ignorance«.

126 Aquinas (1948) vol. 4, Pt. II–II, Q. 150, Art. 4, Reply Obj. 1.

127 Rabin (2004) 78–79.

128 On simple drunkenness, see Rabin (2004) 79; on insanity-drunkenness, see Rabin (2004) 83–85. See also Green (1985) 307 (quoting Martin Madan's observation regarding jury lenience and judge acquiescence in exercising mercy toward some offenders who had been »in liquor« at the time of their offense).

129 Blackstone (1770) 25–26.

130 Hale (1847) 32.

131 Blackstone (1770) 20–21.

such homicides as felonious. In considering whether a particular defendant haled before them merited conviction or acquittal, medieval English jurors considered a range of circumstances. While it is likely that alcohol factored into jury decision-making in individual cases, it is noteworthy that the medieval English common law made no explicit concession to drunken states or, for that matter, any explicit statement condemning crimes committed in a state of inebriation. This can be attributed to the fact that drunkenness, like anger, was treated as a vice that one might choose freely, and yet was also recognized, in extreme circumstances, as a state that might deprive a person of his or her capacity to reason. Rather than take a bright-line approach to alcohol intoxication, the common law left the issue to be sorted by judges and jurors. Given the resulting uncertainty, a man contemplating another drink at the tavern would have been wise to heed the summoner's advice to »drynk moore attemprely« lest he lose not only his »mynde and eek his lymes«,[132] but his very life at the gallows.

■

Bibliography

- Aquinas, Thomas (1948), Summa Theologica, vol. 4, translated by The Fathers of the English Dominican Province, New York
- Aristotle (1927), De Problemata, in: The Works of Aristotle, vol. 7, translated by E. S. Forster, Oxford
- Austin, Gregory A. (1985), Alcohol in Western Society from Antiquity to 1800: A Chronological Survey, Santa Barbara, CA
- Bacon, Francis (1630), The Elements of the Common Lawes of England, vol. 1, London
- Baker, J. H. (ed. and trans.) (1994), Reports from the Lost Notebooks of Sir James Dyer, vol. 2, London
- Bateson, Mary (ed. and trans.) (1904), Borough Customs, vol. 1., London
- Bennett, Judith M. (1996), Ale, Beer, and Brewsters in England: Women's Work in a Changing World, 1300–1600, Oxford
- Benson, Larry D. (ed.) (1987), The Riverside Chaucer, 3rd ed., Boston
- Blackstone, William (1770), Commentaries on the Laws of England, Book IV, Oxford
- Bolland, William Craddock et al. (eds.) (1912), The Eyre of Kent, 6 and 7 Edward II, A.D., 1313–1314, vol. 2, London
- Bromyard, John (1586), Summa praedicantium omni eruditione refertissima, Venice
- Butler, Sara M. (2010), Representing the Middle Ages: The Insanity Defense in Medieval England, in: Turner, Wendy J., Tory Vandeventer Pearman (eds.), The Treatment of Disabled Persons in Medieval Europe, Lewiston, 117–133
- Chobham, Thomas of (1968), Summa Confessorum, edited by F. Broomfield, Louvain
- Clanchy, M.T. (ed. and trans.) (1973), The Roll and Writ File of the Berkshire Eyre of 1248, London
- Coke, Edward (1644), The Third Part of the Institutes of the Laws of England, London
- Corran, Emily (2017), Moral Dilemmas in English Confessors' Manuals, in: Spencer, Andrew M., Carl Watkins (eds.), Thirteenth-Century England XVI: Proceedings of the Cambridge Conference, 1215, Woodbridge, 21–36
- Cox, Edward W. (ed.) (1871), Reports of Cases in Criminal Law Argued and Determined in All the Courts in England and Ireland, vol. 11, London
- Cox, Edward W. (ed.) (1890), Reports of Cases in Criminal Law Argued and Determined in All the Courts in England and Ireland, vol. 16, London
- Cox, Edward W. (ed.) (1921), Reports of Cases in Criminal Law Argued and Determined in the Courts of England, vol. 26, London
- Davis, Natalie Zemon (1987), Fiction in the Archives: Pardon Tales and Their Tellers in Sixteenth-Century France, Stanford
- Dawes, M. C. B. et al. (eds.) (1988), Calendar of Inquisitions Post Mortem, vol. 17, 15–23 Richard II, London
- Duggan, Kenneth F. (2017), The Hue and Cry in Thirteenth-Century England, in: Spencer, Andrew M., Carl Watkins (eds.), Thirteenth Century England XVI: Proceedings of the Cambridge Conference, 2015, Woodbridge, 153–172
- Ekwall, Eilert (1960), The Concise Dictionary of English Place Names, 4th ed., Oxford
- Flamborough, Robert (1971), Liber Poenitentialis: A Critical Edition with Introduction and Notes, edited by J. J. Francis Firth, Toronto
- French, Katherine (1997), Parochial Fund-raising in Late Medieval Somerset, in: French, Katherine et al. (eds.), The Parish in English Life, 1400–1600, Manchester, 115–132
- Gower, John (2003), Confessio Amantis, vol. 2, edited by Russell A. Peck and translated by Andrew Galloway, Kalamazoo
- Gradon, Pamela (ed.) (1965), Dan Michel's Ayenbite of Inwyt, vol. 1, London
- Green, Thomas A. (1985), Verdict According to Conscience: Perspectives on the English Criminal Trial Jury, 1200–1800, Chicago

132 Benson (ed.) (1987) 133 (Canterbury Tales, The Summoner's Tale, III(D).2053).

- Hale, Matthew (1847), The History of the Pleas of the Crown, vol. 2, 1st American ed., Philadelphia
- Hall, Jerome (1944), Intoxication and Criminal Responsibility, in: Harvard Law Review 57,7, 1045–1084
- Hanawalt, Barbara (ed. and trans.) (1976a), Crime in East Anglia in the Fourteenth Century: Norfolk Gaol Delivery Rolls, 1307–1316, Norwich
- Hanawalt, Barbara A. (1976b), Violent Death in Fourteenth- and Early Fifteenth-Century England, in: Comparative Studies in Society and History 18,3, 297–320
- Hanawalt, Barbara A. (1999), The Host, the Law, and the Ambiguous Space of Medieval London Taverns, in: Hanawalt, Barbara A., David Wallace (eds.), Medieval Crime and Social Control, Minneapolis, 204–223
- Harding, Alan (ed. and trans.) (1981), The Roll of the Shropshire Eyre of 1256, London
- Hawke, Michael (1657), The Grounds of the Lawes of England, London
- Helmholz, R. H. (2019), The Profession of Ecclesiastical Lawyers: An Historical Introduction, Cambridge
- Henry, Albert (1986), Un texte œnologique de Jofroi de Waterford et servais copale, in: Romania 425,1, 1–37
- Herrtage, Sidney J. (ed.) (1878), England in the Reign of King Henry the Eighth, Part I, Starkey's Life and Letters, London
- Hicks, Fabian (trans.) (1659), An Exact Abridgement of the Commentaries, or Reports of the Learned and Famous Lawyer, Edmond Plowden, London
- Hunnisett, R. F. (ed. and trans.) (1961), Bedfordshire Coroners' Rolls, Streatley
- Hurnard, Naomi (1969), The King's Pardon for Homicide before A.D. 1307, Oxford
- Ingle, Meghan Paulk (2002), Law on the Rocks: The Intoxication Defenses Are Being Eight-Sixed, in: Vanderbilt Law Review 55, 607–646
- Jenks, Edward (ed.) (1922), Stephen's Commentaries on the Laws of England, vol. 4, 17th ed., London
- Kadish, Sanford H. et al. (2017), Criminal Law and Its Processes: Cases and Materials, 10th ed., New York
- Kamali, Elizabeth Papp (2017), The Devil's Daughter of Hell Fire: Anger's Role in Medieval English Felony Cases, in: Law and History Review 35,1, 155–200
- Kamali, Elizabeth Papp (2019), Felony and the Guilty Mind in Medieval England, Cambridge
- Kamali, Elizabeth Papp, Thomas A. Green (2018), A Crossroads in Criminal Procedure: The Assumptions Underlying England's Adoption of Trial by Jury for Crime, in: Baker, Travis R. (ed.), Law and Society in Later Medieval England and Ireland: Essays in Honour of Paul Brand, Abingdon, 68–74
- Keiter, Mitchell (1997), Just Say No Excuse: The Rise and Fall of the Intoxication Defense, in: The Journal of Criminal Law and Criminology 87,2, 482–520
- Langland, William (2006), Piers Plowman, translated by E. Talbot Donaldson, edited by Elizabeth Robertson, Stephen H. A. Shepherd, New York
- Lyte, H. C. Maxwell (ed.) (1908), Calendar of the Patent Rolls, Henry III, A.D. 1247–1258, London
- Lyte, H. C. Maxwell (ed.) (1910), Calendar of the Patent Rolls, Henry III, A.D. 1258–1266, London
- Lyte, H. C. Maxwell (ed.) (1916), Calendar of Inquisitions Miscellaneous (Chancery), vol. 1, London
- Maitland, F. W. (ed. and trans.) (1889), Select Pleas in Manorial and Other Seignorial Courts: Reigns of Henry III and Edward I, London
- Mannyng, Robert (1983), Handlyng Synne, edited by Idelle Sullens, Binghampton, NY
- Marlowe, Douglas B. et al. (1999), Voluntary Intoxication and Criminal Responsibility, in: Behavioral Sciences and the Law 17, 195–217
- Martin, A. Lynn (2001), Alcohol, Sex, and Gender in Late Medieval and Early Modern Europe, Houndmills
- Martin, A. Lynn (2009), Alcohol, Violence, and Disorder in Traditional Europe, Kirksville, MO
- McAuley, Finbarr (1997), The Intoxication Defense in Criminal Law, in: The Irish Jurist 32, 243–296
- McIntosh, Marjorie Keniston (1998), Controlling Misbehavior in England, 1370–1600, Cambridge
- Mittermaier, C. J. A. (1840), On the Effect of Drunkenness Upon Criminal Responsibility and the Application of Punishment, in: American Jurist and Law Magazine 22,46, 290–333
- The National Archives (TNA)
  TNA JUST 1/664
  TNA JUST 1/1060
  TNA JUST 2/1
  TNA JUST 2/4
  TNA JUST 2/17
  TNA JUST 2/18
  TNA JUST 2/128
  TNA JUST 3/74/3
- Odgers, William Blake, Walter Blake Odgers (1920), The Common Law of England, vol. 2, 2nd ed., London
- Plowden, Edmund (1816), The Commentaries, or Reports of Edmund Plowden, Part I, London
- Powicke, F. M., C. R. Cheney (eds.) (1964), Councils & Synods, with Other Documents Relating to the English Church, II: A.D. 1205–1313, Part I: 1205–1265, Oxford
- Putnam, Bertha Haven (ed.) (1924), Early Treatises on the Practice of Justices of the Peace in the Fifteenth and Sixteenth Centuries, Oxford
- Putnam, Bertha Haven (ed.) (1938), Proceedings before the Justices of the Peace in the Fourteenth and Fifteenth Centuries, London
- Rabin, Dana (2004), Identity, Crime, and Legal Responsibility in Eighteenth-Century England, Houndmills
- Raithby, John (ed.) (1963), The Statutes of the Realm, vol. 1, London

- Riley, Henry Thomas (ed.) (1859), Munimenta Gildhallae Londoniensis; Liber Albus, Liber Custumarum, et Liber Horn, vol. 1, London
- Riley, Henry Thomas (ed.) (1860), Munimenta Gildhallae Londoniensis; Liber Albus, Liber Custumarum, et Liber Horn, vol. 2, part 2, London
- Riley, Henry Thomas (ed.) (1862), Munimenta Gildhallae Londoniensis; Liber Albus, Liber Custumarum, et Liber Horn, vol. 3, London
- Röhrkasten, Jens (ed.) (2008), The Worcester Eyre of 1275, Worcester
- Rosser, Gervase (1994), Going to the Fraternity Feast: Commensality and Social Relations in Late Medieval England, in: Journal of British Studies 33,4, 430–446
- Seabourne, Gwen, Alice Seabourne (2000), The Law on Suicide in Medieval England, in: The Journal of Legal History 21,1, 21–48
- Seneca (1928), Moral Essays, vol. 1, translated by John W. Basore, Cambridge, MA
- Sharpe, Reginald R. (ed.) (1890), Calendar of Wills Proved and Enrolled in the Court of Husting, London, A.D. 1258–A.D. 1688, vol. 2, London
- Sharpe, Reginald R. (ed.) (1899), Calendar of Letter Books Preserved among the Archives of the Corporation of the City of London, Letter-Book A, Circa A.D. 1275–1288, London
- Sharpe, Reginald R. (ed.) (1900), Calendar of Letter-Books Preserved among the Archives of the Corporation of the City of London, Letter-Book B, Circa A.D. 1275–1312, London
- Sharpe, Reginald R. (ed.) (1901), Calendar of Letter-Books Preserved among the Archives of the Corporation of the City of London, Letter-Book C, Circa A.D. 1291–1309, London
- Sharpe, Reginald R. (ed.) (1902), Calendar of Letter-Books Preserved among the Archives of the Corporation of the City of London, Letter-Book D, Circa A.D. 1309–1314, London
- Sharpe, Reginald R. (ed.) (1905), Calendar of Letter-Books Preserved among the Archives of the Corporation of the City of London, Letter-Book G, Circa A.D. 1352–1374, London
- Sharpe, Reginald R. (ed.) (1913), Calendar of Coroners Rolls of the City of London, A.D. 1300–1378, London
- Singh, R.U. (1933), History of the Defence of Drunkenness in English Criminal Law, in: The Law Quarterly Review 196, 528–546
- Skeel, Caroline A.J. (1926), Medieval Wills, in: History 10,40, 300–310
- Stenton, Doris Mary (ed. and trans.) (1937), Rolls of the Justices in Eyre Being the Rolls of Pleas and Assizes for Yorkshire in 3 Henry III (1218–1219), London
- Stenton, Doris Mary (ed. and trans.) (1940), Rolls of the Justices in Eyre for Gloucestershire, Warwickshire and Staffordshire, 1221, 1222, London
- Sutherland, Donald W. (ed. and trans.) (1983), The Eyre of Northamptonshire, 3–4 Edward III, A.D. 1329–1330, vol. 1, London
- Styles, Philip (ed.) (1945), The Victoria History of the County of Warwick, vol. 3, London
- Swain, Warren (2020), Without the Power to Drink or Contract, in: Edinburgh Law Review 24,1, 26–48
- Thorne, Samuel (ed. and trans.) (1968), Bracton On the Laws and Customs of England, vol. 2, Cambridge, MA
- Wenzel, Siegfried (ed. and trans.) (1989), Fasciculus Morum: A Fourteenth-Century Preacher's Handbook, University Park
- Wharton, Francis (1880), A Treatise on Criminal Law, 8th ed., Philadelphia
- Withington, Phil (2011), Intoxicants and Society in Early Modern England, in: The Historical Journal 54,3, 631–657
- Wycliffe, John (1871), Select English Works of John Wyclif, vol. 3, edited by Thomas Arnold, Oxford

Big Apple

Jan Schröder

Zur Bedeutung der Wörter in der Rechts- und Sprachtheorie der frühen Neuzeit*

In dem viel zitierten Abschnitt 43 seiner »Philosophischen Untersuchungen« erklärt Ludwig Wittgenstein: »Die Bedeutung eines Wortes ist sein Gebrauch in der Sprache«.[1] Er wendet sich damit gegen die Vorstellung, Wörter seien (immer gleichbleibende?) »Benennungen von Gegenständen«. Wittgensteins Satz ist auch von Juristen aufgegriffen worden,[2] zuweilen wird sogar gefordert, die Juristen sollten ihre Interpretationslehre nunmehr an der Wittgensteinschen »Gebrauchstheorie« orientieren.[3]

In Wirklichkeit gibt es aber eine Gebrauchstheorie der Wortbedeutung in der deutschen Rechtswissenschaft schon etwa dreihundert Jahre vor Wittgenstein.[4] Diese Tatsache ist an sich bekannt,[5] nicht aber ihre Gründe. Im Folgenden soll dargestellt werden, wie es vor dem Hintergrund einer ganz anders orientierten spätantiken und mittelalterlichen Lehre zu der Gebrauchstheorie gekommen ist. Aus rechtshistorischer Sicht ist diese Frage bisher nicht behandelt worden. In der philosophiegeschichtlichen Literatur ist die umfassendste mir bekannte Untersuchung das Buch von Stephan Meier-Oeser über die Entwicklung der Zeichentheorie von der Spätantike bis zur frühen Neuzeit.[6] Naturgemäß beschränkt sich Meier-Oeser aber auf die philosophischen Quellen und spart die oberen Fakultäten (Theologie, Medizin, Rechtswissenschaft) aus.

Ich fasse zunächst die Entwicklung in der Rechtswissenschaft von Bartolus bis in das 18. Jahrhundert kurz zusammen (I), wende mich dann dem Schicksal der Schlüsselbegriffe Autorität (II) und Etymologie (III) in Philosophie und Rechtswissenschaft zu und schließe mit einer Zusammenfassung (IV). Angesichts der enormen Fülle von Quellen und der schwer zu übersehenden, zersplitterten und hochspezialisierten philosophischen Literatur strebe ich natürlich keine Vollständigkeit an, öfters mag auch eine wichtige Quellen- oder Literaturstelle fehlen. Die Grundzüge der Entwicklung hoffe ich aber richtig gesehen zu haben.

I. Der Ausgangspunkt: Bartolus' Lehre von der »significatio propria« und ihre Verdrängung in der frühen Neuzeit

In seiner Kommentierung von D. 1, 1, 9 (»omnes populi«) fragt Bartolus, wie die eigentliche Bedeutung, die »significatio propria« eines Wortes ermittelt wird. Sie ergibt sich nach seiner Meinung zunächst aus der Autorität, dann aus der Definition und schließlich aus der »Allusion« oder der Ableitung (»derivatio«) des Wortes,[7] wir würden sagen aus der Etymologie. Bartolus' Lehre wird von zahlreichen Juristen noch in das 15. und 16., sogar in das frühe 17. Jahrhundert weiter getragen.

* Ich widme diese Abhandlung, die im März 2021 fertiggestellt wurde, dem Andenken von Sten Gagnér (geboren am 3. März 1921) und von Michael Stolleis (gestorben am 18. März 2021). Die von diesem zum 70. Geburtstag Gagnérs 1991 herausgegebene Festschrift trug den Titel »Die Bedeutung der Wörter«.

1 Wittgenstein (1960), (§) 43, S. 311.

2 Nachweise bei Schröder (2020), II, § 147 I 1, S. 197 f. Wittgensteins Satz wird zitiert z. B. von Fikentscher (1977) 291; Schiffauer (1979) 86; Koch / Rüssmann (1982) 136. Auf Wittgenstein greifen u. a. auch zurück Säcker (1984), Einleitung, Rn. 120; Depenheuer (1988) 39–41; Christensen (1989), s. Register S. 341.

3 So verstehe ich Schiffauer (1979) 86.

4 Ob im Sinne der Wittgensteinschen Theorie, mag hier dahinstehen. Sicherlich herrscht aber seit dem 17. Jahrhundert nicht (mehr) die Vorstellung, Rechtsbegriffe seien unveränderliche »Benennungen von Gegenständen«.

5 Schröder (2020), I, § 31, S. 146.

6 Meier-Oeser (1997) erörtert die Theorie der Wortbedeutung im Rahmen der allgemeineren Lehre vom Zeichen. Die im Folgenden unter III. behandelte Geschichte des etymologischen Gesichtspunkts spielt bei ihm allerdings keine Rolle.

7 Bartolus (1588). Er behandelt zu D. 1, 1, 9, S. 41 ff., die deklarative oder expositive Interpretation von Statuten. Zur significatio propria: »Quaero, unde sumatur ista propria, et qualiter cognoscatur?«. »Primo ab auctoritate […]«, »Item a diffinitione […]«, »Item quando praedicta deficiunt, sumitur propria significatio ex allusione seu derivatione vocabuli […]« (S. 43).

Unter ihnen sind die ersten Verfasser selbständiger Interpretationstraktate wie Constantius Rogerius, Bartholomaeus Caepolla und Valentin Wilhelm Forster,[8] aber auch andere namhafte Autoren wie Andreas Alciatus, Johannes Corasius und Johannes Althusius.[9]

Blickt man dann aber in die Literatur des mittleren und späten 17. sowie des 18. Jahrhunderts, so zeigt sich ein ganz anderes Bild. Mehr und mehr tritt an die Stelle der bartolischen Trias der allgemeine, gewöhnliche Sprachgebrauch. Schon nach Hugo Grotius sind die Wörter im Sinne des »populären Sprachgebrauchs« zu verstehen, und ebenso äußern sich seine naturrechtlichen Nachfolger Samuel Pufendorf und Christian Wolff.[10] Dieselbe Lehre findet sich auch in den zeitgenössischen Schriften über die Gesetzesinterpretation, so in der umfangreichen Dissertation von Johannes Eichel von 1650 und in einem Werk des Hamburger Polyhistors Vincenz Placcius von 1693.[11] In der juristischen Hermeneutik des 18. Jahrhunderts scheint dann unumstritten zu sein, dass der gewöhnliche, übliche Sprachgebrauch maßgeblich ist.[12]

Wie ist diese Neuorientierung der juristischen Bedeutungslehre zu erklären? Offenbar verlieren die Gesichtspunkte, die Bartolus und seine Anhänger für entscheidend hielten – nämlich Autorität, Definition und Etymologie – nach und nach an Gewicht. Unter ihnen kommt es im Grunde nur auf Autorität und Etymologie an, mit deren Hilfe sich eine Wortbedeutung ja erst erkennen läßt, während eine (Real-)Definition[13] voraussetzt, dass die Bedeutung eines Wortes schon auf andere Weise erkannt ist. Auf die beiden Schlüsselbegriffe Autorität (II.) und Etymologie (III.) wollen wir uns deshalb konzentrieren.

II. Die alten Erkenntnismittel und ihr Ansehensverlust in der frühen Neuzeit.

1. Autorität

Bartolus hat seinen Begriff der »Autorität« nicht weiter expliziert. Er bringt aber Beispiele in Gestalt von Worterklärungen aus dem Digestentitel »De verborum significatione« (D. 50, 16), aus denen sich ergibt, dass er an die Autorität römischer Juristen denkt, die diese Regeln über Wortbedeutungen aufgestellt haben oder bezeugen. Autorität haben also angesehene Repräsentanten der Rechtswissenschaft. Autorität hat aber natürlich auch das Gesetz selbst,[14] wenn es Legaldefinitionen kreiert.[15]

8 Rogerius (1549) 23, 27 f., Rn. 5, 6; Caepolla (1551), Sp. 12, Rn. 39; Forster (1613), lib. 2, cap. 4, Nr. 17, S. 353.

9 Alciatus (1530) 6 (im weiteren allerdings sehr kritisch zum etymologischen Argument); Corasius (1603), Bd. 1, S. 437 ff. (S. 439, Rn. 18); Althusius (1649), lib. 1, cap. 17, Rn. 5, S. 52. Weiterhin etwa noch Everardus a Middelburg (1568) 50, Rn. 11; Decianus (1579), vol. 2 resp. 1, Nr. 38, S. 11.

10 Grotius (1680), lib. 2, cap. 16, § II, S. 304: »Si nulla sit conjectura quae ducat alio verba intelligenda sunt ex proprietate, non Grammatica quae est ex origine, sed populari ex usu«; Pufendorf (1672), lib. 5, cap. 12, § 3, S. 525: »verba intelligenda sunt in proprio suo, & famoso, ut loquuntur, significatu, quem ipsis imposuit [...] popularis usus«; Wolff (1746), VI, § 470, S. 327: »a communi usu loquendi recedendum non est«, wenn keine »rationes urgentes in contrarium« vorliegen.

11 Hahn / Eichel (1650), cap. 13, § 11: Die Bedeutung ist »omne ex solo usu & consuetudine desumendum« (zu Eichel s. Schröder (2020), I, § 28, 1, S. 136); Placcius (1693), cap. 8, Rn. 19, S. 221 f.: Der eigentliche Sinn ist der, welcher »nunc omnibus lingua illa sive communione orationis utentibus« als maßgeblich erscheint. Placcius hatte schon in einer unter Pseudonym erschienenen, ebenso betitelten Schrift dieselbe Auffassung vertreten: Nomicus Pacemutus Analyticophilus (1664).

12 Holderrieder (1736), sect. 2, § 12, S. 33: »populari atque vulgato sensui tam diu esse inhaerendum, donec necessitas nos urget ab eo recedere«; Eckhard (1750), lib. 1, cap. 1, § 17, S. 8: Die grammatische Interpretation »sensum verborum ex usu loquendi declarat«; Thibaut (1806), § 2, S. 12: Der »Wortverstand des Gesetzes« sind die »Ideen, welche der gemeine Redegebrauch des Volkes oder der besondere Redegebrauch einer Classe von Personen mit den Worten verbindet«; Glück (1797), § 35, S. 227: Die Bedeutung richtet sich im Zweifel »nach dem gewöhnlichen Sprachgebrauche der Nation, für welche das Gesetz bestimmt war«.

13 *Legaldefinitionen*, wenn sie wirklich eine neue Wortschöpfung darstellen, kann man dagegen auch der Autorität zuordnen, s. den folgenden Text mit den Fn. 14, 15.

14 Von Autorität des *Gesetzes* sprechen denn auch mehrere Juristen, welche die bartolische Trias übernehmen, etwa Rogerius (1547) 27, Rn. 5; Caepolla (1551), Sp. 12, Rn. 39 (»ut si in aliqua lege hoc dicatur«); Decianus (1579).

15 Bartolus (1588), zu D. 1, 1, 9, S. 43, ordnet der »diffinitio« nur verschiedene Legaldefinitionen (Testament, D. 28, 1, 1; tutela, D. 26, 1, 1 pr.; obligatio, Inst. 1, 3, 13 pr.) zu, die er auch bei der »auctoritas« hätte unterbringen können.

1. *Die alte (spätantike und mittelalterliche) Lehre: »Imposition« der eigentlichen Wortbedeutung durch eine Autorität und Irrelevanz eines abweichenden Sprachgebrauchs*

Um Bartolus' Lehre einordnen zu können, muß man sich einige Grundbegriffe der abendländischen Sprachtheorie (die als solche freilich bis zum 19. Jahrhundert noch keine selbständige Wissenschaft ist) vergegenwärtigen. In der griechischen Philosophie war umstritten, ob die Wörter ihre Bedeutung von Natur aus haben (»physei«) oder erst durch menschliche Setzung (»thesei«) bekommen.[16] Platon hatte in seinem Dialog »Kratylos« noch die »physei«-Theorie zu verteidigen versucht. Aber angesichts der biblischen Erzählung von der Sprachverwirrung nach dem Turmbau zu Babel und der tatsächlichen Verschiedenheit der Sprachen war Platons Standpunkt – nach dem ja alle Sprachen gleich sein müßten – offensichtlich unhaltbar. Die weitere Diskussion orientierte sich deshalb an Aristoteles, der in seiner Schrift »Peri hermeneias« (später übersetzt als »De interpretatione«) erklärt hatte, dass die Wörter ihre Bedeutung κατὰ συνθήκην (kata syntheken), nach Vereinbarung, haben.[17] Maßgebend für die spätere Entwicklung wurde die Deutung dieses »kata syntheken« durch Anicius Manlius Severinus Boet(h)ius, den einflußreichen römischen Interpreten und Vermittler der antiken Philosophie. Boetius übersetzte »kata syntheken« mit »secundum placitum«, also »nach Gefallen«,[18] und dieses Verständnis der Wortschöpfung behauptete sich[19] auch in der philosophischen Literatur der Neuzeit.[20] Die Wörter haben ihre Bedeutung nicht von Natur aus, sondern erhalten sie nach dem Gefallen, der Willkür, der Menschen.

Am Anfang steht also eine Bedeutungsverleihung, von den Quellen als »Imposition«[21] bezeichnet. Dabei soll die erste Imposition immer die maßgebliche bleiben. In seinen »Summulae logicales«, der verbreitetsten mittelalterlichen Logik, schreibt Petrus Hispanus, die Wortbedeutung »ad placitum« beruhe auf dem Willen des ersten Wortschöpfers.[22] Warum das so sein muß, erklärt sein Kommentator Johannes Versorius. Wenn einfach das »placitum« jedes beliebigen (späteren) Sprechers den Wortsinn bestimmte, meint Versorius, dann wäre die Bedeutung eines Wortes bis ins Unendliche veränderbar und es gäbe keine sichere Kenntnis. Deshalb muß es auf das »placitum« des

16 Übersichtliche Darstellungen dazu geben Coseriu (1975) 42 ff., 68 ff.; Trabant (2006) 20 ff.

17 Aristoteles (2014), 2. Kap., 16a; 4. Kap., 16b, 17a.

18 Boetius (1847b), Sp. 293 ff. (301 C): »Nomen igitur est vox significativa secundum placitum sine tempore« (im Gegensatz zum Verb, das ein Wort mit Zeitbezug, aber ebenso »ad placitum« ist).

19 Ausführlich dazu Coseriu (1967).

20 An die Stelle von »ad placitum« tritt auch »secundum arbitrium« oder »ex institutione«. Drei Belege aus sehr unterschiedlichen Logiken: Mittelalter: Petrus Hispanus (1572), fol. 7v: »Vocum significativum alia significat naturaliter, alia ad placitum. Vox significativa naturaliter, est illa, quae apud omnes homines idem repraesentat, ut latratus canem, & gemitus infirmorum. Vox significativa ad placitum, est illa, quae ad voluntatem primi instituentis aliquid repraesentat. ut homo, hominem, equus, equum«. – Frühe Neuzeit: Burgersdicius (1666), lib. 1, cap. 24, II 1, S. 78: voces bezeichnen »animi conceptus« und zwar »ex instituto, sive κατὰ συνθήκην«, »ex usu arbitrario hominum eadem societate utentium«; Hobbes (1839) 1 ff.: »I suppose the original of names to be arbitrary« (Kap. 2, 2, S. 14). – Zur allgemeinen Anerkennung der aristotelischen Theorie in der Renaissance und in allen philosophischen Schulen s. auch Demonet (1992). Zu abweichenden »kratylistischen« Tendenzen in der Literaturtheorie der frühen Neuzeit s. jedoch Gardt (1994) 45 ff., 129 ff.

21 Von »positio« spricht Boetius (1847b), Sp. 301 D: Die Bedeutung wird den Wörtern verliehen »secundum positionem, quemadmodum ipsis hominibus placuit, a quibus nomina illa formata sunt«; von »impositio« zum Beispiel Abaelardus (1836) 173 ff. (212) Wortbedeutungen, »quae videlicet, prout libuit ab hominibus format [...] et ad res designandas impositæ«; Alsted (1628), lib. 1, cap. 3, S. 35: »Hinc recte dicimus, omnem vocem esse impositionis [...]«, und viele andere. – Ausführlich zur »impositio« mit einer Fülle von Quellenbelegen Meier-Oeser (1997), vor allem 59–65, 147–153, 263–279, vgl. weiter die Angaben im Register (470).

22 Petrus Hispanus (1572), fol. 7v: »Vox significativa ad placitum, est illa, quae ad voluntatem primi instituentis aliquid repraesentat, ut homo, hominem, equus, equum«.

ersten Imponenten ankommen.[23] Es gibt also nicht weitere, zweite, dritte und vierte usw. Impositionen, die den ursprünglichen Wortsinn abwandeln.[24]

Wer ist nun dieser erste Imponent oder Impositor, auf dessen »placitum« es ankommt? Entsprechend der biblischen Schöpfungsgeschichte konnte man Gott als Sprachschöpfer ansehen, dann auch Adam, der den Tieren und seinem Weib einen Namen gegeben hatte (1. Mose 2, 20 und 3, 20).[25] Aber das galt nur für das Hebräische und nicht für die anderen siebzig oder mehr Sprachen, die man am Beginn der Neuzeit kannte. Sie beruhen offenbar auf menschlichen Impositionen. Der Impositor kann bekannt sein, wie etwa ein Gesetzgeber, der eine Legaldefinition einführt oder ein bedeutender Gelehrter, der ein Wort für einen bestimmten Begriff findet. Soweit man annimmt, das Wort müsse irgendwelche Eigenschaften des bezeichneten Objekts wiedergeben, wird zuweilen überhaupt verlangt, daß der Impositor wissenschaftlich geschult, ein Metaphysiker[26] oder ein Philosoph und Grammatiker[27] ist. Die Imposition erfolgt also durch eine geistige, politische[28] oder sonstige Autorität. Ist der Wortschöpfer unbekannt, dann genügt es wohl auch, wenn eine andere Autorität die Wortbedeutung bezeugt.[29] Allerdings reicht die Autorität allein noch nicht aus, um eine Imposition in der Sprachgemeinschaft durchzusetzen. Es muß eine entsprechende Sprachgewohnheit hinzukommen.[30] Aber der »usus populi«, der Sprachgebrauch des Volkes,

23 Johannes Versorius, in: Petrus Hispanus (1572), fol. 8 r–v: »si vox significet ad placitum, sua significatio erit variabilis in infinitum, et sic nulla erit certa cognitio de significatione vocis significativae«. Variabel ist nur das nicht, »quod determinate sit ad placitum unius, sicut est vox significativa, quae significat solum ad placitum primi instituentis« (auch zitiert bei Meier-Oeser (1997) 273 Anm. 354, aber ohne das letzte »significat«). Die Bedeutung der ersten Imposition betonen ohne weitere Begründung z. B. auch Boetius (1847b), Sp. 301 D: Die nicht naturaliter gebildeten Wörter gehen zurück auf den »Primus qui rebus nomina condidit«; Alsted (1628), lib. 1 cap. 3, S. 35: »Hinc recte dicimus, omnem vocem esse impositionis, vel primae, vel secundae«.

24 Allerdings kennt man neben der ersten auch eine zweite Imposition. Aber sie ändert nicht die Bedeutung der ersten, sondern bezieht sich, anders als diese, nicht auf Dinge und Begriffe, sondern auf Wörter. S. dazu Pinborg (1967) 37 f., 45 f.; Hickman (1976); Kelly (2002) 17–23. Davon abweichend, nämlich als eine Modifikation der Wortbedeutung, scheint hingegen Roger Bacon die zweite Imposition zu verstehen, dazu Fredborg (1981) 168 f. Anders möglicherweise auch der von Meier-Oeser (1997) 149 zitierte Johannes Aznar (1513).

25 Beispiele aus der Literatur der frühesten Neuzeit: *Gott* als Sprachschöpfer: Keckermann (1603), lib. 1, sect. 1, cap. 1, S. 10; Timpler (1612b), lib. 3, cap. 4, problema 12, S. 310; Hornejus (1642), lib. 3, quaestio 3, Rn. 4, S. 304 f. So noch im 18. Jahrhundert Süssmilch (1766); *Adam* als Sprachschöpfer: Timpler (1612b), wie oben. Belege auch bei Gardt (1999) 343–348; Meier-Oeser (1997) 149 (Johannes Aznar 1513).

26 So z. B. Roger Bacon, De signis, § 156, nach Fredborg (1981) 168.

27 So der dänische Grammatiker Boethius de Dacia (ca. 1240–1280), Modi significandi, Q. 12, 52–57: Der Imponent muß Grammatiker sein, um das Wort richtig in die Sprache einzufügen, und Philosoph, um die Eigenschaften des Gegenstandes zu erkennen: »Unde si [sc. impositor] purus grammaticus esset, proprietates rerum non consideraret, et si purus philosophus esset, modos significandi et constructiones non consideraret, et ideo debet esse uterque, ut possit imponere voces ad significandum sub modis significandi designantibus proprietates circa res ipsas significatas«, zitiert nach Beuerle (2010) 185. Ein ähnliches Zitat von Boethius de Dacia bei Meier-Oeser (1997) 75 Anm. 141.

28 S. etwa Johannes a Sancto Thoma (1948), 655b 47 f.: »impositio et destinatio a republica«, zitiert bei Meier-Oeser (1997) 274, und die weiteren Nachweise dort 273 ff.

29 So sind die Autoritäten, die Bartolus aus dem Digestentitel »De verborum significatione« für die Wortbedeutung anführt, wohl eher wortsinnbezeugende als wortschöpfende: D. 50, 16, 83: Güter (bona) kann man nicht die nennen, die größere Nachteile als Vorteile haben (»Javolenus lib. 5 ex Plautio«). D. 50, 16, 235 pr.: Unterscheidung von ferri, portari und agi (»[Gaius] libro tertio ad legem duodecim tabularum«). Hält man allerdings alle »leges« der Digesten für regelrechte Gesetze, dann handelt es sich hier um die Autorität des Gesetzes und nicht um die eines namhaften Autors.

30 Augustinus (2017), S. 69 ff., lib. 3, 3, S. 118: »res omnium mentibus communiter sunt insitae, nomina uero ut cuique placet imponit; quorum uis auctoritate atque consuetudine maxime nititur« (auch zitiert bei Meier-Oeser [1997] 28 Anm. 135, der aber nicht »imponit«, sondern »imposita« schreibt); Valla (1540) 643–761: »Nam quis nescit maximam loquendi partem autoritate niti & consuetudine« (lib. 2, S. 708. Valla erklärt allerdings später die »consuetudo« für maßgeblich, s. u. 2); Manderston (1528), fol. B 4va: »impositio est actus voluntatis per quem terminus imponatur ad significandum [...] quaedam est sufficiens, et ad talem requiruntur duo: scilicet quod fiat ab habente auctoritatem et quod recipiatur apud illos quoad fit illud impositio« (zitiert nach Meier-Oeser [1997] 147 Anm. 127; weitere Belege dort 149 Anm. 131, 274 Anm. 356).

kann die Imposition nur bestätigen, nicht jedoch von sich aus einen Wortsinn schaffen oder verändern. »Das Volk kann nicht machen, dass die eigentliche Bezeichnung [propria significatio] einer Sache wirklich verändert wird«, heißt es bei Bartolus.[31] Ein etwa abweichender volkstümlicher Sprachgebrauch repräsentiert also niemals die eigentliche Bedeutung eines Wortes, die man vielmehr immer auf die ursprüngliche Imposition durch eine Autorität zurückführt.

2. *Übergänge zur neuen Theorie: Die allmähliche Aufwertung des gewöhnlichen Sprachgebrauchs*

Die Lehre, daß ein von den Autoritäten abweichender Sprachgebrauch des Volkes wirkungslos ist und nichts an der »propria significatio« eines Wortes ändert, ist bis in die frühe Neuzeit hinein herrschend. Ganz unumstritten war sie aber schon am Ende des Mittelalters und in der frühesten Neuzeit nicht mehr. Vor allem gab es Widerspruch von humanistischer Seite. Besonders nachdrücklich kritisiert der bedeutende römische Philologe Lorenzo Valla (gest. 1457) die Impositions- und Autoritätstheorie. Das Volk, so sagt er, spreche besser als die Philosophen.[32] Zum Beispiel nennt das Volk ein Faß leer, in dem keine Feuchtigkeit ist, ein Fischbecken leer, in dem kein Wasser oder Fische sind. Der Philosoph dagegen sagt, es sei nicht leer, weil Luft darin ist. Aber wenn alles in der Natur voll wäre, dann gäbe es keine Leere. Oder Aristoteles sagt, eins sei keine Zahl, sondern der Anfang (»principium«) der Zahlen. Aber die Anfänge sind die Sachen selbst: wer den Anfang eines Buches liest, liest das Buch selbst. Wenn zwei Frauen abgezählte Hühnereier verteilen und die eine erhält die mit den geraden, die andere die mit den ungeraden Zahlen, dann bekommt die zweite das Ei, wenn nur ein einziges da ist. »Manchmal haben kleine Frauen eine richtigere Ansicht über die Bedeutung von Wörtern als die größten Philosophen.«[33] Das betont Valla immer wieder: Maßgeblich für die Bedeutung eines Wortes ist der Sprachgebrauch des Volkes, bei ihm liegt (nach einer auch später immer wieder zitierten Horaz-Stelle) die Entscheidung und die Norm der Sprache.[34]

So weit geht die juristische und schulphilosophische Literatur zwar noch nicht. Aber gerade die Juristen waren schon im Spätmittelalter auf die Frage aufmerksam geworden, worauf es ankommen sollte, wenn die »eigentliche« Bedeutung und der Sprachgebrauch auseinandergehen. In diesem Fall hatte sogar schon Bartolus gemeint, bei Statuten gelte der gemeine Sprachgebrauch, sofern sie nicht ausdrücklich auf die »propria significatio« verweisen.[35] Baldus wollte von der »propria significatio« zugunsten des gemeinen Sprachgebrauchs abweichen, wenn die »mens« des Gesetzes es erfordere.[36] Spätere Juristen gehen weiter und meinen, der Sprachgebrauch habe generell Vorrang, und

31 Bartolus (1509) zu D. 33, 10, 7 (»Labeo ait«), Rn. 4–6, fol. 96 r: »Praeterea populus non posset facere, quod [quo?] vere alteretur propria significatio rei«. Vgl. auch Caepolla (1551), Sp. 12, Rn. 42: »Item proprius sensus vocabuli est ille, quem lex ei dat, non quem vulgus imperitum assignat«.

32 Valla (1540), lib. 1, S. 643–761, 684 f.: »Melius igitur populus, quam philosophus loquitur«. Hier auch das im Text folgende Beispiel.

33 Valla (1540), lib. 1, S. 649 (falsch paginiert als 651): »Itaque melius de intellectu verborum mulierculae nonunquam sentiunt, quam summi philosophi.«

34 Valla (1540), lib. 1, S. 685: »Respondeat populus penes se esse arbitrium, et normam loquendi«. Weitere Stellen, an denen Valla die Maßgeblichkeit des gewöhnlichen Sprachgebrauchs betont, finden sich zum Beispiel a. a. O., lib. 1, S. 651 (falsch paginiert als 653): »At philosophia ac dialectica […]«, 656: »Ergo ut veritati […]«; 658: »Quis enim dixerit […]«, 679: »Agamus igitur […]«, 681: »Si alius adhuc […]«; lib. 2, S. 709: »itaque consuetudine tanquam quodam iure civili standum est«; lib. 3, S. 731: »relicta veterum consuetudine […]«, 751: »Id fit consuetudine […]«, 756: »ac quotidianae communique loquendo consuetudine«.). Zu Vallas Sprachtheorie Gerl (1974) 191 ff., 211 ff. (hier auch zahlreiche Belege zum Vorrang des gewöhnlichen Sprachgebrauchs bei Valla); Waswo (1987) 88 ff., 207 ff. Sehr kritisch zu Waswo: Vickers (2002) 320–329.

35 Bartolus (1509). Baldus (1586), zu C. 1, 14, 5 (non dubium), Rn. 8, fol. 65r, versteht ihn allerdings in dem umgekehrten Sinn: auf den »communis usus loquendi« kommt es nur dann an, wenn das Gesetz auf ihn verweist.

36 Baldus (1586), fol. 65v. Er demonstriert das an einem alten rhetorischen Beispiel: Es ist verboten, im Palast Blut zu vergießen. Wie aber, wenn im Palast ein Aderlaß vorgenommen wird? Hier liegt zwar nach der »propria significatio« ein »Blutvergießen« vor, nicht aber nach der »mens« des Gesetzes und dem Verständnis des Wortes »Blutvergießen« im gemeinen Sprachgebrauch.

dies sei auch schon die Ansicht von Bartolus und Baldus gewesen.[37] Für Francisco Suárez ist das dann ein Grund, auch den Sprachgebrauch auf die Ebene der eigentlichen Bedeutung, der »propria significatio«, zu heben. Er zählt drei Arten der »propria significatio« auf: Die erste, »natürliche«, beruht auf »placitum« und Imposition (z. B. »mors« als Tod); neben ihr steht eine zweite »zivile«, welche die natürliche ausdehnt (z. B. »mors civilis« als bürgerlicher Tod); schließlich aber läßt sich noch eine dritte hinzufügen, die man »usualis« nennen kann, die vom Gebrauch und der Sprachgewohnheit herrührt und große Bedeutung in der Rechtswissenschaft hat.[38] Sie tritt sogar an die Stelle der »natürlichen«, wenn sie die ursprüngliche Bedeutung verdrängt, weshalb Suárez aus ihr gar keinen besonderen Einteilungsgesichtspunkt machen möchte.[39] Ebenso äußert sich Georg Frantzke in seinem Pandektenkommentar von 1644.[40] In dieselbe Richtung bewegt sich, ähnlich vorsichtig, die Schulphilosophie der frühesten Neuzeit. So weist etwa Johannes a Sancto Thoma darauf hin, daß Normen ja nicht nur durch ein Gesetz, sondern auch durch Gewohnheit geschaffen werden können.[41] Der Sprachgebrauch erhält jetzt also den Rang der »eigentlichen« (propria) Bedeutung, den man ihm früher verweigert hatte. Aber neben ihm bleibt immer noch die ursprüngliche Imposition maßgeblich.

3. *Der Durchbruch zum »gewöhnlichen Sprachgebrauch« und zur Historizität der Sprache*

Der letzte Entwicklungsschritt im 17. Jahrhundert liegt dann darin, daß sich die »propria significatio« überhaupt nur noch nach dem Sprachgebrauch richten soll. Ein wichtiger Grund dafür dürfte sein, daß sich in der Sprachtheorie allmählich ein historisches Denken verbreitet.[42] Man erkennt die Geschichtlichkeit der Sprache; der Sprachgebrauch kann über die primäre Imposition einer Wortbedeutung hinweggehen und wandelt sich ständig. Besonders deutlich wird der Zusammenhang in der Dissertation von Johannes Eichel über die Gesetzesinterpretation (1650). »Am Anfang«, so sagt er, »sind die Wörter den Dingen durch freien Willen auferlegt worden«. »Aber mit fortschreitender Zeit wurden die Bezeichnungen, die den Dingen nicht richtig zugeteilt erschienen, durch den Gebrauch oder auch die Sachkunde derjenigen, welche die Kunst des Sprechens beherrschten, korrigiert und verändert, so daß wir nun über die eigentliche Bedeutung der Wörter weder aus der ersten Imposition, noch aus der Etymologie und noch viel weniger aus der Allusion urteilen können«,[43] vielmehr »meinen wir, daß die eigentliche Bedeutung eines Wortes in jeder Sprache ganz aus dem Gebrauch und der Gewohnheit

37 Etwa Caepolla (1551), Sp. 10, Rn. 27 (unter Berufung auf Baldus, über den er aber möglicherweise nicht hinausgehen will). Everardus a Middelburg (1568), locus ab etymologia, Rn. 10, S. 50 (Vorrang des gemeinen Sprachgebrauchs bei Statuten, unter Berufung auf Bartolus). Bei Unbekanntheit der eigentlichen Bedeutung bzw. Dunkelheit soll der gemeine Sprachgebrauch auch maßgeblich sein nach Lagus (1592), pars 1, cap. 8, Rn. 6, S. 40, und Althusius (1649), lib. 1, cap. 17, Rn. 9, S. 53 (unter Berufung u. a. auf Bartolus).

38 Suárez (1613), lib. 6, cap. 1, Rn. 9, S. 418: »Quibus [sc. den ersten beiden] addi potest tertia significatio, quae vocari potest usualis, qui est ab usu, & consuetudine loquendi, quae magnam vim habere solet in significatione vocum interpretanda, adeo ut in legum expositione proprietati etiam verborum usus praeferendus sit, ut iuris periti cum Barth. docent«. Allerdings vereinfacht Suárez hier die eben dargestellte juristische Lehre.

39 Suárez, wie vorige Fn.: »nam si usus verbi sit communis totius populi in vulgari modo loquendi, iam illa significatio est facta magis propria magisque naturalis, quam primaeva«.

40 Frantzke (1644), lib. 1, tit. 3, Rn. 17, S. 42: Die natürliche Bedeutung ergibt sich, »quando intelliguntur [sc. verba], uti jacent, & ab initio rebus imposita, *aut* certo communi usu totius populi in vulgari modo loquendi recepta fuerunt« (kursiv von mir). Bei zweideutigen Wörtern soll es sogar allein auf den »communis usus« ankommen (Rn. 23, S. 43).

41 Johannes a Sancto Thoma (1948) 719 b: »consuetudinem habere vim legis. Ergo consuetudo introducens aliquid ad significandum eadem auctoritate introducit rem illa in signum, qua ipsa lex introduceret«, nach Meier-Oeser (1997) 278 Anm. 366. Meier-Oeser spricht in diesem Zusammenhang von einem »juristischen Modell der Begründung sprachlicher Bedeutung« (277).

42 So schon, m. E. zutreffend, Meier-Oeser (1997) 279.

43 Hahn / Eichel (1650), cap. 13, VII, fol. I 2v, I 3r: Nomina »ab initio liberrima voluntate fuerunt imposita, ita procedente tempore ea [sc. nomina], quae haud recte rebus tributa visa sunt, usu vel etiam peritia illorum, qui artem dicendi calluerunt, correcta & mutata sunt, ut adeo de proprietate vocabulorum neque ex prima impositione, neque etymologia, multo minus allusione judicare queamus«.

herzunehmen ist«.[44] Ähnlich hatte schon 25 Jahre vorher Hugo Grotius geäußert, die Wörter seien nach dem populären Gebrauch zu verstehen und nicht nach ihrem ursprünglichen grammatischen Sinn und dazu mit einem Prokop-Zitat angemerkt, die Wörter könnten ihren Sinn verändern.[45] Nur noch kurz schreibt 1746 Christian Wolff: »Durch langen Gebrauch pflegt sich die eigentliche Bedeutung eines Wortes zu verändern, daher sind Verträge zu interpretieren nach dem Sprachgebrauch der Zeit, in der sie entstanden sind«.[46] Die Entdeckung der Geschichtlichkeit der Sprache ist offenbar eine Parallele zu der, gleichfalls im 17. Jahrhundert beginnenden,[47] Entdeckung der historischen Gesetzesinterpretation.

Auch außerhalb der Jurisprudenz verbreitet sich die Einsicht in die Historizität der Sprache und mit ihr die Neigung, nicht mehr nur auf die ursprüngliche Bedeutung eines Wortes, sondern auf den jeweiligen Sprachgebrauch zu sehen. Es ist kein Zufall, daß Lorenzo Valla, der Vorkämpfer des gemeinen Sprachgebrauchs, auch als einer der ersten das Faktum des Sprachwandels wissenschaftlich nutzbar macht. In seiner berühmt gewordenen Schrift über die Konstantinische Schenkung spielt nicht zuletzt der Nachweis eine Rolle, daß die gefälschte Urkunde Wortbedeutungen unterstellt, die es zur Zeit der angeblichen Niederschrift noch gar nicht gab (etwa »papa« als Anrede für den Papst).[48] In der Schulphilosophie weisen schon kurz nach 1600 Bartholomaeus Keckermann und Clemens Timpler auf die Veränderlichkeit der Sprache hin. Für Keckermann ist der Sprachwandel einer von vielen Beweisen dafür, daß die Wortbedeutung nicht »physei« (von Natur), sondern »thesei« (durch Setzung) entsteht,[49] und er erklärt dann, das Wort müsse, um Bezeichnungskraft zu haben, durch allgemeine Zustimmung und Gebrauch aufgenommen sein.[50] Ebenso verwendet Clemens Timpler die Historizität der Sprache als Beweis für Aristoteles' »thesei«-Lehre und leitet die Bedeutung der Wörter aus »Vertrag und Übereinkunft« ab.[51] Beide Autoren bedienen sich auch des alten Vergleichs zwischen dem Sprachsinn und dem Münzwert: der eine wie der andere ist schwankend und vom »Usus« der Menschen abhängig.[52] Auch die ersten fachübergreifenden Interpretationslehren des 17. Jahrhunderts[53] legen entscheidenden Wert auf den »Usus«.

Johann Conrad Dannhauer weist in seiner »Idea boni interpretis [...]« von 1630 immer wieder auf ihn hin: Grundsätzlich besteht die richtige Auslegung in dem allgemeinen (communis) Begriff eines Wortes, es ist auf den »Usus« abzustellen, für dessen Ermittlung die Lexika nützlich sind, aus dem Usus der Menschen und der Imposition sind die Wörter entstanden und aus ihm müssen sie auch verstanden und erklärt werden.[54] Johann

44 Hahn / Eichel (1650), cap. 13, XI, fol. Kr: »Quicquid itaque in ulla lingua propriarum s. κυρίων [kyriōn] vocum deprehendere licet, id *omne ex solo usu & consuetudine desumendum esse* putamus« (kursiv von mir).

45 Grotius (1625). Das griechische Prokop-Zitat (S. 304 Anm. 2) gibt Grotius wie folgt wieder: »longa dies non solet servare voces in quibus primum datae sunt. Sensu vertuntur enim res ipsae, qua volunt homines [...]«. Das Prokop-Zitat benutzt später, mit anderer Übersetzung, in diesem Zusammenhang auch Pufendorf (1662); daneben zitiert er u. a. Quintilians (Institutio oratoria 1, 6, 3) Vergleich von Wort und Münze, dazu auch u. zu Fn. 52.

46 Wolff (1746), VI, § 471, S. 328: »longiore autem usu proprius verborum significatus mutari solet; *pacta interpretanda sunt secundum usum loquendi ejus temporis, quo condita fuerunt*« (kursiv im Original).

47 Dazu Schröder (2003).

48 Setz (1975) 44.

49 Keckermann (1603), lib. 1, sect. 1, cap. 1, S. 11: »at linguas semper varias pati mutationes quis ignorat?«.

50 Keckermann (1603) 26: »vox sit communi consensu & usu recepta«.

51 Timpler (1612b), lib. 3, cap. 4, problema 12, S. 311, und zur Wortbedeutung S. 310 (»ex pacto et consensu«). Zu Timpler auch Meier-Oeser (1997) 278 f.

52 Keckermann (1603) 26: »verba valent usu sicut nummi«; Timpler (1612b) 312. Bezeichnenderweise benutzt auch Valla (1540), lib. 2, S. 708, den Münzvergleich unter Berufung auf Quintilian, Institutio oratoria, 1, 6, 3. In der Rechtsliteratur findet er sich jedenfalls noch am Ende des 18. Jahrhunderts bei Glück (1797), § 35, S. 227. – S. dazu auch Gardt (1994) 334, und die von ihm zitierten Weinrich (1958); Dascal (1976). Hier stehen allerdings andere Vergleichspunkte als die Wertveränderung im Vordergrund.

53 Dazu Danneberg (2001) 98 ff., 106 ff. Als dritten frühen Hermeneutiker, noch vor Dannhauer und Clauberg, nennt Danneberg Bartholomäus Keckermann.

54 Dannhauer (1652): Richtige Auslegung besteht grundsätzlich »in communi vocum notione in intelligendo aliquo scripto« (§ 51, S. 85), sie ergibt sich »ex usu, penes quem vis est & norma loquendi [Horaz-Zitat!] [...] quam ad rem prosunt Lexica« (§ 71, S. 129), »Ex usu hominum & impositione omnes voces natae sunt«, deshalb auch »ex eodem usu cognosci illae & explicari omnes debent« (§ 75, S. 137). Daß es immer *nur* auf die erste Imposition ankommen soll, sagt Dannhauer nicht!

Clauberg sagt schon in den Prolegomena zu seiner »Logica vetus et nova«, daß wir richtig sprechen, wenn wir dem gewöhnlichen (vulgaris) Sprachgebrauch folgen, und an anderer Stelle, es sei der »Usus« zu erklären, den die Wörter im Verständnis derjenigen haben, die sie zu gebrauchen pflegen, also bei allgemein üblichen Ausdrücken das, was alle darunter verstehen.[55] Natürlich wissen Dannhauer und Clauberg, daß Wörter ihren Sinn verändern können.[56] Später weist auch Johann Martin Chladenius darauf hin und will den »eigentlichen Verstand des Wortes« mehr der »Rede des gemeinen Mannes« als der Gelehrten entnehmen,[57] und wie die ihm vorangehenden Hermeneutiker stellt auch Georg Friedrich Meier auf den »Sprachgebrauch im gemeinen Leben und in den Künsten und Wissenschaften ab«.[58] Dasselbe findet sich in deutschen Logiken des späten 17. und frühen 18. Jahrhunderts, etwa bei dem sächsischen Dichter und Gelehrten Christian Weise, der den eigentlichen (proprius) Sinn der Wörter aus dem Gebrauch beurteilen will oder aus dessen Hilfsmitteln, den Lexika,[59] und bei Christian Wolff, der nicht nur in seinem »Ius Naturae« sondern auch in seiner Logik den Sprachgebrauch für maßgeblich erklärt.[60]

Die Überzeugung, daß der Sprachgebrauch die Wortbedeutung bestimmt, scheint sich seit der zweiten Hälfte des 17. Jahrhunderts weit über Deutschland hinaus durchzusetzen. Die bekannte »Logik von Port Royal« unterscheidet willkürliche, zur eigenen Verwendung gebildete Nominaldefinitionen und nicht willkürliche, diese müssen den allgemeinen Gebrauch (usum communem) eines Namens angeben.[61] In England spricht Thomas Hobbes vom »common use« der Wörter,[62] und John Locke erklärt, die verbale Kommunikation unter Menschen setze voraus, daß jeder ein Wort »in the common acceptation of that language« verwende.[63] Überall soll also nicht mehr die autoritative »erste Imposition«, sondern nur noch der wechselnde, gewöhnliche Sprachgebrauch maßgeblich sein.

4. *Die Grenzen der Erklärung aus der Geschichtlichkeit der Sprache: Das Autoritätserfordernis und die Umkehrung von Regel und Ausnahme*

Der Übergang zur »Gebrauchstheorie« läßt sich aber nicht allein aus der Entdeckung der Geschichtlichkeit der Sprache erklären. Aus ihr ergibt sich zwar, daß man nicht bei der »ersten Imposition« stehen bleiben kann. Wenn ein Wort seinen Sinn verändert hat, werden seine erste oder weitere frühere Bedeutungen irrelevant, wie etwa Johannes Eichel ausführlich entwickelt.[64] Aber der Wegfall des Autoritätserfordernisses ist so nicht zu begründen. Die Wandelbarkeit der Sprache eliminiert ja nicht ohne weiteres den Einfluß von Autoritäten. Nicht nur durch den gemeinen Sprachgebrauch, sondern auch durch Autoritäten kann sich die Bedeutung eines Wortes verändern. Es ist zum Beispiel denkbar, daß eine Legaldefinition nicht durch den Sprachgebrauch, sondern durch den Gesetzgeber selbst eingeschränkt oder erweitert wird, oder daß nicht die Gemeinsprache, sondern die Wissenschaft ein Wort in einer neuen, bisher unüblichen Bedeutung verwendet. Es bedarf also der Erklärung, warum mit dem Übergang zu der neuen Gebrauchstheorie der »propria significatio« nicht nur das Erfordernis der ersten

55 Clauberg (1658), Prolegomena, cap. 5, S. 36: »si usum loquendi vulgarem sequamur, recte loquemur«; p. 2, cap. 7, S. 182: »Usus earum est explicare, quid voces tum singulae, tum conjunctae valeant in mente eorum, qui illis uti consueverunt«, bei allgemein üblichen Ausdrücken »quid omnes promiscue intelligere soleant«.

56 Dannhauer (1652), § 74, S. 135 f., der aber darauf hinweist, daß willkürliche individuelle Veränderungen die Zustimmung der Sprachgemeinschaft finden müssen. Deutlich Clauberg (1658), p. 3, cap. 5, S. 272: »Ne autem fallabis, dum significationem vocabuli ex origine investigas, observabis, *originalem significationem saepe differre ab usuali*« (kursiv im Original).

57 Chladenius (1742), §§ 83–84, S. 42.

58 Meier (1757/1996), § 143, S. 56.

59 Weise (1684) p. 2, lib. 3, cap. 4, S. 445: »Sensus vocabulorum priprius [sic] judicatur ex usu, seu ut nominemus potiora usus adminicula, ex Lexicis«.

60 Wolff (1744), 2. Kap., § 16, S. 67: »Wie denn überhaupt nöthig ist, daß, wenn man die eigentliche Bedeutung der Wörter finden will, man sich einige Fälle vorstellet, in denen das Wort gebraucht wird, und dabey auf alles genau acht giebt, was uns selbiges zu brauchen veranlasset«.

61 Arnauld / Nicole (1718), p. 1, cap. 14, S. 71: Nicht willkürliche Nominaldefinitionen sind solche »per quas significationes notantur secundum usum communem« (franz. Ausgabe S. 115: »ce qu'ils signifient dans l'usage«).

62 Hobbes (1839), Kap. 2, 4, S. 16: Aber, »whatsoever the common use of words be«, Philosophen können auch Wörter mit abweichender Bedeutung bilden.

63 Locke (1690), Buch 3, Kap. 2, § 4.

64 Oben zu Fn. 43.

Imposition, sondern auch das Erfordernis der autoritativen Setzung entfällt.

Die Lösung scheint mir darin zu liegen, daß das Autoritätserfordernis nicht wirklich verschwindet, sondern nur einen anderen Platz (außerhalb der Gemeinsprache) zugewiesen bekommt, nämlich im Rahmen der Fachsprachen.[65] Dieser Begriff scheint im Mittelalter noch nicht vorhanden gewesen zu sein. Bei Bartolus und seinen Nachfolgern ist er nicht zu finden, sondern in der alten Vorstellung einer auf autoritativer Imposition beruhenden eigentlichen Wortbedeutung irgendwie mitenthalten. Erst als sich die neue Vorstellung von der durch den gemeinen Sprachgebrauch bestimmten eigentlichen Wortbedeutung durchzusetzen begann, benötigte man eine besondere Rubrik für die Fachsprachen. Sie findet sich denn auch sofort bei den Juristen. Für die »proprietas« eines Wortes, so erklärt Hugo Grotius, ist der populäre Gebrauch maßgeblich, aber für die Wörter der »artes«, die das Volk nicht versteht, die Definition der jeweiligen Fachleute.[66] Johannes Eichel spricht 1650 (als erster Jurist?) schon von »termini technici« und unterscheidet zwischen der Bedeutung alltagssprachlicher Wörter, die »vulgo communis« ist, einerseits, und der »termini technici«, bei denen es auf die Autorität der Fachkundigen ankommt, andererseits.[67] In der folgenden juristischen Literatur wird die Differenzierung zwischen der eigentlichen, umgangssprachlichen und der besonderen fachsprachlichen Bedeutung der Wörter ganz selbstverständlich.[68] – Bei den Philosophen unterscheidet schon 1603 Bartholomaeus Keckermann den allgemeinen Wortgebrauch eines gleichsprachigen Volkes und den besonderen der »artifices« einer Disziplin.[69] Ebenso differenziert ein anderer Logiker wie Christian Weise zwischen den »gemeinsamen« Wörtern, bei denen sich die Bedeutung aus dem »Usus« ergibt, und den Wörtern der Fachdisziplinen, bei denen die Übereinstimmung der wichtigsten Fachleute (consensus artificum praecipiorum) maßgeblich ist.[70] Auch in der allgemeinen Hermeneutik wird so unterschieden.[71] Außerhalb Deutschlands kennt z. B.

65 Allgemein zu deren Geschichte: Seibicke (2003).

66 Grotius (1680), lib. 2, cap. 16, § III, S. 305: »In artium autem vocabuli, quae populus vix capit, adhibenda erit cuiusque prudentum definitio«.

67 Hahn / Eichel (1650), cap. 16, fol. L3v: De proprietate terminorum technicorum [...], und I, fol. Mr: »peculia vocabula, quae a Iurisconsultis solis, frequentantur, & quorum proprietas a nemine, nisi auctoritate prudentium, & si haberi possunt, prudentissimorum desumenda est«.

68 Placcius (1693), cap. 8, Rn. 19, S. 221 f., unterscheidet zwischen der vox propria, die von allen Mitgliedern einer Sprachgemeinschaft benutzt wird, und der »vox technica«, die »omnibus illius artis, vel studii peritis« eigentümlich ist; Pufendorf (1672), lib. 5, cap. 12: einerseits Wörter, die »ex proprietate populari« (popularis usus) zu verstehen (§ 3, S. 525), andererseits »verba artis ex arte«, bei denen die »definitiones prudentum cujusque artis« maßgeblich sind (§ 4, S. 526); Thomasius (1702), lib. 2, cap. 12: Wörter sind entweder »vulgaria seu popularia« oder »technica seu termini artis« (Nr. 14), bei den letzten kommt es auf die »artis periti« an (Nr. 15), bei termini technici muß der fachfremde Ausleger die Regeln und Prinzipien der ars von den artifices lernen (Nr. 16) (alles S. 336); Wolff (1746), § 475, S. 327: Grundsätzlich kommt es auf den gewöhnlichen Sprachgebrauch an. Aber § 478, S. 334: »Vocabula artium, seu termini technici explicandae sunt per definitiones prudentum cujusque artis [...]«; Holderrieder (1736), sect. 2, § 8, S. 26–28: Einerseits gibt es den gewöhnlichen Sprachsinn (»vulgatus significatus«), andererseits »Omnis fere ars peculiaribus utitur vocabulis, usu atque consensu artificium introductis, quae technicorum nomine veniunt« (S. 26).

69 Keckermann (1603), lib. 1, sect. 1, cap. 1, S. 27: »Nunc id observetur inprimis, usum & συνθήκην [syntheken] vocis duplicem esse: publicum nimirum & communem totius populi ὁμογλώττου [homoglottou], & peculiarem artificum in certa disciplina, qui in singulis disciplinis, praesertim instrumentalibus, ut Logica vel Rhetorica, Grammatica suas habent peculiares voces ac terminos«. Da Keckermann sich auf keinen Vorgänger (außer Cicero) beruft, ist er möglicherweise der erste frühneuzeitliche Philosoph, der auf diesen Unterschied hinweist.

70 Weise (1684), p. 3, cap. 4, S. 445: »In vocabulis communibus praevalet usus, in terminis disciplinarum consensus artificum praecipiorum«.

71 Clauberg (1658), p. 2, cap. 7, nr. 47: Einige Wörter sind dem ganzen Menschengeschlecht gemeinsam, andere nur bestimmten Disziplinen, hier richtet sich die Bedeutung nach den Vorstellungen der »Magister«: »Itaque cum quaedam voces sint notionum toto hominum generi communium, aliae vero propriae certas disciplinas profitentium, in illis attendendum, quid omnes promiscue intelligere soleant«, bei den anderen »quid illarum disciplinarum magistri per eas denotare consueverint« (182); Chladenius (1742), §§ 82–83, S. 52 f.: die eigentliche Bedeutung des Worts ist die »im gemeinen Leben«, andererseits gibt es »Kunst-Wörter«, und ein Kunstwort ist ein solches, das »von Künstlern und in Wissenschafften gebraucht (53) wird, einen Begriff anzudeuten, welcher im gemeinen Leben nicht bekannt ist« (S. 52 f.); Meier (1757/1996), § 143, S. 56: »Sprachgebrauch im gemeinen Leben und in den Künsten und Wissenschaften«.

Thomas Hobbes neben dem »common use« der Wörter noch die besondere Sprache der Philosophen, und die Logik von Port Royal, mit anderer Systematik, neben den herkömmlichen Nominaldefinitionen, welche die gewöhnliche Bedeutung eines Wortes angeben, noch eine andere Art von Nominaldefinitionen, die willkürlich und frei gebildet sind, wie die der Mathematiker.[72] Sicherlich gibt es noch viele weitere Belege. In der neuen Sprachtheorie der frühen Neuzeit steht also zwar durchweg der gewöhnliche, populäre Sprachgebrauch im Vordergrund, aber neben ihm gibt es immer auch die Fachsprachen, die auf die Autorität der Fachvertreter zurückweisen. Daß das Wort »Autorität« nicht so oft vorkommt, erklärt sich aus der wachsenden Abneigung der aufgeklärten Wissenschaft gegen Autoritätsargumente.[73] In der Sache bestreitet aber niemand, daß bei den Fachausdrücken das alltägliche Sprachverständnis nicht ausreicht und besondere Fachkunde vorausgesetzt ist.

Wenn also durch die Einführung der »Gebrauchstheorie« nicht nur die erste Imposition, sondern auch das Autoritätserfordernis entfällt, dann liegt darin keine völlige Eliminierung der Sprachautoritäten. Es kehren sich nur Regel und Ausnahme um. Wurde im Mittelalter die »propria significatio«, die eigentliche Bedeutung, eines Wortes durch Autoritäten bestimmt, neben denen die populäre Sprachbedeutung zweitrangig war, so wird in der frühen Neuzeit gerade dieser populäre Sprachgebrauch zur eigentlichen Bedeutung, und die (in der Theorie erst jetzt entdeckten) Fachsprachen der Sachkundigen treten dahinter zurück. Begründungsbedürftig ist also nicht der Ausschluß der Autoritäten, sondern die Rangerhöhung des populären Sprachgebrauchs. Eine quellenmäßig belegbare Erklärung dafür dürfte sich kaum finden lassen. Aber eine Hypothese ist vielleicht möglich. Der populäre Sprachgebrauch ist die »Rede des gemeinen Mannes«[74] und gehört damit der jeweiligen Volkssprache an. Der Bedeutungszuwachs des gemeinen Sprachgebrauchs hängt also vielleicht mit der generellen Aufwertung der Volkssprachen in der frühen Neuzeit zusammen. Diese Entwicklung ist allgemein bekannt und oft beschrieben worden.[75] In Deutschland macht sie sich seit dem 16. Jahrhundert bemerkbar. Es entstehen erste deutsche Wörterbücher und Grammatiken.[76] Die gedruckten Bücher erscheinen mehr und mehr in deutscher Sprache, so daß ausweislich der Meßkataloge schon 1681 mehr deutsche als lateinische Bücher veröffentlicht werden[77] und im Zehnjahresabschnitt 1691–1700 erstmals die deutschsprachige Buchpublikation überwiegt.[78] Die deutsche Sprache dringt allmählich auch in die Wissenschaft ein. Christian Thomasius kündigt 1687 als erster Universitätslehrer offiziell eine deutschsprachige Vorlesung an[79] und veröffentlicht viele seiner Lehrwerke auf Deutsch, ebenso Christian Wolff, der auch in die Philosophie eine zum Teil sehr erfolgreiche deutsche Terminologie einführt.[80] Der neue Vorrang des populären Sprachgebrauchs könnte also eine Erscheinungsform des Aufstiegs der Volkssprachen sein.

Als Zwischenresultat ergibt sich: Im Mittelalter folgte die »eigentliche« Bedeutung eines Wortes aus der ersten Imposition und aus der Autorität. Im Laufe der frühen Neuzeit setzt sich dagegen die Vorstellung durch, die eigentliche Bedeutung sei dem gewöhnlichen Sprachgebrauch zu entnehmen. Der eine Grund für diese Veränderung ist die Einsicht in die Geschichtlichkeit der Sprache, wonach es nicht mehr entscheidend auf die erste Imposition ankommen kann. Der zweite Grund dürfte mit dem Aufstieg der Volkssprachen in der frühen Neuzeit zusammenhängen, der die Autorität in den sekundären Bereich der Fachsprachen zurückdrängt.

72 Hobbes (1655), Kap. 2, 4, S. 16: »whatsoever the common use of words be, yet philosophers, who were to teach their knowledge to others, had always the liberty, and sometimes they both had and will have a necessity, of taking to themselves such names as they please for the signifying of their meaning, if they would have it understood«; Arnauld / Nicole (1718), p. 1, cap. 12, S. 62 f.: frei gebildete Nominaldefinitionen, wie in der Geometrie, cap. 14, S. 71: herkömmliche Nominaldefinitionen, »per quas significationes notantur secundum usum communem«.

73 Dazu Schröder (2020), § 27, I, S. 130 ff.

74 Chladenius (1742), § 83, S. 42.

75 Siehe etwa Pörksen (1983); Gardt (1999) 45–71; Henkel (2004); Klein (2011).

76 Dazu Gardt (1999) 52 ff.; Klein (2011) 480 ff.

77 So Pörksen (1983) 234.

78 Nach der Tabelle bei Paulsen (1885) 787. Zweifel an der Aussagekraft der Meßkataloge äußert allerdings Pörksen (1983) 238 f.

79 Wolf (1951) 382; Pörksen (1983) 231.

80 Dazu Piur (1903); Ricken (1995); Menzel (1996).

III. Die alten Erkenntnismittel und ihr Ansehensverlust in der frühen Neuzeit. 2. Etymologie

Als weiteres Hilfsmittel zur Erkenntnis der Wortbedeutung nennt Bartolus die »allusio seu Derivatio«.[81] »Derivatio«, also die sprachliche Ableitung eines Wortes, kann man mit »Etymologie« übersetzen, obwohl sich dieses Wort in der Jurisprudenz erst seit dem 16. Jahrhundert einzubürgern scheint.[82] Der Begriff der »allusio« (Anspielung) und wie sie sich von der »derivatio« oder Etymologie unterscheidet, ist dagegen unklar: Manche meinen, die »allusio« beziehe sich nur auf das Wort und seinen Klang, die Etymologie dagegen auf den wahren sprachlichen Ursprung des Wortes,[83] andere setzen, wie Bartolus, beides gleich,[84] noch andere erwähnen die Allusion neben der Etymologie schon gar nicht.[85] Einigkeit besteht aber darin, daß die Etymologie (und/oder Allusion) der Definition nicht widersprechen darf:[86] Etymologisch mag z. B. das Testament von »testatio mentis« (Willensbezeugung) herkommen. Aber nicht jede Willensbezeugung ist ein Testament, wie sich aus dessen gesetzlicher Definition in D. 28, 1, 1 ergibt (Äußerung des Willens, was nach unserem Tod geschehen soll); diese hat also Vorrang vor der Etymologie. Davon abgesehen gilt aber die Etymologie als brauchbares Hilfsmittel zur Ermittlung der (aktuellen) Wortbedeutung. Das entspricht einer alten Tradition seit der Antike (1.), die sich erst in der frühen Neuzeit aufzulösen beginnt (2.).

1. *Die alte Lehre von der Wortbedeutung und der Etymologie*

Cicero hatte in seiner Topik drei »loci« genannt, aus denen sich Beweisgründe über einen Gegenstand gewinnen lassen, nämlich Definition, Aufzählung der Teile und »notatio«, »wenn aus der Eigenart des Wortes irgendein Argument gezogen wird«.[87] »Notatio« (ein von ihm neu gebildetes Wort), so erklärt er später, ist das, was die Griechen »Etymologie« nennen.[88] In der Folgezeit verbindet sich die Etymologie mit der Lehre von der Interpretation bzw. der Nominaldefinition oder wird sogar mit ihr gleichgesetzt. Cicero folgend nennt Marius Victorinus in seiner, früher Boetius zugeschriebenen, Schrift »De diffinitione« drei Arten der Definition, nämlich 1) durch Gattung und Art, 2) durch Aufzählung der Teile und 3) aus der »nota«, aus der sich das ergibt, was die Griechen »etymologia« nennen. Allerdings sei nur die erste wirklich (vere) eine Definition, die anderen – denen er noch weitere hinzufügt – nur dem Namen nach.[89] Boetius selbst unterscheidet mit Cicero ebenfalls drei Topoi aus der »Substanz« des Gegenstandes, nämlich Definition, Deskription und Interpretation des Namens, die »ἐτυμολογία« (etymologia) heiße.[90] Man könne die Namensinterpretation in gewissem Sinne auch »Definition« nennen, aber eben nur des Wortes, nicht der Sache selbst.[91] In seinen bekannten »Etymologiae« bezeichnet auch Isidor von Sevilla die Etymologie als Ursprung der Wörter, als Ermittlung der Wortbedeutung durch Interpretation.[92] Die Etymologie

81 Oben Fn. 7.

82 Von »derivatio« sprechen noch Rogerius (1549) 28, Rn. 6; Caepolla (1551), Sp. 12, Rn. 39 f.; Forster (1613), lib. 2, cap. 4, Nr. 17, S. 353. Von »etymologia« aber Alciatus (1530), S. 6; Everardus a Middelburg (1568) 41; Corasius (1603) 439, Rn. 18; Decianus (1779), vol. 2 resp. 1, Nr. 38, S. 11 (»ethimologia«).

83 So Everardus a Middelburg (1568) Rn. 2–5, S. 45 f.; Alciatus (1530) 87.

84 So Rogerius und Caepolla, wie Fn. 82.

85 So Decianus und Corasius, wie Fn. 82.

86 So Bartolus (1588) 43. Ebenso Rogerius und Caepolla, wie Fn. 82, und alle anderen.

87 Cicero (1993), II, Rn. 9 f., S. 10, 12: »notatio, cum ex verbi vi argumentum aliquod elicitur« (Rn. 10, S. 12).

88 Cicero (1993), VIII, Rn. 35, S. 28: notatio »est autem, cum ex vi nominis argumentum elicitur; quam Graeci ἐτυμολογίαν [etymologian] appellant«.

89 Boetius [richtig: Marius Victorinus] (1847a), Sp. 891–910 (901 A–C). Zur Autorschaft von Marius Victorinus (300–379), die 1877 entdeckt wurde, s. Bruce (1946) 135 m. w. N.

90 Boetius (1847c), Sp. 1040 ff. (1111, 1200 f.).

91 Boetius (1847c), Sp. 1200: »Nam interpretatio nominis quaedam ipsius nominis diffinitio est«, aber »a nota vero rem non diffinit, sed nomen interpretatur. Diversa vero sunt res et nomen.«

92 Isidor von Sevilla (1911), lib. 1, Abschnitt 29: »Etymologia est origo vocabulorum, cum vis verbi vel nominis per interpretationem colligitur.«

ist also das maßgebliche Hilfsmittel zur Feststellung eines Wortsinnes, auch wenn sie, wie Isidor bemerkt,[93] nicht überall angewendet werden kann.

Die hoch- und spätmittelalterliche Logik scheint diese Lehre im wesentlichen fortzuführen.[94] Bei den aus der Substanz des Gegenstandes gewonnenen Topoi unterscheidet man nach wie vor zwischen Definition, Deskription (die anstelle von Ciceros »Aufzählung der Teile« tritt) und Interpretation des Namens;[95] erst William Ockham und seine Anhänger ersetzen offenbar die Rubrik »Namensinterpretation« durch »Nominaldefinition«.[96] Die Namensinterpretation oder Nominaldefinition wird jetzt aber nicht mehr ohne weiteres mit der Etymologie gleichgesetzt, vielmehr beschreibt man sie als eine Art der Definition, die ein Wort durch andere (bekanntere) in derselben und/oder einer anderen Sprache erklärt.[97] Sieht man dann aber auf die Erläuterungen, die dazu gegeben werden, so erscheinen sofort wieder die alten etymologischen Beispiele. Allerdings fordern die Logiker, daß diese und das zu erläuternde Wort »konvertibel« sind, also nicht weiter oder enger.[98] Beispiel für eine mit dem Wort nicht konvertible Etymologie ist die im Mittelalter besonders beliebte Herleitung von »lapis« (Stein) aus »laedens pedem« (den Fuß verletzend). Da nicht alles, was den Fuß verletzt, ein Stein ist, können Wort und Etymologie hier nicht ausgetauscht werden. Anders soll es mit φιλόσοφος (Philosophos), d. h. griechisch Freund der Weisheit, liegen.[99]

An der grundsätzlichen Eignung der Etymologie zur Erschließung der Wortbedeutung wird aber nicht gezweifelt, und so bleibt es – nach dem noch konservativeren humanistischen Zwischenspiel[100] – auch in der Schulphilosophie der frühesten Neuzeit. Nur kommt es jetzt offenbar zu einem Kompromiß zwischen der antiken Identifizierung von Namensinterpretation und Etymologie und dem mittelalterlichen Verständnis von Namensinter-

93 Wie vorige Fn.

94 Eine umfassende moderne Untersuchung dazu scheint es nicht zu geben. Wenig ergiebig ist der Artikel »Etymologie« von Trier (1972). Einige Überlegungen zur Etymologie bei Abälard und Thomas von Aquin finden sich bei Grubmüller (1975). Zur »Praxis des Etymologisierens« in der frühen Neuzeit Gardt (1994) 361–364.

95 Abaelardus (1836), p. 3, S. 368 ff., 375; p. 5, S. 490–492; Lambert von Auxerre (1971), fol. 97v, S. 124; William of Sherwood (1995) 80–84; Petrus Hispanus (1572), tract. 5, fol. 147v, 149r, 150r.

96 Ockham (1675), lib. 1, cap. 26, S. 53: Die Definition kann ausdrücken »quid rei« und »quid nominis«. Die erste kann wieder Definition im engeren Sinne oder Deskription sein; Buridanus (2001), tract. 6, cap. 3, S. 411 u. ff.

97 Abaelardus (1836), p. 5, S. 491: »per quam ignotum alterius linguæ vocabulum exponitur«; Lambert von Auxerre (1971), fol. 98r, S. 125: »est expositio unius nominis per alia nomina«; Petrus Hispanus (1572), tract. 5, 3. Abschnitt, fol. 150r: »Interpretatio, est expositio unius nominis minus noti per aliud nomen magis notum vel per integram orationem« (das gilt aber nur für die konvertible Interpretation, s. den folgenden Text); William of Sherwood (1995) 84: »Est autem interpretatio nominis expositio nominis per idem idioma vel per aliud«; Ockham (1675), lib. 3, p. 3, cap. 26, S. 452: Die Nominaldefinition muß nicht »per notiora« gegeben werden, sondern es genügt »per aeque nota«.

98 Lambert von Auxerre (1971), fol. 98r, S. 125; Petrus Hispanus (1572), tract. 5, 3. Abschnitt, fol. 150r. Dagegen meint William of Sherwood (1995) 84, das Interpretierte und das Interpretierende seien immer austauschbar, s. dazu die Erklärung der Herausgeber in Anm. 110 f., S. 254.

99 Auch das bestreitet jedoch Abaelardus (1836), p. 5, S. 492, der überhaupt der Etymologie sehr kritisch gegenübersteht: nicht jeder Liebhaber der Weisheit sei ein Philosoph, sondern nur derjenige, der die »artis doctrina« innehabe. Über Abaelards Einstellung zur Etymologie s. auch Grubmüller (1975) 227.

100 Hier gibt es eine Rückwendung zur spätantiken Lehre, indem die Gleichsetzung von Etymologie und Nominalinterpretation/-definition wieder auflebt, zum Beispiel bei Melanchthon (1536), lib. 1, 2. Abschnitt: »Primum genus [sc. der Definition], definitio nominis est, ea simpliciter ἐτυμολογία [etymologia] vocabuli est«. Allerdings nennt er später (Melanchthon [1548], lib. 1, fol. 47r) die Etymologie von »solstitium« (Sonnenwende) als »solis statio« (Stillstand der Sonne) »knabenhaft« (puerilis). Ebenso die »rhetorisch« orientierte Logik von Ramus (1579), lib. 1, cap. 24, S. 76: »Notatio est nominis interpretatio. Nomina siquidem sunt notae rerum, nominumque vel derivatorum, vel compositorum, si vera notatione fiant, ratio reddi potest ex aliquo argumento primo: ut homo ab humo«. Siehe etwa auch Caesarius (1539), tract. 8, S. 159: Die dritte Art der Definition (nach Cicero) ist die »a nota, ut Cicero, sive ab etymologia […]«.

pretation als Umschreibung: Die Nominaldefinition[101] ist entweder Umschreibung eines Wortes oder Etymologie. So kennen jetzt etwa Keckermann und Jakob Martini zwei Arten der Nominaldefinition, nämlich die κατὰ λέξιν (kata lexin), welche ein Wort durch ein anderes bekannteres umschreibt, und die κατ' ἐτυμολογίαν (kat' etymologian), welche das Wort aus seinem Ursprung erklärt,[102] und Alsted und Timpler unterscheiden bei der Nominaldefinition zwischen der primären (durch Etymologie) und der sekundären (durch andere Wörter).[103]

Schon bei diesen Autoren[104] mehren sich allerdings die Bedenken gegen eine Worterklärung durch Etymologie: Sie funktioniert nicht bei »primitiven«, also nicht irgendwoher abgeleiteten Wörtern,[105] sie kann ungenau, also zu eng oder zu weit sein,[106] manche Wörter haben mehrere Etymologien;[107] überhaupt können Etymologien falsch sein, wie etwa die von »aqua« (Wasser): »a qua sint omnia« (von dem alles kommt)[108] usw.[109]

2. *Die neue Lehre: Nutzlosigkeit der Etymologie für die Ermittlung der (aktuellen) Wortbedeutung*

Der wohl entscheidende Einwand gegen die Etymologie scheint sich aber in der Schulphilosophie um 1600 noch nicht zu finden, nämlich daß sie bestenfalls die erste Bedeutung, nicht jedoch spätere veränderte Bedeutungen eines Wortes erklären kann. Zum Beispiel mag Philosophie etymologisch »Liebe zur Weisheit« sein, sie ist es aber im frühen 21. Jahrhundert, wo jeder Discounter oder Reiseveranstalter seine »Philosophie« hat, sicherlich nicht mehr. Wenn also die Etymologie als Instrument zur Ermittlung des Wortsinnes in der frühen Neuzeit verschwindet, dann kann das nur auf der Einsicht beruhen, daß der Sinn eines Wortes wandelbar ist. Schon 1530 weist Andreas Alciatus (als erster Jurist?) darauf hin, daß die Etymologie versagt, wenn ein Wort seine Bedeutung verändert hat: Die Eheschließung heißt vermutlich deshalb »nuptiae«, weil früher die Frauen bei der Hochzeit ihre Köpfe verhüllt haben (obnubere), aber das ist für die heutige Bedeutung des Wortes nicht mehr relevant.[110]

Bei den Juristen des 17. und 18. Jahrhunderts wird dann die Historizität der Sprache zum maßgeblichen Argument gegen die Etymologie. So verwirft Johannes Eichel, wie wir schon gesehen haben, wegen der Wandelbarkeit des Wortsinnes nicht nur die »erste Imposition«, sondern auch die Etymologie: »so daß wir nun über die eigentliche Bedeutung der Wörter weder aus der ersten Imposition, noch aus der Etymologie […] urteilen können«.[111] Vincentius Placcius erklärt 1664 in seinem unter Pseudonym erschienenen ersten Buch zur Methodenlehre, es sei klar, dass die Etymologie kein ausreichendes Argument ist. Dies

101 Das Wort (Nominal-)Definition tritt jetzt durchweg an die Stelle des älteren »interpretatio nominis«: Martini (1610), lib. 5, cap. 10, S. 99 (»nominis definitio«); Alsted (1628), lib. 4, cap. 3, S. 270 (»definitio verbalis«); Keckermann (1603), lib. 1, sect. 2, cap. 1, S. 208 (»definitio nominis«); Scheibler (1665), S. 35 ff., p. 2, cap. 26, S. 326 (»definitio nominis«); Timpler (1612a), lib. 2, cap. 8, Nr. 11, S. 366 (»definitio nominalis«); Burgersdicius (1666), lib. 2, cap. 4, S. 108 (»definitio nominis«).

102 Keckermann (1603), lib. 1, sect. 2, cap. 1, S. 209; Martini (1610), lib. 5, sect. 2, cap. 10, S. 99.

103 Alsted (1628), lib. 4, cap. 3, S. 270: Verbaldefinition »primaria« und »secundaria«; Timpler (1612a), lib. 2, cap. 8, S. 366 f. – Eine noch etwas andere Terminologie verwenden Scheibler (1665), p. 2, cap. 26, S. 327: Die Nominaldefinition ist »notatio« (Etymologie) oder »transsumptio« (Erklärung eines dunklen Wortes durch ein klareres); Burgersdicius (1666), lib. 2, cap. 4, S. 108 f.: Die Nominaldefinition erklärt das Wort »vel etymologia, vel voce conjugata, vel voce synonyma«.

104 Sehr kritisch schon früher auch Valla (1538), lib 4, cap. 20, S. 286: »plerunque fallax«; ebenso lib. 6, cap. 27, S. 478. Mehrfach auch zu seiner Meinung nach falschen juristischen Etymologien: lib. 6, cap. 26, S. 447 (Testament als »testatio mentis«); lib. 6, cap. 52, S. 501 f.

105 So Keckermann (1603), lib. 1, sect. 2, cap. 1, S. 211; Timpler (1612a), lib. 2, cap. 8, qu. 4, S. 375; Martini (1610), lib. 5, cap. 10, S. 102.

106 Scheibler (1665), p. 2, cap. 26, S. 327, Rn. 3.

107 Timpler (1612a), lib. 2, cap. 8, qu. 4, S. 376; Scheibler (1665), p. 2, cap. 26, S. 331, Rn. 31.

108 Timpler (1612a), lib. 2. cap. 8, qu. 4, S. 375.

109 Noch zahlreiche weitere Regeln führt Scheibler (1665), p. 2, cap. 26, S. 329–331 auf (insgesamt zehn »canones«).

110 Alciatus (1530) 215. Hier auch eine Reihe weiterer Beispiele zur Veränderung von Wortbedeutungen.

111 Hahn / Eichel (1650), wie oben Fn. 43.

könne durch unzählige Beispiele von Wörtern bewiesen werden, die ihren früheren, etymologisch ableitbaren, Sinn verändert und eine ganz andere Bedeutung angenommen hätten. Die Etymologie gelte also nicht, wo sie dem gemeinen Sprachgebrauch widerspricht.[112] Christian Wolff bildet folgende Beweiskette: Bei der Interpretation von Versprechen und Verträgen ist vom gemeinen Sprachgebrauch auszugehen – durch längeren Gebrauch pflegt sich aber die eigentliche Bedeutung der Wörter zu ändern, so dass Verträge nach dem Sprachgebrauch ihrer Entstehungszeit zu interpretieren sind – durch die Etymologie erkennen wir die ursprüngliche Ausprägung eines Wortes – deshalb ist die etymologische Herleitung bei der Interpretation nicht zuzulassen, denn jeder weiß, dass es bei der Bedeutung, die ein Wort im gemeinen Sprachgebrauch hat, nicht auf den Ursprung des Wortes ankommt.[113] Soweit ich sehe, verteidigt im 18. Jahrhundert kein Jurist mehr die etymologische Beweisführung bei der Gesetzesinterpretation.

Auch bei den Philosophen zeigt sich zunehmende Skepsis gegenüber der Etymologie. Blickt man zunächst auf die allgemeine Hermeneutik, so setzt sich zwar deren Begründer Johann Conrad Dannhauer für die »Etymologie« ein, versteht darunter aber nicht die »Ableitung« (derivatio) eines Wortes, sondern dessen »Usus«, der aus Lexika eruiert werden kann.[114] Etymologie ist hier also nicht mehr der historische Ursprung, sondern die aktuelle Bedeutung eines Wortes, dessen »Semantik«.[115] Johann Clauberg verwendet »Etymologie« im alten Sinne und weist darauf hin, daß Wörter ihren Sinn verändern können und dann die ursprüngliche Wortbildung nicht mehr relevant ist.[116] Im Ergebnis warnen also beide Autoren davor, den (etymologischen) Ursprung eines Wortes zur Ermittlung des aktuellen Sinnes heranzuziehen. Dasselbe könnte auch die Ansicht von Johann Martin Chladenius sein, bei dem das Wort »Etymologie« schon gar nicht vorzukommen scheint. Aus dem Rahmen fällt allerdings Georg Friedrich Meier, der den »buchstäblichen Sinn« (das ist auch bei ihm der gewöhnliche Sprachgebrauch) der Wörter durch »die Ableitung derselben von ihren Stammwörtern«, mithin »aus der Etymologie« erkennen will.[117] Freilich läßt Meier in seinem pedantischen Büchlein auch kein Verständnis für die Geschichtlichkeit der Sprache erkennen. – Von anderen Philosophen kann man wieder Christian Weise nennen. Auch Weise will nur mit Vorsicht auf die Etymologie zurückgreifen, hält jedenfalls positive oder negative Schlüsse von der Etymologie auf

112 Nomicus Pacemutus Analyticophilus [Pseudonym von Vincentius Placcius] (1664), Appendix, sect. 6, § 53, S. 257: »Id quod exemplis innumeris vocum probari potest, quae a sententia priori quam habebant, cum primo ab etymo suo derivarentur, in aliam diversissimam transierunt. Ne nunc et a contrario saepe aliquid denominari, & obscurissimas esse, & dubiosas originum divinationes, multis adstruere laborum.« Es werde daher mit Recht gesagt, dass die Etymologie nicht gilt, »ubi repugnat communi usui loquendi […] & non concludere necessario«.

113 Wolff (1746), VI, §§ 470–472, § 474 (S. 327–331). § 474 lautet: »Enimvero nemo est qui nesciat, in significatu, quem vocabulum communi loquendi usu obtinet, minime attendi originem ejus« (S. 331).

114 Dannhauer (1652), p. 1, sect. 3, art. 6, S. 129: Zur grammatischen Interpretation gehört unter anderem »Etymologia, cuius est in vocum significationem, seu definitionem nominalem inquirere, non certe ex *derivatione* vocum, sed ex *usu*, penes quem vis est & norma loquendi [Horaz!] […] quam ad rem prosunt Lexica, quibus hoc seculum utitur instructissima« (kursiv im Original).

115 Auf diesen Bedeutungswandel hat Dascal in seinem Kommentar zu Leibniz (2008) 79 Anm. 5 (Abschnitt »Interpretation and Argumentation in Law«), hingewiesen: »Etymologie« bezieht sich jetzt nicht mehr nur »to the origin of words, but also to their meaning – i. e. to what is today known as ›semantics‹«, zitiert nach Barck (2020) 57 Anm. 258. Auch Leibniz scheint in seiner Abhandlung »De Legum interpretatione, rationibus, applicatione, systemate« (erstmals 1885 gedruckt) diesen neueren Begriff zu verwenden, wenn er zwischen der »Etymologie« eines einzelnen Wortes und der Verbindung der Wörter unterscheidet, s. Barck (2020) 56 f.

116 Clauberg (1658), p. 3, cap. 5, nr. 27, S. 272: »illa [sc. lexica] suppeditant nominum definitiones per vocabula synonyma, vocum homonymias tollunt per distinctiones, denique per etymologias vocabula ex origine declarant«. Aber »Ne autem fallaris, dum significationem vocabuli ex origine ejus investigas, observabis, *originalem significationem saepe differre ab usuali*, h.e. multa vocabula aliud nunc vulgo denotare, aliud olim, cum primum inventa & rebus imposita fuere, sive, usum vocum haud raro ab earum origine recedere« (kursiv im Original). An einer anderen Stelle scheint Clauberg jedoch das neuere Verständnis von »Etymologie« zugrunde zu legen, wenn er von der »Konstruktion« der usualen Bedeutung durch »Etymologie« spricht (p. 2, cap. 7, nr. 47, S. 182 f.).

117 Meier (1757/1996), § 145, S. 56.

den Namen nur beim grammatischen, nicht aber beim gewöhnlichen (»politischen«) Sinn für zulässig.[118] Christian Wolff scheint in seiner Logik weniger auf die Etymologie einzugehen als im Naturrecht, bemerkt aber immerhin, daß die etymologische Auslegung nicht einen dem Autor fremden Wortsinn unterstellen darf.[119] Von nichtdeutschen Logikautoren sagt Thomas Hobbes nichts zur Etymologie, wohl weil er überhaupt keine Nominal-, sondern nur noch Realdefinitionen akzeptiert. Und auch in der Logik von Port Royal spielt die Etymologie kaum eine Rolle. An einer Stelle wird das Wort möglicherweise schon im moderneren »semantischen« Sinne verstanden,[120] an der einzigen anderen – im Rahmen der Topik, die Arnauld und Nicole überhaupt für überflüssig halten[121] – eher ironisch: Mittels der Etymologie könne man beweisen, daß Leute von Welt sich niemals entspannen, weil sie sich niemals mit ernsten Dingen beschäftigen: Entspannen (französisch divertir) bedeute ja etymologisch, sich einmal nicht mit ernsten Dingen zu beschäftigen.[122]

Es lassen sich vermutlich noch weitere Belege finden, aber die hier gegebenen zeigen jedenfalls, daß auch viele Philosophen (bei der Ermittlung der aktuellen Wortbedeutung) der Etymologie nur noch geringen Wert zumessen. Daß auf sie, namentlich in philologisch-historischen Fragen, nicht ganz verzichtet werden kann, ist ebenso klar und wird auch von juristischer Seite nicht bestritten.[123]

IV. Zusammenfassung

Nach Bartolus ist die eigentliche Bedeutung, die »propria significatio«, eines Wortes durch Autoritäten, (Legal-)Definitionen und Etymologie zu ermitteln. Auf den gewöhnlichen Sprachgebrauch kommt es nicht an. Diese Lehre bleibt bis in die frühe Neuzeit hinein herrschend. Im Laufe des 17. Jahrhunderts beginnt die Rechtswissenschaft jedoch, die eigentliche Bedeutung dem gemeinen Sprachgebrauch zu entnehmen.

Ebenso verläuft die Entwicklung in der Philosophie. Die eigentliche Bedeutung eines Wortes soll sich bis zum 16. Jahrhundert aus der Wortschöpfung, der »ersten Imposition«, und aus der dafür verantwortlichen Autorität ergeben (mindestens müssen Autoritäten den Wortsinn bezeugen). Aber wie die Jurisprudenz setzt im 17. Jahrhundert auch die Philosophie den gemeinen Sprachgebrauch an die Stelle der ersten Imposition und der Autoritäten.

Verantwortlich dafür dürften die Einsicht in die Geschichtlichkeit, d. h. Veränderbarkeit der Sprache und der Aufstieg der Volkssprachen sein. Wenn sich die ursprüngliche Bedeutung eines Wortes ändern kann, dann kommt es nicht mehr auf die erste Imposition an. Und wenn der populäre Sprachgebrauch, die Alltagssprache, die eigentliche Bedeutung eines Wortes bestimmt, dann wirkt sich die Meinung der Autoritäten nur noch in den Fachsprachen aus.

Entsprechend wandelt sich bei Juristen und Philosophen die Wertschätzung der Etymologie. Sie gilt bis zum 16. Jahrhundert als brauchbares

118 Weise (1684), p. 2, lib. 1, cap. 5: »Sensus Politicus s. Consuetudinarius« (S. 244), dieser soll keinen Schluß auf den Namen zulassen (S. 245). Weises Etymologiebegriff ist allerdings wenig klar, am Anfang scheint er das Wort im neueren »semantischen« Sinne zu verstehen (S. 242: Etymologie »refertur ad nomen quod significat«), später kommen dann aber wieder die alten Beispiele: testamentum von »testatio mentis«, »mulier« von »mollities« usw.

119 Wolff (1732), § 914, S. 649.

120 Arnauld / Nicole (1718), p. 1, cap. 12, S. 62: Nominaldefinitionen (im traditionellen Sinn) sind »nominis ex vulgari Idiomatis usu, vel Etymologa interpretatio«. Ob »etymologische Interpretation« eine Alternative zur Interpretation aus dem gemeinen Gebrauch oder nur ein anderer Ausdruck dafür sein soll, bleibt offen. Die spätere Stelle spricht aber vielleicht für das erste.

121 Arnauld / Nicole (1718), p. 3, cap. 17, S. 234, cap. 18, S. 245.

122 Arnauld / Nicole (1718), p. 3, cap. 18, S. 239 (franz. Ausgabe p. 3, cap. 17, S. 297: Etymologisch argumentiert man, »quand on dit, par example, que plusieurs personnes du monde ne se divertissent jamais, à proprement parler, parce que se divertir, c'est se desappliquer des occupations serieuses, et qu'ils ne s'occupent jamais serieusement«). Die hier benutzte lateinische Ausgabe gibt das französische »personnes du monde« nicht wieder, so daß die Pointe des Satzes unverständlich ist.

123 Hahn / Eichel (1650), cap. 15, IX, fol. L3v: »non negemus interdum occasionem praebere Etymologia, ad investigandum, quaenam significatio vocabuli primaeva fuerit […]«.

Hilfsmittel zur Ermittlung der aktuellen Wortbedeutung. Auch diese Vorstellung wird mit der Einsicht in die Geschichtlichkeit der Sprache unhaltbar, weil es nicht mehr auf die ursprüngliche Herleitung eines Wortes ankommen kann, wenn dessen Sinn sich verändert hat.

Eine »Gebrauchstheorie« der Sprache, ob nun im Wittgensteinschen Sinne oder nicht, hat sich also schon im 17. Jahrhundert durchgesetzt und bis in die Gegenwart behauptet. ■

Bibliographie

- Abaelardus, Petrus (1836), Dialectica, in: Cousin, Victor (Hg.), Ouvrages inédits d'Abélard, Paris
- Alciatus, Andreas (1530), De verborum significatione libri quatuor, Lugduni
- Alsted, Johann Heinrich (1628), Logicae systema harmonicum, ed. 2, Herborn
- Althusius, Johannes (1649), Dicaeologicae libri tres, 2. Ausg., Frankfurt
- Aristoteles (2014), Peri hermeneias, in: ders., Werke in deutscher Übersetzung, Bd. 1, Teil 2, übersetzt und erläutert von Hermann Weidemann, 3. überarb. Aufl., Berlin
- Arnauld, Antoine, Pierre Nicole (1718), Logica sive ars cogitandi, in qua praeter vulgares regulas plura nova habentur ad rationem dirigendam utilia, ed. nova, Halle
- Augustinus (2017), De musica, hg. von Martin Jacobsson, Berlin
- Baldus (1586), In primum, secundum et tertium Codicis libros commentaria, Venetiis
- Barck, Dorothea (2020), De Legum interpretatione. Gesetzesauslegung bei Gottfried Wilhelm Leibniz, Berlin
- Bartolus (1509), Commentarius super secunda Infortiati, Venetiis
- Bartolus (1588), Digestum vetus, 1. Teil, in: ders., Opera quae nunc exstant omnia, Basel
- Beuerle, Angela (2010), Sprachdenken im Mittelalter. Ein Vergleich mit der Moderne, Berlin
- Boetius [richtig: Marius Victorinus] (1847a), De diffinitione, in: Migne, Jacques-Paul (Hg.), Patrologia latina, Bd. 64, Paris
- Boetius (1847b), In librum Aristotelis de interpretatione libri duo. Editio prima, seu minora commentaria, in: Migne, Jacques-Paul (Hg.), Patrologia latina, Bd. 64, Paris
- Boetius (1847c), In Topica Ciceronis commentariorum libri sex, in: Migne, Jacques-Paul (Hg.), Patrologia latina, Bd. 64, Paris
- Bruce, F. F. (1946), Marius Victorinus and his works, in: The Evangelical Quarterly 18, 132–153
- Burgersdicius, Franco (1666), Institutionum logicarum libri duo, Cambridge
- Buridanus, Johannes (2001), Summulae de dialectica [frühes 14. Jh.], an annotated translation, with a philosophical introduction by Gyula Klima, New Haven
- Caepolla, Bartholomaeus (1551), In titulum de verborum et rerum significatione [...] commentaria, Lugduni
- Caesarius, Johannes (1539), Dialectica, Lugduni
- Chladenius, Johann Martin (1742), Einleitung zur richtigen Auslegung vernünfftiger Reden und Schrifften, Leipzig
- Christensen, Ralph (1989), Was heißt Gesetzesbindung? Eine rechtslinguistische Untersuchung, Berlin
- Cicero (1993), Topica, mit deutscher Übersetzung von Karl Bayer, München
- Clauberg, Johann (1658), Logica vetus et nova, 2. Ausg., Amsterdam
- Corasius Johannes (1603), In rubricam Digestis de servitutibus commentarii, in: ders., Opera quae haberi possunt omnia, hg. von Valentin Wilhelm Forster, Bd. 1, Wittenberg
- Coseriu, Eugenio (1967), L'arbitraire du signe. Zur Spätgeschichte eines aristotelischen Begriffes, in: Archiv für das Studium der neueren Sprachen und Literaturen 204 (119. Jahrgang), 81–112
- Coseriu, Eugenio (1975), Die Geschichte der Sprachphilosophie von der Antike bis zur Gegenwart. Eine Übersicht, Teil I: Von der Antike bis Leibniz. Vorlesung gehalten im Winter-Semester 1968/69 an der Universität Tübingen, Autorisierte Nachschrift von Gunter Narr und Rudolf Windisch, 2. Aufl. von Gunter Narr, Tübingen
- Danneberg, Lutz (2001), Logik und Hermeneutik im 17. Jahrhundert, in: Schröder, Jan (Hg.), Theorie der Interpretation vom Humanismus bis zur Romantik – Rechtswissenschaft, Philosophie, Theologie, Stuttgart, 75–131
- Dannhauer, Johann Conrad (1652), Idea boni interpretis et malitiosi calumniatoris [...] [1630], 4. Ausg., Straßburg
- Dascal, Marcelo (1976), Language and Money. A Simile and its Meaning in 17th Century Philosophy of Language, in: Studia Leibnitiana 8,2, 187–218
- Decianus, Tiberius (1579), Responsa, vol. 2, Venetiis
- Demonet, Marie-Luce (1992), Lex Voix du signe. Nature et origine du langage à la Renaissance, Paris
- Depenheuer, Otto (1988), Der Wortlaut als Grenze. Thesen zu einem Topos der Verfassungsinterpretation, Heidelberg
- Eckhard, Christian Heinrich (1750), Hermeneuticae iuris libri duo, Jena
- Everardus a Middelburg, Nicolaus (1568), Loci argumentorum legales, Lugduni
- Fikentscher, Wolfgang (1977), Methoden des Rechts in vergleichender Darstellung, Bd. IV, Tübingen
- Forster, Valentin Wilhelm (1613), Interpres, sive De interpretatione juris libri duo, Wittenberg
- Frantzke, Georg (1644), Commentarius in viginti et unum libros Pandectarum iuris civilis priores, Straßburg
- Fredborg, Karin Margareta (1981), Roger Bacon on »Impositio vocis ad significandum«, in: Braakhuis, H. A. G. u. a. (Hg.), English Logic and Semantics. From the End of the Twelfth Century to the Time of Ockham and Burleigh, Nijmegen, 167–191
- Gardt, Andreas (1994), Sprachreflexion in Barock und Frühaufklärung. Entwürfe von Böhme bis Leibniz, Berlin

- Gardt, Andreas (1999), Geschichte der Sprachwissenschaft in Deutschland. Vom Mittelalter bis ins 20. Jahrhundert, Berlin
- Gerl, Hanna-Barbara (1974), Rhetorik als Philosophie. Lorenzo Valla, München
- Glück, Christian Friedrich (1797), Ausführliche Erläuterung der Pandecten nach Hellfeld, 1. Theil, 2. Ausg., Erlangen
- Grotius, Hugo (1680), De jure belli ac pacis libri tres [1625], Hagae Comitis
- Grubmüller, Klaus (1975), Etymologie als Schlüssel zur Welt? Bemerkungen zur Sprachtheorie des Mittelalters, in: Fromm, Hans u. a. (Hg.), Verbum et signum, Bd. I, München, 209–230
- Hahn, Heinrich (Praes.), Johannes Eichel (Resp.) (1650), De interpretatione legum pars prima, Helmstedt
- Henkel, Nikolaus (2004), Lateinisch / Deutsch, in: Besch, Werner u. a. (Hg.), Sprachgeschichte. Ein Handbuch zur Geschichte der deutschen Sprache und ihrer Erforschung, 2. Aufl., 4. Teilbd., Berlin etc., 3171–3182
- Hickman, L[arry] (1976), Impositio prima / secunda, in: Ritter, Joachim / Karlfried Gründer (Hg.), Historisches Wörterbuch der Philosophie, Darmstadt, Bd. 4, Sp. 269–270
- Hobbes, Thomas (1839), Computation or Logic [1655], in: Molesworth, William (Hg.), The English Works of Thomas Hobbes, vol. 1, London
- Holderrieder, Johannes Laurentius (1736), De principiis interpretationis legum adaequatis, Leipzig
- Hornejus, Conradus (1642), Institutionum logicarum libri V, 2. Ausg., Hanau
- Isidor von Sevilla (1911), Isidori Hispalensis episcopi etymologiarum sive originum libri XX [um 630], hg. von Wallace Martin Lindsay, 2 Bde., Oxford
- Johannes a Sancto Thoma (1948), Cursus Philosophicus Thomisticus, tomus I: Ars Logica seu De forma et materia ratiocinandi, hg. von Beat Reiser, nova editio, Taurini
- Keckermann, Bartholomaeus (1603), Systema Logicae, 2. Ausg., Hanau
- Kelly, Louis G. (2002), The Mirror of Grammar. Theology, Philosophy and the Modistae, Amsterdam
- Klein, Wolf Peter (2011), Die deutsche Sprache in der Gelehrsamkeit der frühen Neuzeit. Von der lingua barbarica zur HaubtSprache, in: Jaumann, Herbert (Hg.), Diskurse der Gelehrtenkultur in der frühen Neuzeit. Ein Handbuch, Berlin, 465–516
- Koch, Hans-Joachim, Helmut Rüssmann (1982), Juristische Begründungslehre. Eine Einführung in Grundprobleme der Rechtswissenschaft, München
- Lagus, Conrad (1592), Methodica iuris utriusque traditio, in sex partes divisa, Lugduni
- Lambert von Auxerre (1971), Logica (Summa Lamberti um 1250), hg. von Franco Alessio, Florenz
- Leibniz, Gottfried Wilhelm (2008), The Art of Controversies, translated and edited by Marcelo Dascal, Dordrecht
- Locke, John (1690), An Essay concerning Human Understanding, London
- Manderston, William (1528), Compendiosa dialectices epitome, Paris
- Martini, Jacobus (1610), Institutionum logicarum libri VII, Wittenberg
- Meier, Georg Friedrich (1757/1996), Versuch einer allgemeinen Auslegungskunst, Halle; neu hg. von Axel Bühler und Luigi Cataldi Madonna, Hamburg
- Meier-Oeser, Stephan (1997), Die Spur des Zeichens. Das Zeichen und seine Funktion in der Philosophie des Mittelalters und der frühen Neuzeit, Berlin
- Melanchthon, Philipp (1536), De dialectica libri quatuor recogniti, [o. O.]
- Melanchthon, Philipp (1548), Erotemata dialectices, 2. Ausg., Wittenberg
- Menzel, Wolfgang Walter (1996), Vernakuläre Wissenschaft. Christian Wolffs Bedeutung für die Herausbildung und Durchsetzung des Deutschen als Wissenschaftssprache, Tübingen
- Nomicus Pacemutus Analyticophilus [Pseudonym von Vincentius Placcius] (1664), De iurisconsulto perfecto in genere liber unus, Augustae
- Ockham, William (1675), Summa totius Logicae [frühes 14. Jh.], Oxford
- Paulsen, Friedrich (1885), Geschichte des gelehrten Unterrichts auf den deutschen Schulen und Universitäten vom Ausgang des Mittelalters bis zur Gegenwart, Leipzig
- Petrus Hispanus (1572), Summulae logicales, cum Versorii Parisiensis clarissima expositione, Venedig
- Pinborg, Jan (1967), Die Entwicklung der Sprachtheorie im Mittelalter, Münster
- Piur, Paul (1903), Studien zur sprachlichen Würdigung Christian Wolffs, Halle / Saale
- Placcius, Vincentius (1693), De iurisconsulto perfecto, sive interprete atque interpretatione legum liber singularis, Stockholm und Hamburg
- Pörksen, Uwe (1983), Der Übergang vom Gelehrtenlatein zur deutschen Wissenschaftssprache. Zur frühen deutschen Fachliteratur und Fachsprache in den naturwissenschaftlichen und mathematischen Fächern (ca. 1500–1800), in: Zeitschrift für Literaturwissenschaft und Linguistik 51/52, 227–258
- Pufendorf, Samuel (1672), De jure naturae et gentium libri octo, in: ders. (1998), Gesammelte Werke, hg. von Frank Böhling, Bd. IV, Berlin
- Ramus, Petrus (1579), Dialecticae libri duo, ex variis ipsius disputationibus, et multis Audomari Talaei commentariis denuo breviter explicati, Frankfurt
- Ricken, Ulrich (1995), Zum Thema Christian Wolff und die Wissenschaftssprache der deutschen Aufklärung, in: Kretzenbacher, Heinz u. a. (Hg.), Linguistik der Wissenschaftssprache, Berlin, 41–90
- Rogerius, Constantius (1549), Sing. Tractatus de iuris interpretatione, Lugduni
- Säcker, Franz-Jürgen (1984), Einleitung, in: Rebmann, Kurt / ders. (Hg.), Münchener Kommentar zum Bürgerlichen Gesetzbuch, 2. Aufl., München, Bd. 1, 3–78
- Scheibler, Christoph (1665), Opus logicum, in: ders., Opera philosophica, Frankfurt
- Schiffauer, Peter (1979), Wortbedeutung und Rechtserkenntnis. Entwickelt an Hand einer Studie zum Verhältnis von verfassungskonformer Auslegung und Analogie, Berlin

- SCHRÖDER, JAN (2003), Zur Geschichte der historischen Gesetzesauslegung, in: ECKERT, JÖRN (Hg.), Der praktische Nutzen der Rechtsgeschichte. Hans Hattenhauer zum 8. September 2001, Heidelberg, 481–495
- SCHRÖDER, JAN (2020), Recht als Wissenschaft. Geschichte der juristischen Methodenlehre in der Neuzeit, 3. Aufl., München
- SEIBICKE, WILFRIED (2003), Fachsprachen in historischer Entwicklung, in: BESCH, WERNER u. a. (Hg.), Sprachgeschichte. Ein Handbuch zur Geschichte der deutschen Sprache und ihrer Erforschung, 2. Aufl., 3. Teilbd., Berlin, 2377–2391
- SETZ, WOLFRAM (1975), Lorenzo Vallas Schrift gegen die Konstantinische Schenkung, Tübingen
- SUÁREZ, FRANCISCO (1613), Tractatus de legibus ac deo legislatore, Antwerpen
- SÜSSMILCH, JOHANN PETER (1766), Versuch eines Beweises, daß die erste Sprache ihren Ursprung nicht vom Menschen, sondern allein vom Schöpfer erhalten habe, Berlin
- THIBAUT, ANTON FRIEDRICH JUSTUS (1806), Theorie der logischen Auslegung des römischen Rechts, 2. Ausg., Altona
- THOMASIUS, CHRISTIAN (1702), Institutionum jurisprudentiae divinae libri tres, 3. Ausg., Halle
- TIMPLER, CLEMENS (1612a), Logicae systema methodicum, Hanau
- TIMPLER, CLEMENS (1612b), Metaphysicae systema methodicum, Hanau
- TRABANT, JÜRGEN (2006), Europäisches Sprachdenken. Von Platon bis Wittgenstein, München
- TRIER, J[OST] (1972), Artikel »Etymologie«, in: RITTER, JOACHIM / KARLFRIED GRÜNDER (Hg.), Historisches Wörterbuch der Philosophie, Darmstadt, Bd. 2, Sp. 816–818
- VALLA, LAURENTIUS (1538), Elegantiarum latinae linguae libri sex, Lugduni
- VALLA, LAURENTIUS (1540), Dialecticarum disputationum libri 3, in: DERS., Opera, Basel
- VICKERS, BRIAN (2002), »Words and Things« – or »Words, Concepts and Things«? Rhetorical and Linguistic Categories in the Renaissance, in: KESSLER, ECKHARD, IAN MACLEAN (Hg.), Res et verba in der Renaissance, Wiesbaden, 287–335
- WASWO, RICHARD (1987), Language and Meaning in the Renaissance, Princeton
- WEINRICH, HARALD (1958), Münze und Wort. Untersuchungen zu einem Bildfeld, in: LAUSBERG, HEINRICH u. a. (Hg.), Romanica. Festschrift für Gerhard Rohlfs, Halle (Saale), 508–521
- WEISE, CHRISTIAN (1684), Doctrina logica, Leipzig und Frankfurt
- WILLIAM OF SHERWOOD (1995), Introductiones in Logicam / Einführung in die Logik [ca. 1230–1250], hg. von HARTMUT BRANDS und CHRISTOPH KANN, Hamburg
- WITTGENSTEIN, LUDWIG (1960), Philosophische Untersuchungen, Frankfurt am Main
- WOLF, ERIK (1951), Große Rechtsdenker der deutschen Geistesgeschichte, 3. Aufl., Tübingen
- WOLFF, CHRISTIAN (1732), Philosophia rationalis sive Logica, 2. Aufl., Halle
- WOLFF, CHRISTIAN (1744), Vernünftige Gedancken von den Kräfften des menschlichen Verstandes und ihrem richtigen Gebrauche in Erkäntniß der Wahrheit (1713), 12. Aufl., Halle
- WOLFF, CHRISTIAN (1746), Ius Naturae, Bd. VI, Halle

Peter Collin, Wim Decock, Nadine Grotkamp, David von Mayenburg, Anna Seelentag

History of Conflict Resolution in Europe – A Project Report

I. Introductory remarks

This text provides information on a project whose early beginnings date back to 2012, and which ended in 2021 with the publication of the four-volume *Handbuch zur Geschichte der Konfliktlösung in Europa* (Handbook on the history of conflict resolution in Europe).[1] Responsibility for the project lay mainly in the hands of legal historians. Nevertheless, as the handbook's title already makes clear, this has not been a legal history project of the usual kind. Its starting point was conflict and its resolution. As this is not limited to judicial procedures, the project's remit went far beyond an approach concentrating on legal norms and judicial institutions. However, the project did not seek to cover every activity related to conflict management, either, such as unregulated violence. Rather, the aim was to explore conflict resolution as a pattern of action following certain ideas of order. The handbook thus discusses institutionalised and rule-based forms of dealing with conflicting interests and sanctioning norm violations.

The area under investigation is Europe. This requires a little explanation. Not only the nation-state-based approach to legal history is currently under pressure to justify itself; a perspective focused on Europe, too, must question its basic assumptions. This is certainly true with regard to the claim that ideas of liberty, the rule of law, and capitalism arose out of a common European legal tradition,[2] and even more so regarding certain narratives of European legal history that emerged after the Second World War, whose underlying cultural and ideological premises need to be historicised. In the mid-20th century, the assumption of a common Western normative heritage both served as a fulcrum for the new European integration[3] and provided additional legitimatory ammunition during the Cold War. The traditional, Europe-centred approach also limited the scholarly purview: spatially, by concentrating on central, western and south-western Europe; with regard to the sources of law, by leading to a narrow focus on private law as shaped by Roman law; and finally, also regarding the identification of overarching developmental tendencies such as scientisation, professionalisation, rationalisation, and secularisation.[4] More recent developments in legal history, however, have seen such approaches being replaced by global historical perspectives.[5] So why not write a global history of conflict resolution, or at least broaden it to include transnational approaches that go beyond Europe?

The main reason why this route was not taken was pragmatic: there was insufficient capacity for such an undertaking within the framework of this project. However, there are also substantive reasons for limiting the project to Europe. Writing a ›history of conflict resolution in Europe‹ does not have to result in a reproduction of traditional Europe-centred narratives of legal history. Rather, it offers the chance to break new ground – in this case, by including procedures and institutions of conflict resolution that are not shaped by learned and / or codified law. However, there are also limits to how far such a project can be open to new approaches. A uniform methodological and conceptual orientation is hardly enforceable in a four-volume compilation with nearly 200 authors, but it is also not desirable. The handbook is also a reflection of the plurality of research, in which conventional approaches have their place just as much as new trends.

1 Grotkamp / Seelentag (eds.) (2021); Mayenburg (ed.) (2021); Decock (ed.) (2021); Collin (ed.) (2021a).

2 A discussion of these claims can be found in Whitman (2018).

3 Lesaffer (2018), however, has pointed out that (German) attempts to conceptualise a European legal history date back further and were connected with a crisis of Roman law as a scientific discipline.

4 On this, see Duve (2012) 21 ff.

5 Duve (2020) 74.

The handbook's scope does extend to regions on the periphery‹ of geographical Europe, such as to early Israel and ancient Egypt, to Byzantium and the Crusader states, to Russia and other Eastern European states, to the Ottoman Empire and modern Turkey as well as to the European colonies. Limitation to the ›Christian West‹ was thus avoided. The handbook also discusses cultures of conflict resolution of groups that have received little attention in the older Western European legal history tradition, such as American indigenous peoples, Muslims and Jews. Finally, the project's chosen remit is additionally justified by the fact that geographical Europe has been an interconnected space since the end of antiquity at the latest – even if one takes into account its diffuse borders and the links with various Asian and African regions. This interconnected space was based on inner-European migration and expansion, on the unifying power of the Church, on the family ties of the ruling dynasties, on the network of inner-European trade relations, on the exchange of scientific knowledge and, last but not least, on law and certain ideas of institutionalised and rule-governed conflict resolution.

II. Self-reflections of the juridical field

Despite its long history, conflict resolution became the subject of research only relatively recently.[6] The origins of modern conflict research lay in the discipline of psychology in the early 20th century. Morton Deutsch identifies the social psychologist Kurt Lewin (1890–1947) as having pioneered this field of study in the early 1930s.[7] Lewin proposed fundamental definitions and typologies and conducted the first empirical studies to verify them. From the start, research on this topic was always oriented towards practical questions, looking for new ways to resolve conflicts at a time of strong social tensions.

Conflict research did not remain confined to the field of psychology for long, as the scientific examination of conflicts and their resolution is almost inevitably an interdisciplinary enterprise. Overlap soon emerged with the research interests of economists. Though the first studies were presented by outsiders such as Kenneth E. Boulding (1910–1993),[8] it was the game theorists who subsquently studied human behaviour in conflict situations empirically.[9] Since the 1960s, it has been above all sociologists and political scientists who conduct conflict research. Initially, the origin and focus of their interest were the global conflicts of the Cold War and the search for ways to resolve them. Subsequent peace research was also supported by representatives of other disciplines, such as theology.[10]

Historical studies, which had always been very interested in social conflict situations, increasingly resorted to the theoretical and methodological tools developed in the social sciences from the 1970s onwards. Social differences of all kinds manifest in the form of more or less violent conflicts; historical conflict research, therefore, became – albeit relatively late[11] – a central concern of social and cultural history.[12] Historians made use of theories and methods of social science conflict research, such as Gerd Althoff and his students who have analysed strategies of medieval conflict resolution[13] and scholars of early modern history who have worked on ›infrajustice‹ as well as historical crime research.[14] They thus dealt with subject areas similar to those of legal history, though they consciously demarcated their work from it. Since the second half of the 20th century, therefore, conflict research has developed into an important interdisciplinary branch of the social sciences, with its own chairs and research institutions. Its findings are presented in numerous monographs as well as dedicated handbooks and journals.

But how did the juridical field reflect on the problem of conflict resolution? Two preliminary remarks are necessary at this point. Firstly, the term ›juridical field‹ and not ›legal system‹ has been deliberately chosen for this text.[15] In systems

6 The following paragraph (up to and including the phrase »Since the second half …«) is the English translation of a passage from the overall introduction to the handbook.

7 Deutsch (2014) XXXII.

8 Boulding (1962).

9 Deutsch (2014) XXXIII f.

10 On this, see the brief overview in Jahn (2012) 12–17.

11 Volkmann (1972) 551.

12 Dressel (1996) 123.

13 See e. g. Althoff (1997).

14 Garnot (2000); Schwerhoff (2011).

15 It should be emphasised that the following remarks do not outline the theoretical framework of the handbook – which cannot be pressed into a specific theoretical corset, anyway.

theory a legal system is more than a »context of coordinated rules« (which is in any case not capable of self-reflection), namely a »context of communications«.[16] However, this implies a significant limitation of communications, because such a system is operatively closed. Its self-description relates to its own operation and is only to a very limited extent able to include factors and reasons whose rationality lies outside the system rationality of the legal system. While this does not preclude the discussion of, for example, extra-legal justifications and conceptions, it forces them onto the Procrustean bed of legal argumentation.[17] In contrast, Bourdieu's »actor-dependent, constructivist-structural approach« of the juridical field is more open.[18] The juridical field is not merely a context of communications coded in a certain way – as in the case of the systems-theoretical understanding of ›legal system‹ – but a space in which struggles over beliefs and interests are conducted by specialists in the law and their institutions. Without necessarily following further theoretical implications of the Bourdieusian concept of the juridical field,[19] the terminology of the judicial field enables us to broaden the perspective in our investigation of how lawyers – both jurists and practitioners, though in many cases the distinction does not matter – reflect on the problem of conflict resolution.

The debates on judicial reform in Germany in the first half of the 19th century may serve as an example. Here, a comprehensive discussion emerged about the possibilities and limits of judicial conflict resolution – and thus also about the potential of its extrajudicial forms. An important impulse came from the new organisation of the justice system in France, which in the wake of the Napoleonic conquests spread to many European countries, including to large parts of Germany. In this period, French law established modern forms of conflict resolution to complement the ›normal‹ judicial process. Justices of the peace, for example, were an institution that, while also intended to enforce the regulatory claim of state law even in remote areas,[20] was above all meant to create a form of conflict resolution for minor disputes, outside the ›normal‹ judicial system, that was as citizen-oriented, effective and inexpensive as possible.[21] However, the French model of jury courts was even more in the focus of the debates regarding judicial reforms among German lawyers. Here, participatory democratic concepts and distrust of the traditional criminal courts met with the idea that the jurors' sense of justice would lead to an interpretation of the law that corresponded more closely to the needs of practical life than the verdicts of professional judges.[22] Those arguing for the introduction of jury courts hoped they would bridge the »gap between learned law and popular law«.[23]

The first half of the 19th century also saw the beginning of German debates on arbitration, which was similarly expected to take better account of the ›lifeworld‹ of the people concerned. Here the focus lay above all on commercial arbitration.[24]

The debate about the best ways to organise conflict resolution was given new impetus by the enactment of the *Civilprozeßordnung* of 1877, which introduced a uniform civil procedure law for the whole of Germany. The new code was dominated by liberal concepts, which meant that a large part of the procedural actions were placed in the hands of the parties, and the judge's management of the proceedings was restricted. This resulted in an elaborate and complicated procedure that often could only be managed by lawyers and, in addition, carried the possibility of procedural delays.[25] While the discussion of these issues could be conducted on a purely technical-procedural level, in actual fact they also raised fundamental questions. How could conflict resolution be organised in a way that made its institutions easily

16 Luhmann (1995) 40.
17 Ibid. 501 ff.
18 Kretschmann (2019) 15.
19 For a comprehensive discussion, see Guibentif (2019); Sapiro (2019).
20 Boers (2014) 32, 40 f.; D'Antuono (2014) 59 f.
21 Erkens (1994) 31 f.; Mölling (2000), summarising 213–223.
22 Mittermeier (1848) 90; also Heffter (1848) 112: »Der Gesetzgeber muß nämlich dem Geschwornengerichte die Befugnis eröffnen, das Gesetz rein menschlich auszulegen […] nach dem im Volke gewöhnlichen sittlichen Vorstellungen […]« (The legislator must give the jury court the power to interpret the law in a purely humane way, in accordance with the moral conceptions common among the people.)
23 Schwarze (1865) 128.
24 Reyscher (1847).
25 For a summary, see Wilhelm (2010) 252 f.

accessible, offered a procedure that could be easily understood by laypersons and limited costs? It was precisely on these issues that a number of jurists criticised the new German civil procedure. Otto Bähr, one of the most influential players in German legal policy at the time, labelled it »Manchestertum«[26] to emphasise its social imbalance. With his usual eloquence, Otto von Gierke, the most important representative of the Germanist school of jurisprudence, proclaimed: »Our current civil procedure is not German. Nor is it ›of the people‹ [*volkstümlich*]. And least of all is it social.«[27]

At the beginning of the 20th century, the so-called ›free law‹ movement (*Freirechtsbewegung*)[28] concentrated on a different level of the judicial process: instead of debating civil procedure, its members focused on judges' decision-making. Here, the question was whether modern conflict resolution could still take place within the boundaries of statutory law. Based on the premise that there were gaps in positive law, the free law movement demanded that judges be given broad scope for decision-making, unfettered by written law. Its members thus ultimately aimed at the acceptance of an »alternative law«,[29] or in other words, at opening the judicial decision-making basis to normative criteria that were not codified. They argued that the inclusion of such criteria would enable judicial decisions to correspond more closely to the needs of real life.

Contemporary with the free law movement was the so-called ›special courts debate‹ (*Sondergerichtsdebatte*). In such courts, lay assessors were to provide the court with specialist expertise, such as, in particular, in conflicts concerning industrial property rights.[30] However, other special courts were also discussed, including for agricultural disputes, conflicts under tenancy law, construction and real estate law, marital law, for craft trades (*Handwerk*) and even publishers and writers.[31] Not as present in the jurists' debates, but part of its larger context, were other institutions that could also broadly be seen as ›special courts‹: the early labour courts (the so-called *Gewerbegerichte*)[32] and the arbitration courts for workers' insurance (*Schiedsgerichte der Arbeiterversicherung*).[33] The debate centred on the creation of conflict resolution bodies outside the ordinary courts, which was in many respects conceptualised in opposition[34] to the ordinary judicial system: a judicial power guiding the process vs. leaving it to the parties; lay (expert) participation vs. learned professional lawyers; simple, inexpensive and fast proceedings vs. complicated, expensive and protracted civil procedure; a normative taking into account of the practical needs of the lifeworlds concerned vs. strict adherence to dogmatically shaped statutory law; finding compromise through fact-oriented agreement vs. decision by judgement. In short, while the *Sondergerichtsdebatte* did not formulate a coherent proposal for an alternative form of conflict resolution, the outline of one can be reconstructed from various scattered contributions to it, as well as from the concepts that were implemented in practice. It goes without saying that the opening up of judicial decision-making to non-legal rationalities should not be seen solely in a positive light. While such concepts did not completely dispense with the liberal concept of the rule of law, it could no longer necessarily claim primacy.

In Germany, the years around the turn of the last century were the heyday of the debates about an alternative justice system, and thus about more diverse approaches to institutionalised and rule-based conflict resolution. Later discussions did not reach the same breadth or intensity, but rather focused on individual aspects. This was the case during the First World War, when many jurists argued for ending more court proceedings through amicable settlements. This movement was partly motivated by the reduced capacities of the judiciary due to the war, but the desire to strengthen the domestic political »truce« (*Burgfrieden*) through a »legal peace« (*Rechtsfrieden*)[35] in the interest of national unity also played a role. In the course of the democratisation efforts after 1918, the voices for the expansion of lay participation in the judicial

26 Bähr (1885) 341.
27 Gierke (1898) 456.
28 On this, see Riebschläger (1968).
29 Rückert (2008) 200.
30 Franck (2013) 158 ff.
31 Rathenau (1910) 394; Wilhelm (2010) 429 f.; Franck (2013) 159.
32 For a recent overview, see Rudloff / Vogt (2016); Collin (2021b).
33 Ayass (2014) 270 ff.
34 Strictly speaking, such a clear opposition between ordinary and alternative justice institutions applies only if based on the legal concept of ordinary civil justice as it existed at the end of the 19th century. In the 20th century, ordinary courts gradually adopted aspects of alternative dispute resolution that had proven successful.
35 Deinhardt (1916).

system became louder,[36] and many party programmes contained corresponding demands.[37] In the end, however, none of these changes were implemented and the judicial system of conflict resolution remained the same.

Only from the end of the 1960s onwards, as a result of the growing unease with traditional authoritarian structures in politics, law and science, did a fundamental legal discussion about conflict resolution re-emerge in Germany, this time encompassing an even broader range of issues. In the academic and legal policy debate, the demand for judicial decisions to pay greater attention to real-life needs met with increasing approval. Particularly sociologists of law argued for a more comprehensive inclusion of sociological knowledge in legal practice.[38] The call for a reform of the judiciary grew louder. The aim was to dismantle encrusted hierarchies and to take greater account of the ›lifeworld‹ of those affected.[39] Theo Rasehorn, a judge who produced a number of provocative and much-discussed analyses, demanded that judges should take on a *Betreuungsfunktion*, ›taking care‹ of the parties by guiding and accompanying them through the proceedings. »Similar to the arbitrator (*Schiedsmann*) in the big cities today, [the judge] will have a district jurisdiction and will hold talks with those seeking justice in manageable, private locations with a few assistants (*Hilfspersonen*) at a ›round table‹.«[40] In the end, these ideas of far-reaching judiciary reform did not catch on. Instead, the focus of legal sociologists and reform-oriented jurists shifted to extrajudicial forms of conflict resolution (arbitrators, arbitration boards, etc.).[41] However, the general population's demand for such extra-judicial options did not match the academic attention they received, nor did the reform ideas of the left and liberal camps receive much attention outside these circles. In the 1980s, when the literature on this topic had grown in volume, the actual use of such institutions had reached a low point,[42] and there was little demand for them in general.[43]

Since the 1990s, the discussion about alternative justice has intensified once again, though under somewhat different auspices and heavily influenced by international debates.[44] The Alternative Dispute Resolution (ADR) debate – which originated in the USA, where it aimed at broadening and facilitating access to justice[45] – is also gaining ground in Germany. In Europe it has been linked to the need for procedural efficiency and for relieving the courts. Initially driven in part by European legislation, ADR has meanwhile developed numerous institutional manifestations, the most important of which is mediation.[46] In addition, a special form of consumer dispute resolution has established itself.[47] More and more organisations are equipping themselves with ombudspersons, thus creating opportunities for conflict management in advance of judicial conflict resolution.[48] International commercial arbitration has already replaced state jurisdiction in some sectors.[49] Extra-judicial arbitration bodies of various sports associations have recently attracted attention due to a number of controversial decisions.[50] Online platforms, such as eBay, offer their own forms of dispute resolution, Online Dispute Resolution (ODR).[51] Finally, in some Western countries the emergence of ›Islamic justices of the peace‹ has raised fears that an atavistic parallel justice system may develop on a broad scale.[52]

Regardless of whether the above-mentioned developments continue and we really are dealing with a systematic displacement of state justice by extrajudicial or non-state forms of conflict resolution, it is clear that the communication of the juridical field has to a large extent turned to the question of alternative conflict resolution. The number of publications on the various forms of ADR is almost unmanageable, courses in mediation are offered to legal practitioners; and even

36 Le Bouëdec (2018).

37 Zentrumspartei 1918 (pt 29) (in: Lepper (ed.) (1998) 397 ff.); Unabhängige Sozialdemokratische Partei 1919 (pt 12) (in: Treue (ed.) (1954) 108 ff.); Deutsche Volkspartei 1920 (pt 4) (in: ibid. 127 ff.); Sozialdemokratische Partei 1921 (in: ibid. 111 ff.).

38 Bender (1994) 127 ff.

39 Requate (2001).

40 Rasehorn (1969) 281.

41 Rottleuthner (1987) 144.

42 Ibid. 151 (with regard to the arbitrators [*Schiedsmänner*]).

43 Röhl (1987) 518.

44 See on this Schütze (1998).

45 Menkel-Meadow (2016).

46 Masser et al. (2018).

47 Berlin (2014).

48 Hertogh / Kirkham (eds.) (2018).

49 Maurer (2016).

50 Case Pechstein, European Court of Human Rights (3rd Section), 2 October 2018 – 40575/10, 67474/10.

51 Zekoll (2012).

52 Wagner (2011).

lawyers are forced to leave the purely legal discourse and engage with non-legal arguments, for example when Muslim ›justices of the peace‹ raise concerns that traditional Western standards of the rule of law may be eroded, or when transnational investment arbitration tribunals override national sovereignty. In the juridical field, too, we no longer speak only of the resolution of legal conflicts before state courts, but of conflict resolution in the overarching sense – albeit with a special juridical accentuation.

III. Institutional prerequisites of the handbook project

Against the background of this debate, considerations began in the early 2010s to establish a research network on »Extrajudicial and Judicial Conflict Resolution«, in which legal historical issues played an important role. There were special reasons why Frankfurt was the location of these deliberations. On the one hand, this project benefitted from the comparatively high concentration of legal historians in one place. The Goethe University in Frankfurt has five chairs in legal history and the Max Planck Institute for Legal History and Legal Theory (formerly the Max Planck Institute for European Legal History) is also located in Frankfurt. Moreover, Frankfurt could look back on a long tradition of research in the field of the history of conflict resolution. The topic had been formally incorporated into the Max Planck Institute's research programme in 1988. Under the heading of »norm enforcement« (*Normdurchsetzung*), research was to be conducted into »the history of state and private justice, its alternative institutions, and the associated ways of thinking and agents at work in these institutions«.[53] A new book series, *Rechtsprechung*, had already been founded in 1986 and by now comprises 28 volumes.[54] The repertories of printed[55] and unprinted[56] source materials published in other book series focused largely on Europe. After the fall of the Wall in 1989, the project *Normdurchsetzung* was extended to include Eastern Europe.[57] To be sure, the focus of this project lay on the history of the state justice. However, by focussing on procedures, decisions and actors, the project's conceptualisation had already considerably emancipated itself from older fixations on the history of legislation and legal doctrine.

Similar developments had taken place at the Goethe University in Frankfurt. One of the main topics of the Research Training Group (*Graduiertenkolleg*) »European Medieval Legal History, Modern Legal History and Contemporary Legal History«, based at the university from 1988 to 2002, was »The Formation, Dissemination and Enforcement of Norms«,[58] drawing attention to the fact that its approach to legal history also included conflict resolution. A particular focus in Frankfurt was the research on the Imperial Chamber Court (*Reichskammergericht*) of the late medieval and early modern Holy Roman Empire.[59] Another important topic was the study of medieval and early modern commercial conflicts[60] and conflict resolution in the ancient Near East.[61]

This legal-historical focus complemented the research interests of scholars of current law, historians and representatives of other disciplines. It also served the needs of legal practitioners who sought to discuss their own ideas on a broader interdisciplinary basis. In 2012, this resulted in the establishment of the LOEWE Research Focus »Extrajudicial and judicial conflict resolution«,[62] a research network within the framework of the »Funding Programme for the Development of Scientific and Economic Excellence« of the State of Hesse.[63] This provided a broad interdisciplinary platform for research into historical and contemporary manifestations of conflict resolution. As a result, numer-

53 Simon (1988) 201.
54 The first volume of this book series was Ogorek (1986).
55 Ranieri (ed.) (1992).
56 Dölemeyer (1995).
57 Mohnhaupt et al. (eds.) (1997–2003).
58 Rückert (1997) 697.
59 See above all Diestelkamp (1993); Diestelkamp (1995); and various articles in Diestelkamp (1999).
60 Cordes / Dauchy (eds.) (2013); Cordes (2013); Cordes / Höhn (2018). This and the following footnote also include literature published after the start of the LOEWE Research Focus.
61 Pfeifer (2010); Pfeifer (2013a); Pfeifer (2013b); Pfeifer (2015).
62 http://www.konfliktloesung.eu/de.
63 https://wissenschaft.hessen.de/Forschen/Landesprogramm-LOEWE.

ous dissertations, studies and edited volumes were produced;[64] research outcomes were published as part of a working paper series;[65] and a lecture series was held with a focus on conflict resolution under the conditions of cultural diversity,[66] with some of the lectures subsequently published.[67] All in all, it was a project that brought together research questions and work on the topic of extrajudicial and judicial conflict resolution in a quantity and diversity that had not been achieved before.

The funding period of the LOEWE Research Focus ended in 2015. With the end of the project, the need arose to systematically summarise the research findings to date. This intention expanded into the idea of a comprehensive inventory that went beyond the topics and results of the LOEWE Focus – a handbook that was initially conceived as a single volume and then grew to four.

IV. Key concepts

1. *Conflict resolution*

As already stated at the beginning of this article, the handbook project conceptually starts from conflict and its resolution.[68] This avoids the selective and isolating effect of a purely legal approach and overcomes the fixation, typical of conventional legal history, on legal evaluation and judicial decision-making in favour of a broader focus. Starting from typical clashes of interests that manifest themselves in conflicts, the handbook seeks to show the diversity of conflict resolution options available to conflict parties, and with it the numerous institutions, procedures and rationalities of conflict resolution that also exist beyond law and the courts: heads of families, priests or entire village communities could participate in or facilitate dispute settlement processes such as negotiation, mediation and arbitration, reprimand practices, self-help (feud) and magic. These practices also reveal the role of moral or religious norms guiding decision-making in conflict resolution, either alongside the law or indeed in its place. The aim of the handbook is to examine this plurality of conflict resolution strategies, their respective characteristics and their relationship to each other. This approach frees legal history from its exclusive fixation on law and courts, and encompasses the social, cultural, economic, institutional and normative contexts in which partly competing, partly complementary forms of conflict resolution were practised. This opening up of the handbook's purview is apparent in the numerous contributions written by social or cultural historians, political scientists and sociologists, as well as scholars of Jewish, Byzantine and Islamic studies.

Despite the centrality of the concepts of conflict and conflict resolution to the handbook's approach, no single overarching definition of these terms underlies, or emerges from, the contributions. There is neither a uniform social science theory of conflict nor a generally accepted definition of it.[69] What is understood by conflict and conflict resolution dissolves into a multitude of classification criteria, e. g. concerning the levels of analysis (intrapersonal, interpersonal, international conflicts), the objects of conflicts and their structure (indivisible / divisible conflicts), the relative strength of conflict parties (asymmetric / symmetrical conflicts), the degrees of regulation and the functions of conflicts.[70] As a useful starting point for this project, conflict can be understood as a dispute between two or more parties over values, status, power and / or material resources.[71] However, this definition needs to be both expanded and narrowed down in several respects. Firstly, the handbook also takes into account procedures for sanctioning norm violations, i. e. primarily criminal law procedures. This cannot be easily integrated into a classic understanding of conflict. However, it must be borne in mind that, especially for the period before the High Middle Ages, it is often not possible to draw a sharp line between criminal and civil proceedings. By contrast, conflicts between

64 Examples of edited volumes include Zekoll et al. (eds.) (2014); Cordes (2015); Pfeifer / Grotkamp (eds.) (2017); Collin (ed.) (2016). A complete overview (as of 2015) can be found here: http://www.konfliktloesung.eu/de/veroeffentlichungen/.

65 http://www.konfliktloesung.eu/de/veroeffentlichungen/wps/.

66 LOEWE-Ringvorlesung (2013/14) »Die Justiz vor den Herausforderungen der kulturellen Diversität – rechtshistorische Annäherungen«. The programme is available at http://www.konfliktloesung.eu/images/pdf/131205_Ringvorlesung_Programm.pdf.

67 Duve (2013).

68 The following paragraph is the English translation of a passage from the handbook's general introduction.

69 Bonacker (2005) 14 f.

70 Bonacker / Imbusch (2010) 69 ff.

71 Coser (1968) 232; received in historical science, for example, by Mörke (1982) 147.

states – a classic field of peace research – have been largely excluded; however, for the 19th and 20th centuries, both international arbitration and the EU's justice system have been included. In any case, the core of the handbook concentrates on conflicts between citizens and between citizens and the state (or any other superordinate community).

Furthermore, as already mentioned above, the handbook is limited to institutionalised and rule-based conflict resolution. ›Institutionalised‹ means that the process of conflict resolution takes place before persons or institutions who are recognised as legitimate decision-makers or mediators on the basis of legal provisions or social conventions, or it concerns cases in which conflict resolution is placed in the hands of the participants in a generally recognised manner, as in the case of legitimate forms of feud. Spontaneous solutions and unauthorised self-help are thus excluded. ›Rule-governed‹ means that the procedures and decision-making are governed by norms. These can be legal norms, but also norms based on, for example, social conventions, religious beliefs or economic rationalities. Admittedly, this leaves a considerable grey area, especially when groups within a polity practice a type of conflict resolution according to their normative ideas that is either not recognised by the national legal system or operates on the margins of the law. This applies, for example, to the above-mentioned Islamic justices of the peace active in Western countries,[72] the ›thieves' justice‹ (*vorovskaia spravedlivost*) in Russia and the Soviet Union,[73] or the mafia,[74] but also the journeymen's courts at the end of the 18th and the beginning of the 19th century in Germany.[75]

2. *Judicial / extrajudicial*

Even on the basis of the understanding of conflict resolution outlined above, considerable problems remain with regard to internal differentiations. First of all, this concerns the distinction between judicial and extrajudicial conflict resolution – a key distinction of relevance to the handbook, as the regional / national research reports were to contain separate sections for each. The following criteria might be used as indicators of judicial conflict resolution (at least for continental Europe): independence of the decision-making bodies or individual decision-makers, regulation by codified procedural laws (code of civil procedure, code of criminal procedure), legally trained judges, designation as a court. Already for the 19th and 20th centuries, however, some of these criteria fail. For example, the English and French justices of the peace of the 19th century lacked specialised legal training; legal assistance was provided by subordinate employees, in the English case by the clerks.[76] Personal judicial independence remained decidedly precarious in France until the middle of the 20th century.[77] Above all, however, it must be taken into account that the question of what belonged to the judicial system was not answered according to general criteria but on the basis of legal provisions that listed what counted as a court.[78] It is even more difficult to draw the line in the period before the 19th century. The court of the Swabian League in the 16th century, for example, was designed as a court of arbitration, but its institutional organisation and its legally trained staff came very close to a ›real‹ court.[79]

Whether or not a mode of conflict resolution should be considered judicial is not only important for the sake of formal classification. As a result of the constitutional guarantees introduced during the 19th century, courts became subject to certain requirements (e. g. regarding procedure or the judges' qualification), and were at the same time provided with certain protective mechanisms and competences. Distinguishing between judicial / extra-judicial modes is even more difficult for the periods before the emergence of modern notions of the separation of powers. Looking at the variety of conflict resolution institutions over centuries and across many different societies, it may therefore be more productive to understand ›judicial‹ and ›non-judicial‹ not as a dichotomy but rather as the opposite ends of a spectrum.

3. *State / non-state*

Another essential dichotomy – again not merely for classification purposes – is whether, and to what extent, a particular mode of conflict resolution was

72 Rohe / Jaraba (2015) 161 f.
73 Schuppert (2016) 122 ff.
74 Keiser (2011) 140 ff.
75 Deter (1987) 74 ff.
76 Steinmetz (2002) 180 f.
77 Schill (1961).
78 E. g. §§ 12–14 Gerichtsverfassungsgesetz 1877 (Germany).
79 For a comprehensive discussion, see Carl (2000) 370 ff.

organised in state or non-state institutions. This raises the questions of the power constellations in which a mode of conflict resolution is embedded, what ordering principle comes into play, and to what extent the manner and outcome of the process are at the disposal of those affected. Admittedly, in order to determine whether a mode of conflict resolution should be categorised as belonging to the state, we need to clarify our premises. How do we define ›state‹, and to what periods and cultures do we apply this concept? These questions touch on fundamental issues that cannot be pursued here. However, it seems safe to assume that by at least the beginning of the early modern period, European polities had organised themselves as states.[80] For earlier periods, an equivalent role might be attributed to an institutional structure headed by a ruler or ruling body governing a territory or a defined group of people and who, at least in principle, held the monopoly over setting and enforcing norms to which binding force was attributed and which could be enforced with coercive power. Based on these criteria, a mode of conflict resolution can be assigned to the state or the non-state sphere; moreover, one can also – in a more flexible way – make gradations according to its proximity to state institutions or distance from them. This can be done in the form of a typology[81] or according to criteria such as the degree of institutional integration, the staffing, the intensity of state control and state regulation.

4. *Adjudication / conciliation*

Another important pair of words for exploring the inner workings of conflict resolution is that of conciliation / adjudication. Unlike the dichotomies discussed so far, these terms are not opposites; instead, they highlight particular modes of conflict resolution from a more comprehensive set of mechanisms. In the field of ADR, for example, such forms also include arbitration, mediation, negotiation, facilitation, and proceedings before ombudspersons.[82] In legal debates, however, adjudication and conciliation sometimes also appear as a contrasting pair or, more precisely, are seen as representing alternatives. This is particularly the case in discussions of legal policy, where the terms are used to describe two types of judicial problem-solving that are fundamentally differently conceived. In such cases, ›authoritarian‹ adjudication is contrasted with the allegedly positive characteristics of arbitration: the participation of those affected, more flexible solutions, more future-oriented conflict management, and undistorted communication.[83] To some extent, these different perspectives can also be projected back onto historical debates, but they do not really capture the complexity of conflict resolution practice;[84] especially in the Middle Ages, greater authority naturally also promised greater legal certainty.

Looking at the pair of terms from another angle, adjudication and conciliation can also be depicted as complementary. This is the case, for example, when state courts take over cases that are not amenable to conciliation, e. g. because of fundamental normative differences between the parties. This either relieves arbitration institutions from these potential resource-draining proceedings or, because of the state's prohibition of self-help, can actually make the parties more inclined to come to a negotiated agreement.[85] Last but not least, adjudication and conciliation can be identified as components of a uniformly conceived conflict resolution procedure in which judgement is preceded by an attempt to reach an amicable settlement[86] – a concept that can already be observed in pre-modern times. However, the reverse order is also possible: in medieval Japan, a judgement was not the end of the conflict but rather an intermediate step, to be followed by further negotiations. This unusual order can be explained by the lack of a functioning enforcement apparatus within the Japanese legal system at the time.[87]

V. The volumes' thematic structure

In the individual volumes of the handbook, the description of conflict resolution in Europe initially concentrates on examining the formative institutions and structures of the time period covered. However, the overall conception of the

80 See e. g. Duve (2011) 150.
81 Forsyth (2007); similar approaches in Connolly (2005); Kötter (2012) 17 ff.
82 Hopt / Steffek (2008) 16.
83 About this Prütting (1985) 262 f.
84 For a more comprehensive discussion of the following, see Collin (2013).
85 Spittler (1980).
86 § 278 Zivilprozessordnung (Germany).
87 Nishikawa (2001) 109.

handbook that provides the structure of its four volumes also offers the possibility of looking at conflict resolution in a longitudinal view, from antiquity to the present day. This *longue durée* approach allows for the differentiated exploration of both stabilising and dynamic factors and also makes diachronic connections visible. Each volume contains the same thematic sections: »Foundations and fundamental problems«, »Actors of conflict resolution«, »Procedures and institutions« and »Fields of conflict«, which are followed by the research reports on specific regions or countries. While the same main themes can thus be found throughout all four volumes, certain concessions had to be made. These resulted, firstly, from the fact that certain thematic foci had different relevance in the different epochs. For example, while ›revenge‹ is an indispensable key concept for analysing conflict resolution in antiquity, it hardly played a role as an institutionalised form of conflict resolution in 19th- and 20th-century Europe. Secondly, the thematic structure could not always be fully realised, as authors willing and able to write about a certain topic in a European perspective could not always be found. In addition, for certain topics the current state of research simply did not yet provide sufficient material for a handbook article of this nature. Original research would have needed to be performed, which, however, lay outside the scope of a handbook project.

1. *Foundations and fundamental problems*

A number of fundamental questions apply to all forms of conflict resolution, irrespective of period or location. First and foremost, there is the question of the extent to which people had access to institutionalised and rule-based conflict resolution at all. In other words, were there alternatives to unregulated, often violent conflicts or to the arbitrary exercise of the ›law of the strongest‹? Each volume of the handbook thus begins with a discussion of ›access to justice‹ – a modern expression that is nevertheless more generally applicable. Another key theme running through all volumes is ›legal certainty‹. The latter is not only a principle of the modern constitutional state; the topoi of *ius certum* and *certitudo iuris* hint at the older origins of this concept. Legal certainty is about the existence of norms – and not only legal norms – as »counterfactually stabilised expectations«[88] that do not have to prejudice any particular outcomes, but which convey a reliable framework.

Linked to legal certainty is the further fundamental question of how both the normative foundations and the procedure and results of conflict resolution are communicated beyond the narrow circle of those directly involved, and can thus serve as an orientation for other jurists as well as the general public. Under the heading »Media of conflict resolution«, the handbook's authors discuss not only forms of publicising decisions but also, for example, the relationship between written and oral communication.

Another topic dealt with in each of the four volumes is that of the »Sites of conflict resolution«. Where proceedings take place determines not only whether they will be public or not, or how they will be demarcated from everyday life and thus given a certain dignity. The architecture of court locations can also convey a particular understanding of the exercise of justice and, not least, the status one assigns to judicial authorities in relation to other authorities.

Other fundamental questions dealt with in this handbook tend to reflect problems specific to the period covered, such as the topic of »Revenge« for antiquity or that of »Feud« for the Middle Ages, of »Professionalisation« for the early modern period, or that of the distortions of »Justice under National Socialism« in the modern era.

2. *Actors of conflict resolution*

Throughout all four volumes, particular attention is paid to those participating in conflict resolution. Gender-specific problems are addressed, including the position of women not only as plaintiffs or defendants (and whether such a status was granted to them at all), but also the question of the extent to which they could belong to the decision-making personnel or intervene in conflict resolution in other functions. Mostly, however, the groups of actors discussed are period-specific: in antiquity, the focus lies on types of Greek and Roman judicial institutions; for the Middle Ages, on the diversity of actors in the tension-laden duality of secular and ecclesiastical power; for the early modern period, on the inclusion of the indigenous population of the new

88 Luhmann (1969) 37.

European colonies and of Muslim foreigners in Europe; for the 19th and 20th centuries, on the groups of professional and lay judges, who finally came to be distinguished from one other.

3. *Procedures and institutions*

Institutionalised and rule-governed forms of conflict resolution are based on organisations and procedures. Certain structural patterns are visible across all periods covered by the handbook, even if the borders between the categories sometimes blur and the terms vary. In most periods, a fundamental distinction between procedures aimed at penalising misbehaviour and those in which claims were disputed between conflicting parties – that is, between what we label as criminal and civil proceedings – is recognisable. Likewise, it becomes apparent that arbitration as an alternative to judicial decision-making always existed in some form, though its role and character varied. Frequently, its institutions were not open to all but rather accessible only to certain groups or classes. In addition, procedures for mediation also existed throughout the periods studied, though these were only partially formally organised. Of course, this summary is still a rather schematic view based on the thematic foci of the handbook articles in question. A closer look reveals numerous mixed forms and manifestations of ›infrajustice‹ and ›popular justice‹. Furthermore, key elements structuring procedures and influencing or even determining decisions/outcomes were often time-specific and can be presented diachronically only to a limited extent, if at all. Thus, during the period of antiquity we need to pay special attention to magic, and in the Middle Ages to the ordeal. Oath-taking as a procedural element played a prominent role from antiquity up to and including the early modern period. The handbook's volumes also focus on the formative court and procedural structures of each period, such as Roman provincial justice in antiquity, the instruments of dispensations under canon law and appeal procedures in the Late Middle Ages, territorial and imperial jurisdiction in the early modern period, the *ius commune* procedure in the latter two eras, and international arbitration and criminal jurisdiction as well as EU justice in the modern era.

4. *Fields of conflict*

The term ›fields of conflict‹ refers to social areas that have established their own culture of conflict resolution, which are often what Sally Falk Moore termed »semi-autonomous fields«,[89] with their own normative rationalities and specific ideas of authority, consensus and cooperation. That ordinary judicial systems are also active in these fields is clear, but they are partially displaced by specific forms of conflict resolution that attach themselves to them, overlap with them, or operate in semi-legal grey zones. Such social fields can be structured according to the logic of stratified or segmentary order or to the functional rationalities of the modern world. Nevertheless, some constants can be observed (even if the functional mechanisms change over time). Certain groups or social fields tend to develop their own modes and institutions of conflict resolution, such as the military, the nobility, the family and the economic sphere. Religious communities generally produce their own conflict resolution cultures, oriented towards religious normativity. For a long time, there existed also a special kind of rural conflict resolution. The volume on antiquity highlights conflict resolution in Greek competitive sports and in the cities; for the Middle Ages, the authors focus on cities, long-distance trade and universities, among other things, as do the authors of the volume on the early modern period. The latter also examine mining, crafts and guilds. The volume for the 19th and 20th centuries pays special attention to labour relations, state-citizen relations and the European colonies, amongst other things.

5. *Countries, regions and territories – regional research reports*

Each of the handbook's volumes concludes with a section dealing with countries, regions and territories, in the volumes on the early modern and modern periods in the form of country research reports.[90] These are intended, firstly, to overcome the problem that the thematic contributions cannot fully cover the European dimensions either in their breadth or in their depth; in this respect, the

89 Moore (1973).
90 The following passage (up to »development of extrajudicial and judicial conflict resolution«) is the English translation of a passage from the introduction to vol. 4 of the handbook.

country/regional research reports have a supplementary function. Secondly, however, they also have a purpose in their own right. On the one hand, they offer an introduction to the relevant secondary literature, providing starting points for those interested in exploring the issues in greater depth. On the other hand, these chapters provide brief sketches of the specific national or regional development of extrajudicial and judicial conflict resolution. Of course, for many centuries, the polities under consideration were not modern nation-states. The chapters dealing with antiquity, the Middles Ages, as well as some of the early modern period, often focus on empires, the scattered territories held by one dynasty, or regions with weak state institutions. In the volume on antiquity, in addition to the Roman Empire (discussed in detail in the thematic contributions) and classical Greece, the polities discussed include ancient Israel, ancient and Roman Egypt, and the Hellenistic world. The chapters in the volume on the Middle Ages discuss Byzantium, the early medieval ›Germanic‹ world, the Holy Roman Empire, Russia, France, England and Scandinavia. For the early modern period, alongside polities constructed along the lines of nation-states (such as France, the Netherlands, England and Wales, Scotland, Portugal, and to a certain extent Spain), we find composite monarchies (Poland-Lithuania), multiple territories ruled by the same dynasty (Sweden-Finland, Denmark-Norway), confederation-like entities (the Holy Roman Empire), (partially) dependent territories (Ireland, Italy), federations of regions (the Swiss Confederation) and empires (Habsburg and Ottoman). For the 19th and 20th centuries, individual chapters are devoted to most European nation states, although it should be borne in mind that in these 200 years, too, new states were created, old ones ceased to exist and borders were shifted.

VI. Concluding remarks

Of course, the findings of a four-volume handbook can hardly be summarised in a single article. In general, the handbook provides broad information on the basic lines of development and offers an introduction to more detailed research. But what general conclusions can be drawn? In the following, a number of key findings will be highlighted for each individual epoch.

The initial concept of the handbook included the idea of challenging the generally established understanding of conflict resolution in classical antiquity by asking whether the conventional concentration of research on Athens and Rome did not need to be broadened to include other regions as well as possible non-urban ways of dispute settlement. After all, the traditional focus on Athens and Rome is, to a certain extent, a relic of the research interests of scholars in whose contemporary societies the procedural rules of the *Corpus Iuris Civilis* continued to be directly applicable law. As the research progressed, however, it became clear that the traditional focus is actually justified by the central role of cities in ancient life. The authors' attempt to identify separate fields of conflict demonstrated that in antiquity, the city was not one field of conflict among many others but rather the central anchor point, both spatially and institutionally. Supra-regional structures, like the common courts of Greek cities or the different forms of provincial jurisdiction in the Roman Empire, were based on urban structures. Those involved in conflict resolution (parties, judges, arbitrators, etc.) were mainly identified by their city affiliation – their citizenship – even in the Hellenistic kingdoms and the Roman Empire.

Another peculiarity of antiquity that comparison within the project brought to light is that the identifiable functions and structures of conflict resolution appear less independent from roles and structures for other purposes. For example, cult practices were not fundamentally detached from the – in the original sense ›political‹ – structures of city government and administration, and conflict resolution was only rarely performed by ›professional‹ personnel. A person could be a priest or merchant and help others to settle their conflicts, without the notion that any of these tasks should be his principal occupation. This is in line with ancient theoretical thoughts: Aristotle, for example, while distinguishing different aspects of power, did not call for the separation of powers.

The Middle Ages can be described as a kind of laboratory for the development of a highly diverse range of conflict resolution strategies – as diverse as the forms of rule, social structures and political cultures during this period. Sometimes written and oral, ecclesiastical and secular, centuries-old and spontaneously emerging conflict resolution techniques coexisted in close geographical and temporal proximity. Despite this heterogeneity, however, the contributions to the handbook suggest that the development of these multiple modes of conflict resolution did not proceeded at random. Instead, we find some surprising parallels in the history of conflict resolution strategies in very different places in Europe. The handbook's contributions show, for example, that authorities everywhere saw the judicial institutionalisation of instruments of conflict resolution as an important element in securing their rule. Wherever this did not succeed, extrajudicial dispute resolution instruments dominated.

Similar observations apply to the early modern period, which, in many regards, can be considered as perpetuating the medieval paradigm of conflict resolution characterised by normative pluralism and jurisdictional competition. Personal status, religious affiliation and decentralised power structures continued to play a paramount role in shaping particular modes of conflict resolution. For example, in university cities, endless disputes arose about who was competent to judge disputes involving students. The university chancellor, the local bishop, the city alderman's court, the duke's council and the royal high court each asserted their claims. The clergy and nobility enjoyed privileges that challenged the attempts by kings and local governors to centralise power and harmonise procedures – as even Louis XIV came to understand when he prepared his reform of civil and criminal procedure, which prompted hostile reactions by clergy- and noblemen. Well into the 19th century, various forms of conflict resolution outside the normal judicial order remained a »privilege« not only of the nobility and clergy but also of the military and universities. At the same time, by the 18th century the Enlightenment had given impetus to a reform movement that ushered in many of the revolutionary ideas that became reality after 1789. Judges were increasingly expected to motivate their decisions, ecclesiastical authorities were sidelined, and criminal justice, to be applied equally to all citizens, was deemed to be a prerogative belonging exclusively to the state.

In the 19th and 20th centuries, the territorial organisation and professionalisation of the judiciary, begun in the early modern period, continued. In the country research reports, we see how the French system spread throughout most of Europe or at least had a lasting influence on the national development of the judiciary in many areas. At the same time, an enormous push towards juridification can be observed – not only in the sense that legal norms now formed the basis for decision-making, but also in as much as that, due to the requirement of legal bindingness and the independence of the judiciary, only legal communication became permissible in legal decisions. In addition, there is a quantitative aspect: through the gradual establishment of judicial protection of administrative rights throughout Europe, juridification also came to extend to state-citizen relations. Over the same period we also see both judicial and extrajudicial conflict resolution institutions based on the estates or religion either having their competences severely reduced or disappearing altogether. However, with the emergence of the interventionist and welfare state from the end of the 19th century onwards, both the liberal litigation model and the dominance of the ordinary courts entered into a crisis. This manifested itself both in demands for the opening up of judicial decision-making to social and economic concerns and in the emergence of new judicial and extrajudicial conflict resolution institutions – especially in labour relations, social policy and economics – and finally also in an unprecedented internationalisation of justice.

■

Bibliography

- Althoff, Gerd (1997), Königsherrschaft und Konfliktbewältigung im 10. und 11. Jahrhundert, in: idem (ed.), Spielregeln der Politik im Mittelalter. Kommunikation in Frieden und Fehde, Darmstadt, 21–56
- Ayass, Wolfgang (2014), Wege zur Sozialgerichtsbarkeit: Schiedsgerichte und Reichsversicherungsamt bis 1945, in: Masuch, Peter et al. (eds.), Grundlagen und Herausforderungen des Sozialstaats. Denkschrift 60 Jahre Bundessozialgericht, vol. 1, Berlin, 265–282
- Bähr, Otto (1885), Der deutsche Civilprozeß in praktischer Bethätigung, in: Jahrbücher für die Dogmatik des heutigen römischen und deutschen Privatrechts 23, 339–434

- Bender, Gerd (1994), Rechtssoziologie in der alten Bundesrepublik. Prozesse, Kontexte, Zäsuren, in: Simon, Dieter (ed.), Rechtswissenschaft in der Bonner Republik, Frankfurt am Main, 100–144
- Berlin, Christof (2014), Alternative Streitbeilegung in Verbraucherkonflikten, Baden-Baden
- Boers, Michael (2014), The »Juge de Paix« of Napoleonic Europe, in: Delivré, Émilie, Emmanuel Berger (eds.), Popular Justice in Europe (18th–19th Centuries), Bologna, 25–45
- Bonacker, Thorsten (2005), Sozialwissenschaftliche Konflikttheorien – Einleitung und Überblick, in: idem. (ed.), Sozialwissenschaftliche Konflikttheorien, 3rd. ed., Wiesbaden, 9–29
- Bonacker, Thorsten, Peter Imbusch (2010), Zentrale Begriffe der Friedens- und Konfliktforschung: Konflikt, Gewalt, Krieg, Frieden, in: Imbusch, Peter, Ralf Zoll (eds.), Friedens- und Konfliktforschung. Eine Einführung, Wiesbaden, 67–142
- Boulding, Kenneth Ewart (1962), Conflict and Defense: A General Theory, New York
- Carl, Horst (2000), Der Schwäbische Bund 1488–1534. Landfrieden und Genossenschaft im Übergang vom Spätmittelalter zur Reformation, Leinfelden-Echterdingen
- Collin, Peter (2013), Judging and Conciliation – Differentiations and Complementarities. Max Planck Institute for European Legal History Research Paper Series No. 2013-04, available at: https://ssrn.com/abstract=2256508
- Collin, Peter (ed.) (2016), Justice without the State within the State. Judicial Self-Regulation in the Past and Present, Frankfurt am Main 2016
- Collin, Peter (ed.) (2021a), Handbuch zur Geschichte der Konfliktlösung in Europa, vol. 4: Konfliktlösung im 19. und 20. Jahrhundert, Berlin
- Collin, Peter (2021b), Die frühe Arbeitsgerichtsbarkeit – eine Erfolgsgeschichte mit rechtspolitischer Breitenwirkung und rechtspraktischer Vorbildwirkung, in: Deinert, Olaf et al. (eds.), Arbeit, Recht, Politik und Geschichte. Festschrift für Michael Kittner zum 80. Geburtstag, Frankfurt am Main, 118–123
- Connolly, Brynna (2005), Non-State Justice Systems and the State: Proposal for a Recognition Typology, in: Connecticut Law Review 38, 239–294
- Cordes, Albrecht (2013), Litigating abroad – Merchants' expectations regarding procedure before foreign courts according to the Hanseatic privileges (12th–16th c.), in: Andersen, Per et al. (eds.), Law and Disputing in the Middle Ages. Proceeding of the Ninth Carlsberg Academy Conference on Medieval Legal History 2012, Copenhagen, 281–299
- Cordes, Albrecht (ed.) (2015), Mit Freundschaft oder mit Recht? Inner- und außergerichtliche Alternativen zur kontroversen Streitentscheidung im 15.–19. Jahrhundert, Köln
- Cordes, Albrecht, Serge Dauchy (eds.) (2013), Eine Grenze in Bewegung. Öffentliche und private Justiz im Handels- und Seerecht, München
- Cordes, Albrecht, Philipp Höhn (2018), Extra-Legal and Legal Conflict Management among Long-Distance Traders (1250–1650), in: Pihlajamäki, Heikki et al. (eds.), The Oxford Handbook of European Legal History, Oxford, 509–527
- Coser, Lewis (1968), Conflict, Social Aspects, in: Sills, David L. (ed.), International Encyclopedia of the Social Sciences, vol. 3, New York, 232–236
- D'Antuono, Giuseppina (2014), Popular Justice in Europe: The Justice of the Peace, a »popular« French Magistracy in the Kingdom of Naples, in: Delivré, Émilie, Emmanuel Berger (eds.), Popular Justice in Europe (18th–19th Centuries), Bologna, 47–67
- Decock, Wim (ed.) (2021), Handbuch zur Geschichte der Konfliktlösung in Europa, vol. 3: Konfliktlösung in der Frühen Neuzeit, Berlin
- Deinhardt, Richard (1916), Deutscher Rechtsfriede, Leipzig
- Deter, Gerhard (1987), Handwerksgerichtsbarkeit zwischen Absolutismus und Liberalismus. Zur Geschichte der genossenschaftlichen Jurisdiktion in Westfalen im 18. und 19. Jahrhundert, Berlin
- Deutsch, Morton (2014), Introduction, in: Coleman, Peter T. et al. (eds.), The Handbook of Conflict Resolution. Theory and Practice, 3rd ed., San Francisco, XVII–XXXVIII
- Diestelkamp, Bernhard (1993), Die politische Funktion des Reichskammergerichts, Köln
- Diestelkamp, Bernhard (1995), Rechtsfälle aus dem Alten Reich. Denkwürdige Prozesse vor dem Reichskammergericht, München
- Diestelkamp, Bernhard (1999), Recht und Gericht im Heiligen Römischen Reich, Frankfurt am Main
- Dölemeyer, Barbara (1995), Repertorium ungedruckter Quellen zur Rechtsprechung, Bd. 1–2, Frankfurt am Main
- Dressel, Gert (1996), Historische Anthropologie. Eine Einführung, Köln
- Duve, Thomas (2011), Katholisches Kirchenrecht und Moraltheologie im 16. Jahrhundert: Eine globale normative Ordnung im Schatten schwacher Staatlichkeit, in: Kadelbach, Stefan, Klaus Günther (eds.), Recht ohne Staat, Frankfurt am Main, 147–174
- Duve, Thomas (2012), Von der Europäischen Rechtsgeschichte zu einer Rechtsgeschichte Europas in globalhistorischer Perspektive, in: Rechtsgeschichte – Legal History 20, 18–71, http://dx.doi.org/10.12946/rg20/018-071
- Duve, Thomas (2013), Die Justiz vor den Herausforderungen der kulturellen Diversität – rechtshistorische Annäherungen, LOEWE Research Focus »Extrajudicial and Judicial Conflict Resolution«, Working Paper 7, available at: http://www.konfliktloesung.eu/images/pdf/131010_LOEWE_Diversitaet_Einleitung_8102013.pdf
- Duve, Thomas (2020), What is Global Legal History?, in: Comparative Legal History 8, 73–115, DOI: 10.1080/2049677X.2020.1830488
- Erkens, Marcel (1994), Die französische Friedensgerichtsbarkeit 1789–1814 unter besonderer Berücksichtigung der vier rheinischen Departements, Köln
- Forsyth, Miranda (2007), A Typology of Relationships between State and Non-State Justice Systems, in: Journal of Legal Pluralism 56, 67–113

- Franck, Lorenz (2013), Juristen und Sachverständige. Der Diskurs um die rechtliche Ausgestaltung des Verfahrens mit Sachverständigen während der Zeit des Deutschen Reiches, Baden-Baden
- Garnot, Benoit (2000), Justice, infrajustice, parajustice et extrajustice dans la France d'Ancien Régime, in: Crime, Histoire & Sociétés 4, 103–120
- Gierke, Otto von (1898), Rezension zu: Johann Christoph Schwartz, Vierhundert Jahre Civilprozess-Gesetzgebung, in: Zeitschrift für deutschen Zivilprozeß 26, 445–460
- Grotkamp, Nadine, Anna Seelentag (eds.) (2021), Handbuch zur Geschichte der Konfliktlösung in Europa, vol. 1: Konfliktlösung in der Antike, Berlin
- Guibentif, Pierre (2019), Pierre Bourdieu und das Feld des Rechts. Lehren einer unbequemen Beziehung, in: Kretschmann, Andrea (ed.), Das Rechtsdenken Pierre Bourdieus, Weilerswist, 96–111
- Heffter, August Wilhelm (1848), Diskussionsbeitrag, in: Verhandlungen der Germanisten zu Lübeck am 27., 28. und 30. September 1847, Lübeck, 110–117
- Hertogh, Marc, Richard Kirkham (eds.) (2018), Research Handbook on the Ombusman, Cheltenham
- Hopt, Klaus J., Felix Steffek (2008), Mediation: Comparison of Laws, Regulatory Models, Fundamental Issues, in: idem (eds.), Mediation. Rechtstatsachen, Rechtsvergleich, Regelungen, Tübingen, 3–130
- Jahn, Egbart (2012), Frieden und Konflikt, Wiesbaden
- Keiser, Thorsten (2011), Selbstregulierung im entstehenden Nationalstaat: Autogoverno und Corpi intermedi in Italien, in: Collin, Peter et al. (eds.), Selbstregulierung im 19. Jahrhundert – zwischen Autonomie und staatlichen Steuerungsansprüchen, Frankfurt am Main, 127–147
- Kötter, Matthias (2012), Non-State Justice Institutions: A Matter of Fact and a Matter of Legislation (SFB Governance Working Paper Series 43), Berlin
- Kretschmann, Andrea (2019), Pierre Bourdieus Beitrag zur Analyse des Rechts, in: idem (ed.), Das Rechtsdenken Pierre Bourdieus, Weilerswist, 10–26
- Le Bouëdec, Nathalie (2018), Das Gericht als Arena demokratischen Handelns? Ansätze zur Beteiligung des Volkes an der Rechtsprechung in Deutschland in der frühen Weimarer Republik und den ersten Nachkriegsjahren ab 1945, in: Archiv für Sozialgeschichte 58, 163–182
- Lepper, Herbert (ed.) (1998), Volk, Kirche und Vaterland. Wahlaufrufe, Aufrufe, Satzungen und Statuten des Zentrums 1870–1933, Düsseldorf
- Lesaffer, Randall (2018), The Birth of European Legal History, in: Pihlajamäki, Heikki et al. (eds.), The Oxford Handbook of European Legal History, 84–99
- Luhmann, Niklas (1969), Normen in soziologischer Perspektive, in: Soziale Welt 20, 28–48
- Luhmann, Niklas (1995), Das Recht der Gesellschaft, Frankfurt am Main
- Masser, Kai et al. (2018), Die Entwicklung der Mediation in Deutschland. Bestandsaufnahme nach fünf Jahren Mediationsgesetz, Baden-Baden
- Maurer, Andreas (2016), Vanishing Trials in Maritime Law. Why Abitration Replaces Litigation in the Maritime Industry, in: Collin, Peter (ed.), Justice without the State within the State. Judicial Self-Regulation in the Past and Present, Frankfurt am Main, 185–204
- Mayenburg, David von (ed.) (2021), Handbuch zur Geschichte der Konfliktlösung in Europa, vol. 2: Konfliktlösung im Mittelalter, Berlin
- Menkel-Meadow, Carrie (2016), The History and Development of »A« DR (alternative / appropriate dispute resolution), in: Völkerrechtsblog, 1 July, available at: 10.17176/20180220-230945
- Mittermeier, Carl Josef Anton (1848), Bericht, in: Verhandlungen der Germanisten zu Lübeck am 27., 28. und 30. September 1847, Lübeck, 68–91
- Mohnhaupt, Heinz et al. (eds.) (1997–2003), Normdurchsetzung in osteuropäischen Nachkriegsgesellschaften, Bd. 1–5, Frankfurt am Main
- Mölling, Astrid Maria (2000), Der Zivilprozeß vor dem rheinpreußischen Friedensgericht. Die Praxis des Friedensgerichts Xanten (1826 bis 1830), Aachen
- Moore, Sally Falk (1973), Law and social change: the semi-autonomous social field as an appropriate subject of study, in: Law & Society Review 7, 719–746
- Mörke, Olaf (1982), Der »Konflikt« als Kategorie städtischer Sozialgeschichte in der Reformationszeit, in: Diestelkamp, Bernhard (ed.), Beiträge zum spätmittelalterlichen Städtewesen, Wien, 144–161
- Nishikawa, Yoichi (2001), Die gerichtliche Konfliktlösung im europäischen und japanischen Mittelalter, in: Fikentscher, Wolfgang (Hg.), Begegnung und Konflikt. Eine kulturanthropologische Bestandsaufnahme (Bayerische Akademie der Wissenschaften / Philosophisch-Historische Klasse: Abhandlungen N.F., H. 120), München, 106–117
- Ogorek, Regina (1986), Richterkönig oder Subsumtionsautomat? Zur Justiztheorie im 19. Jahrhundert, Frankfurt am Main
- Pfeifer, Guido (2010), Judicial Authority in backlit Perspective: Judges in the Old Babylonian Period (19. August), in: forum historiae iuris, available at: https://forhistiur.net/media/zeitschrift/1103pfeifer.pdf
- Pfeifer, Guido (2013a), Konfliktlösungsmechanismen in altvorderasiatischen Staatsverträgen, in: Zeitschrift für Altorientalische und Biblische Rechtsgeschichte (ZAR) 19, 13–21
- Pfeifer, Guido (2013b), Mechanisms of Conflict and Dispute Resolution in Ancient Near Eastern Treaties, in: LOEWE Research Focus »Extrajudicial and Judicial Conflict Resolution« Working Paper Nr. 9, 1–7, available at: http://publikationen.ub.uni-frankfurt.de/files/32101/131031_Ancient_Near_Eastern_Treaties_Pfeifer.pdf
- Pfeifer, Guido (2015), Klageverzichtsklauseln in altbabylonischen Vertrags- und Prozessurkunden als Instrumentarien der Konfliktvermeidung bzw. Konfliktlösung, in: Barta, Heinz et al. (eds.), Prozeßrecht und Eid: Recht und Rechtsfindung in antiken Kulturen, Wiesbaden, 193–205

- Pfeifer, Guido, Nadine Grotkamp (eds.) (2017), Außergerichtliche Konfliktlösung in der Antike. Beispiele aus drei Jahrtausenden, Frankfurt am Main, available at: http://dx.doi.org/10.12946/gplh9
- Prütting, Hanns (1985), Schlichten statt Richten?, in: Juristenzeitung, 261–269
- Ranieri, Filippo (ed.) (1992), Gedruckte Quellen der Rechtsprechung in Europa, Bd. 1–2, Frankfurt am Main
- Rasehorn, Theo (1969), Von der Klassenjustiz zum Ende der Justiz, in: Kritische Justiz 2, 273–283
- Rathenau, Walther (1910), Gutachten über die Frage: Empfehlen sich Sondergerichte in Streitigkeiten aus dem Gebiete des Gewerblichen Rechtsschutzes?, in: Verhandlungen des Dreißigsten Deutschen Juristentages, Bd. 1, Berlin, 302–488
- Requate, Jörg (2001), Ombudsmann und »Runder Tisch«. Zur Geschichte der Debatte um Alternativen zur Justiz in der Bundesrepublik der sechziger und siebziger Jahre, in: Hof, Hagen, Martin Schulte (eds.), Wirkungsforschung zum Recht III. Folgen von Gerichtsentscheidungen, Baden-Baden, 273–282
- Reyscher (1847), Vortrag über die Schiedsgerichte, in: Verhandlungen der Germanisten in Frankfurt am Main am 24., 25. und 26. September 1846, Frankfurt am Main, 160–166
- Riebschläger, Klaus (1968), Die Freirechtsbewegung. Die Entwicklung einer soziologischen Rechtsschule, Berlin
- Rohe, Mathias, Mahmoud Jaraba (2015), Paralleljustiz. Eine Studie im Auftrag des Landes Berlin. Senatsverwaltung für Justiz und Verbraucherschutz, Berlin, available at: https://digital.zlb.de/viewer/metadata/15965865/1/
- Röhl, Klaus F. (1987), Rechtssoziologie, Köln
- Rottleuthner, Hubert (1987), Einführung in die Rechtssoziologie, Darmstadt
- Rückert, Joachim (1997), Das Graduiertenkolleg »Europäische mittelalterliche Rechtsgeschichte, neuzeitliche Rechtsgeschichte und juristische Zeitgeschichte« an der Johann Wolfgang Goethe-Universität Frankfurt am Main, in: Zeitschrift der Savigny-Stiftung für Rechtsgeschichte (GA) 114, 697–701
- Rückert, Joachim (2008), Vom »Freirecht« zur freien »Wertungsjurisprudenz« – eine Geschichte voller Legenden, in: Zeitschrift der Savigny-Stiftung für Rechtsgeschichte (GA) 125, 199–255
- Rudloff, Wilfried, Dennis Vogt (2016), Parität und Schlichtung: Die Gewerbegerichte als Orte arbeitsrechtlicher Konfliktlösung im Deutschen Kaiserreich, in: Collin, Peter (ed.), Justice without the State within the State. Judicial Self-Regulation in the Past and Present, Frankfurt am Main, 51–90
- Sapiro, Gisèle (2019), Literarisches Feld und juridisches Feld. Von der Differenzierung zur Konfrontation, in: Kretschmann, Andrea (ed.), Das Rechtsdenken Pierre Bourdieus, Weilerswist, 167–185
- Schill, Hans J. (1961), Die Stellung des Richters in Frankreich. Eine rechtshistorische Darstellung unter Einbeziehung der Gerichtsverfassung, Bonn
- Schuppert, Gunnar Folke (2016), The World of Rules: Eine etwas andere Vermessung der Welt, in: Max Planck Institute for European Legal History Research Paper Series No. 2016-01, available at: https://ssrn.com/abstract=2747385
- Schütze, Rolf A. (1998), Alternative Streitschlichtung. Zur Übertragbarkeit ausländischer Erfahrungen, in: Zeitschrift für Vergleichende Rechtswissenschaft 97, 117–123
- Schwarze, Friedrich Oscar (1865), Das deutsche Schwurgericht und dessen Reform, Erlangen
- Schwerhoff, Gerd (2011), Historische Kriminalitätsforschung, Frankfurt am Main
- Simon, Dieter (1988), Normdurchsetzung. Anmerkungen zu einem Forschungsprojekt des Max-Planck-Instituts für europäische Rechtsgeschichte, in: Ius Commune XV, 201–208
- Spittler, Gerd (1980), Streitregelung im Schatten des Leviathan, in: Zeitschrift für Rechtssoziologie 1, 4–32
- Steinmetz, Willibald (2002), Begegnungen vor Gericht. Eine Sozial- und Kulturgeschichte des englischen Arbeitsrechts (1850–1925), München
- Treue, Wolfgang (ed.) (1954), Deutsche Parteiprogramme seit 1861, Zürich
- Volkmann, Heinrich (1972), Wirtschaftlicher Strukturwandel und sozialer Konflikt in der Frühindustrialisierung. Eine Fallstudie zum Aachener Aufruhr von 1830, in: Ludz, Peter Christian (ed.), Soziologie und Sozialgeschichte. Aspekte und Probleme, Wiesbaden, 550–565
- Wagner, Joachim (2011), Richter ohne Gesetz. Islamische Paralleljustiz gefährdet unseren Rechtsstaat, Berlin
- Whitman, James Q. (2018), The World Historical Significance of European Legal History: An Interim Report, in: Pihlajamäki, Heikki et al. (eds.), The Oxford Handbook of European Legal History, 3–21
- Wilhelm, Uwe (2010), Das Deutsche Kaiserreich und seine Justiz. Justizkritik – politische Strafrechtsprechung – Justizpolitik, Berlin
- Zekoll, Joachim (2012), Jurisdiction in Cyberspace, in: Handl, Günther et al. (eds.), Beyond Territoriality. Transnational Legal Authority in an Age of Globalization, Leiden, 341–369
- Zekoll, Joachim et al. (eds.) (2014), Formalisation and Flexibilisation in Dispute Resolution, Leiden

OTEL
CHELSEA

Fokus focus

Karl Härter, Valeria Vegh Weis

Transnational Criminal Law in Transatlantic Perspective (1870–1945): Introductory Notes, Initial Results and Concepts

I. Introduction: Transnational Criminal Law

With the global turn of legal history,[1] researchers have also developed an interest in transnational criminal law, which from a historical perspective can be defined as a »system that attempts to suppress harmful activity that crosses borders or threatens to do so«.[2] It covers various types of crimes with a transboundary effect, is based on transnationally agreed norms and principles as well as on national criminal law, and the states or jurisdictions involved use a variety of transboundary procedures and practices »against harmful activity that affects a given state but occurs in part or whole beyond the state's territory«.[3] Hence, transnational criminal law involved a broad variety of organisations and actors from empires, nation-states and governments to semi- or non-state actors, experts and practitioners.

Whereas the history of modern international criminal law is mostly concerned with war crimes, crimes against humanity, genocide and the establishment of the respective international criminal tribunals from World War II onwards, transnational criminal law has a legal history that dates back to the *ius commune* era and covers a much broader range of norms, crimes, procedures and practices that involve a transboundary dimension. The transnationalisation of criminal law commenced with the French Revolution and lasted over the course of the long nineteenth century up to World War II. It led to the emergence of modern transnational criminal law and related specific regimes that aim at the governance of international crime in the global world.[4]

However, research often focuses on Europe or the more powerful states, whereas the transatlantic dimension of transnational criminal law – and Latin America in particular – constitutes a research field still to be explored by legal history. Therefore, the research project ›Transnational Criminal Law in Transatlantic Perspective (1870–1945)‹ aspires to develop new approaches to the history of transnational criminal law that aim towards a transatlantic dialogue between the Global North and the Global South. This includes a broad range of topics with a particular relevance for Latin American countries, comprising international crimes such as ›anarchist violence‹, ›trafficking of women‹ and ›counterfeiting currency‹, the negotiations of extradition treaties and international suppression conventions, the participation in international conferences and organisations, mutual legal assistance, and cooperation in matters of policing and prosecution as well as the circulation of knowledge in internal discourses of criminal jurisprudence and criminology.

II. Histories of Transnational Criminal Law in Latin America

Some of the topics mentioned above have already been studied as part of the burgeoning research in Latin America on the history of crime, criminal justice, policing and punishment.[5] This has also explored the transatlantic dimension of the transnationalisation of criminal law from the mid-19th to the mid-20th century, in particular:
– the impact of penal codes (especially the French *code pénal*) on the codification of criminal law in Latin American countries;[6]

1 Duve (2016); Duve (2020).
2 Boister (2018) 1.
3 Boister / Currie (2015) 2.
4 Härter / Hannappel / Tyrichter (eds.) (2019); Boister / Gless / Jessberger (eds.) (2021).
5 On the state of research, see Salvatore (1998); Salvatore / Aguirre / Joseph (eds.) (2001); Salvatore / Barreneche (eds.) (2013); Caimari / Sozzo (eds.) (2017); Barreneche (2015); Núñez / González Alvo (2015).
6 Nunes (2018); Agüero / Rosso (2018); Sontag (2014); Duve (1999).

– the importance of criminal jurisprudence, doctrine and criminology, and the participation of Latin American experts in the respective expert discourses;[7]
– the history of transboundary and international crimes, particularly ›anarchist violence‹,[8] ›travelling criminals‹[9] and the ›white slave trade‹;[10]
– the implementation of new methods of policing and identification systems[11] and the establishment of transboundary police cooperation;[12]
– extradition treaties concluded by Latin American countries and the related circulation of transnational criminal law in juridical discourses and international associations.[13]

These pioneering studies demonstrate that, first, issues of transnational criminal law gained in importance in the legal culture of Latin America from the second half of the 19th century onwards.[14] Second, Latin American countries and actors clearly played an active role within these transatlantic developments and were not merely recipients of European knowledge. Their increasing participation in transnational criminal law was not only motivated by the intention to belong to the ›civilised‹ world of political powers and international law,[15] but was also rooted in the tradition of *ius commune* that was still present in most Latin American legal systems and might have influenced the concepts of transnational criminal law.[16]

With the revolutions of 1848/49 and the beginning of the constitutional period in Latin America, the increase in migration from Europe and the growth of transnational trade, international political movements and dissent were increasingly perceived as cross-border, transatlantic threats, which – from the viewpoint of the elites – could endanger order and security.[17] As a consequence, these threats were also labelled as international crimes which transnational criminal law commenced to criminalise with ambiguous concepts such as ›anarchist violence‹, ›white slave trade‹ (trafficking of women), illegal migration and ›travelling criminals‹. From a historical perspective, ›transnational crime‹ refers to different types of criminal activities as well as to specific ›international perpetrators‹ and ›networks of organised crime‹ that operated in secret and across borders to elude national prosecution. This extends to criminal activities that had a cross-border dimension, a foreign connection or a transboundary effect, such as illegal migration, smuggling (drugs, weapons, counterfeit money) and human trafficking as well as various forms of political crime. Regarding the latter, political subversion, protest and revolts in which immigrants or indigenous groups participated gained in importance. American governments perceived the political activities of immigrant or indigenous groups to a certain extent as a transnational threat to the domestic political order and national security because they considered them to be stimulated or incited by international socialist, communist or anarchist ideologies and movements.[18]

Cross-border crime also became an important topic of transnational juridical-political and criminological discourses, in which experts from Europe and the Americas discussed concepts of international crime and related security measures within the framework of transnational criminal law, and in this respect also created labels and narratives of travelling criminals, organised crime and international habitual / professional offenders (*internationale Berufsverbrecher*) and ›dangerousness‹.[19] Recent research has demonstrated that actors from Latin America increasingly participated in these international juridical-political expert discourses and international organisations, particularly in the *Institut de Droit International* (1873), the *International Union of Penal Law* (1889) and, finally, the League of Nations.[20] Furthermore, Latin American countries and experts attended international congresses that developed as key arenas of transnational criminal law. These dealt with techniques of crime control, criminology and policing, all of which gained in importance for Latin America.[21]

7 Olmo (1981); Olmo (1999); Salvatore (2006); Salvatore (2018); Fonseca Rosenblatt / Mell (2018).
8 Albornoz (2017); Albornoz / Galeano (2017).
9 Galeano (2018).
10 Guy (1988); Fischer (2003); Trochon (2006); Ventura (2016); see also the contribution of Paul Knepper in this *Focus*.
11 Galeano / García Ferrari (2011a); Galeano / García Ferrari (2011b); García Ferrari / Galeano (2016); García Ferrari (2016b).
12 Galeano (2009); Galeano (2016); Galeano (2012); Duffau (2017).
13 Yáñez Andrade (2011); Härter (2019b).
14 Sozzo (2011).
15 Obregón (2006); Obregón (2017).
16 Härter (2021).
17 Knepper (2010); Knepper (2011).
18 Albornoz (2017).
19 Pifferi (2016); Härter (2020).
20 Fischer (2012); Scarfi (2017).
21 See the contribution of Elizabeth Gómez Alcorta in this *Focus*.

As early as 1885 and 1889, actors from Latin American countries participated in the first and second congresses of criminal anthropology in Rome and Paris, and brought the new concepts and techniques of criminology and crime control to Latin America, where this knowledge spread to various countries. On the one hand, this transnational circulation of knowledge had an impact on the various countries' domestic policing; for instance, after an office of anthropometric identification was established in 1889 in Buenos Aires, similar institutions were quickly set up in Uruguay, Brazil, Mexico, Ecuador, Peru, and Chile. On the other, it also stimulated the trend to develop transboundary police cooperation. A pivotal actor in this field was Juan Vucetich, an immigrant from the Habsburg Empire who had entered the Argentinian police services in 1888, adapted the Bertillonage method of anthropometric identification and developed fingerprint classification (dactyloscopy). This improved technique of identification and registration not only served national crime control, but was also adopted as a crucial technique of transnational policing, migration control and the prosecution of trans- and international crimes.[22] In general, transboundary security measures of transnational criminal law that included penal transportation/deportation, expulsion, extradition and police cooperation were implemented and used in many Latin American countries.[23]

Although the impact of transnational discourses and concepts on criminology, law-making, policing, punishment and state building in Latin America has been studied,[24] the implementation of the ambiguous concepts and narratives of ›transnational‹ or ›international crime‹ on the domestic level of criminalisation, policing and criminal justice in Latin American countries still needs further research from the perspective of critical criminology, particularly regarding indigenous groups and political movements.

In many Latin American countries, both the actual threats and the narratives of international crime – particularly of anarchist violence – were closely intertwined with transnational policing, expulsion and extradition. For instance, Argentina and Italy established a transatlantic police cooperation to monitor Italian anarchists who had migrated to Argentina. The cooperation was not only aiming at the prevention of political violence (›terrorism‹), but, to some extent, included the exchange of intelligence as well as the monitoring of transatlantic migration.[25] These activities were part of an overall rise of South American police cooperation in the second half of the 19th century and increased on the international level between 1905 and 1920, which was related to similar developments in Europe.[26] Already a cursory glance at the international police conferences in Monaco (1914), Vienna (1923) and Berlin (1926) reveals the importance of transnational criminal law and transatlantic relations. Topics such as expulsion, extradition and the creation of international criminal registers (also by using the records of criminal courts) were discussed at length, as well as ›international crime‹ and ›transnationally operating and organised criminals‹, who were perceived as a new kind of threat to international as well as national security. At the *First International Criminal Police Congress* in Monaco in 1914, delegates from Brazil, Cuba, Guatemala, Mexico and San Salvador participated; representatives from Argentina, Bolivia, Brazil, Cuba and Peru were present in Berlin in 1926. However, little is known about the role of these delegates, what they reported back to whom in their respective countries, and how this might have influenced policing and security discourses in Latin America.

Actors from Latin America not only participated in European-based discourses, organisations and conferences but also themselves organised activities in the field of transnational criminal law. From 1877 to 1914, several Latin and Pan-American congresses, conventions and collaborations dealt with issues of transnational criminal law, extradition and policing in the Americas and

22 Galeano / García Ferrari (2011a); Galeano / García Ferrari (2011b); García Ferrari / Galeano (2016); García Ferrari (2016b).

23 See, for example, Salvatore / Aguirre (2016); Albornoz / Galeano (2016); Duffau (2017).

24 Aguirre (1998); Dias (2016); Sozzo (2017); Salvatore (2006); Salvatore (2018); Fonseca Rosenblatt / Mell (2018).

25 Jensen (2015); see also the article by Nicolás Duffau in this *Focus*.

26 Schettini (2017); Galeano (2009); Galeano (2012).

beyond, including the transatlantic threat of anarchist violence.[27] After the *International Anti-Anarchist Conference* in Rome (1898), the *Second Pan-American Conference* (Mexico 1901–1902) concluded the *Tratado de Extradición y Protección contra el Anarquismo*.[28] This was not only the first multilateral extradition treaty worldwide, but also comprised the ›anarchist clause‹ that excluded anarchist acts and violent political crimes from the political offence exception (and therefore political asylum) and defined them as extraditable transnational crimes. Although the *Institut de Droit International* and the *International Anti-Anarchist Conference* had already proposed such a provision in 1880 and 1898, based on the Belgian assassination clause, it was the Latin American states that implemented it in transnational criminal law.[29] Already in 1897, Brazil and Chile had concluded a treaty that comprised the clause, and Paraguay successfully implemented it in the extradition treaty it concluded with Germany in 1909. This example demonstrates that states and actors in Latin America were not only well aware of the discourses and concepts developed by international associations; they even pioneered the adoption of notions of transnational crime and the anarchist clause years before European states implemented them. Although the German Empire had promoted the international fight against anarchism since the late 19th century, it was the extradition treaty with Paraguay that introduced the anarchist clause into German transnational law.[30]

Already since the 1850s, we can observe the increasing importance of extradition as an essential component of transnational criminal law, manifesting in various extradition treaties that Latin American and European countries concluded, as, for instance, Brazil (1877), Uruguay (1880) and Paraguay (1909) with Germany. The provisions listed forgery and fraudulent distribution of official documents (passports etc.) or counterfeit money, criminal acts committed by ship captains and crews, piracy, child abandonment, formation of criminal gangs, procuring of minors, bribery of public officials, and damaging of public transport and public facilities as having a transboundary dimension and affecting international security.[31] Thus, they were not only stipulated as extraditable crimes but also required some kind of transboundary cooperation such as immediate provisional arrest in urgent cases, the exchange or delivery of evidence and witnesses, the exchange of verdicts and practical implementation measures. As a consequence, the treaties both established practices of mutual legal assistance and influenced the practices of transnational policing.

Similar to police agencies in Europe, several states in Latin American (in particular Argentina, Brazil and Uruguay) started to build a network of police cooperation that culminated in the police conferences held in 1905, 1912 and 1920, two of them referred to as *Conferencia Internacional de Policía*. Like the *International Police Conferences* in Europe in 1914, 1923 and 1926, the Latin American conferences dealt with various issues of police cooperation, extradition, and international crime.[32] Moreover, at the *Congreso Científico Internacional Americano* (Montevideo 1901), the inventor of dactyloscopy, Juan Vucetich, propagated an international police cooperation based on his new identification system. The next *Congreso Científico Internacional Americano* (Buenos Aires 1910) followed this path and discussed cross-border crime, ›travelling criminals‹ and the foundation of a Universal Police Union, proposed by Vucetich's student Luis Reyna Almandos. The interrelations between the various international, Latin American and European conferences – and the ones organised in the same period in the US – have not been explored in detail, and little is known about how they influenced transatlantic criminal law.[33]

III. Further Research and Initial Results

As briefly outlined, existing research has already yielded important results, but pertinent aspects of the transatlantic dimension of transnational criminal law still require further interdisciplinary study. The application of integrative concepts, particularly regime theory and critical criminology, would enable further clarification of the historical role / function of the ›Global South‹ (and Latin America in particular) within the emerging transnational criminal law regimes and the global governance of transnational crime in the crucial period between

27 For an overview, see Inman (1965).
28 Yáñez Andrade (2011); Jensen (2014); Jensen (2015).
29 Nunes (2019).
30 Härter (2019b).
31 Härter (2019b).
32 Galeano (2009).
33 García Ferrari (2016a); García Ferrari (2016b).

the middle of the 19th century and World War II. The research project ›Transnational Criminal Law in Transatlantic Perspective (1870–1945): Towards a dialogue between the Global North and the Global South‹ intends to overcome the current gaps in this area of research by exploring the historical context of transnational crimes and transnational criminal law regimes, and by clarifying how the historical links between European and Latin American legal frameworks operated in terms of crime and criminal law, justice and punishment. Based on these initial considerations and the state of research, the papers presented at the workshop ›Transnational Criminal Law in Transatlantic Perspective (1870–1945)‹ further explored the transatlantic dimensions of transnational criminal law.[34] Three of these are published in this *Focus* and provide exemplary case studies.

In her closer look at international criminological congresses held between 1870 and 1945, Elizabeth Gómez Alcorta studies different issues of transnational criminal law and their impact on penal law in Latin America. Even when they were announced as ›transnational‹, most of these congresses were carried out almost entirely in Europe and followed a European agenda. To rectify this misleading image, Gómez Alcorta examines both the topics discussed at the conferences and the Latin American delegates' role at them in order to investigate the actual emergence of transnational interactions and draw first conclusions about the consequences and impact of these congresses in Latin America. Her study analyses the congresses' impact on domestic legislation with a focus on how ›dangerousness‹ was incorporated in the discursive and normative framework they created. The chapter shows that despite the cultural diversity of each of the countries or regions, these meetings became tools for the universalisation of norms, ranging from legislative proposals linked to the ›social question‹ to criminal procedure and the penal and penitentiary system. At the same time, the study examines the role played by a certain part of the scientific elite in Central Europe in the discursive elaboration that would become dominant in criminology in the late 19th and early 20th centuries. Finally, Gómez Alcorta asks whether the construction of ›dangerousness‹ as a cross-border legal-political concept could constitute a tool for global governance and explores its extensive reception in Latin America as an instrument of social and criminal control. Overall, her contribution demonstrates the impact of transnational criminal law regimes in Latin America and thus contributes to seeing crime and criminals in a historical and transatlantic perspective.

The article by Nicolás Duffau analyses the ›Volpi-Patroni Case‹ (1882) as an example for the transnational regime of Italian immigration, crime, and police actions in Uruguay. Raffaele Volpi and Vicenzo Patroni – Italian immigrants unfairly accused of murder – were tortured by the Uruguayan police. As a result, the Kingdom of Italy suspended diplomatic relations with the Republic of Uruguay in March 1882. At that time, criminals and marginalised people were frequently stigmatised and persecuted by the authorities, who accused them of blocking the political and cultural development of ›modern‹ Uruguay. Through the historical analysis of the Patroni-Volpi case and its broad press coverage and transnational dimension, Duffau examines the complex process of social identity formation in the period of immigration and the inclusion of foreigners into the Uruguayan society in the late 19th century and thus demonstrates the interdependencies between transnational criminal law and migration regimes.

Exploring the regime that the League of Nations established to fight the international crime of the ›white slave trade‹ (traffic in women), Paul Knepper also demonstrates the transnationalisation of criminal law. During the 1920s, the League of Nations sent undercover researchers into more than a hundred cities across Europe, North and South America as part of the first ›worldwide‹ investigation into the traffic in women. The League's investigation illustrates the transnationalisation of criminal law. John D. Rockefeller, Jr., who funded the project, had the idea for an undercover inquiry before the First World War. His role demonstrates the ›entangled history‹ of trafficking. Grace Abbott, the American representative to Geneva, organised an inquiry that displays multiple characteristics of transnational law regimes. One of the first assignments to the researchers was to investigate reports of a plot to send several hundred women aboard a single ship from Germany to South American brothels. This report,

34 Workshop (2019).

which turned out to be false, had such importance because it referenced the white slave trade narrative as part of the wider cultural, political, and social contexts in which transnational law regimes operate. Another report of a New York theatrical agent believed to have trafficked several hundred women to Panama, demonstrates the meanings of ›transnational criminal‹ and ›transnational crime victim‹.

IV. Approaches and Concepts: Transnational Regimes and Global Legal History

The broad range of topics as well as the transatlantic dimension of transnational crime call for an interdisciplinary approach and sophisticated concepts. Overall, the project on ›Transnational Criminal Law in Transatlantic Perspective (1870–1945)‹ aims to apply the concepts of historical regimes of normativity and global legal history. From a methodological perspective, both interdisciplinary and inter-regional research are core elements of the project. Complex global and transnational phenomena require refined interdisciplinary analyses, which can only be achieved through the collaborative work of researchers coming from different disciplinary backgrounds, in this case legal and social history, criminology, international law, political science and sociology. In particular, understanding criminal justice systems not only from a normative perspective but through the concepts of ›practices‹, ›normative knowledge‹ and ›regimes‹ allows for a multidimensional understanding of the diverse phenomena of transnational crime and criminal law that have been mostly studied by scholars from the Global North. Thus, research should not only incorporate scholars from the Global South to think through these topics; it should also foster a collaborative dialogue between academics from both sides of the globe. In this regard, transnational criminal law constitutes an important topic of historical regimes of normativity and global legal history, the latter understood as »legal history in a global perspective […] especially interested in the reconstruction of the historical interaction between actors and actants – often remote from one another – or even in the interaction between members of different historiographic communities«.[35]

From the viewpoint of historical regimes of normativity, transnational criminal law hardly forms a coherent international normative order based on the rule of law, but can rather be conceptualised as a historically changing, flexible criminal law regime which developed mechanisms for the global governance of crime and punishment. Transnational regimes can be defined as more or less stabilised historical arrangements or agglomerations of norms, discourses and practices, in which a broad variety of actors from more than one state or jurisdiction respond to specific threats or a particular complex of problems, form a particular field of action and pursue general purposes such as ›security‹ or the ›governance of crime‹.[36] The regime concept enables a »form of observation to overcome the basic model of legal history centred on the nation-state […] and understands norms as part and product of historically consolidated structures (therefore, normativity regimes)«.[37] Regime theory was developed in the context of international law and relations[38] and is thus particularly appropriate for analysing the history of transnational criminal law as the evolution of a legal framework that extended to international, multilateral and national levels.[39] Transnational criminal law regimes can further be differentiated with regard to their various levels and actors, by considering the interdependencies of international, transnational and national levels on which laws, discourses and practices could be interpreted differently or serve different purposes and functions. Furthermore, transnational regimes involve various judicial and administrative, formal and informal transboundary procedures and practices and are therefore also characterised by legal pluralism, multinormativity, legal collisions and conflicts of jurisdiction.

The formation of transnational criminal law regimes in the second half of the 19th century involved a multiplicity of legal norms (ranging from international suppression conventions and

35 Duve (2018).
36 Härter (2011); Härter (2013).
37 Historical Regimes of Normativity – Part 1 (2021).
38 Haggard / Simmons (1987); Zangl (2006).
39 Boister / Gless / Jessberger (2021) 2.

bilateral treaties to national criminal law), international discourses and congresses, and various cross-border public / governmental institutions and non-state actors, experts and practitioners. International organisations such as the *Institut de Droit International*, the *International Union of Penal Law* and the *League of Nations* as well as a variety of different conventions such as the *International Prison Congresses* (1872, 1895), the *International Congress on Prostitution* (1877), the conferences of the *International Abolitionist Federation* (since 1878), the *Criminal Anthropology Conferences* (since 1885), the *International Congresses on the White Slave Trade* (1899, 1904, 1910), the *International Anti-Anarchist Conferences* (1898, 1904), the *Pan-American Conference* (1901/02), the *Congreso Sudamericano de Derecho Internacional* (1888/89), the *International Conference of American States* (1889/90), the *Congresos Científicos Internacionales Americanos* (1901, 1905, 1910), the *Conferencia Internacional de Policía* (1905) and the *International Police Congresses* (1909, 1912, 1914) periodically dealt with various matters of transnational crime and criminal law. In all of them, governmental and non-governmental experts, jurists, committees, associations from the Global North and the Global South participated, exchanged experiences and knowledge and influenced normativity and narratives.[40]

As stabilised historical arrangements or agglomerations of norms, discourses and practices, these transnational regimes (or their various manifestations) dealt with international crimes, criminals and threats (or narratives thereof) that were of high importance for the countries / actors involved and also implied a transatlantic dimension. Specific regimes evolved for several international / transnational crimes, such as for the trafficking of slaves and women, anarchism and political crime, drug trafficking, the smuggling of counterfeit currency and illicit arms. Although actors from Latin America participated in these transnational criminal law regimes, only a few studies on the history of transnational crime have included Latin America, and these mostly cover contemporary developments.[41] Moreover, the theoretical conceptualisation of transnational regimes is still mainly modelled on the blueprint of the Global North and to some extent neglects the equivalent consideration of the Global South as well as the perspective of global legal history.

It seems particularly appropriate to analyse how actors from both the Global North and the Global South responded to transboundary threats and international crimes and developed as well as exchanged normativity, knowledge, and practices of transnational criminal law in a transnational-transatlantic setting. Hence, a fundamental component of the regime concept is the international circulation of law, principles, knowledge and technologies that are applied or agreed by two or more states / jurisdictions and deal with cross-border or transboundary procedures and practices that extended to the national level. For Latin American countries, the domestic incorporation of principles, knowledge and technologies of transnational criminal law constituted a way of belonging to the ›civilised‹ world. In the core period of the formation of transnational criminal law regimes, the transatlantic relations between the newly formed nation-states in Latin America and Europe were framed by the idea of civilisation (knowledge coming from Europe) versus barbarism (the local indigenous cultures in Latin America). However, beyond the deconstruction of such narratives, research needs to clarify the specific motives and interests of Latin American states as well as their role in transnational criminal law regimes and transatlantic activities as vital actors and not mere recipients of European knowledge. Particularly, Latin American devotion to techniques of crime control and criminology (such as statistics and fingerprinting methods) that subsequently gained transnational importance could be considered as an effort to participate in transnational criminal law regimes as ›civilised‹ and active states.

By looking at actors, research can not only consider nation-states but also non-governmental actors, experts and the ›target groups‹ of transnational criminal law activities, such as political dissenters, protesters, anarchists, foreigners / migrants, marginal and indigenous groups. This could also contribute to overcoming the still pre-

40 For Latin America, see the contribution of Elizabeth Gómez Alcorta to this *Focus*; further examples: González / Núñez (2020).

41 Farer (ed.) (1999); Lloyd (2018).

dominant focus on the European nation-state and demonstrate that the historical development of penal law was influenced by other – both non-state and non-European – actors as well. Based on the concept of ›global legal history‹, the outlined project focuses on the transatlantic perspective and the transboundary interaction and exchange between European and Latin American states as well as on the exchange, interdependence and activities of states and non-state ›transnational actors‹ in the sphere of transnational criminal law. A comparative approach is therefore essential for analysing the transboundary practices and activities of transnational / transatlantic actors regarding the direct exchange between at least two states or the participation of individual actors in international discourses, associations and conferences.

As a consequence, the regime concept and the transatlantic approach to the history of transnational criminal law enhance the common approaches of legal history and international law and allow us to integrate the history of transnational policing and ›global governance‹ of crime as well as concepts such as ›critical criminology‹ and ›criminal selectivity‹,[42] the labelling approach, the global circulation of legal knowledge and the transnational creation and dissemination of security threats and narratives.[43] In particular, including the critical criminology, criminal selectivity and labelling approaches into the framework of transnational criminal regimes permits us to examine specific threats, narratives, labels and images of transnational criminals and security created and disseminated in intersected international expert and security discourses.[44] These narratives and labels also had an impact on domestic criminal agencies and the labelling and selection processes that extended to political dissenters, protesters, anarchists, foreigners, migrants, marginal and indigenous groups. In turn, the model of the security dispositif and critical discourse analysis as conceptualised by Foucault[45] is useful for unearthing the underlying transnational / transatlantic power relations and constitutes an essential approach as well, particularly concerning security discourses, security threats and ›securitisation narratives‹ related to (or constituting) processes of (de)securitisation as historical developments of transnational criminal law regimes.

Taking a long-term perspective, studying transnational-transatlantic criminal law regimes allows us to trace the roots of modern global governance of crime and security by investigating if the normativity, knowledge and practices of these regimes were transformed into a ›global regime‹. This, in turn, can help us determine if the modern phenomenon of the global governance of crime is new or can be traced back to the 19th century or even the pre-modern era. It could furthermore contribute to refining the notions of ›global governance‹ and ›globalisation‹ regarding the development and current status of ›power balances‹ and related legal interdependencies between Latin American and European countries.[46] The transnationalisation of criminal law and the formation of transatlantic criminal law regimes in the period between 1870 and 1945 were also characterised by international conflicts, contradictory interests, competing nation-states and historical (dis)continuities. Hence, the formation of transnational criminal law regimes was related to complex and contradictory historical changes and by no means a uniform process of modernisation at the transnational level. The observation of historical transnational-transatlantic criminal law regimes therefore provides an analytical basis to further discuss current worldwide problematics of the global governance of crime. This includes questions such as whether transnational crimes should be addressed exclusively from an international or criminological perspective; whether countries that are not affected by a particular transnational crime should be compelled to pass legislation and enforce policies to deter that offence as part of a global strategy; and which level of collective self-determination of developing countries is appropriate for contesting and even rejecting legislative proposals from international organisations.[47] Studying legal phenom-

42 For an attempt to conceptualise the contemporary prosecution of international crime as a selective criminal law regime, see Cryer (2008).

43 On the history of security regimes, see Daase (2013); Härter (2019a).

44 Vegh Weis (2014).

45 Dillon / Neal (eds.) (2008); for a comparison of Foucault's model of the security dispositif and the regime concept, see: Härter (2013).

46 Jakobi / Wolf (2013).

47 Vegh Weis (2020).

ena from the perspective of historical regimes of normativity thus allows us to understand the genesis of the current state of transnational crime and criminal law, to compare different historical processes with ambiguous outcomes that are still influencing current opportunities, to comprehend *longue durée* processes, to conduct broader and interdisciplinary analyses of legal concepts, to acknowledge cultural diversity and to reflect on the past to avoid the repetition of painful historical events.[48]

■

Bibliography

- Agüero, Alejandro, Matías Rosso (2018), Codifying the Criminal Law in Argentina: Provincial and National Codification in the Genesis of the First Penal Code, in: Masferrer (ed.), 297–322
- Aguirre, Carlos (1998), Crime, Race, and Morals: The Development of Criminology in Peru 1890–1930, in: Crime, History & Societies 2, 73–90
- Albornoz, Martín (2017), Policías, cónsules y anarquistas: la dimensión transatlántica de la lucha contra el anarquismo en Buenos Aires (1889–1913), in: Iberoamericana 17, 57–79, online: https://journals.iai.spk-berlin.de/index.php/iberoamericana/article/view/2234
- Albornoz, Martín, Diego Galeano (2016), El momento beastly. La policía de buenos aires y la expulsión de extranjeros (1896–1904), in: Astrolabio Nueva Época: Revista digital del Centro de Investigaciones y Estudios sobre Cultura y Sociedad 17, 6–41
- Albornoz, Martín, Diego Galeano (2017), Anarquistas y policías en el atlántico sudamericano: una red transnacional, 1890–1910, in: Boletín del Instituto de Historia Argentina y Americana »Dr. Emilio Ravignani«, Tercera serie, núm. 47, 101–134
- Barreneche, Osvaldo (2015), Las Instituciones de seguridad y del castigo en Argentina y América Latina. Recorrido historiográfico, desafíos y propuestas de diálogo con la historia del derecho, in: Max Planck Institute for European Legal History Research Paper Series No. 2015-04, online https://ssrn.com/abstract=2645608
- Boister, Neil (2018), An Introduction to Transnational Criminal Law, 2nd ed., Oxford (first ed. 2012)
- Boister, Neil, Robert J. Currie (2015), Introduction, in: idem (eds.), Routledge Handbook of Transnational Criminal Law, London / New York, 1–7
- Boister, Neil, Sabine Gless, Florian Jessberger (2021), Introduction, in: idem (eds.), 1–13
- Boister, Neil, Sabine Gless, Florian Jessberger (eds.) (2021), Histories of Transnational Criminal Law, Oxford
- Caimari, Lila, Máximo Sozzo (eds.) (2017), Historia de la Cuestión Criminal en América Latina, Rosario
- Cryer, Robert (2008), Prosecuting International Crimes. Selectivity and the International Criminal Law Regime, Cambridge
- Daase, Christopher (2013), Politische und rechtliche Konsequenzen der erweiterten Sicherheit, in: Fischer-Lescano, Andreas, Peter Mayer (eds.), Recht und Politik globaler Sicherheit, Frankfurt am Main, 11–42
- Dias, Rebeca (2016), Brazilian Criminological Thinking During the First Republic (1889–1930), in: Max Planck Institute for European Legal History Research Paper Series No. 2016-13, online: https://ssrn.com/abstract=2874851
- Dillon, Michael, Andrew W. Neal (eds.) (2008), Foucault on Politics, Security, and War, Basingstoke
- Duffau, Nicolás (2017), Propuestas orientales, concreciones rioplatenses. Redes delictivas, extradición criminal y colaboración policial en el Río de la Plata (1854–1865), in: Revista Historia y Justicia 8, 138–165, online: https://journals.openedition.org/rhj/898
- Duve, Thomas (1999), ¿Del absolutismo ilustrado al liberalismo reformista? La recepción del Código Penal Bávaro de 1813 de P. J. A. von Feuerbach en Argentina y el debate sobre la reforma del derecho penal hasta 1921, in: Revista Historia del Derecho 27, 125–152
- Duve, Thomas (2016), Global Legal History: A Methodological Approach, in: Max Planck Institute for European Legal History Research Paper Series No. 2016-04, http://dx.doi.org/10.2139/ssrn.2781104 and Oxford Handbooks Online – Law, Jan. 2017, DOI: 10.1093/oxfordhb/9780199935352.013.25
- Duve, Thomas (2018), Global Legal History: Setting Europe in Perspective, in: Philajamäki, Heikki, Markus D. Dubber, Mark Godfrey (eds.), The Oxford Handbook of European Legal History, online: http://www.oxfordhandbooks.com/view/10.1093/oxfordhb/9780198785521.001.0001/oxfordhb-9780198785521-e-5
- Duve, Thomas (2020), What is Global Legal History?, in: Comparative Legal History 8, 73–115, DOI: 10.1080/2049677X.2020.1830488
- Farer, Tom J. (ed.) (1999), Transnational Crimes in the Americas, New York
- Fischer, Thomas (2003), Der Weg nach Buenos Aires – Frauenhandel und Prostitution in den 1920er Jahren, in: Comparativ 13, 138–154
- Fischer, Thomas (2012), Die Souveränität der Schwachen. Lateinamerika und der Völkerbund, 1920–1936, Stuttgart
- Fonseca Rosenblatt, Fernanda, Marília Montenegro Pessoa de Mell (2018), Criminology in Brazil: Beyond »Made-in-the-North« Criminological Narratives, in: Triplett (ed.), 345–359

48 Duve (2016) 10.

- Galeano, Diego (2009), Las conferencias sudamericanas de policías y la problemática de los delincuentes viajeros, 1905–1920, in: Bohoslavsky, Ernesto, Lila Caimari, Cristiana Schettini (eds.), La policía en perspectiva histórica. Argentina y Brasil (del siglo XIX a la actualidad), Buenos Aires, online: http://www.crimenysociedad.com.ar/files/submenu5-item1.html
- Galeano, Diego (2012), Voyages de policiers: Une route entre Paris et les villes sud américaines, 1880–1905, in: Denys, Catherine (ed.), Circulations policières 1750–1914, Villeneuve-d'Ascq, 41–62
- Galeano, Diego (2016), Traveling Criminals and Transnational Police Cooperation in South America, 1890–1920, in: Huertas, Luz E., Bonnie A. Lucero, Gregory J. Swedberg (eds.), Voices of Crime. Constructing and Contesting Social Control in Modern Latin America, Tucson (AZ), 17–50
- Galeano, Diego (2018), Delincuentes viajeros. Estafadores, punguistas y polícias en el Atlántico sudamericano, Buenos Aires
- Galeano, Diego, Mercedes García Ferrari (2011a), Cartographie du bertillonnage. Le système anthropometrique en Amérique latine: circuits de diffusion, usages et résistances, in: Piazza, Pierre (ed.), Aux origines de la police scientifique. Alphonse Bertillon, précurseur de la science du crime, Paris, 308–329
- Galeano, Diego, Mercedes García Ferrari (2011b), The bertillonage in the South American Atlantic World, in: Criminocorpus: Identification, contrôle et surveillance des personnes, online: http://journals.openedition.org/criminocorpus/402
- García Ferrari, Mercedes (2016a), El gabinete de Juan Vucetich: un laboratorio de experimentación. La Plata, Argentina: 1891–1901 in: Estudios Interdisciplinarios de América Latina y el Caribe 27, 7–28, online: http://eial.tau.ac.il/index.php/eial/article/view/1436
- García Ferrari, Mercedes (2016b), Un saber »sudamericano«. La dactiloscopia en el Congreso Científico Latinoamericano, 1901–1909, in: Historia Crítica 60, 81–101, online: dx.doi.org/10.7440/histcrit60
- García Ferrari, Mercedes, Diego Galeano (2016), Police, Anthropometry, and Fingerprinting: Transnational History of Identification systems from Río de la Plata to Brazil, in: História, Ciências, Saúde – Manguinhos 23, online: http://www.scielo.br/hcsm
- González, Esteban, Jorge Núñez (2020), Argentina's Participation in the International Penal and Penitentiary Congress (1872–1950), in: GLOSSAE. European Journal of Legal History 17, 83–118, available at http://www.glossae.eu
- Guy, Donna J. (1988), White Slavery, Public Health, and the Socialist Position on Legalized Prostitution in Argentina, 1913–1936, in: Latin American Research Review 23, 60–80
- Haggard, Stephan, Beth A. Simmons (1987), Theories of International Regimes, in: International Organization 41, 491–517
- Härter, Karl (2011), Die Formierung transnationaler Strafrechtsregime: Auslieferung, Asyl und grenzübergreifende Kriminalität im Übergang von gemeinem Recht zum nationalstaatlichen Strafrecht, in: Rechtsgeschichte – Legal History 18, 36–65, online: http://dx.doi.org/10.12946/rg18/036-065
- Härter, Karl (2013), Security and Cross-border Political Crime: The Formation of Transnational Security Regimes in 18th and 19th Century Europe, in: Historical Social Research 38, Special Issue: Security and Conspiracy in History, 16th to 21st Century, ed. by Beatrice de Graaf, Cornel Zwierlein, 96–106
- Härter, Karl (2019a), Security and Transnational Policing of Political Subversion and International Crime in the German Confederation after 1815, in: Graaf, Beatrice de, Ido de Haan, Brian Vick (eds.), Securing Europe after Napoleon. 1815 and the New European Security Culture, Cambridge, 193–213
- Härter, Karl (2019b), The Circulation of Transnational Criminal Law between the Americas and Germany (1848–1914) in Extradition Treaties, Juridical Discourses and International Associations, in: Revista da Faculdade de Direito da Universidade Federal de Minas Gerais 74, 353–378, online: https://www.direito.ufmg.br/revista/index.php/revista/article/view/1988
- Härter, Karl (2020), Zweckgedanke, Social Defence and Transnational Criminal Law: Franz von Liszt and the Network of Positivist Criminology (1871–1918), in: GLOSSAE. European Journal of Legal History 17, 150–175
- Härter, Karl (2021), Norms, Procedures and Practices of Transnational Criminal Law in 18th and Early 19th-Century Europe, in: Boister / Gless / Jessberger (eds.), 14–26
- Härter, Karl, Tina Hannappel, Jean Conrad Tyrichter (eds.) (2019), The Transnationalisation of Criminal Law in the Nineteenth and Twentieth Century. Political Crime, Police Cooperation, Security Regimes and Normative Orders, Frankfurt am Main
- Historical Regimes of Normativity – Part 1 (2021), Historical Regimes of Normativity – Part 1, written by Regime Theory Working Group, June 28, 2021, https://legalhistoryinsights.com/historical-regimes-of-normativity-part-1/
- Inman, Samuel Guy (1965), Inter-American Conferences 1826–1954. History and Problems, Washington
- Jakobi, Anja P., Klaus Dieter Wolf (2013), The Transnational Governance of Violence and Crime: Non-State Actors in Security, New York
- Jensen, Richard Bach (2014), The Battle against Anarchist Terrorism. An International History, 1878–1934, Cambridge
- Jensen, Richard Bach (2015), Global Terrorism and Transnational Counterterrorism: Policing Anarchist Migration across the Atlantic: Italy and Argentina, 1890–1914, in: Dietze, Carola, Claudia Verhoeven (eds.), The Oxford Handbook of the History of Terrorism, Oxford, online: DOI:10.1093/oxfordhb/9780199858569.013.027
- Knepper, Paul (2010), The Invention of International Crime. A Global Issue in the Making, 1881–1914, London
- Knepper, Paul (2011), International Crime in the 20th Century. The League of Nations Era, 1919–1939, London
- Lloyd, Marshall B. (2018), Transnational Crimes in the Americas. Law, Policy and Institutions, London / New York
- Masferrer, Aniceto (ed.) (2018), The Western Codification of Criminal Law. A Revision of the Myth of its Predominant French Influence, Cham
- Nunes, Diego (2018), The ›Code Pénal‹ in the Itinerary of the Criminal Codification in America and Europe: ›Influence‹ and Circularity of Models, in: Masferrer (ed.), 281–295
- Nunes, Diego (2019), Extradition and Political Crimes in the ›International Fight against Crime‹: Western Europe and Latin America 1833–1933, in: Härter / Hannappel / Tyrichter (eds.), 41–63

- Núñez, Jorge, Luis González Alvo (2015), El porvenir del pasado penitenciario. Sobre la construcción de una agenda de trabajo para la historia de la prisión en la Argentina (1860–1950), in: Max Planck Institute for European Legal History Research Paper Series No. 2015-06, online: https://ssrn.com/abstract=2648960
- Obregón, Liliana (2006), Between Civilisation and Barbarism: Creole Interventions in International Law, in: Third World Quarterly 27, 815–832
- Obregón, Liliana (2017), Identity Formation, Theorization and Decline of a Latin American International Law, in: Wojcikiewicz Almeida, Paula, Jean-Marc Sorel (eds.), Latin America and the International Court of Justice: Contributions to International Law, London, 3–14
- Olmo, Rosa del (1981), América Latina y su criminología, México
- Olmo, Rosa del (1999), The Development of Criminology in Latin America, in: Social Justice 26, 19–45
- Pifferi, Michele (2016), Reinventing Punishment. A Comparative History of Criminology and Penology in the Nineteenth and Twentieth Centuries, Oxford
- Salvatore, Ricardo D. (1998), Criminal Justice History in Latin America: Promising Notes, in: Crime, History & Societies 2, 5–14
- Salvatore, Ricardo D. (2006), Positivist Criminology and State Formation in Modern Argentina, 1890–1940, in: Becker, Peter, Richard F. Wetzell (eds.), Criminals and Their Scientists. The History of Criminology in International Perspective, Washington D. C., 253–279
- Salvatore, Ricardo D. (2018), Criminology in Argentina, 1870–1960, in: Triplett (ed.), 309–320
- Salvatore, Ricardo D., Carlos Aguirre (2016), Colonies of Settlement or Places of Banishment and Torment? Penal Colonies and Convict Labour in Latin America, c. 1800–1940, in: De Vito, Christian G., Alex Lichtenstein (eds.), Global Convict Labour, Leiden, 273–309
- Salvatore, Ricardo D., Carlos Aguirre, Gilbert M. Joseph (eds.) (2001), Crime and Punishment in Latin America. Law and Society Since Late Colonial Times, Durham
- Salvatore, Ricardo, Osvaldo Barreneche (eds.) (2013), El delito y el orden en perspectiva histórica, Rosario
- Scarfi, Juan Pablo (2017), The Hidden History of International Law in the Americas: Empire and Legal Networks, New York
- Schettini, Cristiana (2017), En búsqueda de América del Sur: agentes secretos, policías y proxenetas en la Liga de las Naciones en la década de 1920, in: Iberoamericana 64, 81–103
- Schwöbel, Christine (ed.) (2014), Critical Approaches to International Criminal Law. An Introduction, Oxford
- Sontag, Ricardo (2014), Código Criminológico? Ciência Jurídica e codificação penal do Brasil 1889–1899, Rio de Janeiro
- Sozzo, Máximo (2011), Cultural Travels and Crime Prevention in Argentina, in: Melossi, Dario, Máximo Sozzo, Richard Sparks (eds.), Travels of the Criminal Question. Cultural Embeddedness and Diffusion, Oxford, 185–215
- Sozzo, Máximo (2017), Los usos de Lombroso. Tres variantes en el nacimiento de la criminología positivista en Argentina, in: Caimari / Sozzo (eds.), 27–69
- Triplett, Ruth Ann (ed.) (2018), The Handbook of the History and Philosophy of Criminology, Hoboken / Oxford
- Trochon, Yvette (2006), Las rutas de eros. La trata de blancas en el Atlántico Sur. Argentina, Brasil y Uruguay (1880–1932), Montevideo
- Vegh Weis, Valeria (2017), Marxism and Criminology. A History of Criminal Selectivity, Leiden
- Vegh Weis, Valeria (2020), Policing in Times of Globalization. Counterterrorism Legislation as a Platform for the Militarization of Policing in Argentina, in: Nagy, Veronika, Klára Kerezsi (eds.), A Critical Approach to Police Science: New Perspectives in Post-Transitional Policing Studies, The Hague, 245–272
- Ventura, Iris (2016), The Rise of Human Trafficking in Central America, Law School Student Scholarship 739, Seton Hall University, South Orange (NJ), online: https://scholarship.shu.edu/student_scholarship/739
- Workshop (2019), ›Transnational Criminal Law in Transatlantic Perspective (1870–1945): Towards a dialogue between the Global North and the Global South‹, organised by Karl Härter and Valeria Vegh Weis, Frankfurt am Main, May 23–24, online: https://www.lhlt.mpg.de/1695551/event-2019-05-23-transnational-criminal-law
- Yáñez Andrade, Juan Carlos (2011), Tratado de extradición y protección contra el anarquismo (1901–1902), in: Relaciones. Estudios de historia y sociedad 32, 125–136
- Zangl, Bernhard (2006), Regimetheorie, in: Schieder, Siegfried, Manuela Spindler (eds.), Theorien der Internationalen Beziehungen, Opladen, 121–144

Elizabeth Gómez Alcorta

Congresos criminológicos internacionales y su impacto en los códigos penales de América Latina (1870–1945)

I. Introducción

El presente artículo desarrollará una aproximación a los distintos congresos criminológicos (o que abordan la cuestión criminal) denominados internacionales pero llevados a cabo casi en su totalidad en Europa, en el periodo de 1870 a 1945, a fin de determinar cuáles fueron los ejes temáticos abordados y cuál fue la participación de delegados de países latinoamericanos. Con ello se busca investigar las incipientes interacciones transnacionales.

Asimismo, se aspira esbozar una primera conclusión sobre las consecuencias y el impacto de aquellos congresos en América Latina y, en particular, cuál ha sido la huella en materia legislativa y cómo se ha traducido el *estado de peligrosidad* a nivel discursivo y normativo.

De este modo, plantearemos el análisis de los diferentes congresos, entendiéndolos como producciones teoréticas y discursivas en torno a la cuestión criminal. En este sentido, se analizará cómo estos encuentros fueron herramientas para la universalización de normas, a partir de propuestas legislativas vinculadas a la cuestión social, al proceso penal, al régimen penal y penitenciario, más allá de la diversidad cultural de cada uno de los países o regiones. A la vez, se estudiará el rol que cierta parte de la élite científica del centro de Europa tuvo en la elaboración discursiva y en la narrativa que regiría durante fines del siglo XIX y comienzos del XX en las cuestiones vinculadas a la criminología.[1] Asimismo, se verá como aquella producción y subjetividad eurocéntrica basada en una clasificación social racista tuvo amplia acogida por la élite criolla ›blanqueada‹.

Por último, se interrogará si la construcción del *estado de peligrosidad* como concepto jurídico-político transnacional podría constituir una herramienta de gobernanza global vinculada a una etapa del capitalismo, resultando su vasta recepción en América Latina tanto un modo de formar parte del mundo civilizado como un instrumento de control de las clases dominantes a los transgresores y perturbadores del orden.

Metodológicamente hemos acudido a diversas fuentes: primero para reconstruir parcialmente lo acontecido en los distintos congresos, así como también para acercarnos a los contextos en los que ellos se llevaron adelante. Así, trabajamos a partir del método arqueológico de Michel Foucault, quien atiende a las formaciones y prácticas discursivas y a los documentos como materiales de trabajo, a la vez que recusa todo intento de concebir la linealidad y la continuidad del acontecer social. De ese modo, podremos indagar los modos de problematización de la criminología en tanto integrantes y dependientes de la estructura de poder y de la dinámica de clases de la sociedad en que se plantean. En tal sentido los documentos que dan cuenta de los diferentes congresos, se presentan como restos arqueológicos que sugieren formas de ver y pensar la producción teórica y discursiva en torno al saber criminal y a su transnacionalización.

No ha sido sencillo encontrar fuentes directas o material y bibliografía sobre los diferentes encuentros que se llevaron adelante en el periodo mencio-

1 A los fines de este trabajo definimos criminología como diferentes elaboraciones teóricas discursivas que abordan una heterogeneidad de objetos y de métodos no homogeneizables entre sí, pero orientados hacia la solución de un problema común: cómo garantizar el orden social. Ver Pavarini (1983).

nado: Congresos Penitenciarios Internacionales; Congresos Internacionales de Antropología Criminal; Congresos de la Unión Internacional de Derecho Penal y Congreso Internacional de Criminología. Por ello, el presente trabajo deberá ser continuado en base a nuevas fuentes.

En fin, este estudio busca realizar un aporte sobre el trasfondo histórico de la transnacionalización de los regímenes de derecho penal, identificando algunos de los modos de elaboración y difusión de los discursos vinculados a la criminología y a la cuestión criminal en Europa, tanto como su impacto en América Latina. Asimismo, busca contribuir a asignarle una historicidad a la categoría de delito y de delincuencia.

En cuanto a la temporalidad, la criminología comienza a ser considerada en Europa una ciencia a partir de las últimas décadas del siglo XIX,[2] logrando una importante difusión, tanto dentro del continente como en América Latina, y ello a partir de la creación de sociedades internacionales y de congresos internacionales (muchos de ellos organizados por esas sociedades) para estudiar el problema delictivo. En aquel periodo las principales ideas vinculadas a la prevención del delito y el tratamiento del delincuente tuvieron varias vías de difusión, más allá de los congresos y encuentros internacionales, resultando primordiales también las revistas especializadas y abundante material bibliográfico. Aquí nos abocaremos exclusivamente a los primeros.

Desde mediados del siglo XIX el problema del orden y el progreso se vinculó a la relación entre capital y trabajo, pasando a ocupar un lugar destacado como objeto de estudio de las ciencias del hombre. La delincuencia es uno de los factores desestabilizadores del orden social y fue abordado a partir de aquel momento mediante la psiquiatría y la antropología, de acuerdo al método positivista que se impuso a partir de 1880, a pesar de la disputa con la teoría clásica. El nacimiento de la antropología criminal o ciencia criminal obedeció no solo al nuevo panorama científico, sino también a ciertos cambios que se produjeron con la expansión del capitalismo y con el surgimiento de su etapa imperialista.

En las últimas décadas del siglo XIX, »el capitalismo se convertía en una economía genuinamente mundial y por lo mismo el globo se transformó de expresión geográfica en constante realidad operativa. En lo sucesivo la historia sería historia del mundo«.[3]

Así, a partir de 1870 se inicia una nueva era histórica, política y económica que socavó al liberalismo que había sido el modelo hegemónico durante la primera mitad del siglo XIX:

> La expansión industrial trajo como resultado que surgieran potencias no-europeas, como el caso de los Estados Unidos, que ingresaron a la arena para disputarse la hegemonía del mundo. Este hecho tendría sus repercusiones también en el campo del delito y específicamente en la forma de controlarlo. Ya no se haría dentro de los límites del Estado nacional, sino que se buscarían soluciones universales.[4]

En este marco es que veremos el rol que cumplieron los congresos internacionales, los que contaban con el sostén gubernamental, como espacios de encuentro para la difusión de normas universales para el control social.

En 1870 se llevó adelante el Congreso Nacional sobre la Disciplina de las Penitenciarías y Establecimientos de Reforma en la ciudad de Cincinnati, Ohio, Estados Unidos, organizado por la Asociación Nacional de Prisiones de los Estados Unidos y, en particular, por Enoch Wines – filántropo y reformador – y por Rutherford Haynes, iniciando una práctica (que se replicará tanto en Europa como en Latinoamérica) de encuentros que buscan fomentar cambios a nivel internacional.[5] Una de las resoluciones que se tomó en aquella reunión fue la de convocar a un Congreso Penitenciario Internacional. Para ello, el Congreso de los Estados Unidos de América resolvió que un comisionado[6]

2 Se puede situar el inicio de la criminología a partir de los estudios de Lombroso, más precisamente con su obra *El hombre delincuente*, que fue publicada en 1876.

3 Hobsbawm (1977) 72.

4 Olmo (1999) 50.

5 En la primeras décadas del Siglo XIX se llevaron adelante otros congresos o encuentros, como por ejemplo el Congreso Penitenciario de Frankfurt de 1846, Bruselas de 1847, y de Frankfurt de 1857, pero no eran sostenidos desde ámbitos gubernamentales.

6 Finalmente, el Presidente de Estados Unidos comisionó a Enoch Wines para tal tarea.

	Congreso Penitenciario Internacional	Congreso Internacional de Antropología Criminal	Congreso de la Unión Internacional de Derecho Penal	Congreso Internacional de Derecho Penal	Congreso Internacional de Criminología
1872	Londres				
1878	Estocolmo				
1885	Roma	Roma			
1889		Paris	Bruselas		
1890	San Petersburgo		Berna		
1891			Kristina		
1892		Bruselas			
1893			Paris		
1894			Amberes		
1895	Paris		Linz		
1896		Ginebra			
1897			Lisboa		
1899			Budapest		
1900	Bruselas				
1901		Amsterdam			
1902			San Petersburgo		
1905			Hamburgo		
1906		Torino			
1910	Washington D.C.		Bruselas		
1911		Colonia			
1913			Copenhague		
1925	Londres				
1926				Bruselas	
1929				Bucarest	
1930	Praga				
1932				Palermo	
1935	Berlín				
1937				Paris	
1938					Roma

Cuadro 1

convocara a otros gobiernos al encuentro internacional que se llevaría a cabo en Londres, dos años después.

A partir de 1872 y hasta 1938 se llevaron adelante treinta y cinco (35) congresos y, a excepción de uno que se desarrolló en Washington, el resto tuvieron lugar en Europa (ver cuadro 1).

Los encuentros, salvo los primeros, tuvieron una frecuencia anual. En el periodo 1913/1925 se vieron suspendidos debido a la Gran Guerra que interrumpió toda colaboración internacional. La organización de cada uno de los congresos tuvo en general un fuerte apoyo gubernamental, a la vez que se crearon organizaciones o comisiones que tenían entre sus funciones la organización de los encuentros, la compilación de información, el intercambio de ideas y la universalización de ciertos postulados.

Luego del primer Congreso Penitenciario en Londres (1872) se designó una Comisión Penitenciaria Internacional que tenía entre sus funciones la organización del próximo encuentro, así como también recolectar estadísticas penitenciarias de diferentes países. Finalmente, aquella comisión se constituyó de modo permanente y estableció relaciones entre los gobiernos para formular un plan uniforme de trabajo. Luego de su primera reunión en Bruselas en 1974, los organizadores entendieron indispensable que la comisión tuviera un carácter oficial, para lo cual se dirigieron a los gobiernos con el fin de solicitarles que nombraran delegados para asistir a la próxima sesión de la comisión que se llevó a cabo un año después en Bruchsal.[7] Luego de algunos años, en 1878, se aprobó el Estatuto o Reglamento de la Comisión Penitenciaria Internacional. Desde aquella fecha fueron adhiriendo otros países a la Comisión que, en 1900, estaba ya integrada por representantes de Inglaterra, Baden, Baviera, Bélgica, Bulgaria, Dinamarca, Estados Unidos, Francia, Grecia, Hungría, Países Bajos, Rusia y Suiza. A los pocos años adhirieron Serbia, España, Luxemburgo, Japón y Sudáfrica. Después de la primera guerra mundial, se integraron Checoslovaquia, las Indias Británicas, Nueva Zelanda, Alemania, Austria, Polonia, Egipto, Finlandia, Chile, Lituania, Rumania, Argentina, Letonia, Estonia y Portugal.[8]

En paralelo, la Unión Internacional de Derecho Penal fue constituida en 1888 con la finalidad de coordinar las tendencias reformadoras que estaban surgiendo y dar mayor autoridad a los cambios legislativos. Su principal promotor fue Von Liszt junto a Van Hanel y Prins. El art. 1 del Estatuto rezaba:

La Unión Internacional de Derecho Penal, estima que la criminalidad y la represión deben ser analizados tanto desde el punto de vista social como del jurídico. Ello persigue la consagración de este principio y de sus consecuencias en la ciencia del derecho criminal y en las legislaciones penales.

Si bien la Unión pretendió presentarse con una posición ecléctica entre las teorías clásicas y el positivismo criminológico,[9] lo cierto es que primaba el segundo. La Unión Internacional pretendió, además, introducir una serie de instituciones y criterios en la legislación punitiva de los distintos Estados en vistas a la posible unificación de los códigos penales.

Luego del XII Congreso llevado adelante en Copenhague en 1913 y ya iniciada la primera guerra mundial, una serie de intercambios de opiniones entre miembros de la Unión, vinculados a cuestiones nacionalistas, motivó las renuncias de varios de ellos, lo que llevó a la desaparición del organismo internacional. A ello se suma que, en 1917, falleció Van Hamel y en 1919 Liszt y Prins.

Sin embargo, en 1924 en París, se formó la Asociación Internacional de Derecho Penal (AIDP-IAPL) como refundación de la Unión Internacional de Derecho Penal, constituyéndose como una asociación de especialistas en ciencias penales con la meta de promover

7 A aquella reunión asistieron representantes oficiales de Alemania y el Gran ducado de Baden, Bélgica, Dinamarca, Estados Unidos, Francia, Holanda, Italia, Noruega, Rusia, Suecia y Suiza.

8 Ver: La Obra de la Comisión Internacional Penal y Penitenciaria 1872–1942 (1943) 247, 269.

9 El art. 2 del estatuto enuncia nueve tesis: »1 – La misión del Derecho Penal es la lucha contra la criminalidad contemplada como fenómeno social. 2 – La ciencia y la legislación penal deben tener en cuenta los resultados de los estudios antropológicos y sociológicos. 3 – La pena es uno de los medios más eficaces que dispone el estado contra la criminalidad. No es el único medio. Ello no debe aislarse de los demás medios sociales y particularmente no debe hacer olvidar las medidas preventivas. 4 – La distinción entre los delincuentes accidentales y habituales es esencial tanto en la práctica como en la teoría; debe ser la base de las disposiciones de la ley penal. 5 – Como los tribunales represivos y la administración penitenciaria concurren al mismo fin y puesto que la condena no es válida más que por su forma de ejecución, la separación consagrada por nuestro derecho moderno entre la función represiva y la función penitenciaria es irracional y perjudicial. 6 – La pena privativa de libertad ocupa justamente el primer lugar de nuestro sistema de penas. La Unión decide una atención especial a todo lo que concierne a la mejora de las prisiones y de las instituciones que a ella se refieren. 7 – En lo que concierne, sin embargo, a las penas de prisión de corta duración, la Unión considera que la sustitución de la prisión por medidas de una eficacia equivalente es posible y deseable. 8 – En lo que concierne a las penas de prisión de larga duración, la Unión estima que es necesario hacer defender la duración de la prisión, no únicamente de la gravedad material y moral de la infracción cometida, sino también de los resultados obtenidos por el régimen penitenciario. 9 – En lo que concierne a los delincuentes habituales incorregibles, la Unión estima que independientemente de la gravedad de la infracción e incluso cuando se trate de reiteración de pequeños delitos, el sistema penal debe ante todo tener por objetivo poner a estos delincuentes fuera del esta do de perjudicar el mayor tiempo posible.«

el intercambio y la colaboración entre cuantos, en los diferentes países, se consagran al estudio del Derecho penal o participan en su aplicación, estudiar la criminalidad, sus causas y remedios, y favorecer el desarrollo teórico y práctico del Derecho penal internacional.[10]

Por otro lado, en 1934, luego del VII Congreso de Antropología Criminal – Colonia 1911 – se creó la Sociedad de Antropología y Psicología Criminal que contaba con un comité internacional con el mandato de formar la Federación Internacional de Criminología. Estaba integrado por representantes de Alemania, Bélgica, España, Gran Bretaña, Italia y Argentina.[11] Finalmente, en 1937 se creó la Sociedad Internacional de Criminología, la que convocó para el año siguiente al I Congreso Internacional de Criminología en Roma.

Esta breve mención a las asociaciones u organizaciones que daban vida a los diferentes encuentros tiene como finalidad marcar algunas líneas de continuidad. A ello se suma que varios miembros tenían activa intervención en más de una organización: Van Hamel integraba la Unión Internacional de Derecho Penal y asistió a la mayoría de los Congresos Internacionales de Antropología Criminal; Von Liszt y Prins, fundadores de la Unión Internacional, asistieron al III Congreso de Antropología Criminal y el segundo de ellos también lo hizo al IV; Garófalo asistió a los Congresos de Antropología Criminal y al III Congreso de la Unión Internacional, y junto a Lombroso concurrió al IV Congreso Penitenciario de San Petersburgo, solo por mencionar algunos casos.

En 1872 sesionó el primer Congreso Penitenciario Internacional, en Londres, a los que siguió el primer Congreso de Antropología Criminal (Roma, 1885) y el primer Congreso de la Unión Internacional de Derecho Penal (Bruselas, 1889), en los que Lombroso expuso los lineamientos de la escuela positivista italiana y la necesidad de coordinar la nuevas tendencias y reformas legislativas.

Más allá de las distintas especialidades de cada una de las organizaciones y de los encuentros, como veremos, las agendas eran muy similares e incluso se trataban paralelamente idénticos temas. Por ejemplo, el V Congreso Penitenciario Internacional (París, 1895) se pronunció a favor de la pena de deportación, al igual que lo hizo el VII Congreso de la Unión Internacional de Derecho Penal (Lisboa, 1897). También, el VII Congreso Penitenciario Internacional (Budapest, 1905) consolidó la pena de multa, al mismo momento que los Congresos de la Unión Internacional de Derecho Penal la discutían. En el VIII Congreso Penitenciario Internacional (Washington, 1910) se aprobó la sentencia indeterminada, al igual que en el Congreso Internacional de Antropología Criminal (Colonia, 1911).

En el periodo analizado se llevaron adelante once Congresos Penitenciarios, siete Congresos de Antropología Criminal que luego fueron retomados en 1938 por el Congreso de Criminología, doce congresos de la Unión Internacional de Derecho Penal que fueron continuados, después de la primera guerra mundial, en cuatro Congresos Internacionales de Derecho Penal.

El primer Congreso Penitenciario Internacional,[12] al que se lo denominó Primer Congreso sobre Prevención y Represión del Delito incluyendo el Tratamiento Penal y Reformatorio, organizado por Wines, fue celebrado en Londres en 1872 y se invitó a participar a representantes gubernamentales elegidos por el gobierno norteamericano – la invitación oficial era distribuida vía diplomática por aquel país. En este primer encuentro se tomó la *Declaración de Principios* – que había promulgado el Congreso de Cincinnati –, donde se fijaron treinta y siete (37) principios de política penal difundidos como una plataforma internacional de la institucionalización del control social. De hecho, aquellos principios se convirtieron en un »manual« en diferentes países, siendo Wines quien sugirió a diplomáticos de América Latina la edición del folleto en español. Asimismo, al presentarle el informe final del primer Congreso al gobierno mexicano, se le sugirió publicarlo allí debido a que podía ser de utilidad para las reformas

10 Cuesta / Blanco Cordero (2015) 459 (Prefacio de José Luis de la Cuesta y John Vervaele).

11 Representada por Tito Foppa y Francisco La Plaza.

12 Los once congresos que se llevaron adelante se diferenciaron de otros congresos penitenciarios que se habían llevado adelante desde 1841 (Frankfurt, 1846; Bruselas, 1847 y Frankfurt, 1857), en razón del carácter privado de estos y con un fuerte contenido filantrópico.

penitenciarias nacionales y de otros países hispanoamericanos.[13]

Enrique Cortés, secretario de la delegación de Colombia en Washington tuvo a su cargo la edición que incluía la Declaración de Principios y tres trabajos, a saber, E. C. Wines, »El sistema penitenciario irlandés«; Z. B. Brockway, »El ideal de un sistema penal« y J. B. Bittinger, »De la responsabilidad social por las causas del delito«. Este folleto circuló ampliamente por América Latina.[14]

A Londres asistieron representantes diplomáticos de Brasil y de Chile (P. de Andrade y Carlos Morales Vicuña); a la vez que México respondió el cuestionario que había sido enviado previamente y fue representado en el encuentro por el propio Wines. Luis Jiménez de Asúa afirmó que aquel primer Congreso »hace nacer una conciencia universal frente al problema de la delincuencia y de las cárceles y llegar así a internacionalizar ciertos principios«.[15] Entre los principios se fijó como objetivo del tratamiento penitenciario al criminal y no al crimen.

Los Congresos dividían sus agendas en diferentes secciones: i) Legislación penal; ii) administración carcelaria, iii) prevención de la delincuencia, y, luego se sumó iv) la infancia delincuente. Entre los puntos de los diversos programas que promovió la Comisión en los encuentros, encontramos: la regeneración moral del delincuente, la clasificación de los detenidos, la individualización del tratamiento, la organización del trabajo en las cárceles, la formación profesional del personal de los detenidos liberados.[16]

Si bien el primero de los Congresos se presentó como un espacio de recolección de estadísticas e información de diferentes países, evitando discusiones teóricas, en las sucesivas reuniones se tomaron resoluciones que se alineaban con la *Declaración de principios* y con las posiciones del Movimiento Reformador Norteamericano representado por Wines. De ese modo, se van perfilando diferentes resoluciones vinculadas a los siguientes puntos:

a) El tratamiento que impone a los criminales la sociedad es para ésta una medida de protección; b) El fin esencial de la pena consiste en reformar al criminal y no en imponerle un sufrimiento por espíritu de venganza; c) El criminal no debería ser condenado por tiempo determinado en la sentencia. Sería más conveniente consignar en ella que se le mantendría en prisión hasta el momento en que demuestre enmienda. Sería preciso, sustituir a las sentencias condenatorias, por sentencias de reforma. En síntesis, parece apreciarse a través de esta serie de principios, que se impulsaba que el tratamiento de los criminales fuera de protección y reforma, y se reclamaba la sentencia indeterminada como único medio de lograr su objetivo.[17]

La comisión contaba para cumplir con sus objetivos, aparte de los Congresos, con su Boletín – publicado regularmente desde 1880 – y con el *Bureau* permanente que se estableció en Berna en 1926.

En el segundo de los Congresos, realizado en Estocolmo en 1878, la delegación argentina presentó un informe en el que reconoce que las conclusiones del encuentro de Londres retoman las líneas del Congreso de Cincinnati de 1870 y la importancia de la *Declaración de principios* que fueron enviados para ser estudiados por todos los pueblos. Luego afirma que el informe sobre el estado de las prisiones en Argentina será de interés porque »mostrarán que admitimos en nuestro país los principios formulados por el Congreso de Cincinnati«[18] reconociendo la eficacia de aquellos, afirmando luego que »las resoluciones aprobadas [en el Congreso de Estocolmo] serán como el tratamiento que el médico indica para combatir cualquier enfermedad«.[19] El informe contenía varias citas del artículo de Bittinger que integraba el folleto en español de la *Declaración de Principios*, al que hicimos referencia.

Al III Congreso, celebrado en Roma en 1885, asistieron Lombroso, Garófalo y Ferri, los que a la vez para aquel año participaron activamente en el I Congreso Internacional de Antropología Criminal, también con sede en Roma. Si bien la concepción sobre la delincuencia y el delito que pregonaba el Movimiento Reformador Norteamericano

13 Ver García Basalo (1972), citado por Olmo (1999) 61.
14 Olmo (1999) 50.
15 Jiménez de Asúa (1957).
16 Ver La Obra de la Comisión Internacional Penal y Penitenciaria 1872–1942 (1943).
17 Milla (2014) 101.
18 Ver »République Argentine« en Guillaume (1878) 447–449, citado también por Olmo (1999) 63.
19 Olmo (1999) 63.

era independiente a la escuela positivista italiana, ambos tenían miradas comunes, comenzando a partir de este año a tener mayores niveles de coincidencias.

En el V Congreso (París, 1895) se avanzó con la internacionalización del control social, al requerir la validez internacional de las sentencias penales, como la necesidad de unificar los procedimientos antropométricos.

En cuanto a la influencia transnacional de estos encuentros,

> ha sido tendencia de los congresos y de la Comisión la de hacer poco a poco, por los esfuerzos combinados de los representantes oficiales, de los prácticos y de la ciencia penal teórica y de las organizaciones filantrópicas, una conciencia universal, por así decir, frente al problema de la delincuencia y de las cárceles; y llegar así a internacionalizar ciertos principios que, sometidos en forma de proposiciones a los gobiernos que las examinaron, las hicieron pasar sucesivamente a sus respectivas legislaciones.[20]

Según José María Paz Anchorena, la participación en los Congresos Penitenciarios Internacionales de representantes o delegados de Argentina había sido irregular, adjudicándolo a diversas cuestiones: es posible que las comisiones organizadoras hayan enviado con tardanza las invitaciones y como es natural, se hayan dirigido al Ministerio de Relaciones Exteriores, y éste, a su vez, al de Justicia, o quizá debe achacarse esta aparente indiferencia de nuestros gobiernos, al desconocimiento de la importancia de estas reuniones.[21]

Al encuentro de 1878 se presentó como delegado oficial de Argentina el doctor Ernst Georg Åberg, de origen suizo, pero con gran participación en la labor pública argentina.[22] Al III Congreso Penitenciario Internacional (Roma, 1885) asistió en representación de Argentina el doctor Ángel Rojas. En el siguiente encuentro (San Petersburgo, 1890) participaron Eduardo Ybarbalz y Eduardo García Mansilla, quienes mostraron una representación de una celda celular de la Penitenciaría Nacional, además de otros artículos fabricados en sus talleres. Recién vuelve a estar representada Argentina en el VI Congreso Penitenciario Internacional en la ciudad de Bruselas, al cual viajaron como delegados oficiales Marco Avellaneda, Juan Belgrano y Joaquín Lemoine. En el VIII Congreso reunido en Washington en 1910 participó Armando Claros, Director de la Penitenciaría Nacional.

> Claros publicó un informe titulado *Nuevas tendencias penales en el Congreso Penitenciario de Washington* (1911), en donde se remarca la adscripción de la CIPP a la aplicación de la sentencia por tiempo indeterminado, una de las principales banderas de la criminología positivista de la *scuola italiana*, así como el tratamiento individualizado. En este mismo sentido, se apoyó la idea de que todo penado podía alcanzar la regeneración, enfatizando el compromiso con los tratamientos penitenciarios.[23]

En el próximo Congreso, que se llevó a cabo recién en 1925 en Londres, asistió una comisión integrada por Eusebio Gómez, José María Paz Anchorena y Juan P. Ramos. Los tres contaban con un perfil similar en cuanto tenían un importante reconocimiento académico, a la vez que ocupaban altos cargos directivos de instituciones argentinas. Eusebio Gómez, que era para la época director de la Penitenciaría Nacional, realizó una presentación en aquel Congreso en la que

> reafirmaba el compromiso del penalista en la gestión penitenciaría, que solo ocupaba desde hacía dos años. La reforma penitenciaria fue pensada por el delegado oficial en términos

20 La Obra de la Comisión Internacional Penal y Penitenciaria 1872–1942 (1943) 253.

21 Paz Anchorena (1936) 25.

22 El informe presentado por Åberg considera que representan el esquema nacional de castigo penitenciario los edificios de Santa Fe y Mendoza, cuyos informes son remitidos por Severo Basavilbaso – presidente del Tribunal Supremo de Santa Fe – y José Zapata, – miembro de la Cámara de Justicia mendocina –. Paz Anchorena calificará negativamente estos informes: en el caso del texto de Åberg, por lamentar el desconocimiento de la situación penitenciaria que impidió completar de manera oportuna el cuestionario remitido por la CPI. Los reportes de Basavilbaso y Zapata fueron leídos con sorpresa por el penalista, quien cuestionó la »ligereza« con que el Ministerio de Justicia aprobó los informes. Ver González (2018) 36.

23 González (2018) 37.

más bien disruptivos con el positivismo criminológico hegemónico entre los claustros, lo que revela que en las prácticas institucionales durante los años veinte se impulsó una gestión penitenciaria más arraigada en los lineamientos del emergente penitenciarismo que reconocía entre sus bases las ideas de la Comisión Penal y Penitenciaria Internacional.[24]

En paralelo, comienzan en 1885 a llevarse a cabo los Congresos Internacionales de Antropología Criminal (inicialmente denominado Congreso de Antropología Criminal, Biología y Sociología), que tendrían siete ediciones hasta 1911. Desde sus inicios, estos encuentros tuvieron como finalidad discutir las ideas de la escuela positivista italiana, doctrina que ya se había comenzado a difundir en diferentes ámbitos y que finalizará con la consagración del estudio científico del individuo delincuente.

En el primer encuentro tuvo centralidad la obra reciente de Lombroso, *El hombre delincuente* (1876). Esta ordenó las sesiones en dos ejes: una biológica bajo la orientación del médico italiano que analizó la relación entre la epilepsia, la locura moral y la criminalidad congénita; la otra jurídica bajo la dirección de Ferri y Garófalo que estuvo centrado en analizar la posibilidad de aplicar las ideas de la escuela positivista a la legislación penal.

En los sucesivos encuentros, hubo en su seno una clara puja entre los penalistas clásicos y los partidarios de la escuela positivista, y entre estos y los representantes de la Escuela Francesa de Sociología, que sostenían una mayor influencia de los factores sociales en la delincuencia.

La presencia de Lombroso, Garófalo y Ferri en la mayoría de los encuentros tuvo un peso fundamental en las distintas sesiones. En este sentido, la escuela positivista no admitía reformulaciones a los métodos de la justicia penal, sino una utilización de un nuevo método »científico« que debía estudiar al individuo y establecer su peligrosidad como principal herramienta para la defensa social del delito. De esta manera, parte de las discusiones se centraron en los modos de diferenciar a los individuos delincuentes de los que no-delincuentes. Para ello, la Antropología era la ciencia indicada para realizar los estudios que se debían llevar a cabo, centralmente, en las prisiones.[25]

En los sucesivos programas de los encuentros se trataron la relación entre la Antropología Criminal y la investigación de la policía; así como también su aplicación jurídica a las legislaciones y su vinculación con el delito político; la degeneración y la vagancia; el tratamiento del delincuente alienado; las anomalías psíquicas; la identificación del delincuente y la policía científica. Asimismo, se centró la atención en los delitos de las muchedumbres y en las actividades anarquistas. En el IV Congreso (Ginebra, 1896) el holandés Van Hamel, quien, como hemos referido, era uno de los fundadores de la Unión Internacional de Derecho Penal, presentó una ponencia sobre el vínculo entre el anarquismo y la Antropología Criminal.

A lo largo de los años, los Congresos fueron acompañando las modificaciones o reformulaciones que vivió la escuela positivista, al ampliar la visión de que el delincuente nato no tenía su etiología exclusivamente en razones biológicas o anatómicas, sino en factores del medio ambiente y del medio social. De este modo, se abrió un camino para trabajar en relación al tratamiento del delincuente, el que será un eje central a partir del V Congreso.

A los diferentes Congresos asistió Norberto Piñero, uno de los representantes más influyentes de la escuela positivista argentina; así, a partir del quinto encuentro y por intermedio suyo, Argentina estuvo representada en la Comisión Internacional. De igual manera, diferentes países de América Latina habían enviado representantes al siguiente congreso.[26] También señala Rosa del Olmo que

> [l]a revisión general de los siete congresos de Antropología Criminal, celebrados entre 1885 y 1911, refleja la dirección que tomaría el control de la delincuencia en esa época, control que sólo lo lograría, según la escuela positivista, por medio del estudio ›científico‹ del individuo delincuente. Este nuevo instrumento ideológi-

24 González (2018) 45.

25 En el II Congreso (París, 1889) se formó una comisión integrada por Bertillón, Benedikt, Lacassagne, Lombroso, Magnan, Manouvrier y Semal para que estudiaran a cien individuos criminales y a cien personas no delincuentes, y presentaran sus conclusiones en el evento siguiente. Finalmente, la comisión no se reunió y ese estudio no se llevó adelante.

26 Olmo (1999) 69.

co, resultaba útil, logrando institucionalizarse internacionalmente a causa de la expansión del capitalismo en todos los campos.[27]

En 1937, en Italia, se formó la Sociedad Internacional de Criminología, que tenía entre sus objetivos

> asegurar la colaboración de las diversas técnicas con la ciencia del Derecho Penal, permitiendo así que las llamadas ciencias penales, y especialmente las que se ocupan del estudio del delincuente y del problema de la delincuencia, bajo el punto de vista biológico y social, puedan colaborar mejor con los organismos administrativos y el órgano jurisdiccional para poder así asegurar la adaptación de la ley penal a las necesidades de la prevención de la delincuencia, de la reeducación del delincuentes y de la defensa social contra el crimen.[28]

La Sociedad estaba integrada por representantes de Alemania, Bélgica, España, Gran Bretaña, Italia y Argentina (representada por Tito Foppa y Francisco La Plaza). Se convocó a un primer encuentro para el año siguiente en Roma, continuando, de ese modo, con el lugar que habían dejado vacante a nivel internacional los Congresos de Antropología Criminal.

Al primer encuentro concurrieron representantes de diferentes lugares del mundo, entre ellos Arturo Rocco por Italia; A. de Marisco, profesor de la Universidad de Nápoles; G. Mariani, Profesor de la Universidad de Roma; A. Santoro profesor de la Universidad de Niza; E. Mezger, Profesor de la Universidad de Múnich; L. Verbaeck antropólogo belga; P. de Casablanca miembro de la Suprema Corte de París. De Latinoamérica asistieron representantes de Argentina, Bolivia, Brasil, Chile, Colombia, Costa Rica, Cuba, Ecuador, Guatemala, México, Nicaragua, Perú, Uruguay y Venezuela. Los temas que fueron abordados en aquel encuentro se centraron en: 1) etiología y diagnóstico de la criminalidad de los menores e influencia en las disposiciones jurídicas; 2) el estudio de la personalidad del delincuente; 3) el papel del Juez en la lucha contra la criminalidad y su preparación en criminología; 4) organización de la profilaxis criminal en diversos países; 5) etnología y criminología, y 6) la experiencia de las medidas de seguridad en diversos países.[29]

A partir de 1889, se llevarán adelante los trece Congresos o reuniones de la Unión Internacional de Derecho Penal que buscaron dar una nueva orientación al derecho penal de acuerdo a las necesidades de la política criminal. La Unión dictó un Estatuto – al que se ha hecho referencia – que rigió a la asociación durante los primeros seis encuentros, luego de los cuales fue modificado. De este modo la Unión sostenía un enfoque en el estudio de la criminalidad y la represión, que suponía una toma de postura que intentaba ser conciliador y un reconocimiento de posible validez y coexistencia de los dos enfoques sobre el problema de la criminalidad, pretendiendo evitar el alejamiento de la realidad de las teorías clásicas, como la des-juridización de la escuela positivista. En este sentido, faltaba crear una normativa jurídica que sostuviera al positivismo y de algún modo la Unión intentó cumplió esa función. De allí que una de las principales preocupaciones que tuvo fue de la de reformar los cuerpos legales, pretendiendo la aplicación de los mismos principios a las distintas legislaciones.

Las principales exposiciones en los Congresos estuvieron concentradas en: i) la posibilidad de unificación del Derecho Penal, para ellos se propiciaron estudios comparativos de derecho penal; ii) las causas del delito, trabajando tanto en la organización de estadísticas sobre reincidencia, como en el estudio de la vejez en la delincuencia; iii) el cambio de orientación en la lucha contra la criminalidad: abordando el problema del estado peligroso, las medidas de seguridad y la sentencia indeterminada, a la vez que orientando sus estudios a los jóvenes delincuentes, la multa, la deportación, el patronato, la mendicidad, la vagancia y la trata de blanca; y iv) el procedimiento penal.

La influencia de las reuniones de la Unión Internacional en América Latina es de gran relevancia. En 1891 asistieron representantes de seis países. De Argentina, concurrieron Luis María Drago, José Matienzo y Norberto Piñero; de Brasil, Joao Vieira de Araujo; de Chile, Aníbal Echeverría

27 Olmo (1999) 69.
28 Garrido (1939) 255.
29 Garrido (1939) 256.

y Reyes; de Costa Rica, Octavio Beeche; de Guatemala, Agustín Gómez Carrillo, Manuel Echeverría y Baltasar Estupinam y de Venezuela, Francisco Ochoa.

En definitiva,

> la Unión Internacional de Derecho Penal dejó establecido que: 1. el delito no es solo una entidad abstracta de orden jurídico, sino también un fenómeno social de carácter patológico influido por factores individuales congénitos o adquiridos. La lucha debe adelantarse mediante la investigación científica de tales causas. 2. El derecho penal debe estudiar a los delincuentes en dos categorías: a) los que sucumben ante poderosas influencias exteriores como la miseria y el alcoholismo y b) los que mantienen hábitos derivados de su género de vida. Los primeros son ocasionales; los segundos, los habituales o de naturaleza. 3. La pena no es suficientes en la lucha contra el delito, sino que son indispensables medidas preventivas sin que estas puedan separarse de aquellas. Las penas largas privativas de la libertad deben depender no solo del delito sino del resultado penitenciario y en lo que concierne a las de corta duración o de naturaleza benigna, pueden suplantarse por medidas equivalentes, en todo caso, los incorregibles deben quedar en situación de no dañar el mayor tiempo posible, pero es necesario que el régimen de prisiones responda a los dictados de una sana política criminal.[30]

Como ya mencionamos, luego de la que Unión se disolvió, tomó su lugar la Asociación Internacional de Derecho Penal (que fue creada en 1924 y continúa vigente en la actualidad), llevando adelante los Congresos, cuya celebración fue quinquenal – a excepción de algún periodo –, donde se reunieron profesores de derecho penal y de derecho procesal penal, magistrados, expertos, provenientes de muchos países. Los encuentros contaban con cuatro secciones tradicionales: derecho penal, parte general; derecho penal, parte especial; proceso penal y derecho penal internacional. En el periodo objeto de investigación se llevaron adelante cuatro congresos, en Bruselas en 1926; en Bucarest en 1929, en Palermo en 1932 y en París en 1937. Algunos de los temas que fueron abordados en ellos fueron: las medidas de seguridad, como sustituto de la pena o como pena complementaria; la necesidad de la creación de una Corte Criminal Internacional; la responsabilidad penal de las personas jurídicas; la aplicación judicial de leyes penales extranjeras, la jurisdicción universal; el intercambio internacional de informaciones concerniente a los antecedentes judiciales de los inculpados. Al primero de los encuentros asistieron los argentinos Juan P. Ramos y Jorge Coll; este último presentó un informe sobre el estado de las leyes penales argentinas. »Como resultado de las deliberaciones del congreso, Coll, sugirió al gobierno argentino la necesidad de celebrar un congreso de derecho penal internacional argentino.«[31]

En el Congreso de Bruselas se votó a favor de la unificación del derecho penal en los siguientes términos:

> considerando altamente deseable la unificación de las ideas fundamentales sobre el ejercicio de la represión en los proyectos de los diferentes Estados con vistas al reconocimiento de los principios que la ciencia contemporánea del Derecho penal ha consagrado de manera unánime. Visto que en muchos Estados se procede actualmente a la elaboración de nuevos proyectos, expresa el deseo de que: Las comisiones encargadas por los gobiernos de la redacción de los proyectos de Códigos penales se reúnan en una conferencia internacional. Esta conferencia debería servir para discutir y unificar los principios que se encuentran en la base de los proyectos elaborados por las comisiones, y para insertar en ellos, en la medida de lo posible, principios comunes para el ejercicio de la represión. A tal fin, el Congreso encarga al secretario general de la Asociación Internacional de Derecho Penal que haga llegar el presente deseo a todos los gobiernos de los Estados en donde hay proyectos de Código penal en curso de elaboración.[32]

A este fin, en 1932 se constituyó una Junta Internacional con representación de varios Estados;

30 Olmo (1999) 73 s.
31 Olmo (1999) 84.
32 Cuesta / Blanco Cordero (2015) 465 s.

para 1939 la integraban dieciséis países, entre ellos varios de Latinoamérica.

En el transcurso de unas pocas décadas, se había cambiado radicalmente el eje del control social y el modo de enfrentar al delito. El delincuente pasó a ser un individuo que no era normal, cuyas causas debían ser estudiadas a fin de conocer el *estado de peligrosidad*, por lo que debe ser sometido a un tratamiento que requiera individualizar la pena y una sentencia indeterminada. Las medidas de seguridad devinieron en las herramientas necesarias en aquel tratamiento, al igual que la pena de multa y *la probation* como alternativas a la pena de prisión.

El nuevo discurso se presentó como científico – tanto del saber médico, como jurídico – y como más humanitario, a la vez dirigido al control social de los disidentes o resistentes al orden. Estas ideas, producidas en el seno de Europa, fueron rápidamente difundidas a diferentes latitudes, teniendo una amplia recepción en América Latina:

> Una vez establecida las características del control social en el seno de las sociedades internacionales y la estrecha conexión entre los congresos de las diferentes sociedades como difusores de ›normas universales‹ para la prevención del delito y el tratamiento del delincuente, hay que estudiar cómo se reciben esas normas en América Latina, primero a través de los latinoamericanos que asisten a esas reuniones y el papel que desempeñan en sus respectivas sociedades en diferentes épocas como portavoces de esas ›normas universales‹, y posteriormente, en la acogida que tendrán éstas en los respectivos países, ya sea como simple discurso académico o como medio de solución de los problemas locales de criminalidad.[33]

II. El impacto de la universalización del discurso y las normas en América Latina

La criminología positivista tuvo una amplia y rápida recepción en América Latina. En el ámbito académico, se crearon asociaciones profesionales, se publicaron revistas especializadas, se editaron abundantes libros y se organizaron congresos regionales que abordaron el nuevo orden social, de modo que muy rápidamente se consolidaron sus postulados. La admiración por las teorías y posiciones europeas era una constante en la región, a la vez que la nueva teoría resultaba de utilidad para las elites políticas dominantes locales con vistas al nuevo momento de expansión del capitalismo y los problemas que implicaba en términos sociales:

> Fundamentalmente a causa de su carácter dependiente y a la necesidad de buscar soluciones en estos momentos, son los latinoamericanos los primeros países de la periferia capitalista dispuestos a acoger los planteamientos de estos congresos.[34]

Sin embargo, como hemos desarrollado, la presencia de delegados de los diferentes países en los encuentros internacionales no fue uniforme, sino que dependían del grado de integración que tuviera cada nación en la división internacional del trabajo y del desarrollo de conformación del Estado liberal. De ese modo se puede explicar la prominente presencia de delegaciones de Argentina, Brasil, Chile y México. Su difusión latinoamericana, como lo hemos dicho, coincide con un momento de estrechamiento de las relaciones económicas de complementariedad y subordinación con el poder central, particularmente en la década del ochenta del siglo pasado, en que se produce la concentración terrateniente en el »porfirismo« mexicano; la decadencia total de la esclavitud y del poder »esclavócrata« en beneficio de la economía exportadora sureña en el Brasil, que culmina con la »República Velha«, nacida bajo signo expresamente positivista; el establecimiento del »roquismo« en la Argentina y el reforzamiento de las corrientes inmigratorias la consolidación de la dependencia financiera en el Perú, después de las »guerra del salitre«, etc., es decir, en general, el periodo de consolidación de las »economías de exportación«.[35]

Como señala Beatriz Ruibal, el discurso criminológico no se acotaba al problema de la cuestión criminal, sino que a la vez abarcaba un amplio abanico de acciones que se reputaban peligrosas

33 Olmo (1999) 13.
34 Olmo (1999) 124.
35 Zaffaroni (1993) 171.

para el orden social – acciones que implicaban »mala vida«, como el alcohol, la prostitución, el vagabundeo y la mendicidad, entre otras – superponiéndose la criminalidad con la protesta obrera y el anarquismo. Las nuevas teorías que se asentaban en métodos científicos habilitaban dispositivos de saber-poder que permitían regular y combatir todos los comportamientos que atentaban contra el nuevo orden económico y social; separando a aquellos individuos considerados perturbadores del desarrollo.[36]

Sin embargo, cabe mencionar que, si bien existió un proceso complejo de importación cultural, no se trató de un puro traspasamiento teórico, sino que aquel marco se mixturó con la producción discursiva local. Desde la edición en 1878 de la obra de José María Ramos Mejía, *La neurosis de los hombres célebres en la historia argentina*, en adelante, se publicaron una vasta cantidad de libros y revistas en Argentina, México, Brasil, Costa Rica, Chile, Cuba y Uruguay.[37] Asimismo, se fundó en 1888 la Sociedad de Antropología Criminal en Buenos Aires, por la iniciativa de Luis María Drago, Piñero y Ramos Mejía, quienes además dirigieron un boletín que publicó los estudios de esas Sociedad. En 1889, en Río de Janeiro se creó la Asociación Antropológica y de Asistencia Criminal. En 1907 se creó un Gabinete de Psicología Clínica y Experimental destinado al estudio de los delincuentes, denominado Instituto de Criminología en el ámbito de la Penitenciaría Nacional en Argentina.[38] En 1912 se fundó en Chile el Instituto de Criminología a semejanza al de Buenos Aires; en 1933 se fundó la Sociedad Argentina de Criminología, a los pocos años se creó su par mexicana.

La Sociedad de Antropología Jurídica que se constituyó en Buenos Aires, estaba integrada por parte de la elite intelectual de la ciudad, como Norberto Piñero, Francisco y José María Ramos Mejía, Luis María Drago, José Nicolás Matienzo y Rodolfo Rivarola. Esta aspiraba, por un lado, a »completar la ciencia europea con los datos de la antropología y la sociología argentinas y de la América indígena«, y por otro, a »estudiar la personalidad del delincuente como base para preparar la reforma de las leyes penales«.[39]

La producción intelectual de los criminólogos argentinos se incrementó a partir de tomar contacto directo con Lombroso y Ferri. En 1887, las aulas universitarias de la Universidad de Buenos Aires tuvieron la primera cátedra de Derecho Penal, a cargo de Piñeiro, en las que se impartieron las ideas de la Escuela positivista que habían sido formuladas en el I Congreso de Antropología Criminal celebrado en Roma en 1885. Asimismo, en 1897, la Facultad de Medicina de aquella Universidad inauguró el primer curso de Antropología y Sociología Criminal, dictado por el médico Francisco de Veyga.

En paralelo, a partir de 1898 se comienzan a llevar adelante una serie de Congresos Científicos Latinoamericanos que tendrán ocho ediciones hasta 1940. Los primeros tres – el I en Buenos Aires en 1898; el II en Montevideo, en 1901 y el III en Río de Janeiro, en 1905 – lo harán con esa denominación; luego con la inclusión de Estados Unidos entre sus participantes, pasó a llamarse Congreso Científico Panamericano – Chile 1909, Washington 1915/1916, Lima 1924, México 1936 y Washington 1940 – donde se abordaron las más diversas temáticas, entre ellas algunas vinculadas al control social.

Así, por ejemplo, en el primero de los Congresos se dividen siete áreas: 1. Ciencias Exactas. 2. Ingeniería, 3. Ciencias Físico Químicas, 4. Ciencias Naturales, 5. Ciencias médicas, 6. Ciencias Antropológicas y 7. Sociología. Esta última área abordaba: a) sociología general, b) estadística y demografía; c) antropología y sociología criminal, d) economía política y e) geografía americana. Asimismo, finalmente se presentaron estudios vinculados a la emigración y la inmigración; caracteres de la criminalidad en la América Latina y sus medios preventivos y represivos.

Entre las resoluciones que fueron adoptadas por el Congreso se encuentran aquellas »Sobre Legislación penal«:

36 Ruibal (1993) 14.
37 Puede consultarse la extensa lista en Aniyar de Castro/Codino (2013) 93, 94 y en Zaffaroni (1993) 172.
38 Aquel gabinete estuvo bajo la inicial dirección de José Ingenieros y Argentina se convirtió en el primer país en poner en práctica la criminología clínica en el campo penitenciario.
39 Olmo (1999) 135.

El congreso declara: 1°. Que verían complacido que los gobiernos de América Latina dedicaran preferente atención al establecimiento de colonias penales en sus territorios; 2°. Que es conveniente adoptar, para el tratamiento de la reincidencia, el sistema de deportación por largo tiempo, como pena accesoria del último delito cometido por el reincidente; 3°. Que sería conducente, como medida preventiva, una intervención legal en las informaciones sobre criminalidad que suministra la prensa diaria; 4°. El Congreso hace votos para que en la América latina haya sociedades de protección a los penados cumplidos, como medio de regeneración moral de los delincuentes y de prevenir reincidencia.[40]

No abordaremos aquí cada uno de los Congresos, pero haremos algunas menciones a diferentes cuestiones que fueron tratados en ellos. Así, fue materia de un fuerte debate los sistemas de identificación criminal – existiendo tensiones entre la antropometría francesa de Alphonse Bertillon y la dactiloscopia suramericana de Juan Vucetich. En la reunión de Montevideo se concluyó que la dactiloscopia era sólo un auxiliar en el proceso de identificación antropométrica, cuyas fichas serían la base de la cooperación policíaca a nivel internacional.[41]

El Congreso en Santiago de Chile de 1909, acordó el intercambio de antecedentes personales entre Chile, Argentina, Brasil y Uruguay, lo que significó la implantación de la dactiloscopia como medio de identificación jurídico-legal en casi todo el sur del continente americano. Unos años más tarde, la técnica de Vucetich sería adoptada con leves modificaciones en Francia y en todos los países de América Latina. A la vez, la agenda de ese Congreso incluyó el problema de los menores delincuentes, de las lesiones corporales, recomendando tomar en cuenta la peligrosidad del sujeto para su clasificación y de la necesidad de reformar, cuando fuese necesario, la legislación penal de los países. Finalmente, el Congreso sancionó un voto expresando el deseo de que el sistema de trabajo de la Penitenciaría de Buenos Aires se aplique a los demás establecimientos.[42]

En el encuentro que se llevó adelante en Lima, en 1924, se tomaron resoluciones sobre las siguientes cuestiones: toxicomanías, formación del Juez Penal, escuelas penitenciarias, la dirección técnicas de los establecimientos penitenciarios, el delito sanitario, el infanticidio, el registro de reincidentes, la creación de un Instituto Internacional de Derecho Penal, el Patronato de Liberados, los Tribunales de Menores, la creación de laboratorios, de cátedras de Antropología Criminal, criminalística, etc.

La Sociedad Argentina de Criminología, creada en 1933 por el médico Osvaldo Loudet, fue la encargada de convocar al I Congreso Latinoamericano de Criminología, que se llevó adelante en 1938 en Buenos Aires, apenas unos meses antes del Internacional, que se desarrollaría en Roma. Tal como lo señala Rosa del Olmo la comparación de los temarios de ambos congresos refleja el estrecho vínculo entre quien los organizaban – por ejemplo, Francisco de La Plaza fue delegado argentino en la reunión que se realizó en París en 1934 en la que se fundó la Federación Internacional de Criminología, llamada Sociedad Internacional de Criminología y en la que se fijó el temario para el Congreso que posteriormente convocó a Roma en 1938.[43]

El Congreso llevado adelante en Buenos Aires – al que asistieron más de seiscientos latinoamericanos[44] – abordó los siguientes tópicos: la valoración de los factores biológicos y sociológicos en las reacciones antisociales de los menores; la formación científica del Juez del Crimen; los índices médico-psicológicos y legales de la peligrosidad; la peligrosidad como fundamento y medida de la responsabilidad; la culpabilidad y la teoría de la imputabilidad legal; la analogía en el derecho penal. Dentro de las resoluciones que se dictaron,

40 Ver los anales de la Primera reunión del Congreso Científico latino americano celebrada en Buenos Aires del 10 al 20 de abril de 1898 por iniciativa de la Sociedad científica argentina, online: https://archive.org/details/primerareunind121898cong/page/n101 (último acceso 18.12.2020).

41 El Congreso fue el trampolín para la difusión internacional de identificación dactilar: Vucetich fue considerado como una gloria de América que había hecho sucumbir las pretensiones universalistas de la antropometría europea, y su sistema dactiloscópico fue valorado como »una conquista de la civilización y de la mentalidad latina suramericana«. Ver Calvo Isaza (2001) 107.

42 Ver Calvo Isaza (2001).

43 Ver Olmo (1999) 158, 160.

44 Asistieron delegaciones de Argentina, Bolivia, Brasil, Colombia, Costa Rica, Cuba, Chile, Ecuador, El Salvador, Guatemala, Haití, Honduras, México, Nicaragua, Panamá, Paraguay, Perú, Uruguay, Venezuela.

destacamos la necesidad de incorporar a la legislación penal el estado peligroso y los modos de establecer los criterios médico-psicológicos que expliquen los índices legales.

A los pocos años, en 1941, se llevó adelante el II Congreso de Criminología Latinoamericano de Santiago de Chile,[45] el que abordó dieciocho temas, de los cuales sólo seis eran la agenda oficial. Se debatió sobre la necesidad de una reforma integral de las legislaciones penales, que incluyera no sólo las leyes sustantivas, sino también las procedimentales y administrativas.

> Que existe la posibilidad de uniformar, respecto de algunas materias, la legislación penal vigente en los países de América Latina; esas materias podrían ser, entre otras: la referente a la especial defensa contra la actividad de los delincuentes habituales, profesionales y reincidentes peligrosos, teniendo en cuenta las sentencias pronunciadas por los Tribunales de cualquier otro país; la lucha contra la delincuencia internacional.[46]

También se recomendó que las nociones de delito políticos y de delito social se observe en virtud del criterio subjetivo, de acuerdo al móvil determinante de aquellos hechos; que se coordinen todos los Institutos de policía técnica de la región y designar con el nombre de Instituto de Criminología a los organismos técnicos penitenciarios, encargados del examen de la personalidad de los delincuentes; y organizarlos tomando en consideración los fundamentos jurídicos, antropológicos y sociológicos de cada uno; entre otras cuestiones. Previo a la edición de los Congresos Latinoamericanos, diferentes países ya habían celebrado reuniones de encuentros o congresos a nivel nacional.[47]

Los diversos canales de difusión de las enseñanzas de la antropología criminal nacida en Italia, sumados a la receptividad en ámbitos académicos y la asistencia a los congresos internacionales de delegados y representantes de América Latina, a la par de la celebración de encuentros regionales con cierta regularidad, explican el afianzamiento de esta posición criminológica en muchos países de la región.

III. El estado de peligrosidad y la legislación penal

Tal como hemos enunciado la doctrina positivista se extendió y arraigó en Latinoamérica en el periodo estudiado, lo que permitió a partir de un método científico racionalizar las desigualdades generadas por los nuevos desafíos que el capitalismo le exigía a la región. Su acogida comulgó con un discurso racista que imperaba en la ideología del colonialismo central y de las oligarquías locales. De ese modo, la justificación de que »los pobres eran pobres porque eran biológicamente inferiores«,[48] apoyaba la idea de que la superioridad era el resultado del evolucionismo.

Es por ello que el concepto de *estado peligroso*, acuñado por esta escuela, era aplicable a todos los individuos que fueran considerados anormales, delincuentes, pobres, vagabundos, enfermos mentales. En definitiva, los anormales y degenerados eran peligrosos y el Estado debía corregirlos, de ser ello posible, y si no neutralizarlos para su bien, pero sobre todo para el bien de la sociedad. La peligrosidad se convirtió en el fundamento del *ius puniendi*, pero también en su medida:

> El delito se consideró como una entidad en sí, debido a que apareció por los síntomas biológicos, psicológicos y sociales del delincuente. Lo aplicable a esta persona anormal, debía relacionarse conforme a la perversidad. Era una sanción adaptada a la cantidad y calidad del delincuente para dañarse a él y a la sociedad.[49]

45 Asistieron al Segundo Congreso las delegaciones oficiales de estos catorce países: Argentina, Bolivia, Brasil, Colombia, Costa Rica, Chile, Ecuador, Guatemala, Haití, México, Nicaragua, Perú, República Dominicana, Uruguay.

46 Medrano Ossio (1940) 42.

47 Por ejemplo, en Argentina en 1914 se celebró el I Congreso Penitenciario Nacional y en 1922, la I Conferencia para organizar el Patronato de Liberados; en México, para 1923 se lleva adelante el I congreso Criminológico y Penitenciario y en 1932 el I Congreso Penitenciario; en Brasil, 1930 se celebra la I Conferencia Penal y Penitenciaria Brasileña y en 1936 la I congreso Conferencia de Criminología.

48 Olmo (1999) 30.

49 Agudelo Betancur (1991) 14 s.

Respecto de la recepción de esta doctrina a los Códigos Penales, por un lado, analizaremos los primeros códigos penales latinoamericanos, y, por otro lado, aquellos que fueron modificados hasta 1945. Veremos como todos los países de la región adoptaron códigos de países europeos, en muchos casos, casi de forma íntegra y absoluta, a la vez que todos ellos se mantienen ajenos a los postulados del positivismo y sobre todo del *estado peligroso*. Así, el Código de la República del Salvador, del 13 de abril de 1826, y el de Bolivia, del 28 de octubre de 1830, siguieron al Código de España de 1820 y 1822. El Código Francés (Código Napoleón) de 1810 fue adoptado por Haití el 31 de julio de 1835 y una década después, traducido al castellano, por la República Dominicana. El Código bávaro de 1813 fue modelo para Argentina con el llamado Proyecto de Tejedor de 1865[50] y por Paraguay en 1871. El Código brasileño del 16 de diciembre de 1830, se basó en los códigos francés, bávaro y napolitano y en el Proyecto para la Luisiana. Venezuela y Perú en 1863, México en 1871, Cuba en 1872, Chile en 1874, Nicaragua en 1879, Costa Rica en 1880, Colombia en 1887, Guatemala y Uruguay en 1889 y Honduras en 1898 adoptan Códigos bajos las influencias de los Códigos españoles de 1822, 1850 y 1870. Por último, el código de Ecuador seguirá al Código belga de 1867.[51]

Tal como lo afirmó Jiménez de Asúa, el clasicismo fue la doctrina que imperó en los códigos penales redactados hasta 1881, tanto en la rama legislativa latina como en la germánica. En ellos,

> el delito es solo punto de mira de estas viejas leyes, y el sujeto hombre queda en un plano de olvido y de sombra, de desconocimiento más bien; la inimputabilidad, basada en el libre albedrío, late en cada uno de los artículos de estos códigos, anteriores al de los Países Bajos, y la pena es un medio intimidante, represivo, expiatorio, nunca una sencilla y útil sanción de defensa social.[52]

Según Rosa del Olmo,

> una de las características de nuestro continente, que merece mencionarse, es que a nivel legislativo – salvo muy contadas excepciones – jamás se aceptaron postulados positivistas. La legislación sería de tendencia clásica e incluso los códigos modernos son de corte neoclásico.[53]

Más allá de esta afirmación, diversos países han incluido en sus códigos penales nociones de peligrosidad y de medidas de seguridad, adoptando sistemas dualistas de culpabilidad y peligrosidad.

De este modo, Jiménez de Asúa refiere que la escuela político-criminal representada en Franz von Liszt supone una fisonomía ecléctica entre las teorías clásicas y las positivistas, con una naturaleza componedora y pragmática. De este modo, se postula el mantenimiento simultáneo de la imputabilidad y culpabilidad y del estado peligroso, solo para ciertas categorías de delincuentes temibles; no niega que el delito sea un fenómeno natural, pero sostienen la labor técnica de la dogmática jurídica; a la vez, prevén como doble medio de lucha contra el crimen a las penas y a las medidas de seguridad.[54] En América latina, varios códigos penales exhiben el eclecticismo de esta escuela, entre ellos el de Costa Rica, del 29 de noviembre de 1918,[55] y el de Argentina de 1921.[56] Este último, prevé las medidas de seguridad para casos de inimputabilidad; a la vez que establece a la peligrosidad en las circunstancias atenuantes y agravantes de la pena (Art. 41, inciso 2 del Código Penal) y como parámetro para establecer la posibi-

50 Inicialmente fue adoptado por diversas provincias y recién en 1886 fue la base principal del Código Penal que regirá en todo el territorio nacional.

51 Ver Rivacoba y Rivacoba (2001) y Olmo (1999) 134.

52 Jiménez de Asúa (1928) 35.

53 Olmo (1999) 133.

54 Jiménez de Asúa (1928) 89 ss.

55 Entró en vigencia el 11 de abril de 1919.

56 Jiménez de Asúa refería sobre el Código Penal argentino »a pesar del fuerte arraigo en el país de las teorías del positivismo penal, no se hallan en el Código de 1922 los rasgos fisonómicos que caracterizan a la escuela [...] Para que una ley sancionadora pueda filiarse en el positivismo, precisa presentar, entre otros caracteres, las siguientes notas esenciales: a) la aceptación de la llamada responsabilidad social y de la peligrosidad del delincuente; b) la multiplicidad de sanciones para poder individualizar el tratamiento penal y defensivo; y c) la recepción de la sentencia indeterminada. [...] Si analizamos ahora el Código argentino en referencia a estos tres puntos fundamentales, llegaremos a la conclusión de que el positivismo ha ejercido nulo influjo sobre el nuevo cuerpo legal«. Más adelante matiza esta afirmación reconociendo »que muchos de los preceptos del reciente Código argentino se hallan sombreados de positivismo«, Jiménez de Asúa (1928) 178, 184.

lidad de la reducción o eximición de la pena en casos de delito imposible (Art. 44, Párrafo 2). En la misma orientación se encuentran el Código de México de 1931 que recogió algunas instituciones jurídicas importantes de corte positivista, como la reincidencia y la habitualidad, acudiendo al criterio de la peligrosidad para individualizar la pena,[57] y el Código Penal de Uruguay que entró en vigencia en 1934 y tenía diversas previsiones referidas a la peligrosidad por tendencia.[58] A la vez, se establecían

> los elementos que se tienen que tener en cuenta en el juicio de peligrosidad, y que constituyen a su vez el diagnóstico de personalidad sobre el cual se apoyará, precisamente, el pronóstico de futuros hechos delictuosos.[59]

Por otro lado, el código tomaba en cuenta la peligrosidad para la determinación de la pena[60] y la posibilidad de aplicar medidas de seguridad que se aplicaban a delincuentes habituales y a los homicidas que por la excepcional gravedad del hecho denuncien su gran peligrosidad (Art. 92, inciso 39); entre otras previsiones.

Por último, el Código Penal de 1936 de Colombia fue influenciado por la escuela positivista, centralmente con previsiones vinculadas a las medidas de seguridad y el tratamiento de personas inimputables en el país.

> La declarada simbiosis de los delincuentes psicópatas, se ve materializada a partir de los años 30' en donde, con la promulgación de las medidas de seguridad dentro de un sistema dualista, se empezó a entender la inimputabilidad. Esa nueva concepción creó características inherentes a la psiquiatría y a algunos conceptos emanados por la criminología. En primer lugar, se recurrió a la noción de peligrosidad para auxiliar la intervención represiva del Estado; como segundo elemento, se declaró la irresponsabilidad del inimputable, como consecuencia de las medidas de seguridad de carácter terapéutico.[61]

Jiménez de Asúa expresaba en 1928 que

> América ha tenido también, aunque con menos intensidad, el anhelo renovador de las leyes penales. Cumplido ya en Costa Rica y Argentina, se halla en proyecto en otros Estados; pero, al atravesar los mares, buena parte de las más nuevas instituciones han quedado rezagadas o fenecidas en la travesía. Mencionaré algunos de estos proyectos americanos. Cuba compuso, en 1908, un Proyecto que ha quedado sin terminar, en el que se halla una moderna orientación, aunque sea estimable la técnica. En Méjico se terminó, en 11 de junio de 1912, un Proyecto de Código penal que se publicó en 1914, que, al revés del anterior, muestra, frente a una técnica deficiente, algunos atisbos de certeras medidas aseguradoras. Finalmente, debo mencionar el proyecto peruano de 1916, debido a Víctor Manuel Maúrtua, que es una de las obras más perfectas y avanzadas, y que constituyen el más notable documento penal redactado en América hispana.[62]

IV. Las leyes inmigratorias y de extranjería

Más allá de la escasa recepción de la doctrina positivista en los códigos penales latinoamericanos, la mayoría de las legislaciones latinoamericanas encontraron en las políticas de inmigración[63] y en las leyes de extranjería un canal para la utilización de la categoría de personas peligrosas como

57 Ver Malo Camacho (1997).

58 Art. 48 numeral 39 expresa: »Debe ser considerado habitual el que además de hallarse en las condiciones especificadas en el inciso precedente, acusare una tendencia definida al delito en concepto del Juez, por el género de vida que lleva, su inclinación a la ociosidad, la inferioridad moral del medio en que actúa, las relaciones que cultiva y todos los demás antecedentes de análogo carácter.«

59 Schurmann Pacheco (1958) 896.

60 Art. 50 inciso 29 expresa: »Para elevar o rebajar la: pena, el Juez atenderá, preferentemente, a la calidad de las circunstancias concurrentes y a las conclusiones que ellas permitan derivar acerca de la mayor o menor peligrosidad del agente« y art. 53 expresa: »Cuando concurran circunstancias agravantes y atenuantes en el mismo hecho, el Juez, teniendo en cuenta su valor esencialmente sintomático, tratará de formarse conciencia acerca de la peligrosidad del agente, fijando a pena entre el máximo y el mínimo de acuerdo, con las indicaciones que dicho examen le sugiera.«

61 Parada Gamboa (2012) 225.

62 Jiménez de Asúa (1928) 96.

63 Se debe tener en cuenta que en el periodo analizado en esta investigación la mayoría de los países de la región tenían una amplia política migratoria, optando toda América Latina por mantener un criterio de *ius soli* para otorgar la nacionalidad.

extranjeros indeseables. En este sentido se dictaron normas con contenido punitivo que se enmarcan en la peligrosidad del individuo para su expulsión de algún país.

> La ›expulsión de extranjeros‹ se configuró como una eficaz herramienta de control social. Una cuestión central que plantea el artículo es que la producción y circulación de la deportación o ›expulsión de los extranjeros‹ tuvo lugar en el marco de la organización y las luchas del movimiento obrero contra la explotación capitalista y, particularmente, con la expansión del anarquismo a través de las corrientes migratorias de alcance intercontinental que protagonizaron (italianos y españoles principalmente) y de las redes transnacionales que establecieron.[64]

Antes de presentar un breve relevamiento de las legislaciones nacionales, veremos cuáles fueron las instancias internacionales que trataron la cuestión de la pena de deportación y del control social de la inmigración. En 1897, el VII Congreso de la Unión Internacional de Derecho Penal (Lisboa) se pronunció a favor de la pena de deportación y, un año después, el I Congreso Científico Latino Americano, llevado adelante en Buenos Aires, adoptó entre sus resoluciones »que es conveniente adoptar, para el tratamiento de la reincidencia, el sistema de deportación por largo tiempo, como pena accesoria del último delito cometido por el reincidente«.

En 1902, se firmó en América el *Tratado de extradición y protección contra el anarquismo*, promovido por Estados Unidos. Aquel instrumento de cooperación internacional fue parte de una política estadounidense de acercamiento a los estados latinoamericanos y tuvo su gestación en la Segunda Conferencia Panamericana, llevada adelante entre diciembre de 1901 y enero de 1902. Este fue, sin lugar a dudas, un hito en la cooperación para enfrentar al anarquismo a nivel regional.

Unas décadas después, la Conferencia Internacional Sudamericana de Policía, llevada adelante en Buenos Aires en 1920, con la asistencia de delegados de Argentina, Bolivia, Brasil, Chile, Paraguay, Perú y Uruguay, presentaron conclusiones sobre: la extradición de delincuentes; la policía fronteriza y la entrada de extranjeros. La conferencia tenía la finalidad de acordar procedimientos que sirvan a la defensa social y como un medio de estrechar aún más las vinculaciones entre las respectivas policías. Todos los temas que se trataron estaban dirigidos a un control más efectivo y directo de los posibles grupos resistentes. Por último, el II Congreso Latinoamericano de Criminología en Santiago de Chile en 1941 también abordó el tema y entre sus conclusiones afirmó que debería establecerse en cada país un comité de inmigración constituido por economistas y especializados en los problemas básicos de la eugenesia, a fin de dictar las disposiciones según las cuales se pueden admitir inmigrantes de un país extraño; asimismo que no debe aceptarse inmigraciones de individuos distintos de la raza blanca, para no agravar el problema ya inquietante de la mestización americana; deben conocerse los antecedentes de moralidad y buena conducta social de los presuntos inmigrantes, siendo rechazados los que tengan asuntos relacionados con la criminalidad.

Esta cuestión es muy delicada, ya que muchos delincuentes comunes se van a otro país alejado, huyendo de la justicia, y entonces no debe primar el concepto de humanitarismo, sino el de profilaxis social. Las leyes de extradición deber ser generales.[65]

Brasil dictó en 1907 un decreto sobre expulsión de extranjeros del territorio nacional que tenía un fuerte contenido biologicista, en cuanto afirmaba que se debía expulsar a aquellos que podían amenazar »el cuerpo nacional« como por ejemplo los enfermos, locos, vagos, anarquistas y criminales.[66] Argentina dictó en la primera década del siglo XX dos normas en la que delimitan el carácter peligroso de ciertos extranjeros. En 1902, la Ley de Residencia otorgaba al poder ejecutivo facultades para expulsar a los extranjeros cuya conducta com-

64 Domenech (2015) 170.
65 Segundo Congreso Latinoamericano de Criminología. Santiago de Chile, 19–26 de enero, 1941, ver https://www.dipublico.org/101525/segundo-congreso-latinoamericano-de-criminologia-santiago-de-chile-19-26-de-enero-1941/ (último acceso 18.12.2020).
66 Lacerda (1907) 63–85.

prometan la seguridad nacional o perturbe el orden público. Unos años más tarde, en 1910 se sanciona la Ley de Defensa Social[67] que prohíbe el ingreso al país a »los anarquistas y demás personas que profesan o preconizan el ataque por medio de fuerza o violencia contra los funcionarios públicos o los gobiernos en general o contra las instituciones de la sociedad«.

> Las argumentaciones que componían el discurso de la clase dirigente, particularmente en los debates parlamentarios, estaba inspirado en ideas europeas, especialmente del romanticismo, como también de las teorías de Spencer, Comte, la nueva disciplina denominada criminología que intentaba explicar las causas de la delincuencia, entre otras.[68]

En 1911 se dictó en Bolivia la Ley de Residencia que fijaba restricciones de ingreso y de expulsión a extranjeros. Permitía al poder ejecutivo »ordenar la salida del territorio de la Nación« e »impedir la entrada al territorio de la República« a todo extranjero que hubiera sido condenado o perseguido por tribunales extranjeros debido a crímenes o delitos comunes o que comprometiera la »seguridad nacional« o perturbara el »orden público«.[69]

En Chile, en 1918 se sancionó una Ley de Residencia, que estableció la expulsión de los extranjeros. A la vez, prohibía el ingreso de extranjeros que practicaran o enseñaran »la alteración del orden social o político por medio de la violencia« y la radicación de aquellos que difundieran »doctrinas incompatibles con la unidad o individualidad« de la nación, provocaran »manifestaciones contrarias al orden establecido«, o se dedicaran a »tráficos ilícitos que pugnan con las buenas costumbres o el orden público«.[70]

Venezuela introdujo en 1919 en la ley de Extranjería una lista de impedimentos para el ingreso al país, enumerando a aquellos que »puedan turbar el orden público interior«, »que pertenezca a sociedades o fines opuestos al orden público o civil«.[71] En 1920, Colombia dicta una legislación similar a la de Venezuela, incluyendo en las listas a los pobres, enfermos, criminales y anarquistas y comunistas que atenten contra el derecho de propiedad.

Uruguay dictó en 1932 la ley de inmigración que prohibía el ingreso a extranjeros que hubieran sido condenados por delitos en el país o en el exterior, como a vagos, maleantes, toxicómanos, ebrios consuetudinarios, personas expulsadas de cualquier otro país y los que sufran enfermedades mentales. Esta norma fue sucesivamente ampliada, en 1934 un decreto presidencial estableció el »control sanitario de extranjeros« que implicaba una obligatoria pericia psiquiátrica para quienes quisieran radicarse en el país. Dos años después, la ley 9.604 identificó como sujetos indeseables a todos aquellos pertenecientes a »organismos sociales o políticos que por medio de la violencia tiendan a destruir las bases fundamentales de la nacionalidad«, como los que padezcan enfermedades crónicas de los centros nerviosos, epilépticos, toxicómanos y ebrios consuetudinarios y mendigos.

El concepto de peligrosidad tuvo una amplia recepción en las leyes vinculadas con la inmigración, en una región que llevó adelante políticas activas migratorias entre fines del siglo XIX y comienzos del XX. Junto con el concepto de extranjero indeseable se acuñan una serie de exclusiones raciales explícitas:

> Comparando las políticas de exclusión de *extranjeros indeseables*, hay que señalar que no solo las políticas se desarrollan paralelamente, a veces de manera sincrónica, debido a procesos estructurales paralelos, sino que también pueden destacarse conexiones transnacionales en la génesis de las leyes nacionales.[72]

67 Esta ley fue dictada en junio de 1910, en el marco de los festejos del Centenario de la Revolución de Mayo, como respuesta estatal a una explosión de una bomba colocada en el Teatro Colón, en la Ciudad de Buenos Aires.

68 Costanzo (2009) 15.

69 Ley de Residencia del 18 de enero de 1911, Bolivia.

70 Domenech (2015) 179.

71 Schwarz (2012) 55.

72 Schwarz (2012) 67.

V. Conclusión preliminar

Desde 1870 y en adelante, con el cambio de la estructura económica a nivel mundial se produce una transformación social y cultural que impacta de diferentes maneras en las regiones, de acuerdo al nivel de desarrollo de la organización estatal y de su inclusión en la división internacional del trabajo. Es en este periodo en el que el Estado asume como una responsabilidad primaria el control social, como la única manera de poder intervenir frente a los resistentes a la disciplina que se impone en el nuevo orden mundial, surgiendo en Italia una escuela teórica, con discurso científico, que legitima racionalmente aquel control.

A partir de allí, por un lado, se inicia una interacción transnacional por medio de la creación de diferentes sociedades y entidades – sostenidas por los países centrales de Europa – con vocación universal y con una fuerte interacción entre ellas y con influencia directa a ciertos países de Latinoamérica. Estas tendrán entre sus principales objetivos: i) universalizar la legislación punitiva (unificación de códigos penales, etc.); ii) universalizar la creación de una serie de instituciones vinculadas al control social (patronatos de liberados, gabinetes antropológicos, etc.); iii) universalizar ciertos métodos de tratamiento del delincuente (de observación experimental), o de identificación de los delincuentes, etc.; iv) consolidar y desarrollar un mismo marco teórico para el control social (la escuela positivista); es decir, llevar adelante una institucionalización internacional del control social. De este modo, se da inicio a los regímenes de derecho penal trasnacional, entendido como una forma de gobierno global del crimen y de la seguridad.

Desde el inicio de aquella interacción, el flujo o intercambio fue asimétrico entre Europa y América Latina, siendo uno de los canales o medios de difusión y de discusión de aquellos postulados los diversos congresos que se desarrollaron en el seno de Europa, a los que asistieron delegaciones americanas. De allí brotarán una serie de instrumentos conceptuales y teóricos que crean la categoría del delincuente, que legitimaron la intervención estatal a aquellos individuos degenerados o resistentes al nuevo orden con una rápida recepción en parte de América Latina. Como hemos reconstruido, se trató de un proceso de interacción entre actores estatales y no estatales, a menudo alejados uno de otros.

Sin embargo, podemos afirmar que no se trató de una simple traducción teórica ya que no sólo no fueron adoptados aquellos postulados acríticamente,[73] sino que a la vez se elaboraron posiciones novedosas al adaptarlas a las necesidades locales:[74]

> Así, el proceso de incorporación de la matriz criminológica implicó apropiaciones y, al mismo tiempo, reformulaciones: las ideas fueron adaptadas a las condiciones del suelo nacional, adquiriendo entonces nuevos significados.[75]

Por otro lado, más allá del extenso alcance en el mundo académico, político y jurídico de los postulados positivistas, estos no fueron receptados ampliamente en las legislaciones latinoamericanas, a pesar de la inclusión de diversas normas vinculadas a la peligrosidad para la determinación de la pena, para evaluar la capacidad psíquica del delito y la adopción de sistemas dualista de culpabilidad y peligrosidad.

El dictado de leyes con contenido punitivo que se basó en los postulados del *estado peligrosidad* tuvo su centralidad en materia migratoria para prohibir el ingreso o para expulsar a extranjeros. Este concepto ha sido acogido en diferentes países y regiones por su utilidad en cuanto fundamento de diferentes prácticas de control social, como de discursos y narrativas habilitantes para enfrentar ciertos problemas sociales (vagancia, grupos mar-

73 Así, Sozzo plantea tres tipos de actitudes de los intelectuales locales en relación con los conceptos y argumentos de Lombroso: por un lado, la adopción en que se toman los núcleos fundamentales del pensamiento lombrosiano determinismo y abandono del libre albedrío, idea del criminal nato, imperativo de la defensa social, etc.; por el otro, la transacción donde se utilizan ideas del pensador italiano, pero se descartan ciertos tópicos – rechazo del atavismo, la embriología del crimen, la idea de degeneración producto de factores hereditarios y ambientales, etc. –; por último, el rechazo, en donde se argumenta que no se puede negar el libre albedrío y que »si bien existen criminales natos o por instinto, ello no implica descartar su responsabilidad subjetiva«. Núñez (2018) 141.

74 Por ejemplo el aporte de José Ingenieros, quien integró las causas biológicas y sociales del crimen y las vinculó con los factores psicológicos – ampliando de este modo los postulados de la antropología criminal incorporando el análisis de su estructura y funcionamiento psíquico.

75 Portelli (2017) 174.

ginales) como políticos (anarquismo, manifestantes), y consolidar el nuevo orden social.

A pesar de que en el periodo analizado el mundo no se encontraba globalizado, podemos esbozar que la conjunción entre un determinado marco teórico, la sistematicidad y organicidad de ciertas herramientas de difusión internacional, y la universalización de ciertos métodos vinculados al control social, representan el germen de un gobierno global del crimen.

■

Bibliografía

- Agudelo Betancur, Nódier (1991), Grandes corrientes del derecho penal. Escuela positivista (Introducción a la lectura de César Lombroso, Rafael Garófalo y Enrique Ferri), Bogotá
- Aniyar de Castro, Lola, Rodrigo Codino (2013), Manual de criminología sociopolítica, Buenos Aires
- Calvo Isaza, Oscar (2001), Conocimiento desinteresado y ciencia americana. El Congreso Científico (1898–1916), in: Historia Crítica. Revista del Departamento de Historia de la Facultad de Ciencias Sociales de la Universidad de los Andes 45, 87–113
- Costanzo, Gabriela (2009), Los indeseables: las Leyes de Residencia y Defensa Social, Buenos Aires
- Cuesta, José Luis de la, Isidoro Blanco Cordero (eds.) (2015), Resoluciones de los Congresos de la Asociación Internacional de Derecho Penal (1926–2014), in: Revista Internacional de Derecho Penal, nouvelle série 86, 1er/2e trimestres, online: https://www.penal.org/sites/default/files/RIDP86%201-2%202015%20ESP.pdf (último acceso 19.04.2022)
- Domenech, Eduardo (2015), Inmigración, anarquismo y deportación: la criminalización de los extranjeros ›indeseables‹ en tiempos de las ›grandes migraciones‹, in: Revista Interdisciplinar da Mobilidade Humana, vol. 23, núm. 45, 169–196
- García Basalo, Juan Carlos (1972), Las prisiones de México ante el Congreso Penitenciario Internacional de 1872, in: Revista Mexicana de Prevención y Readaptación Social, núm. 6, 5–20
- Garrido, Luis (1939), El Primer Congreso Internacional de Criminología, in: Revista de la Escuela Nacional de Jurisprudencia, vol. I, núm. 2, 255–262
- González, Esteban (2018), El trabajo de los penados argentinos alrededor del mundo. Eusebio Gómez en el IX Congreso Penitenciario Internacional (Londres, 1925), in: Revista de Historia de las Prisiones 7, 28–48
- Guillaume, Louis (1879), Le Congrès Pénitentiaire International de Stockholm [1878], Mémoires et Rapports, Bureau de la Commission Pénitentiaire International, vol. 2, Estocolmo
- Hobsbawm, Eric (1977), La era del capitalismo, vol. 1, Madrid
- Jiménez de Asúa, Luis (1928), El nuevo Código Penal Argentino y los recientes proyectos complementarios ante las modernas direcciones del Derecho Penal, Madrid
- Jiménez de Asúa, Luis (1957), Tratado de derecho penal, vol. 2, Buenos Aires
- La Obra de la Comisión Internacional Penal y Penitenciaria 1872–1942 (1943), in: Revista Penal y Penitenciaria, año VII, núm. 24, 247–270
- Lacerda, Francisco de Paula (1907), O decreto nº 1641 de 7 de Janeiro de 1907 sobre a expulsão de extrangeiros do território nacional (ligeiramente comentado o precedido de alguns capítulos doutrinários sobre o fundamento jurídico e aplicação prática do direito de expulsão com referencia aos autores nacionais e à jurisprudência prática), Rio de Janeiro: Typographia da Revista dos Tribunais
- Malo Camacho, Gustavo (1997), Derecho penal mexicano, México
- Medrano Ossio, José (1940), Responsabilidad penal de los indígenas, Potosí: Universidad Autónoma »Tomás Frías«
- Milla, Diana Gisella (2014), Los beneficios penitenciarios como instrumentos de acercamiento a la libertad. Análisis desde la legislación Iberoamericana, Alcalá, online: https://ebuah.uah.es/dspace/bitstream/handle/10017/22579/Tesis%20Diana%20G.%20Milla.pdf?sequence=1&isAllowed=y (último acceso 18.12.2020)
- Núñez, Jorge (2018), Comentario a Lila Caimari y Máximo Sozzo (eds.), Historia de la cuestión criminal en América Latina, in: Delito y Sociedad 45,1, 141–145
- Olmo, Rosa del (1999), América Latina y su criminología, Madrid
- Parada Gamboa, Marcela (2012), El peligrosísimo positivista: un discurso vigente en el Código Penal de 1980 en Colombia, in: Memorando de derecho 3,3, 219–228
- Pavarini, Massimo (1983), Control y Dominación. Teorías Criminológicas burguesas y proyecto hegemónico, México
- Paz Anchorena, José María (1936), Origen y desarrollo de los Congresos Penitenciarios Internacionales, in: Boletín del Patronato de Recluidas y Liberada, año III, núm. 9, 3–30
- Portelli, María Belén (2017), »Apasionado por ese movimiento científico«: Cornelio Moyano Gacitúa y el estudio empírico de la delincuencia argentina a comienzos del siglo XX, in: Revista Historia y Justicia 8, 166–194, online: http://revista.historiayjusticia.org/varia/apasionado-por-ese-movimiento-cientifico-cornelio-moyano-gacitua-y-el-estudio-empirico-de-la-delincuencia-argentina-comienzos-del-siglo-xx/ (último acceso 18.12.2020)
- Rivacoba y Rivacoba, Manuel de (2001), El Derecho Penal en América Latina a finales del siglo XX, in: Direito e Cidadania, año IV, núm. 10–11, 33–54, online: https://blog.uclm.es/cienciaspenales/files/2016/07/2.1.12el-derecho-penal-en-america-latina-a-finales-del-siglo-xx-rivacoba.pdf (último acceso 18.12.2020)
- Ruibal, Beatriz Celina (1993), Ideología del control social: Buenos Aires 1880–1920, Buenos Aires

- Schurmann Pacheco, Rodolfo (1958), Concepto científico y función jurídica de la peligrosidad en el código penal uruguayo, in: Revista de la Facultad de Derecho y Ciencias Sociales 9,4, 883 ss.
- Schwarz, Tobias (2012), Políticas de inmigración en América Latina: el extranjero indeseable en las normas nacionales de la Independencia hasta los años 1930, in: PROCESOS. Revista Ecuatoriana de Historia 36, 39–72
- Zaffaroni, Raúl (1993), Criminología. Aproximación desde un margen, Bogotá

Nicolás Duffau

Italian Immigration, Crime, and Police Actions in Uruguay: The Volpi-Patroni Case (1882)

I. Introduction

On February 7, 1882, the newspaper *La Democracia* cautioned against the advisability of certain proposed measures to »limit and restrict the rights enjoyed by foreigners in the collective life of the country«. According to the editorial of this daily, which generally supported the views of the National Party (in opposition at the time), these proposals were contrary to »the principles of equality on which any good political system rests« and went »against the true social and economic interests of the nation«. Curtailing the social and political rights of foreigners, the editorial argued, was tantamount to ignoring the existence of »14,500 Spaniards, 13,600 Italians, 6,720 French nationals, 1,820 Brazilians, 3,750 Argentines, 1,290 English nationals, 462 Germans, and 2,858 people of other nationalities« in the Department of Montevideo alone, in addition to the significant amount of capital brought in by foreigners. The journalist concluded that »foreigners who have thus settled in our country, and who have tied their fortunes and dearest affections to it, have as much of an interest as nationals in seeing that the rule of law prevails and that all the guarantees promised by our institutions are effectively granted«. In this way, one of the newspapers that opposed the government, and which championed ›work‹ and ›industry‹, demanded that foreigners – and in particular those who contributed to the country's economic development – be eligible to vote, as they represented »the greatest sum of material and moral interests«.[1]

Some days later, these views, echoed by other Montevideo newspapers,[2] became the focus of an intense debate when, in his statement to the police, the leading suspect in a murder case incriminated two Italian immigrants, triggering a major diplomatic incident with the Kingdom of Italy that lasted over a month. Under the prevailing political climate, rumors that the suspects detained for this crime had been tortured sparked public outrage. The Volpi-Patroni case, as it was known at the time, prompted heated discussions in the Montevideo press over the naturalization of foreigners.

Uruguayan historiography has dealt with the subject of international relations through the study of various treaties governing trade matters and sanitary or scientific cooperation, but the relationship between immigration and crime has not been sufficiently addressed, with the exception of research in the field of law that has examined extradition as a purely legal phenomenon.[3] The objective of this chapter is to combine the history of transnational criminal law with a social history that seeks to analyze the representations of criminals and foreigners by looking at narratives surrounding immigration and the role of immigrants – and of their countries of origin – during Uruguayan nation-building.[4] I will examine some of the salient aspects of the Volpi-Patroni case in order to shed light on the conflicts underlying an incident prosecuted as a crime, their torture, whose transnational dimension has largely been overlooked by Uruguayan historiography. To that end, as primary sources I will draw on press media from both Montevideo and the rest of the country (*El Bien Público*, *El Ferrocarril*, *El Norte*, *L'Italia*, *La Democracia*, *La Opinión Nacional*, *La Prensa*, *La Razón*, and *La Tribuna Popular*), covering a range of political and ideological tendencies, as well as on diplomatic documents held by Uruguay's General National Archive (*Archivo General de la Nación de Uruguay*).[5]

1 El extranjero (editorial), in: *La Democracia*, February 7, 1882, 1.

2 The newspaper *La Razón* used the same arguments as *La Democracia* in a series of editorials published on February 8 and 9, 1882 (El patriotismo y los extranjeros, El trabajo y los extranjeros), which were written in response to the vilification of immigrants in *El Nacional*, the newspaper loyal to the government of President Máximo Santos.

3 Olarte (1942) vol. 1.

4 For an initial study, see Duffau (2017). See also Härter / Hannappel / Tyrichter (eds.) (2019) especially 1–19; Boister (2012) especially 3–23; Andreas / Nadelmann (2008) 7–13.

5 Some of the newspapers mentioned here, such as *La Tribuna Popular*, *El Ferrocarril* or *El Norte*, labeled immigrants as transnational criminals and as a threat to society.

My approach to this incident is aimed at finding out what reactions it triggered in the press, among the authorities of the time, and among the population. As an event that involved immigrants, it can throw light on the complex processes of the construction of social identities experienced by Uruguayan society during the massive influx of foreigners into the country in the final quarter of the 19th century.

II. Uruguay: A Burgeoning Nation

In 1860, the government of Bernardo Prudencio Berro conducted Uruguay's second population census. While there are undoubtedly numerous gaps in the data gathered, given the state's inability to cover every area of the nation's territory and the roaming nature of many of the country's rural inhabitants, some useful conclusions can be drawn. The census figures show that since the previous official count in 1852, Uruguay's population had shot up from 132,000 people to 221,000 in 1860.[6] In less than ten years, Montevideo's population had increased from 34,000 to 58,000 inhabitants.[7] Immigration data reveals the role foreigners played in this growth, as their share rose from 21.6 % to 35 % of the total population in 1860. In Montevideo that percentage was even higher, as immigrants (not including descendants) accounted for 48 % of the capital's inhabitants. Twenty-two years later, in 1882, the population had more than doubled, totaling 505,207 for the entire territory, and, while precise figures are not available for Montevideo, it is safe to say that a significant number of Uruguay's population was concentrated in the capital.[8]

The contribution of foreign capital and, more importantly, cheap and efficient labor was a key component of the country's economic policy. Backed by the state, private enterprise put in place various schemes for recruiting workers, such as subsidizing fares, distributing land, and granting jobs, which in the vast majority of cases concealed forms of exploitation and abuse.[9] With the establishment of the Immigration Committee (*Comisión de Inmigración*) at the end of 1865, the government fostered the promotion and protection of foreign immigrants and launched an active campaign in Mediterranean ports and cities to attract workers to the country. At the same time that the significance of France, Germany and England as the countries from which most migrant workers originated waned, the Río de la Plata region began to attract an increasing number of Italians, drawn by the promise of work. This promise was reason enough for them to abandon a land devastated by war, economic crisis, and overpopulation. Given the circumstances that prevailed in their homeland, it is not surprising that a motley stream of unemployed workers and tradeless outcasts came to Montevideo from Italian as well as Spanish peninsular ports. These immigrants sparked concern among local authorities and animosity in the ruling classes, who feared that the incomers would turn the Uruguayan capital into a city of shoe polishers, street peddlers, invalids, musicians, and beggars.[10]

According to the 1860 census, there were 7,582 Italians in Montevideo, accounting for 27 % of all immigrants and only exceeded in number by their Spanish counterparts, who at 7,811 represented 28.22 % of the total.[11] By 1884, the number of Italians had risen to 32,829 (45.11 % of all immigrants), now surpassing by more than ten thousand the number of Spanish immigrants (22,122). Between 1879 and 1880, an estimated 8,824 Italians migrated to Uruguay, and over the following five years a further 26,473 immigrants from the Italian peninsula entered the country through the port of Montevideo. Between 1882 and 1886, the total number of foreigners in the Department of Montevideo stood at 72,781, compared to 91,247 Uruguayans.[12]

6 The data is taken from Silva / Witter / Santos (1990).

7 Without denying the importance of immigration in the process, 19th-century Uruguay was also characterized by what the historian José Pedro Barrán has called a »demography of excesses«, with a young population and a high birth rate. Barrán (1990) 29.

8 For a detailed study on migration, see Duffau / Pellegrino (2016) especially 196–199.

9 On employment contracts for immigrants in the preceding period, see Thul (2014).

10 Half of the 16,367 individuals who applied for work to the Committee between 1867 and 1876 declared that they had no trade. Data taken from Pacheco (1892) 105.

11 Silva / Witter / Santos (1990) 301.

12 Silva / Witter / Santos (1990) 302.

Region	1882–1886
Piedmont	335
Lombardy	718
Liguria	1260
Veneto	43
Emilia-Romagna	32
Tuscany	166
Marche	35
Lazio	No data
Umbria	No data
Abruzzo and Molise	12
Campania	876
Apulia	1
Basilicata	1451
Calabria	519
Sicily	25
Sardinia	No data
Total	**5473**

Italian immigration to Uruguay by region of origin.
Source: Devoto (1993) 33.

As shown in the above table, from 1882 to 1886 the Campania region – which was where Volpi and Patroni were from – contributed 866 people to the inflow of Italian immigrants (about 16 % of those whose origins we can trace), thus making it one of the leading regions of origin for immigrants from that country. The figures do not show how many of those Campania immigrants came from Naples, the region's capital. However, the terms *napolitano* (Neapolitan) and *gringo* (disparaging slang for ›foreigner‹) soon spread and were widely used to refer to any Italian living in Montevideo at the time. The historian Juan Oddone has noted that, in the case of the urban upper class, the attitude of contempt toward *gringos* did not extend to all foreigners but instead expressly excluded immigrant groups from countries that were considered to be at the forefront of modern political or economic development (France, Germany, Britain, and the United States). In contrast, the urban upper classes scorned immigrants from Italy, and to a lesser extent those from Spain, because of their social class and their supposed economic preferences, seeing them as potential criminals and a threat to order and security.[13]

The historian Silvia Rodríguez Villamil has pointed out that opponents of immigration were strongly influenced by the *Criollo* (Creole) mentality, which, among other basic features, was characterized by its connection with rural life, the idealization of the past (in particular the colonial past), and a rejection of all things new. The defenders of the Creole mentality were the old patrician upper class and associated families as well as urban lower-class sectors.[14] The most evident aspects of ›foreignness‹ – the presence of the immigrant and the prctice of European customs and ways of life – sparked a strong hostility among the sectors where *Criollo* mentality predominated. According to Rodríguez Villamil, that hostility can be traced to the *Criollos'* view of immigration as an invasion of their world by outside elements, as well as their disdain for the social class of most immigrants. Behind these stereotypes we can locate upper-class fears, in which immigrants figured as mostly belonging to the lower classes and as deviants or potential criminals threatening law and order. In this sense, the attitude of upper-class opponents of immigration was clearly conservative: they saw the prevailing social hierarchy as just, and the presence of immigrants alarmed those who defended a static image of society.

It is difficult to determine exactly how widespread these ideas were among the population of late 19th-century Uruguay. However, one possible working hypothesis could be to consider the Volpi-Patroni case as the culmination of a process of open violence against foreigners, as a number of high-profile incidents had already preceded it. These included the Paso Hondo incident in 1880, in which Brazilian officers were executed without trial because they allegedly planned to invade Uruguay; the beating of Italian immigrant Noe Scampieri by the chief of police of the town of Sauce (Department of Canelones); the disappearance of Manuel Sánchez Caballero in 1881,[15] and the subsequent killing of Silverio Sarrasina because

13 Oddone (1969) 16.
14 Villamil (2008) 44.
15 The Spaniard Manuel Sánchez Caballero, who had a feud with the Political Chief of the Department of Tacuarembó, Manuel Suárez, disappeared from his home in late 1881 and was never seen again. His disappearance caused a conflict between Uruguay and Spain, but neither the Political Chief nor other suspects were ever put on trial. For an account, see Acevedo (1934) 165 and 166.

he had signed a petition calling for an investigation into the fate of Sánchez Caballero. These incidents were closely observed by the Italian community, which objected to the methods of the police but also accused the government of arbitrariness, and society of meeting immigrants with contempt at every level.

III. The Crime

On the night of February 16, 1882, Juan Bentancour, a 19-year-old employee of the money exchange house *Francisco Platero y Hermanos*, located on Juncal Street in downtown Montevideo, was murdered by burglars as they attempted to rob the business. Days later, Uruguayan national José Carbajal, a forty-year-old legal assistant, was arrested as the main suspect. He confessed to the crime, and in his statement to the police implicated two Italian immigrants as his accomplices: the forty-year-old Raffaele Volpi di Giovanni and Vicenzo Patroni, a forty-eight-year-old street hawker, both originally from Padula, in Salerno.[16]

The Montevideo press immediately reported the news of the crime. One of the most widely read and more affordable newspapers, *La Tribuna Popular*, was known for featuring the most detailed coverage of violent crimes, and within twenty-four hours of Carbajal's arrest it had published an elaborate account of his crime. The reporter had either had access to the accused man's statement – difficult but not improbable – or simply made up the facts. Either way, his account was later repeated by other newspapers as a reliable version of what had happened.

According to this version, Carbajal was »short of funds« and went to see Volpi and Patroni who owed him a significant amount of money for legal services rendered by him in the Department of Soriano. They »told him they had no cash, but had a good business deal in the works, which would bring them a large sum of money«. The deal turned out to be a plan to rob the money exchange house. Around 8:30 p.m. on February 16, as the young employee was preparing to close up, Carbajal, »who had been watching him from across the street, saw his chance and went into the office first, with the two Neapolitans close behind. Once inside, he took a bill out of his pocket and said to his unfortunate victim, ›Hey, will you change this peso for me?‹« At that point, the two Italians went into the shop and »grabbed the money, filling their pockets with everything they could find, and then joined Carbajal in stabbing the victim to death«.[17]

The best-selling newspaper at that time was *El Ferrocarril*. Its popularity had to do with its price and its coverage of police news, which were written in a simple language that made them the most widely read. The paper's crime reporting style had a novel-like quality with an engaging and colloquial prose style.[18] Its dramatic portrayal of the suspects – Carbajal, Volpi, and Patroni – stirred the public's curiosity. Under the title »Famous Case«, it began a thorough coverage aimed at captivating readers. It started out by highlighting the exceptionality of the crime perpetrated at the *Francisco Platero y Hermanos* money exchange. It described it as very uncommon »in our country, and that is something we must congratulate ourselves on. Because despite the many turbulent times that the inhabitants of this republic have had to suffer, it has only been on rare – very rare – occasions that the press has had to report crimes such as this one, whose perpetrators, it is plain to see, have a soul darker than the depths of hell.«[19] In the following editions, over the months of February and March, *El Ferrocarril* continued its detailed account of the Bentancour crime, in a tone that was more in line with the ›true crime‹ stories of pulp magazines than with information featured in the pages of a newspaper. Both *El Ferrocarril* and *La Tribuna Popular* employed literary devices in their police chronicles to achieve a more realistic narrative, but they failed to clearly indicate that dialogues and facts might have been invented for effect.

La Democracia, more moderate in its coverage of police news, was against releasing information on crimes that were still under investigation. It cautioned that to do so would be to disregard »the most serious guarantees afforded by law to suspects of crimes or offenses who have been brought to

16 It was impossible to find the case files of the suspects in the Judicial Section of the General National Archive of Uruguay. Thus, we lack data of when they emigrated to Uruguay.

17 *La Tribuna Popular*, February 19, 1882, 1.

18 For a more comprehensive analysis of *El Ferrocarril*, see Duffau (2014) especially 63–83.

19 Causa célebre, *El Ferrocarril*, February 22, 1882, 1.

justice and are awaiting trial«, and that, it said, was dangerous. It therefore urged all the other press media to observe the discretion and reserve required by »the process on which are dependent the life and reputation of men who are accused of a criminal act and fall under the actions of the authorities«. *La Democracia* argued that it was necessary to protect the personal safety of all defendants, who were to be considered innocent »until they have been found guilty in a judgment handed down by a competent judge which has become final«. The press had a duty to cooperate with the judges so that the ruling in the Volpi and Patroni case, as in others, was not made »amidst the din and pandemonium [surrounding the crime] and under the initial impressions formed when the whole criminal plot and its perpetrators and various degrees of accomplices are discovered, or are believed to be discovered«.[20]

On February 19, police authorities released an alleged confession from Volpi in which he admitted that he had participated in the crime and said he was willing to cooperate. As a result he was taken to his home where he intended to return the stolen money. Once there, however, according to the media, »Volpi tried to take advantage of the situation by making a scene, inciting his neighbors against the authorities, and asking for help with cries of ›Long Live Italy!‹«[21] After he was taken back to jail, rumors that torture had been inflicted on him and the other detainees were picked up by some newspapers, which denounced the methods used by the police to force confessions under duress. The Italian community protested through its associations, in particular the *Circolo Napolitano*, and the newspaper *L'Italia*.[22]

El Ferrocarril did not limit its coverage to an account of the facts. As in other ›famous cases‹ of the time, it gave its opinion with respect to the treatment of perpetrators. A week after the crime, and in direct reference to the rumors of torture suffered by Carbajal, Volpi, and Patroni, the daily stated: »We have no knowledge of coercive methods being used – as some newspapers claim – to force a confession from these despicable murderers, these perpetrators of the heinous crime on Juncal Street. However, we must bear in mind that these are criminals who are very careful to conceal any evidence of their crimes, but not so much that they can fool the vigorous efforts of police investigators.« The newspaper asked if criminals should be shown consideration, and while it did not respond to the question directly, its answer was implicit when it continued by asking if the three accused had had any consideration »when they committed the premeditated, brutal homicide they had been hatching in their minds for more than a month?«[23]

The rumors of torture continued, prompting the Italian vice consul, Enrico Perrod, to insistently request that he be allowed to visit the prisoners to check on their state of health. Here the case enters the transnational level, because the suspects were still considered Italian nationals by Uruguayan authorities, and Italy demanded that the Uruguayan government should act within the rule of law according to their citizenship.

On February 27, the Italian diplomat, accompanied by a doctor from the gunship *Sicilia*, visited the Central Jail, housed in the Cabildo of Montevideo, and met with the detainees, who did not show any signs of torture or physical punishment.[24] In his statements to the press, Perrod affirmed that he had »found the accused men in good health«, while the Italian physician declared that »their bodies did not present any traces of having suffered torture«.[25]

This did not stop the rumors, however, and twenty days after he had visited the prisoners, the Italian diplomat sent a new letter requesting that the situation of his fellow countrymen, who were still being held in solitary confinement, be promptly resolved. Some years earlier, on April 14, 1879, Uruguay had entered into an extradition agreement with Italy. Under that treaty, which had been signed by the Uruguayan ambassador to Italy, Pablo Antonini y Diez, and ratified in 1881, each party agreed to hand over any nationals of the

20 Las garantías de la justicia (editorial), *La Democracia*, February 23, 1882, 1.
21 *El Bien Público*, March 25, 1882, 1.
22 Calma e fermezza (editorial), *L'Italia*, February 23, 1882, 1.
23 *El Ferrocarril*, February 23, 1882, 2.
24 The Italian gunship *Sicilia* was stationed in Montevideo at the express request of Perrod, who, after a series of crimes, attacks against newspapers, and a robbery suffered by the Brazilian Embassy in May 1881, all of which had been perpetrated by gangs loyal to President Máximo Santos, joined other diplomatic missions in demanding that a »permanent naval station« be allowed to »guard important interests of our community«. Letter from Eduardo Perrod to the Minister of Foreign Affairs of the Kingdom of Italy, May 25, 1881, in: Oddone (1965) 84–87.
25 *La Tribuna Popular*, February 28, 1882, 1.

other party taken into custody if the other party issued a diplomatic request for their extradition.[26] The fact that these diplomatic provisions were not observed should not be understood as a lack of concern on the part of the Uruguayan government for the international treaties it had ratified. While a norm was blatantly disregarded, this breach violation also illustrates the nature of state-building processes, which are not always linear, nor do they adjust rapidly to regulations. The existence of a law or treaty does not mean it will be immediately respected or enforced, as local circumstances could lead the authorities to disregard the rules. The conflict surrounding the Volpi-Patroni case also happened during the period when the characteristics of transnational law were still being defined, and criminal matters were precisely one of the areas in which full agreement did not yet exist. Moreover, it would be some years before Uruguay adopted a Criminal Code (in 1889), so that at this time criminal law consisted mostly of provisions dating back to the colonial period and some new regulations governing the administration of justice.[27]

In his letter addressed to the Uruguayan Foreign Minister, Manuel Herrera y Obes, the Italian diplomat noted, »I cannot ignore the persistent rumors of the barbaric treatment to which the police is subjecting these individuals by the name of Volpi and Patroni.« He also warned the minister about »the general outrage these rumors have sparked among the public, in particular the Italian community«, which is »in a state of alarm and concern over the arbitrary refusal of the authorities to allow me to verify with my own eyes« the state of the prisoners.[28] Uruguay's foreign minister replied the next day. As reported in *El Bien Público*, Herrera y Obes told Perrod that »if there are any complaints of torture – which is prohibited under the laws of this country – to which Volpi and Patroni are said to have been subjected, it is these men themselves who must bring those complaints directly to the attention of the judge in charge of the proceedings, so that he is made aware of them and can take appropriate action«. In addition, he cautioned the vice consul that »his diplomatic status does not grant him power to represent the defendants, as he can rest assured that all the regulations established by the laws of the country are being applied in their case«.[29]

The Italian community, however, did not back down from its demands. In subsequent letters to the press and in complaints filed with the Uruguayan government – but not always approved by the diplomatic authorities – its members continued to call for the immediate release or trial of the two prisoners. On March 21, Volpi and Patroni were released due to lack of evidence, after Carbajal recanted his statement against them.[30] The following day, *L'Italia* published a long article in which it gave an account of the month the »Neapolitans« had spent behind bars, describing what it called the »various torments« they suffered, including being placed in a clamp, held in a shackle bar, and beaten with riding crops and canes.[31] The Italian community accused their diplomatic representatives of having been fooled by the Uruguayan prison wardens. The latter had allegedly shown them two other Italians, in jail for other crimes, who were made to pretend they were Volpi and Patroni.[32]

Once freed, the two Italians, accompanied by the *Circolo Napolitano* Steering Committee, told their story in the headquarters of the Italian Diplomatic Mission, where they were examined by two doctors, Karl Brendel (a German physician who was a resident of Uruguay) and Vicente Stajano (an Italian). The medical report, which was disclosed a few days later, revealed that Raffaele Volpi had injuries on his body that he attributed »to the clamp torture, which he suffered on three consecutive days and at designated hours during

26 Italia. Convenio internacional de extradición de criminales con la República Oriental del Uruguay (1879), in: Criado (ed.) (1881) 432–439. In the same year, Uruguay also signed extradition agreements with Argentina, Peru, Chile, Bolivia, Ecuador, Venezuela, Costa Rica, and Guatemala. Olarte (1942) vol. 2, 21–22.

27 On this subject, see Fessler (2012).

28 Letter from Enrico Perrod to the Uruguayan Foreign Office, March 17, 1882. Archivo General de la Nación, Documentos de la Administración Central, Ministerio de Relaciones Exteriores (hereinafter AGN-MRE), box 405, folder 338.

29 *El Bien Público*, March 28, 1882, 2.

30 *L'Italia*, March 22, 1882, 1; *El Bien Público*, March 22, 1882, 2.

31 Gravissimo, *L'Italia*, March 22, 1882, 1.

32 They were further ridiculed because thousands of lithograph portraits of the accused had been sold throughout the capital during the month the men spent in jail, so that their faces were familiar to the public and should have been recognized by the diplomatic authorities. Some press media denounced the sale of these portraits as they thought it exposed the alleged murderers. See Las garantías de la justicia (editorial), *La Democracia*, February 23, 1882, 1.

the previous month«.[33] The medical examination also showed that he had scars on various parts of his body caused by blows, burns, and knife stabs, in addition to suffering paralysis in his arms and having lost several teeth, which had been pulled by the mouth gag. Vicenzo Patroni presented »a small but deep and irregular wound between his eyebrows, on the left side, which he says was caused by a kick he received when he was in the clamp«, and like his fellow countryman he suffered arm paralysis and had had several molars pulled out.[34]

On March 24, *L'Italia* published the complete statements of the two Italians. In addition to describing the torture they had suffered, they denied having seen Perrod, thus confirming that the Italian diplomat and doctor had been shown other prisoners. Several Uruguayan press media also denounced the torture. Among them was the ›Europeanizing‹ and ›civilized‹ newspaper *La Razón*, which, under the title »The Crime at the Cabildo«, devoted its March 23 editorial to the matter. It apologized to all foreigners in the country, as, it said, »never before have our public officials been possessed by such evil, such great cynicism, such shameless impunity«. On behalf of the Uruguayan people, it declared, »we beg your forgiveness [...] for the atrocities that have been committed against you«.[35]

During the month that Volpi and Patroni were in prison, the newspaper *El Ferrocarril*, which insisted on their guilt, published an ongoing, detailed account of the case. This featured dialogues between the killers and their victim that had supposedly taken place in the money exchange house on the night of the murder, which it claimed were taken from different confessions. But once the statements of the two Italians were released, the newspaper accused the national authorities of being like »the blacks of Mozambique or the court of Kana-kana«. For this newspaper, however, the torture inflicted by the police during the jailing of the two Italians was not the issue; rather, it was concerned with safeguarding the ›fatherland‹ from being tarnished by foreign claims.[36] For its part, *La Tribuna Popular*, the other newspaper that had seemed certain that Volpi and Patroni were guilty, published an editorial the day after their release highlighting »the noble sentiments of our people« who saw foreigners as »brothers«, so that »the Volpi and Patroni cause is not just an Italian cause, it is eminently national, because we are interested in protecting the dignity of the country, compromised as it was by individuals who we hope will answer to justice for their punishable actions«.[37]

On March 23, the Italian Diplomatic Mission sent a letter of complaint to Uruguay's Foreign Office, attaching the statements given by Volpi and Patroni. In the letter, it requested that the Uruguayan government prosecute the individuals responsible for the torture. Foreign Minister Herrera y Obes dismissed the statements because they had been given on the premises of the Italian Diplomatic Mission and not before a Uruguayan judge, who »under the laws of the Republic is the only one authorized to hear such statements and consider them for the purposes of adopting a judicial decision«.[38] This is also an interesting issue of transnational law, since the diplomatic mission was clearly considered extraterritorial and thus outside the jurisdiction of Uruguayan law.

The following day, representatives of all the Italian associations in the capital signed a letter of complaint addressed to the diplomatic authorities of the Kingdom of Italy. Francisco Passano, speaking on behalf of the Italian community, declared that it was »an insult to our dignity as men and Italians that we should have to protest as we are protesting on behalf [of the Italian authorities] against the disregard for the natural rights of Man and the obligations established by the laws of the People, which has of late been committed by the recognized Authority of a region that prides itself on being civilized and claims to be a friend of Italy«.[39]

33 *El Bien Público*, March 25, 1882, 2.
34 *El Bien Público*, March 25, 1882, 2.
35 El crimen de Cabildo (editorial), *La Razón*, March 23, 1882, 1.
36 Hágase justicia, pero sálvese la dignidad nacional, *El Ferrocarril*, March 24, 1882, 1.
37 Calma y justicia (editorial), *La Tribuna Popular*, March 23, 1882, 1.
38 *El Bien Público*, March 28, 1882, 2.
39 Passano's speech was reproduced in the March 28, 1882 edition of *La Democracia* (page 1). The exact number of Italian organizations in Montevideo and their membership at the time are not known. According to estimates by Luigi Favero and Alicia Bernasconi based on Italian consular information, in 1879 there were fourteen organizations in Montevideo that gathered Italian immigrants or their descendants. In 1885, according to figures from these authors, the four most important organizations (*Societa di mutuo socorros Operai italiani*, *Lega lombarda d'istruzione*, *Lega lombarda corale instrumentale*, and *Circolo Napolitano*) had a total of 2,793 members, with 850 in the *Circolo Napolitano* alone. Favero / Bernasconi (1993) 382.

No doubt due to these pressures from the Italian community and following the declarations of the Uruguayan Foreign Minister, on March 25 the Italian Diplomatic Mission sent an ultimatum threatening to break diplomatic relations. On March 26, Italian diplomatic officials, escorted by Naval Captain Carlo de Amézaga, took down the Italian coat of arms and flag from the front of the diplomatic headquarters, and all diplomatic personnel abandoned the premises.[40]

While to the press and the Italian community, the authorities appeared unresponsive to Italian demands, these events did not just cause a diplomatic incident, they also called into question the stability of the Uruguayan government. Even though in the late 19th century, Italy was still new to the international concert of nations, it formed part of a group of countries that were considered global powers, so that starting a conflict with it represented a risk for the Uruguayan government. Some press media feared that the breaking of diplomatic relations would spark a war, especially considering that the recently unified European country was starting to exhibit its first imperialistic aspirations.

El Bien Público[41] held the Italian Diplomatic Mission responsible because it refused to have Volpi and Patroni give a statement before a Uruguayan judge, which the newspaper saw as demonstrating »a disregard for [Uruguay's] national jurisdiction«.[42] On March 27, this newspaper analyzed a manifesto published by Amézaga, in which he justified the Italian diplomats' actions and reiterated the Italian demands. Taking a clearly anti-Italian stance, *El Bien Público* stated that »a breakdown of relations means probable war, and if one of the nations rupturing relations is weak and cannot sustain a war, the breakdown foreshadows humiliation or sacrifice for that nation«. The latter was probably what this Catholic newspaper predicted would happen to Uruguay, so that it called for »serene and patriotic reflection« to solve the dispute.[43]

For their part, government supporters considered that the Italian demand was »a gratuitous and despicable offense«, contrived merely »to slander General Santos and his government«.[44] According to this view, the ruling Colorado Party was Italy's »brother in arms«, while »those who preach uproar and scandal are the same who, having come out of ranks that have gone as far as sanctifying crime, now seek to rally together in order to bring confusion and distress to the spirit of the people«. In response to what he considered inappropriate statements by Amézaga, President Santos banned »all diplomatic agents accredited in the Republic from publishing anything of a political nature and related to pending international issues which may incite their fellow nationals to disturb the public order«.[45] Nevertheless, on March 26, Santos issued a decree discharging the Political Chief of the capital, Francisco Barreto, and the First Officer, Bernardo Dupuy, from their respective positions.[46] In addition, Police Chiefs Rufino Larraya and Juan Charlone were arrested.[47] In another communication, Santos undertook to provide every guarantee for the two Italians to give a statement in a Uruguayan court, but this offer was once again rejected by the Italian Diplomatic Mission.

In the diplomatic sphere, before receiving the Italian Diplomatic Mission's ultimatum on March 25, the Foreign Minister Herrera y Obes had asked

40 *El Bien Público*, March 28, 1882, 2. Amézaga later published his view of events in a memoir which he wrote after returning to Rome from the trip that had taken him around the world and brought him to Montevideo in March 1882. Amézaga (1885).

41 *El Bien Público* was the unofficial mouthpiece of the Catholic Church. It is not surprising, then, that its opinion regarding the conflict with Italy was influenced by the loss of the papal territories suffered by the Church during the Italian unification process of the 1860s.

42 Nuestro puesto de honor (editorial), *El Bien Público*, March 28, 1882, 1.

43 En el crepúsculo (editorial), *El Bien Público*, March 29, 1882, 1.

44 Hechos y no palabras, *La Opinión Nacional*, March 31, 1882, 1.

45 *El Bien Público*, March 29, 1882, 3.

46 Decree issued by Máximo Santos on March 26, 1882. AGN-MRE, box 405, folder 338. Perhaps reflecting the Santos administration's reluctance in making this decision, *La Opinión Nacional* opposed their arrest and published a series of editorials offering supposed evidence of Barreto's innocence. See, for example, La justicia y la oposición and El arresto del Señor Barreto, *La Opinión Nacional*, April 8 and 10, 1882, 1.

47 *El Bien Público*, March 28, 1882, 2. On April 5, the police doctor, Diego Pérez, was charged with covering up the torture. *La Tribuna Popular*, April 5, 1882, 2. In his defense brief, Pérez argued that the Montevideo Chief of Police had forced him to sign a statement asserting that the two imprisoned Italians were in good health. *La Democracia*, March 30, 1882, 1.

Uruguay's ambassador in Rome, Pablo Antonini y Diez, to take the necessary steps to ensure the withdrawal of the Italian war fleet from the Bay of Montevideo, as its captain »was printing out manifestos directed at the Italian community, increasing their state of excitement and using terms that are offensive to the President of the Republic, who should not and cannot tolerate them«.[48]

The Montevideo press and a group of citizens also published manifestos denouncing the Volpi and Patroni case, although the incident may be considered to have served them as a pretext to comment on the country's political situation, in particular the rising authoritarianism that had begun in the early 1880s and intensified with the inauguration of President Santos in March 1882. According to one of these manifestos, torture was »a product of an anomalous and violent inclination, which is not subject to rule or restraint, and when it has crossed moral barriers, there can be no hope of its resuming the path of the law by its own devices«.[49]

A letter written in the newsroom of *La Democracia* and signed by various political personalities claimed that the attacks perpetrated by law enforcement agents were »the predictable and inevitable consequence of the system of force and arbitrariness introduced years ago«, so that opposing that growing authoritarianism was an »act of patriotism […] positioned in time within the realm of truth and justice to condemn the crimes that are being committed«. The letter expressed some views regarding international politics and recognized Italy's status as one of the European powers, arguing that it was therefore necessary to strengthen »in the minds of our fellow citizens the conviction that relatively weak peoples can only win the consideration and respect of the powerful by being fair and dignified, and that only through the establishment of institutional rule can they satisfactorily respond to international demands caused by arbitrariness and force«.[50]

Meanwhile, the judge on criminal matters summoned the two Italians to give a statement. Volpi agreed to appear before the judge at the British Embassy, but the hearing, scheduled for March 30, was canceled by the President Santos, who ordered the judge to immediately leave the embassy, insisting that the investigation be conducted on Uruguayan soil.[51] On March 29, Interior Minister José L. Terra was summoned by legislators to give an explanation of the government's conduct. In his statement to Congress, the representative of the executive branch highlighted the inappropriate behavior of the Italian diplomats, who had failed to respect Uruguay's domestic laws and had obstructed the actions of the national courts.[52] Regarding the alleged slowness to act on the part of the justice system and the delay in arresting the officers implicated in the tortures, Terra maintained that »to suspend a civil servant under the weight of an accusation [of torture] was to discredit from day one the civil servant who was suspended«.[53]

The Kingdom of Italy sent the Marquis de Cova as its special envoy to solve the conflict.[54] He traveled to Montevideo from Buenos Aires and on April 4 held a confidential meeting in which he presented Italy's demands. In a subsequent letter cited by *El Bien Público*, de Cova summarized these as including: the arrest of all the individuals responsible for the treatment to which Volpi and Patroni had been subjected in prison; a payment of 50,000 francs in gold »as proof of the Uruguayan Government's deep regret at the actions that have been verified«; a public apology, »worded appropriately and given by His Excellency, the Minister of Foreign Affairs of the Republic of Uruguay in the response to this letter, retracting the statements contained in official publications with respect to the [Italian] royal authorities«; an official visit by the President of the Republic of Uruguay to the Special Envoy and the Plenipotentiary Minister of Italy on mission in Montevideo; and a »reciprocal salute pursuant to marine rules«.[55] Facing Italian pressure, the Uruguayan government accepted these conditions on April 6.[56] The following day the two nations reached an agreement and reestab-

48 Letter from Manuel Herrera y Obes to Pablo Antonini y Diez, March 25, 1882. AGN-MRE, box 338, folder 405.

49 La cuestión del día, *La Democracia*, March 28, 1882, 1.

50 *La Democracia*, March 31, 1882, 1.

51 *El Bien Público*, March 31, 1882, 2; *La Opinión Nacional*, March 31, 1882, 1.

52 Diario (1885) 205 and 206.

53 Diario (1885) 207.

54 Telegram to the Ministry of Foreign Affairs from the Uruguayan representative accredited in Rome, March 30, 1882. AGN-MRE, box 405, folder 338.

55 *El Bien Público*, April 9, 1882, 2.

56 Telegram from Manuel Herrera y Obes to the Uruguayan representative in Italy, April 6, 1882. AGN-MRE, box 405, folder 338.

lished relations, with Uruguay promising that the officers implicated in the Volpi-Patroni case would be brought to justice[57] and that the injured parties – who had by then left the country – would be compensated financially.[58]

La Tribuna Popular viewed the imposition of Italy's conditions and their acceptance by the Uruguayan government as an affront to national sovereignty. »We must understand that the nation's dignity has been disgraced by the agreement signed and that there is a great risk that the justice system will not have the freedom of action necessary to finally deliver that famous superior order that all accused cite but whose origin nobody knows.«[59] In contrast, the newspapers loyal to the government considered that it had reached »an honorable agreement for both parties«.[60]

These articles were likely fueled by some editorials published in *L'Italia*, the unofficial mouthpiece of the Italian community, which was still attacking the local authorities. On April 13, *L'Italia* took up the conflict again and defended the Italian community. Although the agreement reached five days earlier seemed to indicate that calm would be restored and a conciliatory tone would reign, the paper called for President Santos to be jailed, accusing him of being ultimately and primarily responsible for the torture of Volpi and Patroni. The newspaper vowed to warn its countrymen of the disadvantages that Uruguay presented as a destination country for immigrants.[61] Later, in a special edition published on April 17, *L'Italia* called for the resignation of Herrera y Obes.[62] The article sparked a heated reaction from the minister, who sent a letter to the Italian Diplomatic Mission protesting »the seditious attitude adopted by a sector of the Italian population in the presence of the Agents of His Majesty the King toward this Government, which has shown them a tolerance that is excessive and taxing on the national sovereignty of the Republic and the respect due to the authorities that represent it«.[63]

Once the case was settled, the press reconstructed the events in various serialized stories that depicted the murder at Juncal Street. *La Patria Argentina*, a newspaper of the city of Buenos Aires, began publishing »The Story of the Gruesome Crime«, written by the journalist »Mr. González Bonovino, Secretary of the Editorial Board of [*El Ferrocaril*]«, who had interviewed the murderer ›Caravajal‹[64] in jail. Volpi and Patroni were not mentioned in these accounts, except as the victims of the incriminating statements made by ›Caravajal‹. The story featured in *La Patria Argentina* was reprinted in Montevideo's *El Ferrocarril* under the name »The Montevideo Drama: The Bentancour Murder«. The story generated great reader interest and was published as a book not long after.[65]

Starting on May 22, and in what can be considered the first steps in positivist criminology in Uruguay, *El Ferrocarril* began printing portraits of Carbajal accompanied by an analysis of the link between physical features and behavior.[66] These views were also connected with the ideas that identified immigrants, in particular Latin immigrants, as the direct cause of the growing crime rate.[67] In this way, a decisive importance was attributed to a criminal's origins and to the natural characteristics that made an individual prone to inclinations that would turn them into »famous criminals, who merited being studied by those who investigate the abilities of those monsters who from time to time shock a society by perpetrating vicious attacks«. According to *La Patria*

57 Record drawn up at the Italian Diplomatic Mission upon delivery of the monetary compensation to Volpi and Patroni. AGN-MRE, box 405, folder 338.

58 José Carbajal (who had implicated Volpi and Patroni) was found guilty and sentenced to death. However, in September 1882, the day before he was to be executed, President Santos paid a visit to the Central Jail and the execution was postponed and eventually commuted for a prison sentence.

59 La espada de Damocles (editorial), *La Tribuna Popular*, April 12, 1882, 1.

60 *La Opinión Nacional*, April 8, 1882, 2.

61 *L'Italia*, April 13, 1882, 1.

62 *L'Italia – Bollettino Straordinario*, April 17, 1882, 1. AGN-MRE, box 405, folder 338.

63 Letter from Manuel Herrera y Obes to Barón de Cova, April 18, 1882. AGN-MRE, box 405, folder 338. This did not put an end to the discussion and the mutual recriminations, with the opinion pieces on the Volpi-Patroni case continuing throughout 1882 and part of 1883.

64 This is how the name of the murderer appears in the issues of *El Ferrocarril*.

65 *El Ferrocarril*, April 24, 1882, 2.

66 *El Ferrocarril*, May 22, 1882, 1.

67 Pesavento (2009) 5–24; Scarzanella (2007) 30 and 31. See, for example, a study by Héctor Miranda, a young Uruguayan legal expert who would later become a well-known politician of the Colorado Party, in which he examined the causes of Uruguay's rising crime rate and suggested some prevention policies. Miranda (1907).

Argentina – as reproduced by *El Ferrocarril* – »Caravajal's crime is not one of those simple homicides perpetrated to carry out a robbery; there are details and circumstances that make the murderer a character in the annals of barbarism and expose him for what he is: a monster of perversity, cunning, and cynicism, one who calculates the probabilities, coldly ponders the difficulties, the consequences, and the contingencies, and prepares everything in such a way as to escape punishment for his crime.«[68]

The renewed publicity of the incident sparked new confrontations between Italians and the police. On the one hand, this reflected the police's hostile attitude toward the Italian community, who were accused of being dangerous immigrants. On the other, the Volpi-Patroni case demonstrates a general way of dealing with crime and criminals that was not necessarily linked to racist or xenophobic views. As the events of this case unfolded, excesses, arrests, tortures, and beatings were also being committed against the Uruguayan population, in response to both criminal acts and political unrest.[69]

IV. Final Considerations

In this chapter I have attempted to examine the history of a series of related transgressions – a murder and the subsequent torture of suspects – and its different social, political, cultural, and transnational implications. The intended focus was not the crime itself but its representations (how the crime was viewed), which I hoped would allow us to see the more salient features of Uruguayan society at the time, in particular with respect to immigration and crime. The ramifications of the Volpi and Patroni case are an interesting starting point for the study of views that called for a halt to immigration, and a contribution to the necessary ›transatlantic‹ approach that will allow us to examine the criminal history of the 19th century and the first decades of the 20th century from a different perspective.

At the same time, this is an analysis of the press as it began to perform a thorough public examination of criminals and immigrants with reconstructions of the most famous cases through the lens of international positivist criminology. In this way, the press sketched profiles and established stereotypes of Italian immigrants from the lower (working) classes that were directly associated with social disorder and decline. This last aspect is interesting in order to analyze the emergence of social marginality in ›civilized‹ Uruguay: the rural or urban criminal and the poor immigrant, who became the preferred targets when it came to stigmatizing the enemies of the new order imposed by the upper classes. This chapter also reveals how countries dealt with a transnational conflict, issues of sovereign territorial integrity, and civil liberties for citizens and immigrants during the process of nation-building. The existence of diplomatic relations and the approval of an extradition treaty was interpreted differently by the Uruguayan and Italian authorities. In the Volpi-Patroni case, the Uruguayan rulers ignored the provisions in force. Italy, in turn, did not recognize the Uruguayan judicial authorities and put pressure on the government of President Santos in order to achieve extradition. This aspect is central because it occurred at the time of the incorporation of the two countries into transnational criminal law, although it is important to note that being part of the system did not imply direct compliance with the provisions. In other words, on the one hand there was the law, and on the other the local practices and historical contexts that have to be taken into account in order to understand the transnational dimension of the application of criminal law in Uruguay.

■

68 *El Ferrocarril*, April 18, 1882, 1. On this kind of portrayals, see Sozzo (2007).

69 On repression in this period, see Duffau (2013).

Bibliography

- Acevedo, Eduardo (1934), Anales históricos del Uruguay, vol. 5, Montevideo
- Amézaga, Carlo de (1885), Viaggio di circumnavigazione della regia corvetta »Caracciolo« negli anni 1881–82–83–84, vol. 1, Rome
- Andreas, Peter, Ethan Nadelmann (2008), Policing the Globe: Criminalization and Crime Control in International Relations, New York
- Barrán, José Pedro (1990), Historia de la sensibilidad en el Uruguay, vol. 1, Montevideo
- Boister, Neil (2012), An Introduction to Transnational Crime, Oxford
- Criado, J. Manuel Alonso (ed.) (1881), Colección Legislativa de la República Oriental del Uruguay por Matías Alonso Criado, vol. 7, Montevideo
- Devoto, Fernando (1993), Un caso di migrazione precoce. Gli italiani in Uruguay nel secolo XIX, in: idem et al. (eds.) 1–36
- Devoto, Fernando et al. (eds.) (1993), L'emigrazione italiana e la formazione dell'Uruguay moderno, Turin
- Diario (1885) = Diario de sesiones de la Cámara de Representantes, vol. 47 (March 29, 1882 session), Montevideo
- Duffau, Nicolás (2013), Armar el bandido: delito, prensa y folletines en el Uruguay de la modernización. El caso de El Clinudo (1882–1886), Montevideo
- Duffau, Nicolás (2014), Armar al bandido. Prensa, folletines y delincuentes en el Uruguay de la modernización. El caso de El Clinudo (1882–1886), Montevideo
- Duffau, Nicolás (2017), Propuestas orientales, concreciones rioplatenses. Redes delictivas, extradición criminal y colaboración policial en el Río de la Plata (1854–1865), in: Revista Historia y Justicia 8, 138–165
- Duffau, Nicolás, Adela Pellegrino (2016), Población y Sociedad, in: Caetano, Gerardo (ed.), Uruguay. Reforma social y democracia de partidos. 1880–1930, vol. 2, Montevideo
- Favero, Luigi, Alicia Bernasconi (1993), Le associazioni italiane in Uruguay fra il 1860 e il 1930, in: Devoto et al. (eds.) 375–429
- Fessler, Daniel (2012), Derecho penal y castigo en Uruguay (1878–1907), Montevideo
- Härter, Karl, Tina Hannappel, Jean Conrad Tyrichter (eds.) (2019), The Transnationalisation of Criminal Law in the Nineteenth and Twentieth Century: Political Crime, Police Cooperation, Security Regimes and Normative Orders, Frankfurt am Main
- Miranda, Héctor (1907), El clima y el delito, Montevideo
- Oddone, Juan (1965), Una perspectiva europea del Uruguay. Los informes diplomáticos y consulares italianos. 1862–1914, Montevideo
- Oddone, Juan (1969), Los gringos, in: Rama, Ángel (ed.), Enciclopedia Uruguaya, vol. 26, Montevideo, 1–18
- Olarte, Julio María de (1942), Extradición. Doctrina. Legislación. Jurisprudencia, vol. 1 and 2, Montevideo
- Pacheco, Álvaro (1892), Consideraciones sobre inmigración y colonización, Montevideo
- Pesavento, Sandra Jathay (2009), Visoes do Cárcere, Porto Alegre
- Scarzanella, Eugenia (2007), Italiani malagente. Inmigrazione, crminalitá, razzismo in Argentina, 1890–1940, 7th ed., Milan
- Silva, Hernán A., José Sebastião Witter, Alvaro Brandão Santos (1990), Inmigración y estadísticas en el Cono Sur de América. Argentina, Brasil, Chile, Uruguay, Montevideo
- Sozzo, Máximo (2007), Retratando al ›homo criminalis‹. Esencialismo y diferencia en las representaciones ›profanas‹ del delincuente en la Revista Criminal (Buenos Aires, 1873), in: Caimari, Lila (ed.), La ley de los profanos. Delito, justicia y cultura en Buenos Aires (1870–1940), Buenos Aires, 23–65
- Thul, Florencia (2014), Coerción y relaciones de trabajo en el Montevideo independiente. 1829–1842, Montevideo
- Villamil, Silvia Rodríguez (2008), Las mentalidades dominantes en Montevideo (1850–1900), Montevideo

WHAT

Paul Knepper

The League of Nations, Traffic in Women and the Transnationalization of Criminal Law

During the 1920s, the League of Nations pursued a campaign against trafficking in women built around a ›worldwide‹ investigation. The Advisory Committee on the Traffic in Women and Children sent undercover investigators to more than a hundred cities in nearly thirty countries across Europe, the Mediterranean and the Americas. The investigators conducted 5000 covert interviews with persons knowledgeable of the sex trade at brothels, hotels, cafés and music halls, in addition to 1500 official interviews with representatives from police departments, immigration authorities, and shipping lines.[1]

The League's campaign, and particularly the investigation, advanced the idea of the traffic in women as an international crime. From the perspective of crime history, international crime can be identified as an activity such as drug smuggling, assassination, counterfeiting or financial fraud that crossed a border, or threatened to, and attracted concern from multiple nation states. Police, in particular, used this language to refer to such crimes. During the 1920s, the International Criminal Police Commission (to become known as INTERPOL) alerted governments to »a new class of criminal – the international criminal« that made use of technological advances in communication and transportation to perpetrate organized forms of cross-border criminality.[2]

From the perspective of global legal history, however, the term ›international crime‹ is less than satisfactory because it confuses an important distinction between international criminal law and transnational criminal law. As Neil Boister explains, international criminal law refers to law directly applicable to international criminal tribunals, such as the International Criminal Court, and criminal responsibility directly applied under international law. International criminal law concerns war crimes, crimes against humanity, and genocide. Transnational criminal law forms a broader system that aims to suppress harmful activity across national boundaries. Nation states enforce their own criminal laws, but must rely on other states if they are to enforce their laws against criminals operating across shared borders. ›Transnational criminal law‹ provides a clearer description for crimes such as drug smuggling, terrorism, etc., than ›international criminal law‹ because transnational criminal law operates indirectly by means of vocabularies, procedures, and practices that range from formal cooperation to informal coordination of police or other authorities.[3]

This essay will explore how the League of Nations' Advisory Committee on Traffic in Women (ACTW) operated as a legal regime in the realm of transnational criminal law. The essay has four parts. Part one introduces the League's campaign against the traffic from the perspective of entangled history. Part two explains how the organization of the investigation as envisioned by Grace Abbott fits the definition of a ›transnational law regime‹. Part three examines the wider cultural, political and social contexts in which such regimes operate with a look at the *SS Cap Polonio* case and South America. Part four examines the legal status of the League and the meaning of ›transnational criminal‹ within the controversy surrounding the alleged trafficker known as 18-R.

I. The League of Nations and the Traffic in Women

At the end of the First World War, the international campaign against the white slave trade succeeded in inserting Article 23c into the Covenant of the League of Nations, in which the League assumed responsibility for monitoring treaties concerning the white slave trade and drug smuggling agreed before the war. The first woman to address the Assembly spoke about the traffic in women.

1 Leppanen (2007); Pliley (2010); Limoncelli (2010); Chaumont (2009).

2 Deflem (2002). See, further, Knepper (2011); Gorman (2012); Jäger (2006).

3 Boister/Currie (2015).

Henni Forchhammer, a member of the Danish legation, emphasized that the illicit trade in women's bodies could not be suppressed without multinational intervention coordinated via the League.[4] The Assembly directed the Secretariat to survey the member states about the present status of legislation and their future plans. In 1921, the League of Nations convened an international conference on the traffic in women. Representatives from 34 nations met in Geneva to review progress on the two existing international agreements concerning the white slave trade: the International Agreement of 18 May 1904 and International Convention of 4 May 1910. The conferees agreed to a series of resolutions, which became known as the Final Act of the conference. The Final Act became a multilateral treaty, the International Convention for the Suppression of the Traffic in Women, signed by 27 countries, including several from South America.[5]

Two resolutions passed at the 1921 conference proved to be of particular significance. First, the conference inaugurated the conceptual language of *trafficking*. Resolution 13 provided that the phrase ›white slave trade‹ in international agreements should be replaced with the words ›traffic in women‹. The language provided for a new category of criminal activity that became part of the League's concern because it took place across national borders. H. Wilson Harris, who popularized the League's campaign against the traffic in women in his 1928 book *Human Merchandise*, recognized the significance of the new vocabulary. The new language had come about as a convenient reference in Article 23c which had, perhaps unintentionally, linked the sex trade and drug smuggling, »but«, Harris wrote, »it is impossible to follow the course of the League's activities in either field without being impressed by the extent of the common terminology habitually applied to both evils – traffic in drugs, traffic in human bodies and souls«.[6] Eric Ambler captured the logic of this new threat of cross-border criminality in his 1939 novel *The Mask of Dimitrios*. Drawing on the popular conception of the League's efforts, the character of Dimitrios is not merely a principal in the white slave trade, but also in drug smuggling, political assassination, spying and financial fraud.[7] In other words, the concept of *trafficker* enabled the League of Nations to claim ownership over a range of cross-border activities.

Second, the 1921 conference institutionalized the international anti-traffic campaign. Resolution 11 of the Final Act created the Advisory Committee on the Traffic in Women and Children (ACTW). The Council invited France, Great Britain, Japan, Poland, Spain, Romania, Denmark, Italy and Uruguay to appoint representatives. In addition, there would be five unofficial representatives or ›assessors‹ from the voluntary agencies: the International Bureau for the Suppression of the Traffic in Women and Children, the International Women's Organization, the International Catholic Association for the Protection of Women and Girls, and the Jewish Association for the Protection of Girls and Women. Ostensibly, the ACTW was a technical organization within the League framework, and as such, an organization with limited scope and influence. However, as Susan Pedersen points out, the technical organizations claimed particular success as intergovernmental organizations. The ›institutional entrepreneurs‹ that led these technical committees built ever larger empires, so that by the 1930s, more than half the League's budget went for ›technical work‹.[8] Rachel Crowdy, head of the League's Social Questions and Opium Traffic Section, led the ACTW. During the war, she had joined the Voluntary Aid Detachment (VAD), organized to support the British army, and became the principal commandant of VADs on the Continent. In 1919, she received the equivalent of a knighthood from King George V (Dame Commander of the Most Excellent Order of the British Empire) for her work during the war organizing medical support centres and ambulance stations. Crowdy was the only woman to lead a department within the League Secretariat. She was particularly effective at building networks of women's groups, voluntary associations and member states to advance the ›Geneva dream‹.[9]

Reading the texts of politicians, journalists, academics and other League advocates, it is easy

4 Henni Forchhammer spoke against trafficking in women and children at the League of Nations session in December 1920.

5 Boeckel (1929).

6 Harris (1928) 26.

7 Ambler (1939).

8 Pedersen (2007) 1092.

9 Gorman (2012) 62.

to see the campaign against the traffic in women waged by the League of Nations as an abrupt transition in the history of crime, the moment when the League abandoned the 19th-century concept of ›white slave trade‹ and introduced the 21st-century concept of ›traffic in women‹. The League of Nations has received good marks from historians for discarding the antiquated language of *white* slavery with its racist implication that only European women mattered. This fits with the leading historiographical view of the development of international society as a progressive advance from power politics to a global community.[10] In practice, however, the League's continuing concern with European women taken to brothels in South America and the Middle East remained less universalist / human rights oriented and more European / colonialist.[11] The League's campaign in the 1920s is more a story of continuity. On the one hand, it takes place in a much longer history of internationalism, transnationalization of criminal law, extension of concepts of criminal behaviour.[12] On the other, while the League brought significant innovation in the form of a transcontinental investigation, even this had its origins in the decades when the problem was conceptualised as the white slave trade. This is also why the concept of entangled history fits so well. The story of traffic in women is not unique to the present age, but has a longer provenance. Each generation sees coerced prostitution through a lens of anxiety about the immediate future, and the impact of broader social, cultural, economic, and technological changes in society. Entangled histories do not offer a single point of departure, but complex intertwined networks without a clear beginning or end.[13]

The idea for an investigation into the traffic in women did not emerge from discussions in Paris in 1919 when the League of Nations added the ›white slave trade‹ to the Covenant but from legal proceedings in New York City a decade before.[14] In 1909, *McClure's*, a popular magazine with a national circulation, printed an exposé of the white slave trade that portrayed New York City as the capital of the international underworld. Under the protection of corrupt politicians, white slavers supposedly procured girls from East Side tenements and villages of Eastern Europe for brothels throughout the United States, West Indies and South America. The white slave trade became the leading issue in municipal elections that year, and a grand jury was called to determine the truth of the reports. To lead the grand jury, the judge appointed billionaire John D. Rockefeller Jr.[15]

Rockefeller pursued his task with missionary zeal. He secured $25,000 from the mayor's office for an undercover investigation in which operatives attempted to buy women. Among the operatives were three women who posed as decoys, a private investigator, and investigators from the district attorney's office. Although the grand jury concluded that a clandestine trade in women's bodies did exist, they turned up »no evidence« of »incorporated syndicates« or »international bands« of criminals.[16] Rockefeller planned to urge the mayor to set up a permanent commission, staffed with an investigator, to carry on the work of the grand jury. But then he had another idea. The publicity surrounding the investigation and the political wrangling over the findings convinced him of the need for a new strategy. Rockefeller registered a corporation known as the Bureau of Social Hygiene, which initially operated out of rooms in the Stand-

10 Wertheim (2012) 211. As Wertheim explains, the teleological view of history, banished from national histories, has found a home in international history. See, for example, Ikenberry (2001); Iriye (2002); Kennedy (2006).

11 Knepper (2009).

12 See, for example, Mazower (2012).

13 Duve (2014) 7–8.

14 The 1899 convention passed at that year's International Congress on the White Slave Trade in London resulted in the 1904 international convention on administrative measures and special police activities / branches that should investigate the crime. Also in 1904, the *Nationale Zentralstelle Mädchenhandel* was established in Germany, and in 1905 the Reichstag passed the corresponding Abkommen zwischen dem Deutschen Reiche und anderen Staaten über Verwaltungsmaßregeln zur Gewährung wirksamen Schutzes gegen den Mädchenhandel, 18. Mai 1904, Deutsches Reichsgesetzblatt 1905, vol. 33, 695–705.

15 Knepper (2012).

16 Presentment in the Matter of the Investigation as to the Alleged Existence in the County of New York of an Organized Traffic in Women for Immoral Purposes, 2 January 1910, Rockefeller Archives, RG 2, Series 0, Box 8, Folder 56.

ard Oil Building at 26 Broadway, New York City. During the next two decades, the Bureau would pour more than $5 million into the moral war against the »social evil« of prostitution.[17]

One of the organizations funded by Rockefeller's Bureau, the American Social Hygiene Association (ASHA), would figure prominently in the League's worldwide investigation. The ASHA, formed in 1914 from an amalgamation of several organizations set up to promote public morality, was one of a number of private organizations that conducted secret investigations into vice districts of cities across the United States. These organizations relied on undercover investigators to break down the collusion between corrupt officials and criminal elements believed to support wide scale prostitution. The investigators prepared reports that were presented to city officials on the understanding that this information would be handed over to the press if officials failed to act.[18] The investigations blurred the distinction between public and private, legal and social inquiry. The organizations' leaders displayed an enthusiasm for covert investigation with little regard for legal rights; they believed they were justified in doing so by the need to address pressing social problems.[19]

II. Abbott's Proposal for a Worldwide Investigation

At the 1923 meeting of the ACTW, the American representative, Grace Abbott, proposed a comprehensive study. From the 19th century onwards, stories had circulated about girls trapped into prostitution; girls drugged with chocolates, spirited away in motor cars, or lured with offers of careers on stage. So many incidents were reported to have occurred in a few years it strained credulity. The reports always appeared second-hand; there was never a victim's account sworn before the police or a magistrate. The emotional appeal of the ›white slave‹ narrative was meant to convince readers about the urgency of the problem; there was no need to ask for proof.[20] Abbott insisted that the League's effort would not have credibility without a systematic inquiry to »establish the facts« of the traffic: the extent of the traffic in women for prostitution; the methods and routes used by traffickers; and the effectiveness of national controls. Skilled investigators would need to visit cities regarded as key sites. It would be difficult and dangerous work, but essential to provide an »intelligent basis« for international cooperation.[21]

Abbott's proposal is interesting on several levels. The United States did not join the League of Nations. President Wilson's opponents in the US Senate defeated his international agenda, and the US Congress refused to ratify the agreement, so Abbott's proposal did not represent that of a member state. At the initial meeting of the ACTW, the members decided to invite the United States (and Germany) to send representatives to serve in an informal capacity. The Harding Administration sent Abbott, director of the child-labour division of the US Children's Bureau in Washington, DC. Abbott had been a resident of Hull House in Chicago, the pioneering immigrant settlement organization. She completed a doctorate in political science at the University of Chicago, and in 1910 joined the faculty of its School of Civics and Philanthropy. Further, Abbott's proposal did not represent the initiative of the Harding Administration, but rather that of a private individual, Rockefeller. The British representative welcomed the proposal. The French countered with a bid for each country to carry out an enquiry within its own borders, but Abbott insisted this would fail to produce »official and accurate« data about cross-border activity. When Abbott promised that she could find the money to fund the investigation, she won the argument. She brokered a grant of $75,000 from Rockefeller's Bureau of Social Hygiene in New York City.[22]

17 The Origin, Work and Plans of the Bureau of Social Hygiene, 27 January 1913, Rockefeller Archives, Series 1, Box 2, Folder 25; Helen Spencer to Edward Robinson, 26 November 1949, Rockefeller Archives, RG 2, Series 0, Box 9, Folder 72.

18 *First Annual Report 1913–1914*, New York: American Social Hygiene Association, 1914, Social Welfare History Archives, Elmer Andersen Library, University of Minnesota (Box 170).

19 Fronc (2009); Robertson (2009); Knepper (2012).

20 Billington-Greig (June 1913).

21 ACTW (1923a) 27; Grace Abbott, Recommendations submitted as a possible subject for discussion by the Committee on Traffic in Women and Children, Edith and Grace Abbott Papers, Regenstein Library, University of Chicago (Box 61).

22 ACTW (1923b) 3–4.

The relationship between Rockefeller, Abbott and the ACTW can be understood within what Karl Härter defines as a »transnational law regime«. The ACTW brought together government and non-state actors, experts and practitioners, extending to transnational as well as national levels, characterized by varying legal and administrative procedures.[23] Or, as Boister puts it, transnational criminal law includes all forms of criminal law with an international dimension. It is distinguished by its indirect nature, which contrasts with the direct nature of international law, but forms a »distinct system«.[24] In examining the work of the ACTW, we also see the role of private initiatives in a transnational law regime. Daniel Gorman refers to Rockefeller's contribution as »private internationalism«, a significant aspect of the American contribution to international society.[25]

The Council of the League of Nations agreed to Abbott's proposal and appointed a Special Body of Experts to carry out the investigation.[26] To lead the Special Body of Experts, Abbott secured William F. Snow, a trained physician who was professor of preventive medicine at Stanford University. He also led the ASHA, which, Abbott realized, was less than ideal from the standpoint of conducting objective fact-finding.[27] To lead the field investigation, Snow chose Bascom Johnson, the ASHA's legal director. Johnson had completed his law degree at the University of Pennsylvania and practiced law in Philadelphia before becoming legal counsel at the ASHA. During the First World War, both Johnson and Snow had served with the US Commission on Training Camp Activities. Major Johnson and Colonel Snow had together campaigned to close down red light districts adjacent to military camps across the western United States.[28]

Johnson planned the field investigation along the lines established by the ASHA for its work in cities. The ASHA's method might be described as an ›undercover policing model‹. As Jean-Michel Chaumont, Magaly Rodríguez García and Paul Servais point out, Johnson referred to police methods to justify this strategy in addressing the Special Body of Experts.[29] But the fact that these investigations targeted corruption by police and other authorities meant that they necessarily relied on private investigators, and thus legal requirements concerning procedure, evidence, and prosecution that would extend to the police did not apply. What Johnson did not tell the Special Body of Experts is that the ASHA had been criticized for their undercover methods. The District Attorney's office in New York City had accused ASHA investigators of entrapment; the *New York Evening Graphic* newspaper had said they engaged in »sneaky, slimy spy work«.[30]

Abbott's proposal projected an understanding of the law known as ›sociological jurisprudence‹, or more precisely, the American version of it. During the 1920s, Harvard law professor Roscoe Pound challenged the philosophical basis of international law. He argued that international law did not represent a separate form of law and that international lawyers made so little progress because they had conceived of international law as a »closed metaphysical system«. Proponents of international law adopted rules, then imagined social realities would conform to them. According to Pound, the failure of international law, which had become apparent with the First World War, was due to its reliance on an outworn philosophy that refused to adapt the developing techniques of the social sciences for understanding social realties. American sociological jurisprudence originally targeted

23 Härter (2019) 3.
24 Boister (2003) 956–958.
25 Gorman (2012) 180–187.
26 The experts making up the Special Body were: Alfred de Meuron, head of the International Bureau for the Suppression of the White Slave Traffic; Princess Cristina Guistiniani Bandini, social worker and leader of the Catholic women's movement; Isidore Maus, head of the child welfare division of the Belgian government; Joseph Louis Hennequin, director of the French anti-traffic society; Yotaro Sugimura, from the Japanese Ministry of Foreign Affairs; Paulina Luisi, physician and professor at the University of Montevideo; and Sidney Harris, a specialist in child welfare at Britain's Home Office.
27 Grace Abbott to Raymond Fosdick, 8 January 1924, Edith and Grace Abbott Papers, Regenstein Library, University of Chicago (Box 61). Professor Abraham Flexner, who had carried out research on prostitution in Europe, had been the first choice but declined due to illness.
28 Sandos (1980).
29 See Chaumont / Rodríguez García / Servais (2017b) 10.
30 Knepper (2012) 790–791. See, further, Pivar (2002); Fronc (2009); Robertson (2009).

municipal law; Pound insisted that like municipal law, international law remained mechanical and formalistic.[31] He encouraged international lawyers to borrow methods of the social sciences and to pursue active social engineering. The way forward for international law would be found in »new philosophies of action« and pursuit of »social control«.[32]

To say that Abbott intended her proposal as an application of sociological jurisprudence would be a step too far. She never said this was what she was doing. But her approach followed from Pound's theory, and she had a close working relationship with him. Pound graduated from the University of Nebraska, studied law at Harvard University, and returned to Lincoln, where he practiced law and taught at the university. He went on to professorships in law at the University of Nebraska, Northwestern University, and the University of Chicago, before settling at Harvard, where he served as dean of the law school for twenty years. Like Pound, Abbott was originally from Nebraska. Before her move to Chicago, she received her undergraduate degree at the University of Nebraska and completed a graduate course taught by Pound. She corresponded with him throughout her career, sought his advice on child labour legislation, and was part of his network of »progressive-pragmatists«.[33] She made her proposal to the ACTW in Geneva in 1923, about a year after Pound's lecture at the University of Leiden in which he advocated sociological jurisprudence as a foundation for international law.[34]

III. The *SS Cap Polonio* episode

About the time the investigation into the traffic in women got underway, a story appeared in various newspapers about a trafficking operation on an industrial scale. The *New York Evening Post* reported the discovery of a plot to ship 500 girls to the United States via Antwerp, Hamburg, and Rotterdam. According to the newspaper, the police in Antwerp had »definite proof« that Hans Braun (or Mr Brown), who led the Girls' Protection Society in Berlin, was actually operating a white slave traffic ring. The authorities discovered his false identity, but he escaped from Germany before the police could make an arrest.[35] When Rachel Crowdy heard the story, she wrote to Grace Abbott in Washington, DC, and to Annie Baker at the International Bureau in London. Abbot had no further information, but Baker had information from the German National Society for the Suppression of the Traffic in Women and Children. Dr Jung, president of the society, reported that Braun had in September 1923 sent five girls from Romania to South America. A young woman named Anna Gertler had told him the women had sailed on the steamship *SS Cap Polonio*.[36]

The ACTW's work on the Cap Polonio case illustrates political, cultural, and other social aspects of transnational law. International criminal law implies a community of nation states guided by shared values and committed to cooperation. Transnational criminal law implies sovereign states committed to selective cooperation depending on perceived self-interest. The degree of cooperation varies from crime to crime, depending on the level of harm, or perceived threat of harm. Transnational criminal law encourages us to think about the construction of transnational threats and the appropriateness of transnational responses, that is, the political, social and cultural contexts from which transnational law regimes form and operate.[37]

When Crowdy heard the story, she immediately contacted the South American Bureau within the League's Secretariat to see if the destination of the *SS Cap Polonio* could be determined. She learned that the Cap Polonio had indeed left Hamburg for Buenos Aires on 30 September, and that eight days had elapsed between Gertler calling on Jung and the Cap Polonio's departure. Had the information from Jung reached the Secretariat in a timely manner, Crowdy explained to the Secretary General, Eric Drummond, »steps could have been

31 Astorino (1995–96); Geis (1963–64).
32 Pound (1923).
33 Costin (1983) 19.
34 In his 1908 critique of the philosophical approach to the study of law, Pound said that American legislation often failed because it had »not been the product of preliminary study for the conditions to which it was to apply«. Pound (1908) 613.
35 *New York Evening Post*, 1 November 1923.
36 ACTW (1924) 24.
37 Boister (2015) 10–11.

taken which might have led to the liberation of the girls and the arrest of those responsible«. Crowdy emphasized that none of the South American countries had sent their annual reports on the prosecution of trafficking cases for 1922 (as had been agreed in 1921). »Unless member states submitted these reports, it was impossible to take prompt action when information of supposed or actual traffic reaches the Secretariat.« She said she would bring this issue to the ACTW.[38]

Britain's representative on the ACTW, Sidney Harris, agreed it was important to act on such information. Rumours circulated in the press, and the best response was to investigate them. In the future, he proposed, the national organizations should not only share information with each other, but work with the voluntary agencies and the police to substantiate rumours before reporting them to the ACTW.[39] Samuel Cohen of the Jewish Association for the Protection of Girls and Women disagreed. The Jewish Association had investigated the Braun report because Anna Gertler was Jewish. Cohen discovered that in her case, and that of the other girls, there had never been any suspicion of trafficking. From his inquiries at steamship companies in Antwerp, Hamburg and Rotterdam, he learned »how impossible the case was«. He found no record that Gertler had sailed as Jung had claimed. Although three women from Czernowitz had left for South America several months later, all had been of legal age, had worked as prostitutes, and intended to emigrate. The story of 500 girls was an exaggeration he traced to a statement Jung had made at a London conference in 1923. Cohen said the Jewish Association investigated all the reports because of the great harm to the voluntary associations brought by »wild rumours«.[40]

The *SS Cap Polonio* case received significant attention from the Special Body of Experts. When they met in April 1924 for the first time, they discussed a memorandum the Secretariat had received concerning trafficking cases that included the *New York Evening Post* report of a »vast white slave enterprise« exporting hundreds of girls from Eastern Europe for prostitution.[41] Given the publicity the story had received, Dr Snow felt they could not dismiss it. Either it should be included in their investigation to the League as evidence of the traffic in women, or dismissed as a rumour circulated in the press. He directed Bascom Johnson to make a special investigation.[42] Johnson sent his German-speaking investigator, Samuel Auerbach, to talk with Dr Jung. Jung confirmed that Anna Gertler had visited his office in September 1923. She said that shortly after losing her job as a clerk in Czernowitz, she met Hans Braun. He suggested she could find work in South America and told her that his organization, the Bureau of Aid to Emigration, would pay advance passage for her and several friends. She lost contact with Braun and missed her opportunity, but knew of five girls from Czernowitz who had left with him. Jung suspected Braun was a trafficker, notified the police, and when they caught up with Gertler, found that she was carrying a fake passport. Jung learned from sources in Hamburg that her five friends had sailed. Auerbach pressed Jung for details: the names of the five girls, Gertler's address in Czernowitz and present whereabouts, but Jung did not have this information.[43]

In April 1924, Auerbach met with the Aid Society of German Jews in Berlin. He located a report about Gertler from 1 Oct 1923 in which she gave a similar account, but added that her friends had not travelled with Braun, but one of his associates. She could not remember the man's name. The file contained a letter from the Aid Society's Hamburg branch stating there was no truth to the report of 500 sex slaves shipped from Germany. The branch had examined the passenger list of 13 September 1923 and found no evidence of trafficking, although there were five women from

38 Rachel Crowdy, Memorandum by the Secretary on the Case of the Alleged Traffic Reported in the New York Evening Post 1 November 1923, 4 February 1924, League of Nations Archives, United Nations Library, Geneva, Box S181.
39 ACTW (1923b) 24.
40 ACTW (1923b) 24.
41 Chaumont / Rodríguez García / Servais (2017a).
42 Special Body of Experts on the Traffic in Women and Children: Sixth Session, Verbatim Report of the Fifth Meeting, February 9, 1927, 2. League of Nations Archives, United Nations Library, Geneva, Box S169.
43 Samuel Auerbach, In re Cap Polonio Case, 28 April 1924. League of Nations Archives, United Nations Library, Geneva, Box S181.

Romania who travelled on the *SS Cap Polonio*.[44] In September 1924, another of Johnson's investigators, Paul Kinsie, found Anna Gertler in Antwerp. She was working as a governess. She re-told her version of events, but again changed some aspects. This time she said Braun had promised to take her and her sister to New York. She wished she had left with her friends. Her employers said their house had been »in turmoil« since her arrival. She had been caught lying, stealing, and spent her time reading »trashy« stories. Kinsie decided that Anna was »demented«. »My opinion of Anna's story«, Kinsie concluded, »is that the girl never met a man named Braun.« She admitted she did not know the man's name until she heard it from the police. Kinsie surmised that several friends had told her of a mythological organization who paid advance fare for overseas travel and that she invented the rest.[45]

Gertler, Johnson reported to Snow, was not a victim of the traffic. She had never heard of the *SS Cap Polonio*, had never met a man named Braun nor the other girls as Jung had claimed. Johnson learned of two similar cases: reports of a Dutch trafficker named van Gulpen and another named Swan. It was possible that van Gulpen and Swan were the same man, but this could not be established. Johnson concluded that the Braun case as reported in the New York papers was an amalgamation of three different reports. Journalists had tied together unrelated information from the reports of police and protection societies into a narrative of an international criminal who became the illusive Mr. Braun.[46]

The Cap Polonio case proved to be such a vexing issue because it was just the sort of exaggerated story circulating in the newspapers the ACTW wanted to distance itself from. Yet, it was framed within a larger narrative, the so-called »Road to Buenos Aires«, that guided Abbott, Crowdy, Snow and Johnson in their investigation.

Johnson had initiated the fieldwork for the worldwide investigation by following the alleged route of white slavers from ports in Europe to the brothels of South America. In May 1924, Johnson and Auerbach, along with their most experienced undercover investigator, Paul Kinsie, sailed from France to Argentina. They visited Buenos Aires, Montevideo, and Rio de Janeiro. While Johnson and Auerbach interviewed public officials, Kinsie explored the cabarets, late-night cafés, theatres and brothels. From these interviews, Johnson and associates ›worked backwards‹. They identified the ›source‹ countries from the nationalities of foreign women working in the brothels of the leading ›destination‹ country. In writing their official publications, Snow and Johnson described two major routes of the white slave trade. The first led from Eastern Europe to South America; specifically, from Poland, Romania, France, and Germany to Argentina. The second route operated through Eastern Europe to North Africa, through Tunis and Alexandria to Cairo.

This is what white slave trade campaigners from English-speaking countries already believed to be the case. As early as 1920, three years before the investigation began, the ASHA had alerted the public to the situation in South America. The *Social Hygiene Bulletin*, a newsletter distributed to the Association's supporters and well-wishers, described Buenos Aires as the »Paris of America«, the most »wide open« city in the Americas.[47] In a 1923 letter, Annie Baker of the International Bureau for the Suppression of the International Traffic in Women in London wrote to Johnson that, given legislation in the United States and Canada prohibiting prostitution, it could be »fully assumed« these countries would not attract traffickers. »As in former days«, she wrote, »their eyes will doubtless be directed to South American ports even more than to Egypt.«[48]

Not surprisingly, the *Report of the Special Body of Experts into the Traffic in Women*, released in February 1927, met with criticism, and critics challenged the conclusions about South America in particular. »The chief complaints made against the American chairman, William F. Snow«, the *New York Times* summed up for its readers, »are, in effect, that the expert investigators were handpicked by himself

44 Auerbach, In Re Cap Polonio Case, Box S181 (n. 43) 5.
45 Paul Kinsie, S.S. Cap Polonio Case: In Re Anna Gertler, 25–26 September 1924.
46 Special Body of Experts, Report of the Fifth Meeting (n. 42) 5.
47 Buenos Aires Clamps Lid on Commercial Vice, in: *Social Hygiene Bulletin* 8 (1920) 3, copy in the Social Welfare Collection, Elmer Andersen Library, University of Minnesota.
48 Johnson (1923) 204.

and have given a rough white-washing to the Anglo-Saxon nations while the Latin nations come in for bitter criticism.«[49] Paulina Luisi, the representative from Uruguay on the ACTW and the Special Body of Experts, emerged as the most severe critic. A professor at the University of Montevideo, Luisi led a successful campaign to urge the Uruguayan government to accept the 1921 League Convention on the traffic in women. In the months before publication of the *Report*, she made clear her opposition. She boycotted the fourth, fifth and sixth sessions of the Special Body of Experts, and at the seventh meeting, fired a volley of criticism about the text. She declined to sign the final product and went so far as to propose that it appear only with her statement that it was unsatisfactory from the point of view of South America. In a letter to Secretary General Eric Drummond, Luisi charged that the research in South America was »very insufficient and somewhat superficial«. Field researchers had limited their investigations to cities with comfortable hotels.[50]

IV. The Case of 18-R

On 4 December 1927, the *New York World* announced that it would present an »uncensored« version of the *Report of the Special Body of Experts on the Traffic in Women* acquired by its Geneva Correspondent, which included portions of the report that, the paper alleged, governments had hoped to suppress.[51] The fourth article in this series ignited a political controversy that challenged the legal standing of the League, but also anticipated a modern understanding of the ›transnational criminal‹.[52]

In discussing trafficking within the United States, the *World* quoted the unrevised version of the report as saying girls were found to have left New Orleans and cities in Florida for cabarets in Mexico and Cuba. An agent working with a New York theatrical agency, referred to in the report as 18-R, boasted to the League's investigator that he had sent many girls to Panama. »If you'd been here five minutes ago you'd have seen the swellest flock of blonds you ever laid eyes on. In the next room is the guy who's taking them to Panama tomorrow.« The report charted the route through which women from Europe came into Panama, through a launch from Bocas del Toro to a tiny strip of beach beyond the jurisdiction of the United States.[53]

The reference to 18-R in the published version of the *Report* was even more dramatic. It says the manager of a cabaret in Panama told the League's investigator that 18-R, a theatrical employment agent in New York, had furnished him with all the American girls in his establishment. The cabaret encouraged the artistes to drink with the customers and accompany them to hotels after hours. The League's investigator subsequently interviewed the agent in New York City and, posing as an entrepreneur considering Panama, asked him about acquiring girls for his music hall. The report says that 18-R claimed he had »sent over 300 girls down there«.[54]

The references to 18-R in the news embroiled the Secretary General, Eric Drummond, in a controversy that tested the legal authority of the League of Nations. As Stephen Legg explains, its technical committees, such as the ACTW, took particular concern with ordinary problems in the lives of individuals in addition to the efforts to address social, economic and health problems affecting national populations.[55] Rachel Crowdy certainly believed in the authority of the League of Nations to intervene in individual cases of trafficking in women; she wanted the ACTW to decide when and how to involve local police. Not surprisingly, a number of member states disagreed. The French government, for example, insisted the

49 Commission Revises White Slave Report, *New York Times* 27 November 1927, 27.
50 William F Snow to Eric Drummond, 5 December 1927. League of Nations Archives, United Nations Library Geneva, Box S181.
51 Originally, Snow and Johnson intended to keep some information confidential, to be seen only by representatives of member states. But the Council decided in June 1927 that all material in what became part 2 of the Report should be made public and that governments would have until September of that year to review it. The *New York World* claimed to print what the League Secretariat had tried to suppress at the insistence of angry governments: The World to Print Facts League Vice Inquiry Found, *New York World*, 4 December 1927, 1.
52 U.S. Fares Well in Exposure of White Slavery, *New York World*, 8 December 1927, 6.
53 U.S. Fares Well (n. 52).
54 *Report of the Special Body of Experts on the Traffic in Women and Children*, part 2, Geneva: League of Nations, 1927, 165.
55 Legg (2012).

League of Nations investigators had no legal standing vis-à-vis national governments. Traffic in women, like prostitution, was a matter for domestic regulation. This issue represents a dilemma typical for transnational criminal law regimes; they organize around international agreements, but enforcement is left to national governments, as specified in the international agreements of 1904 and 1910. But as Johnson, Snow, Crowdy and Drummond were about to discover, it was not the French but their own government that would challenge the ability of the ACTW to function as a legal regime.[56]

In response to statements in the *World* about the scale of 18-R's activities, Charles Tuttle, the US Attorney for the Southern District of New York, announced his own inquiry. He had been recently appointed to his position as federal prosecutor by President Coolidge and created an image of himself as a man who had left a highly successful legal practice with a Wall Street firm to become a humble servant of the people dedicated to ferreting out corruption.[57] He appointed Assistant US Attorney Henry Gerson to investigate the claims made by the mysterious theatrical agent. Gerson began by asking Johnson for the identity of 18-R, and Johnson refused. Johnson believed that Tuttle was trying to take advantage of the fact that he and Snow were American citizens and their office (the ASHA) happened to be located within New York City.[58]

Tuttle demanded a copy of the *full* report, that is, with the names of cities, establishments, and actual persons rather than code words. Johnson protested that the information had been protected with codes because it remained confidential. The names of cities, establishments and persons could only be obtained from the League Secretariat in Geneva. He had been acting in an official capacity for the League of Nations and requests for information could only be approved by the League Secretariat. Further, he did not turn over the report to Gerson because he believed it would not be useful. The report did not contain information sufficient for prosecution, and 18-R's theatrical agency no longer operated in New York City. From Tuttle's point of view, this made no difference. If crimes had been committed in New York City and they were punishable within the statute of limitations, he would issue subpoenas and make arrests. If the investigation required statements from persons in Panama, he would bring them to New York City to make such statements.[59]

In January 1928, Drummond received a letter from William R. Castle, Assistant Secretary of State in Washington, DC, that requested, on behalf of Tuttle, the name of the theatrical agent referred to in Part 2 of the report as 18-R. There was »considerable pressure« on the US government to indict this man, Castle explained, and if the League did not furnish the name, Tuttle was determined to subpoena Snow and Johnson to appear before a New York grand jury.[60]

Tuttle's grand jury threat pressed the question about what authority the League actually had to conduct its investigation. In a letter to Snow, Drummond made its position clear. The material collected for the League's investigation into the traffic in women stood on »very special footing« because it could only be obtained through facilities of the League of Nations and only with the permission of states in which the investigations had been made. Releasing this information would »create justifiable complaints« from governments who permitted the investigators to work in their territory and make further inquiries much more difficult. »It would not be right for an investigator to make public information received as an international official and regarded as confidential [...]«, Drummond wrote. »Mr Johnson, we think, is not entitled, and ought not be forced, to disclose in any kind of public proceedings information not contained in the published report.«[61] Rachel Crowdy wrote to Drummond to express a different view. The demand for information raised »a question not only of principle but possibly of politics«. She did

56 As Boister points out, transnational criminal law must be produced by »an authentic political process in order to justify the use of state and interstate authority against individuals«. Boister (2003) 957.

57 Tuttle (2002).

58 Tuttle Starts Inquiry, *New York Herald Tribune*, 29 December 1927, 8.

59 White Slave Inquiry Here Blocked by League Agent, *New York Herald Tribune* 30 December 1927, 14; White Slave Inquiry Here, *New York Times*, 29 December 1927, 40.

60 William R. Castle to Eric Drummond, 9 February 1928, League of Nations Archives, United Nations Library, Geneva, Box R3024.

61 Eric Drummond to William Snow, 9 February 1928, League of Nations Archives, United Nations Library, Geneva, Box R3024.

not see how the League of Nations could deny someone from the United States government access to »source material« at the League's office in Geneva if they wished. She did not think Johnson should testify before a New York grand jury, as it would involve revealing information which had been kept secret from League member states to a government that was not a member of the League of Nations.[62]

Drummond accepted the wisdom of Crowdy's position. To avoid being drawn into public legal proceedings, he agreed to give Tuttle what he wanted: the identity of the notorious white slave trafficker known as 18-R. He had no objection to Tuttle learning that 18-R was Harry Walker, but asked that this be regarded as what the English police referred to as *information received*, avoiding public disclosure about the source of the information. Drummond agreed to allow someone from the American consulate in Geneva to inspect material at the Secretariat and make notes for use by the US Secretary of State on the condition it would not become evidence in any public legal proceeding.[63]

In March 1928, Tuttle released his own report on the alleged traffic from New York City to Panama. The claims made in the *Report of the Special Body of Experts on the Traffic in Women and Children* about traffic in women from New York City to Panama, the report concluded, had »no foundation in fact«. The findings in the report amounted to »uncorroborated statements of an investigator [...] that in August 1924 [...] he had from certain persons, some of whom could not be identified, certain verbal admissions, which inevitably, such persons would deny, and, so far as we have been able to reach them, have denied«.[64] Tuttle's investigation may have been designed more for political gain than to secure a prosecution, but it raised an important question about what sort of facts the League's investigation was meant to uncover: evidence that could be used in criminal proceedings within a particular jurisdiction, or sociological facts about a form of criminality but without specific illegal acts?[65]

In an effort to preserve the credibility of the League's campaign against the traffic, Johnson engaged Tuttle's concerns about the prosecution of Harry Walker. He drafted a statement he hoped Tuttle would give to the press. Johnson suggested that Tuttle should say the League's investigation »was not designed to secure legal evidence« that would be »sufficient to insure successful prosecution of criminals«. Rather, it was meant to »determine between what countries and in what manner women were transported for purposes of prostitution«. Tuttle was to say he had learned of Walker's activities too late to bring a successful prosecution in federal court, but that the evidence gathered by the League's investigators in the report was of sufficient quality to enable prosecution if he had decided to pursue this. Johnson preferred that Tuttle respond to press inquiries by saying: »These admissions, if it were possible to have them reported before a jury by persons alleged to have made them, would in my judgment, be sufficient to convict under our criminal laws.«[66]

The League's investigators had, in fact, discarded the »legalistic definition« of traffic and formed their own working definition. As Johnson explained, the legal definition was too narrow in that it limited traffic to cases of women under twenty-two years of age or, if over that age, those procured by force or fraud.[67] For their inquiry, they regarded »international traffic« as »direct or indirect procuration and transportation for gain to a foreign country of women or girls for the sexual gratification of one or more other persons«. It included employment agents obtaining women as entertainers and artistes and profiting from their

62 Rachel Crowdy to Eric Drummond, 10 February 1928, League of Nations Archives, United Nations Library, Geneva, Box R3024.

63 Eric Drummond to Gilson Blake, 11 February 1928, League of Nations Archives, United Nations Library, Geneva, Box R3024.

64 White Slave Data Refuted by Tuttle, *New York Times* 9 March 1928, 26.

65 This contradiction can be seen in other issues of concern to transnational criminal law regimes, such as anarchism, in which the goal is not to commit to enforcement but to acquire information informally from other states. Knepper (2011) 163.

66 Bascom Johnson to Eric Drummond, in: Draft of points to be considered by US Attorney Charles H Tuttle for inclusion in any statement he may feel necessary to give to newspapers concerning the League of Nations report on traffic in women and children, 2 March 1928, League of Nations Archives, United Nations Library, Geneva, Box R3024.

67 Johnson (1928) 68.

prostitution.[68] This was an important insight because it meant they could explain international trafficking without relying on professional criminality. Crowdy made it clear in 1927 that the investigators had explored the possibility of »what one might call a ring with a super-trafficker sitting at the head making profits out of a big organisation« and »found nothing of the kind«.[69]

The League's investigation had shown how *trafficking* could take place without *traffickers*. In the portion of the devoted to the United States, Johnson used the Walker case as an example. A young woman argued with her roommate, lost access to her apartment, and decided she wanted to get away from New York City. She met a theatrical agent who offered her a new life as a jazz singer at a cabaret in Panama and told her she could make extra money by having sex with Navy officers. Having arrived in Panama, it was not what she expected, and she wanted to return home. But she could not afford the return fare until completing her contract. The proprietor of the cabaret did not allow the women to use rooms at his club, but encouraged them to drink with customers. The proprietor had an understanding with the theatrical agent about sending girls willing to drink with customers and spend the night with them afterwards. The agent made money by sending girls willing to engage in casual sex, and the proprietor made money from the additional customers attracted by the presence sexually available females. The young woman turned to prostitution and eventually agreed to a second contract. As Snow and Johnson explained, most of the cabarets overseas amounted to little more than houses of prostitution, and the recruiting of American girls for them under the guise of entertainers and artistes »is international traffic«.[70]

The controversy surrounding the identity of 18-R diminished the ACTW's authority in the arena of transnational criminal law, but also diverted attention from innovative work on the definition of transnational crime. Tuttle wanted to find a way to stop transnational criminals involved in the sex trade but the League's investigation had a different problem in mind: how to address an inter-continental system of prostitution that moved women on a wide scale without any bureaucratic structure. Johnson's field investigators were not looking for rings or ringleaders to prosecute, or seeking to bring individuals to justice, but rather, trying to destroy a wide-scale system of exploitation. The report of the Special Body of Experts argued that trafficking would be abolished not by making arrests in individual cases but by extending regulation over the sex trade. The system of toleration, or licensed houses in certain cities, created a demand for »fresh attractions«. Trafficking in women represented the supply. Essentially, the laws to abolish prostitution in the United States should be extended to other countries. Closing down licensed houses in Buenos Aires, Cairo, and Paris would undermine the demand, the market for women would diminish, and the sinister business of trafficking in women would slide into a terminal recession.[71]

V. Conclusions

In 1933, the International Criminal Police Commission (ICPC) attempted to define ›international criminal‹ and ›international crime‹. Their discussion began with a definition formulated in 1905 by the International Penal Law Union which essentially said that any crime could be considered international if any element of it (planned, facilitated, or carried out) had an effect in more than one country. The discussion focused, however, on the hunt for ›professional criminals‹. Dr Antonio Pizzuto of the Italian Federal Police insisted that international crime could not be distinguished from the international criminal. It was necessary to »control and register the criminals of an international kind«; the international kind of criminal differed from ordinary criminals through habitual behaviour and attempts to evade criminal penalty.[72] The ICPC became an advisory organization to

68 *Report of the Special Body of Experts*, part 1 (n. 54) 9.
69 Crowdy (1927) 157.
70 *Report of the Special Body of Experts*, part 1 (n. 54) 12.
71 *Report of the Special Body of Experts*, part 1 (n. 54).
72 International Criminal Police Commission, Report on the Present Conditions of Investigations Undertaken with the Purpose of Finding a Practical Definition of the ›International Criminal‹. Ninth Meeting, Rome, May 15–20. Geneva: United Nations Library, League of Nations Archives, Box R5665, 1–3.

the League of Nations in 1929, by which time the ACTW had conducted the first transcontinental investigation into one of the leading cross-border crimes and advanced the understanding of transnational criminal law beyond notions of professional or habitual criminality.[73]

The investigation carried out by the ACTW initiated the conceptual language of ›trafficking‹ as a ›transnational crime‹. The exchange between Bascom Johnson and Charles Tuttle over the identity of 18-R diminished the legal authority of the League of Nations, and previewed a challenge that would become evident during the planning of the second investigation, in Asia, during the 1930s.[74] Yet Tuttle did more to undermine the League's campaign against traffic in women by portraying the point of the investigation to be the effort to find super-traffickers such as 18-R. Instead, Johnson and the investigators had conceptualised trafficking in women as a ›social network‹ or ›criminal network‹, an understanding of transnational crime that would become increasingly important throughout the 20th century.[75]

The ACTW operated as a legal regime in the realm of transnational criminal law. The rationale for, and methodology of, the ›worldwide‹ investigation was not new or novel but part of a longer history. The idea for the investigation originated in John D Rockefeller's campaign against the white slave trade initiated before the First World War. Yet the ACTW carried out the first attempt to measure the white slave trade on an international scale and this effort contributed significantly to the use of *trafficking* as a concept for understanding transnational crime. As a transnational law regime, it may have been guided by sociological jurisprudence. Grace Abbott's proposal reflects this approach. The ACTW certainly involved state and non-state entities, including that of a private individual – Rockefeller. The investigation demonstrates the significance of wider social, political and cultural contexts to the formation of transnational criminal law. Ostensibly, the investigation was meant to determine the routes of trafficking in women. Yet in pointing to Buenos Aires and other South American cities as the primary destinations for trafficked women, the investigators pursued what they believed to be true based on their understanding of urban prostitution. It is important to understand the wider extra-legal contexts in which legal regimes operate.

■

Bibliography

- ACTW (1923a) = Advisory Committee on the Traffic in Women and Children: Minutes of the Second Session. March 22–27, Geneva: League of Nations
- ACTW (1923b) = Advisory Committee on the Traffic in Women and Children: Report on the Work of the Third Session, Geneva: League of Nations
- ACTW (1924) = Advisory Committee on the Traffic in Women and Children: Minutes of the Third Session. April 7–11, Geneva: League of Nations
- Ambler, Eric (1939), The Mask of Dimitrios, London
- Astorino, Samuel J. (1995–96), The Impact of Sociological Jurisprudence on International Law in the Inter-War Period: The American Experience, in: Duquesne Law Review 34, 277–298
- Billington-Greig, Teresa (June 1913), The Truth About White Slavery, in: English Review 14, 428–446

73 Other concepts circulating within the League of Nations framework relied on theories of ›social defence‹ and ›criminal science‹. These were, for example, discussed by the lawyers of the committee appointed by the Assembly to work towards the unification of criminal law. The Committee for the Unification of Criminal Law, Gradual Unification of Criminal Law and Co-operation of States in the Prevention and Suppression of Crime: Report of the First Committee to the Assembly, 30 May 1933, Geneva 1933. This effort, led by V.V. Pella, combined the resources of several international organizations: International Penal Law Association, International Bureau for the Unification of Criminal Law, International Criminal Police Commission, Howard League for Penal Reform, International Law Association, and the International Penal Law Union.

74 Knepper (2012) 795–800.

75 Kleemans (2014).

- Boeckel, Florence (1929), Women in International Affairs, in: Annals of the American Academy of Political and Social Science 143, 230–248
- Boister, Neil (2003), Transnational Criminal Law?, in: European Journal of International Law 14, 953–978
- Boister, Neil (2015), Further Reflections on the Concept of Transnational Criminal Law, in: Transnational Legal Theory 6, 9–30
- Boister, Neil, Robert J. Currie (2015), Introduction, in: idem (eds.), Routledge Handbook of Transnational Criminal Law, New York, 1–7
- Chaumont, Jean-Michel (2009), Le mythe de la traite des blanches. Enquête sur la fabrication d'un fléau, Paris
- Chaumont, Jean-Michel, Magaly Rodríguez García, Paul Servais (2017a), Anna Gertler and the *Cap Polonia* Affair, in: idem (2017b) 345–349
- Chaumont, Jean-Michel, Magaly Rodríguez García, Paul Servais (2017b), Trafficking in Women 1924–1926: The Paul Kinsie Reports for the League of Nations, Vol. 1, Geneva
- Costin, Lela B. (1983), Two Sisters for Social Justice: A Biography of Grace and Edith Abbott, Urbana, IL
- Crowdy, Rachel (1927), The Humanitarian Activities of the League of Nations, in: Journal of the Royal Institute of International Affairs 6, 153–169
- Deflem, Mathieu (2002), Policing World Society: Historical Foundations of International Police Cooperation, Oxford
- Duve, Thomas (2014), Entanglements in Legal History. Introductory Remarks, in: idem (ed.), Entanglements in Legal History: Conceptual Approaches, Frankfurt am Main, 3–25, http://dx.doi.org/10.12946/gplh1
- Fronc, Jennifer (2009), New York Undercover: Private Surveillance in the Progressive Era, Chicago
- Geis, Gilbert (1963–64), Sociology and Sociological Jurisprudence: Admixture of Lore and Law, in: Kentucky Law Journal 52, 267–293
- Gorman, Daniel (2012), The Emergence of International Society in the 1920s, Cambridge
- Härter, Karl (2019), The Transnationalisation of Criminal Law in the Nineteenth and Twentieth Century: Political Crime, Police Cooperation, Security Regimes and Normative Orders – An Introduction, in: idem et al. (eds.), The Transnationalisation of Criminal Law in the Nineteenth and Twentieth Century, Frankfurt am Main, 1–19
- Harris, H. Wilson (1928), Human Merchandise: A Study of International Traffic in Women, London
- Ikenberry, G. John (2001), After Victory: Institutions, Strategic Restraint and the Rebuilding of Order after Wars, Princeton
- Iriye, Akira (2002), Global Community: The Role of International Organizations in the Making of the Contemporary World, Berkeley, CA
- Jäger, Jens (2006), Verfolgung durch Verwaltung: Internationales Verbrechen und Internationale Polizeikooperation 1880–1933, Konstanz
- Johnson, Bascom (1923), International Efforts for the Prevention of Traffic in Women and Children, in: Journal of Social Hygiene 9, 200–215
- Johnson, Bascom (1928), International Traffic in Women and Children, in: Journal of Social Hygiene 14, 67–75
- Kennedy, Paul (2006), The Parliament of Man: The Past, Present and Future of the United Nations, New York
- Kleemans, Edward (2014), Theoretical Perspectives on Organized Crime, in: Paoli, Letizia (ed.), The Oxford Handbook of Organized Crime, New York, 32–52
- Knepper, Paul (2009), The »White Slave Trade« and the Music Hall Affair in 1930s Malta, in: Journal of Contemporary History 44, 205–220
- Knepper, Paul (2011), International Crime in the Twentieth Century: The League of Nations Era, 1919–1939, London
- Knepper, Paul (2012), Measuring the Threat of Global Crime: Insights from Research by the League of Nations into the Traffic in Women, in: Criminology 50, 777–809
- Legg, Stephen (2012), »The Life of Individuals as well as of Nations«: International Law and the League of Nations' Anti-Trafficking Governmentalities, in: Leiden Journal of International Law 25, 647–664
- Leppanen, Katarina (2007), Movement of Women: Trafficking in the Interwar Era, in: Women's Studies International Forum 30, 523–533
- Limoncelli, Stephanie (2010), The Politics of Trafficking: The First International Movement to Combat the Social Exploitation of Women, Stanford
- Mazower, Mark (2012), Governing the World: The History of an Idea, New York
- Pedersen, Susan (2007), Back to the League of Nations, in: American Historical Review 112, 1091–1117
- Pivar, David J. (2002), Purity and Hygiene: Women, Prostitution and the »American Plan«, 1900–1930, Westport, CT
- Pliley, Jessica (2010), Claims to Protection: The Rise and Fall of Feminist Abolitionism in the League of Nations' Committee on the Traffic in Women and Children, 1919–1936, in: Journal of Women's History 22, 90–113
- Pound, Roscoe (1908), Mechanical Jurisprudence, in: Columbia Law Review 8, 605–623
- Pound, Roscoe (1923), Philosophical Theory and International Law, in: Bibliotheca Visseriana 73, 73–90
- Robertson, Stephen (2009), Harlem Undercover: Vice Investigators, Race and Prostitution, in: Journal of Urban History 35, 486–504
- Sandos, James (1980), Prostitution and Drugs: The United States Army on the Mexican-American Border, 1916–1917, in: Pacific Historical Review 49, 621–645
- Tuttle, Charles H. (2002), Life Stories of a Celebrated Lawyer in New York and Lake George, Clifton Corners, NY
- Wertheim, Stephen (2012), The League of Nations: A Retreat from International Law?, in: Journal of Global History 7, 210–232

Truth.
Long Island Rail Road
A C E 1 2 3
The truth is
The truth is

THINK

AMERICA

Gerd Bender

Duale Autonomie. Zur Rechtsgeschichte des Arbeitsmarktregimes*

I. Perspektive

Als Otto Kahn-Freund, zu diesem Zeitpunkt als Arbeitsrechtswissenschaftler längst schon zu großem Ruhm gelangt, auf einen Text zurückblickte, den sein Lehrer und Mentor Hugo Sinzheimer viele Jahrzehnte zuvor in die frühe Weimarer Debatte um das Arbeitsmarktregime[1] eingebracht hatte, war diese Rückschau von einer gewissen Fassungslosigkeit gekennzeichnet. Er erachtete Sinzheimers Aufsatz über die Zukunft der Arbeiterräte von 1919[2] »ganz einfach als eine Verirrung«,[3] die quer lag zu dem, was der Autor des fundamentalen Werks über den »Korporativen Arbeitsnormenvertrag« von 1907[4] jemals – vor 1919 und danach – für richtig und zukunftsträchtig gehalten hatte. In diesem Werk hatte Sinzheimer in einer aufwändigen arbeitsrechtstheoretischen Anstrengung versucht, die normative, also unmittelbare und zwingende Wirkung der Tarifvertragsbestimmungen auf die Einzelarbeitsverhältnisse zu begründen: Normsetzung durch die frei gebildeten Koalitionen der Arbeitsmarktparteien im Wege des Kollektivvertrags als Königsweg aus der Unter-Regulierung des industriellen Arbeitsverhältnisses mit all ihren explosiven Folgen, die damals als gesellschaftliches Großrisiko empfunden und in den unermüdlichen Foren der Sozialpolitik aufs Breiteste debattiert wurden.

Nun, im Chaos der Revolutionszeit,[5] rückte Sinzheimer – in einer publizistischen Sekunde – von diesem Modell des freien kollektiven Verhandelns der freien Arbeitsmarktkoalitionen ab, das er mit Vehemenz verfochten hatte. Plötzlich schien Sinzheimer dieses voluntaristische Modell, als dessen vielleicht bedeutendster Promotor er bis heute gilt, zu verwerfen. Jetzt sollten »Arbeiterräte« ins Zentrum der Normsetzung einziehen und gemeinsam mit den Vertretungen der Arbeitgeber über die Arbeitsnormen beschließen. Die Gewerkschaften wurden als Zwangsverbände konzipiert, die ihre Delegierten in die arbeitskammerähnlichen Räte entsandten. Gewerkschaften und Arbeitgeberverbände galten nun also als die auf Zwangsmitgliedschaft begründete Basis einer korporatistischen Organisation neben dem Staat im hoheitlichen Rahmen.

Über die Gründe, die Sinzheimer zu diesem »Ausreißer« bewogen haben, lässt sich spekulieren. Man kann mit Kahn-Freund auf Erklärungen verzichten. Oder mit einem hochrangigen sozialdemokratischen Rechtspolitiker jener Zeit vermuten, »daß man die Räte nur deshalb auf die Tarifbewegung loslassen und irgendwie unterbringen will, weil sie auf politischem Gebiet unbequem sind«.[6] Was man aber sagen kann: In Hinblick auf Sinzheimer speziell mochte man den Vorschlag, auf Korporatismus zu setzen und die Idee der Ordnung durch freies kollektives Verhandeln zu verabschieden, als befremdlich empfinden. In der allgemeinen Debatte, die man im Reich seit den 1890er Jahren führte, war die Idee einer korporatistischen Version von *Governance* allerdings durchaus weit verbreitet. Im Kaiserreich, auch im Reichstag selbst, wurde eine intensive Debatte über Arbeitskammern geführt;[7] im Verein für Socialpoli-

* Überarbeitete Fassung des Vortrags »*Systembildung. 1890–1920*«. Jahrestagung »*Geschichte der Betriebsverfassung*« des Kooperationsprojekts »Initiative Arbeitsrechtsgeschichte« (MPI für Rechtsgeschichte und Rechtstheorie / Hugo Sinzheimer Institut), 2021.

1 Zum Regimebegriff im Kontext des Governance-Konzepts Benz / Dose (2010) insbes. 264–270; speziell zu »Arbeitsmarktregime« Lessenich (1995) 49–98 und Wood (2001); zum umfassenderen Konzept »Produktionsregime« kurz Teubner (2014) 7; Duve (2021) zu Dimensionen des Regimebegriffs in der rechtshistorischen Forschung.

2 Sinzheimer (1976).

3 Kahn-Freund (1976) 18.

4 Sinzheimer (1977).

5 Sinzheimer (1921) 7.

6 Heinemann (1919) 417. Es folgt eine signifikante Konkretisierung der Kritik: »Was Sinzheimer ausführt, löst das Problem der Arbeiterräte nicht. Damit vernichtet man nur das Wesen des Tarifvertrags (was Sinzheimer, der verdienstvolle Theoretiker des Tarifvertrags, der auf diesem Gebiet Bahnbrechendes und Grundlegendes geleistet hat, natürlich nicht im entferntesten will) und greift in das ureigene Gebiet der Gewerkschaften ein […].«

7 Siehe Däubler / Kittner (2020) 113–116.

tik, der bedeutendsten sozialpolitischen Bühne des Kaiserreichs, sorgte die Frage für scharfe Kontroversen.[8] Und noch im Übergang vom Kaiserreich zur Weimarer Republik brachte Brentano – mit Unterstützung aus den Freien Gewerkschaften, wie betont werden muss – ein Modell in die Debatte um die kommende Tarifautonomie ein, das, Sinzheimers »Abweg« von 1919 nicht ganz unähnlich, korporatistisch geprägt gewesen ist.[9]

Historisch »durchgesetzt« hat sich das Tarifrechtsmuster, wie wir es heute kennen, mit freien Assoziationen als Akteuren und freien kollektiven Verträgen als normerzeugendem Instrument. Verschwunden ist die Option Korporatismus aber nicht zur Gänze, wie die viel später angestoßene große Debatte um »Neo-Korporatimus«[10] als Fall einer hybriden *Governance* es belegen mag. Vor allem aber – und im Kontext unserer Skizze Gegenstand – wurden die »großen« Vereinigungen von Kapital und Arbeit, die das Assoziationsmodell tragen, von Anfang an von den »kleinen« betriebsbezogenen Räten flankiert, wie immer die Kompetenzen zwischen den Arenen zu verschiedenen historischen Zeiten auch konkret verteilt sein mochten. Gemeinsam und miteinander verflochten trugen diese ungleichen Organisationen das Regime des Arbeitsmarkts, das für den neuartigen Interventionsstaat mitentscheidend werden sollte. Dieses Regime wurde überaus relevant für die Gesellschaften des expansiven Kapitalismus, in denen sich, wie Osterhammel in seinem fulminanten Buch über »Die Verwandlung der Welt« notiert,

> »das Ideal des einfachen Regierens und des kleinen Staates verflüchtigte. Neuartige Mittlerinstanzen machten sich breit. Zwischen Volk und Regierende schoben sich nicht länger altertümliche Stände, sondern Bürokratien, politische Parteien, Syndikate, Gewerkschaften, Interessenverbände und Lobbies aller Art. [...] Die so rationellen und einfachen politischen Systeme des klassischen Liberalismus wurden zu ziemlich komplizierten Angelegenheiten.«[11]

Wir blicken in diesem Beitrag – anhand deutscher Geschichte, wie man betonen muss – auf Konturen des sich formierenden Regimes, auf einen prägnanten Aspekt dieser von Osterhammel beschriebenen großen Komplizierung, also auf das Ensemble aus Regeln, Praktiken und Theorie der kollektiven Arbeitsbeziehungen. Wir behandeln in groben Zügen die Historizität des »dualen Systems der industriellen Beziehungen«,[12] jener historisch überaus voraussetzungsvollen Konfiguration, in der die arbeitsmarktpolitischen Koalitionen (Gewerkschaften, Arbeitgeberverbände) als Kräfte der sektoralen Mesoebene mit den auf der Mikroebene der Unternehmen agierenden Betriebsräten koexistieren, koordiniert durch selbstproduzierte, praxisgenerierte Normativität und durch das kollektive Arbeitsrecht des Staates.[13]

Dieses duale System gehörte seit den frühen Zeiten der industriellen Ordnung zur Realität, ja mehr und mehr zum Kernbestand des Arbeitsmarktregimes, das dem ökonomischen Handeln einen Rahmen vorgab und vorgibt – trotz aller Krisen und Bifurkationspunkte, die es während dieser langen Dauer gegeben hat. Diese Struktur begleitet den »wirtschaftspolitisch aktiven Interventionsstaat«, der sich noch während des Kaiserreichs formierte, bis in unsere Gegenwart hinein. Sie ist bezogen auf das Basisproblem dieser ambitionierten Staatlichkeit, das Stolleis beschrieben hat:

8 Zum »Verein« aus arbeitsrechtshistorischer Sicht Becker (1995) 151–218.

9 Dazu Preller (1949) 256 und wiederum Heinemann (1919) 414–416. Brentanos Vorschlag sah freilich von Zwangsverbänden ab und bejahte die Möglichkeit von Arbeitskämpfen als Ultima Ratio ausdrücklich.

10 Die Debatte um »Neo-Korporatismus« oder »Liberalen Korporatismus« oder »Bargained Coporatism« hat die politische Wissenschaft des ausgehenden 20. Jahrhunderts in außerordentlicher Weise bewegt. Sie hatte die intensivierte Interaktion zwischen Staat und Verbänden zum Gegenstand. Anders als im »klassischen« Korporatismus bleiben die Verbände im Neo-Korporatismus als freie Organisationen dem Assoziationsprinzip verpflichtet. Sie werden aber durch Anreize und rechtliche Steuerungsmaßnahmen in die Politik des Staates (»regulierte Selbstregulierung«) eingebettet, dessen Förderung ihrer Organisationsinteressen sie sich im Gegenzug gewiss sein können. Das duale System der industriellen Beziehungen, dessen Evolution wir beobachten, begünstigte die neo-korporatistische Integration der Arbeitsmarktkoalitionen zusätzlich. Zum Ganzen Streeck (1999); zur historischen Dimension Nocken (1981).

11 Osterhammel (2009) 906.

12 Zu diesem bedeutenden Themenfeld der Industriesoziologie das Standardwerk von Keller (1995) 78–81.

13 Zur historischen Dimension Bender (2007) 247–258.

»Während der liberale Staat sich auf die Gefahrenabwehr beschränken und die freie Gesellschaft im Übrigen ihrer eigenen Dynamik überlassen wollte, übernahm der Interventionsstaat wieder die Verantwortung für Funktionsfähigkeit und Wohlstand der Gesellschaft. Das verschafft ihm, wie wir heute am Anfang des 21. Jahrhunderts viel deutlicher sehen, einen unerhörten Zuwachs an Macht. Auf der anderen Seite wurde er dadurch in neuer Weise schwach und anfällig, angewiesen auf die Gesellschaft, die er hoheitlich zu steuern hatte.«[14]

Mit dem arbeitspolitischen Verhandlungssystem erwuchs dieser großen Komplikation, mit ihren typischen Verschränkungen von Macht und Ohnmacht, eine tragende Säule. Zuständig für die Anwendungsbedingungen, besonders aber für den Ertrag der abhängigen Arbeit, wurde es für das neuartige wohlfahrtsstaatliche Großregime wesentlich – im strikten Sinne »systemrelevant«, wie man im Tonfall unserer Jetztzeit vielleicht sagen würde. Schon sehr früh, fast noch am Anfang der Entwicklungen, die wir beobachten, hat das sozialpolitische *Mastermind* Gustav Schmoller – erfasst von zeittypischer Revolutionsangst – das Erfordernis eines funktionsfähigen Arbeitsmarktregimes in drastischer Weise zum Ausdruck gebracht. Man habe »heute nur die Wahl zwischen der kommenden socialen Revolution, welche unsere ganze wirtschaftliche Kultur begraben kann, und zwischen einem Mitreden der Arbeiter in Form der englischen Gewerkvereine und in Form der bescheidenen Arbeiterausschüsse.«[15] Im Kontext des »Neuen Kurses«, am Anfang der Ausdifferenzierung der neuartigen Institutionen, postuliert Schmoller den arbeitspolitischen Aufbruch. Und er zeigt auf, an wen man sich dabei in besonderer Weise zu halten haben wird. Es sind die industriellen Koalitionen und die Räte, deren Koexistenz und Kombination die Trift des kommenden Verhandlungssystems und des Arbeitsmarktregimes in der langen Geschichte, die folgen sollte, bestimmten.

II. Dualismus: Tarifautonomie und Betriebsautonomie

Im Zentrum der kollektiven Arbeitsbeziehungen und deren Recht steht zuvörderst die Tarifautonomie der industriellen Koalitionen als basale Einrichtung – nach zögerlichen, ja im hohen Maße fragilen Anfängen im 19. Jahrhundert und immer wieder aufflammenden Krisen und so mancher Ermüdung, wie man hinzufügen sollte.[16]

Dort, wo Tarifverträge Geltung erlangen, verfügt das ökonomische System über einen Mechanismus der Selbstregulierung, der eine Alternative sowohl zum freien Arbeitsvertrag als auch zum staatlichen Eingriff anbietet. Die Anreicherung des ökonomischen Systems durch Tarifautonomie schafft die Möglichkeit einer subsysteminternen Politik der Wirtschaft. Die selbstregulative Begrenzung der individuellen Vertragsfreiheit ermöglicht es, die evolutionäre Errungenschaft der Vertragsfreiheit auch mit Blick auf die Arbeitswelt zu konsolidieren. Das heißt: Je legitimer und effektiver die Ordnung ist, die so entsteht, umso geringer der Anreiz zu öffentlich-rechtlichen Lösungen, für die Lohngesetzgebung des Sozialstaats, für staatliche Zwangsschlichtung, für Experimente mit hartem, »öffentlich-rechtlichem« Korporatismus; Tarifautonomie statt guther Policey in noch so neuzeitlich wirkenden Erscheinungsformen, soziale Autonomie auch und gerade als Bastion des ökonomischen Systems gegen sozialstaatliche Expansion, als Palliativ gegen politische Fremdsteuerung, als interne Politik[17] des Wirtschaftssystems. In der Welt der industriellen Verbände und der Verträge, die sie schließen, ihrer Kämpfe, ihrer Dispute und der Konventionen, die sie dem Verhandlungssystem zu Grunde legen, verteidigt man

14 Stolleis (2001) 14.

15 Schmoller (1890) 436 f.

16 Zur Institutionengeschichte jetzt Rückert (2019); insgesamt Kittner (2005); zur Theorieseite etwa Bender (2006).

17 Zu diesem Konzept Luhmann (2010) und dort das Kapitel »Politik in der Gesellschaft und in anderen Sozialsystemen«.

den ökonomischen Eigensinn und deckelt politische Steuerungsambitionen.

Zugleich aber entstehen mit dem industriellen Verhandlungssystem neue, indirektere Chancen des Staates, auf wirtschaftliche Abläufe einzuwirken. Der Staat konditioniert das Verhandlungssystem mit seinem Arbeitsrecht, in Deutschland anders als in England eine zu keinem Zeitpunkt via »Immunity« verworfene Option.[18] Im Gegenteil: Die Politik der Einbettung des kollektiven Verhandelns in eine juridische Ordnung wurde noch zu Zeiten der Reichsgewerbeordnung durch Wissenschaft und Rechtsprechung auf den Weg gebracht und im Laufe der Institutionengeschichte immer weiter ausgebaut.

Jenseits dieser Verrechtlichung der industriellen Beziehungen wurden die neuen Organisationen aber auch noch auf einer anderen, weicheren Ebene zum Gegenstand eines inklusiven Staates. Der post-liberale Staat lernte es, den wirtschafts- und arbeitsmarktpolitischen Erfolg zu suchen, indem er die Verbände am Prozess der Politik beteiligte. In dieser dynamischen Konstellation des »Semisovereign State«[19] sehen wir einen tiefgreifenden Wandel des Politischen. Das politische System nimmt an Komplexität und innerer Differenziertheit zu. Seine zentrale Organisation, der Staat, bildet das Zentrum des Systems. Die politische Peripherie ist mit intermediären Verbänden besiedelt, die sich als Kollektivpersonen im Wege der Inklusion ins politische System verwickelt sehen, ohne ihre Position im Wirtschaftssystem einzubüßen.[20]

Aber, wie bereits hervorgehoben: Gewerkschaften und Arbeitgeberverbände befinden sich in der industriellen Arena mit ihrer Tarifautonomie eben nicht allein auf weiter Flur. Der Pfad, auf dem das Institutionengefüge seit Kaisers Zeiten prozessiert, ist schon bald durch den Dualismus von Gewerkschaft und Betriebsrat, von Tarifautonomie und Betriebsautonomie, von Tarifvertrag und Betriebsvereinbarung, von sektoraler und unternehmensbezogener Regulation geprägt: von einer komplexen Autonomielage, wenn man so will.[21]

Wichtiges an dieser Betriebsautonomie erinnert an die tarifautonome Sphäre: Die Verrechtlichung, von der wir sprachen, ist auch hier an allen Ecken und Enden präsent – und dies noch viel eindringlicher, als es bei der verrechtlichten Tarifautonomie der Fall ist. In der Regie des Betriebsverfassungsrechts entfaltet die Betriebsvereinbarung, der wichtigste Kontrakt, den die Betriebsautonomie generieren kann, unmittelbare und – heutzutage, wie zu betonen wäre – zwingende Wirkungen ganz so wie der Tarifvertrag auch, so dass sich die regulatorischen Verhältnisse gleichsam verdoppeln.

In anderen Hinsichten befinden wir uns allerdings in einer distinkten Welt der Regulierung.

Dies gilt für die unbedingte Friedenspflicht, die Arbeitskämpfe zwischen den Betriebsparteien ausschließt. Dies gilt für die Zulässigkeit einer Zwangsschlichtung, wie sie aus dieser Friedenspflichtkonzeption notwendigerweise resultiert. Und dies gilt für die Zwangsrepräsentation, die sich die Mitglieder der Belegschaft gefallen lassen müssen, gleich, ob sie eine Vertretung durch den Betriebsrat und die Geltung der Betriebsvereinbarungen für sich wünschen oder nicht, wenn und solange ein Betriebsrat überhaupt gewählt worden ist. Anders als bei den industriellen Koalitionen der Fall, stehen Exit-Optionen den Teilnehmern an der Betriebsautonomie nicht zur Verfügung. Etwas anderes als »Voice« – bei den Betriebsratswahlen und anderen mehr informellen Gelegenheiten – wird nicht geboten. Die Inklusion der Arbeitnehmer in die Interessenvertretung ist in diesem Regimebereich weit vorangetrieben.

III. Formierung

Wie wir gezeigt haben, besteht dieses im Ländervergleich ziemlich einzigartige duale System aus zwei Komponenten, die sich – beide dem Ziel der Arbeitsmarktregulierung verschrieben – in wichtigen Punkten unterscheiden. Vor allem folgen sie unterschiedlichen Prinzipien der Repräsentation. Die Tarifautonomie basiert auf dem Ge-

18 Zur differenten englischen Arbeitsverfassung etwa Steinmetz (1999) insbes. 92–94.

19 Katzenstein (1987).

20 Zu Gewerkschaften als Organisationen mit mehrfacher teilsystemischer Zuordnung Luhmann (2017) 256.

21 Siehe jetzt zur Geschichte der Betriebsverfassung auch im Folgenden die Gesamtdarstellung Däubler / Kittner (2020) mit umfassenden Informationen.

danken der Assoziation, der freien Vereinigung also, während die Betriebsautonomie jenseits des Voluntarismus existiert, als mikro-korporatistische Institution im strikten Sinne. So entgegengesetzt die Prinzipien aber auch sind, die den Regelungsmechanismen zugrunde liegen: Es handelt sich eben doch um Komponenten *eines* Systems. Sie stehen nicht einfach nebeneinander wie Konkurrenten in der Arena der Regulation. Sie sind hingegen aufs engste verflochten und treten normativ koordiniert in Erscheinung.

Dieses duale Verhandlungssystem der verbundenen Autonomien war dabei nicht etwa die Frucht eines Masterplans, den eine arbeitspolitische Zentrale entwickelt und implementiert hätte, so bedeutsam politische Inputs an verschiedenen Stellen des Pfades auch gewesen sind. Es war die Mühle der Geschichte, notorisch rücksichtslos gegenüber Prinzipien und für jede Volte zu haben, die dieses komplizierte Geflecht der Institutionen produzierte.

Die Geschichte dieses Mehrebenensystems[22] führt, wie so viele andere Institutionen der Arbeits- und Sozialpolitik auch, zurück ins deutsche Kaiserreich, genau genommen in die post-bismarckschen Jahre, eine Zeit der Chancen für große sozialpolitische Innovationen und Institutionalisierungen. An diesem historischen Ort – in den programmatischen Zeugnissen des Kathedersozialismus zumal – lässt sich eine außergewöhnliche Varianz der arbeitspolitischen Möglichkeiten beobachten, die Abelshauser vom Kaiserreich als Laboratorium der Sozialpolitik sprechen ließ.[23] Im arbeitspolitischen Repertoire fehlte es nicht an der Vielfalt der Ideen und Konzepte. Es mangelte aber spürbar an der Fähigkeit, zu selektieren und die getroffenen Entscheidungen zu stabilisieren.

Das Bild einer Disparität von großem Diskurs, bestenfalls minimalistischer Implementation und gegenläufiger Politiken der Desintegration und Exklusion, das sich von jener arbeitspolitischen Epoche zeichnen lässt und das von einer auf »Arbeiterbewegung« fokussierenden Sozialgeschichte lange gepflegt und zugespitzt wurde, darf aber den Blick auf die andere Seite, die es auch gab, und damit auf die Ambivalenz des Arbeitsmarktregimes nicht verstellen. Das Tarifvertragswesen war auf dem Vormarsch, nicht in der Schwerindustrie, aber in den Sektoren des Konkurrenzkapitalismus mit einiger Verve, wo die Gewerkschaften nach dem Ende des Sozialistengesetzes trotz starken Widerstands der Gegenseite zu Großorganisationen heranwuchsen. In rechtlicher Hinsicht lassen sich inklusionsfreundliche Veränderungen des Vereinsrechts ebenso verzeichnen wie erste zukunftsweisende Modernisierungsschritte des privatrechtlichen Arbeitskampfrechts, bei Fortbestand der strafrechtlichen Probleme freilich, über die in der Arbeitsrechtsgeschichte so viel geschrieben worden ist.[24] Die 1890 geregelte und auf Konsens gepolte Gewerbegerichtsbarkeit florierte. Die schuldrechtliche Verbindlichkeit der Tarifverträge wurde vom Reichsgericht noch vor dem Weltkrieg festgestellt, ohne dass aber eine rechtlich ausreichende Lösung für das Problem der normativen Wirkung gefunden werden konnte.[25]

Nicht zuletzt brachte der viel beschriebene Neue Kurs, der mit dem Übergang der Reichskanzlerschaft von Bismarck auf Caprivi im Jahre 1890 einsetzte, den Einstieg in die betriebliche Interessenvertretung durch Ausschüsse, die von der Belegschaft bestimmt werden.[26] Der Schritt, der nach der kaiserlichen Botschaft des Jahres 1890 gegangen wurde, war zögerlich und ohne große Kraft, wie in den Verhandlungen klar zutage trat. Gleichwohl: Die sozialpolitische Entscheidung für die Ausschüsse war doch ein signifikanter Beitrag zu einer Arbeitspolitik neuen Stils, die sich *step by step*, fast schon inkrementell, in den Gründerjahren des Mehrebenensystems herauskristallisierte.

Die neuen §§ 134 a–h GewO brachten keine zwingende betriebliche Interessenvertretung mit sich. Vom Bergbau abgesehen, blieb es bis zum Hilfsdienstgesetz von 1916 dabei, dass die Einrichtung von Arbeiterausschüssen zur Disposition des Unternehmens stand. Immerhin mochte die neu begründete Pflicht, die Belegschaft vor Erlass der jetzt zwingend vorgeschriebenen Arbeitsordnung anzuhören, und die Möglichkeit, diese Anhörung durch die Anhörung des Arbeiterausschusses zu ersetzen, schon aus Zweckmäßigkeitsgründen für die Ausschüsse sprechen. Dort, wo sie bestanden,

22 Zum Konzept des Mehrebenensystems Benz (2010).

23 Abelshauser (2003), Kapitel II: Das Kaiserreich – Treibhaus der Institutionen (23 ff.).

24 Zur ambivalenten Situation im späten Kaiserreich z. B. Bender (2021) 277–280.

25 Siehe zum Tarifrecht im späten Kaiserreich nur Ramm (1961) 36–47.

26 Siehe dazu auch die rechtshistorische Pionierleistung von Rückert / Friedrich (1979).

blieben ihre Befugnisse, von diesem Anhörungsrecht abgesehen, von Rechts wegen rudimentär. Aber von der Rechtslage abgesehen: Die Frage danach, wie es in der betrieblichen Praxis in den vielzähligen Einzelfällen aussah, eröffnet ein interessantes Feld der wissenschaftlichen Vertiefung.[27]

Nicht nur die – geradezu modern wirkende – Entscheidung des Gesetzgebers für die Regelungsvariante des *soft law*, auch die abwehrende Grundhaltung vieler Arbeitgeber, besonders aber die zunächst ganz unverhüllte Gegnerschaft der sozialistischen Arbeiterbewegung standen einem schnellen Avancement der Räte entgegen.[28] Man fürchtete die Ausschüsse als Kristallisationspunkte für »gelbe« Tendenzen und als Mittel, die »freien« Gewerkschaften aus den Betrieben zu exkludieren. Teuteberg hat in seiner großen Arbeit zur industriellen Mitbestimmung[29] gezeigt, wie diese Aversionen allmählich in den Hintergrund traten. Soweit Betriebsvertretungen bestanden, lernten die Gewerkschaften die dezentralen Institutionen als Instrumente ihrer eigenen Tarifpolitik zunehmend schätzen. Die Sicht auf die Räte als »verlängerter Arm der Gewerkschaft im Betrieb«[30] fand immer mehr Anhänger. Die Gewerkschaften setzten den Ausschüssen gegenüber auf Inklusion und schufen so die koalitionsinternen Voraussetzungen des dualen Systems.

Der Durchbruch zu einer obligatorischen Betriebsvertretung wurde durch das berühmte Gesetz über den Vaterländischen Hilfsdienst von 1916 und das nicht minder prominente Arbeitsgemeinschaftsabkommen vom November 1918 erzielt. Das Hilfsdienstgesetz verfügte die zwingende Errichtung ständiger, von den Arbeitnehmern gewählter Arbeiterausschüsse in den kriegswichtigen Betrieben der gewerblichen Wirtschaft, sofern diese mindestens 50 Arbeiter beschäftigten. Zugleich wurden Ausschüsse und Arbeitgeber auf Kooperation und »gutes Einvernehmen« festgelegt.

Das Arbeitsgemeinschaftsabkommen vom November 1918[31] hat den Errichtungszwang für die Friedenswirtschaft aufrechterhalten, vor allem aber die Verhältnisse zwischen Gewerkschaften und Betriebsräten jetzt ganz offen im Sinne einer Dominanz der Tarifautonomie strukturiert und wurde mit dieser Entscheidung wegweisend für alles, was später kommen sollte. Der Ausschuss habe die Aufgabe, »in Gemeinschaft mit dem Betriebsunternehmer darüber zu wachen […], daß die Verhältnisse des Betriebes nach Maßgabe der Kollektivvereinbarungen geregelt werden«. Damit hatte das gewerkschaftliche Idealbild des kollektiven Verhandlungssystems in der viel beschworenen »Magna Charta der deutschen Gewerkschaften« seinen gleichsam reinen Ausdruck gefunden. Die Betriebsvertretungen spielten als »Tarifpolizei«[32] eine nützliche, dem vorherrschenden Regulativ Tarifautonomie aber dienend nachgeordnete Rolle. Eigenständige Kompetenzen waren nicht vorgesehen, schon gar nicht in Form von Mitbestimmungsrechten, die dem von den Arbeitgebern nun endlich bewilligten Vertretungsmonopol der Gewerkschaften hätten Konkurrenz machen können. Als die Tarifvertragsverordnung vom Dezember 1918 diese Regelungsmuster in ihrem betriebsverfassungsrechtlichen Teil ratifizierte, war im revolutionären Deutschland ein kollektives Arbeitsrecht entstanden, das die Gewerkschaften als Sieger auf ganzer Linie erscheinen ließ. Von Staat und Arbeitgebern anerkannt und ausgestattet mit umfassenden Garantien der Tarifautonomie, schien der Weg, den die Legiensche Generalkommission seit den 1890er Jahren beschritten hatte, von Erfolg gekrönt. Und dass jetzt eine betriebliche Zwangsvertretung im Dienst der Tarifautonomie und der Gewerkschaften bestand, schien das Bild der Befestigung der Verbandsmacht zu runden.

IV. Betriebsrätegesetz

Die weitere Entwicklung ließ den Gewerkschaften nur wenig Zeit, sich auf den Organisationserfolgen auszuruhen. Die emergente revolutionäre Betriebsrätebewegung gefährdete das mit dem Stinnes-Legien-Abkommen und der Tarifvertragsverordnung eben erst konsolidierte Mehrebenensystem in gravierender Weise. Schon bald aber, und bereits im anlaufenden Prozess der Weimarer

27 Einen empirischen Zugriff versucht ein neues Forschungsprojekt des MPI für Rechtsgeschichte und Rechtstheorie; dazu Wolf et al. (2022) in diesem Heft. Wegweisend Plumpe (1999).

28 Für charakteristische Kritik siehe den einflussreichen Beitrag von Schippel (1890/91).

29 Teuteberg (1961) 490–498. Dort (493) auch zur zwischenzeitlich veränderten Position Schippels.

30 Flatow (1924) 398.

31 Zu diesem Abkommen umfassend Krüger (2018). Einordnungsversuch durch Bender (2021) 282–285.

32 Fraenkel (1966) 107.

Verfassungsgebung nicht mehr zu negieren,[33] zeigte sich, dass es sich nicht wirklich um den Aufstieg eines gefährlichen Rivalen in der Arena der industriellen Regulation handelte, sondern um ein zunächst vehementes, dann aber schnell abflauendes Kurzzeitproblem. Bereits das Betriebsrätegesetz von 1920 atmete wieder den Geist der Normalisierung und unterstrich das Modell der dualen Autonomie, das im Arbeitsgemeinschaftsabkommen kodifiziert worden war. Es folgte in seinen Grundzügen den gewerkschaftlichen Vorstellungen. Kurz gesagt: Das Gesetz hielt an der »Subordination des Betriebsrates gegenüber der Gewerkschaft, seiner Stempelung zum gewerkschaftlichen Vorwerk im Betriebe« fest.[34]

So wurde den Koalitionen ein Konfliktaustragungsmonopol eingeräumt, während die Räte durch § 66 in ihrer Interaktion mit dem Arbeitgeber auf Wirtschaftsfriedlichkeit und Kooperationsgeist verpflichtet wurden. Neben dieser Festlegung der Räte auf eine Interessenvertretung mit gebremstem Schaum wurde die Suprematie des Tarifvertragssystems aber vor allem durch die Kompetenzverteilungsnormen unterstrichen.[35] Über die grundsätzliche Bestimmung des § 8[36] hinaus fanden sich im Gesetz »zahlreiche Sicherungsbestimmungen der Gewerkschaften dagegen, dass die Organisationen durch die Betriebsräte verdrängt oder in ihrem Aufgabenkreis beeinträchtigt werden«.[37] In dieser Hinsicht von größtem Belang waren die Regeln des § 78 Ziff. 2.[38] Diese Norm räumte den Räten zwar einerseits die Befugnis ein, Betriebsvereinbarungen über materielle Arbeitsbedingungen zu schließen und führte damit ein tragendes Element des dualen Systems, wie wir es heute kennen, in die betriebsverfassungsrechtliche Ordnung ein. Zugleich aber wurde die Kompetenz, betriebliche Kollektivverträge zu schließen, auf tarifvertragsfreie Räume begrenzt und setzte auch dort das Benehmen mit den zuständigen Koalitionen voraus. Und schließlich ebenfalls wichtig und das Bild der untergeordneten Betriebsautonomie abrundend: Die Betriebsvereinbarung wirkte zwar unmittelbar auf die Arbeitsverhältnisse ein, so wie der Tarifvertrag dies tat. Ihre Normen waren aber – anders als später durch die Gesetzgebung der Bundesrepublik vorgesehen – nicht zwingend, sodass sie von Rechts wegen durch arbeitsvertragliche Vereinbarungen zulasten des Arbeitnehmers abbedungen werden konnten, wenn die Machtverhältnisse dies zuließen.

Diese gleichsam unvollständige Normativität der Betriebsvereinbarung unterstreicht noch einmal das Gesamtbild, das sich nach dem Niedergang der revolutionären Rätebewegung ergab. Von der großen Ambition dieser im strikten Sinne autonomen Räte war kaum etwas in die postrevolutionäre Zeit und deren Konzeption des dualen Systems hinübergerettet worden.[39] Das, was das Betriebsrätegesetz auf der Ebene des Rechts und die gewerkschaftliche Betriebsrätepolitik auf der Ebene der Praxis fixierten, erinnerte mehr an die kooperativen Räte des Kaiserreichs als an den Impetus der Revolution. Deren Irritationen und die damit eng verbundene Legitimationskrise des gewerkschaftlichen Vertretungsprimats schienen spätestens mit der Legislation von 1920 überwunden. Die juridische und die praktische Version des dualen Systems waren weitestgehend unbelastet durch revolutionäre Ablagerungen. Georg Flatow, der bedeutende Experte des frühen Betriebsverfassungsrechts hat dazu in seinem Rückblick des Jahres 1924 das Fazit gezogen:

> »Der Kampf zwischen Betriebsräten und Gewerkschaften ist damit arbeitsrechtlich in der

33 Prägnant Ramm (1980); siehe insgesamt Bender (2021).

34 Winschuh (1922) 17. Zusammen mit der Arbeit von Brigl-Matthiass (1926) stellt Winschuhs Schrift eine besonders inspirierende Quelle zur Frühgeschichte des dualen Systems dar.

35 Auch zum Gesetzesinhalt klar und instruktiv das bereits erwähnte grundlegende Werk von Däubler/Kittner (2020) hier 164–192.

36 »Die Befugnis der wirtschaftlichen Vereinigungen von Arbeitern und Angestellten, die Interessen ihrer Mitglieder zu vertreten, wird durch die Vorschriften dieses Gesetzes nicht berührt.«

37 Fraenkel (1966) 103.

38 »Der Arbeiterrat und der Angestelltenrat oder, wo ein solcher nicht besteht, der Betriebsrat hat die Aufgabe, soweit eine tarifvertragliche Regelung nicht besteht, im Benehmen mit den beteiligten wirtschaftlichen Vereinigungen der Arbeitnehmer bei der Regelung der Löhne und sonstigen Arbeitsverhältnisse mitzuwirken, namentlich auch bei der Festsetzung der Akkord- und Stücklohnsätze oder der für ihre Festsetzung maßgebenden Grundsätze, bei der Einführung neuer Lösungsmethoden, bei der Festsetzung der Arbeitszeit […].«

39 Zur Frage des Räteartikels der WRV siehe Stolleis (2018), speziell 215 zur Verfassungsgebung zwischen Räteminimalismus und symbolischer Gesetzgebung.

gleichen Weise entschieden worden, wie ihn die Arbeiterbewegung selbst in den Jahren 1918–1920 entschieden hat, indem sie die Betriebsrätebewegung zu einem Glied der Gewerkschaftsbewegung gemacht und damit verhindert hat, dass die im BRG schlummernde Tendenz des Betriebsegoismus, des Syndikalismus und seines Widerparts, des (gelben) Werkvereins, über den gewerkschaftlichen Gedanken einer beruflichen Arbeiterpolitik siegte.«[40]

V. Turbulenzen

1. Von der Agenda der Arbeitspolitik ist die Kontroverse um das Mehrebenensystem trotz der Befestigungsleistung der frühen Jahre gleichwohl nicht verschwunden. Der Zerfall der Zentralarbeitsgemeinschaft der Koalitionen, der 1924 besiegelt wurde,[41] die Dominanz der staatlichen Zwangsschlichtung,[42] die immer weitere Kreise zog, die scharfe Polemik einer neo-klassisch inspirierten Nationalökonomie gegen »politische Löhne«, die bereits im Zusammenhang mit dem Gesetz über Arbeitsvermittlung und Arbeitslosenversicherung von 1926,[43] also noch in den ökonomisch guten Jahren, eskalierte, die schwindende Fähigkeit des Staates überhaupt, die Effektivität und Legitimität der Sozialpolitik zu verteidigen: All dies formte den Rahmen der Dauerkrise des Arbeitsmarktregimes, die Weimar nicht mehr auflösen konnte.[44] In deren Kontext entstand in den letzten Jahren Weimars eine große Debatte über »Tariffesseln«,[45] die man als eine zweite, die Tarifautonomie konkret betreffende Kündigung der Arbeitsgemeinschaft von 1918 und ihres Konsensmodells verstehen durfte. Jetzt war in der Sicht der Gewerkschaft das Betriebsräteproblem, das Problem der Entkoppelung des dualen Systems wieder da, wenn auch unter gänzlich anderen Vorzeichen, als dies zu Zeiten der Revolution der Fall gewesen ist. Fraenkel erschien die Kampagne getragen vom »Bestreben des Unternehmertums, durch Verhandlung mit den Betriebsräten die Gewerkschaften auszuschalten«.[46] Im Kern ging es um eine Umstellung der Regulationsweise auf Betriebsbezogenheit und betrieblichen Korporatismus zulasten der Tarifautonomie, nicht als Folge eines revolutionären Syndikalismus, der 1918/19 zur Debatte stand, sondern jetzt als Folge eines Umbruchs der Perspektive mit einem radikal verbetrieblichten Arbeitsmarktregime als arbeitspolitischem Ziel.

Außer einer veritablen Literaturflut hat diese Kampagne dann wenig Zählbares erbracht. Sie ist im beschleunigten Prozess des Weimarer Verschwindens untergegangen, wie so manche andere späte Reformidee auch. An Makroregulierung orientierte Zeitgenossen gaben nichts auf die Dekonstruktion des dualen Systems und auf die Verbetrieblichung der Normsetzung als Krisenlösung und verfolgten die Debatte mit Argwohn und Kritik.[47] Und als die letzten wirkungslosen Veröffentlichungen pro Dezentralität endlich erscheinen konnten, befand sich die Notverordnungspolitik mit ihrem harschen etatistischen Akzent bereits auf einem anderen Weg,[48] bevor die Kontroverse um die duale Autonomie im Nationalsozialismus verebbte.

2. Angesichts des kläglichen Ausgangs könnte man über dieses letzte Gefecht, das zu Zeiten Weimars um das duale System und seinen Platz im Arbeitsmarktregime geführt wurde, die Akten schließen und sich – das Scheitern des Weimarer Konsensmodells und dessen fatale Folgen beklagend – einfach vom Thema abwenden. Das kann man natürlich nicht, zumindest nicht ohne Weiteres, denn die Geschichte der dualen Autonomie ist mit Weimar nicht zu Ende, und am Ende angelangt ist auch und gerade nicht der wiederkehrende Versuch, die Balance der Systemkomponenten neu zu justieren, um mit einer unternehmensnäheren Normsetzung den Krisen des Arbeitsmarkts zu entrinnen.

40 Flatow (1924) 388.
41 Zusammenfassend Bender (2021) 289–291.
42 Becker (2005) 103–110. Zur differenten Situation in unterschiedlichen Branchen aber Plumpe (2004).
43 Zum Thema »Politischer Lohn« und zur sogenannten Cassel-Kontroverse Bender (1991) 155–160.
44 Die Eskalation des Ruhreisenstreits war das unübersehbare Krisenfanal. Dazu Preller (1949) 399–406.
45 Dazu ausführlich Weisbrod (1985) 295–325.
46 Fraenkel (1966) 103.
47 Exemplarisch Huber (1932).
48 Instruktive Skizze bei Kittner (2005) 487–495.

Die jüngste Zeitgeschichte des Arbeitsmarktregimes birgt eine lange diskursive Sequenz, in der über die historisch gewordene Vorherrschaft der Tarifautonomie gestritten wurde wie über kaum etwas anderes sonst.[49] Sie führt von dem sehr speziellen und intrikaten Dezentralisierungssignal des spektakulären Leber-Rüthers-Kompromisses von 1984 mit anwachsender Heftigkeit hinein in die beiden ersten Jahrzehnte der neuen Berliner Republik, bevor sich die Kombattanten, von der Regierung mit deutlichen Hinweisen animiert, wieder in einen Zustand einer gewissen und womöglich trügerischen Ruhe versetzten. Nachdem man über zwei quälende Diskursjahrzehnte hinweg die »Krise der Tarifautonomie« und die Forderung nach einer grundlegenden »Flexibilisierung« und »Verbetrieblichung« des Arbeitsmarktregimes geradezu zelebriert hatte, schien die Legitimationskontroverse mit dem ersten Jahrzehnt des 21. Jahrhunderts beendet. Auf der Ebene des Rechts war der projektierte Paradigmenwechsel hin zu einer »Dezentralisierung und, womöglich, auch der Entgewerkschaftung der Lohnfindung«[50] ausgefallen. Das Recht des Verhandlungssystems war in diesen beiden Jahrzehnten zwar unter Druck wie seit seinen Weimarer Tagen nicht mehr. Es hat diesem Druck aber widerstanden, fast schon wie ein Fels in der Brandung.[51] Der Finanz- und Wirtschaftskrise entrann man auf stabiler Rechtsgrundlage mit neo-korporatistisch vereinten Kräften im Staat-Verbände-Verbund – und nicht zuletzt auch mit klugen Dezentralisierungsstrategien, die die Praxis der Arbeitspolitik veränderten.[52] Nun wusste man wieder zu würdigen, was man dem tradierten Regime, dem sich unser Beitrag gewidmet hat, verdankte. Teubners treffliches Resümee:

> »Nach der Wirtschaftskrise erscheinen für viele Beobachter die neo-korporatistischen Arrangements heute weltweit aufgrund ihres ›historical comparative advantage‹, angesichts ihrer höheren Produktivität und ihrer gesteigerten gesellschaftlichen Legitimität als die attraktiveren Produktionsregimes.«[53]

3. Mit dem Lobpreis der Re-Stabilisierung nach der großen Irritation sollte die Bilanz der jüngsten Turbulenz aber nicht ihr Bewenden haben. Zu vielzählig sind die Fragezeichen, die das tradierte Arbeitsmarktregime, seine normativen Strukturen und den Gesundheitszustand seiner institutionellen Akteure heute betreffen. Insbesondere die Regimekomponente Tarifautonomie bietet Anlass zu Zweifeln. Bei allem rechtspolitischem Erfolg, bei allen gelungenen Anpassungsleistungen der Tarifpolitik, mit denen ein wichtiger Beitrag zur Resilienz der Wirtschaft geleistet und fast schon verlorenes Ansehen und Legitimität zurückgewonnen wurde: Es erscheint auch jetzt noch immer zweifelhaft, ob die kommende Geschichte des Arbeitsmarktregimes als Stabilitätsgeschichte geschrieben werden kann.

Man ist, wie die Dinge heute liegen, von der Stabilisierung der Autonomie der Koalitionen nicht wirklich überzeugt. Denn es lässt sich schwerlich übersehen, dass die Erfolgsgaranten von eben, Gewerkschaften und Arbeitgeberverbände gleichermaßen, um die sozialen Prämissen ihrer Tarifautonomie hart zu kämpfen haben, wie schwächelnde Organisationsgrade und tariffreie Räume belegen. Sogar dort, wo man – wie vor allem in den traditionsgeprägten Sektoren der Industrie des alten Westens und im öffentlichen Sektor – noch über Bindungskraft verfügt, mehrt sich die Skepsis, ob die exponierte Position im Arbeitsmarktregime gehalten werden kann. In den enttraditionalisierten Regionen des Beitrittsgebiets, in den neuen post-industriellen Branchen, in der sich entfaltenden *Gig Ecomomy*[54] der Plattformen schon gar, tun sich die Koalitionen und ihre Statusverträge mehr als schwer damit, überhaupt irgendwie Fuß zu fassen. Das Prinzip der freien Assoziationen als Produzent von Normativität gerät von unten her ins Wanken. Gleichzeitig steht die Tarifautonomie bei staatlichen und suprastaatlichen Akteuren als Problemlöser und Ordnungsgarant hoch im Kurs, fast so, als habe sich seit den Glanzzeiten des Regimes nichts geändert. So lässt die Europäische Union keine Gelegenheit

49 Dazu ausführlich Bender (2018).
50 Streeck (2013) 57.
51 Zu Persistenz trotz starkem Veränderungsdruck Pierson (1998).
52 »Kontrollierte Dezentralisierung«. Zu dieser neuen Tarifpolitik etwa Bahnmüller (2010) und zusammenfassend Bender (2018) 712–714.
53 Teubner (2014) 218.
54 Zu den Konturen Crouch (2019).

aus, die Bedeutung des Tarifvertrags für die Zügelung und Einbettung der neuen Formen der Arbeit zu betonen.[55] Und auch der in Deutschland abgeschlossene Koalitionsvertrag bestätigte die Institution Tarifautonomie als unverzichtbar. Nur Weniges findet sich freilich zu den Problemen der prospektiven Problemlöser, zu den fragilen sozialen Voraussetzungen der Kollektivverträge und dazu, ob die ordnungspolitischen Erwartungen angesichts der unübersehbaren Schwierigkeiten noch realistisch sind. Nicht von ungefähr widmen sich hochmögende Initiativen und Foren verstärkt der Frage, was man zur Sanierung der angeschlagenen Institution Tarifautonomie unternehmen könnte. So ist die Uraltdebatte über tarifvertragliche Differenzierungsklauseln als Anreiz für Mitgliedschaft jetzt wieder entflammt,[56] und der altehrwürdige Deutsche Juristentag verhandelte, auf den historischen Wegen von 1908 wandelnd, über die »Stärkung der Tarifautonomie« und über »Änderungen des Tarifvertragsrechts«, die sich zu diesem Zweck »empfehlen«.[57]

Jenseits des Stärkungs-Diskurses sind noch handfestere Anzeichen für eine tiefgreifende Veränderung kaum zu übersehen. Das Avancement der staatlichen Lohnpolitik, die immer stärker in Gang kommt, ist in diesem Zusammenhang besonders auffällig. Der Staatsanteil des Arbeitsmarktregimes wächst. Das Instrument der Allgemeinverbindlichkeitserklärung wird forciert, wo immer dies möglich ist. Und man setzt im Niedriglohnsektor auf gesetzliche Mindestlöhne, die man in Deutschland über ein Jahrhundert hinweg vermieden hatte.[58] Im Bundestagswahlkampf von 2021 wurde die Höhe des Mindestlohns zum Kampagnenschlager und im Vollzug des Wahlergebnisses – an der korporatistisch konzipierten Mindestlohnkommission vorbei – sogleich zum Gegenstand der Lohngesetzgebung des direkten Staates.[59] Diesem vorrückenden Staat im Geiste eines überkommenen kollektiven Liberalismus in seinem eigenen wohlverstandenen Interesse zur Abstinenz zu raten, scheint indessen wenig hilf- und aussichtsreich. Die Defizite des tradierten Arbeitsmarktregimes, die sich auftun, können dem auf Intervention festgelegten Wohlfahrtsstaat einfach nicht gleichgültig sein. Arbeitseinkommen, die trotz Arbeit in Armut münden, aber auch »ungerechte Entlohnung« überhaupt, der das Tarifvertragssystem nichts Überzeugendes entgegenzusetzen hat, kann dieser Staat nicht ohne große Schwierigkeiten durchhalten; den Übergang zur Direktregulierung auf breiter Front zu einem gründlich »entkomplizierten« Regime angesichts der dann allfälligen Legitimations- und Überlastprobleme womöglich aber auch nicht. Das Problem der nicht-staatlichen Ressourcen des interventionistischen Staats, das wir – auf historische Ausgangspunkte blickend – aufgeworfen haben,[60] wird unter den Umständen unserer Zeit wieder zusehends akut.

VI. Schlussbemerkung

Mit Prognosen hat sich die Normativitätsgeschichte zurückzuhalten. Was man aber vielleicht doch sagen darf: Es könnte angesichts der Funktionsprobleme die Frage nach einer Veränderung des Arbeitsmarktregimes nicht so fern liegen, wie man, beeindruckt von großer Regimegeschichte und Blütezeiten der Institution, noch gerne glauben mag. In welchem modernisierten Gewand auch immer: Mit dem Thema Regimereform könnte jene Komponente ins Spiel kommen, die ein »atypischer« Sinzheimer unter zugespitzten gesellschaftlichen Umständen einst erwogen hatte: »Räte« über die Mikroebene des Betriebs hinausgreifend als bestimmende Kraft im Regime des Arbeitsmarkts, als korporatistische Variante der »Autonomie«. Im beginnenden 20. Jahrhundert stand sie als Alternative zu Interventionsstaat und

55 Siehe die Pressemitteilung der Europäischen Kommission vom 30. Juni 2020: »Europäische Kommission leitet Verfahren zur Klärung der Frage von Tarifverhandlungen für Selbständige ein.« Ziel der Initiative ist es zu gewährleisten, »dass die Arbeitsbedingungen durch Tarifverträge nicht nur für Arbeitnehmer, sondern auch für schutzbedürftige Selbständige verbessert werden können.« Dabei gehe es nicht zuletzt auch darum, die kollektivvertragliche Regulierung mit den Wettbewerbsvorschriften der EU zu harmonisieren. Zugleich – und dies ist in unserem Zusammenhang zu unterstreichen – kommt aber auch die Debatte um »Europäische Betriebsräte« in Fahrt. Zu dieser Institution Kocher (2020) 224–227.

56 Vgl. den Gesetzesentwurf von Benecke u. a. (2021).

57 Gutachten von Bepler (2014).

58 Siehe z. B. Schubert u. a. (2015).

59 Laut »BDA-Agenda 4/22: Tarifautonomie schützen« erwägt der Arbeitgeberverband, gestützt auf ein Gutachten des Staatsrechtlers Schorkopf, Verfassungsklage wegen Verstoßes gegen die Tarifautonomie des Art. 9 III GG einzureichen.

60 Oben bei Anm. 14.

freiem kollektiven Verhandeln hoch im Kurs, wie wir am Anfang des Beitrags erwähnten. Korporatismus als dritter Weg zwischen Staat und Assoziation hat damals viele Teilnehmer am sozial- und rechtspolitischen Diskurs fasziniert und hatte in der großen Soziologie Durkheims eine besonders brillante Fürsprecherin.[61] Als große Lösung wurde »Korporatismus« damals aber nicht implementiert, sieht man von den steckengebliebenen Reminiszenzen im Räteartikel der Weimarer Reichsverfassung, die wir erwähnt haben, und von dem einen oder anderen späteren Denkansatz pro Wiederbelebung einmal ab. Im Systemgedächtnis blieb die Variante zwischen Etatismus und Pluralismus vor allem als *verworfene Möglichkeit* verankert. Zumindest in den dezentralen Betriebsräten des dualen Systems, an das wir erinnert haben, ist sie über das Jahrhundert des Arbeitsmarktregimes hinweg aber als *vitale Struktur* stets präsent geblieben.

■

Bibliographie

- Abelshauser, Werner (2003), Kulturkampf: der deutsche Weg in die Neue Wirtschaft und die amerikanische Herausforderung, Berlin
- Bahnmüller, Reinhard (2010), Dezentralisierung der Tarifpolitik – Re-Stabilisierung des Tarifsystems, in: Bispinck, Reinhard, Thorsten Schulten (Hg.), Zukunft der Tarifautonomie, Hamburg, 81–113
- Becker, Martin (1995), Arbeitsvertrag und Arbeitsverhältnis in Deutschland. Vom Beginn der Industrialisierung bis zum Ende des Kaiserreichs, Frankfurt am Main
- Becker, Martin (2005), Arbeitsvertrag und Arbeitsverhältnis in der Weimarer Republik und in der Zeit des Nationalsozialismus, Frankfurt am Main
- Bender, Gerd (1991), Arbeitsvermittlung und Arbeitslosenversicherung in der Weimarer Republik, in: Benöhr, Hans-Peter (Hg.), Arbeitsvermittlung und Arbeitslosenversorgung in der neueren deutschen Rechtsgeschichte, Tübingen, 137–169
- Bender, Gerd (2006), Regulierte Selbstregulierung. Der Fall Tarifautonomie, in: Vec, Miloš (Hg.), Selbstorganisation. Ein Denksystem für Natur und Gesellschaft, Köln, 355–371
- Bender, Gerd (2007), Gewerkschaft und Betriebsrat, in: Stolleis, Michael, Wolfgang Streeck (Hg.), Aktuelle Fragen zu politischer Steuerung im Kontext der Globalisierung, Baden-Baden, 245–258
- Bender, Gerd (2018), Herausforderung Tarifautonomie. Normative Ordnung als Problem, in: Duve, Thomas, Stefan Ruppert (Hg.), Rechtswissenschaft in der Berliner Republik, Berlin, 697–725
- Bender, Gerd (2021), Inklusive Arbeitspolitik – Strukturen der kollektiven Arbeitsverfassung, in: Schumann, Dirk u. a. (Hg.), Demokratie versuchen. Die Verfassung in der politischen Kultur der Weimarer Republik, Göttingen, 274–294
- Benecke, Martina u. a. (2021), Entwurf eines Gesetzes über Differenzierungsklauseln in Tarifverträgen (Differenzierungsklauselgesetz – DiffklausG), in: Arbeit und Recht 7–8, 310–318
- Benz, Arthur (2010), Multilevel Governance – Governance in Mehrebenensystemen, in: ders., Nicolai Dose (Hg.), 111–136
- Benz, Arthur, Nicolai Dose (2010), Von der Governance-Analyse zur Policytheorie, in: dies. (Hg.), 244–276
- Benz, Arthur, Nicolai Dose (Hg.) (2010), Governance – Regieren in komplexen Regelsystemen. Eine Einführung, 2. Aufl., Wiesbaden
- Bepler, Klaus (2014), Stärkung der Tarifautonomie – Welche Änderungen des Tarifrechts empfehlen sich? Gutachten B zum 70. Deutschen Juristentag, München
- Brigl-Matthiass, Kurt (1926), Das Betriebsräteproblem in der Weimarer Republik, Berlin
- Crouch, Colin (2019), Gig Economy. Prekäre Arbeit im Zeitalter von Uber, Minijobs & Co., Berlin
- Däubler, Wolfgang, Michael Kittner (2020), Geschichte der Betriebsverfassung, Frankfurt am Main
- Durkheim, Emile (1988), Über soziale Arbeitsteilung. Studie über die Organisation höherer Gesellschaften, 2. Aufl., Frankfurt am Main
- Duve, Thomas (2021), Rechtsgeschichte als Geschichte von Normativitätswissen?, in: Rechtsgeschichte – Legal History 29, 41–68, online: http://dx.doi.org/10.12946/rg29/041-068
- Flatow, Georg (1924), Betriebsräte und Gewerkschaften, in: Neue Zeitschrift für Arbeitsrecht 4, 386–395
- Fraenkel, Ernst (1966), Zehn Jahre Betriebsrätegesetz, in: Ramm, Thilo (Hg.), Arbeitsrecht und Politik. Quellentexte 1918–1933, Neuwied, 97–112
- Heinemann, Hugo (1919), Rechtswissenschaft, in: Sozialistische Monatshefte 52, 414–417

61 Durkheim (1988), mit seinem herausragenden Vorwort zur zweiten Auflage: »Einige Bemerkungen über die Berufsgruppen«, 41–75, insbes. 46–47. Siehe zu »Durkheims Hoffnung auf ein Wiedererstarken professionell-korporativer Bindungen« auch die Einleitung durch Luhmann (1988) 34.

- Huber, Ernst Rudolf (1932), Lockerung der Tarifverträge, in: Neue Zeitschrift für Arbeitsrecht 12, 211–218
- Kahn-Freund, Otto (1976), Hugo Sinzheimer (1875–1945), in: ders., Ramm (Hg.) 1–31
- Kahn-Freund, Otto, Thilo Ramm (Hg.) (1976), Hugo Sinzheimer, Arbeitsrecht und Rechtssoziologie. Gesammelte Reden und Aufsätze, Bd. 1, Frankfurt am Main
- Katzenstein, Peter J. (1987), Policy and Politics in West Germany. The Growth of a Semisovereign State, Philadelphia
- Keller, Berndt (1995), Einführung in die Arbeitspolitik. Arbeitsbeziehungen und Arbeitsmarkt in sozialwissenschaftlicher Perspektive, 4. Aufl., München
- Kocher, Eva (2020), Europäisches Arbeitsrecht, 2. Aufl., Baden-Baden
- Kittner, Michael (2005), Arbeitskampf. Geschichte, Recht, Gegenwart, München
- Krüger, Dieter (2018), Das Stinnes-Legien-Abkommen 1918–1924, Berlin
- Lessenich, Stephan (1995), Wohlfahrtsstaat, Arbeitsmarkt und Sozialpolitik in Spanien. Eine exemplarische Analyse postautoritären Wandels, Opladen
- Luhmann, Niklas (1988), Arbeitsteilung und Moral. Durkheims Theorie, in: Durkheim, 19–38
- Luhmann, Niklas (2010), Politische Soziologie, Berlin
- Luhmann, Niklas (2017), Systemtheorie der Gesellschaft, Berlin
- Nocken, Ulrich (1981), Korporatistische Theorien und Strukturen in der deutschen Geschichte des 19. und frühen 20. Jahrhunderts, in: Alemann, Ulrich von (Hg.), Neokorporatismus, Frankfurt am Main, 17–42
- Osterhammel, Jürgen (2009), Die Verwandlung der Welt. Eine Geschichte des 19. Jahrhunderts, München
- Pierson, Paul (1998), Irresistible forces, immovable objects: post-industrial welfare states confront permanent austerity, in: Journal of European Public Policy 5, 539–560
- Plumpe, Werner (1999), Betriebliche Mitbestimmung in der Weimarer Republik. Fallstudien zum Ruhrbergbau und zur chemischen Industrie, München
- Plumpe, Werner (2004), Tarifsystem und innerbetriebliche Konflikte in der Weimarer Republik, in: Führer, Karl Christian (Hg.), Tarifbeziehungen und innerbetriebliche Konflikte in Deutschland im historischen Wandel, Bonn, 26–63
- Preller, Ludwig (1949), Sozialpolitik in der Weimarer Republik, Stuttgart
- Ramm, Thilo (1961), Die Parteien des Tarifvertrags, Stuttgart
- Ramm, Thilo (1980), Die Arbeitsverfassung der Weimarer Republik, in: Gamillscheg, Franz et al. (Hg.), In Memoriam Sir Otto Kahn-Freund, München, 225–246
- Rückert, Joachim (2019), Koalitionsrecht, Tarifverträge, kollektives Arbeitsrecht und ihr Prinzip in Deutschland, in: Zeitschrift für Arbeitsrecht 50, 515–578
- Rückert, Joachim, Wolfgang Friedrich (1979), Betriebliche Arbeiterausschüsse in Deutschland, Großbritannien und Frankreich im späten 19. und frühen 20. Jahrhundert, Frankfurt am Main
- Schippel, Max (1890), Arbeiterausschüsse, in: Neue Zeit 1, 129–133
- Schmoller, Gustav (1890), Zur Social- und Gewerbepolitik der Gegenwart, Leipzig
- Schubert, Jens M. u. a. (2015), Das neue Mindestlohngesetz. Grundlagen und Auswirkungen, Baden-Baden
- Sinzheimer, Hugo (1921), Grundzüge des Arbeitsrechts. Eine Einführung, Jena
- Sinzheimer, Hugo (1976), Die Zukunft der Arbeiterräte, in: Kahn-Freund, Ramm (Hg.) 351–355
- Sinzheimer, Hugo (1977), Der korporative Arbeitsnormenvertrag. Eine privatrechtliche Untersuchung, 2. Aufl., Berlin
- Steinmetz, Willibald (1999), Theorie und Praxis des Arbeitsrechts in Deutschland und England (1850–1930). Annäherung an einen Vergleich verschiedener Rechtskulturen, in: Moving the Social 22, 85–113
- Stolleis, Michael (2001), Konstitution und Intervention. Studien zur Geschichte des öffentlichen Rechts im 19. Jahrhundert, Frankfurt am Main
- Stolleis, Michael (2018), Die soziale Programmatik der Weimarer Reichsverfassung, in: Dreier, Horst, Christian Waldhoff (Hg.), Das Wagnis der Demokratie. Eine Anatomie der Reichsverfassung, München, 195–218
- Streeck, Wolfgang (1999), Korporatismus in Deutschland, Frankfurt am Main
- Streeck, Wolfgang (2013), Gekaufte Zeit. Die vertagte Krise des demokratischen Kapitalismus, Berlin
- Teubner, Gunther (2014), Transnationale Wirtschaftsverfassung: Franz Böhm und Hugo Sinzheimer jenseits des Nationalstaats, in: Zeitschrift für ausländisches öffentliches Recht und Völkerrecht 74, 733–761
- Teuteberg, Hans Jürgen (1961), Geschichte der Mitbestimmung in Deutschland, Tübingen
- Weisbrod, Bernd (1985), Die Befreiung von den »Tariffesseln«, in: Geschichte und Gesellschaft 11, 295–325
- Winschuh, Josef (1922), Betriebsrat oder Gewerkschaft? Beiträge zur Soziologie des Betriebsrätewesens, Essen
- Wolf, Johanna, Tim-Niklas Vesper, Benjamin Spendrin, Matthias Ebbertz (2022), Neue Ansätze in der Arbeitsrechtsgeschichte. Ein digitales Quelleneditionsprojekt am Max-Planck-Institut für Rechtsgeschichte und Rechtstheorie, in: Rechtsgeschichte – Legal History 30, 199–213
- Wood, Stewart (2001), Labour Market Regimes under Threat? Sources of Continuity in Germany, Britain and Sweden, in: Pierson, Paul (Hg.), The New Politics of the Welfare State, Oxford, 369–409

RADIO CITY
RADIO CITY
MUSIC HALL

Rebecca Zahn

Industrial Democracy in the UK: Precursors to the Bullock Report

I. Introduction

Industrial democracy is an elusive idea in the UK. It has served as an umbrella term for different ways of extending political democracy to the workplace in order to minimise the economic exploitation of workers and limit employers' arbitrary decision-making.[1] Many of the debates in the labour movement on how to ensure and implement industrial democracy through worker representatives on company boards reached their peak during two periods of the twentieth century: between the two World Wars and in the 1970s.[2] The Report of the Committee of Inquiry on Industrial Democracy (»the Bullock Report«) – the last serious attempt by the state to introduce »industrial democracy« – generated considerable controversy when it was published in 1977. It was generally accepted that the Report's recommendations – to appoint worker representatives to the boards of directors of companies for which they work – would result in a fundamental change to Britain's industrial landscape. No consensus could be found on the Report's implementation, and the political and industrial turbulence that followed in the late 1970s and throughout the 1980s resulted in the abandonment of the recommendations. Even though debates over how much »say« workers should have in the running of their employers' business and what form this »voice« should take have not subsided, the UK remains without statutory provision for board-level representation of workers.[3]

This article uses the Bullock Report as an entry point to reconsider the feasibility of worker representation on company boards in the UK from a labour law perspective. It does so by comparing the Report with debates which took place between the two World Wars – an intellectually rich but often neglected period when the British trade union movement was at a critical point in its development. Insights from labour law history and comparative law reveal the points at which historical factors led to certain choices. An awareness of these historical factors and choices facilitates a reassessment of traditional narratives. This text is based on a presentation given at the annual conference of the »Initiative Arbeitsrechtsgeschichte«, an initiative of the Hugo Sinzheimer Institute and the Max Planck Institute for Legal History and Legal Theory, on the topic *Geschichte der Betriebsverfassung* (*History of the Works Constitution*) on 18 June 2021.

The article proceeds as follows. Section II situates the topic within British labour law history and explains the author's methodology. Section III provides an overview of the literature on British industrial democracy, including the findings of the Bullock Report. Section IV explores the debates taking place within the trade union movement in-between the two World Wars. A final section concludes the article.

II. Methodology

Labour law history in the UK lives at the margins and intersections of a number of different fields – including labour history, legal history, labour law, and industrial relations. Despite the rich scholarly output that exists on British labour law history,[4] few contemporary academic labour lawyers would identify as labour law historians.[5] Labour law history emerged, along with labour history, in the late nineteenth and early twentieth centuries among scholars interested in the »labour

1 Clegg (1951).

2 There were also debates taking place during this time about the feasibility and necessity of a statute-based system of workplace worker representation below the board-level. While these debates raise a number of interesting questions about the meaning of industrial democracy, space precludes a detailed discussion of the topic. See further for an overview, for example, Dukes (2008).

3 Recent (non-statutory) developments include the introduction of provision 5 into the UK Corporate Governance Code (2018) which sets out methods for engagement with the workforce, including the possibility of a director appointed from the workforce.

4 For an overview see Zahn (2020).

5 See generally Tucker (2017).

question« which was centred on the role of workers' collective action. Early labour law histories traced the legal regulation of trade unions. Labour law history has thus traditionally been situated within an industrial relations rather than a legal history framework. Labour law historians analyse the history of labour law in relation to wider social forces and are receptive to socio-legal methods – going beyond doctrinal legal sources.[6]

The question of whether and how to draw on other disciplines in order to undertake a comparison also permeates comparative law. Recent scholarship has sought to move away from what Pierre Legrand described as »positivist« comparative law, towards the contextualised analysis of legal rules, their active interpretation, and engagement with interdisciplinary study.[7] As part of this trend, scholars have applied different methodological lenses in order to give a voice to individuals and social groups whose views are not part of mainstream narratives.[8] In an article published in 2015, Sherally Munshi borrowed from comparative literature to propose the idea of a minor comparativism.[9] A minor comparativism retains the general tenor of comparative law, which is »to reveal something about our immediate world that would not reveal itself but through the practice of adopting a foreign perspective«, but it seeks that foreign perspective »within« one's own country.[10] It »sets the official image of a particular state *against* the reflections of its minority subjects«.[11] A minor comparativism acknowledges that the minority – to be understood in the sense of foreign or not belonging to the majority – is not peripheral but central to the formation of laws, the state, and the nation. A consequence of this is that a minor comparativism resists regurgitating authorised representations of the law. While traditional approaches to comparative law tend to identify and isolate particular rules or institutions across legal systems, a minor comparativism seeks to disrupt received understandings of the law and its development. For labour lawyers, the use of such an approach opens up traditional narratives to reinterpretation. As Munshi explains:

> »The purpose of such investigation is not merely ethnographic or to thicken our account of a culture, but liberatory. By recognizing that authoritative declarations of law do not exhaust our own understanding or experience of law, we proliferate opportunities to transform the laws that give shape and meaning to our shared circumstances.«[12]

The question arises as to who, in the eyes of labour law scholars, is »the minority«. Different possibilities arise. For the purposes of this article, the focus is on discovering the historical factors which have shaped contemporary labour law. As a first step, this necessitates recognising that this shape depends on the outcome of power struggles. As Bob Hepple explains, the development of labour law »is the product of a variety of historical factors, which are neither ›necessary‹ nor ›natural‹ […]. The choices made were not inevitable solutions to the social problems created by the workings of the market.«[13] According to Hepple, the demands were unsuccessful because, »they were unacceptable to those with greater economic and political power […]. [T]he powerfulness of the opponents of reform was the decisive factor in the making of labour law.«[14] The views of the individuals or groups who lost out in the power struggles – social reformers and labour movements who were unsuccessful – have been erased from the legal record and, by extension, are the subject of study of legal or labour historians but are often neglected by comparative law and labour law scholars. Yet their demands held sway at particular moments in history even if they were not translated into law in the end – the outcome of power struggles was neither inevitable nor predetermined. Rediscovering their viewpoints disrupts and reframes received understandings of the historical development of labour law. Such an exer-

6 For an overview see Zahn (2020).
7 See generally Legrand (2017); as well as the other contributions in the 2017 special issue of the American Journal of Comparative Law.
8 For an overview, see the *Decolonial Comparative Law* project led by Professor Dr Ralf Michaels and Dr Lena Salaymeh at the Max Planck Institute for Comparative and International Private Law (Hamburg), available at https://www.mpipriv.de/decolonial.
9 Munshi (2015) 665.
10 Munshi (2015) 664.
11 Munshi (2015) 665.
12 Munshi (2015).
13 Hepple (1986) 4.
14 Hepple (1986) 5.

cise requires scholars to engage seriously with the discourse of minorities and to set it against the traditional narrative. This, in turn, enables scholars to identify, question, and challenge conventional assumptions about the legal system by rendering those conventional assumptions foreign to themselves.

Such an approach has not hitherto been applied to labour law. It allows scholars to consider the possibilities of what could have been, to think about law in a different framework to the norm, and to develop alternative approaches to legal regulation. Accordingly, in the next sections I will explore the topic of board-level representation of workers by first explaining the traditional narrative on industrial democracy leading to the Bullock Report and then rediscovering the debates which took place within the trade union movement in the 1920s and 1930s. In a final section I compare these debates in order to draw some initial conclusions.

III. Industrial Democracy and the Bullock Report

Writing in 1897, Beatrice and Sidney Webb observed that the organisation of workmen within trade unions amounted to the formation of a spontaneous democracy within a state.[15] The object of such trade unionism was the deliberate regulation of the conditions of employment in such a way as to protect workers from the evil effects of industrial competition from workers. In order to do this effectively and without threatening the democratic state, trade unions would operate within a framework of industrial democracy, to be understood in a two-fold manner: first, it had an internal dimension that referred to trade-union democracy,[16] and, second, it had an external dimension, which the Webbs understood as effective collective bargaining.[17] They considered collective bargaining as a pure instrument of trade union action, without giving thought to the regulatory interest that it might have for employers. »[F]or the Webbs, collective bargaining was exactly what the words imply: a collective equivalent and alternative to individual bargaining«,[18] the primary aim of which was to reduce potentially disastrous competition among workers. Although the Webbs later included an element of worker representation in management in their understanding of industrial democracy,[19] this was merged with the idea of public ownership. Thus, the socialisation of ownership would also socialise economic participation and complement collective bargaining.

Worker interests – and by extension industrial democracy – would thus primarily be protected by independent trade unions engaging in collective bargaining. This so-called single-channel model became the defining feature of the industrial pluralist model of worker representation, particularly following World War II, which was informed by the idea of equality of bargaining power and an acceptance of a conflictual relationship between employers and trade unions.[20] Writing in 1959, Otto Kahn-Freund, the »founding father« of British labour law and one-time student of the German socio-legal labour law scholar Hugo Sinzheimer,[21] described this state of affairs as *collective laissez-faire*. He defined this to mean »allowing free play to the collective forces of society, and to limit the intervention of the law to those marginal areas in which the disparity of these forces – those of organised labour and management – is so great as to prevent the successful operation of the negotiating machinery«. He went on to say that the main characteristic of the British trade union movement was its »aversion to legislative intervention, its disinclination to rely on legal sanctions, its almost passionate belief in the autonomy of industrial forces«.[22] Within this system of *collective laissez-faire*, collective bargaining in the second half of the twentieth century became a political institution, given its two fundamental features as norm-producing and as involving power relations among organisations. Modern collective bargaining – that of the age of full industrial development – was therefore primarily a process of joint regulation in which the trade unions performed twofold action, »as power or pressure groups certainly but also, together with employers, as private legislators«.[23] The latter was based on the observation that »the effects of [the trade union's] action extend beyond the securing

15 Webb/Webb (1897).
16 Webb/Webb (1897) part 1.
17 Webb/Webb (1897) part 2.
18 Flanders (1968) 3.
19 Webb/Webb (1920) 760.
20 See further Dukes (2008).
21 See generally Dukes (2009).
22 Kahn-Freund (1959) 224.
23 Flanders (1968) 12.

of material gains to the establishment *of rights* in industry; the right to a defined rate of wages, the right not to have to work longer than a certain number of hours, the right to be paid for holidays, and so on«.[24] As such, collective bargaining was seen to promote the »›rule of law‹ in employment relationships«,[25] albeit within a channel of conflict.

As a consequence, workers' representation in management or their involvement in controlling industry could not serve as a fundamental underpinning in post-war understandings of industrial democracy. Trade unions could only represent the industrial interests of workers, and participation in management was »unacceptable« as it threatened trade-union independence.[26] In 1968, the Donovan Commission asserted that »collective bargaining is the most effective means of giving workers the right to representation in decisions affecting their working lives«.[27]

Yet as the post-war economic boom slowed, successive UK governments began to advocate industrial rationalisation, which in turn »creat[ed] a need to extend the sphere of workers' influence«.[28] By the late 1960s, mainstream union figures, in particular Jack Jones of the Transport and General Workers' Union (TGWU), were arguing that »Industrial Democracy is a natural extension of trade unionism«.[29] Jones's assessment of trade union power and influence in the UK was that unions were very strong on the »low ground«, at workplace and plant levels, through a strong shop steward movement and collective bargaining, and on the »high ground« through their involvement in economic and industrial planning. However, they were weak on the »middle ground«, at company/corporate level, where company policy and strategy were formulated. For Jones, worker representatives on company boards would be in a position to rectify this gap and would enable workers to make a meaningful contribution and consent to their employer's decision-making.[30] The Trades Union Congress (TUC) and its affiliates largely backed Jones, although there remained a fear that having worker representatives on boards could weaken collective bargaining and undermine trade unions. Left-wing intellectuals and academics remained sceptical of the fit between worker representation on boards, at least when imposed through legislation, and collective laissez-faire.[31]

At a political level, both the Labour and Conservative parties proposed plans for worker participation in company decision-making in the early 1970s. The Labour Party's manifesto of February 1974 promised to introduce »an Industrial Democracy Act [...] to increase the control of industry by the people [...] [and to] take steps to make the management of existing nationalised industries more responsible to the workers in the industry«.[32] Simultaneously, the TUC had proposed legislation to achieve 50/50 worker representation on company and nationalised industry boards. Yet despite all the enthusiasm for »industrial democracy«, the concept remained elusive. As a union leader pointed out, there were »probably as many meanings for each term [used] as there are people who use it«.[33]

Labour was elected as a minority government in February 1974 and obtained a small majority in the October 1974 election. The government was under pressure to respond to the demands for industrial democracy, and in early 1975 a bill introduced by a backbench MP proposing 50% worker representation on nationalised industry boards as well as the introduction of parity supervisory boards forced the government to set up a Committee of Inquiry to further consider the issue.[34]

The Committee – chaired by Lord Bullock and therefore also known as the Bullock Committee – was set up by the Department of Trade in December 1975. The Committee was directed to consider only one aspect of industrial democracy, namely the representation of employees on the boards of companies for which they work.

Over the course of a year, the Committee gathered a wide range of written evidence from stakeholders and commissioned two papers on the

24 Flanders (1968) 12.
25 Flanders (1968) 12.
26 Clegg (1960) 22.
27 Report (1968) 27.
28 Williamson (2016).
29 Jones at the 1968 TUC Congress, quoted in Williamson (2016) 123.
30 Williamson (2016) 129 quoting an interview with George Bain, 14 March 2015.
31 Williamson (2016) 129.
32 Labour Party (1974).
33 Roberts (1973) 22.
34 Report (1977).

»European experience« of having workers represented on boards of directors. The majority report (the Bullock Report), which was signed by all members except the three industrialists on the Committee and delivered in January 1977, proposed that all boards of directors of companies with more than 2,000 employees should be reconstituted to be composed of three elements – an equal number of employee and shareholder representatives plus a third group comprising an uneven number of additional directors (but less than a third of the overall board). The employee representatives were expected to *represent* the workforce rather than act as delegates of their trade union; meaning that they should be »free to express [their] opinions and to reach [their] own conclusions about which policies will work for the greater good of the company, not as a delegate, told how to vote by [their] constituents«.[35] The rationale for this so-called 2x+y approach – as opposed to parity representation between workers and shareholders – was that it would bring special expertise and experience into the boardroom and accommodate broader public interest concerns. The proposed rules for worker representation on boards were to be implemented where a union made a request for representation and that request was endorsed by a majority of the whole (unionised and non-unionised) workforce voting in a secret ballot. The Bullock Report did not support universally mandatory legislation. It stressed that it did not want to undermine the unions' representative capacity and that it considered collective bargaining as the most effective means of giving workers a voice in decision-making both within the company and within wider society. In its recommendations, the Bullock Report can be seen to strive for a balance between avoiding the transformation of the single-channel model – that is, accepting that collective bargaining should remain the primary means of workplace representation – and recognising the need for some representation of the workforce at company level. This tension between trade unions as a channel of conflict and trade unions as partners remained unresolved both in the Bullock Report and subsequently.

The Bullock Report generated considerable controversy and received a mixed reception from all sides of the political and intellectual spectrum.[36] The Confederation of British Industry did not approve of it, with many Conservative activists holding the view that trade unionists »did not [...] understand the legal implications of being a director«.[37] The TUC endorsed the Bullock Report, with Jones reporting that »the General Council [of the TUC] had had three representatives on the Bullock Committee and [...] the majority report would be seen largely to conform to Congress policy«.[38] Other voices on the Left, including in the trade union movement and amongst labour law scholars, were more muted, focusing specifically on the threat of board-level representation to collective bargaining.[39] The 2x+y formula (as opposed to parity representation) also drew criticism as »virtually [guaranteeing] the hostility of a majority of board members to labour interests at key times in all cases«.[40] Clive Jenkins of the Association of Scientific, Technical and Managerial Staffs (ASTMS) opposed the recommendations of the Report and argued instead for the extension of collective bargaining as the most effective way of securing worker interests in the workplace.[41]

Kahn-Freund, too, criticised the Bullock Report, observing that board-level employee representation was »an idea originally alien to the trade union movement«.[42] Although recognising that the Bullock Committee's remit precluded it from considering the issue, Kahn-Freund questioned whether the purpose of the Committee's purpose could not have been »equally well or better attained by an expansion of collective negotiations«.[43] He was sceptical whether board-level employee representation as proposed by Bullock would be effective as long as there was a legal duty for the board to take decisions »in the company's overall best interest«, with the expectation being that »a company's best interest« would align with that of the shareholders. This would expose em-

35 Report (1977) chapter 8, para 40.
36 For an overview see Williamson (2016).
37 Agenda (1977). On the resistance of employers to the proposals see Phillips (2011).
38 TUC (1977).
39 See Coates / Topham (1977) from 113 onwards.
40 Coates / Topham (1977) 113.
41 ASTMS (1977).
42 Kahn-Freund (1977) 71.
43 Kahn-Freund (1977) 75.

ployee representatives on a board to »a conflict of duties which is simply insoluble«.[44] Other scholars disagreed, suggesting that the phrase »the company's best interests« was a shorthand for »the interests of both employees and shareholders, i. e. ›the company‹ is to be defined as embracing the interests of both of these groups«.[45] This argument rested on the assumption that a company may have legitimate goals which go beyond profit maximisation, thereby allowing directors to take different interests into account in determining a company's *overall* best interests. As to the compatibility of collective bargaining with board-level worker representation, Davies and Wedderburn suggested that:

> »Collective bargaining is one form of joint regulation. The extent to which participation in the institutions of the enterprise causes workers to integrate themselves into that enterprise, depends upon the concrete terms of their participation. [...] Account must be taken of the nature of the participation proposed – and above all of its relationship to the independent trade unions that constitute the labour movement and represent workers' interests in that country. The proposals of the T.U.C. in 1974 [which went beyond the Bullock Report's proposals] implied a self-confidence on the part of British unions that, *so long as* the conditions of the participation were acceptable, new forms of joint regulation could be entertained.«[46]

There were some subsequent experiments in appointing worker-directors in the public sector, notably at British Steel and in the Post Office.[47] The verdict on these experiments was not, however, very positive and they were quickly abandoned. No consensus could be found within the government, who by the time the Bullock Report had been delivered had lost their parliamentary majority, as to how to implement the Report more widely and it was ultimately shelved.

Overall, statutory provision for worker representation on management boards was not only anathema to Conservatives and employers but also to many on the Left, including trade unions whose strength in many sectors was at its peak during this period and who preferred to maintain the status quo.[48] The single-channel model, which assumed that collective laissez-faire was the most effective means of regulating work relationships, complicated the reconciliation of worker representation on management boards with collective bargaining. Without a fundamental shift in thinking, including an acceptance of a more overt role for the state in regulating industrial relations,[49] it was difficult to see how to alleviate the tension between trade unions playing a conflictual role through collective bargaining and then becoming partners/aligning interests with employers for the purposes of board-level representation in order to take company-wide strategic decisions. Although the landscape of British industrial relations has changed significantly since the 1970s, contemporary debates over worker representation on company boards continue to be tainted by these tensions. By using a minor comparativism, the next section focuses on an earlier period, before the single-channel model became the dominant narrative describing industrial relations, to explore some of the rich intellectual debates that took place during the inter-war years, particularly after the 1926 General Strike, which had led some unions and their leaders to explore alternative ways of industrial cooperation and participation. Setting the Bullock Report against this earlier period reveals alternative starting points for worker representation on company boards by focussing on the views of a »minority«.

IV. The Inter-War Years

Starting from Hepple's observation that »the powerfulness of the opponents of reform was the decisive factor in the making of labour law«,[50] this section looks in more detail at the demands made by a number of British trade unionists who (unsuccessfully) advocated worker participation in

44 Kahn-Freund (1977) 77. Kahn-Freund also criticised the absence of a suitable sub-structure below board level which could support board-level representation. Davies and Wedderburn in Davies/Wedderburn (1977) offered a response to this. This line of argumentation is beyond the scope of this paper and is therefore not dealt with in more detail.
45 Davies/Wedderburn (1977) 198.
46 Davies/Wedderburn (1977) 203.
47 Williamson (2016) 137.
48 Crouch (1986) 107–109.
49 Although Ewing argues in Ewing (1998) that the state has always played a greater – albeit indirect – role in collective laissez-faire than has generally been recognised.
50 Hepple (1986) 5.

workplace decision-making throughout the 1920s and 1930s. Although they constituted a minority in the sense of a minor comparativism because their views did not become part of the dominant narrative, these trade unionists made an important contribution to a rich intellectual debate at a time when the British trade union movement was reassessing its purpose in the wake of the General Strike. These trade unionists were influenced by various ideas on ownership and management of industry circulating in between the two World Wars. For example, thinkers like GDH Cole, Harold Laski and RH Tawney initiated a radical-utopian variety of British pluralism which sought to gradually devolve functions from central government and managerial authority down to workers' control within the firm. This was also referred to as guild socialism – a British version of syndicalism (although unlike syndicalism, guild socialism was not opposed to the continued existence of a political state).[51] A grass-roots campaign in the form of the Shop Stewards Movement, originating in the Glasgow shipbuilding industries, advocated the nationalisation of industry with equal participation of workers in management. Some of these debates spilt over into trade unions. The General Strike of 1926, in particular, appears to have had a formidable influence on some trade union leaders such as Walter Citrine, the general secretary of the TUC from 1925–1946, in showing the limits of union power when not directed at a revolutionary challenge. The failure of the General Strike and the fraught relationship with the Labour Party during that period led Citrine to view politics as a complementary but by no means primary sphere in which to pursue trade union aims. He recognised that the conflictual model of industrial relations must be replaced by one that made more extensive use »of the machinery for joint consultation and negotiation between employers and employed«.[52] Citrine's formative years had been heavily influenced by the Independent Labour Party, and there is evidence of syndicalist influences until at least 1921 although later, after the General Strike, he advocated a »New Union« approach which proposed industrial cooperation. This approach was supported by Ernest Bevin, the powerful general secretary of the TGWU at the time. Its implementation was attempted by both during the »Mond-Turner« talks in 1928–1929 between the industrialist Alfred Mond and 21 other employers and the TUC, represented by its president Ben Turner, which explored possibilities for substituting joint consultation and co-operation for conflict in British industry.[53]

The issue of worker representation on the boards of nationalised industry – and how this may be implemented in practice – preoccupied the TUC's Research and Economic Department during this time.[54] Until 1932, the TUC's standing orders had called for »the General Council [to] endeavour to establish … public ownership and control of natural resources and of services with proper provision for the adequate participation of the workers in the control and management of public services and industries«.[55] An Industrial Workers' Charter adopted at the 1924 Congress had advocated proper provision to be made for worker representation through trade unions on nationalised industry management boards. The TUC's Research and Economic department was established and operated under the leadership of Walter Milne-Bailey until his death in 1935. Milne-Bailey had been strongly influenced by guild socialism and favoured democratic corporatist government of industry. He, along with the general secretary of the TUC at the time – Walter Citrine – foresaw a new role for trade unions, moving away from confrontational industrial action towards a more wide-ranging and constructive corporatist approach.[56] In 1931, the TUC's Economic Committee began to draft a report on »Public Control and Regulation of Industry and Trade« which considered the question of labour representation on the boards of nationalised industries.[57]

That draft TUC report ended up in similar terms to that espoused by the Labour Party who were also, at the same time, preparing reports on the socialisation of several industries. The Labour Party's discussions on worker participation in man-

51 For a general overview see Pribićević (1959) and also Ackers / Reid (eds.) (2016).

52 The words of George Hicks, president of the Trades Union Congress in 1927, quoted in Clegg (1976) 130.

53 For an overview see Mcdonald / Gospel (1973).

54 See Barry (1965) 320–322.

55 See, for example, TUC (1932b) 450.

56 Ackers / Reid (2016) 10–11.

57 TUC (1932a).

agement had been dominated by Herbert Morrison, the post-war deputy to Prime Minister Clement Attlee. Morrison strongly advocated the public corporation, where members of the board were appointed by the relevant minister from among suitably qualified individuals. He refused any claims for direct representation, stating:

> »I was not convinced that the statutory right of the representation of labour in the industry would necessarily provide the best man from the ranks of labour; it would involve a difficult and embarrassing business of selection from the names submitted by the various Trades Unions in the industry; and if I conceded the statutory right of representation to labour in the industry, I should ... inevitably be involved in almost irresistible demands for the right of representation from other elements of interests.«[58]

This view was not undisputed amongst left wing intellectuals. For example, 18 prominent unionists and socialists in 1932 provided a memorandum to the TUC Economic Committee and the Labour Party Executive on »Workers Control and Self-Government in Industry«, which took public ownership as its starting point and advocated for equal representation of trade unions on a nationalised industry's governing board.[59] The pamphlet recognised that this kind of reshaping would require »large changes in the structure and workings of Trade Unionism« as well as appropriate training for worker representatives if they were to play an effective role.[60] This memorandum was not, however, taken into consideration by the TUC or the Labour Party.

Both the TUC and the Labour Party Executive presented their reports on public control of industry in 1932 to Congress and Conference respectively, where both were confronted with severe criticism. To avoid defeat at the TUC Congress, it was agreed that a draft of the report would be circulated widely for comments to affiliated unions and to friendly unions in other countries.[61]

The tenor of the responses and the criticisms were to the effect that workers should have direct representation on boards of management of publicly owned industries. TGWU general secretary Ernest Bevin insisted that socialised boards should include a *statutory* right to worker representation chosen by the unions concerned.[62] Bevin described Morrison's proposal of the public corporation as »positively the worst form of public control«.[63] He argued that »Labour is [not] an interest occupying a like position with a group of other interests. [Labour] occupies a special position and should be so dealt with«.[64] For the TGWU, this implied that workers should have »effective representation [...] through their Trade Unions on any controlling board. [...] We claim the right to be where policy is determined.«[65]

In arguing in favour of statutory worker representation on management boards, Bevin was supported not only by the TGWU but also by the Miners' Federation of Great Britain, the Associated Society of Locomotive Engineers and Firemen and the National Union of General and Municipal Workers (NUGMW).[66] In a questionnaire circulated on the draft report in 1932 amongst TUC affiliates, 18 out of 27 unions with a combined membership of just under 2 million workers opposed the report; only 9 unions with a membership of 160,000 were in favour.[67] A range of amendments were suggested to the section of the report on trade union representation on management boards, and there were calls for the final report to be delayed until a broader discussion on the meaning and purpose of industrial democracy could be had. Although the opinions on the purpose of industrial democracy differed, overall, there was a general agreement within the trade union movement that the public corporation proposed by Morrison did not guarantee socialisation and that the public corporation did not adequately provide for worker control inside individual undertakings. There was recognition that state ownership in a capitalist system is worth little unless accompanied by effective trade union participation in direction and management at all levels. The question of control should therefore be distinct from that of ownership. Adequate provision should be made for parity or even majority worker representation both on industry-wide governing boards and within individual enterprises regardless of the owner-

58 Morrison (1933) 191.
59 Cole/Mellor (eds.) (1933).
60 Cole/Mellor (eds.) (1933) 4.
61 TUC (1933) 256.
62 Bullock (1960) 459.
63 Note circulated to members of the Committee dated 21 December 1931. See Bullock (1960) 510.
64 Letter (1933).
65 Ibid.
66 See further Zahn (2015).
67 TUC (1933).

ship structures. This would guarantee giving workers a voice, endow them with responsibility, and also in some sectors reduce antagonism between employers and employees.[68]

However, in spite of the opposition to the report, joint TUC-Labour Party committees in early 1933 worked out a compromise statement which recognised:

> »Organised labour claims for Trade Unions in the industry the right to nominate persons for appointment to such a Board [of Management and Control]. This claim of organised labour that it shall have its place in the control and direction of publicly owned industries is accepted. It is agreed that in order to give effect to this object there shall be consultation between the responsible Minister and the Trade Unions concerned.«[69]

A resolution brought by the NUGMW and passed at the 1934 TUC Congress called on the TUC Economic Committee to reconsider its position. It demanded that:

> »[W]age earners of all grades and occupations have a right, which ought to be acknowledged by law, to an effective share in the control and direction of the industries which their labour sustains. [...] [T]his right should be exercised by adequate representation on the Central Board of Management.«[70]

The resolution also did not just refer to socialised industries but claimed a statutory right of 50% representation for trade unions on boards of management, managerial committees, and in industries in the capitalist system.

The resolution was never, however, acted upon; the reference to private industry ignored; and international issues dominated the discussions after 1934. The TUC General Council did not debate the opposing ideological views on labour participation and instead used delaying tactics to avoid the issue. The question of participation was not taken up again until 1944 in post-war planning, and at that time, references to the earlier debate on participation in management were largely deleted or ignored. Morrison's public corporation became the dominant approach of the post-war Labour government when it pursued large scale nationalisation (incidentally, Morrison became the Minister for Nationalisation in that government).

V. Conclusion

What then is the usefulness of this minor comparativism, of comparing the Bullock Report to earlier debates on worker representation on company boards? First, the debates which took place within the TUC in the 1920s and 1930s foresaw many of the challenges the Bullock Report would encounter. The biggest among those was how to reconcile collective bargaining as a conflictual method with worker representation as necessarily based on cooperation and partnership. The 1931 TUC Report and the subsequent arguments from different trade unions advocating board-level representation had the foresight to distinguish between management and control, and to recognise that worker representation was another form of joint regulation, one that served a different purpose to that of collective bargaining. In particular, it was seen as having the potential to involve workers in strategic decision-making, thereby giving them both greater control over and responsibility for decisions affecting the workplace. There was also recognition that within an enterprise, employees have a special status which is not comparable to that of other interest groups, and which justifies at least parity representation on boards where important decisions are taken. Finally, the TUC Report acknowledged that, in order to be effective, there had to be a statutory mechanism to mandate representation.

More generally, the minor comparativism applied in this article shines a light on the earlier debates on industrial democracy, which constitute an important – albeit under-researched – period of British labour law history. It reopens common assumptions that worker representation on company boards »is an idea originally alien to the trade

68 TUC (1933).
69 Labour Party (1933).
70 TUC (1934).

union movement«,[71] thereby complicating our understanding of how labour law developed and providing different starting points for a debate within the field of labour law as to the future shape and feasibility of board-level worker representation. Looking at the rich and under-researched debate within the trade union movement on this topic throughout the 1920s and early 1930s, a time when unions had suffered from a decline in strength and were reassessing their purpose and mode of operation following the General Strike allows scholars to consider different ideas of trade union power, how and where this should be exercised. It also enables an exploration of different perspectives on the role of co-operation and joint regulation in industrial relations. There are thus some potentially useful starting points for contemporary debates on the future of British trade unions. Overall, the debates of the inter-war years, especially compared with the Bullock Report, which has been extensively discussed in the literature, provide fertile intellectual ground for labour law scholars interested in considering different starting points to develop a contemporary model for worker participation – one grounded in labour law.

■

Bibliography

- Ackers, Peter, Alastair Reid (eds.) (2016), Alternatives to State-Socialism in Britain, Basingstoke
- Agenda (1977) = Agenda for the 153rd Meeting of Advisor Committee of Policy, 9 November 1977, Cambridge, Churchill Archives Centre, the Papers of Lord Howell, HWLL 2/4/1/9
- ASTMS (1977) = ASTMS Conference Resolution, 2 June 1977, the Papers of Clive Jenkins, Modern Records Centre, MSS.79/6/CJ/3/52
- Barry, E. Eldon (1965), Nationalisation in British Politics, London
- Bullock, Alan (1960), The Life and Times of Ernest Bevin, Vol. 1: Trade Union Leader 1881–1940, London
- Clegg, Hugh (1951), Industrial Democracy and Nationalization: A Study Prepared for the Fabian Society, London
- Clegg, Hugh (1960), A New Approach to Industrial Democracy, Oxford
- Clegg, Hugh (1976), The System of Industrial Relations in Great Britain, Oxford
- Coates, Ken, Tony Topham (1977), The Shop Steward's Guide to the Bullock Report, Nottingham
- Cole, George Douglas Howard, William Mellor (eds.) (1933), Workers' Control and Self-Government in Industry, London
- Crouch, Colin (1986), Politics of Industrial Relations, Manchester
- Davies, Paul, Lord Wedderburn Of Charlton (1977), The Land of Industrial Democracy, in: Industrial Law Journal 6, 197–221
- Dukes, Ruth (2008), Voluntarism and the Single Channel: the Development of Single-Channel Worker Representation in the UK, in: International Journal of Comparative Labour Law and Industrial Relations 24, 87–121
- Dukes, Ruth (2009), Otto Kahn-Freund and Collective Laissez-Faire: An Edifice without a Keystone?, in: Modern Law Review 72, 220–246
- Ewing, Keith (1998), The State and Industrial Relations: ›Collective Laissez-Faire‹ Revisited, in: Historical Studies in Industrial Relations 5, 1–31
- Flanders, Allan (1968), Collective Bargaining: A Theoretical Analysis, in: British Journal of Industrial Relations 6, 1–26
- Hepple, Bob (1986), The Making of Labour Law in Europe: A Comparative Study of Nine Countries up to 1945, London
- Kahn-Freund, Otto (1959), Labour Law, in: Ginsberg, Morris (ed.), Law and Opinion in England in the 20th Century, London, 215–263
- Kahn-Freund, Otto (1977), Industrial Democracy, in: Industrial Law Journal 6, 65–84
- Labour Party (1933) = Joint Meeting of the Economic Committee of the Trades Unions Congress and the Policy Committee of the Labour Party, 08.03.1933: Labour Party NEC Minutes
- Labour Party (1974) = Labour Party Manifesto February 1974. Let us work together – Labour's way out of the crisis, available at http://www.labour-party.org.uk/manifestos/1974/Feb/1974-feb-labour-manifesto.shtml
- Legrand, Pierre (2017), Jameses at Play: A Tractation on the Comparison of Laws, in: American Journal of Comparative Law 65, 1–132
- Letter (1933) = Letter Ernest Bevin to Walter Citrine on ›Public Control and Regulation of Industry and Trade 3 January 1933 MSS.292/574.1/4
- Mcdonald, G. W., Howard F. Gospel (1973), The Mond-Turner Talks, 1927–1933: A Study in Industrial Co-Operation, in: The Historical Journal 16, 807–829
- Morrison, Herbert (1933), Socialisation and Transport, London

71 Kahn-Freund (1977) 71.

- MUNSHI, SHERALLY (2015), You Will See My Family Become so American: Toward a Minor Comparativism, in: American Journal of Comparative Law 63, 655–718
- PHILLIPS, JIM (2011), UK Business Power and Opposition to the Bullock Committee's 1977 Proposals on Worker Directors, in: Historical Studies in Industrial Relations 31–32,1, 1–30
- PRIBIĆEVIĆ, BORIS (1959), The Shop Stewards' Movement and Workers' Control, 1910–1922, Oxford
- Report (1968) = Report of the Royal Commission on Trade Unions and Employers' Associations, H.M.S.O, Cmnd. 3623, London
- Report (1977) = Report of the Committee of Inquiry on Industrial Democracy, H.M.S.O., Cmnd. 6706, London
- ROBERTS, ERNIE (1973), Workers' Control, London
- TUC (1932a) = TUC Report on Public Control and Regulation of Industry and Trade, submitted to the TUC Congress at Newcastle
- TUC (1932b) = TUC Standing Orders, Appendix B, 64th Annual Report of the Trades Union Congress, London
- TUC (1933) = Economic Committee, General Council's Report of Public Control and Regulation of Industry, Economic Committee 3/2 3 January 1933, Modern Records Centre, MSS.292/574.1/4
- TUC (1934) = Economic Committee, Workers' Control in Industry, Economic Committee 1/2 12 December 1934, Modern Records Centre, MSS.292/574.1/3
- TUC (1977) = TUC General Council Minutes, 26 January 1977, item 42, TUC MSS.292D/574.93/4
- TUCKER, ERIC (2017), On Writing Labour Law History: A Reconnaissance, in: International Journal of Comparative Labour Law and Industrial Relations 33, 39–57
- WEBB, SIDNEY, BEATRICE WEBB (1897), Industrial Democracy, London
- WEBB, SIDNEY, BEATRICE WEBB (1920), The History of British Trade Unionism, London
- WILLIAMSON, ADRIAN (2016), The Bullock Report on Industrial Democracy and the Post-War Consensus, in: Contemporary British History 30, 119–149
- ZAHN, REBECCA (2015), German Codetermination without Nationalization, and British Nationalization without Codetermination: Retelling the Story, in: Historical Studies in Industrial Relations 36, 1–27
- ZAHN, REBECCA (2020), Finding New Ways of »Doing« Socio-Legal Labor Law History in Germany and the UK: Introducing a »Minor Comparativism«, in: German Law Journal 21, 1378–1392

HILLS OF BROOKLYN
THROB

Thorsten Keiser

Angestellte zwischen Rechts- und Sozialgeschichte: Forschungsfragen zur Entstehung einer Arbeitnehmerkategorie[1]

I. Einleitung

Die Entwicklung der Kategorie der Angestellten fällt in eine Zeit, in der Arbeitsrecht in erster Linie berufsständisch geprägtes Statusrecht war. Die Welt der Arbeit erwies sich als ziemlich resistent gegen die naturrechtlichen Abstraktionen, die seit etwa 1800 zu einer Überwindung der ständischen Gliederung des Rechts geführt hatten. Sie implizierte eine Neuorganisation unter Berücksichtigung der Bedürfnisse und Pflichten von »Individuen«, die eben grundsätzlich nicht bestimmten Kategorien zugeordnet werden sollten. Statt Personen auf bestimmten sozialen Stufen zu erfassen, stellte man rechtsfähige Menschen in den Mittelpunkt. Im Bereich der Arbeit war eine Auffächerung in normativ geprägte Standesmodelle jedoch nach wie vor relevant. Auch in der zunehmend industrialisierten Privatrechtsgesellschaft des 19. Jahrhunderts gab es deutliche Grenzen zwischen Gesinde, Gesellen, gewerblichen Arbeitern oder Heimarbeiterinnen. Berufsständisch geprägtes Recht ist nicht denkbar ohne ein bestimmtes Selbstverständnis. Immer wieder wird beschrieben, wie Angestellte neue variable Identitäten in Abgrenzung zum Klassenbewusstsein der Arbeiter herausbildeten.[2] »Angestellter« war in der ökonomisch-sozialwissenschaftlichen Terminologie ein Begriff, der sich erst nach dem des Arbeiters im allgemeinen Sprachgebrauch als Sammelbezeichnung für verschiedene, nicht körperliche Arbeiten etabliert hatte.[3] Zum Rechtsbegriff wurde »Angestellter« zuerst im Versicherungsrecht, mit dem Gesetz über die Angestelltenversicherung vom 20. Dezember 1911.[4] Hierbei ging es zunächst um Ausgleich für eine als unbefriedigend empfundene Altersversorgung von Menschen, die Bürotätigkeiten ausübten.[5] Klar war dabei aber auch, dass man eine eigene Regelung für den »Mittelstand« schaffen wollte, der sich damit von der Lohnarbeiterschaft abgrenzte.[6]

Das Eigentümliche daran ist, dass kategoriale Einteilung arbeitender Menschen immer auch einen sozialen Konsens darüber voraussetzt, wer zu welcher Gruppe gehört. Soziale Rollenbilder prägten die Arbeitswelt und ihr Recht viel stärker als heute. Ohne klare Rollenerwartungen an Dienstboten, die sich über Jahrhunderte hinweg stabilisiert hatten, wäre etwa kein Gesinderecht denkbar gewesen. Bei dieser Herausbildung von Standesvorstellungen konstituierten Arbeitnehmer- und Arbeitgeberperspektiven die Basis für bestimmte soziale Rollenbilder. Nicht unerheblich ist dabei die Prägung durch informelle Normen. Insofern ist klar, dass bei der Erforschung des Rechts der Angestellten besondere Synergien zwischen Rechts- und Sozialgeschichte zu erwarten sind. In den folgenden Ausführungen soll daher der Versuch gemacht werden, neue Anregungen für einen weiteren Dialog zwischen Rechts- und Sozialgeschichte auf einem Feld zu entwickeln, das von der Rechtsgeschichte weitgehend ignoriert wurde, während sozialgeschichtliche Literatur dazu zahlreich existiert.[7]

1 Einführungsvortrag, gehalten auf der Jahrestagung des Arbeitskreises Arbeitsrechtsgeschichte (Max-Planck-Institut für europäische Rechtsgeschichte / Hugo-Sinzheimer-Institut Frankfurt am Main) »Die Rechtsgeschichte des Angestelltenverhältnisses« am 6. Dezember 2019. Der Vortragsstil wurde im Wesentlichen beibehalten.

2 Siehe unten III. 1. a) und b).

3 Glootz (1999) 26 f.

4 Versicherungsgesetz für Angestellte vom 20. Dezember 1911, RGBl. I, 989–1061.

5 Zum Versicherungsstatus der Angestellten vor 1911 Apitz (1967) 69 ff.

6 Zu den Motiven etwa zeitgenössisch Manes / Königsberger (1912) 9 f.

7 Bibliographisch Schulz (2000). Über den Ansatz, Gerichtsurteile als Quelle für die sozialen Verhältnisse der Angestellten zu erschließen, vgl. Haupt (2018).

II. Angestellte zwischen Individualismus und kollektivem Selbstbewusstsein

Wenn man die Kategorie der Angestellten als rechthistorischen Forschungsgegenstand erfassen will, kann man sich über soziologische Literatur annähern. Angestellte waren Träger einer eigenen Kultur, bestimmter Konsummöglichkeiten, die man als typisch für die Moderne ansah.[8] Aus Sicht der Rechtsgeschichte ist noch ein weiterer Umstand bemerkenswert: Die Kategorie der Angestellten im Sinne eines »Standes« erhielt gerade besondere Konturen in einer Zeit, in der auch die Idee berufsständischen Rechts zunehmend relativiert werden sollte. Walter Kaskel beschrieb in seinem Lehrbuch des Arbeitsrechts zu Beginn der Weimarer Republik, wie das Arbeitsrecht seiner Zeit von der Suche nach Vereinheitlichung im Sinne einer »einfachen Formel« geprägt war,[9] muss dann aber konstatieren, dass das »neue Recht« letztlich ein »Sonderrecht bestimmter Berufsstände« geblieben sei und als »neues Arbeitsrecht« in ein »Arbeiterrecht und ein Angestelltenrecht« zerfalle.[10]

Auf anderen Ebenen erlebte der berufsständische Gedanke andererseits eine Renaissance. Manche wünschten sich als Reaktion auf die Massengesellschaft eine Rückbindung von Menschen an ihr soziales Umfeld, um ein Auseinanderdriften der durch den Individualismus angeblich atomisierten Gesellschaft zu verhindern. In Ansätzen einer organischen Neuformierung des Rechts sollten auch Stände wieder eine Rolle spielen. Mit ständischer Neugliederung wurde die Hoffnung verbunden, den Gegensatz zwischen Arbeit und Kapital überwinden zu können und gleichzeitig die als problematisch empfundene Entfernung von Staat und Gesellschaft. In der Weimarer Verfassung wurde der Reichswirtschaftsrat zum Anknüpfungspunkt solcher Überlegungen einer Etablierung des ständischen Gedankens in der Wirtschaft.[11]

Angestellte passen in dieses Schema nicht hinein. Sie entwickelten zwar ein Gruppenbewusstsein, dieses war aber keineswegs antiindividualistisch. Angestellte waren abhängig arbeitende Menschen, orientierten sich aber tendenziell an Selbständigen. Exemplarisch dafür kann ein Gerichtsurteil aus dem Jahr 1905 angeführt werden. Das Kaufmannsgericht München hatte über den Fall eines Handlungsgehilfen zu entscheiden, der die Bezahlung von Überstunden verlangte.[12] Er behauptete, in einem Zeitraum von Januar bis März 180 ½ Überstunden geleistet zu haben und verlangte dafür einen Stundenlohn von 0,75 Pfennigen. Zur Begründung berief sich der Handlungsgehilfe auf eine in München bestehende »Handelsusance«, nach welcher für Überstunden Entschädigung gewährt werde.[13] Das ist bemerkenswert, denn der Handelsbrauch ist bekanntlich eine Figur des Gewohnheitsrechts, das zwischen selbstständigen Kaufleuten entsteht. Der klagende Handlungsgehilfe war aber lediglich kleiner Angestellter in einem Warenhaus. Sozial stand er auf keiner sehr hohen Stufe.[14] Womöglich hatte er keine Chance, jemals ein selbständiges Handelsgewerbe zu begründen, es sei denn, er stammte selbst aus einer Kaufmannsfamilie, was ihm die Aussicht auf späteren Eintritt in das elterliche Geschäft verschafft hätte. Das hinderte ihn aber nicht daran, vor Gericht mit dem Selbstverständnis eines Kaufmanns aufzutreten. Gerade diese Haltung wurde ihm jedoch im vorliegenden Fall zum Nachteil. Bei seiner Entscheidung stellte das Gericht auf ortsübliche Gepflogenheiten ab. Es kam zu dem Ergebnis, dass in München bei Überstunden in der Regel nur ein Abendessen oder stattdessen eine Entschädigung von einer Mark pro Tag zu beanspruchen sei.[15] Das Gericht bezeichnete diese Gewohnheit nicht als Handelsbrauch, sondern als »Ortsgebrauch«. Bemerkenswert ist nicht dieser Umstand, sondern die weitere Argumentation: Der Handlungsgehilfe sei im Gegensatz zu den Gewerbegehilfen besser bezahlt, erhalte längeren Urlaub und habe eine mehrstündige Tischzeit.[16] Auch sei er gegen Monatslohn angestellt, anders als der Gewerbegehilfe, der mit Tagelohn bezahlt werde. Beim Tagelohn sei die Vergütung von Überstunden angemessen, bei Monatslohn aber nicht. Hier sieht man klar die berühmte »Kragenlinie«. Sie verläuft zwischen Gewerbe und Handel. Darüber hinaus habe der Kläger im vorliegenden Fall

8 Vgl. unten III. 1. b).
9 Zur Vereinheitlichung in Bezug auf das Angestelltenrecht siehe unten III. 1. a).
10 Kaskel (1921) 26 f.
11 Zeitgenössisch Hauschild (1926).
12 Urteil des KG-München vom 19. Juni 1905, in: Baum (Hg.) (1912) 442 f.
13 Baum (Hg.) (1912).
14 Zu Lohnmodalitäten und sozialer Stellung der Handlungsgehilfen um 1900: Pierenkemper (1987) 128 ff.
15 Pierenkemper (1987) 443.
16 Baum (Hg.) (1912) 442 f.

bei der Neueinrichtung eines großen Warenhauses mitgearbeitet.[17] So hätte ihm von vornherein klar sein müssen, dass mäßige Überschreitungen der gewöhnlichen Arbeitszeit unvermeidlich seien. Sie wurden hier auch von einem einfachen Angestellten verlangt. Der privilegierte Status, welchen der Angestellte reklamierte, auf den er vielleicht auch stolz war, führte letztlich zu einer Schlechterstellung in Bezug auf die Überstunden. Man erwartete von ihm persönliches Engagement, dass man beim Lohnarbeiter eben nicht erwartete.

Individualismus und die prinzipielle Orientierung an höheren Ebenen der sozialen Hierarchie bedeutete freilich nicht, dass Angestellte sich nicht in Verbänden zusammenschlossen. Der Deutsche Handlungsgehilfenverband war die bekannteste Organisation dieser Art.[18] Solche Verbände hatten es sich aber gerade zur Aufgabe gemacht, die Sonderstellung des Angestelltenverhältnisses zu verteidigen. Angestellte wollten gerade nicht in der Masse der arbeitenden Menschen aufgehen, sondern ihre eigenen Spielräume bewahren. Sie waren somit Individualisten in anti-individualistischer Zeit.

III. Sozialwissenschaft und Sozialgeschichte

Bei der sozialgeschichtlichen Annäherung kann man in zwei Literaturgattungen unterscheiden. Zum einen ist die zeitgenössische Sozialwissenschaft relevant, die sich den Angestellten schon seit dem späteren 19. Jahrhundert widmete.[19] Diese Richtung war eindeutig interdisziplinär. Ökonomische, juristische und soziologische Argumentationsmuster gingen dabei oft Hand in Hand. Auf der anderen Seite setzte in den siebziger Jahren des 20. Jahrhunderts eine bemerkenswerte Forschungstätigkeit auf Seiten der Sozialgeschichte der Bundesrepublik Deutschland zu den Angestellten ein.

1. *Zeitgenössische Betrachtungen*

a) Sozialreform und Arbeitsrecht vor dem Ersten Weltkrieg

Unter zeitgenössischer Sozialwissenschaft kann man empirische Untersuchungen eines bestimmten Wirtschaftsbereichs fassen, die oft durch Umfragen beteiligter Akteure durchgeführt wurden. Solche Studien sind aus dem Umfeld des Vereins für Socialpolitik bekannt. Sie dokumentieren den Erfahrungsaustausch von Wissenschaft und Praxis. Im Bereich der Angestellten entfaltete vor allem die 1901 gegründete Gesellschaft für soziale Reform solche Aktivitäten.[20] Anders als beim von sog. »Kathedersozialisten« getragenen Verein für Socialpolitik waren hier nicht Wissenschaftler federführend, sondern eher bürgerliche, den »gewerblichen Frieden« betonende Sozialpolitiker, wie der Freiherr von Berlepsch. Die vierte Generalversammlung der Gesellschaft für soziale Reform widmete sich 1909 bei einem Kongress in Frankfurt am Main dem »Recht der Privatbeamten« und deren Pensionsversicherung.[21] Bei der Eröffnung von Bürgermeister Franz Adickes und dem Freiherrn von Berlepsch wurden zunächst die anwesenden Frauen begrüßt, die zum ersten Mal an den Verhandlungen der Gesellschaft teilnehmen durften. Zuvor waren sie in abgegrenzte Räume verwiesen worden, wo sie zwar »zuhören, aber nicht mitsprechen« durften.[22] Hier wird schon ein erstes charakteristisches Merkmal der Beobachtungen des Angestelltenverhältnisses deutlich: Es wurden auch weibliche Erwerbsbiografien dabei berücksichtigt. Zuvor war das in dieser Form nur bei den Heimarbeiterinnen der Fall gewesen, in gewissem Maße auch beim Gesinderecht, das männliche und weibliche Rollenbilder normiert hatte.

Mit der Zunahme weiblicher Arbeitskräfte im Bereich der Angestelltenverhältnisse entstanden neue Möglichkeiten zum Vergleich zwischen der

17 Baum (Hg.) (1912) 442 f.

18 Dazu Martin Otto in diesem Rg-Fokus: Otto (2022).

19 Überblick bei Mangold (1981) 13 ff.

20 Zur Gesellschaft für Soziale Reform Bruch (2005) 248 ff.

21 Die Ergebnisse sind dokumentiert in: Vorstand der Gesellschaft für Soziale Reform (Hg.) (1909). Ein Jahr zuvor waren bereits zwei Bände mit dem Titel »Der Dienstvertrag der Privatangestellten« erschienen: Baum et al. (1908).

22 Vorstand der Gesellschaft für Soziale Reform (Hg.) (1909) 2441.

Entlohnung männlicher und weiblicher Arbeitskräfte. Zwar gab es auch im Bereich der Angestellten unterschiedliche Rollenbilder männlicher und weiblicher Arbeit, jedoch zahlreiche von beiden Geschlechtern wahrgenommene Tätigkeitsbereiche, was die Möglichkeit zum direkten Gehaltsvergleich eröffnete, mit dem Ergebnis, dass die weiblichen Arbeitskräfte oft weniger verdienten.[23] Bei Tätigkeiten der Angestellten konnte man die ungleiche Bezahlung nicht mehr mit einem weniger an Arbeitseffizienz aufgrund geringerer körperlicher Leistungskraft rechtfertigen, wie das bei anderen Bereichen über Jahrhunderte hinweg getan wurde.

Ein Anliegen der Gesellschaft für soziale Reform war es, den Arbeiterschutz auszuweiten und sich dabei nicht mehr nur auf die »lohnarbeitenden Handarbeiter« zu beschränken.[24] Wie die Arbeiter seien auch die Angestellten Hilfskräfte der Industrie, und wie sie seien sie auch erst mit der Großindustrie entstanden. Man konstatierte das stetige Anwachsen einer Gruppe abhängig Beschäftigter, die, anders als die Arbeiter, bisher von Rechtswissenschaft und Sozialpolitik noch nicht genügend beachtet worden seien.[25] Eine umfangreiche Diskussion zu arbeitsrechtlichen Fragen der Angestellten mit vielen Beiträgen von Praktikern sollte diese Lücke füllen. Sie wurde eingeleitet von dem Arbeitsrechtler und Sozialpolitiker Heinz Potthoff, der damals liberaler Reichstagsabgeordneter war.[26] Potthoff arbeitete die sozialen und rechtlichen Unterschiede zwischen Arbeitern und Angestellten heraus und stellte fest, dass für die Arbeiterschaft der Kampf um mehr Lohn zentral gewesen sei, während für die Angestellten die Sicherheit des Arbeitsverhältnisses in Form von Kündigungsschutz im Vordergrund stand.[27] Der Arbeiter lege »auf die Freiheit im Arbeitsvertrage das Hauptgewicht«, während dem Angestellten eher an der Sicherheit des Arbeitsverhältnisses gelegen sei.[28] Hier ist ein plausibler Unterschied herausgearbeitet, der seine Ursache im überlieferten Rollenverständnis der unterschiedlichen Arbeitnehmerkategorien hat. Die gewerblichen Arbeiter des 19. Jahrhunderts sind erwachsen aus den Gesellen des alten Handwerks und versuchten einen guten Teil der zünftigen Traditionen in die Fabrik hinüber zu retten. Frei sollte der Geselle sein, seinen Meister nach Möglichkeit selbst auszuwählen und die Arbeitsstelle schnell wechseln zu dürfen, wenn es günstig oder notwendig erschien. Gesellen hatten sich gegen die Fesselung an das Arbeitsverhältnis durch zu harte Vertragsbruchvorschriften gewendet.[29] Man wollte keine Sanktionen bei Austritt aus dem Arbeitsverhältnis. Genau diese Forderung ließ sich dann später in die Forderung nach Streikrecht umwandeln, denn Streik war ursprünglich aus Sicht der Gesetzgebung nichts anderes als Kontraktbruch, also Nichtleistung.[30] Flexibilität und Dynamik, sowie die Möglichkeit zu kollektiven Protesten, waren ein Anliegen der Gesellen und später der Industriearbeiter.

Für die Angestellten wird auch von der späteren sozialhistorischen Literatur festgestellt, dass der Kündigungsschutz einer ihrer großen Vorteile gewesen sei.[31] Dabei ging es aber zunächst noch nicht um materiellen Kündigungsschutz, nach heutigem Verständnis, sondern lediglich um »Zeitschutz«.[32] Mehr Kündigungsschutz bedeutete längere Kündigungsfristen bei der ordentlichen Kündigung und womöglich eine für den Arbeitnehmer günstige Handhabung der Voraussetzungen einer außerordentlichen Kündigung.

Insgesamt deutet sich hier schon ein großer Unterschied an, der das Verständnis des Angestelltenrechts im 20. Jahrhundert generell prägen sollte. Streikrecht war darin keine zentrale rechtspolitische Forderung. Man dachte eher vom Individuum her, als vom Kollektiv. Deutlich wird das auch in einer Sammlung von Berichten aus der Praxis zum »Dienstvertrag der Privatangestellten« von 1908. Dort werden u. a. die »Wünsche« verschiedener Gruppen von Angestellten zusammen-

23 In Bezug auf Handlungsgehilfen Pierenkemper (1987) 132 f. m.w.N. auch zum Problemkreis der Lohnkonkurrenz zwischen Männern und Frauen.
24 Pierenkemper (1987) 2442.
25 Pierenkemper (1987).
26 Biographisch Seelig (2008), insbes. 160 ff.
27 Vorstand der Gesellschaft für Soziale Reform (Hg.) (1909) 2460.
28 Potthoff (1908).
29 Insgesamt Keiser (2013) 329 ff.
30 Keiser (2013) 284 ff.
31 Siehe unten III. 2.
32 Als Beispiel siehe einen Bericht über eine Forderung von »Mindestkündigungsfristen« bei technischen Angestellten in: Baum et al. (1908) Bd. 1, 100.

gefasst. Eine Erweiterung des Koalitionsrechts kommt vor,[33] aber eher als ein Wunsch unter vielen, wie Lohnfortzahlung im Krankheitsfall oder die Regelung von Ruhepausen.[34] Manche der rechtspolitischen Themen spiegelten auch den Wunsch nach Anerkennung individueller Leistungen, wie das oft diskutierte Thema des Erfinderschutzes bei den technischen Angestellten,[35] oder individuelle Statusfragen, wie die Versuche der Verwaltungsangestellten auf Gutshöfen, sog. »Güterbeamten«, sich vom Gesinderecht abzugrenzen.[36]

Heinz Potthoff schien die marginale Rolle des Streiks bei seinem Referat auf der Konferenz der Gesellschaft für Soziale Reform von 1909 als selbstverständliche Voraussetzung von Angestelltenrecht ebenfalls zu Grunde zu legen. Die Forderung nach Lohngerechtigkeit für Angestellte wurde bei ihm vornehmlich als Problem des § 138 BGB diskutiert,[37] nicht als Frage kollektiven Arbeitsrechts.[38] Potthoff begrüßte, dass das Kaufmannsgericht Berlin erste Schritte gemacht habe, über die Sittenwidrigkeitsklausel für gerechtere Lohnverhältnisse zu sorgen. Wenn eine Ladenangestellte oder ein Familienvater sich weit unter Wert anstellen ließen, geschehe das wohl aus einer Notlage heraus, was die Rechtsprechung berücksichtigen müsse.[39]

Ein weiteres typisches Problem des Angestelltenrechts sah man im nachvertraglichen Konkurrenzverbot.[40] Blickt man in die Praxis, zeigt sich, dass Streitigkeiten über die Wirksamkeit von Konkurrenzklauseln vor dem Ersten Weltkrieg einen der Schwerpunkte der Tätigkeit der Kaufmannsgerichte ausmachten.[41] Autoren wie Potthoff plädierten dafür, die Konkurrenzklausel zumindest stark zu beschränken. Abzulehnen sei die Behinderung des Fortkommens der Angestellten »im rein privaten Vermögensinteresse des früheren Arbeitgebers«.[42] Abhilfe sollten Rechtsprechung und Gesetzgebung schaffen.

Letztlich sah man sich aber immer mit demselben Grundproblem konfrontiert: Die wirksame Umsetzung der Forderungen eines sozialeren Angestelltenrechts war nicht möglich ohne eine rechtssichere Statuszuweisung. Somit mündete die von den empirischen Untersuchungen konstatierte Differenzierung verschiedener Verhältnisse stets in die rechtspolitische Forderung einer konsequenten Rechtsvereinheitlichung.[43]

Diese Forderung wurde auch von Hugo Sinzheimer geteilt und mit praktischen Beispielen untermauert.[44] Auch Sinzheimer sah es als Nachteil an, dass etwa der Handlungsgehilfe sein Recht »zunächst durch das Handlungsgehilfenrecht des Handelsgesetzbuchs, desweiteren durch die Vorschriften der Reichsgewerbeordnung und des Bürgerlichen Gesetzbuchs« empfange.[45] Wer bei einem Kaufmann die Bücher führe, unterliege dem Handlungsgehilfenrecht des HGB. Wer aber dieselbe Arbeit auf einem landwirtschaftlichen Gut verrichte, bei einem Rechtsanwalt oder einem Berufsverband, verliere den Handlungsgehilfenstatus und unterliege lediglich dem (weniger spezifischen) Recht des BGB, da kein Handelsgewerbe vorliege.[46] Wirft man einen Blick auf die Rechtsprechung, zeigt sich die praktische Tragweite dieser Statuszuordnungsprobleme. Unzählige Urteile finden sich zur Frage, wer überhaupt Handlungsgehilfe sei. Man begegnet Handlangern, Berichterstattern, Stenographen, Kolporteuren, Schaufensterdekorateuren, Milchkutschern, Platzanweisern und Detektiven etc., die alle Handlungsgehilfen sein wollen.[47] Die Kritik an solchen Abgrenzungsproblemen erfolgte jedoch bei Sinzheimer mit anderen Akzenten als bei Potthoff. Sinzheimer forderte nachdrücklich – im Gegensatz zu

33 Etwa bei den technischen Angestellten, siehe Baum et al. (1908) Bd. 1, 98.

34 Siehe dazu die Zusammenstellung der Forderungen von technischen Angestellten in gewerblichen Betrieben in: Baum et al. (1908) Bd. 2, 18.

35 Siehe Baum et al. (1908) Bd. 2, 49 ff.

36 Baum et al. (1908) Bd. 1, 111 ff.

37 Zu entsprechenden Entscheidungen aus der Gewerbegerichtsbarkeit demnächst ausführlich Allstadt.

38 Vorstand der Gesellschaft für Soziale Reform (Hg.) (1909) 2463.

39 Vorstand der Gesellschaft für Soziale Reform (Hg.) (1909).

40 Umfassend dazu Baum et al. (1908) Bd. 1, 131 ff.; Seelig (2008) 2461. Weitere Urteilsanalysen zum Konkurrenzverbot demnächst in Allstadt.

41 Zusammenfassend zur Tendenz der Rechtsprechung vgl. Baum et al. (1908) Bd. 1, 152.

42 Vorstand der Gesellschaft für Soziale Reform (Hg.) (1909).

43 So auch die zentrale Aussage von Potthoff (1908).

44 Sinzheimer (1914).

45 Sinzheimer (1914) 7.

46 Sinzheimer (1914) 11.

47 Zu weiteren Urteilen, auch im Hinblick auf die Abgrenzung von Angestelltenverhältnissen zu selbständiger Arbeit, gerade bei Reisenden oder Kellnern demnächst Allstadt.

Potthoff – Arbeiterausschüsse, also Mitbestimmung, zur Sicherung der Freiheit des arbeitenden Menschen.[48] Bei den Angestellten sah auch Sinzheimer die große Gefahr für die Freiheit des Arbeitsvertrags in den Konkurrenzklauseln. Während diese nach Ansicht von Potthoff jedoch durch zwingendes Vertragsrecht einzudämmen waren, bemerkte Sinzheimer, dass der Gesetzgeber nicht der alleinige und vielleicht nicht einmal der zentrale Akteur zur Vereinheitlichung des Arbeitsrechts sein könne.[49] Wie es seiner zentralen Argumentationslinie aus dieser Zeit entsprach, forderte er auch hier eine Rechtsschöpfung durch »die gesellschaftlichen Kräfte«, denen man objektive Rechtswirkung zuerkennen müsse.[50] Entscheidend ist dann natürlich der Tarifvertrag. Dezentralisierung und Vereinheitlichung seien eben kein Widerspruch, sondern sich gegenseitig ergänzende Elemente. Bei Potthoffs Ansatz, der sich auf Gesetzgebung und Rechtsprechung konzentriert, spielt der Tarifvertrag hingegen eine geringere Rolle.

Wie man insgesamt beobachten kann, erhielt die Forderung nach Vereinheitlichung des Arbeitsrechts wichtige Impulse von einer nach 1900 einsetzenden Debatte um das Angestelltenrecht.[51] Soziale Forderungen wurden auch für die Angestellten immer deutlicher formuliert, mit eher invidualvertraglichen (Potthoff) oder kollektiven Tendenzen (Sinzheimer). Auch im Kontext eines einheitlichen Arbeitsrechts sollte Angestelltenrecht jedoch mit spezifischen Konturen erkennbar bleiben.[52] Die berühmte »Kragenlinie«[53] erwies sich als hartnäckig, auch im Bereich der Rechtswissenschaft.

b) Siegfried Kracauers »Angestellte« – eine Analyse aus der Weimarer Zeit

Die berühmteste Analyse der Angestellten überhaupt ist das Werk von Siegfried Kracauer, das 1929 zum ersten Mal in der Frankfurter Zeitung veröffentlicht wurde.[54] Es faszinierte und fasziniert als Buch über die Großstadt, die Moderne, die Kultur der Massen, das Lebensgefühl einer neuen Mittelschicht, die Suche nach Identität, Selbstverwirklichung, Radikalität, Konformismus und Rebellion. Davon abgesehen wurden darin aber auch die großen Themen der soziologischen Studien über die Angestellten bereits vorgezeichnet, die in der Zeit nach dem Zweiten Weltkrieg ausführlich wieder aufgegriffen und eingehend diskutiert worden sind.[55] Kracauer beschrieb schon die politische Einstellung der Angestellten und ihrer Interessenvertretungen. Den Gesamtverband deutscher Angestelltengewerkschaften ordnete Kracauer dem christlich nationalen Flügel der Gewerkschaften zu und beschrieb ihn als Gegner des Sozialismus, der darüber hinaus mit antisemitischen Einstellungen behaftet sei.[56] Zu erforschen wäre, wo Spuren politischer Einstellungen von Angestellten sich in der Rechtspraxis auswirkten. In einem Urteil des Kaufmannsgerichts Mannheim von 1907 ging es beispielsweise um die Kündigung eines Angestellten eines »jüdischen Prinzipals«, der Kunden seines Arbeitgebers antisemitisch beleidigt und sich darauf berufen hatte, dass er als Angehöriger des Deutschnationalen Handlungsgehilfenverbands Juden nicht bediene. Das Gericht sah die Kündigung als rechtmäßig an, da der Prinzipal nicht dulden müsse, dass ein Angestellter sich antisemitischer Tendenzen rühme.[57]

Hier war schon der soziologisch-analytische Zusammenhang gekennzeichnet, der gerade nach 1960 für intensive Diskussionen sorgte, nämlich die Frage nach der politischen Tendenz der Angestellten, denen man gemeinhin Gewerkschaftsferne, Staatsnähe und teilweise Neigungen zu Positionen aus dem rechten politischen Spektrum zuschrieb.[58] Wie Walter Benjamin in einer Rezension zu Kracauers »Angestellten« ausführte, charakterisiert dieser die Ideologie der Angestellten als eine »einzigartige Überblendung der gegebenen ökonomischen Wirklichkeit, die der des Proletariats sehr nah kommt, durch Erinnerungs- und Wunschbilder aus dem Bürgertum«.[59] Oft bestä-

48 Sinzheimer (1914) 29.
49 Sinzheimer (1914) 35.
50 Sinzheimer (1914).
51 Siehe auch das Fazit von Bohle (1990) 136 f.
52 So auch 1914 in der Konzeption Sinzheimers (1914) 35.
53 Zum Begriff Kocka (1981b).
54 Als Buchausgabe: Kracauer (1930).
55 Siehe dazu den folgenden Abschnitt.
56 Kracauer (1930) 14.
57 Urteil des Kaufmannsgerichts Mannheim vom 20. August 1907, in: Baum (Hg.) (1912) 513.
58 Ausführlich Kocka (1981a) 148 ff.
59 Benjamin (1930/1971) 117.

tigt ist die während der Weimarer Republik schon mehrfach geäußerte, von Kracauer aufgenommene These, dass die Angestellten eine neue »industrielle Reservearmee«[60] bildeten, welche einen unerfüllbaren Traum vom Mittelstand träumte. Geistig und emotional seien sie somit heimatlos, da sie weder in der Welt des klassenbewussten Proletariats, noch der des Bürgertums ihren Platz finden konnten.[61] Auch wenn die Ebene der politischen Einstellung bei Kracauer nur *en passant* erwähnt wird, leuchtet unmittelbar ein, dass diese Akzentuierung der Heimatlosigkeit mit Verführbarkeit zu politischen Extremen assoziiert werden kann.

2. *Rechtshistorische Beobachtungen der Sozialgeschichte nach 1945*

In der Sozialgeschichtsschreibung der 1970er Jahre wurde die Frage nach den politischen Tendenzen der Angestellten nachdrücklicher gestellt. Angestelltenforschung wurde immer expliziter zur Ursachenforschung für das Abgleiten einer Personengruppe in die Nähe zur Diktatur, das etwa in der Studie von Jürgen Kocka über Angestellte zwischen Faschismus und Demokratie erörtert wurde.[62] Bemerkenswert ist das Werk auch aus rechtshistorischer Perspektive. Es gibt Aufschluss über eine Wechselwirkung der schon in den 1930er Jahren viel beschriebenen, kulturell herausgebildeten Angestelltenmentalität, oder des Angestelltenbewusstseins, und bestimmten Rechtsfiguren oder normativen Grundeigenschaften von Angestelltenverhältnissen. Begibt man sich auf diese Beobachtungsebene, erlangt man Erkenntnisse über das Zusammenspiel von Sein und Sollen, über die Verbindung soziologisch feststellbarer Faktoren und gesetzgeberischer oder richterlicher Gestaltung von Recht.

Eine sozialhistorische Beobachtung bezieht sich auf den Unterschied zwischen Lohn und Gehalt.[63] Gehalt sei feststehend, nicht markt- und leistungsabhängig.[64] Das Gehalt sei somit keinen Schwankungen unterworfen. Das mache die Leistung des Angestellten weniger messbar, weniger kontrollierbar. Somit mussten Angestellte eine Art Vertrauensvorschuss genießen, da sie eine eher abstrakte Gegenleistung erhielten, die zunächst einmal gerechtfertigt werden musste. Das alles rückt das Verhältnis der Angestellten eher in die Nähe des freien Dienstvertrages als in die Nähe des Lohnarbeitsverhältnisses. Mentalitäten prägen Statusvorstellungen und diese prägen Vertragsinhalte, die sich wiederum gewohnheitsrechtlich verdichten. Die Idee des Vertrauensvorsprungs, die in der Terminologie des Gehalts zum Ausdruck kommen soll, spiegelt sich auch in der ehemals versicherungsrechtlich relevanten Bezeichnung der Angestellten als »Privatbeamte«. Diese mochte impliziert haben, dass Angestellte sich als loyale Verbündete ihres Arbeitgebers fühlen wollten, die sich – gleich Staatsbediensteten – in Pflichtbindungen und Treueverhältnissen sahen.[65] In der Praxis dürfte sich der Unterschied zwischen Leistungslohn und Gehalt freilich relativiert haben, da die besondere Leistung von Angestellten oft in Form besonderer Provisionen honoriert wurde. Jedenfalls musste, was unter dem Gehalt der Angestellten zu verstehen war, im Laufe der Zeit richterrechtlich konkretisiert werden. 1904 hatte das Kammergericht Berlin etwa zu entscheiden, ob eine Umsatzprovision, sowie Kost und Wohnung zum Gehalt gezählt werden sollten.[66] Schon vom Sprachgebrauch her sei Gehalt etwas anderes als eine Provision, meine das Gericht, aber auch zu unterscheiden vom Unterhalt, weshalb Naturalbezüge und Gehalt zu trennen seien. Kost und Logis durften im vorliegenden Fall also nicht in das Bargehalt mit einberechnet werden.

Ansonsten weist auch das Verständnis von Leistung und Gegenleistung bereits vor dem Ersten Weltkrieg Parallelen zum heute geltenden Arbeitsrecht auf. Das Kaufmannsgericht Hamburg hatte etwa 1908 festgestellt, dass Gratifikationen eines Prinzipals an den Handlungsgehilfen keine unverbindlichen Leistungen waren, sondern, sofern sie sich wiederholten oder zugesichert wurden,

60 Kracauer (1930) 13.
61 Kracauer (1930) 91.
62 Kocka (1977) insbes. 17–57.
63 Kocka (1977) 49.
64 Kocka (1977).
65 Zur ursprünglichen Nähe des Angestellten- zum Beamtenbegriff Kocka (1981a) 116 ff.
66 Urteil des Kammergerichts Berlin vom 14. Mai 1904, in: Baum (Hg.) (1912) Bd. 2, 490; allerdings im Kontext einer Norm (§ 68 HGB), welche den vertraglichen Regelungsspielraum einer Kündigungsfrist gestaltet.

als Vertragsbestandteil aufgefasst werden mussten, und damit zum Teil des Gehalts wurden.[67]

Weiterhin erwähnt auch die neuere sozialgeschichtliche Literatur die besondere Relevanz von Kündigungsschutz – ein Aspekt, der schon in zeitgenössischer Perspektive hervorgehoben wurde. Kündigungsschutz sei eine typische Forderung der auf Sicherheit bedachten Angestellten gewesen.[68] Während des Ersten Weltkriegs hätten die Arbeiter dann auch immer mehr Kündigungsschutz verlangt, sich also rechtspolitisch in eine Richtung bewegt, die zuvor typisch für die Angestellten gewesen sei.[69] Dass die Angestellten in gewisser Weise zu den Vorreitern bei den Forderungen nach Kündigungsschutz gehörten, erscheint plausibel, ebenso wie die Differenzierung der Zeit vor und nach dem Ersten Weltkrieg. 1861 wurden im Allgemeinen Deutschen Handelsgesetzbuch spezielle Schutzbestimmungen für Handlungsgehilfen eingeführt. Diese betrafen die – freilich nicht abschließende – Normierung konkreter Gründe für eine außerordentliche Kündigung (§ 71 und § 72 HGB) seitens und gegenüber dem Handlungsgehilfen. Auch wenn erhebliche Auslegungsspielräume verblieben, war ein gewisser Schutz gewährleistet.

Außerordentliche Kündigungsgründe wurden in dieser Zeit auch in die vielen Gesindeordnungen der deutschen Bundesstaaten aufgenommen.[70] Das damit erreichte Maß an Rechtssicherheit und Willkürverhinderung war also keineswegs ein Privileg der Handlungsgehilfen, die übrigens im 19. Jahrhundert auch nicht selten im Haushalt ihres Dienstherren lebten, weshalb das Handelsgesetzbuch auch Vorschriften zum Schutz ihres Status in dieser Situation vorgesehen hatte (§ 62 ADHGB). Beim Schutz von »Sittlichkeit und religiösen Bedürfnissen« arbeitender Menschen zeigt sich also tatsächlich eine Parallele zwischen Gesinde und Handlungsgehilfen.

Was die ordentliche Kündigung anging, ergaben sich bei den Handlungsgehilfen schon früh Unterschiede zu den gewerblichen Arbeitskräften. Das Handlungsgehilfenverhältnis konnte zum Schluss eines Kalendervierteljahres unter Einhaltung einer Kündigungsfrist von sechs Wochen gekündigt werden (§ 66 HGB). Bei den Fabrikarbeitern ging man von einer 14-tägigen Kündigungsfrist für beide Teile aus, die vertraglich abbedungen werden konnte. Solche Regelungen fanden sich bereits in den Zunftsordnungen des alten Handwerks, von dort gelangten sie dann in die preußische Gewerbeordnung von 1845 und schließlich in die Reichsgewerbeordnung.[71] Erneut zeigen sich hier konkrete rechtliche Auswirkungen der unterschiedlichen Prägungen der Berufsstände. Das Fabrikarbeitsverhältnis erwuchs teilweise aus Normbeständen alten Handwerksrechts. Beim Handlungsgehilfenrecht, das Grundlage für viele Angestellte war, knüpfte man nicht an diese Basis an und gelangte zu anderen Lösungen. Dieses freilich marginale Beispiel verdeutlicht, dass die vieldiskutierte »Kragenlinie« ihre Ursachen auch in weiter zurückreichenden Unterschieden der Rechtsquellenbasis verschiedener Statusbereiche hat.[72]

In der Weimarer Republik kämpften die Angestellten dann weiter um Kündigungsschutz. Ein Schwerpunkt der Debatte war hier der Kündigungsschutz für sogenannte ältere Angestellte. Über deren Probleme hatte bereits Siegfried Kracauer berichtet.[73] Sie werden bei ihm als die ersten Opfer der Rationalisierung des Angestelltenverhältnisses dargestellt. Auf den ersten Blick würde man die Verdrängung älterer Menschen aus dem Arbeitsmarkt aber eher bei Berufen vermuten, wo ein Verlust körperlicher Leistungsfähigkeit eine Einschränkung der Arbeitsproduktivität bewirkt. Gerade die Angestellten müssten die Chance gehabt haben, bis ins höhere Alter auf gleichem Niveau zu arbeiten. »Behaglich altern« ließ es sich aber laut Kracauer nur in den höheren Ebenen des Angestelltendaseins, nämlich dort, wo es den Betreffenden gelungen war, sich für den Fall der Kündigung eine Abfindung auszubedingen.[74] Heute steht man vor der Herausforderung der

67 Urteil des Kaufmannsgerichts Hamburg vom 20. Februar 1908, in: Baum (Hg.) (1912) Bd. 2, 449 f.

68 Zum am Beamtenleitbild orientierten Sicherheitsbedürfnis auch Kocka (1981a) 173.

69 Kocka (1977) 51.

70 Deutsch / Keiser (2013) §§ 620 ff., Rn. 95.

71 Deutsch / Keiser (2013) §§ 620 ff., Rn. 73.

72 Zu sozialhistorischen Erklärungen für die in Deutschland wirkmächtige Unterscheidung zwischen Arbeitern und Angestellten: Kocka (1981a) 175 ff.

73 Kracauer (1930) 44 ff.

74 Kracauer (1930) 47.

Digitalisierung und sieht ähnliche Entwicklungen und Gefährdungen. Mitte der Zwanzigerjahre waren es verschiedene Maßnahmen, welche unter Rationalisierung verstanden werden konnten, sicherlich die Mechanisierung der Büroarbeit, aber vor allem die Zusammenlegung von Büros zur Kostenersparnis. Motiv für die Rationalisierung waren der Druck der Wirtschaftskrise, aber auch die Übernahme technischer Neuerungen. Weil dabei zunehmend ältere Angestellte das Nachsehen hatten, erreichte man eine Verbesserung des Kündigungsschutzes (wiederum in zeitlicher Hinsicht) durch ein Gesetz von 1926,[75] demzufolge die Kündigungsfristen nach Betriebszugehörigkeit gestaffelt von drei bis zu sechs Monaten betragen konnten.

Diese Beispiele zeigen erneut, dass sich die Dynamik im Recht des Angestelltenverhältnisses auf das Individualarbeitsrecht konzentrierte. Schon vor dem Ersten Weltkrieg wurde das mit dem berühmt-berüchtigten Angestelltenbewusstsein begründet. Dieses war natürlich ein Stein des Anstoßes für alle, denen an einer Bündelung von Arbeitnehmerinteressen im Rahmen einer einheitlichen Interessenorganisation gelegen war. Tatsächlich sollte auch die Sozialversicherung für Angestellte aus dem Jahr 1911 dazu beitragen, die Angestellten vor den sog. »Sirenentönen der Sozialdemokratie« abzuschirmen.[76] Selten war es aber gelungen, die Angestellten zur Aufgabe ihres besonderen berufsständischen Selbstverständnisses zu bewegen. Die Trennung zwischen Arbeitern und Angestellten war schließlich auch im Recht der Bundesrepublik Deutschland in § 5 des Betriebsverfassungsgesetzes von 1952 bekräftigt worden. Zwar spielte sie eine geringere Rolle als in der Weimarer Republik, da es einen Gesamtbetriebsrat gab, in dem Vertreter beider Gruppen zusammenkamen. Dennoch wurde die Differenzierung nach der »Kragenlinie« beibehalten, obwohl man sie bereits 1952 als »soziologisch überholt« betrachtete.[77]

IV. Fazit

Dieser Überblick verdeutlicht, dass die Rechtsgeschichte an viele Felder der Sozialgeschichte anknüpfen kann. Zahlreiche Einzelfragen gewinnen in der Zusammenschau von rechts- und sozialhistorischen Anknüpfungspunkten an Profil, so etwa die Pionierrolle des Angestelltenrechts beim Kündigungsschutz oder einzelne Rechtsentwicklungen, die man in der juristischen Literatur und in der Praxis vor den Kaufmanns- und Gewerbegerichten beobachten kann. Relevant ist aber auch, wie sich innerhalb des Angestelltenrechts verschiedene Bereiche herausbilden. Rechtliche Sonderprobleme weiblicher Angestellter sind eine weitere Beobachtungskategorie, aber natürlich auch das (hier nicht erwähnte) Recht der leitenden Angestellten, sowie die Verknüpfungen zwischen Arbeits- und Sozialversicherungsrecht. Ein weiteres wichtiges Praxisfeld war die Frage von Gehaltsgestaltung und Gratifikationen.[78] Womöglich ersetzten diese funktional zum Teil den im Gewerbe üblichen Leistungslohn. Anhand von Gerichtsurteilen lässt sich beobachten, dass sie aber immer mehr zum normalen Gehaltsbestandteil wurden, der, wenn er einmal zugesichert war, auch nicht mehr modifiziert wurde. Ein weiterer, näher zu untersuchender Schwerpunkt wäre das Wettbewerbsverbot, bei dem schon vor dem 2. Weltkrieg sich zahlreiche Urteile auf die Wirksamkeit oder Unwirksamkeit einer Konkurrenzklausel bezogen.

Insgesamt wird man bei solchen Untersuchungen auf juristischer Ebene beobachten können, wie und warum sich eine soziale Gruppe als »Mittelstand« formieren konnte, welche Widerstände dabei überwunden wurden und welche Konsequenzen das für die Rechts- und Gesellschaftsordnung insgesamt hatte. Wie aktuell diese Frage heute ist, zeigt die Debatte um die kultursoziologische Beobachtung einer »Gesellschaft der Singularitäten«, in der die Herausbildung einer neuen Mittelklasse anhand von Kriterien wie Kreativität und Vertrautheit mit der digitalen Welt beschrieben wird.[79]

75 Gesetz über die Fristen für die Kündigung von Angestellten vom 9. Juli 1926, RGBl. I Nr. 46, 399, Nr. 48, 412. Bei der Vorbereitung spielten auch Leitsätze des sozialpolitischen Ausschusses des vorläufigen Reichswirtschaftsrats eine Rolle. Abgedruckt in: Sitzler / Goldschmidt (1930) 129.

76 Zur politischen Motivlage zur Zeit der Entstehung der Sozialversicherung m.w.N. vgl. Glootz (1999) 21 f.

77 Dietz (1952) § 5 Rn. 1.

78 Zu diesem besonderen Aspekt der Lohngerechtigkeit im Hinblick auf das Angestelltenverhältnis demnächst Allstadt.

79 Reckwitz (2019) 181 ff.

Auch in der neuen Mittelklasse entsteht ein neues Bewusstsein, das – wie zu Beginn des 20. Jahrhunderts das Angestelltenbewusstsein – neue Rechts- und Vertragsformen prägen kann. Somit führt das Thema der Angestellten auch zu juristisch soziologischen Vergleichsebenen zwischen der Gegenwart und der industrialisierten Gesellschaft der Zwischenkriegszeit. Ein Grundkonflikt wird dabei nach wie vor zu beobachten sein, nämlich das Spannungsverhältnis von Streben nach Individualität und der im Arbeitsrecht der Moderne angelegten Forderung nach kollektiver Interessenartikulation.

■

Bibliographie

- Allstadt, Anne (demnächst), Lohnkonflikte vor den Gewerbe- und Kaufmannsgerichten. Eine historische Rechtsprechungsanalyse im Hinblick auf das Verständnis von Lohngerechtigkeit
- Apitz, Hans Joachim (1967), Entstehung und Bedeutung der Deutschen Sozialgesetzgebung für Heimarbeiter und Angestellte in den Jahren 1896 bis 1914, Berlin
- Baum, Georg (Hg.) (1912), Handbuch des Gewerbe- und Kaufmannsgerichts, Berlin
- Baum, Georg, Willi Cuno et al. (1908), Der Dienstvertrag der Privatangestellten, 2 Bde., Jena
- Benjamin, Walter (1930/1971), Politisierung der Intelligenz. Zu S. Kracauer, »Die Angestellten«, in: Kracauer, Siegfried, Die Angestellten. Erweiterte Ausgabe, mit einer Rezension von Walter Benjamin, Frankfurt am Main, 116–123
- Bohle, Thomas (1990), Einheitliches Arbeitsrecht in der Weimarer Republik, Tübingen
- Bruch, Rüdiger vom (2005), Bürgerlichkeit, Staat und Kultur im Deutschen Kaiserreich, Stuttgart
- Deutsch, Andreas, Thorsten Keiser (2013), §§ 620–630. Beendigung des Dienstverhältnisses, in: Historisch-kritischer Kommentar zum BGB, hg. von Mathias Schmoeckel, Joachim Rückert, Reinhard Zimmermann, Bd. III: Schuldrecht: Besonderer Teil, §§ 433–853, Tübingen, 1271–1351
- Dietz, Rolf (1952), Kommentar, Betriebsverfassungsgesetz mit Wahlordnung, München
- Glootz, Tanja Anette (1999), Geschichte der Angestelltenversicherung des 20. Jahrhunderts, Berlin
- Haupt, Heinz-Gerhard (2018), Angestellte vor Gericht. Ein Beitrag zur Verrechtlichung von Arbeitsbeziehungen in Deutschland und Frankreich um 1900, in: ders., Klassen im sozialen Raum, Göttingen, 325–341
- Hauschild, Harry (1926), Der vorläufige Reichswirtschaftsrat, Berlin
- Kaskel, Walter (1921), Das neue Arbeitsrecht, 3. Aufl., Berlin
- Keiser, Thorsten (2013), Vertragszwang und Vertragsfreiheit im Recht der Arbeit von der Frühen Neuzeit bis in die Moderne, Frankfurt am Main
- Kocka, Jürgen (1977), Angestellte zwischen Faschismus und Demokratie, Göttingen
- Kocka, Jürgen (1981a), Die Angestellten in der deutschen Geschichte: 1850–1890; vom Privatbeamten zum angestellten Arbeitnehmer, Göttingen
- Kocka, Jürgen (1981b), Einleitende Bemerkungen, in: ders. (Hg.) (1981c) 7
- Kocka, Jürgen (Hg.) (1981c), Angestellte im europäischen Vergleich, Göttingen
- Kracauer, Siegfried (1930), Die Angestellten. Aus dem neuesten Deutschland, Frankfurt am Main
- Manes, Alfred, Paul Königsberger (1912), Kommentar zum Versicherungsgesetz für Angestellte vom 20. Dezember 1911, Berlin
- Mangold, Werner (1981), Angestelltengeschichte und Angestelltensoziologie, in: Kocka (Hg.) (1981c) 11–38
- Otto, Martin (2022), Auch eine Gewerkschaft? Der Deutschnationale Handlungsgehilfenverband und die Angestellten, in: Rechtsgeschichte – Legal History 30, 184–196
- Pierenkemper, Toni (1987), Arbeitsmarkt der Angestellten im Deutschen Kaiserreich 1880–1913, Stuttgart
- Potthoff, Heinz (1908), Einheitliches Privatbeamtenrecht, in: Baum et al., Bd. 2, 91–142
- Reckwitz, Andreas (2019), Die Gesellschaft der Singularitäten, Berlin
- Schulz, Günther (2000), Die Angestellten seit dem 19. Jahrhundert, München
- Seelig, Marie Louise (2008), Heinz Potthoff (1875–1945) – Arbeitsrecht als volkswirtschaftliches und sozialpolitisches Gestaltungsinstrument, Berlin
- Sinzheimer, Hugo (1914), Über den Grundgedanken und die Möglichkeit eines einheitlichen Arbeitsrechts in Deutschland, Berlin
- Sitzler, Friedrich, Heinz Goldschmidt (1930), Der Kündigungsschutz für Angestellte, Berlin
- Vorstand der Gesellschaft für Soziale Reform (Hg.) (1909), Das Recht der Privatbeamten und die Pensionsversicherung der Privatbeamten, Jena

Martin Otto

Auch eine Gewerkschaft? Der Deutschnationale Handlungsgehilfenverband und die Angestellten*

I. Die Architektur der Angestelltengewerkschaft

Das Gebäude ist bis heute repräsentativ. Die Hauptverwaltung des »Deutschnationalen Handlungsgehilfenverbandes« (DHV) am Holstenwall in Hamburg am Rande der Neustadt wurde 1927 bis 1931 von Ferdinand Sckopp und Wilhelm Vortmann im norddeutschen Backsteinexpressionismus erbaut.[1] Das im Krieg fast unzerstörte Bürogebäude gilt als erstes Hamburger Hochhaus und war lange der höchste Profanbau der Hansestadt; nur die fünf stadtbildprägenden lutherischen Hauptkirchen waren größer.[2] Der Bauherr DHV verstand sich ausdrücklich als christliche Gewerkschaft. Von 1965 bis 2005 befand sich hier, nach zwischenzeitiger Nutzung als Sitz der englischen Militärregierung, Versicherungszentrale und Polizeipräsidium, die Hauptverwaltung der »Deutschen Angestellten-Gewerkschaft« (DAG).[3] Die Bedeutung des Gebäudes für die deutsche Gewerkschaftsgeschichte steht außer Zweifel. In seiner Baugeschichte, erbaut während der »guten« Jahre der Weimarer Republik, spiegelt sich der Bedeutungszuwachs der »Angestellten«.[4] Zählte das Deutsche Reich im Jahr 1907 noch 1,5 Millionen Angestellte, waren es bei einer leicht gesunkenen Gesamtbevölkerung im Jahr 1930 mit 3,9 Millionen mehr als doppelt so viele. 65 % davon waren kaufmännische Angestellte, nach damaligem Sprachgebrauch »Handlungsgehilfen«. Die große Mehrheit von ihnen war in nichtsozialistischen Gewerkschaften organisiert, der DHV die bei weitem größte. An der politischen Orientierung des DHV ließ die aufwändige bauliche Gestaltung der Hauptverwaltung keine Zweifel aufkommen. Bis heute vorhandene Wappen aus farbigen Kacheln erinnern in den Arkaden des Gebäudes an die Städte Danzig, Kattowitz, Malmedy, Memel, Metz, Posen, Straßburg, Thorn und Tondern, die das Deutsche Reich nach dem Ersten Weltkrieg abtreten musste. In der Ablehnung der Friedensbedingungen bestand zwar kein prinzipieller Unterschied zu den »freien« Gewerkschaften oder der großen Mehrheit der Bevölkerung, aber die besondere bauliche Berücksichtigung war noch einmal ein politischer Akzent. Hinzu kam ein Bronzeelefant des Bildhauers Ludwig Kunstmann, der an die ehemaligen Kolonien erinnert.

II. Angestellte und Gewerkschaften

Die Zahl der Angestellten fand auch Niederschlag in ihrer gewerkschaftlichen Organisation.[5]

1. Angestelltengewerkschaften in der Weimarer Republik

Der streng berufsständische DHV war mit 400.000 Mitgliedern nicht nur in der Weimarer Republik die größte deutsche und europäische Angestelltengewerkschaft.[6] Der SPD-nahe »Zentralverband der Angestellten« (ZdA) im »Allgemeinen freien Angestellten-Bund« (AfA-Bund),[7] der mit dem »Allgemeinen Deutschen Gewerkschaftsbund« (ADGB) kooperierte, kam mit knapp 200.000 Mitgliedern gerade auf die Hälfte, der linksliberale »Gewerkschaftsbund der Angestellten« (GDA) auf knapp 300.000. Während der Weimarer Republik bestanden zeitweilig 91 Angestelltenverbände in den drei Gewerkschaftsverbänden. Die freigewerkschaftlich-sozialistische »Arbeitsgemeinschaft freier Angestelltenverbände« (seit 1921 AfA-Bund) hatte 1921 ein Kooperationsabkommen mit dem ADGB geschlossen. Sie stand

* Dem Andenken meines Lehrers Michael Stolleis, verstorben am 18. März 2021, der in der Diskussion des diesem Beitrag zugrundeliegenden Vortrags auf der 5. Tagung der »Initiative Arbeitsrechtsgeschichte« in Frankfurt am Main am 6. Dezember 2019 wichtige Anregungen gab. Die Vortragsform wurde weitgehend beibehalten, das Schrifttum ist auf dem Stand vom 31. März 2022.

1 Meyhöfer (2007) 93 f.

2 Skrentny (1986) 37.

3 Halberstadt (1991).

4 Kocka (1969); Kocka (1977); Schulz (2000). Anders akzentuiert auch Stegmann (1972) 365 ff.

5 Übersicht auch bei Schulz (2000) 24 ff.

6 Brockhaus (1925) 711.

7 Palberg-Landwehr (1993).

wie die »freien« Gewerkschaften insgesamt der SPD nahe und war ein Dachverband von 14 Einzelgewerkschaften, darunter der mit dem DHV unmittelbar konkurrierende ZdA und der »Bund technischer Angestellter und Beamten« (BUTAB); Angestellte in künstlerischen Berufen waren selbständig organisiert. Insgesamt kamen »freie« Angestelltengewerkschaften 1928 auf 428.000 Mitglieder. Dabei bestand bei allen Gewerkschaften Fluktuation, da Lehrlinge oft nach Abschluss der Lehre austraten. Nur wenig schwächer war der linksliberale GDA, der im gleichen Zeitraum auf knapp 300.000 Mitglieder kam; die tatsächliche Zahl der bei »Hirsch-Duncker« organisierten Angestellten war größer, es bestanden zusätzlich Gewerkschaften für Bank- und Versicherungsangestellte. Erheblich stärker war bei den »national-christlichen« Gewerkschaften der »Gesamtverband der deutschen Angestellten-Gewerkschaften« (GEDAG) mit stabil 550.000 Mitgliedern. Ihm gehörte als bei weitem größte Gewerkschaft der DHV an. Die meisten Angestellten waren in nichtsozialistischen Gewerkschaften organisiert. Lediglich technische Angestellte (»Werkmeister«) tendierten zur SPD und »freien« Gewerkschaften mit dem BUTAB, der über 100.000 Mitglieder zählte,[8] nur 20.000 waren im GEDAG organisiert. Offensichtlich war die soziale Distinktion der technischen Angestellten weniger ausgeprägt.[9]

2. *Umgekehrte Organisationsverhältnisse*

Noch 1920 waren »freie« Angestelltengewerkschaften erheblich stärker; die gewerkschaftlichen Verhältnisse der Angestellten entwickelten sich in der Weimarer Republik umgekehrt zur gesamten Organisation der Arbeitnehmer. Die »Freien Gewerkschaften« im ADGB kamen 1928 auf 5,2 Millionen Mitglieder, nur ein Bruchteil waren Angestellte.[10] Ein deutliches Übergewicht besaßen Angestellte bei den »Hirsch-Dunckerschen« Gewerkvereinen im »Freiheitlich-Nationalen Gewerkschaftsring deutscher Arbeiter-, Angestellten und Beamtenvereine«, die der DDP nahestanden und 1928 auf knapp 600.000 Mitglieder kamen.[11] Die im »Deutschen Gewerkschaftsbund« (DGB) organisierten christlichen Gewerkschaften, die bis 1930 überwiegend Zentrum, DNVP und DVP nahestanden, kamen 1928 auf 1,3 Millionen Mitglieder, die sich auf drei Unterorganisationen verteilten.[12] Dies waren der »Gesamtverband der Christlichen Gewerkschaften«, 18 Fachgewerkschaften für Arbeiter mit 600.000 überwiegend katholischen Mitgliedern, der eher unbedeutende »Gesamtverband Deutscher Beamtengewerkschaften« (150.000 Mitglieder), der sich 1926 zudem gespalten hatte, und eben der GEDAG.[13] Von einer gewissen Bedeutung waren hier neben dem DHV sein weibliches Pendant, der »Verband der weiblichen Handels- und Büroangestellten« mit bis zu 100.000 Mitgliedern, der »Deutsche Bankbeamten-Verein« mit 86.000 Mitgliedern, der aber 1923 aus dem GEDAG ausgeschieden war. Hinzu kamen als kleinere Gewerkschaften der mit dem BUTAB konkurrierende »Deutsche Werkmeisterbund« mit höchstens 18.000 Mitgliedern, der »Verband Deutscher Techniker« zwischen 4500 und 13.000, der »Reichsverband der Büroangestellten und Beamten« zwischen 2000 und 10.000 sowie der bereits aus strukturellen Gründen politisch konservative »Verband der Gut- und Forstbeamten« mit 10.000 Mitgliedern und weitere, zum Teil sehr kleinteilige Gewerkschaften mit unter 1000 Mitgliedern. Es bestanden erhebliche Schwankungen.

III. »Die größte Angestelltengewerkschaft der Welt«

Diese betrafen aber zu keinem Zeitpunkt den DHV, der nicht nur die größte christliche und nichtsozialistische, sondern auch eine der größten Gewerkschaften im Deutschen Reich und im internationalen Maßstab war. Er wurde als größte Angestelltengewerkschaft Europas, sogar der Welt bezeichnet. Dabei nahm er nur männliche christliche Angestellte auf, doch seine Mitgliederzahl war, anders als bei vielen Gewerkschaften, auch gegenüber Inflation und Weltwirtschaftskrise konstant. In der Weimarer Republik konnte er einen Zuwachs verzeichnen. Eine Besonderheit war die beschränkte Mitgliedschaft. Weiblichen Hand-

8 Der BUTAB war ein 1919 gegründeter Gewerkschaftsverband für technische und verwaltende Angestellte und gehörte dem AfA-Bund an. Zu diesem etwa Sander (2009) 169 ff. Die Mitgliederzahl wird hier für das Jahr 1919 mit 106.000 angegeben; Sander (2009) 170.

9 Dazu auch Stegmann (1972) 367.

10 Huber (1981) 1119.

11 Huber (1981) 1122.

12 Huber (1981) 1120.

13 Huber (1981) 1121.

lungsgehilfen stand allerdings als Schwestergewerkschaft der gleichfalls mitgliederstarke »Verband der weiblichen Handels- und Büroangestellten« offen.[14] Schwerwiegender war der offene Antisemitismus des Verbandes: »Juden und im bewussten Gegensatz zum Deutschtum stehende Angehörige anderer Nationen oder Rassen können keinerlei Mitgliedsrechte erwerben.«[15]

Stand der DHV in der Tradition eines »Sozialismus der dummen Kerls«[16]? Sieht man von der beschränkten Mitgliedschaft ab, war der DHV im zeitgenössischen Kontext durchaus eine »normale« Gewerkschaft, politisch konservativ, aber nicht gewerkschaftsfeindlich oder »gelb«. Er nahm an Tarifverhandlungen teil und war eindeutig auf der Arbeitnehmerseite angesiedelt. Zur gewerkschaftlichen Arbeit gehörte die effektive Überwachung von Ladenschlusszeiten und Sonntagsruhe, er befürwortete ein Verbot der Sonntagsarbeit.[17] Der Hauptunterschied zu den »freien« Gewerkschaften war dabei, dass die religiöse Bedeutung des Sonntags betont wurde.[18] Der DHV befürwortete Arbeitszeitverkürzungen und lehnte, in Übereinstimmung mit anderen Gewerkschaften, »Lehrlingszüchterei«,[19] die Verwendung von Lehrlingen als billige Arbeitskräfte ohne Aussicht auf Weiterbeschäftigung nach Abschluss der Lehre, ab. Gewerkschaftliche Selbsthilfe wurde in großem Umfang betrieben.

1. *Antisozialdemokratisch und antisemitisch*

Der DHV wurde am 7. September 1893 in Hamburg »im Hinterzimmer einer mittleren Bierwirtschaft« in der Schauenburger Straße 44 durch 23 junge Handlungsgehilfen gegründet.[20] Erster Vorsitzender war der Pfarrerssohn Johannes Irwahn.[21] Es war eine Initiative in Anschluss an die »Kaiserliche Botschaft« von 1881.[22] Die Zahl der Handlungsgehilfen war rasant angestiegen, in einer Stadt wie Hamburg besonders; insgesamt hatte sie sich im Deutschen Reich von 1887 (468.591) bis 1907 (835.303) fast verdoppelt. Es war eine neue Schicht entstanden; nur wenige Handlungsgehilfen hatten die Aussicht, einmal selbständiger Kaufmann zu werden.[23] Die Sozialdemokraten waren in diesem Milieu zunächst erfolgreich. Mit dem betont als »Kampfverein der Handlungsgehilfen gegen die Sozialdemokratie« gegründeten DHV verloren die Sozialdemokraten erheblich an Einfluss. 1909 warb der DHV als »größter kaufmännischer Verein der Welt«. »Deutschnational« verstand sich nicht parteipolitisch; bei Bedarf wurde auch Zusammenarbeit mit dem Zentrum gesucht. Es bestand Nähe zu Organisationen wie dem »Alldeutschen Verband«, dem »Bund der Landwirte« und dem »Deutschen Schulverein«, die sich auch in Doppelmitgliedschaften manifestierte, aber kein politischer Gleichlauf; Interessenkonflikte, etwa über angemessene Lebensmittelpreise, bestanden. Zur frühen Gewerkschaftsarbeit gehörten »Überwachungsausschüsse«[24] für das zum 1. Oktober 1900 in Kraft getretene Ladenschlussgesetz[25] und erfolgreiche Kandidaturen für Kaufmannsgerichte ab 1904.[26] Der DHV war von evangelischen Mitgliedern dominiert, verstand sich aber überkonfessionell. Antikatholische Tendenzen bestanden nicht; auf katholische Funktionäre wurde Wert gelegt. Er besaß viele Mitglieder mit aktiver kirchlicher Bindung und hochkirchlichen Ausrei-

14 Der Organisationsgrad weiblicher Angestellter war bereits im Kaiserreich sehr hoch; hierzu mit bis heute berechtigtem Hinweis auf Desiderate der Forschung nur Nienhaus (1981) 320 ff.

15 Hamel (1967) 53.

16 August Bebel zugeschrieben, tatsächlich aber von dem österreichischen Politiker Ferdinand Kronawitter; Bahr (1894) 21. Ferner Bebel (1894).

17 Hierzu Heckmann (1986); dies spielte seit dem Inkrafttreten der »Verordnung, betreffend das Inkrafttreten der auf die Sonntagsruhe im Handelsgewerbe bezüglichen Bestimmungen der Gewerbeordnungsnovelle vom 1. Juni 1891« (RGBl. 1892, 339) jedoch nur noch eine untergeordnete Rolle.

18 Hamel (1967) 25, 53 f. u.ö.; zeitgenössisch Hörbrand (1926).

19 Hamel (1967) 17 f. Vom sozialistischen zeitgenössischen Standpunkt: Deutsch (1904).

20 Dazu Hamel (1967) 25 ff.

21 Johannes Wilhelm Heinrich Irwahn (1868–1948), Kaufmann, Sohn eines Pastors (Leiter Hamburger Stadtmission) in Rothenburgsort, Neffe des Bürgerschaftsabgeordneten Friedrich Raab, 1893 bis 1896 erster Vorsteher des DHV. Vgl. Kimmel (2009a).

22 Tennstedt (1981) 663.

23 Vgl. etwa Sozialpolitische Abteilung (1925).

24 Hamel (1967) 17.

25 D. i. Gesetz betreffend die Abänderung der Gewerbeordnung vom 30. Juni 1900 (RGBl. 321). Hierzu insgesamt etwa Spiekermann (2004).

26 Hamel (1967) 115. Zu den Kaufmannsgerichten Collin (2016); nunmehr auch Vogt (im Druck).

ßern.[27] Innerhalb des katholisch geprägten DGB war er die größte Einzelgewerkschaft. Wie bereits aus dem Namen hervorging, war der DHV »großdeutsch«, bestand also auch in Österreich, ab 1920 in der Tschechoslowakei (späteres »Sudetenland«); dort war er aus verschiedenen Gründen aber von erheblich geringerer Bedeutung. Das Interesse an »Volks-« und »Auslandsdeutschen«[28] als Mitgliedern war keine Besonderheit des DHV, die meisten größeren Gewerkschaften besaßen vergleichbare Organisationen.[29] Ein wichtiges soziales Bindeglied der Mitglieder war Standesstolz, die Abgrenzung gegenüber dem »Proletariat«. Freihandel und Frauenemanzipation wurden abgelehnt, doch in der praktischen Gewerkschafsarbeit spielte dies eine Nebenrolle. Der DHV wurde in seiner Gründungsphase stark vom christlich-sozialen Gedankengut Adolf Stoeckers beeinflusst;[30] auch Antisemitismus gehört zu diesem zweifelhaften Erbe. Dabei wurde nicht klar zwischen religiösem oder »biologischem« Antisemitismus unterschieden; darin bestand eine Parallele zum studentischen Antisemitismus.[31] Stoecker und die antisemitischen Parteien hatten bei Gründung des DHV ihren Zenit überschritten, ab 1905 trat dort der Antisemitismus in den Hintergrund.[32] 1909 musste der erste Vorsitzende Wilhelm Schack[33] nach einem Sexskandal zurücktreten.[34]

2. *Von Schack zu Bechly: Sozialpolitik und Sachlichkeit*

Unter dem ab 1911 amtierenden Nachfolger Hans Bechly[35] trat an Stelle der antisemitischen die sozialpolitische Agitation.[36] Die Verbandsarbeit war seitdem von einer pragmatischen Linie geprägt. »Aber die größere Sachlichkeit und Rationalität in der Argumentation bedeutete nicht die Preisgabe der antisemitisch-deutschnationalen Vorstellungen.«[37]

Auch wenn sicher überproportional viele DHV-Mitglieder gegenüber der Monarchie sentimentale Gefühle aufbrachten und der Revolution skeptisch begegneten, dominierte ein konservativer Vernunftrepublikanismus, der für die frühe Weimarer Republik nicht untypisch war. Die Möglichkeit einer Restauration war ausgeschlossen, dem Kampf gegen Revolution und Anarchie wurde Priorität eingeräumt. Auch aus eigennützigen Gründen gab sich der DHV pragmatisch, akzeptierte früh die Republik und nannte sich ab 1921 ganz offiziell »Gewerkschaft der deutschen Kaufmannsgehilfen«. Und er handelte im kollektiven Arbeitsrecht wie andere Gewerkschaften auch. Er besaß Tariffähigkeit, nicht nur aufgrund seiner beeindruckenden Größe, sondern auch wegen der grundsätzlichen Bejahung des Arbeitskampfes. Viele Tarifverträge wurden gemeinsam mit den freien Gewerkschaften, insbesondere dem AfA-Bund, ausgehandelt und unterzeichnet, allein 1929 über 1.000.[38] Streik wurde als »letztes Mittel« restriktiver gehandhabt als von »freien« Gewerkschaften, im Fall des Arbeitskampfes etwa gegen Akkordarbeit oder untertarifliche Entlohnung dann aber gemeinsam mit diesen.[39] Für die »Sozialpolitische Abteilung« des DHV war das kollektive Arbeitsrecht »Grundlage des heutigen sozialen Zusammenlebens«.[40] Auch um Abwanderung zu den »freien« Gewerkschaften zu verhindern, wurde die sozialpolitische Arbeit betont, dazu gehörten Mitbestimmungs- und Gewinnbeteiligungsmodelle. Der DHV profitierte von der Weimarer Republik wie keine zweite Gewerkschaft, was auch an seiner Doppelrolle als »Völkischer Verband und nationale Gewerkschaft«, so der Titel der von Iris Hamel bei Fritz Fischer an der Universität Hamburg 1964/65 entstandenen ersten wissenschaftlichen Monographie,[41] lag. Sozialpolitisch bestanden zwischen DHV und »freien« Gewerkschaften zahlreiche Übereinstimmungen, doch die »poli-

27 Fenske (2009) 32 f.
28 Zur Auslandsarbeit des DHV in den USA etwa Wilhelm (1998) 52 ff.
29 Vgl. etwa den 1922 gegründeten »AfA-Bund Polnisch-Oberschlesien« mit Sitz in Kattowitz.
30 Kupisch (1970).
31 Kampe (1988).
32 Bergsträsser (1928) 133 ff.
33 Wilhelm Schack (1869–1944), 1896–1909 Vorsitzender des DHV, Rücktritt nach Sexaffäre; Hansen / Tennstedt (Hg.) (2010); Kimmel (2009b).
34 Kasischke (1997) 400 ff.
35 Hans Bechly (1871–1954), 1911–1933 Vorsitzender des DHV, nach 1945 Mitbegründer DAG. Umfassend noch immer Hamel (1967) 117–122; zeitgenössisch Thiel (1931).
36 Hamel (1967) 54 ff.
37 Hamel (1967) 119.
38 Nerger / Zimmermann (2006) 8.
39 Beispiele aus Hannover (Streik bei den Continental-Gummiwerken gegen Akkordarbeit und Streik gegen den Einzelhandel wegen untertariflicher Bezahlung) bei Anders / Riesche (1985) 32 ff.
40 Gerber (1926) 6 (Vorwort).
41 Hamel (1967) 7. Zu der Rolle von Fritz Fischer vor 1945 etwa Vordermayer (2022).

tisch-weltanschauliche« Konzeption des DHV war »diametral entgegengesetzt«.[42] Für viele Angestellte war der DHV durch seine Mischung aus konventionellen Gewerkschaftsforderungen und Nationalismus attraktiv, die Ablehnung des Klassenkampfes war standesbewussten Angestellten bei der Abgrenzung vom »Proletariat« hilfreich. Der Erfolg des DHV kann als Symptom für die Abstiegsängste des Bürger- und Kleinbürgertums gesehen werden, für das Gefühl, »etwas Besseres« zu sein.[43] Entsprechend lautete eine frühe Selbstbeschreibung des DHV: »Den großen Teil des deutschen Mittelstandes, den unser Stand bildet, vor der Proletarisierung, vor dem Untergang zu bewahren.«[44]

Als monokausale Erklärung griffe dies aber zu kurz. Allein aus politischen Sympathien sind die wenigsten Beitritte zu Gewerkschaften erfolgt, auch nicht in den »freien« Gewerkschaften, bei denen auch ein bestimmtes »Milieu« hinzukam. Zum Teil bestand aber auch ein Desinteresse der »freien« Gewerkschaften und der SPD an der besonderen Situation der Handlungsgehilfen.[45]

3. *Das Milieu der Handlungsgehilfen*

Zum DHV gehörte ein weitgefächertes Milieu mit gemeinsamer Freizeitgestaltung (Sport, Gesang, Reisen). Das Bildungsangebot (»Fichte-Gesellschaft«[46]) war hochwertig und stand qualitativ und quantitativ den freien Gewerkschaften nicht nach.[47] In der Jugendarbeit, die unter dem romantischen Namen »Fahrendes Volk« firmierte, bestanden personelle und inhaltliche Überschneidungen mit der Bündischen Jugend, zahlreihe Elemente des »Wandervogel« wurden sichtbar aufgegriffen. Daneben wurde aber auch traditionelle Gewerkschaftsarbeit betrieben, so bestanden zahlreiche Lehrlingsgruppen; allerdings war hier, wie auch bei anderen Gewerkschaften, eine hohe Fluktuation zu beobachten. Der DHV war zudem unternehmerisch tätig. Das war eine weitere Gemeinsamkeit mit den »freien« Gewerkschaften, auch wenn eine ideologische Begründung wie »Gemeinwirtschaft« damit nicht verbunden war. Umgekehrt arbeiteten Unternehmen der freien Gewerkschaften wie die Versicherungsgesellschaft »Volksfürsorge«, die »Bank der Deutschen Arbeit« oder die Konsumgenossenschaft »Produktion« nach den gleichen kaufmännischen Maßstäben wie »kapitalistische« Unternehmen. Auch der DHV bot mit dem 1913 gegründeten »Deutschen Ring« Versicherungen an.[48] Zu weiteren Unternehmen gehörten die 1899 gegründete »Deutschnationale Kranken- und Begräbniskasse«, 1930 in der »Deutschen Angestellten Krankenkasse« (DAK)[49] aufgegangen und die 1918 gegründete »Gemeinnützige Aktiengesellschaft für Angestellten-Heimstätten« (GAGFAH).[50] In engem Zusammenhang mit der Bildungsarbeit stand die verlegerische Tätigkeit, insbesondere über die »Hanseatische Verlagsanstalt« Hamburg,[51] die innerhalb der »Konservativen Revolution« Bedeutung besaß.[52] Verbunden war die Buchgemeinschaft »Deutsche Hausbücherei«; in der Sache bestand kein Unterschied zu den »freien« Gewerkschaften und der »Büchergilde Gutenberg«. 1928 wurden der »Georg Müller Verlag«, 1931 der »Albert Langen Verlag«, beide in München, vom DHV erworben.[53] Durch die »Verlagsfusion Langen-Müller« war ein »nationaler« Verlagskonzern von erheblicher Bedeutung entstanden; hier erschien etwa »Volk ohne Raum« von Hans Grimm,[54] ein Autor des »Albert Langen Verlages«. Der nationalistische Bestseller, von Kurt Tucholsky 1928 in der Weltbühne als »Grimms Märchen« verspottet,[55] war aber wahrscheinlich mehr wegen seines Namens als seines Inhalts be-

42 Hamel (1967) 54.
43 Vgl. auch den Beitrag von Keiser in diesem Fokus, 173–182.
44 Mitteilungen des Deutschen Handlungsgehilfen-Verbandes vom 1. November 1894, hier zitiert nach Hamel (1967) 10.
45 Nipperdey (1990) 379.
46 Zu der 1916 gegründeten »Fichte-Gesellschaft« insbesondere Gossler (2001) 81 ff.
47 Hamel (1967) 123 ff.
48 Deutscher Ring (1963).
49 Böge / Stein (1999) 79 ff.
50 Börsch-Supan (1993). Zu der GAGFAH-Siedlung »Fischtalgrund« in Berlin (1929; Paul Schmitthenner, Heinrich Tessenow u. a.), exemplarisch für die Bautätigkeit der GAGFAH, Rave / Knöfel (1968) Nr. 146.4–29.
51 Lokatis (1992).
52 Mohler / Weissmann (2005) 280.
53 Insgesamt hierzu Meyer (1989).
54 Grimm (1926). Zu diesem Autor auch Lattmann (1969).
55 Wrobel [d. i. Tucholsky] (2001). Dort aber auch: »Anzumerken, daß Grimm ein im tiefsten Kern anständiger Mann ist; die üble Ausnutzung, die der Roman durch deutsch-nationale Annexions-Politiker erfahren hat, mag ihm selber nicht sehr behaglich sein […].« Wrobel (2001) 358.

kannt. Verlagsarbeit wurde aber als politisches Kampfmittel verstanden. Über die »Deutsche Hausbücherei« hieß es in einer Selbstdarstellung:

»Sie bringt keine Werke volksfremder Bücherschreiber. Deutschen kann nur von Deutschen geholfen werden. Sie will keine Welt-, sondern Nationalliteratur unter Einschluss des germanischen Nordens. […] Nicht jedes in deutscher Sprache geschriebene Buch ist auch ein deutsches Buch; nicht jeder in deutscher Sprache schreibende Schriftsteller ist auch ein deutscher Schriftsteller.«[56]

Zu diesen »deutschen Schriftstellern« zählte Ernst Jünger, der über Hans Grimm zur »Hanseatischen Verlagsanstalt« gekommen war,[57] dessen kultureller Horizont selbst in seiner nationalistischen Phase aber deutlich weiter war.[58] Den Verlagsvertrag über seinen politischen Großessay »Der Arbeiter« unterzeichnete Jünger im DHV-Hochhaus in Hamburg am 9. März 1932.[59]

IV. Juristische Bildungsarbeit und Netzwerke

Von Anfang an betrieb der DHV eine anspruchsvolle juristische Veröffentlichungspolitik. Die Schriften richteten sich an Mitglieder. Politische Agitation war die Ausnahme. Von 1922 bis 1931 wurde die juristische Fachzeitschrift »Der Kaufmann in Wirtschaft und Recht« publiziert. Neben den von Karl Bott[60] herausgegebenen populärwissenschaftlichen »Hamburger Kaufmannsbüchern« mit volkswirtschaftlichen und rechtswissenschaftlichen Inhalten bestanden weitere Schriftenreihen mit praktischem Bezug ohne ideologischen Beifang und Autoren wie Philipp Allfeld[61] und Emil Sehling;[62] Hochschullehrer waren als Autoren aber die Ausnahme. Eine besondere Nähe zum DHV besaß das »Institut für öffentliches Recht und Arbeitsrecht« der Universität Marburg, kleiner als die bekannteren Institute in Jena, Köln oder Leipzig.[63] Seine Mitglieder Friedrich André[64] und Felix Genzmer[65] nahmen einen betont »berufsständischen« Standpunkt ein, zu ihren Schülern gehörten Hans Gerber, Edgar Tatarin-Tarnheyden[66] und der »sozialpolitische Mitarbeiter« des DHV Hermann Kandeler.[67] In seiner Dissertation betrachtete er Arbeitgeberverbände und Gewerkschaften als »öffentliche Körperschaften«, eine Minderheitenposition, selbst im betont berufsständischen[68] DHV.

1. *Das Problem der »gewollten Tarifunfähigkeit«*

Als Kandeler 1924 einen Widerspruch der »gewollten Tarifunfähigkeit« zur Schlichtungsverordnung vom 30. Oktober 1923 feststellte, wurde dies auch außerhalb des DHV geteilt.[69] »Gewollte Tarifunfähigkeit« betraf alle Gewerkschaften und war ein Kernproblem des kollektiven Arbeitsrechts der Weimarer Republik.[70] Zunehmend hatten Arbeit-

56 Undatierte Werbung, zitiert nach Meyer (1989) 15.
57 Meyer (1989) 148.
58 Ähnlich wie hier Lokatis (2019) 11.
59 Lokatis (2019) 12.
60 Karl Bott (1883–1964), aus der Lehrlingsarbeit des DHV, Funktionär für kaufmännische Berufsausbildung beim DHV, Dr. rer. pol. h. c., ab 1907 zahlreiche Veröffentlichungen (»Der große Bott«) auch lange nach 1945 zur kaufmännischen Büroorganisation; Generaldirektor Hanseatische Verlagsanstalt. Vgl. Meyer (1989) 35 f.
61 Allfeld (1924). Philipp Allfeld (1852–1940), Professor für Straf- und Völkerrecht in Erlangen, große Bedeutung im Urheberrecht; Struwe-Urbanczyk (2017).
62 Sehling (1924). Emil Sehling (1850–1928), Professor für Kirchenrecht, Handels- und Privatrecht in Erlangen; heute in erster Linie als Kirchenrechtler bekannt (Edition der Kirchenordnungen des 16. Jahrhunderts), allerdings auch rege Tätigkeit im Handelsrecht, Vorlesungen ab 1919 auch an der Handelshochschule Nürnberg; Arend (2011).
63 Dubischar (1990) 83.
64 Friedrich (Fritz) André (1859–1927), seit 1922 Direktor am Institut für öffentliches Recht und Arbeitsrecht Marburg, romanistischer Rechtshistoriker; Auerbach (1979) 76–77.
65 Felix Genzmer (1878–1959), Professor für Öffentliches Recht in Marburg, germanistischer Rechtshistoriker; Kuhn (1964).
66 Vgl. Tatarin-Tarnheyden (1930), erstmals im Sammelwerk »Die Grundrechte« von Hans Carl Nipperdey; vgl. auch Bender (2021) 286. Zu diesem Autor auch Otto (2013).
67 Kandeler (1925); Kandeler (1927); kritisch dazu Jacobi (1927) 258, 393 u. ö.; vgl. Otto (2008) 155 mit Hinweis auf den damaligen ADGB-Justitiar Clemens Nörpel (mit Kandeler »italienischen oder russischen Zuständen entgegen«). Hermann Kandeler (1901–1990), 1936 Beamter im Reichsmarineamt, 1940 Marineoffizier; vgl. Otto (2021) 302.
68 Brockhaus (1925); Hering (2005).
69 Kandeler (1924).
70 Hierzu etwa Bähr (1989) 154, 180. Sie wurde von Erich Melsbach, Heinrich Potthoff, Rudolf Joerges, Anton Erdel, Walter Kaskel und Hugo Sinzheimer abgelehnt, befürwortet von Hans Carl Nipperdey, Paul Oertmann, Lutz Richter, Heinrich Göppert und Wilhelm Silberschmidt.

geberverbände durch ihre Satzungen Tarifverträge ausgeschlossen. Umstritten war, ob trotzdem ein Schlichtungsverfahren durchführbar war. Als der »Arbeitgeberverband für Velbert und Umgebung« den Tarifabschluss von einem Quorum der Mitgliederversammlung abhängig machte, sprach sich der Schlichtungsausschuss Barmen am 5. September 1924 dagegen aus; der Schiedsspruch wurde durch den Schlichter Ernst Mehlich (SPD)[71] für verbindlich erklärt. Dies war das einzige Mal, dass ein Schiedsspruch, der die gewollte Tarifunfähigkeit ablehnte, für verbindlich erklärt wurde. Hans-Carl Nipperdey befürwortete dagegen prominent die »gewollte Tarifunfähigkeit«;[72] auch staatliche Schlichter nahmen zunehmend diesen Standpunkt ein. Die Entscheidung des Schlichtungsausschusses Neumünster gegen den das Quorum für Tariffähigkeit verfehlenden »Arbeitgeberverband für Rendsburg und Umgebung« wurde vom staatlichen Schlichter in Lübeck nicht für verbindlich erklärt, ebenso eine ähnlich gelagerte Kölner Entscheidung gegen die »Arbeitgeber der Metall- und Feuerstein-Industrie«. Im Reichsarbeitsministerium wies Schlichter Ewald Kuttig[73] alle Zuständigkeit von sich, als sich die »Vereinigung Braunschweigischer Metallindustrieller« im laufenden Verfahren tariffähig erklärte; gegen die »Norddeutsche Gruppe des Gesamtverbandes Deutscher Metallindustrieller Abteilung Seeschifffahrtswesen« hatte Schlichter Paul Grabein[74] sämtliche Angestelltenverbände zur Rücknahme ihrer Anträge bewegt. Der Einschätzung der »Sozialpolitischen Abteilung« des DHV dürften die »freien« Gewerkschaften kaum widersprochen haben:

> »Die gegenwärtige ungünstige Wirtschaftslage hat zur Folge, daß gewisse Kreise der Arbeitgeber versuchen, die sozialen Einrichtungen, die in jahrzehntelanger Entwicklung unter stärkstem Einfluß der Kräfte der Arbeitnehmerschaft entstanden sind, zu beseitigen oder in ihrer Bedeutung herabzumindern.«[75]

Der DHV gab ein Gutachten in Marburg in Auftrag. Ausdrücklich wurde betont, dass das dortige Institut »bisher in Streitfragen zwischen der Arbeitgeber- und Arbeitnehmerschaft noch nicht eingegriffen hat, so dass es als absolut unvoreingenommen gelten kann.«[76]

2. *Hans Gerber*

Wichtigster Autor des Gutachtens war Hans Gerber,[77] der als Vertreter des Öffentlichen Rechts bekannt ist, doch in seiner Bedeutung für das Arbeitsrecht der Weimarer Republik keineswegs unterschätzt werden darf. Geboren 1899 im thüringischen Altenburg, studierte er nach dem Abitur Rechtswissenschaften in Jena und schloss sich dabei dem national-sozialen »Verein Deutscher Studenten« an, der ähnlich wie der DHV in Anschluss an die »Soziale Botschaft« gegründet worden war.[78] 1913 wurde Gerber bei dem Strafrechtler Heinrich Gerland[79] zum Dr. iur. promoviert. Nach dem Kriegsdienst war er ab 1919 Herausgeber der »Jungdeutschen Stimmen« des »Jungdeutschen Ordens«[80] und wurde Referent der Berliner Verwaltung des DHV; seine Gutachter- und Referententätigkeit, auch in der gewerkschaftlichen Bildungsarbeit setzte er bis 1933 fort. 1923 habilitierte sich Gerber in Marburg bei Felix Genzmer am »Institut für öffentliches Recht und Arbeitsrecht« und wurde 1927 außerplanmäßiger Professor in Marburg, im gleichen Jahr dann Professor in

71 Ernst Mehlich (1882–1926), Buchdrucker, Gewerkschafter und revisionistischer Sozialdemokrat (auch in der proletarischen Abstinenzbewegung aktiv), nach 1920 bis zu seinem frühen Tod (Eisenbahnunglück) häufig Schlichter, vgl. etwa Bähr (1989) 82–86 u. ö.

72 Nipperdey (1923). Vgl. auch Hollstein (2007) 29.

73 Ewald Kuttig (1888–1946); Oberregierungsrat im Reichsarbeitsministerium, 1929 Ministerialrat; Bähr (1989) 119 ff. Hansen / Tennstedt (Hg.) (2018) 108 f.

74 Paul Grabein (1869–1945), Dr. phil., Journalist, ab 1921 Referent Schifffahrtsangelegenheiten Reichsarbeitsministerium, Ministerialrat; häufiger Schlichter, Bähr (1989) 125, 209; Mechow (o. J.) 78 f.

75 Gerber (1926) 3 (Vorwort).

76 Gerber (1926) 5 (Vorwort).

77 Stolleis (1999) 285 ff.; Bullinger (1981); Braun / Grünzinger (Hg.) (2006) 86; Brunner (2020) 151, 163 f.

78 Zirlewagen (2014) 250–253.

79 Heinrich Gerland (1874–1944), Professor für Straf- und Prozessrecht in Jena, 1924–1928 MdR (DDP), Schwiegersohn von Otto Schott; Eisser (1964).

80 Mohler / Weissmann (2005) 298 f. m. w. N.

Tübingen. 1934 wurde Gerber auf den Lehrstuhl für öffentliches Recht und Arbeitsrecht in Leipzig berufen. Er trat die Nachfolge von Erwin Jacobi an, der seinen Lehrstuhl wegen »nichtarischer Herkunft« verloren hatte; es bestand jedoch weiterhin Kontakt zum Lehrstuhlvorgänger.[81] 1934 wurde Gerber Vorsitzender des evangelischen »Gustav-Adolf-Vereins«, 1941 erhielt er einen Lehrstuhl in Freiburg, den er 1945 zunächst verlor. In den Nachkriegsjahren war Rudolf Smend ein wichtiger Förderer, der Tätigkeiten im »Evangelischen Hilfswerk« vermittelte;[82] es kam auch zur Wiederaufnahme der Lehrtätigkeit in Freiburg. 1957 wurde Gerber emeritiert und verstarb 1981 in Bad Krozingen.

3. *Das »Gutachten über die Frage der gewollten Tarifunfähigkeit von Arbeitgeberorganisationen«*

Im November 1925 lag das »in Einvernehmen« mit den Marburger Professoren Fritz André, Felix Genzmer und Rudolf Schulz-Schäffer[83] erstellte »Gutachten über die Frage der gewollten Tarifunfähigkeit von Arbeitgeberorganisationen« vor.[84] Der Meinungsstreit wurde objektiv dargestellt. Das Ergebnis war ausdrücklich gegen Nipperdey und weitere »privatrechtlich befangene Rechtsgelehrte« wie den Bonner Handelsrechtler Heinrich Göppert,[85] Lehrer von Ernst Rudolf Huber. Gerber war keine antiindividualistische Volte zu schade:

> »Es muss aber einseitig privatrechtlich befangenen Rechtsgelehrten immer wieder gesagt werden, dass die im Sinne eines weltanschaulichen Individualismus vorgenommene Verselbständigung ein bedenklicher Irrtum ist.«[86]

Die »bürgerliche Freiheit« war bei Gerber »im Bereich des Privatrechts ein jederzeit (siehe Mieterschutzgesetzgebung!) widerrufbares und abänderbares Geschenk der staatlichen Gemeinschaft an ihre Glieder«.

Auch wenn in der Bildungsarbeit des DHV der deutsche Idealismus eine große Rolle spielte und der hochkirchlichen Strömungen nahestehende Gerber eine »Jugendschrift« Wilhelm von Humboldts aus der »Berlinischen Monatsschrift« 1792 zitierte,[87] war für ihn das Bestehen einer »natürlichen« Freiheit[88] »im ursprünglichen Sinne der Grund- und Freiheitsrechte«[89] allein eine Frage von Weltanschauung und Politik: »Das sind alles politische Erwägungen über die gerechte Ausgestaltung des von uns gezeigten Verhältnisses und setzen dieses so, wie klargelegt, voraus.«

Dabei bejahte Gerber ein »unbedingtes Wesen des Staates«; »staatliches Eingreifen vom Willen der Tarifparteien abhängig« zu machen, erniedrige »den Staat in altbekannter Weise zum Nachtwächter und Büttel von Privatinteressen«.[90] Eine Aussage des aus dem Umfeld Nipperdeys stammenden Juristen Erich Lange,[91] der die Satzungsautonomie der Koalitionen mit der Autonomie der »Landesfürsten« im Mittelalter verglichen hatte, war für Gerber Steilvorlage, die Tarifautonomie mit »mittelalterlichen Zuständen« in Verbindung zu bringen:

> »Wenn wir also nicht wollen, dass das nach schwerem Ringen wieder geeinte und mit letzten Opfern in seiner Einheit erhaltene Deutschland aufs Neue in sich zerbricht durch die Autonomie der modernen Landesherren, Ritter, Grafen und Städte, Ritterbündnisse und Städtebündnisse – dann mögen wir aufmerken, daß nicht das, was heute auf der Grundlage des geltenden Tarifrechts unmöglich ist, durch eine neue Formulierung im geplanten Arbeitstarifgesetze Wirklichkeit werde!«[92]

Das perhorreszierte »einartige« Recht des Mittelalters war ein damals beliebtes rechtspolitisches

81 Otto (2008) 247.
82 Wischnath (1986) 150–153.
83 Rudolf Schulz-Schäffer (1885–1966), 1921 außerordentlicher, 1936 ordentlicher Professor für Bürgerliches Recht in Marburg; Nagel (2000) 544.
84 Dazu auch Otto (2021) 303–305.
85 Heinrich Göppert (1867–1937), zunächst preußischer Beamter (Geheimer Regierungsrat), 1919–1935 Professor für Arbeits-, Handels- und Wirtschaftsverwaltungsrecht in Bonn; Wolff (2004).
86 Gerber (1926) 55.
87 Humboldt (1903).
88 Klippel (1975).
89 Zu Humboldt in diesem Kontext Klippel (1976) 132 f.; Klippel (1990) 206.
90 Gerber (1926) 59.
91 Lange (1925).
92 Gerber (1926) 61.

Argument.[93] Anders als Kandeler befürwortete Gerber aber grundsätzlich die privatrechtliche Organisationsform der Koalitionen. In einem Gutachten für den mit dem DHV kooperierenden »Verband der weiblichen Büro- und Hausangestellten« hatte Wilhelm Silberschmidt[94] dagegen den privatrechtlichen Charakter der Schlichtung betont.[95] Gerbers Ergebnis lag auf Linie der »Arbeitnehmerseite«. Rechtspolitisch bestand kein Unterschied zwischen »freien« und »nationalen« Gewerkschaften. Das eigenwillige, aber sachliche Gutachten kann als Indiz für das Potential des DHV als »deutsche Tories«, als konservative, aber die Republik bejahende Gewerkschaft gesehen werden. Dies ist aber letztlich eine kontrafaktische Fragestellung; eine erste Maßnahme des ab 1928 amtierenden DNVP-Vorsitzenden Alfred Hugenberg war die Entmachtung der aus dem DHV stammenden Parteifunktionäre.[96]

V. Parteipolitik und Auflösung

Der DHV war seit 1911 offiziell parteipolitisch nicht festgelegt.[97] Die Eigenbezeichnung »deutschnational« wurde in der Weimarer Republik behalten, doch exklusive Nähe zur »Deutschnationalen Volkspartei« nie gesucht, wenn auch der DHV als »Vorfeldorganisation« in den ersten Jahren der DNVP eine wichtige Rolle spielte.[98] Bevorzugt wurde aktiver Lobbyismus, etwa in Form finanzieller Unterstützung von Abgeordneten. Gegenüber SPD, von Bedeutung wegen der Konkurrenzsituation zum »AfA-Bund«, und KPD bestand ein Unvereinbarkeitsbeschluss,[99] die Nähe zur DVP war größer als zur DNVP. Nicht ohne Stolz verwies der Verband nach den Reichstagswahlen vom 14. September 1930 auf Abgeordnete in fünf Fraktionen, allerdings auch in der NSDAP.[100] 1931 kam der DHV nach eigenen Angaben auf 1.088 Parlamentarier (Reichs- und Landtage einschließlich preußischer Provinziallandtage), davon 210 der NSDAP. In der DNVP spielte der DHV seit 1929 keine Rolle mehr. Das Verhältnis zwischen DHV und NSDAP war ambivalent. Ab 1921 bestand innerhalb der Gewerkschaft der explizit rechtsstehende »Ring der Getreuen«, der allerdings immer Minderheit blieb. Hakenkreuze, die sich vor 1918 zuweilen auf Werbematerial des DHV befanden, wurden in der Weimarer Republik nicht benutzt. Ein früher Nationalsozialist im DHV war Franz Stöhr,[101] der 1925 erstmals in den Reichstag gewählt wurde; innerhalb der NSDAP stand er dem linken »Strasser-Flügel« nahe, dessen Rolle komplex ist.[102] Vom extremen rechten Rand hielt sich der DHV eher fern, seine Spitze tendierte schließlich zu den Abspaltungen der Hugenberg-DNVP (»Christlich-sozialer Volksdienst«, »Volkskonservative«). Der DHV befürwortete die Diktatur des Reichspräsidenten und die Politik Schleichers. Am 9. April 1933 erfolgte die Selbstgleichschaltung des Vorstandes, am 10. April 1933 die Entmachtung von Vorstandsmitglied Max Habermann, eines überzeugten und exponierten Gegners

93 Jacobi (1927), dazu Otto (2008) 164; weitere Nachweise, darunter Molitor und Sinzheimer, bei Blanke (2005) 109. Das Argument war auch noch in der zweiten Jahrhunderthälfte beliebt; ein Vergleich mit der »Verbreitung mittelalterlicher Stadtrechte« für das Recht des nachehelichen Unterhalts etwa bei Gernhuber (1983) 1072.

94 Wilhelm Silberschmidt (1862–1939), Richter am Bayerischen Obersten Landesgericht; Becker (2005) 176–183.

95 Gerber (1926) 57.

96 Mergel (2003) 346.

97 Stegmann (1972) 366 f. m. w. N.

98 Mergel (2003) 328 (»Organisationsstruktur, die der DNVP unterlegt werden konnte«).

99 Wirsching (2014) 17 f.

100 »Unsere Reichstagsabgeordneten« in »Deutsche Handelswacht« 1930, 355, hier zitiert nach Anders / Riesche (1985) 9. Nämlich für das Zentrum Otto Gerig (1885–1944, MdR 1923–1933, ermordet im KZ Buchenwald), für die DVP Otto Thiel (1884–1959, MdR 1920–1932) und Frank Glatzel (1892–1958; MdR 1930–1932), für die »Volkskonservativen« von der »Konservativen Volkspartei«, eine verfassungstreue Abspaltung der DNVP, Walther Lambach (1885–1943, 1920–1932 MdR, bis 1930 DNVP), für den »Christlichsozialen Volksdienst« (CSVD) Otto Rippel (1878–1957; MdR 1924–1928 und 1930–1932, bis 1929 DNVP), für die NSDAP Franz Stöhr (1879–1938, MdR 1924–1938, 1930/31 Reichstagsvizepräsident, 1924–1928 noch NSFP, starb nach Suizidversuch) und Albert Forster (1902–1952, MdR 1930–1945, hingerichtet). Bei Stöhr ist von »einem gewissen sozialpolitischen Rang«, so Huber (1981) 1122, die Rede.

101 Franz Stöhr (1879–1938), aus Böhmen, Buchhalter, ab 1906 hauptberuflich DHV-Funktionär, ab 1924 MdR, zunächst für die »Deutschvölkische Freiheitspartei«, ab 1927 NSDAP, 1930/31 Vizepräsident des Reichstags; nach 1933 nur nachgeordnete Funktionen, Vorwurf der Unterschlagung, Freitod. Huber (1981) 1122; Hamel (1967) 239 f.

102 Kissenkötter (1979) 130.

des Nationalsozialismus. Kurzzeitig hoffte der DHV, »Träger des Angestelltengedankens« in der »Deutschen Arbeitsfront« (DAF) zu werden, doch dies erwies sich als illusorisch. Das Gewerkschaftsvermögen fiel an den DAF, die offizielle Auflösung war am 20. Februar 1934. Der »Deutsche Ring« warb in Anzeigen bald ausdrücklich um SA-Männer.[103]

VI. Jenseits der Einheitsgewerkschaft? Nachspiel nach 1945

Der DHV wurde nach 1945 zunächst nicht wiederbegründet; wegen seiner antisemitischen Vergangenheit war er den Alliierten suspekt. Zahlreiche frühere Mitglieder nahmen aber aktiv am gewerkschaftlichen Neubeginn teil. Der in Haft verstorbene Max Habermann[104] hatte sich im Widerstand mit Wilhelm Leuschner und Jakob Kaiser für die Einheitsgewerkschaft eingesetzt. Hans Bechly rief zum Beitritt zu der neugegründeten DAG auf und verließ 1948 mit dieser den DGB;[105] gerade die Angestellten sollten in den ersten Nachkriegsjahren die Einheitsgewerkschaft faktisch opponieren. Aber auch in der DGB-Gewerkschaft Handel, Banken und Versicherungen (HBV) waren zahlreiche ehemalige DHV-Mitglieder. 1950 kam es zu einer Wiederbegründung des DHV (»DHV-neu«) im Christlichen Gewerkschaftsbund Deutschlands (CGB), der wie alle konfessionellen Gewerkschaften in der Bundesrepublik randständig blieb. Die 1933 zwangsweise in die DAF überführten Immobilien des wohlhabenden DHV wurden auf DAG und DGB, später auch HBV neu verteilt; in Hannover etwa fiel das »Haus der Kaufmannsgehilfen« an den DGB.[106] Das DHV-Haus in Hamburg wurde 1945 von der britischen Militärverwaltung beschlagnahmt und diente auch als Sitz der Versicherungsgesellschaft »Neue Welt«, wie der »Deutsche Ring« bis 1953 firmierte, und der »Deutschen Angestellten-Krankenkasse«, die Übertragung 1956 an die DAG war umstritten. 1958 entschied das Landgericht Hamburg endgültig für die Rückerstattung des Grundstücks an die Vermögensverwaltung der DAG. In den 1950er Jahren kam es zu mehreren Rechtsstreitigkeiten um frühere Immobilien des DHV.[107] Auch ein »DHV – neu« war vor einigen Gerichten überraschend erfolgreich, dessen Bedeutungslosigkeit konnte es jedoch nicht verhindern. In den ersten Jahrzehnten der Bundesrepublik erinnerte die Großgewerkschaft DAG außerhalb des DGB an eine Sonderrolle der Angestellten in den Gewerkschaften, an ein Sonderbewusstsein der Angestellten als vermeintliches Stiefkind der organisierten Arbeitnehmer. Dass diese Gewerkschaft ihren Sitz in der alten Hauptverwaltung des DHV hatte, die durch ihre Architektur ein Standesbewusstsein der Angestellten verkörperte, war kein Zufall, auch wenn der DAG sicher zu keinem Zeitpunkt das politische Erbe des DHV antrat. Mit dem Aufgehen der DAG in der neuen Großgewerkschaft ver.di im DGB endete endgültig 2001 ein berufsständischer Sonderweg der Angestellten, für den der DHV wie keine andere Gewerkschaft stand. Es bedarf keiner weiteren Erklärung, dass nach 1945 an das politische Erbe des DHV nicht angeknüpft wurde. Dennoch wäre es zu eng, den Erfolg des DHV im Milieu der Angestellten allein aus seiner politischen Rolle zu erklären. In der Weimarer Republik äußerte sich die Sonderrolle dieser Gewerkschaft weniger in politischen Aktionen als in dem Gutachten von Hans Gerber, das in seiner extrem berufsständischen und paternalistischen Begründung für die Koalitionsfreiheit der Bundesrepublik kaum als Vorbild oder auch nur Bezugspunkt geeignet ist. Allerdings: Gerbers Argumentation war politisch konservativ, aber nicht radikal oder extremistisch, er setzte sich mit anderen Ansichten fair auseinander und im Ergebnis, der Ablehnung der gewollten Tarifunfähigkeit, war er dicht bei Hugo Sinzheimer,[108] aber weit von Hans Carl Nipperdey entfernt. Und auch in der praktischen Gewerkschaftsarbeit war der DHV ein-

103 Abbildung bei Skrentny (1986) 37.
104 Max Habermann (1885–1944), Buchhändler, ab 1906 hauptamtlicher Funktionär DHV, Schriftleiter »Deutsche Handelswacht«, ab 1933 explizite Gegnerschaft zum Nationalsozialismus, wiederholt inhaftiert, im Widerstand tätig, in Gefangenschaft verstorben; Krebs (1966); Rütters (2009) 81.
105 Hierzu knapp auch Müller (2011) 31 ff.
106 Anders / Riesche (1985) 27.
107 Vgl. etwa »Erbschaft mit Saugnäpfchen« in »Der Spiegel«, Ausgabe vom 22. April 1949; Bericht über einen Streit zwischen Hans Bechly und dem früheren DHV-Geschäftsführer Hans Sube über das Gewerkschaftsvermögen.
108 Zur »gewollten Tarifunfähigkeit« Blanke (2005) 181; zeitgenössisch etwa Jacobi (1927) 213 (ausdrücklich gegen Gerber (1926)).

deutig auf der Arbeitnehmerseite positioniert und arbeitete mit den anderen Gewerkschaften durchaus pragmatisch zusammen. Insofern lässt sich die Frage »Auch eine Gewerkschaft?« für den DHV bejahen. Die 1930 stolz beworbenen Reichstagsabgeordneten des DHV decken ein Spektrum ab, das sich von dem aktiven Widerstandskämpfer Otto Gerig, 1944 ermordet im KZ Buchenwald, bis zu dem ausgesprochenen »Täter« und langjährigen Gauleiter Albert Forster, 1952 in Warschau als vielfacher Mörder hingerichtet, erstreckt. Dies dürfte die politischen Strömungen der Angestellten in der Weimarer Republik ziemlich exakt beschreiben. Der DHV war als Gewerkschaft beliebt, weil sich die Mehrheit der Angestellten in ihm wiedererkennen konnte. ■

Bibliographie

- Allfeld, Philipp (1924), Gewerblicher Rechtsschutz, Hamburg
- Anders, Bernd, Hans-Peter Riesche (1985), Gewerkschaft im »Volkskörper« – Der Deutschnationale Handlungsgehilfen-Verband (DHV) in der zweiten Hälfte der Weimarer Republik insbesondere in Niedersachsen, Hannover
- Arend, Sabine (2011), Emil Sehling (1860–1928) – zum 150. Geburtstag des Erlanger Ordinarius für Kirchenrecht, in: Zeitschrift der Savigny-Stiftung für Rechtsgeschichte (KA) 97, 411–439
- Auerbach, Inge (1979), Catalogus professorum academiae Marburgensis, Bd. 2: Von 1911 bis 1971, Marburg
- Bahr, Hermann (1894), Der Antisemitismus. Ein internationales Interview, Berlin
- Bähr, Johannes (1989), Staatliche Schlichtung in der Weimarer Republik. Tarifpolitik, Korporatismus und industrieller Konflikt zwischen Inflation und Deflation. 1919–1932, Berlin
- Bebel, August (1894), Sozialdemokratie und Antisemitismus. Rede auf dem IV. Parteitag der Sozialdemokratischen Partei zu Köln am Rhein. Nebst einem Nachtrag, Berlin
- Becker, Martin (2005), Arbeitsvertrag und Arbeitsverhältnis während der Weimarer Republik und in der Zeit des Nationalsozialismus, Frankfurt am Main
- Bender, Gerd (2021), Inklusive Arbeitspolitik – Strukturen der kollektiven Arbeitsverfassung, in: Schumann, Dirk u. a. (Hg.), Demokratie versuchen. Die Verfassung in der politischen Kultur der Weimarer Republik, Göttingen, 274–294
- Benz, Wolfgang (Hg.) (2009), Handbuch des Antisemitismus, Bd. 2, Berlin
- Bergsträsser, Ludwig (1928), Geschichte der politischen Parteien in Deutschland, 5. Aufl., Mannheim
- Blanke, Sandro (2005), Soziales Recht oder kollektive Privatautonomie? Hugo Sinzheimer im Kontext nach 1900, Tübingen
- Böge, Volker, Hartwig Stein (1999), 225 Jahre DAK. Gesundheit und soziale Verantwortung, Hamburg
- Börsch-Supan, Axel (1993), 1918–1993. 75 Jahre GAGFAH, Essen
- Braun, Hannelore, Gertraud Grünzinger (Hg.) (2006), Personenlexikon zum deutschen Protestantismus, Göttingen
- Brockhaus (1925), Der Große Brockhaus. Handbuch des Wissens in 20 Bänden, Bd. 4, 15. Aufl., Leipzig
- Brunner, Benedikt (2020), Volkskirche. Zur Geschichte eines evangelischen Grundbegriffs (1918–1960), Göttingen
- Bullinger, Martin (1981), Hans Gerber †, in: Archiv des öffentlichen Rechts 106, 651–654
- Collin, Peter (2016), Privat-staatliche Regelungsstrukturen im frühen Industrie- und Sozialstaat, Berlin
- Deutsch, Julius (1904), Der Kampf gegen die Lehrlingszüchterei, in: Sozialistische Monatshefte 12, 984–987
- Deutscher Ring (1963), Deutscher Ring, Lebensversicherungs-Aktiengesellschaft: 1913–1963, Hamburg
- Dubischar, Roland (1990), Zur Entstehung der Arbeitsrechtswissenschaft als scientific community, in: Recht der Arbeit 43, 83–97
- Eisser, Georg (1964), Heinrich Ernst Karl Balthasar Gerland, in: Neue Deutsche Biographie, Bd. 6, Berlin, 306
- Fenske, Wolfgang (2009), Innerung und Ahmung. Meditation und Liturgie in der hermetischen Theologie Karl Bernhard Ritters, Frankfurt am Main
- Gerber, Hans (1926), Gutachten über die Frage der gewollten Tarifunfähigkeit von Arbeitnehmerorganisationen, Hamburg
- Gernhuber, Joachim (1983), Der Richter und das Unterhaltsrecht, in: Zeitschrift für das gesamte Familienrecht 30, 1069–1079
- Gossler, Ascan (2001), Publizistik und konservative Revolution. Das »Deutsche Volkstum« als Organ des Rechtsintellektualismus 1918–1933, Hamburg
- Grimm, Hans (1926), Volk ohne Raum, München
- Halberstadt, Gerhard (1991), Die Angestellten und ihre Gewerkschaft. Stationen einer bewegten Geschichte, Freiburg (Br.)
- Hamel, Iris (1967), Völkischer Verband und nationale Gewerkschaft. Der Deutschnationale Handlungsgehilfen-Verband 1893–1933, Frankfurt am Main
- Hansen, Eckhard, Florian Tennstedt (Hg.) (2010), Biographisches Lexikon zur Geschichte der deutschen Sozialpolitik 1871 bis 1945, Bd. 1: Sozialpolitiker im Deutschen Kaiserreich 1871 bis 1918, Kassel
- Hansen, Eckhard, Florian Tennstedt (Hg.) (2018), Biographisches Lexikon zur Geschichte der deutschen Sozialpolitik 1871 bis 1945, Bd. 2: Sozialpolitiker in der Weimarer Republik und im Nationalsozialismus 1919 bis 1945, Kassel
- Heckmann, Friedrich (1986), Arbeitszeit und Sonntagsruhe. Stellungnahmen zur Sonntagsarbeit als Beitrag kirchlicher Sozialpolitik im 19. Jahrhundert, Essen

- Hering, Rainer (2005), Deutschnationaler Handlungsgehilfenverband (DHV), in: Kopitzsch, Franklin, Daniel Tilgner (Hg.), Hamburg Lexikon, 3. Aufl., Hamburg, 127–128
- Hollstein, Thorsten (2007), Die Verfassung als »Allgemeiner Teil«. Privatrechtsmethode und Privatrechtskonzeption bei Hans Carl Nipperdey (1895–1968), Tübingen
- Hörbrand, Maria (1926), Die Sonntagsruhe im Handelsgewerbe, Berlin-Wilmersdorf
- Huber, Ernst Rudolf (1981), Deutsche Verfassungsgeschichte seit 1789, Bd. 6: Die Weimarer Reichsverfassung, Stuttgart
- Humboldt, Wilhelm von (1903), Ideen zu einem Versuch, die Grenzen der Wirksamkeit des Staates zu bestimmen [1792], in: Leitzmann, Albert (Hg.), Wilhelm von Humboldts Werke, Bd. 1: 1785–1795, Berlin, 99–254
- Jacobi, Erwin (1927), Grundlehren des Arbeitsrechts, Leipzig
- Kampe, Norbert (1988), Studenten und »Judenfrage« im deutschen Kaiserreich. Die Entstehung einer akademischen Trägerschicht des Antisemitismus, Göttingen
- Kandeler, Hermann (1924), Gibt es eine gewollte Tarifunfähigkeit?, in: Der Kaufmann in Wirtschaft und Recht 3, 414–416
- Kandeler, Hermann (1925), Streik oder Aussperrung und Tarifvertrag, in: Kaskel, Walter (Hg.), Koalitionen und Koalitionskampfmittel, Berlin, 99–108
- Kandeler, Hermann (1927), Die Stellung der Berufsverbände im öffentlichen Recht, Berlin
- Kasischke, Daniela (1997), Antisemitismus im Spiegel der Hamburger Presse während des Kaiserreichs, Hamburg
- Kimmel, Elke (2009a), Johannes Irwahn, in: Benz (Hg.) 398
- Kimmel, Elke (2009b), Friedrich Schack, in: Benz (Hg.) 723
- Kissenkötter, Udo (1979), Gregor Strasser und die NSDAP, Stuttgart
- Klippel, Diethelm (1975), Freiheit VI. Der politische Freiheitsbegriff im modernen Naturrecht (17./18. Jahrhundert), in: Geschichtliche Grundbegriffe. Historisches Lexikon zur politisch-sozialen Sprache in Deutschland, Bd. 2, Stuttgart, 469–488
- Klippel, Diethelm (1976), Politische Freiheit und Freiheitsrechte im deutschen Naturrecht des 18. Jahrhunderts, Paderborn
- Klippel, Diethelm (1990), Von der Aufklärung der Herrscher zur Herrschaft der Aufklärung, in: Zeitschrift für Historische Forschung (ZHF) 17, 193–210
- Kocka, Jürgen (1969), Unternehmensverwaltung und Angestelltenschaft am Beispiel Siemens 1847–1914. Zum Verhältnis von Kapitalismus und Bürokratie in der deutschen Industrialisierung, Stuttgart
- Kocka, Jürgen (1977), Angestellte zwischen Faschismus und Demokratie. Zur politischen Sozialgeschichte der Angestellten. USA 1890–1940 im internationalen Vergleich, Göttingen
- Krebs, Albert (1966), Hans Max Habermann, in: Neue Deutsche Biographie, Bd. 7, Berlin, 397–398
- Kuhn, Hugo (1964), Felix Stephan Hermann Genzmer, in: Neue Deutsche Biographie, Bd. 6, Berlin, 195–196
- Kupisch, Karl (1970), Adolf Stoecker. Hofprediger und Volkstribun. Ein biographisches Porträt, Berlin
- Lange, Erich (1925), Nochmals: Zwangstarif und gewollte Tarifunfähigkeit, in: Das Schlichtungswesen. Monatsschrift für Arbeitsrecht und Schlichtung 7, 122–123
- Lattmann, Dieter (1969), Raum als Traum. Hans Grimm und seine Saga von der Volkheit, in: Schwedhelm, Karl (Hg.), Propheten des Nationalismus, München, 243–263
- Lokatis, Siegfried (1992), Hanseatische Verlagsanstalt. Politisches Buchmarketing im »Dritten Reich«, in: Archiv für Geschichte des Buchwesens 38, 1–189
- Lokatis, Siegfried (2019), Ernst Jüngers Marmorklippen. Benno Ziegler und die Hanseatische Verlagsanstalt, in: Jünger-Debatte 2, 9–28
- Mechow, Max (o. J. [d. i. 1969]), Namhafte CCer. Kurzbiographien verstorbener Landsmannschafter und Turnerschafter, Stuttgart-Möhringen
- Mergel, Thomas (2003), Das Scheitern des deutschen Tory-Konservatismus. Die Umformung der DNVP zu einer rechtsradikalen Partei 1928–1932, in: Historische Zeitschrift 276, 323–368
- Meyer, Andreas (1989), Die Verlagsfusion Langen-Müller. Zur Buchmarkt- und Kulturpolitik des Deutschnationalen Handlungsgehilfen-Verbands in der Endphase der Weimarer Republik, Frankfurt am Main
- Meyhöfer, Dirk (2007), Hamburg. Der Architekturführer, Berlin
- Mohler, Armin, Karlheinz Weissmann (2005), Die konservative Revolution in Deutschland 1918–1932, 6. Aufl., Graz
- Müller, Hans Peter (2011), Die Deutsche Angestellten-Gewerkschaft im Wettbewerb mit dem DGB. Geschichte der DAG 1947–2001, Baden-Baden
- Nagel, Anne Chr. (2000), Die Philipps-Universität Marburg im Nationalsozialismus: Dokumente zu ihrer Geschichte, Stuttgart
- Nerger, Katja, Rüdiger Zimmermann (2006), Zwischen Antisemitismus und Interessenvertretung. Periodika und Festschriften des Deutschnationalen Handlungsgehilfen-Verbands in der Bibliothek der Friedrich-Ebert-Stiftung. Ein Bestandsverzeichnis, Bonn
- Nienhaus, Ursula (1981), Von Töchtern und Schwestern. Zur vergessenen Geschichte der weiblichen Angestellten im deutschen Kaiserreich, in: Kocka, Jürgen (Hg.), Angestellte im europäischen Vergleich. Die Herausbildung angestellter Mittelschichten seit dem späten 19. Jahrhundert, Göttingen, 309–330
- Nipperdey, Hans Carl (1923), Beiträge zum Tarifrecht, Mannheim
- Nipperdey, Thomas (1990), Deutsche Geschichte 1866–1918, Bd. 1: Arbeitswelt und Bürgergeist, München
- Otto, Martin (2008), Von der Eigenkirche zum Volkseigenen Betrieb. Erwin Jacobi (1884–1965). Arbeits-, Staats- und Kirchenrecht zwischen Kaiserreich und DDR, Tübingen
- Otto, Martin (2013), Edgar Tatarin-Tarnheyden, in: Neue Deutsche Biographie, Bd. 25, Berlin, 794–796
- Otto, Martin (2021), Tarifautonomie als »Geschenk der staatlichen Gemeinschaft an ihre Glieder«. Hans Gerber und das Arbeitsrecht im »Deutschnationalen Handlungsgehilfenverband«, in: Deinert, Olaf et al. (Hg.), Arbeit, Recht, Politik und Geschichte. Festschrift für Michael Kittner, Frankfurt am Main, 298–305

- Palberg-Landwehr, Joachim (1993), Die Freien Angestelltengewerkschaften zwischen Arbeiterbewegung und bürgerlicher Konkurrenz. Eine historisch-soziologische Studie über den Afa-Bund. 1921–1933, Paderborn
- Rave, Rolf, Hans-Joachim Knöfel (1968), Bauen seit 1900 in Berlin, Berlin
- Rütters, Peter (2009), Der Deutschnationale Handlungsgehilfen-Verband (DHV) und der Nationalsozialismus, in: Historisch Politische Mitteilungen 16, 81–108
- Sander, Tobias (2009), Die doppelte Defensive. Soziale Lage, Mentalitäten und Politik der Ingenieure in Deutschland 1890–1933, Wiesbaden
- Schulz, Günther (2000), Die Angestellten seit dem 19. Jahrhundert, München
- Sehling, Emil (1924), Deutsches Handelsrecht, Hamburg
- Skrentny, Werner (1986), Hamburg zu Fuß. 20 Stadtteilrundgänge durch Geschichte und Gegenwart, Hamburg
- Sozialpolitische Abteilung (1925), Die Stellenlosigkeit der Kaufmannsgehilfen. Untersuchungen und Forderungen des Deutschnationalen Handlungsgehilfen-Verbandes, Hamburg
- Spiekermann, Uwe (2004), Freier Konsum und soziale Verantwortung. Zur Geschichte des Ladenschlusses in Deutschland im 19. und 20. Jahrhundert, in: Zeitschrift für Unternehmensgeschichte 49, 26–44
- Stegmann, Dirk (1972), Zwischen Repression und Manipulation. Konservative Machteliten und Arbeiter- und Angestelltenbewegung 1910–1918. Ein Beitrag zur Vorgeschichte der DAP/NSDAP, in: Archiv für Sozialgeschichte 12, 351–432
- Stolleis, Michael (1999), Geschichte des öffentlichen Rechts in Deutschland, Bd. 3: Staats- und Verwaltungsrechtswissenschaft in Republik und Diktatur 1914–1945, München
- Struwe-Urbanczyk, Alice (2017), Philipp Allfeld (1852–1940), in: Apel, Simon (Hg.), Biographisches Handbuch des Geistigen Eigentums, Tübingen, 27–29
- Tatarin-Tarnheyden, Edgar (1930), Berufsverbände und Wirtschaftsdemokratie. Ein Kommentar zu Artikel 165 der Reichsverfassung, Berlin
- Tennstedt, Florian (1981), Vorgeschichte und Entstehung der Kaiserlichen Botschaft vom 17. November 1881, in: Zeitschrift für Sozialreform 27, 663–710
- Thiel, Otto (1931), Hans Bechly, in: Heyde, Ludwig (Hg.), Internationales Handwörterbuch des Gewerkschaftswesens, Bd. 1, Berlin, 171
- Vogt, Dennis (im Druck), Arbeit am Konflikt. Die Lösung individueller Arbeitsstreitigkeiten im Deutschen Kaiserreich. 1890–1918, Frankfurt am Main
- Vordermayer, Thomas (2022), Fritz Fischer, in: NDB-online, https://www.deutsche-biographie.de/dbo044254.html#dbocontent (letzter Zugriff am 24. März 2022)
- Wilhelm, Cornelia (1998), Bewegung oder Verein? Nationalsozialistische Volkstumspolitik in den USA, Stuttgart
- Wirsching, Andreas (2014), Antikommunismus als Querschnittsphänomen politischer Kultur 1917–1945, in: Creuzberger, Stefan, Dierk Hoffmann (Hg.), »Geistige Gefahr« und »Immunisierung der Gesellschaft«. Antikommunismus und politische Kultur in der frühen Bundesrepublik, München
- Wischnath, Johannes Michael (1986), Kirche in Aktion. Das Evangelische Hilfswerk 1945–1957 und sein Verhältnis zu Kirche und Innerer Mission, Göttingen
- Wolff, Oliver (2004), Heinrich Göppert, in: Schmoeckel, Mathias (Hg.), Die Juristen der Universität Bonn im »Dritten Reich«, Köln, 233–250
- Wrobel, Ignaz [d.i. Kurt Tucholsky] (2001), Grimms Märchen [1928], in: Maack, Ute (Hg.), Kurt Tucholsky Gesamtausgabe, Bd. 10: Texte 1928, Reinbek, 358–368
- Zirlewagen, Marc (2014), Biographisches Lexikon der Vereine Deutscher Studenten, Bd. 1: Mitglieder A–L, Norderstedt

Johanna Wolf, Tim-Niklas Vesper, Benjamin Spendrin, Matthias Ebbertz

Neue Ansätze in der Arbeitsrechtsgeschichte. Ein digitales Quelleneditionsprojekt am Max-Planck-Institut für Rechtsgeschichte und Rechtstheorie

§ 1
Wer in Arbeit tritt, hat sich von dem Augenblick seines Eintritts an nach folgenden Gesetz zu richten.

§ 2
Während des zweiten Michaelis und Ostern ablaufenden Jahres wird wöchentlich 72 volle Stunden gearbeitet. Montags von früh 7 bis Abends 8 Uhr, Sonnabends von früh 6 bis Abends 5 Uhr, alle übrigen Arbeitstage von früh 6 bis Abends 8 Uhr. [...]

§ 4
Wenn jemand außerstande wäre, seine Arbeit wie es sich gehört anfangen und bis zur bestimmten Zeit fortführen zu können, hat er dies auf dem Comtoire mit der Bemerkung wie lang und aus welchen Gründen er bei der Arbeit fehlte, anzuzeigen. Wer diese Vorschrift nicht befolgt, ist des Lohnes auf denjenigen Theil des Tages, an welchem er gearbeitet hat, verlustig. Im Wiederholungsfall verliert er ein volles Tageslohn.[1]

Die hier niedergeschriebenen Regelungen zur Arbeitszeit aus dem Jahr 1834 stammen von einem der führenden Maschinenbauer seiner Zeit, Carl Gottlieb Haubold in Chemnitz. Nach dem Anschluss Sachsens an den Zollverein 1833 hatte der sächsische Unternehmer eine ältere Fabrik übernommen, die rasch in die Aktiengesellschaft Sächsische Maschinenbau-Compagnie überführt wurde und sich zu den »am besten eingerichteten Werken Deutschlands« entwickelte.[2] Haubold war bald nicht nur Pionier technologischer Neuerungen, sondern auch einer der ersten, der für seine Werkstätten ein sogenanntes Hausgesetz[3] erließ.[4] Für seine rund 300 Beschäftigten schrieb er eine Ordnung vor, um den Arbeitsablauf in den Werkstätten zu regeln, die Arbeiter[5] zur Arbeitsdisziplin zu erziehen, vor allem aber, um die Arbeitszeit um täglich eine Stunde zu erhöhen und damit die vom Staat aufgenommenen Kredite zu erwirtschaften.[6]

Dass der Fall Haubold in der Forschung so viel Aufmerksamkeit erlangte, liegt nicht nur an seiner Rolle als Vorläufer, sondern auch an der guten Ausgangslage. Das Hausgesetz von Haubold gelangte ins Stadtarchiv Chemnitz, da sich kurz nach

1 Abgedruckt in Forberger (1999) 420.
2 Strauss (1960) 57.
3 Diese Ordnungen firmierten je nach historischem Kontext unter unterschiedlichen Begriffen, wie Fabrik-, Arbeits- oder Betriebsordnung, Hausgesetz oder General-Regulativ. Trotz ihrer sehr unterschiedlichen Ausgestaltung war allen gemein, dass sie die Grundsätze der innerbetrieblichen Zusammenarbeit regelten, siehe Fischer (1950). Wenn durch den jeweiligen Kontext nicht anders vorgegeben, verwenden wir im Artikel den Begriff »Arbeitsordnung«.
4 Auch in den ersten Jahrzehnten des 19. Jahrhunderts existierten vermutlich schon Arbeitsordnungen. Da diese nicht dem Rat der Stadt vorgelegt werden mussten, ist darüber allerdings wenig bekannt, Uhlmann (1996) 166.
5 Wir haben uns entschieden, im Artikel das generische Maskulinum zu verwenden. In der Metallindustrie arbeiteten außer während der beiden Weltkriege mehrheitlich Männer. Durch die Berichte von Fabrikinspektoren wissen wir, dass unter den jugendlichen Arbeitern auch einige weibliche waren, allerdings fällt die Zahl im Vergleich zur Textilindustrie ebenfalls weitaus geringer aus. In der Analyse der Quellen arbeiten wir gesondert mit der Kategorie »Frauen« bzw. »weibliche Arbeiter«.
6 Uhlmann (1996) 166.

seiner Verkündung der Rat der Stadt als Schlichter einschalten musste. Die Arbeiter hatten dem Hausgesetz nicht zugestimmt und in Folge die Arbeit verweigert. Erst nach Einschaltung der Kommunalgarde und anschließender Verhandlung, die die Bezahlung der zusätzlichen Arbeit erreichte, nahmen die Arbeiter ihre Beschäftigung wieder auf.[7] Von den 218 dokumentierten Arbeitsordnungen sind im Stadtarchiv Chemnitz 157 erhalten.[8] Damit war für die Forschung auch der Vergleich verschiedener zu dieser Zeit und später entstandener Arbeitsordnungen möglich.[9] Über die Entwicklung von Arbeitsordnungen in bestimmten Regionen oder zu einzelnen, eher größeren Unternehmen gibt es vergleichbare historische Arbeiten.[10] Diese sind bisher allerdings noch nicht in einer übergreifenden Studie zusammengeführt worden und waren in diesem Sinne auch nicht Gegenstand der Arbeitsrechtsgeschichte. Dabei sind betriebliche Regulierungen für die Arbeitsrechtsgeschichte von außerordentlichem Wert.

Der folgende Artikel ist ein Werkstattbericht aus dem Projekt *Nichtstaatliches Recht der Wirtschaft. Die normative Ordnung der Arbeitsbeziehungen in der Metallindustrie vom Kaiserreich bis in die frühe Bundesrepublik* dar, durchgeführt am Max-Planck-Institut für Rechtsgeschichte und Rechtstheorie (mpilhlt).[11] Ziel des Projektes ist die Erstellung einer digitalen, annotierten Quellenedition, in der Arbeitsordnungen einen außerordentlichen Stellenwert haben. Sie sind nicht allein auf Grund ihrer Anzahl von Bedeutung, sondern auch wegen der Vielfalt ihrer Regelungsmaterien. Der Artikel geht zunächst auf ihre arbeitsrechtshistorische Bedeutung ein. Anschließend wird ein Einblick in das gesamte Forschungsprojekt gegeben und dessen Bedeutung für die Arbeitsrechtsgeschichte sowie seine Anschlussfähigkeit an das mpilhlt. Im zweiten Teil loten wir mit Hilfe eines Pilotprojekts zur Arbeitszeit die Möglichkeiten der Analyse einer digitalen Quellenedition aus und stellen nach methodischen Vorüberlegungen vier Beispiele aus diesem Pilotprojekt vor, die verdeutlichen sollen, welchen Mehrwert Annotationen in digitalen Quelleneditionen haben können, wie die Annotationskategorien mit Hilfe der Literatur und Stichproben der Quellen definiert werden und welche Forschungsfragen sich aus diesen Analysen explorieren lassen. Dabei soll betont werden, dass wir am Anfang dieses Annotationsprozesses stehen und alle Beobachtungen einen vorläufigen Charakter haben, der sich erst mit entsprechender Quellenbasis und Bearbeitung der Quellen bestätigen lassen wird.

I. Die Bedeutung von Arbeitsordnungen für die Arbeitsrechtsgeschichte

Arbeitsordnungen schrieben Arbeitsbedingungen und Verhaltensansprüche an die Arbeiter fest und stellten im 19. Jahrhundert die einzig formalisierte und schriftlich festgehaltene Rechtsgrundlage für betriebliche Arbeitsverhältnisse dar.[12] Wolfgang Wüst schreibt, Arbeitsordnungen seien »Schlüsseldokumente zum Verständnis von regionalen Arbeits- und Lebenswelten« gewesen, vergleichbar mit Gerichts- und Policeyordnungen der vorindustriellen Zeit.[13] Sie hatten im industriell produzierenden Betrieb eine disziplinierende

7 Ebd. 168.

8 Ebd. 166.

9 Über das Unternehmen Haubold und die Entwicklung des Chemnitzer Maschinenbaus allgemein gibt es zahlreiche Werke, siehe Strauss (1960); Stöbe (1962); Barth (1972).

10 Zwahr (1973); Metzger (2006); Wirtz (1982). Übergreifender, aber mit Fokus auf das 19. Jahrhundert Machtan (1981) sowie das Grundlagenwerk von Teuteberg (1961).

11 Siehe https://www.lhlt.mpg.de/forschungsprojekt/nichtstaatliches-recht-der-wirtschaft. Das Projekt unter Leitung von Peter Collin wird gefördert von der Hans-Böckler-Stiftung, dem Verband der Metall- und Elektroindustrie NRW e.V. und dem Institut der deutschen Wirtschaft, Köln. Im Rahmen der »Initiative Arbeitsrechtsgeschichte« erfolgt eine Kooperation mit dem Hugo-Sinzheimer-Institut. Die Projektarbeit wird begleitet von einem Fachbeirat, der aus folgenden Mitgliedern besteht: Prof. Dr. Astrid Wallrabenstein (Goethe-Universität Frankfurt am Main / Bundesverfassungsgericht) (Beiratsvorsitzende); Prof. Dr. Boris Gehlen (Universität Stuttgart); Prof. Dr. Thorsten Keiser (Universität Gießen); Prof. Dr. Michael Kittner (Hugo-Sinzheimer-Institut, Frankfurt am Main); Prof. Dr. Nina Kleinöder (Universität Bamberg); Dr. Hagen Lesch (Institut der Deutschen Wirtschaft, Köln); Dr. Luitwin Mallmann (Verband der Metall- und Elektro-Industrie NRW, Düsseldorf). An dieser Stelle sei allen Beteiligten herzlich gedankt für die Begleitung und Unterstützung des Projekts.

12 Arbeitsordnungen stellen damit – auch durch die im 19. Jahrhundert langanhaltende Nicht-Existenz von schriftlichen Arbeits- und Tarifverträgen – die einzige Quelle dar, die uns über die normative Ordnung der Arbeitswelt informieren, siehe auch Flohr (1981) 9–10.

13 Wüst (2010) 257.

Funktion.[14] Sie regulierten den Arbeitstag, dessen Länge und Pausen, die Anfangs- und Endzeiten. Zugleich spiegelte sich im Regelungsbemühen ein viel umfassenderer Anspruch des Arbeitgebers auf das (Arbeits-)Leben der Beschäftigten. Arbeitsordnungen regelten den Aufenthalt auf dem Betriebsgelände und am Arbeitsplatz, das Putzen von Maschinen, die Pausen, Toilettengänge, das Waschen, Umkleiden, Essen, Trinken, Rauchen. Erlaubte und unerlaubte Abwesenheit wurden ebenso geregelt, wie Pünktlichkeit oder blaue Montage.[15] Außerdem wurde festgelegt, wer die Regelungen kontrollieren und gegebenenfalls sanktionieren durfte. Arbeitsordnungen stellten Strafordnungen auf, wie das Beispiel des Hausgesetzes von Haubold zeigt: Sechs der 20 Paragrafen beinhalteten Strafmaßnahmen, in der Regel Lohnabzug, aber auch Kündigung, die bei Nichteinhaltung der vorgesehenen Arbeitszeiten oder einem Zuwiderhandeln gegen betriebliche Regeln eingesetzt wurden. Das konnte das Zuspätkommen betreffen, Trunkenheit oder Widerstand gegen Anordnungen des Vorgesetzten. Später wurden den Arbeitsordnungen Strafkataloge angehängt, die Vergehen und Strafe detailliert regelten. Damit dokumentieren sie Herrschafts- und Machtverhältnisse und die dadurch entstehenden Konflikte zwischen Fabrikbesitzern und Arbeitern – ablesbar auch an den mehrfach überarbeiteten Arbeitsordnungen, die in der Quellenedition gesammelt werden. Denn das Hinzukommen oder Wegfallen bestimmter Regulierungen war häufig das Resultat von Aushandlungsprozessen innerhalb der Fabrikgemeinschaft bzw. des industriellen Interessenkonflikts.[16]

Ähnlich wie es Gerd Bender für die Tarifautonomie diskutiert hat,[17] kann auch die Geschichte der Arbeitsordnung als Geschichte regulierter Selbstregulierung verstanden werden, denn einerseits ging die Normsetzung und Normdurchsetzung maßgeblich von Wirtschaftsorganisationen bzw. wirtschaftlichen Interessenvertretern aus, zunächst vornehmlich von Unternehmen, später auch von der erstarkenden Arbeiterbewegung. Andererseits war diese wirtschaftliche Selbstorganisation aber immer auch – und seit der Proklamation des Kaiserreichs um so stärker – staatlichen Steuerungsprozessen unterworfen.[18] Zwar war die Ausgestaltung der betrieblichen Arbeitsverhältnisse laut Reichsgewerbeordnung »Gegenstand freier Übereinkunft« und somit »staatlich geschützter, gesellschaftlicher Freiraum«,[19] doch zeigte sich, dass der Staat – auch schon vor 1869 – eine gewisse Beobachtungsfunktion innehatte.[20] Auch im Fall von Konflikten beanspruchte er Entscheidungsbefugnisse für sich. So legte § 19 des Hausgesetzes von Haubold fest, dass bei Konflikten zwischen Unternehmer und Arbeiter der Chemnitzer Stadtrat »auf polizeilichem Wege« entscheiden sollte, was wie oben berichtet bereits bei Bekanntgabe geschehen war.[21] Nicht zuletzt ist diesen staatlichen Vorgaben zu verdanken, dass heute eine solche Fülle an Arbeitsordnungen in den Archiven existiert. 1861 schrieb die sächsische Gewerbeordnung vor, dass ein Unternehmen ab 20 Arbeitern

14 Zwar setzte die Arbeitsordnung das Disziplinierungspotential schon voraus, durch Standardisierung und Objektivierung wurden Verhaltenskontrolle und -sanktionierung uniformiert und in verbindliche Regeln transformiert. Durch das Festschreiben dieser Regeln mussten diese nicht jedes Mal neu legitimiert und konstituiert werden und konnten sich als Bestandteil eines überdauernden Ordnungsgefüges für die Arbeiter durchsetzen, siehe Flohr (1981) 82.

15 Oskar Negt analysiert diese umfassende Regelungstätigkeit als Teil einer Machtpolitik, klar abgegrenzte funktionale Orte zu schaffen. Raum- und Zeitbestimmungen befinden sich in jeweils unterschiedlichen Abhängigkeiten, deren Grad sich durch die jeweiligen körperlichen Bewegungsspielräume beschreiben lasse. Negt (1984) 21–22.

16 Lüdtke argumentiert, dass Regulierungen, die in Arbeitsordnungen hinzukamen, häufig Ergebnis von betrieblichen Auseinandersetzungen waren bzw. der Versuch der Eindämmung widerständigen Verhaltens, Lüdtke (1993) 92. Auch Flohr weist darauf hin, dass die immer präziseren Regelungen der Arbeitsordnungen Resultat der Kämpfe der Arbeiterbewegung waren, in deren Ergebnis die Willkür der Generalklausel, die dem Fabrikherrn die jeweilige Auslegung überließ, einem ausdifferenzierten, verlässlicheren Normensystem wich, das Handlungen und deren Strafbarkeit schließlich für beide Seiten kalkulierbar machte. Siehe Flohr (1981) 21.

17 Bender (2012).

18 Collin (2011a) 5.

19 Machtan (1981) 180.

20 Die Ursprünge der freien Übereinkunft zwischen Arbeitgeber und Arbeitnehmer waren bereits im preußischen Gesetz über die polizeilichen Verhältnisse der Gewerbe aus dem Jahr 1811 geregelt, mit der Reinhard Richardi den Beginn der modernen Arbeitsverfassung in Deutschland fasst, siehe Richardi (2002) 24.

21 Strauss (1960) 66.

eine Arbeitsordnung zu verfassen habe und diese auch einer »obrigkeitlichen Genehmigung bedurfte«,[22] weshalb gerade für den sächsischen Raum eine Vielzahl an Arbeitsordnungen aus den Jahren 1861/1862 im Sächsischen Staatsarchiv zu finden waren.

Für das Kaiserreich kam diese Vorgabe erst mit der Gewerbeordnungsnovelle 1891 zustande, die nun ebenfalls ab 20 Arbeitern eine Arbeitsordnung vorschrieb.[23] Mit dem Inkrafttreten des Betriebsrätegesetzes 1920 wurde schließlich festgelegt, dass Arbeitsordnungen mit dem Betriebsrat abzustimmen und von diesem zu unterzeichnen seien.[24] Für diesen Zeitraum ist in den Archiven fast in jedem der dort archivierten Unternehmensbestände eine Arbeitsordnung zu finden. Viele der Unternehmer orientierten sich dabei an den von den Arbeitgeber- und Arbeitnehmervertretungen ausgehandelten, sektoralen Arbeitsordnungen.[25] Eine letzte Welle neuer Arbeitsordnungen erklärt sich aus dem Gesetz zur Ordnung der nationalen Arbeit 1934. Laut Arbeitsordnungsgesetz hatte der »Führer des Betriebes« über die Ordnung des Betriebes zu entscheiden und schriftlich eine nun als Betriebsordnung bezeichnete Arbeitsordnung zu erlassen.[26]

II. Forschungsstand und Einblick in ein Forschungsprojekt des mpilhlt zum nicht-staatlichen Recht der Wirtschaft

Arbeitsordnungen sind also nicht nur wegen ihrer frühen Existenz für die Arbeitsrechtsgeschichte interessant, sondern auch wegen ihrer Langlebigkeit, auch wenn sich im Laufe der Jahrhunderte ihre Funktion veränderte. Stellten sie im frühen 19. Jahrhundert die einzig formalisierte Rechtsquelle zur Regulierung von betrieblichen Arbeitsverhältnissen dar, waren sie im 20. Jahrhundert neben Tarifnormen und Gesetzesrecht eine von vielen. Dass wir keine umfassenden Kenntnisse über die Regulierung von Arbeitsbeziehungen im 19. Jahrhundert haben, liegt nicht zuletzt an der fehlenden Quellenbasis[27] und ist einer der Gründe, weshalb die Arbeitsrechtsgeschichte häufig erst mit der Betrachtung des Kaiserreichs beginnt bzw. hier sogar die Wurzeln des heutigen Arbeitsrechts gesehen werden.[28] Es fehle an eigenständigen, quellengestützten Gesamtdarstellungen und überhaupt an einer zusammenfassenden Darstellung des Rechts der Arbeitswelt, so der Arbeitsrechtshistoriker Joachim Rückert und meint damit auch die Leerstellen im 19. Jahrhundert.[29] Diese fehlen-

22 Gesetz- und Verordnungsblatt für das Königreich Sachsen 1861, 217, nach: Däubler / Kittner (2020) 73.

23 Große Novelle zur Reichsgewerbeordnung vom 1. Juli 1891 (RGBl. 141). Richardi sieht darin eine Neuausrichtung der Arbeiterschutzpolitik. Sie ging zurück auf den Erlass des Kaisers vom Februar 1890, der die Wahrung der Gesundheit, Sittlichkeit und der wirtschaftlichen Bedürfnisse des Arbeiters zur Aufgabe des Staates erklärte. Die Novelle der Reichsgewerbeordnung gab dem Arbeiterausschuss im Betrieb nun die Gelegenheit, sich zum Inhalt von Arbeitsordnungen zu äußern, siehe Richardi (2002) 29. Thilo Ramm sieht darin auch die »Geburtsstunde des Dualismus im kollektiven Arbeitsrecht Deutschlands«. Siehe Ramm (1978) 207.

24 § 104 Abs. 5–7 Betriebsrätegesetz vom 4. Februar 1920 (RGBl. 145).

25 Siehe z. B. Sächsisches Staatsarchiv, Staatsarchiv Chemnitz (im Folgenden: SächsStA-C), 31029 Deutsche NILES Werke AG, Werk Siegmar, Nr. 8, Arbeitsordnung für die Metallindustrie vereinbart zwischen dem Gesamtverband Deutscher Metallindustrie, Berlin, einerseits, und dem Deutschen Metallarbeiterverband, Stuttgart, dem Christlichen Metallarbeiterverband, Duisburg, und dem Gewerksverein Deutscher Metallarbeiter, Berlin, andererseits. Mit ergänzenden Vereinbarungen zwischen dem Chemnitzer Bezirksverband Deutscher Metallindustrieller und dem Deutschen Metallarbeiter-Verband, Verwaltungsstelle Chemnitz u. a., vom 6. September 1920.

26 §§ 26 ff. Gesetz zur Ordnung der Nationalen Arbeit vom 20. Januar 1934 (RGBl. I, 45).

27 Laut Jürgen Brand sei die Ordnung und Regelung gewerblicher Produktion, dem Bereich, der unter das heutige Arbeitsrecht fällt, für dieses Jahrhundert weitgehend unbekannt. Siehe Brand (2011) 134.

28 Thilo Ramm konstatiert, dass viele Vorschriften der Gewerbeordnung, des Handelsgesetzbuchs, des Bürgerlichen Gesetzbuchs oder des preußischen Berggesetzes aus dieser Zeit stammen. Wenn man die Novelle zur Gewerbeordnung von 1891 hinsichtlich einiger Grundgedanken als Vorläufer des Betriebsverfassungsgesetzes fasst, lassen sich auch die Ursprünge des BRG in dieser Linie interpretieren, siehe Ramm (1978) 191.

29 Rückert (2015) 8.

de Quellengrundlage war Anlass am mpilhlt über eine Quellenedition nachzudenken, die die Normativität industrieller Beziehungen in ihrer Vielgestaltigkeit abbilden sollte – vom frühen 19. Jahrhundert bis zur Mitte des 20. Jahrhunderts.[30] Dabei wird nicht nur nach Arbeitsordnungen recherchiert, sondern auch nach anderen Quellen, die die Arbeitsbeziehungen in der Metallindustrie regulierten.[31] Die Quellen werden in Staats-, Stadt- und Wirtschaftsarchiven recherchiert,[32] digitalisiert[33] und anschließend für die computergestützte Weiterverarbeitung und Publikation vorbereitet. Die mit Hilfe eines automatischen Textkennungsprogramms (OCR, Optical Character Recognition) gesammelten Normtexte werden anschließend in mehreren teils automatischen, teils manuellen Schritten ediert.[34] Die Quellenedition beinhaltet momentan 417 Quellen, dabei haben Arbeitsordnungen (140) und Tarifverträge (99) den größten Anteil.[35]

Das Projekt knüpft an eine Vielzahl bisheriger Forschungen am mpilhlt an. In der Wissenschaft steht eine ausführliche Diskussion über die Möglichkeiten der Zusammenführung noch aus.[36] Der Aufsatz verortet das Projekt zunächst im Kontext der *Multinormativität*. Multinormativität geht von der »Koexistenz verschiedener *modi* von Normativität« im selben sozialen Raum aus und greift dabei auf einen weiten Kreis von Rechtsquellen zurück.[37] In Bezug auf unser Projekt heißt das zwar nicht, dass mit der Quellenedition alle Texte erfasst werden (können), die alle Änderungen von Arbeitsordnungen dokumentieren – wie beispielsweise die wöchentlichen Ankündigungen über Mehrarbeit –, und ebenso wenig kann Material dokumentiert werden, das die Aushandlungen oder Praktiken dieser Regulierungen betrifft.[38] Es bedeutet aber dennoch, dass wir alle Formen von Arbeitsordnungen, von den frühen Hausgesetzen der 1830er Jahre bis zu den Betriebs-

30 Die Gründe für die Wahl des Zeitraums, des Sektors und des Untersuchungsraums (verschiedene vom Projektteam definierte Regionen im Gebiet der heutigen Bundesrepublik) werden aus Platzgründen an anderer Stelle ausgeführt.

31 Zu den Normtexten zählen neben den Arbeitsordnungen u. a. Statuten von Betriebs- und Pensionskassen, Lehrverträge, Tarifverträge (mit ihren unterschiedlichen Bezeichnungen) sowie Satzungen von Interessenvertretungsorganisationen (Arbeitgeber und Arbeitnehmer).

32 Dazu wurden im Projektteam bestimmte Stichworte definiert, die bei der Suche in den Archiven Orientierung bieten. In den sehr unterschiedlichen Suchmaschinen der Archive wird zunächst automatisch gesucht und anschließend bei der Durchsicht der Bestände händisch geprüft.

33 Je nach Umfang und Möglichkeit werden die Quellen mit Hilfe eines Scan-Tents und entsprechender Kamera von den Wissenschaftler*innen eigenständig aufgenommen oder es wird ein Reproduktionsauftrag an das Archiv gestellt.

34 Im Einzelnen wird für das OCR die Software OCR4all (Reul et al. (2019)) eingesetzt, für die automatische Transformation aus dem Ausgabeformat der OCR-Software in das TEI/XML-Format eine angepasste Variante des XSLT-Programms page2tei (Kampkaspar (2022)), und für die manuelle Überarbeitung (etwa die Eintragung der hierarchischen Textstruktur von Abschnitten und Unterabschnitten sowie die orthographische Korrektur) das Programm oXygen XML Editor, https://www.oxygenxml.com/ (zuletzt abgerufen am 11. April 2022).

35 Mit Stand vom 5. April 2022. Die Suche der Quellen erfolgte nach einer Schwerpunktsetzung, die sich auf vom Projekt definierte Regionen konzentriert, darunter Sachsen, das Ruhrgebiet (Rheinland und Westfalen), Berlin, Nürnberg / Fürth. Die Recherche für die Region Sachsen ist mit der Durchsicht der drei Hauptstandorte des Sächsischen Staatsarchivs – Dresden, Leipzig und Chemnitz – beinahe abgeschlossen, während die anderen Regionen derzeit bearbeitet werden.

36 An dieser Stelle soll nur der Ansatz der Multinormativität erwähnt werden. Das Projekt ist aber gleichzeitig Teil des am mpilhlt angesiedelten Forschungsfeldes *Sonderordnungen* (www.lhlt.mpg.de/forschungsfeld/sonderordnungen) und leistet einen Beitrag zum Forschungsansatz *Historische Normativitätsregime*.

37 Duve (2017) 90. Im Prinzip ist dieser Rechtspluralismus dem Arbeitsrecht inhärent. Viele Definitionen zum Arbeitsrecht bzw. der Arbeitsverfassung gehen von einem weiten Verständnis des Begriffes aus. So schreibt Ramm, dass es »die gesamten Arbeitsbeziehungen auf allen Ebenen« umfasse: »der individuellen mit dem Arbeitsvertrag, der kollektiven mit den kollektiven Vereinbarungen, den Tarifverträgen und den Betriebsvereinbarungen und endlich den Arbeitsmarkt und die staatlichen Regelungen.« Ramm (1978) 195. Allgemeiner, aber mit gleicher Intention formuliert Richardi, die Arbeitsverfassung sei die Gesamtheit der geschriebenen und ungeschriebenen Normen, die »das Arbeitsleben als Bestandteil der wirtschaftlichen Ordnung in sachlicher, personeller und funktioneller Beziehung regeln.« Siehe Richardi (2002) 22.

38 Das beschriebene Erkenntnisinteresse und projektökonomische Zwänge bewogen uns ebenfalls, editorische Aspekte wie die Aufzeichnung einer diplomatischen Erfassung der Quellen oder die Anzeige von Bilddigitalisaten zugunsten der Quellenbreite und -anzahl sowie zugunsten der im Folgenden beschriebenen Erschließungsanstrengungen zurückzustellen.

vereinbarungen im 20. Jahrhundert, als Rechtsquellen ernst nehmen und damit über traditionelle Quellen der Arbeitsrechtsgeschichte hinausgehen.[39] Im Fokus der Multinormativität stehen besonders Interaktionen und Dynamiken, Austausch- und Verschmelzungsprozesse.[40] Das bedeutet für unser Projekt, den Einflüssen von Gesetzen auf betriebliche Regulierungen nachzugehen. Welchen Einfluss hatten beispielsweise die Regelungen zu Arbeits- und Pausenzeiten für jugendliche Arbeiter seit dem Preußischen Regulativ von 1839? Fand durch die gesetzlichen oder durch die von Interessenvertretern ausgehandelten Vorgaben zu Arbeitsordnungen eine Homogenisierung der Arbeitsordnungen statt oder behielten es sich die Unternehmer auch im 20. Jahrhundert noch vor, über Details ihrer Betriebsordnung – so gering die Differenzen auch sein mochten – selbst zu entscheiden? Wo lagen hier die Frei- und Spielräume? Indem wir von einem praxeologischen Verständnis von Recht ausgehen, das die vielfältigen Bedingungen und Regeln der Normerzeugung berücksichtigt, finden auch Forschungsfragen der Sozial- und Wirtschaftsgeschichte Berücksichtigung,[41] wenn wir beispielsweise untersuchen, ob der allgemeine Anstieg des Tabakkonsums in der Gesellschaft Einfluss auf die Regulierung oder ggf. das Verbot des Rauchens auf dem Fabrikgelände hatte.

III. Pilotprojekt über die Regulierung von Arbeitszeit in Arbeitsordnungen

Da die Durchsetzung und Normierung von *Arbeitszeit* ein durchgängiges Ordnungsproblem in industrialisierten Gesellschaften darstellt und sich diese Bemühungen in allen Arbeitsordnungen widerspiegeln, haben wir uns im Projekt entschieden, auf diesen Teilaspekt genauer einzugehen. Bestimmungen zur Arbeitszeit finden sich in allen Arbeitsordnungen, unabhängig von Zeit, Ort und Unternehmen. Ihre verbindliche Festsetzung und vor allem ihre erfolgreiche Durchsetzung waren zentral für den wirtschaftlichen Betrieb einer komplexen Fertigung. Auch in der Sozial- und Wirtschaftsgeschichte sind die Entwicklung und die Auseinandersetzung um Arbeitszeit ein zentrales und bis heute viel diskutiertes Thema.[42]

Frühe Arbeitsordnungen definierten zunächst Anfang und Ende der Arbeitszeit für verschiedene Jahreszeiten sowie Wochen-, Wochenend- und Feiertage, was durch die Regulierung von Pausenzeiten später ergänzt wurde. Die Arbeitszeit verdichtete sich, während die verschiedenen Tätigkeiten, die auf und außerhalb des Fabrikgeländes ausgeübt wurden, ausdifferenziert wurden: Arbeit, Freizeit, Reproduktionsarbeit wurden voneinander getrennt und der intermittierende Arbeitsprozess der handwerklichen Produktionsweise wurde normiert und homogenisiert.[43] Dieser Normierungsprozess kann in den Arbeitsordnungen nachvollzogen und anhand der umfassenden Quellensammlung für unterschiedliche Regionen räumlich und zeitlich vergleichend untersucht werden. Ziel des Pilotprojektes ist es, am Beispiel der Regulierung von Arbeitszeit die Möglichkeiten der digitalen Quellenedition auszuloten und dafür Schlagworte zu entwickeln, die die Normtexte strukturell erschließen.

IV. Methodische Überlegungen zur Verschlagwortung der digitalisierten Quellenedition am Beispiel der Arbeitszeit

Durch die umfassende Datengrundlage und die Digitalisierung der Quellen ist erstmals die Darstellung ihrer Normenvielfalt, ihrer Transformation und ihrer historischen Entwicklung möglich.[44] Bei Durchsicht der Quellen im Hinblick auf

39 Trotz aller Bemühungen, in den Archiven so viele Quellen wie möglich zur Regulierung von Arbeitsbeziehungen auszuheben, ist uns bewusst, dass wir unvollständig bleiben und der Reiz der Quellenedition darin liegt, beständig zu wachsen und für weitere Quellenprojekte anschlussfähig zu sein.

40 Duve (2017) 93.

41 Ebd. 94.

42 So organisiert die German Labour History Association für das Jahr 2022 eine Konferenz zu diesem Thema, siehe: Arbeit/Zeit. Globale Perspektiven (https://www.hsozkult.de/event/id/event-95216).

43 Tätigkeiten, die zuvor während der Anwesenheit in der Fabrik ausgeübt wurden, wurden aus der Fabrikzeit in die private Zeit verschoben und damit die tatsächliche Arbeitszeit geregelt, siehe auch Deutschmann (1982) 36.

44 Duve (2014) 33–34. Weitere Möglichkeiten der Digitalisierung sind statistische Analysemethoden, Nachnutzungsmöglichkeiten für andere Forschungsrichtungen, wie korpuslinguistische Untersuchungen, die in diesem Projekt bisher noch nicht Berücksichtigung finden konnten. Insgesamt sind Forschungsergebnisse für

die Forschungsfragen ist deutlich geworden, dass sich mit den Möglichkeiten der Digitalisierung auch neue Herausforderungen ergeben. So ist es zur Bearbeitung und Anwendung digitaler Projekte zunächst notwendig, die Struktur der digitalisierten Texte zu erfassen und ein möglichst auf alle Texte anwendbares Strukturschema zu entwickeln.[45] Die uns vorliegenden Texte sind zwar nach einer normativen Logik aufgebaut und beinhalten gliedernde Überschriften und Absätze, doch ist ihre Struktur nicht quellenübergreifend gleich. So erschien es notwendig, nach äquivalenten Regelungsmaterien zu suchen und sie für spätere Nutzer*innen auch verständlich und in ihrem Entstehungsprozess nachvollziehbar zu machen.[46] Diese Idee mündete in die Entwicklung eines Schlagwortbaumes mit dem Fokus auf Arbeitszeit, was bedeutete, die Erkenntnisinteressen der Projektbeteiligten einzubeziehen, mögliche Forschungsinteressen zu antizipieren und zu reflektieren, wo eine (scheinbar) *objektive* Datenerfassung endet.[47] Ein Ansatz dafür ergab sich aus der Analyse exemplarisch ausgewählter Arbeitsordnungen. Ausgehend von der Frage, welche Erkenntnismöglichkeiten digital edierte Quellen für die Arbeitsrechtsgeschichte bieten können, haben wir vier Regelungskomplexe ausgemacht, die in nahezu allen Arbeitsordnungen vorkamen. Dies sind

1. Formale *Regelungsbegriffe*, worunter Arbeitszeit, Überarbeit, Kontrolle und Strafen fallen,
2. *Tätigkeiten*, wie Essen, Rauchen oder der Konsum von Alkohol,[48]
3. *Rollen*, darunter erwachsener und jugendlicher Arbeiter und Arbeiterinnen, Meister oder Pförtner[49] und
4. *Physische Objekte*, wie Fabrikuhr, Maschine, Werkzeug oder besondere Räumlichkeiten wie Werkstätten, Pausenräume, Wege oder Tore.

In einem mehrstufigen, iterativen Prozess haben wir die Schlagworte hierarchisiert und zusammengeführt.[50] Ziel dieser Hierarchisierung ist es, Inhalte mit ähnlicher Bedeutung zusammenzufassen, somit die Komplexität zu reduzieren und eine umfassende Auswertung zu ermöglichen.[51] Im TEI/XML-Standard, der die Kodierung unserer Quellen beschreibt, können zusammenhängende Textabschnitte mit Schlagworten markiert werden, von einzelnen Worten bis hin zu ganzen Absätzen. Ein Textabschnitt kann dabei auch mehrere Schlagworte enthalten. Das Programm TEI Publisher, das wir als Plattform für die Darstellung der Quellen für die Nutzenden gewählt haben, verfügt neuerdings über die Funktion, ausgewählten Textpassagen ein Schlagwort aus unserem Katalog zuzu-

Dritte leichter nachvollziehbar und damit transparenter, siehe Sukhondyaeva (2016); Thaller (2016). Siehe auch das Editionsprojekt des mpilhlt *Policeyordnungen der Frühen Neuzeit* (https://policey.lhlt.mpg.de/web/).

45 Birr (2016) 331.

46 Schwandt (2016) 337; Schlauwitz (2016) 350.

47 Drucker (2011); Küsters / Volkind / Wagner (2019) 256–257.

48 Die Zuordnung einer Tätigkeits- oder Verhaltensbeschreibung zur ersten oder zweiten Kategorie orientierte sich an der Frage, ob die Tätigkeit bzw. das Verhalten auch unabhängig vom normativen Kontext (Arbeitsregime) vorstellbar ist. Dies gilt für das »Schlafen«, nicht aber für »Strafen«.

49 Hiermit sind Rollen gemeint, die durch die Berufsbezeichnung (»Pförtner«), die Funktion im allgemeinen Betrieb (»Vorarbeiter«) oder den sozialen Kontext (»jugendliche Arbeiter«) bestimmt werden und die letztlich Erwartungen definieren, die von der aktuellen Handlung unabhängig sind. Davon zu unterscheiden sind Rollen, die die Aufgabenverteilung in konkreten Interaktionen bestimmen (»Käufer«, »Verkäufer«). Erstere werden in der Literatur häufig als »soziale Rollen« diskutiert, letztere als »thematische Rollen«. Häufig beziehen sich normative Regelungen darauf, dass die Wahrnehmung bestimmter thematischer Rollen an die soziale Rolle gebunden ist (z.B. mag die thematische Rolle des »Meldungsempfängers« in bestimmten Kontexten der Meldung von Abwesenheit den »Meistern« vorbehalten sein. Siehe Goy / Magro / Rovera (2018); Masolo et al. (2004)).

50 Zur Veranschaulichung des Schlagwortbaumes und seiner Tiefe, hier ein Beispiel: 0 Regelungsbegriff / 0.1 Arbeitszeit / 0.1.1 Arbeitstage / 0.1.1.2 Sonderwerktag / 0.1.1.2.2 Sonnabend.

51 Beispielsweise sind in der Gruppe 3.1 Signaleinrichtungen, Fabrik- und Stechuhren sowie Glocken zusammengefasst. Durch die Zuordnung zu einer gemeinsamen Oberkategorie soll es in der Edition möglich werden, diese Regelungen gesammelt auszugeben.

weisen; somit ist es für uns nicht mehr nur eine Präsentations-, sondern auch eine Annotationsplattform zum projektinternen Gebrauch.[52]

Im Folgenden stellen wir exemplarisch vier Schlagworte vor, die im Kontext des Pilotprojektes Arbeitszeit diskutiert und stichprobenartig in den Arbeitsordnungen gesucht wurden. Damit soll veranschaulicht werden, wie Schlagworte durch ein antizipiertes Forschungsinteresse generiert, kontextualisiert und definiert werden können und welcher Mehrwert durch die Verschlagwortung einer digitalen Quellenedition entstehen kann. Dabei ist zu beachten, dass die hier ausformulierten Beispiele erste Beobachtungen darstellen und die aufgestellten Hypothesen aus der Literatur und aus den Stichproben der bereits vorhandenen Arbeitsordnungen stammen. Ein darauffolgender Arbeitsschritt wird dann sein, die Annotation *aller* Arbeitsordnungen der digitalen Quellenedition vorzunehmen und sie anschließend auszuwerten, worauf in diesem Artikel auf Grund des Arbeitsstandes nicht genauer eingegangen wird.

V. Beispiele aus der Verschlagwortung von Arbeitsordnungen zum Thema Arbeitszeit

1. *Pausen*

In der Literatur sind Arbeitspausen als betrieblich regulierte Form der Freizeit dargestellt worden, die kollektiven und konventionalisierten Regeln gehorchte.[53] Ihre wirkliche Ausgestaltung in Fabriken des 19. und 20. Jahrhunderts lässt sich zwar aus den vorliegenden Rechtsquellen nicht exakt rekonstruieren, dennoch ermöglichen sie einen Einblick in den Umgang mit und das Verhältnis von Arbeitszeit und Pause und deren Veränderung. So sind Angaben von Pausen und Pausenzeiten in den Arbeitsordnungen des frühen 19. Jahrhunderts nur selten zu finden.[54] Es ist jedoch nicht anzunehmen, dass Arbeiter ohne Unterbrechung arbeiteten, vielmehr ist aus den sehr langen Arbeitszeiten zu schließen, dass die Arbeiter je nach Bedarf individuelle Pausen einlegten, um Bedürfnissen wie Essen oder Kinderbetreuung nachzugehen.[55] Arbeitsordnungen der 1840/50er Jahre enthalten erste Festlegungen für Unterbrechungen der Arbeit zu einem bestimmten Zweck, wie Frühstück oder Mittagessen, legen allerdings nur eine Dauer, keine konkreten Uhrzeiten fest.[56] Formulierungen wie »übliche Frühstückszeit« weisen darauf hin, dass diese Pausen einem gewissen Gewohnheitsrecht unterlagen, welches keiner Konkretisierung in der entsprechenden Regulierung bedurfte – ganz anders in den Arbeitsordnungen nach 1900. Hier ist nun nicht nur von Pausen, Pausendauer und exakten Uhrzeiten die Rede, sondern es werden auch separate Angaben zu besonderen Gruppen, wie jugendlichen Arbeitern, gemacht.[57] Diese erste, auf Stichproben beruhende Beobachtung bedarf einer genaueren Analyse der annotierten Quellen und könnte interessante Befunde zutage fördern. Indem alle Pausenarten (vormittags, mittags und nachmittags) einzeln annotiert werden, können Rückschlüsse auf deren Entwicklung und Veränderung gezogen werden. Gab es Verschiebungen? Sind Pausen weggefallen oder haben vulnerable Gruppen besondere Pausenregelungen erhalten? Dies sind einige Fragen, die in diesem Kontext gestellt werden können. Durch Hinzuziehung weiterer Rechtsquellen, wie Schutzbestimmungen durch den Staat, kann danach gefragt werden, ob sie Einfluss auf die Regulierung von Pausen in Arbeitsordnungen hatten oder sogar dazu führten, dass Regulierungen wegfielen, weil sie in anderen

52 Siehe TEI Publisher. The instant publishing toolbox, https://teipublisher.com/index.html (zuletzt abgerufen am 12. April 2022).

53 Muri (2004) 65.

54 Die *Fabrikordnung C.G. Haubold AG, Maschinenfabrik, Chemnitz* gibt 1834 72 Arbeitsstunden für eine 6-Tage-Woche vor, ohne Pausen festzulegen, was 12 Stunden pro Tag entspricht. Abgedruckt in: Forberger (1999) 220.

55 Deutschmann (1985) 90–93.

56 Arbeitsordnung des Metallwarenfabrikanten Arnold Gerdes in Altena, 1840, abgedruckt in: Ellerbrock (2017) 295; Reglement für die Arbeiter der Maschinen-Bau-Anstalt und Eisengießerei der Seehandlung in Moabit [Berlin], 1844, DZA Rep. 109 A XXIV f., Nr. 6, Vol. I, fol. 10–12, abgedruckt in: Schröter / Becker (1962) 112–117; Entwurf einer Fabrikordnung für die Maschinenfabrik Richard Hartmann, Chemnitz, 1862, abgedruckt in: Ludwig (1980) 41–51.

57 SächsStA, Staatsarchiv Leipzig, 20835 G. A. Schütz, Maschinenfabrik und Eisengießerei, Wurzen, Nr. 32, Arbeits-Ordnung für die Fabrik der Firma G. A. Schütz, Wurzen i. S., 14. April 1913, 2.

Rechtsquellen geregelt wurden. Mit Hilfe der Annotierung – auch bei der Nichterwähnung von Pausen – ließen sich diese Veränderungen darstellen.

2. *Rauchen*

Als besonders interessant erschien uns das Thema Rauchen, das im Kontext der Arbeitsordnungen meist einschränkend reguliert wurde.[58] Wir wollten die Regelungen zum Rauchen im Sinne des Teilprojektes aus arbeitszeitökonomischer Perspektive betrachten.[59] Anhand der Genese der Rauchordnung bei Bayer hat Tom Reichard aufgezeigt, dass die Regulierung des Rauchens aufgrund der Sorge um eine mögliche Verkürzung der realen Arbeitszeit eine Rolle spielte.[60] Durch die im Projekt vorhandene Vielzahl an Arbeitsordnungen können Erkenntnisse in größerer Breite gewonnen und eine Antwort darauf gegeben werden, welche Normierungen des Tabakkonsums in der Metallindustrie verbreitet waren und wie diese im Kontext von Arbeitszeit zu bewerten sind.

Die Schlagwortannotation bietet im Vergleich zu einer herkömmlichen Volltextsuche gerade in der Kombination von Stichworten wertvolle Ansatzpunkte für eine tiefergehende Analyse der Rauchregulierungen. Eine Kernidee war es, das Rauchen im Zusammenhang mit Arbeitspausen zu betrachten. Es erwies sich aber als nicht praktikabel, die Rauchbestimmungen als Variante von Regelungen zur Arbeitspause im Schlagwortkatalog zu kategorisieren und sie damit als Stichwort unterzuordnen.[61] Insofern schien eine selbstständige Annotation geeigneter. Damit sind die Bestimmungen zum Rauchen in Arbeitsordnungen schnell ausfindig zu machen und es kann zwischen Arbeits- und Pausenzeiten differenziert werden und damit ein detaillierter Einblick in die zugeschriebene Funktionslogik des Rauchens zu verschiedenen Abschnitten des Fabrikalltags gewonnen werden.[62] In Kombination mit dem räumlichen Aspekt könnte weiterführend gefragt werden, für welche Orte auf dem Fabrikgelände das Rauchen erlaubt, eingeschränkt oder verboten wurde, wo der Tabakkonsum letztendlich im Fabrikalltag stattfand oder zumindest stattfinden durfte.[63] Durch die örtliche und zeitliche Integration bzw. Exklusion des Rauchens in den Arbeitsordnungen sind somit im Fortgang der Arbeit weitere Rückwirkungen auf das industrielle Zeitregiment aufzuzeigen.

Aus einer Durchsicht der bis jetzt vorliegenden Arbeitsordnungen und einer zeitlichen Einordnung derselben ergaben sich folgende Eindrücke. Bereits während der Frühindustrialisierung scheint das Rauchen im Betrieb keine Randerscheinung gewesen zu sein, da ein unternehmerischer Regulierungsanspruch in einigen frühen Arbeitsordnungen nachzuweisen ist. Die Vorschriften enthielten teilweise individuelle Sondergenehmigungen für den Tabakgenuss während der Arbeitszeit in den Fabrikräumen,[64] auch wenn das Rauchen allgemein bereits eingeschränkt oder sogar komplett verboten wurde. Seit dem späten 19. Jahrhundert wurden mit dem Anstieg des Tabakkonsums die Verbotsbestimmungen universeller. In Reaktion auf die zunehmende gesellschaftliche Verbreitung

58 Der Tabakkonsum der Arbeiterschaft mit Pfeifen und Zigarren war schon im 19. Jahrhundert nicht unüblich. Besonders in Form der Zigarette verbreitete sich das Rauchen zu Beginn des 20. Jahrhunderts auch im Fabrikalltag breitflächig. Siehe auch Schürmann (2017) 42–43.

59 In vielen Arbeitsordnungen kommt zum Ausdruck, dass die Regulierung des Rauchens im Betrieb daneben natürlich auch dem Sicherheitsaspekt durch Brandgefahr Rechnung trug.

60 Siehe Reichard (2015) 111–113.

61 Der geringe Anteil der Ordnungen mit direktem Regelungsverweis auf das Rauchen in der Pause und das Vorhandensein von Raucherlaubnissen während der Arbeitszeit etwa an Arbeitsplätzen mit offenem Feuer, wie in den Gießereien, sprachen gegen eine so gerichtete Verengung des Blicks auf die Rauchbestimmungen. Auch im Sinne der Praktikabilität der Einordnung weiterer Handlungsweisen im Arbeitsumfeld haben wir das Rauchen daher dem Oberbegriff *Tätigkeit* zugeordnet.

62 Siehe Muri (2004) 66–67.

63 So ließe sich abfragen, welche der Paragraphen, in denen das Rauchen reguliert wurde, auch Schlagworte zu Räumlichkeiten und Wegen enthalten. Die Ergebnisliste könnte mit den Ergebnissen einer Suche nach Rauchen insgesamt verglichen werden und dahingehend überprüft werden, wie das Verhältnis von einschränkenden und erlaubenden Normen ist, oder wie es sich zur Erwähnung von Pausenzeiten verhält.

64 Siehe z. B. Hausgesetze für die mechanischen Werkstätten Haubold, C. G. Haubold AG, Maschinenfabrik, Chemnitz 1834, abgedruckt in Forberger (1999) 421: »Niemand ist es erlaubt, ohne vorherige Erlaubnis, welche jedoch nur älteren Personen und mit Rücksicht auf besondere Umstände erteilt wird, Tabak zu rauchen« (§ 12).

der Zigarette wurde das Rauchen sowohl während der Arbeitszeit als auch auf dem gesamten Werksgelände verboten.[65] Durch großflächige generelle Verbote versuchten die Werksleitungen produktive Arbeitszeit in den Produktionsräumen und das Rauchen in der Pausen- oder Feierabendzeit auf dem Fabrikhof oder vor den Fabriktoren räumlich zu trennen. Anhand der Rauchregelungen in der Weimarer Republik zeigt sich daran anschließend, dass in vielen Betrieben der mittlerweile gesellschaftlichen Durchdringung und öffentlichen Akzeptanz des Zigarettenrauchens nicht allein durch die normative Verbannung des Tabakkonsums begegnet werden konnte. Gegen generelle Rauchverbote regte sich zum Teil Widerstand in der Arbeiterschaft.[66] Allgemeine Rauchverbote auf dem gesamten Fabrikgelände ließen sich gegen die Gewohnheiten der Arbeiter nicht konsequent überwachen und umsetzen. In den Arbeitsordnungen fällt deshalb nun neben dem lokalen Fokus auf die Fabrikräume explizit ein zeitlicher Fokus auf die offizielle Arbeitszeit auf.[67] Dies kann als Versuch zu werten sein, zumindest den Produktionsprozess gegen befürchtete Dispositionen abzusichern. Auch hierin verdeutlicht sich der bereits aufgegriffene Homogenisierungs- und Intensivierungsprozess der eigentlichen Arbeitszeit. Die Arbeitsordnungen im Dritten Reich schließlich zeichnen sich, zwar nicht durchweg, aber auffallend häufig durch einen hohen Grad der Angleichung von Formulierungen und Regelungen aus. Sie basieren auf den gleichen Vorlagen für Arbeitsordnungen, in denen es häufig ohne weitere Differenzierung heißt: »Untersagt ist: […] das Rauchen im Betrieb.«[68]

3. *Zeitmessung und Zeitkontrolle*

Zu den Oberkategorien für den Schlagwortbaum haben wir im Projekt das Schlagwort *Objekte* definiert, worunter neben Materialien und Räumen die Einrichtungen für Anzeige und Kontrolle der Arbeitszeit fallen.[69] Darunter ist auch die *Uhr* zu fassen, die die Zeit – mit Einschränkungen[70] – objektiv kontrollierbar macht. Im Konfliktfall kann sich sowohl von Arbeitgeber- als auch Arbeitnehmerseite auf sie berufen werden. Für das Projekt ist es interessant zu beobachten, wie sich die Bedeutung der Uhr in den Arbeitsordnungen widerspiegelt, welche Regelungen zu Signalen und Zeitanzeigern getroffen wurden und wie sich diese entwickelten. Dafür haben wir die Arbeitsordnungen zunächst in einer Stichprobe gezielt nach dem Regelungskomplex *Uhr* durchsucht. Es fällt auf, dass Uhren und auch andere Zeitanzeiger in frühen Arbeitsordnungen nicht erwähnt werden, obwohl das Problem der Kontrolle und Durchsetzung der Arbeitszeit in diesen Ordnungen schon im Zentrum steht. So bestimmt eine sächsische Fabrikordnung von 1862, dass die Festsetzung des Endes der Arbeitszeit im Ermessen des Fabrikherrn liege,[71] zumeist waren die Arbeitszeiten aber in den Ordnungen schon früh mit genauen Uhrzeiten geregelt. Damit fand zumindest der Anspruch

65 Siehe z. B. Bayerisches Wirtschaftsarchiv, S 12 / 2140, Arbeitsordnung der Firma Keller & Knappich G.m.b.H. Augsburg, den 1. November 1904, 5: »Das Rauchen ist nicht allein in den Arbeitsräumen, sondern im Fabrikterrain überhaupt streng verboten.«

66 Dies äußerte sich z. B. bei Bayer anhand von zahlreichen Verstößen gegen das Rauchverbot. Aber auch der Arbeiterausschuss versuchte auf die Werksleitung einzuwirken, das Rauchverbot zu lockern. Siehe Reichard (2015) 109–110.

67 Siehe z. B. SächsStA-C, 31077 C. F. Hutschenreuther & Co. KG, Aue, Nr. 36. Arbeitsordnung der Metallwarenfabrik C. F. Hutschenreuter & Co. Aue i. Erzgeb., den 15. Juni 1924, 14: »Verboten ist: […] das Rauchen in den Fabrikräumen während der Arbeitszeit und an feuergefährlichen Stellen, sowie auch das Anstecken von Tabakspfeifen, Zigarren und Zigaretten innerhalb der Fabrikräume beim Verlassen derselben.«

68 SächsStA-C, 31035 Sächsische Textilmaschinenfabrik vorm. Richard Hartmann AG, Chemnitz, Nr. 134, Betriebs-Ordnung der Firma sächsische Textilmaschinenfabrik vorm. Rich. Hartmann AG, Chemnitz, den 1. Juli 1934, 14.

69 Für Lewis Mumford war die Entwicklung der Uhr – nicht die Dampfmaschine – zentral für die Entstehung des industriellen Kapitalismus, siehe Mumford (2010/1934). Insbes. Edward P. Thompson hat die Uhr in den Mittelpunkt seines Werkes über die Sozialdisziplinierung und den Übergang von agrarischen zu industrialisierten Gesellschaften gestellt. Siehe Thompson (1967). Siehe auch Dohrn-van Rossum (1995), insbes. das Kapitel Arbeitszeit und Stundenlohn, 372–414.

70 Berichte über Konflikte mit Fabrikherren, denen Uhrenmanipulation vorgeworfen wird, ziehen sich durch die gesamte entsprechende Literatur des 19. und selbst noch des 20. Jahrhunderts. Siehe Dohrn-van Rossum (1995) 408.

71 Entwurf einer Fabrikordnung für die Maschinenfabrik Richard Hartmann, Chemnitz, 1862, abgedruckt in: Ludwig (1980) 44: »Den Schluß der Arbeitszeit an den einzelnen Tagen bestimmt der Fabrikherr je nach seinem Ermessen«.

einer geregelten Arbeitszeit in die Ordnungen Eingang. Doch erst im Verlauf des 19. Jahrhunderts kamen Regelungen hinzu, die die akustische oder optische Anzeige der Arbeits- und Pausenzeiten auf dem Fabrikgelände bzw. an den Arbeitsplätzen vorschrieben. Vor den Uhren waren das etwa Werksglocken oder andere, nicht weiter ausgeführte Signalgeber.

Wurde in früheren Arbeitsordnungen die Unpünktlichkeit noch durch das Aussperren vom Fabrikgelände sanktioniert, so scheint diese Maßnahme gegenüber anderen Kontrolleinrichtungen abzunehmen. Dafür kommen in den Arbeitsordnungen Regelungen zur Kontrolle der Arbeitszeit hinzu, wie Marken zur Überprüfung der Anwesenheit, das handschriftliche Notieren durch den Pförtner oder die Einführung von Stechuhren, die mittels eines Zeitstempels den Arbeitsbeginn individuell darstellbar machten. Außerdem findet sich spätestens um die Jahrhundertwende in den Arbeitsordnungen zunehmend die Formulierung, dass ausschlaggebend für die Arbeitszeit allein die Fabrikuhr oder die Uhr im Pförtnerhaus sei. Interessant sind in diesem Zusammenhang die Verbote von individuellen Chronometern für Arbeiter, wovon auch Thompson berichtet.[72] In deutschen Arbeitsordnungen lassen sich dazu zwar keine ausdrücklichen Verbote finden. Doch der sich Anfang des 20. Jahrhunderts verbreitende und 1920 in der Musterarbeitsordnung der Weimarer Republik aufgenommene Satz, dass die Werksuhr maßgeblich sei, deutet bereits auf mögliche Konflikte und das Bedürfnis, Rechtssicherheit zu schaffen, hin. Mithilfe der digitalen Quellenedition lässt sich nachvollziehen, wo diese Regelung als erstes auftaucht und wie sie sich verbreitet, sodass in einer Tiefenbohrung gezielt nach dem Kontext gesucht werden kann.

4. *Jugendliche Arbeiter*

Teil unseres Schlagwortbaumes sind Akteure, hier als Rollen bezeichnet, die in verschiedenen Funktionen in den Arbeitsordnungen auftreten. Das reicht von Betriebsführern, Vorgesetzten und Meistern bis zu erwachsenen Arbeitern und Arbeiterinnen, Portiers und betriebsfremden Personen. Ein besonderes Augenmerk wollten wir auf marginalisierte Gruppen in den Fabriken lenken, darunter Frauen und Jugendliche. Dabei war uns bewusst, dass sie in der Metallindustrie eine zahlenmäßig untergeordnete Rolle spielten, aber nichtsdestotrotz in einigen Branchen tätig waren und dementsprechend – so unsere Annahme – in den Regulierungen Berücksichtigung finden mussten. Im Kontext der Arbeitsrechtsgeschichte sind beide Gruppen unter den Sonderrechten zu finden und ihre Arbeitstätigkeit ist auf Grund ihrer Schutzbedürftigkeit bereits früh staatlich reguliert worden.[73]

Als erste Regelung zur Kinderarbeit ist das Preußische Regulativ aus dem Jahr 1839 über die Beschäftigung jugendlicher Arbeiter in Fabriken[74] zu sehen. Dabei wurde der Schutz der Kinder und Jugendlichen vor allem durch kürzere Arbeitszeiten festgeschrieben. Die Arbeitszeit der 9- bis 16-Jährigen wurde im Regulativ auf maximal zehn Stunden täglich – und zwar in der Zeit zwischen 5 und 21 Uhr – begrenzt (§ 3).[75] Eine stichprobenartige Durchsicht unserer Quellen, die in die Regionen der Preußischen Provinzen fielen, ergab, dass jugendliche Arbeiter in den frühen Arbeitsordnungen kaum, meistens gar nicht erwähnt wurden. Dabei hätte mindestens die Begrenzung der Arbeitszeit von täglich zehn Stunden gesondert aufgeführt werden müssen, denn in den meisten Fällen lag die Arbeitszeit mit Abzug der Pausen eine Stunde über diesen Vorgaben.[76] Wenn Ju-

72 Siehe Thompson (1967) 85. Mitte des 18. Jahrhunderts hatten in England vor allem Meister, höhere Angestellte und die Oberklasse Uhren im privaten Besitz, während sie im Verlauf des 19. Jahrhunderts mehr und mehr auch bei Arbeitern als Statussymbol Verbreitung fanden, siehe Thompson (1967) 67.

73 Rückert (1998) 215.

74 Regulativ über die jugendlichen Arbeiter in Fabriken vom 9. März 1839, Gesetzsammlung für die Preußischen Staaten 1839, 156.

75 Boentert (2007) 62.

76 Siehe z. B. Reglement für die Arbeiter der Maschinen-Bau-Anstalt und Eisengießerei der Seehandlung in Moabit von 1844, DZA Rep. 109 A XXIV f., Nr. 6, Vol. I, fol. 10 12, abgedruckt in: Schröter / Becker (1962) 112–117.

gendliche erwähnt wurden, dann nur, wenn sie von der Beschäftigung allgemein ausgeschlossen waren, wie in den *Allgemeinen Bestimmungen zur Aufrechterhaltung der Ordnung* des Hörder Bergwerks- und Hütten-Vereins von 1853, in der es hieß: »Wer nicht das Alter von 15 Jahren erreicht hat, wird zur Arbeit nicht angenommen« (Artikel 2).[77] Diesen Befund gilt es mit Hilfe der digitalen Quellenedition zu verifizieren, denn erst mit einer entsprechen Quellengrundlage kann gezeigt werden, ob die Arbeitszeit von jugendlichen Arbeitern tatsächlich keinen Eingang in frühe Arbeitsordnungen fand.

Die Interpretationsmöglichkeiten, warum Unternehmer die Arbeitszeiten von jugendlichen Arbeitern in ihren Arbeitsordnungen nicht (oder nicht genau) definierten, sind vielfältig. Zum einen konnte es bedeuten, dass ein Gesetz, das über den lokalen, betrieblichen Normierungen lag, keiner weiteren Erwähnung bedurfte, da die Angelegenheit als geregelt galt. Ein Hinweis darauf findet sich in einer späteren Arbeitsordnung von 1920, in der es heißt: »Die Arbeitszeit der jugendlichen Arbeiter wird nach den gesetzlichen Bestimmungen geregelt und durch Anschlag bekanntgegeben« (§ 9).[78] Dass hinter der Nicht-Erwähnung auch praktische Erwägungen lagen, zeigt die in der Arbeitsordnung versehene handschriftliche Notiz: »Es wurde von der Verhandlungskommission nicht für zweckmäßig angesehen, die gesetzlich festgelegte Arbeitszeit der Jugendlichen in die Arbeitsordnung aufzunehmen, da jede behördliche Neuregelung der Arbeitszeit für die Jugendlichen eine Änderung der Arbeitsordnung bedingen würde.«[79] Diese Äußerungen stammen aus einer Zeit, als die Regelung der Arbeitszeit Jugendlicher über die Gewerbeordnung nicht nur genau geregelt, sondern auch kontrolliert wurde, denn der in der Gewerbeordnungsnovelle des Norddeutschen Bundes 1878 festgehaltene § 139b »übertrug die Aufsicht über die gesetzlichen Kinderschutzbestimmungen im gesamten Reichsgebiet den Beamten einer neu zu errichtenden, staatlichen Fabrikinspektion.«[80] Diese hatte es im frühen 19. Jahrhundert noch nicht gegeben, weshalb Annika Boentert als Grund für die systematischen Verstöße gegen das Regulativ von 1839 die geringen Kontrollinstanzen und die unwirksamen Strafmaßnahmen sieht.[81] Am ehesten ist wohl davon auszugehen, dass die Unternehmer sich über die gesetzlichen Regulierungen stillschweigend hinwegsetzten. Klar ist: Die Begründungen für die Nicht-Erwähnung der Arbeitszeiten für Jugendliche müssen durch andere Quellen gefunden werden. Dass Jugendliche Anfang des 20. Jahrhunderts aber vermehrt in Arbeitsordnungen angesprochen und ihre Arbeitszeiten und Pausen festgelegt wurden, spricht für einen Bedeutungszuwachs dieses Themas, einer verstärkten Kontrolle durch den Staat und einer breiteren gesellschaftlichen Akzeptanz.

VI. Zusammenfassung und Ausblick

Dieser Artikel hat einen Einblick in die Entwicklung eines digitalen Quelleneditionsprojektes gegeben. Am Beispiel der Arbeitsordnung, die nicht nur eine zentrale quantitative, sondern auch qualitative Bedeutung in der Quellenedition haben wird, wurde eruiert, welche Möglichkeiten die Digitalisierung von Rechtsquellen bietet, welche Forschungsfragen entwickelt werden können, wenn eine solche Fülle an neu ausgehobenen Normtexten zur Verfügung steht, und welchen Mehrwert Annotationen bieten, die sich an ein bestimmtes Forschungsinteresse richten.

Am Beispiel der Arbeitszeit wurden einzelne Schlagworte diskutiert, die über die Arbeitsrechtsgeschichte hinaus in der Forschung interessant sind und in der Literatur bereits größere Aufmerksamkeit erhielten. Durch die Verschlagwortung einer Vielzahl an Quellen sollte ein neuer Forschungszugang zu Themen wie die Entwicklung von Arbeitspausen, die Regulierung des Rauchens, die normative Einführung einer verbindlichen Zeitanzeige und Zeitsignalgebung und deren Kontrolle sowie der Umgang mit bestimmten Gruppen

77 Abgedruckt in: Ellerbrock (1990) 34–37.
78 SächsStA-C, 30942 Eisengießerei G. Krautheim AG, Chemnitz, Nr. 485, Normal-Arbeits-Ordnung für die Betriebe des Chemnitzer Bezirksverbandes deutscher Metallindustrieller. Arbeits-Ordnung der Firma G. Krautheim, Berlin, den 1. Juli 1920, 8.
79 Ebd., Notiz zu § 9, 25.
80 Boentert (2007) 88.
81 Ebd., 64–65.

wie jugendlichen Arbeitern entwickelt werden. Dabei konnte gezeigt werden, dass das Rauchen, welches auf den ersten Blick keine Verbindung zur Arbeitszeit aufweist, sich durch die Kontextualisierung mit dem Ort (verschiedene innerhalb oder außerhalb des Fabrikgeländes definierte Orte) mit dieser in Zusammenhang bringen lässt. Es wurde ebenfalls deutlich, wie Fragen anderer Disziplinen – wie der Konsumgeschichte – in der Arbeitsrechtsgeschichte Berücksichtigung finden können. Denn wie dargelegt werden konnte, hatte die zunehmende gesellschaftliche Akzeptanz des Rauchens seit dem Ersten Weltkrieg Einfluss auf die Regulierung des Rauchens in Arbeitsordnungen.

Am Beispiel der Pausen wurde deutlich, dass durch die Verschlagwortung der Quellen auch der Wandel bestimmter Regelungsmaterien sichtbar gemacht werden kann. Die Annotation der verschiedenen Pausenarten bietet den Nutzer*innen der Edition die Möglichkeit, die Nicht-Regulierung oder den Wegfall bestimmter Pausen nachzuvollziehen sowie sich eine quantitative Veränderung von Pausenzeiten einerseits und Arbeitszeiten andererseits anzeigen zu lassen. Mit dem Beispiel der jugendlichen Arbeiter wurde thematisiert, wie autark betriebliche Regulierungen im Verhältnis zu staatlichen Vorgaben existierten. Die rechtlichen Vorgaben zum Schutz der Kinder und Jugendlichen in den Fabriken fanden kaum Eingang in die Arbeitsordnungen. Diese Beobachtung ist ein interessanter Ausgangspunkt für eine Vielzahl weiterer Forschungsfragen zur wechselseitigen Beziehung zwischen Staat, Unternehmen und gesellschaftlichen Akteuren. Das Beispiel der Uhr enthält viele der bereits angesprochenen Punkte. Auch hier kann der Einfluss der technischen und gesellschaftlichen Entwicklungen zur Zeitregulierung und -kontrolle nachvollzogen werden. Es lässt sich durch die Vielzahl an Rechtsquellen zeigen, wann etwas hinzukam, wegfiel oder ganz neu und anders reguliert wurde.

Im nächsten Schritt gilt es nun, diese Quellen zu annotieren und Abfragen im Sinne der oben gestellten Fragen zu generieren. Die hier noch gar nicht angesprochenen geographischen Unterschiede bilden eine weitere interessante Ausgangslage der digitalen Quellenedition. Denn mit Hilfe der in den Metadaten festgehaltenen Ortsdaten wird der zeitliche Längsschnitt durch eine geographische Breite ergänzt und kann ebenfalls interessante Ergebnisse zu Tage fördern. Fiel beispielsweise eine Region durch eine frühe Regulierung bestimmter Regelungsmaterien auf? Gab es Ähnlichkeiten, die auf Verbindungen oder gegenseitige Beeinflussung hindeuten? Dies sind nur einige Fragen, die durch den Blick auf räumliche Unterschiede oder Gemeinsamkeiten gestellt werden können.

Es ist sicher deutlich geworden, dass die digitale Quellenedition zum *Nichtstaatlichen Recht der Wirtschaft* nach Fertigstellung eine große Bereicherung für die Arbeitsrechtsgeschichte darstellen wird. Sie bringt erstmals Rechtsquellen zusammen, die in der Arbeitsrechtsgeschichte aufgrund ihrer Vielfalt, aber auch der Schwierigkeiten, sie auszuheben, bisher keine Berücksichtigung finden konnten, und versucht damit gleichzeitig dem auf die Untersuchung von Multinormativität zielenden Forschungsanspruch des mpilhlt gerecht zu werden. Die Verschlagwortung der digitalisierten Quellen bringt zusätzlich neue Möglichkeiten der wissenschaftlichen Erkenntnis. Entwicklungen können im historischen Längsschnitt und in ihren geographischen Besonderheiten (quantitativ) dargestellt werden. Durch die Kombination verschiedener Schlagworte oder der Markierung von Materien, die nicht reguliert wurden, lassen sich Abfragen generieren, die über eine einfache Volltextsuche hinausgehen. Ob die hier diskutierten Aspekte am Ende alle Eingang in die jeweiligen Forschungsarbeiten des Projektteams finden werden, ist zum jetzigen Zeitpunkt noch nicht auszumachen. Dass sie auf Grund der genannten Möglichkeiten einen besonderen Reiz darstellen, dürfte hingegen deutlich geworden sein.

■

Bibliographie

- Barth, Ernst (1972), Fabrikordnungen im alten Chemnitz, in: Der Heimatfreund für das Erzgebirge, Stollberg 17,1, 16–19
- Bender, Gerd (2012), Tarifautonomie, Regulierte Selbstregulierung, Korporatismus. Eine Skizze, in: Collin, Peter et al. (Hg.), Regulierte Selbstregulierung im frühen Interventions- und Sozialstaat, Frankfurt am Main, 53–67
- Birr, Christiane (2016), Die geisteswissenschaftliche Perspektive: Welche Forschungsergebnisse lassen Digital Humanities erwarten?, in: Rechtsgeschichte – Legal History 24, 330–334, http://dx.doi.org/10.12946/rg24/330-334 (zuletzt abgerufen am 25. Mai 2022)
- Boentert, Annika (2007), Kinderarbeit im Kaiserreich 1871–1914, Paderborn
- Brand, Jürgen (2011), Arbeitsrecht. Gesellschaftliche Selbstregulierung in der Welt der Arbeit des 19. Jahrhunderts, oder: Im Westen nichts Neues, in: Collin et al. (Hg.) (2011b) 133–176
- Collin, Peter (2011a), »Gesellschaftliche Selbstregulierung« und »Regulierte Selbstregulierung« – ertragreiche Analysekategorien für eine (rechts-)historische Perspektive?, in: ders. et al. (Hg.) 3–31
- Collin, Peter et al. (Hg.) (2011b), Selbstregulierung im 19. Jahrhundert. Zwischen Autonomie und staatlichen Steuerungsansprüchen, Frankfurt am Main
- Däubler, Wolfgang, Michael Kittner (2020), Geschichte der Betriebsverfassung, Frankfurt am Main
- Deutschmann, Christoph (1982), Zeitflexibilität und Arbeitsmarkt. Zur Entstehungsgeschichte und Funktion des Normalarbeitstages, in: Offe, Claus (Hg.), Arbeitszeitpolitik. Formen und Folgen einer Neuverteilung der Arbeitszeit, Frankfurt am Main, 32–45
- Deutschmann, Christoph (1985), Der Weg zum Normalarbeitstag. Die Entwicklung der Arbeitszeiten in der deutschen Industrie bis 1918. Studienreihe des Instituts für Sozialforschung Frankfurt am Main, Frankfurt am Main
- Dohrn-van Rossum, Gerhard (1995), Die Geschichte der Stunde. Uhren und moderne Zeitordnungen, München
- Drucker, Johanna (2011), Humanities Approaches to Graphical Display, in: Digital Humanities Quarterly 5,1, http://www.digitalhumanities.org/dhq/vol/5/1/000091/000091.html (zuletzt abgerufen am 11. April 2022)
- Duve, Thomas (2014), German Legal History. National Traditions and Transnational Perspectives, in: Rechtsgeschichte – Legal History 22, 16–48, http://dx.doi.org/10.12946/rg22/016-048 (zuletzt abgerufen am 25. Mai 2022)
- Duve, Thomas (2017), Was ist ›Multinormativität‹? – Einführende Bemerkungen, in: Rechtsgeschichte – Legal History 25, 88–101, http://dx.doi.org/10.12946/rg25/088-101 (zuletzt abgerufen am 25. Mai 2022)
- Ellerbrock, Karl-Peter (1990), Von Piepenstock zum »Phoenix«. Geschichte der Hermannshütte (1841–1906), Dortmund
- Ellerbrock, Karl-Peter (2017), Quellen zur Wirtschaft, Gesellschaft und Technik vom 18. bis 20. Jahrhundert aus dem Westfälischen Wirtschaftsarchiv, Münster
- Fischer, Guido (1950), Betriebsordnung und Betriebsvereinbarung, in: Mensch und Arbeit 2,4, 75–78
- Flohr, Bernd (1981), Arbeiter nach Maß. Die Disziplinierung der Fabrikarbeiterschaft während der Industrialisierung Deutschlands im Spiegel von Arbeitsordnungen, Frankfurt am Main
- Forberger, Rudolf (1999), Die Industrielle Revolution in Sachsen 1800–1861, Bd. 2, Erster Halbband: Die Revolution der Produktivkräfte in Sachsen 1831–1861, Stuttgart
- Goy, Anna, Diego Magro et al. (2018), On the role of thematic roles in a historical event ontology, in: Applied Ontology 13,1, 9–39
- Kampkaspar, Dario (2022), Page2TEI, https://github.com/dariok/page2tei (zuletzt abgerufen am 11. April 2022)
- Küsters, Anselm, Laura Volkind, Andreas Wagner (2019), Digital Humanities and the State of Legal History. A Text Mining Perspective, in: Rechtsgeschichte – Legal History 27, 244–259, http://dx.doi.org/10.12946/rg27/244-259 (zuletzt abgerufen am 25. Mai 2022)
- Lüdtke, Alf (1993), Eigen-Sinn. Fabrikalltag, Arbeitererfahrungen und Politik vom Kaiserreich bis in den Faschismus, Hamburg
- Ludwig, Kurt (1980), Zu Problemen der Konstituierung des Proletariats in Chemnitz um die Mitte des 19. Jahrhunderts, dargestellt am Beispiel der Maschinenfabrik Richard Hartmann, in: Beiträge zur Heimatgeschichte von Karl-Marx-Stadt 24, 5–56
- Machtan, Lothar (1981), Zum Innenleben deutscher Fabriken im 19. Jahrhundert. Die formelle und die informelle Verfassung von Industriebetrieben anhand von Beispielen aus dem Bereich der Textil- und Maschinenbauproduktion (1869–1891), in: Archiv für Sozialgeschichte 21, 179–236
- Masolo, Claudio, Laure Vieu et al. (2004), Social Roles and Their Descriptions, in: Dubois, Didier, Christopher A. Welty et al. (eds.), Principles of Knowledge Representation and Reasoning: Proceedings of the Ninth International Conference, (KR2004), Palo Alto, 267–277, http://www.loa.istc.cnr.it/old/Papers/KR04MasoloC.pdf (zuletzt abgerufen am 11. April 2022)
- Metzger, Pascal (2006), Die ersten Nürnberger Fabrikarbeiter. Die Lebenswelt der Arbeiterschaft der Maschinenbauanstalt Johann Wilhelm Spaeth im Spiegel der Fabrikordnung von 1838, in: Jahrbuch für fränkische Landesforschung 66, 285–299
- Mumford, Lewis (2010), Technics and Civilization, Chicago
- Muri, Gabriela (2004), Pause! Zeitordnung und Auszeiten aus alltagskultureller Sicht, Frankfurt am Main
- Negt, Oskar (1984), Lebendige Zeit, enteignete Zeit. Politische und kulturelle Dimensionen des Kampfes um die Arbeitszeit, Frankfurt am Main
- Ramm, Thilo (1978), Die Arbeitsverfassung des Kaiserreichs, in: Triffterer, Otto, Friedrich von Zezschwitz (Hg.), Festschrift für Walter Mallmann, Baden-Baden, 191–211
- Reichard, Tom (2015), Die Zeit der Zigarette. Rauchen und Temporalität in der ersten Hälfte des 20. Jahrhunderts, in: Geschichte und Gesellschaft, Sonderheft 25: Obsession der Gegenwart. Zeit im 20. Jahrhundert, 92–122
- Reul, Christian, D. Christ et al. (2019), OCR4all – An Open-Source Tool Providing a (Semi-)Automatic OCR Workflow for Historical Printings, in: Applied Sciences 9,22, https://doi.org/10.3390/app9224853 (zuletzt abgerufen am 25. Mai 2022)

- Richardi, Reinhard (2002), Arbeitsrecht als Teil freiheitlicher Ordnung. Von der Zwangsordnung im Arbeitsleben zur Arbeitsverfassung der Bundesrepublik Deutschland, Baden-Baden
- Rückert, Joachim (1998), Die Verrechtlichung der Arbeitsbeziehungen in Deutschland seit dem frühen 19. Jahrhundert, in: Nutzinger, Hans G. (Hg.), Die Entstehung des Arbeitsrechts in Deutschland, Marburg, 211–229
- Rückert, Joachim (2015), Einleitung, in: ders. (Hg.), Arbeit und Recht seit 1800. Historisch und vergleichend, europäisch und global, Köln, 7–20
- Schlauwitz, Thorsten (2016), Chancen und Grenzen der automatischen Schriftanalyse und -erkennung, in: Rechtsgeschichte – Legal History 24, 349–350, http://dx.doi.org/10.12946/rg24/349-350 (zuletzt abgerufen am 25. Mai 2022)
- Schröter, Alfred, Walter Becker (1962), Die deutsche Maschinenbauindustrie in der industriellen Revolution, Berlin
- Schürmann, Sandra et al. (2017), Die Welt in einer Zigarettenschachtel. Transnationale Horizonte eines deutschen Produkts, Kromsdorf
- Schwandt, Silke (2016), Digitale Objektivität in der Geschichtswissenschaft? Oder: Kann man finden, was man nicht sucht?, in: Rechtsgeschichte – Legal History 24, 337–338, http://dx.doi.org/10.12946/rg24/337-338 (zuletzt abgerufen am 25. Mai 2022)
- Stöbe, Herbert (1962), Der große Streik der Chemnitzer Metallarbeiter zur Durchsetzung des Zehnstundentages im Jahr 1871, Karl-Marx-Stadt
- Strauss, Rudolph (1960), Die Lage und die Bewegung der Chemnitzer Arbeiter in der ersten Hälfte des 19. Jahrhunderts, Berlin
- Sukhondyaeva, Tatiana (2016), Digital Possibilities and Availability of Original Sources on Military Legislation of the 16th–19th Centuries, in: Rechtsgeschichte – Legal History 24, 356–357, http://dx.doi.org/10.12946/rg24/356-357 (zuletzt abgerufen am 25. Mai 2022)
- Teuteberg, Hans Jürgen (1961), Geschichte der industriellen Mitbestimmung in Deutschland, Tübingen
- Thaller, Manfred (2016), Was sind (keine) methodischen Implikationen der Digital Humanities?, in: Rechtsgeschichte – Legal History 24, 335–336, http://dx.doi.org/10.12946/rg24/335-336 (zuletzt abgerufen am 25. Mai 2022)
- Thompson, Edward Palmer (1967), Time, Work-Discipline, and Industrial Capitalism, in: Past & Present 38, 56–97
- Uhlmann, Wolfgang (1996), Chemnitzer Fabrikordnungen im 19. Jahrhundert, in: Sächsische Heimatblätter 42,3, 166–172
- Wirtz, Rainer (1982), Die Ordnung der Fabrik ist nicht die Fabrikordnung. Bemerkungen zur Erziehung in der Fabrik während der frühen Industrialisierung an südwestdeutschen Beispielen, in: Haumann, Heiko (Hg.), Arbeiteralltag in Stadt und Land. Neue Wege der Geschichtsschreibung, Berlin, 61–88
- Wüst, Wolfgang (2010), Fabrikordnungen zwischen sozialer Disziplinierung und patriarchalischer Fürsorge, in: Murr, Karl Borromäus et al. (Hg.), Die süddeutsche Textillandschaft. Geschichte und Erinnerung von der Frühen Neuzeit bis in die Gegenwart, Augsburg, 257–282
- Zwahr, Hartmut (1973), Ausbeutung und gesellschaftliche Stellung des Fabrik- und Manufakturproletariats am Ende der Industriellen Revolution im Spiegel Leipziger Fabrikordnungen, in: Jacobeit, Wolfgang, Ute Mohrmann (Hg.), Kultur und Lebensweise des Proletariats. Kulturhistorisch-volkskundliche Studien und Materialien, Berlin, 85–136

Kritik critique

Steffen M. Jauß

Institutiones Hammurapi?*

Innerhalb des von der Öffentlichkeit wahrgenommenen Ausschnitts der keilschriftlichen Überlieferung kommt dem Codex Hammurapi eine herausragende Bedeutung zu, die wohl selbst das Gilgamesch-Epos mit seiner Sintfluterzählung in ihren Schatten stellt. Dementsprechend umfangreich wurde der Codex Hammurapi durch die Fachwissenschaft gewürdigt. Wie so oft bedingt dies eine gewisse Iteration der im Schrifttum anzutreffenden Aussagen. In diesem Sinne bietet auch vorliegender Band jedenfalls in seinen Details wenig Neues.

Barmash, die ihre Studie als *histoire totale* begriffen haben will, präsentiert den Codex Hammurapi in der Einleitung (1–17) einerseits als Kulminationspunkt einer in Herrscherinschriften und älteren Rechtssammlungen fassbaren Traditionslinie. Andererseits soll er als über ein Jahrtausend tradierter und fixierter Text eine kopernikanische Wende im intellektuellen Leben Mesopotamiens markieren und zum Startpunkt eines neuen Traditionsstroms geworden sein. Letztere Idee wird indes erst im abschließenden 7. Kapitel (251–277) wieder aufgegriffen, wo Barmash eine Rezeption zumindest gewisser Denkmuster in den Nachbarregionen Mesopotamiens wahrscheinlich macht. Verheißungsvoll angekündigt, gelangt die Betrachtung des Einflusses, den der Text auf das antike griechische oder gar römische Recht ausgeübt haben soll, hingegen zum altbekannten Ergebnis, dass ihr die nötige Quellengrundlage fehlt. Insgesamt bildet die Rezeptionsgeschichte aber eher einen Nebenaspekt der Arbeit. In ihrem Zentrum steht die gleichfalls schon in der Einleitung skizzierte Debatte um die Natur jenes Textes, deren Beantwortung seiner Einordnung in ältere Traditionen dient:

Kapitel 1 (19–47) ist zunächst der Materialität der im Louvre ausgestellten Stele, dem wichtigsten, aber nicht einzigen Textzeugen, gewidmet. Hinsichtlich der Ikonographie stützt sich Barmash überwiegend auf eine Arbeit Schmandt-Besserats, blendet aber die kurz zuvor erschienene Studie von Elsen-Novák / Novák[1] aus. Die hier gebotene Interpretation der bildlichen Szene am Stelenkopf überspannt den Bogen: Zum einen überbetont Barmash die Innovativität und Einzigartigkeit der Darstellung eines dem Sonnengott Šamaš direkt und ohne störendes Zwischenelement gegenüberstehenden Hammurapi, die ihre besondere Verbundenheit symbolisieren soll. Weitere Beispiele solcher Darstellungen hat Seidl bereits vor Jahrzehnten zusammengestellt.[2] Zum anderen wird die szenische Darstellung am Stelenkopf bloß mit der Erwähnung Šamaš' im sog. Prolog kontextualisiert. Auf diese Weise nivelliert Barmash geflissentlich die Diskrepanz zwischen Bild und Text, die sich aus der im Text dargestellten Einsetzung Hammurapis durch den Stadtgott Marduk statt durch Šamaš ergibt. Daneben illustriert Barmash anhand von Textbeispielen die Verbindung der Götter mit dem Recht im Denken Mesopotamiens. Im Übrigen beschränkt sie sich auf Plattitüden der Art, dass die Stele in ihrer Monumentalität der Manifestation von Macht diene. Soweit sie dabei auf die Erhaltung von Hammurapis Namen abstellt, kann sich Barmash wiederum auf ein breites Schrifttum stützen, das sie aber nur ausschnittsweise berücksichtigt.[3]

Die folgenden Kapitel bilden eine inhaltliche Einheit. Auf abstrakterer Ebene adressiert Kapitel 2 (49–86) das Recht als Aspekt mesopotamischer Herrscherideologie. Einmal mehr weist auch Barmash auf die zentralen Konzepte *kittum* und *mīšarum* hin, von welchen ersteres eine Art (statisches) Naturrecht adressiere,[4] letzteres hingegen die (dynamische) Herbeiführung eines jenem Na-

* Pamela Barmash, The Laws of Hammurabi at the Confluence of Royal & Scribal Traditions, New York: Oxford University Press 2020, X + 320 S., ISBN 978-0-19-752540-1

1 Gabriele Elsen-Novák, Mirko Novák, Der »König der Gerechtigkeit«, in: Baghdader Mitteilungen 37 (2006) 131–151.

2 Ursula Seidl, Babylonische und Assyrische Flachbildkunst des 2. Jahrtausends v. Chr., in: Winfried Orthmann (Hg.), Der Alte Orient (Propyläen Kunstgeschichte 18), 2. Aufl., Berlin 1985, 298–327, dort etwa Nrn. 183, 184b, 187.

3 Unerwähnt bleibt etwa Karen Radner, Die Macht des Namens (SANTAG 8), Wiesbaden 2006.

4 Weitere Anregungen hierfür hätte die Arbeit von Kai Lämmerhirt, Wahrheit und Trug (Alter Orient und Altes Testament 348), Münster 2010, bieten können.

turrecht entsprechenden Zustands. Als diesem Zweck dienende Instrumente begegnen in der Überlieferung neben einer judiziellen Tätigkeit des Königs selbst vor allem sog. Gerechtigkeitserlasse und Codizes, für welche Barmash jeweils Quellenbeispiele nennt. Erstere will sie chronologisch in zwei Gruppen unterteilen: In vor-altbabylonischer Zeit seien solche Erlasse zum einen vorwiegend durch Inschriften sowie Hymnen bezeugt und hätten zum anderen der Sicherung sozialen Friedens gedient; ab altbabylonischer Zeit seien sie als regulatorische Eingriffe in das Wirtschaftsleben überliefert. Zentrales Anliegen dieses Kapitels ist aber die Diskussion des Verhältnisses jener Quellengattungen zueinander. Anknüpfend an und in Abgrenzung zu entsprechenden Ansätzen Finkelsteins und Veenhofs zeigt Barmash auf, dass Prolog und Epilog des Codex Hammurapi in Rhetorik und Inhalt gewisse Ähnlichkeiten zu Hymnen und Inschriften aufweisen, während die sog. Rechtssätze zumindest formale Ähnlichkeiten mit den Gerechtigkeitserlassen haben.

Hieran anknüpfend analysiert Barmash den Codex Hammurapi in Kapitel 3 (87–135) als eigentliche Herrscherinschrift, deren Aussagen durch die Rechtssätze bloß ausgemalt erscheinen. Diese Feststellung ist wichtig, weil sie der seit dem frühen 20. Jahrhundert beobachtbaren Tendenz entgegenwirkt, die Rechtssätze als eigentlichen Inhalt des Textes, Prolog und Epilog gleichsam nur als Beiwerk zu begreifen. Auf Grundlage von Arbeiten Ries', vor allem aber Hurowitz' werden sowohl Vorlagen als auch die kunstvolle Komposition jener Textabschnitte analysiert. In Kapitel 4 (137–201) rücken dann die Rechtssätze in den Fokus, die Barmash in enger Verknüpfung zur Schreiberausbildung behandelt: So wie Schreiber juristische Konzepte, Institute und Begriffe anhand von Beispielsfällen erlernten, dienten auch die Rechtssätze als *exempla*, die bestimmte Rechtsprinzipien nicht benennen, aber demonstrieren sollten. Darauf, dass sich dies insbesondere durch geschickte Kombination verschiedener Beispielsfälle resp. Rechtssätze erreichen ließ, hat in anderem Kontext auch schon der Rezensent hingewiesen.[5] Zum einen ordnet Barmash dies in den weiteren Kontext literarischer Traditionen ein, die sich einerseits in der listenartigen Zusammenstellung der Rechtssätze und andererseits in der Präsentation von Wissen im Konditionalschema niederschlage.[6] Zum anderen skizziert sie die Zusammenstellung paradigmatischer Regelungskomplexe, deren Arrangement zu Clustern, thematische Gruppierung sowie die gruppierungsübergreifende Anordnung identischer Rechtsfolgen als Techniken zur Verdeutlichung solcher Prinzipien und zugleich Ausdruck altmesopotamischen Rechtsdenkens. Auch hierbei kann sie sich auf ein breites Schrifttum stützen, das seinerseits auf bahnbrechenden Vorarbeiten Koschakers und Petschows beruht. Diese Deutung wird durch einen Exkurs (203–218) plausibel gemacht, der vor allem die Schreiberausbildung beleuchtet. Anhand der Rechtssätze zur Adoption lässt Barmash jene Perspektive auf die altorientalischen Codizes im kurzen 5. Kapitel konkret werden (219–229).

Sodann wendet sie sich im 6. Kapitel (231–250) dem zentralen Problem der Rechtsnatur des Codex Hammurapi zu. Die Feststellung, dass nur vereinzelte, den Rechtssätzen allenfalls sinngemäß entsprechende Rechtsfälle überliefert sind, führt zur altbekannten Einsicht, dass sich nicht belegen lässt, ob der Text anwendbares Recht setzt oder zumindest angewandtes Recht reflektiert. In Abgrenzung zur bisherigen Diskussion betont Barmash, dass Zitation eines Gesetzes keine Voraussetzung für die Berufung auf seine Geltung ist. Der Text, so meint sie, stelle keine allgemeinen Regeln auf, sondern drücke exemplarisch aus, was als angemessen empfunden wurde. Weil Schreiber jenes Rechtsempfinden verinnerlichten, hätten sie als judiziell tätige Funktionäre dann im Sinne des Codex entschieden. Damit verwechselt Barmash Rechtsnatur mit Rechtstechnik. Die Idee, Recht durch Normierung von Ausbildungsmaterial zu setzen, lässt sich etwa auch zweieinhalb Jahrtausende später in Ost-Rom fassen. Ob der von Barmash als Ausbildungsmaterial verstandene Text nun im Sinne von ›Institutiones Hammurapi‹ auf eine Anordnung mit Geltungsanspruch oder doch auf freie Willkür des

5 Steffen M. Jauss, Kasuistik – Systematik – Reflexion über Recht, in: Zeitschrift für Altorientalische und Biblische Rechtsgeschichte 21 (2015) 185–216, 186 f.

6 Vgl. Guido Pfeifer, Das Recht im Kontext normativer Ordnungen des Alten Orients, in: ZRG (RA) 135 (2018) 17–19.

jeweiligen Schreibers oder gelehrte Diskussion zurückführbar ist, ist damit keineswegs entschieden – und wird wohl nie entschieden werden.

Von großem Wert ist hingegen die monographische Zusammenführung der disparate Aspekte betreffenden und über viele Fachmedien verstreut geführten Diskussion. Sie steht als besonderes Verdienst der Autorin für sich.

■

Ulrike Babusiaux

Häresie(n) zum und im spätantiken Recht*

Die 2019 an der Juristischen Fakultät der Eberhard Karls Universität Tübingen abgenommene Dissertation umfasst nicht nur stolze 898 Seiten, sondern ist auch in ihrer Anlage ein mehrbändiges Werk. Der erste Band (19–252) widmet sich den »Prinzipien spätantiker Gesetzgebung und der Codex-Theodosianus-Kompilation«, der zweite Band betrachtet das Erbrecht der Spätantike und dort spezifisch »Erbrechtliche und verwandte Sanktionen außerhalb der Heterodoxengesetzgebung« (253–408), während sich ein dritter Band mit den erbrechtlichen Sanktionen gegenüber heterodoxen Gruppen, namentlich gegenüber Manichäern, Donatisten, Eunomianern und Apostaten befasst (409–764). Ein Annex untersucht die »erbrechtlichen Sanktionen nach 428« (765–810). Dem Autor (R.) ist diese Überfrachtung durchaus bewusst, er rechtfertigt sie in der »Hinführung« mit der Überlegung: »Nicht wenige Codex-Theodosianus-Studien machen sich durch eine strenge Scheidung zwischen Generellem und Speziellem angreifbar« (14). Daher will er seine allgemeinen Überlegungen zur spätantiken Gesetzgebung an einem konkreten Beispiel – der Gesetzgebung gegen häretische Lehren – überprüfen.

Besondere Aufmerksamkeit verdient aus Sicht der Rezensentin vor allem der erste, auch titelgebende Teil zu den spätantiken Konstitutionen, denn er vermag einige in der Forschung allgemein akzeptierte Paradigmata zu erschüttern, wie auch Reaktionen auf das Werk gezeigt haben.[1]

Hinsichtlich der »Typologie spätantiker Kaisernormen« (26–77) verfährt R. zunächst in überkommenen Bahnen, wenn er »Einzelfallerlasse«, die er als »Reskripte im weiteren Sinne« bezeichnet, und »Konstitutionen« unterscheidet, zu denen er die an die Bevölkerung gerichteten Edikte und die an Amtsträger gerichteten Briefe zählt. Als Vorläufer dieser Briefe, die mit Publikationsvermerk versehen waren und daher meist durch den Empfänger der Öffentlichkeit bekannt gemacht wurden, erkennt er die kaiserzeitlichen *mandata* (59). Als dritten Typus der »Konstitutionen« ordnet er die Oratio ein (63), – in der hier interessierenden Zeit – ein an den Senat in Rom oder Konstantinopel verfasster Brief mit Normcharakter. Diese Typologie vermag freilich die Vielfalt des spätantiken Kaiserrechts nicht vollständig zu erklären: Wie R. zutreffend erläutert, wird das Bild durch verschiedene Ausfertigungen, vor allem von Briefen der Kaiser und ganz unterschiedlichen »Verteilerlisten«, mit denen die Adressaten für jeden Einzelfall festgelegt wurden (72 f.), weiter verkompliziert. Hinzu treten Situationen, in denen ein Text z. B. als Edikt ergeht und zusätzlich als Brief an andere Würdenträger verschickt wird. Man könnte angesichts dieser Fluidität der Begrifflichkeiten sogar noch weiter gehen als R., indem man beachtet, was

* Peter Riedlberger, Prolegomena zu den spätantiken Konstitutionen. Nebst einer Analyse der erbrechtlichen und verwandten Sanktionen gegen Heterodoxe, Stuttgart/Bad Cannstatt: frommann-holzboog 2020, 898 S., ISBN 978-3-7728-2886-7

1 Vgl. Boudewijn Sirks, Did the published Theodosian Code include obsolete constitutions?, in: Tijdschrift voor Rechtgeschiedenis 89 (2021) 70–92; Dirk Rohmann, Rez., in: GFA 23 (2020) 1091–1097; Matthijs Wibier, Rez., in: ZRG (RA) 138 (2021) 771–776.

Anna Plisecka bereits für die severischen Apokrimata festgestellt hat:[2] Die antiken Termini für kaiserliche Anordnungen dürfen keineswegs im Sinne moderner Normtheorien missverstanden werden, ein Aspekt, der sich nach den Ausführungen von R. auch für das von ihm untersuchte Material aufdrängt.

Vergleichbares gilt für das Stichwort »Geltung« (77–112), unter dem R. vor allem den Geltungs*bereich* der Konstitutionen in der Spätantike diskutiert. Zu diesem Zweck untersucht er zunächst den Begriff *promulgare*, den er mit »erlassen« übersetzt und damit zu Recht von der modernen Promulgation von Gesetzen abgrenzt. Die sich damit stellende Frage: »Gab es ein Publikationserfordernis?« (82) verneint R. Er argumentiert u. a. mit dem Befund, dass viele Normen auch Amtsträgern unbekannt bleiben konnten. Hingegen erscheint es zweifelhaft, ob man – wie R. – aus Libanios or. 48, 15 f. (24, 87) wirklich ableiten kann, dass die Publikation *keine* Voraussetzung für die Beachtung des Gesetzes sei, denn offenbar bezweifelt der Redner die Existenz des Gesetzes über den Eintritt von Ratsmitgliedern vor allem deshalb, *weil* es nicht veröffentlicht wurde.

Vorrangig aber bekämpft R. die in der Forschung vorherrschende Vorstellung, die »Geltung« einer Konstitution sei auf den westlichen oder östlichen Reichsteil beschränkt gewesen. Zu recht verweist er darauf, dass schon die mit der Geltung implizierte Idee des *iura novit curia* für die Antike verfehlt ist und ihre anachronistische Übernahme die rechtshistorische Diskussion verfälscht hat: »Kaiser erlassen Gesetze nicht mit Geltung für ihren Reichsteil, sondern schicken Briefe an einzelne Würdenträger, möglicherweise regelmäßig in identischer Kopie an andere Würdenträger.« (108). Zentral sei hingegen die Berufung auf ein Gesetz vor Gericht, das dann von der begünstigten Partei vorgelegt werde.

Man könnte angesichts dieser bedenkenswerten Dekonstruktion der herrschenden Lehre auch fragen, ob nicht schon der Begriff der »Geltung« zu vermeiden ist, und zwar nicht nur für das spätantike, sondern auch schon für das kaiserzeitliche Recht.[3] Natürlich gibt es – wie schon Dieter Nörr bemerkte – in der Kaiserzeit einen »Gesetzespositivismus« derart, dass die Gesetze, die bekannt sind, auch beachtet werden, d. h. vor Gericht zitiert und berücksichtigt werden müssen; dies heißt aber gerade nicht, dass sie – in einem modernen abstraktrechtlichen Sinne – »Geltung« beanspruchen. Vielmehr lässt sich zeigen, dass andere Argumente und zwar nicht nur (im modernen Sinne) »normativer« Natur die Entscheidung beeinflussen. Dazu gehören nicht nur die Aspekte der Einzelfallgerechtigkeit, sondern auch Maß und Umfang der Jurisdiktionsgewalt des Entscheiders sowie die Autorität der Juristen als Ausleger des Rechts in seiner Gesamtheit.

Eine Hauptfrage des zweiten Teils ist, warum die Heterodoxengesetzgebung nicht – wie etwa die *lex Iulia et Papia* – die Erwerbsfähigkeit (*capacitas*) der Erben beschränkt, sondern den Häretikern die Testierfähigkeit genommen habe. R. diskutiert zunächst die Erklärungen der bisherigen Literatur, die von der Annahme einer symbolischen, dem Bürgerrechtsentzug vergleichbaren Sanktion bis hin zum Ausschluss der Heterodoxen aus dem sozialen Zeremoniell der Testamentserrichtung als letztem Urteil reichten. Er verwirft diese Ansätze als nicht stichhaltig; auch das schon zur Prinzipatszeit immer wieder beklagte Delatorenunwesen könne die erbrechtliche Maßnahme nicht erklären. Die eigene Antwort im dritten Teil differenziert: Die Einschränkung der Testierfreiheit sei von Theodosius I. zunächst als Maßnahme gegen die Manichäer erdacht worden, da bei diesen die für die Missionierung zuständigen Kleriker hauptsächlich von den Almosen der »Hörer« gelebt hätten. Erst ein Einzelfall habe dazu geführt, die für diese spezifische Gruppe durchaus passende Bestrafung auf die Donatisten zu übertragen. Hiermit vertrage sich auch, dass die Eunomianer nur anlassweise mit erbrechtlichen Sanktionen und bei den Apostaten vorrangig Kleriker mit entsprechenden Strafen versehen worden seien. Insgesamt widerspricht R. der Vorstellung, die spätantike Gesetzgebung sei chronologisch und inhaltlich geordnet gegen »Häretiker« als Gruppe vorgegangen. Vielmehr er-

2 Anna Plisecka, Material Aspects of Severan Legislation in the Light of Documentary Papyri, in: Cornelia Ritter-Schmalz / Raphael Schwitter (Hg.), Antike Texte und ihre Materialität. Alltägliche Präsenz, mediale Semantik, literarische Reflexion, Berlin / New York 2019, 287–308.

3 So Ulrike Babusiaux, § 6 – Die römischen Rechtsschichten, in: dies. et al. (Hg.), Handbuch des Römischen Privatrechts, Tübingen 2022, 114–191.

weise sich die spätantike Gesetzgebung als anlassbezogen und sei – wie er in seinen Ergebnissen betont – »mit einem stemmatischen Modell« (814) erklärbar.

In der Tat erweist sich das Stemma als ein gutes Bild, um die Abhängigkeit von und die Variation früherer Texte in späterer Gesetzgebung zu erklären, wobei sich erwägen ließe, dieses Modell auch auf die Rechtsetzung im Prinzipat zu übertragen. Die oben vorgeschlagene Infragestellung der »Geltung« von antiken und spätantiken Gesetzen ist damit sehr gut vereinbar, denn die innergesetzliche Referenzierung zeigt, dass die Anordnungen zwar möglicherweise bekannt und einschlägig waren, keineswegs aber die »Geltungskraft« einer modernen Norm für sich beanspruchen konnten. Somit erweist sich die Neubewertung der spätantiken Gesetzgebung durch R. als äußerst fruchtbar. Zudem finden sich in Rs. Werk immer wieder ertragreiche Exkurse und wichtige Nebenerkenntnisse. So bildet das Kapitel »Vererben und Erben in der Spätantike« (264–290) einen Abriss über die Entwicklung des Testamentrechts bis zum 4. Jh., wobei nicht die rechtlichen Aspekte, sondern die sozialen Realitäten im Vordergrund stehen; darüber hinaus finden sich weiterführende Passagen zu *deportatio*, *relegatio* und *exilium* (321–341) sowie zur spätantiken Infamie (353–405).

Selbst wenn man nicht in allem den emphatischen Aufrufen von R. zur Abkehr von der bisherigen Lehre folgen wird, machen der Gedankenreichtum, die konsequente Quellennähe und die intellektuelle Eigenständigkeit der Darstellung das Werk zu einer in jeder Hinsicht anregenden und überaus gewinnbringenden Lektüre.

■

Marie Seong-Hak Kim

The Legal Past of Asia When It Was the World*

Professor Janos Jany discloses at the beginning of his *Legal Traditions in Asia* that »one of the most important inspirations to writing this book was the late Professor H. Patrick Glenn's magnum opus, *The Legal Traditions of the World*«. Glenn's book, first published in 2000, is a global account of laws, separated into »traditions« in the context of world history. *Legal Traditions in Asia*, written by a specialist of Jewish, Islamic, and Zoroastrian law, focuses on Asian laws, which Jany breaks down into Ancient Near Eastern, Islamic, Hindu, Chinese, and customary law »legal circles«. Glenn's work has been acclaimed for demonstrating that the disciplines of comparative law and legal history are one and the same. Jany's reaffirms the significance of history, religion, and philosophy in comparative law research. Yet the two books are rather different in spirit, structure, and approach.

Professor Jany states that his organizing scheme of the concept of »legal circle« is »identical to neither legal tradition nor legal system« (6). He defines a legal system as »a totality of laws in a particular state«, whereas a legal tradition is composed of laws which »are not a product of political law making and their boundaries are less clear cut as that of a legal system« (6). The »legal circles«, each composed of a »dominant« legal culture to which »satellite« legal cultures were attached, can help group local variants of legal traditions, he argues. The satellite legal cultures of the Ancient Near Eastern legal circle include cuneiform law, Jewish law, Persian law, and the law of the Church of the East. Jany separates the Islamic legal circle into pre-Islamic Arabia and classical Islamic law. The Hindu legal circle comprises Hindu law in India as well as the Buddhist Thai-Lao and the Mon-Burmese legal traditions in Southeast Asia. Societies belonging to the Chinese legal circle, embodying Confucian thought, are Vietnam, Korea, and Japan.

* Janos Jany, Legal Traditions in Asia. History, Concepts and Laws, Cham: Springer 2020, viii + 496 p., ISBN 978-3-030-43727-5

The author identifies three models of how the ties between the dominant and satellite legal cultures in these four legal circles were created: through cultural and religious expansions in the cases of the ancient Near East and of Hindu law in Southeast Asia; through political and military influences in East Asia; and through commercial relations and economic activities, as witnessed in Islam's gaining footholds in Central Asia and the archipelago of Southeast Asia. Jany's fifth and final legal circle of customary laws does not fit into the dominant / subordinate framework, and the laws of many localities, such as *adat* law, could have been placed under one of the four dominant legal circles. But the author chose to group them together to form a separate legal circle, because they display a variety of similarities that elaborate »a new, Asia-specific classification of customary laws« (8).

The introductory chapter in *Legal Traditions in Asia* is brief, and readers who expect an extended prolegomenon offering central themes and arguments are recommended to read the Concluding Remarks first, where the author articulates the book's main theme in terms of the immutability of legal traditions. Jany writes: »The status quo between the spheres of influence among Asian legal systems and circles were [*sic*] constant throughout the entire legal history of Asia and no Asian legal circle was able to or willing to influence other legal circles to the extent of shaking their foundations and base them on different underlying principles. […] Asian legal circles remained constant and stable without any cross-fertilisation among them.« (461) According to him, changelessness prevailed in the internal working of each legal circle as well: the relationship between a dominant and a satellite legal tradition, once formed, remained largely frozen. This thesis, while persuasive to an extent, seems to downplay the fact that the diffusion of a foreign religion, moral philosophy, or laws based on them took place through encounters and contacts, a normal process of historical development, to which Asia was no exception.

The Asian continent was one well-connected world. The Silk Road passed through Mesopotamia, Syria, Persia, the Arabian Peninsula, Central Asia, north India, and to China, serving as a path for the transmission of religions, ideas, and technology. Maritime trade linked the Indian Ocean with the Red Sea and the Mediterranean, connecting East Africa and southern Europe to Eurasia, and this was how Islam supplanted Buddhism in most of India and Southeast Asia. The author notes that Hindu and Chinese laws »adopted nothing from each other, despite their connection through various channels (trade, Buddhist missionaries)« (462). Yet, it is not clear which time period the author is referring to. What exactly is Hindu law and what is Chinese law, defined in which era? Jany says that »the status quo lasted for a remarkably long historic period and each legal circle was closed and inward looking without any intent to learn or adopt anything from another Asian legal circle« (461–462). This statement would benefit from a more specific temporal reference. Legal history should privilege the time dimension.

This book explains the constancy of Asian laws in terms of legal pluralism. Legal pluralism was common in societies where religious law was dominant, for example in Muslim countries, which delicately sustained an »equilibrium lasting for long centuries« (467) in the region. According to Jany, it shielded individual legal circles from being affected by one another, until this state of balance was destroyed by Western colonization. Yet, highlighting the presumed plurality and innate cultural elasticity or adaptability should not obscure the dynamic forces of exchange underlying this vast continent over thousands of years before the coming of European colonialism. Here, Jany's view contrasts with that of Glenn, who defined »tradition« as information and declared that his goal was to study the transmission of information, that is, the irrepressible communication of ideas over time, both within and without legal traditions.

The author's discussion of »legal pluralism and politics« in modern China is of interest. After Mao's death, »the centralised state allowed Chinese society for [*sic*] a limited (legal) pluralism in some areas of law in exchange for not interfering to [*sic*] politics at all«, and »with this new policy of statism in economy, China emerged as one of the most important players globally which created a new relationship between society and the centralised state (entrepreneurship)« (465–466). But does the policy of allowing limited rights to private property as part of state *dirigisme* really evince a pluralistic legal order? The Chinese Communist Party has had no intention to recognize a legal order other than the unitary state law. The party leadership's sincerity in reviving Confucian philosophy is suspect, too, as it features, at best, a muscular

Confucianism that combines the rhetoric of persuasion with the threat of force to support the status quo.

Jany's dense book is packed with highly interesting details. The discussions of laws in the Near East and Middle East are doubtless thorough and authoritative. The author's analysis of Jewish and Islamic scholars' discourses, jurisprudence, and legal training are insightful and perceptive. Less so are the latter parts of the book dealing with South Asia, East Asia, and Southeast Asia, which draw mainly on Western-language secondary sources. Some sections read as if they were from a survey history book. The overall coverage is thus uneven. Some errors are expected when personal and geographical names as well as terms in so many different languages appear, but there are more than the usual number of infelicities. It is regrettable that deficiencies in copyediting and proofreading have diminished the readability of this important contribution to comparative legal history. There are handy glossaries for selected chapters, yet the absence of an index must be pointed out as a major defect in a book of this nature – at least in its print version.

The significance of this book is clear, nonetheless. Not many can write a book like this one, pulling together a daunting amount of information. Professor Jany's ambitious and painstaking work offers readers essential reference materials and a much-needed foundation for linking a great diversity of legal traditions to one another. His book marks a timely and welcome occasion to promote a dialogue among jurists, historians, theologians, philosophers, anthropologists, and anyone else interested in the evolution of laws when Asia, borrowing Stewart Gordon's words, was the world. Professor Glenn reminded us that »comparing is thus becoming no longer a process of simple, allegedly factual, determination of similarities and differences, but [...] an ongoing and dynamic process of co-existence, of (potentially different) equals«. We anticipate continued explorations of influences across the legal circles as set forth in *Legal Traditions in Asia*.

■

Helwig Schmidt-Glintzer

Das Recht der Mitte*

Drei Bände mit einer Darstellung der Geschichte des Rechts in China, oder besser: Geschichte der chinesischen Rechtskultur sind hier anzuzeigen. Herausgegeben von Chinas Doyen der Rechtsgeschichte Zhang Jinfang, Jahrgang 1930, wird die Rechtskultur von den Anfängen bis in die Gegenwart in ihrer Entwicklung nachgezeichnet. Es ist eine Darstellung aus chinesischer Perspektive, die sich auf die Theorie des Marxismus-Leninismus als ihre Grundlage beruft, ohne weiter darauf Bezug zu nehmen, wenn man von Formulierungen absieht wie: »The economic pattern of agrarianism, the political system of despotism, the social structure of family-centered patriarchy, the stable blood and geographical relationships, [...] have constituted a unique national condition which has further determined the main feature of Chinese legal civilization« (I, v). Für eine westliche Leserschaft wiegt schwerer, dass, von einigen japanischen Ausnahmen abgesehen, in keiner Weise die internationale rechtshistorische Forschung berücksichtigt und auch an keiner Stelle auf sie verwiesen wird. Neben der umfangreichen angelsächsischen Forschungs- und Übersetzungsliteratur ist immer noch nützlich Robert Heuser, *Einführung in die chinesische Rechtskultur* (1999) und ders., *Grundriß der Geschichte und Modernisierung des chinesischen Rechts* (2013).

* Jinfan Zhang, The History of Chinese Legal Civilization. Ancient China – From About 21st Century B.C. to 1840 A.D., vol. 1 + 2, Singapore: Springer 2020, xxi + 1308 S., ISBN 978-981-10-1027-9 [zitiert als I + II]

Jinfan Zhang, The History of Chinese Legal Civilization. Modern and Contemporary China (From 1840 –), Singapore: Springer 2020, xv + 903 S., ISBN 978-981-10-1030-9 [zitiert als III]

Die ohne Register vorgelegten Bände erschließen sich dem Leser erst, wenn er sich auf eine geduldige Lektüre einlässt. Dann aber entfalten sich die zahlreichen Themen der Rechts- ebenso wie der Verwaltungskultur und der Maßnahmen zur öffentlichen Ordnung, und man wird einen vertiefenden Einblick in die Regelungstraditionen Chinas erhalten. Auch wenn eine Lektüre der etwas holzschnittartigen (im Band 2 nochmals abgedruckten) Einleitung entbehrlich ist, so offenbart sie doch einen sinozentrischen Blick, den das ganze Werk kennzeichnet, auch wenn es in der chronologischen und dem Ablauf der Dynastien folgenden Darstellung dann erheblich differenzierter im Detail ist.

Die den dritten Band einleitende Behauptung, die chinesische Rechtsentwicklung sei bis ins 19. Jahrhundert ein ausschließlich innerchinesischer Prozess, muss man bezweifeln. China hatte immer Austausch mit seinen Nachbarn, nicht nur während der Zeiten der Fremddynastien im frühen Mittelalter, sondern in besondere Weise auch in den Dynastien Liao, Jin, Yuan und Qing. Der Satz »[...] in the long process of historical development, there is only lengthways inheritance, but no horizontal comparison and absorption. The legal exchange between China and the neighboring countries is actually a single-direction export of Chinese laws.« (III, 3) wäre angesichts der von Rechtshistorikern innerhalb und außerhalb Chinas vorgetragenen Erkenntnisse zu überprüfen. Paul Heng-chao Ch'en (*Chinese Legal Tradition under the Mongols. The Code of 1291 as Reconstructed*, 1979) etwa hat gezeigt, dass der Beitrag der Mongolen zum chinesischen Rechtssystem größer war und bedeutungsvoller als bisher zumeist vermutet. Die Behauptung, mit den »Barbaren« habe kein Austausch stattgefunden, wobei der hier als »Barbaren« gefasste Begriff zunächst nichts als die Randvölker bezeichnete, muss also stark relativiert werden. Die Leugnung dieser Prägung unter der Mongolenherrschaft verstellt übrigens die Einsicht in ein wesentliches Charakteristikum der in der Mongolenzeit begründeten und von der Mandschu-Herrschaft beerbten und dann im 20. Jahrhundert verfolgten Einheitsstaats- und Herrschaftsideologie. Hier schlägt die fehlende Berücksichtigung der internationalen, auf China bezogenen rechtshistorischen Forschung besonders zu Buche.

Für die Einbettung der Publikation in die gegenwärtigen Bemühungen um eine Definition der angestrebten Rolle Chinas in der Welt ist dann vor allem das Nachwort im dritten, der Moderne und der Gegenwart gewidmeten Band aufschlussreich: »Postscript: The Formation and Experience of the Socialist Legal System with Chinese Characteristics« (III, 901–903). Danach wird die Geschichte der chinesischen Rechtskultur als Vorgeschichte zu einer noch langwierigen Entwicklung einer zukünftigen spezifisch chinesischen Rechtskultur verstanden: »we should be fully aware that we still have a long way to go in the future to build a country ruled by law, because it requires our constant hard work and unyielding spirit« (III, 901). Von der ganzen Welt wolle man einerseits lernen, von der »advanced legal culture of the rest of the world«, und zugleich solle die Kultur Chinas weiter entwickelt werden und dabei »in conformity with the inherent mindset of the Chinese Nation« bleiben (III, 902).

Während man tatsächlich, so wie es den Reformern zu Beginn des 20. Jahrhunderts deutlich vor Augen stand, auch heute noch von einem andauernden Nationsbildungsprozess in China sprechen muss, spricht das vorliegende Werk von einer immer schon bestehenden »Nation«, wenn in der Einleitung von einem stabilen und geeinten Reich und einem bereits länger als viertausend Jahre anhaltenden zivilisatorischen Prozess und von einer »unified and multi-ethnic national composition« (I, v) die Rede ist. Dieses Konzept einer auf Riten (*li*) und Rechtsnormen (*fa*) basierten Rechtskultur wird in der Einleitung (I, vi–xii) aufgerufen, mündend in der Feststellung: »because Chinese law not only had its uniqueness but also its progressiveness in legal culture, it is universally acknowledged in the world as one of the most important legal systems« (I, xii). Die Darstellung der Rechtsgeschichte stützt sich auf Berichte in den offiziellen Dynastiegeschichten und einer Vielfalt von Kompendien wie Text- und Fallsammlungen. Die Frage nach Differenzen zwischen dem Rechtssystem und der Rechtspraxis bleibt weitgehend ausgeblendet, obwohl doch gerade die Späte Kaiserzeit hierzu eine Vielzahl von Quellen und Dokumenten jenseits der kanonischen Literatur bietet. Allerdings werden zahlreiche Dokumente, etwa Throneingaben und Memoranden, angeführt, die als Reaktion auf bestimmte Missstände gelesen werden und als ein wesentlicher Teil der Rechtsentwicklungsdynamik angesehen werden können.

Während das Rechtssystem des die Reichseinigung verwirklichenden Staates Qin und der folgenden Han-Dynastie (bis 220 n. Chr.) auch unter

Einbeziehung neuerer Textfunde – auf Bambus oder Seide – ausführlicher geschildert wird, werden der Zeit der Reichsteilung bis zur Wiedervereinigung unter der Dynastie Sui (220–581 n. Chr.) nur knapp 90 Seiten gewidmet (I, 381–470). Diese Darstellung ist jedoch schon allein deswegen zu begrüßen, weil sonst die Rechtssysteme dieser Periode eher stiefmütterlich behandelt werden. So kommt Recht als Thema in dem diese Epoche behandelnden Band der *Cambridge History of China* (Vol. 2, 2019) nicht vor. Durch die Auswertung der Dynastiegeschichten als Quelle, insbesondere darin enthaltener Berichte und Dokumentenauszüge, ohne diese allerdings quellenkritisch zu diskutieren, erfährt man dann doch viel über Veränderungen, Reformen und die Durchführung einzelner Regelungen, so dass trotz der eingangs beschworenen Einheitlichkeit und Kontinuität ein buntes Panorama entsteht, etwa wenn für die Zeit der Reichsteilung im frühen chinesischen Mittelalter (3.–6. Jahrhundert) über die im Gegensatz zu den Südstaaten größere Reformfreudigkeit im nördlichen Staat Wei gesprochen wird (I, 433). Einflüsse von nach China gelangten Regelungen anderer Völker und Kulturen werden aber in dieser frühen Zeit gar nicht erst gesucht, sondern erst im dritten Band thematisiert, wo ihnen streckenweise dann sogar das Hauptaugenmerk gilt.

Eine wirklich gewinnbringende Beschäftigung mit dem Werk wird jedoch ohne sinologischen Fachbeistand kaum gelingen, weil zu viele Bezugspunkte weiterer Erläuterung bedürfen. Trotz aller Vorbehalte ist das Werk dazu geeignet, einen ersten Einstieg in das wichtige Gebiet der chinesischen Rechtsgeschichte zu ermöglichen und zugleich zur Gewinnung eines »pluriversalen Rechtsverständnisses« (Ralf Michaels in: Max Planck Forschung 4/2021) beizutragen. Um aber überhaupt erst zu einer gemeinsamen Verständigung über Gemeinsames und Trennendes in den jeweiligen Rechtstraditionen zu gelangen, ist noch ein weiter Weg zu gehen. Die Aussichten hierfür dürften wesentlich davon abhängen, wie intensiv jeweils die Bereitschaft ausgeprägt ist, sich auf die Besonderheiten der jeweiligen Traditionen einzulassen. Vor allem wird China, selbst wenn es wie bekundet eine spezifisch chinesische eigene Rechtskultur anstrebt, eine neue Moderne nicht mehr ganz ohne die Erfahrungen »des Westens« erreichen, weil die Auseinandersetzung damit, wie vor allem der dritte Band belegt, inzwischen ein Teil der chinesischen Rechtsidentität geworden ist. Solche Studien wie die sich vor allem mit den Verhältnissen im 19. Jahrhundert beschäftigende von Anselm Stolte (*Gesellschaftsunternehmen und Gesellschaftsrecht in China und Europa. Ein Beitrag zur Max Weber-Forschung*, 2014) bleiben ganz außer Betracht, und doch wäre gerade eine derartige multiperspektivische Betrachtung im dritten Band besonders wünschenswert gewesen.

Die größte Gefahr in dem dominanten Narrativ von der weitgehenden Eigenständigkeit chinesischer Rechtsentwicklung liegt in einer neuen Selbstisolierung und einer damit verbundenen Leugnung der bisherigen Austauschbeziehungen. Diese Gefahr ist keineswegs gebannt, und die gegenwärtige Parole von China als einem »systemischen Rivalen« könnte einem solchen Trend zu einem »decoupling« noch weiteren Vorschub leisten. Deswegen bleibt es geboten, rechtshistorische Fragen immer wieder erneut aufzurufen. Besonders reizvoll könnte es sein, Rechtsbegriffe zu thematisieren, die, obwohl sie durch Beschäftigung mit nicht-chinesischen Rechtstraditionen geprägt bzw. gefärbt sind, im Chinesischen dann nicht mehr auf den ersten Blick als solche erkennbar sind, weil die chinesische Schrift diese Prägungen oft verhüllt.

So ist es unbestreitbar, dass der Reformer Liang Qichao (1873–1929), um nur ein Beispiel zu nennen, stark von den Werken Rudolf von Jherings (1818–1892) beeinflusst war. Jherings Schrift »Der Kampf um's Recht« von 1872, die mit dem Satz beginnt: »Das Ziel des Rechts ist der Friede, das Mittel dazu der Kampf« (Rudolf von Jhering: *Der Kampf um's Recht*, 1872, zitiert nach der 11. Aufl., Wien 1894, 1), hatte Liang beeindruckt, und er könnte dort auch den Satz gelesen haben: »Die politische Stellung eines Volkes nach Innen und nach Außen entspricht stets seiner moralischen Kraft – das Reich der Mitte mit seinem Bambus, der Ruthe für erwachsene Kinder, wird trotz seiner Hunderte von Millionen den fremden Nationen gegenüber niemals die geachtete völkerrechtliche Stellung der kleinen Schweiz einnehmen« (ebd., 70). Derart provokative Positionen mögen für die China-Zentriertheit der vorliegenden Rechtsgeschichte Zhangs ein weiteres Motiv und Antrieb gewesen sein; doch tatsächliche Verbindungen freizulegen wird die Aufgabe einer zukünftigen Darstellung der Rechtsgeschichte Chinas sein, die ihren hybriden Charakter eingesteht und nicht verhüllt.

■

Anselm Küsters

Eine allumfassende Geschichtstheorie ohne Geschichte*

Das neueste Buch des Harvard-Anthropologen Joseph Henrich, *The WEIRDest People in the World*, bietet eine allumfassende Theorie der modernen Welt, der zufolge sich die sozialen, ökonomischen, und rechtlichen Spezifika jeder Kultur auf ihre Verwandtschaftsinstitutionen und die sich daraus ergebenden psychologischen Muster zurückführen lassen. Gekonnt führt Henrich diese Theorie mit anthropologischer und psychologischer Evidenz zusammen, um daraus zu folgern, dass die europäische Kultur aufgrund von psychologischen Eigenschaften, die ihren Ursprung im Christentum haben, im Laufe der Zeit westlich, gebildet, industrialisiert, reich und demokratisch wurde – sie wurde WEIRD (*Western*, *Educated*, *Industrialized*, *Rich*, *Democratic*). Im Unterschied zu Max Weber identifiziert er den Geist des modernen Kapitalismus nicht mit okzidentalem Rationalismus und protestantischer Ethik, sondern hebt auf einen viel älteren, aber wenig beachteten Grundsatz des frühen westlichen Christentums ab, nämlich dass es für Cousins und Cousinen falsch sei, einander zu heiraten. Durch reines Eigeninteresse habe die katholische Kirche mit diesem Inzestverbot und weiteren Familienvorschriften die früheren, auf Verwandtschaft basierenden Machtnetzwerke aufgelöst und damit die Entwicklung der europäischen Gesellschaft auf einen einzigartigen Weg gelenkt. Obwohl Henrichs Argumentation die historische Institutionalismus-Literatur um eine erfrischende psychologische Basis erweitert, kommen aus rechts- und wirtschaftsgeschichtlicher Perspektive die konkrete geschichtliche Erfahrung sowie die geschichtswissenschaftliche Methodik oftmals zu kurz.

Der Autor hat viel vor. Auf rund 700 Seiten beschreibt das Buch die Eigenschaften von in WEIRD-Kulturen aufwachsenden Menschen (Abschnitt 1), zeigt, dass frühe Gesellschaften universalistische Religionen nutzten, um sich zu vergrößern, und damit einen folgeschweren Prozess der kumulativen kulturellen Evolution einleiteten (Abschnitt 2), und illustriert, wie das Christentum die psychologische und institutionelle Landschaft in westlichen Gesellschaften geprägt hat (Abschnitt 3). Das durch kirchliche Heiratsverordnungen in Europa geschaffene »psychological package of individualism, analytic orientation, positive-sum thinking, and impersonal prosociality« (465) habe zu Vertrauen, Mobilität und Unternehmertum geführt, was dann wiederum – vermittelt über typisch westliche Institutionen wie Universitäten, Gerichte und akademische Zeitschriften – in einem unvergleichlichen Anstieg der Prosperität endete. Der von Max Weber hervorgehobene Protestantismus ist in dieser Perspektive nur ein »booster shot« (418) für WEIRD-typische psychologische Muster, deren Entwicklung bereits im vierten Jahrhundert mit den Briefen des Augustinus eingesetzt hätte (für eine hilfreiche Auflistung aller relevanten kirchlichen Entscheidungen und Dekrete, siehe: 168–171 und 491–498). Im Kontrast dazu fühlten sich die Menschen außerhalb Europas, so suggeriert Henrich, noch länger lokalen Gemeinschaften verpflichtet, was ihre institutionelle Entwicklung in eine andere Richtung präfigurierte.

Gerade die anthropologischen und psychologischen Ergebnisse der ersten beiden Buchabschnitte, die die empirische Grundlage für Henrichs weitreichende Behauptungen im dritten Abschnitt bilden, bereichern die rechts- und wirtschaftsgeschichtliche Debatte. Sie belegen, dass viele westliche Normen und Verhaltensweisen – wie Geduld, Vertrauen, analytisches Denken, Leistungsdrang und Innovationsfreudigkeit – überhaupt nicht so universell sind, wie das in vielen experimentellen Studien oder theoretischen Argumenten vorausgesetzt wird. Man denke nur an den oft belächelten *homo oeconomicus*, der nach wie vor die

* Joseph Henrich, The WEIRDest People in the World: How the West Became Psychologically Peculiar and Particularly Prosperous, New York: Farrar, Straus and Giroux 2020, xxv + 680 S., ISBN 978-0-374-17322-7

Konjunkturmodelle von Makroökonomen lenkt. Westliche Juristen wiederum wachsen mit der Vorstellung von individuellen, unveräußerlichen Rechten und einem von persönlichen Relationen unabhängigen Rechtssystem auf, die Henrich zufolge ebenfalls nur ein Spiegelbild der nicht verallgemeinerbaren WEIRD-Psychologie ist (395–429). Die breite, oftmals aus eigenen Feldexperimenten gewonnene quantitative Evidenz demonstriert, dass Menschen in nicht-westlichen, nicht-elitären Umgebungen viel stärker in die Forschung einbezogen werden müssen – nicht nur aus anthropologischem oder historischem Interesse, sondern auch, um theoretische Argumente zu nuancieren und zu passenderen Politikempfehlungen zu gelangen. Dieser empirische Fokus bietet Anknüpfungspunkte etwa zu den »glokalgeschichtlichen« Ansätzen in der Rechtsgeschichte oder den »history from below«- und »local varieties of capitalism«-Studien der Wirtschaftsgeschichte. Zugleich bieten die vielfältigen Ergebnisse dieser Forschungsbereiche eine notwendige Differenzierung gegenüber dem monotonen und recht pauschalen Bild, das Henrich implizit von den in nicht-WEIRD-Gebieten lebenden Bevölkerungen zeichnet.

Die Frage, warum gerade Europa in den letzten Jahrhunderten eine unvergleichliche Prosperität erreicht hat, beschäftigt Geistes- und SozialwissenschaftlerInnen seit langem. Beliebte Erklärungen reichen von der Entwicklung repräsentativer Regierungen, dem Aufstieg des Handels und der Verfügbarkeit englischer Kohle bis zur Intensität der europäischen Kriegsführung, dem relativen Preis britischer Arbeitskräfte und der Entwicklung einer rationalen Wissenschaftskultur. Henrichs Erläuterungen zu dem Einfluss des »Marriage and Family Program« der Kirche (165) weisen auf tiefere soziale und psychologische Grundlagen hin, auf denen die meisten Erklärungen der Industriellen Revolution aufbauen. Für WirtschaftshistorikerInnen ist hierbei die ökonometrische Überprüfung von Henrichs Thesen durch den US-Ökonomen Jonathan Schulz relevant, der mithilfe eines historischen Differenz-von-Differenzen-Ansatzes belegen konnte, dass der Kontakt zur Kirche zur Bildung von partizipatorischen Institutionen beigetragen hat.

Aus geschichtswissenschaftlicher Perspektive sind die bei einem solch umfassenden Erklärungsansatz wohl fast notwendigerweise zu kurz kommenden chronologischen Einordnungen und historischen Kontextualisierungen zu monieren. Henrichs Erzählung springt zu mühelos vom fünften Jahrhundert ins Hochmittelalter oder direkt in die heutige Zeit. RechtshistorikerInnen könnten den Fokus auf schriftliche Gesetze um eine differenziertere Diskussion von zwischen Oralität und Schriftkultur angesiedelten mittelalterlichen Normen bereichern. Bereits 2008 zeigte Karl Ubl in seiner Tübinger Habilitationsschrift, dass es sich beim Inzestverbot entgegen der älteren Forschung um keine kirchliche Strategie zur Zerstörung der germanischen Sippen handelte, sondern um einen Versuch, die Gesellschaft zu stabilisieren. Gewichtiger ist die fehlende Berücksichtigung der Schattenseiten der WEIRD-Kultur, die eben nicht nur Aufklärung und Industrialisierung, sondern auch Kolonialismus und Weltkriege hervorgebracht hat. Inwieweit diese Aspekte mit der von Henrich propagierten Entwicklung zusammenhängen, wird nicht reflektiert. Zudem illustrieren die verflechtungsgeschichtlichen Studien der letzten Jahrzehnte, wie sehr die im Buch behandelte Periode durch wirtschaftlichen, kulturellen und nicht zuletzt personellen Austausch geprägt war. Das erschwert es, wie Henrich von »disparate societies« zu sprechen, deren unterschiedliche kulturelle Psychologie ihre Entwicklungsmöglichkeiten wie »dark matter« bestimme (470) – zu sehr erinnert eine solch binäre und deterministische Einteilung in WEIRD- und nicht-WEIRD-Kulturen an die mittlerweile verfemten Thesen eines »Zusammenpralls der Zivilisationen« (Samuel Huntington). So wie die von Physikern vermutete dunkle Materie Sterne auf ihren Bahnen hält, so droht eine solche Unterteilung ganze Gesellschaften auf geschichtliche Pfade festzuschreiben und damit einen, sicherlich ungewollten, Fatalismus zu befördern.

Zum Schluss eine methodische Beobachtung. Henrich betont, dass die von der Kirche initiierten Veränderungen als »unintended success« (485) zu verstehen seien. Seine Argumentation basiert zwar auf vielen interessanten Korrelationen zwischen Schätzungen der historischen Verwandtschaftsintensität und der Kirchenexposition auf der einen und heutigen Umfrageergebnissen auf der anderen Seite (exemplarisch: 193–232), kann aber nur selten tatsächliche Transmissionsmechanismen beschreiben. Die im Buch häufig verwendete Semantik vom »accidental genius« (161) der Kirche verdeckt dieses methodische Problem eher, als dass sie hilft – auch zufällig ablaufende Wirkungsketten lassen sich historisch rekonstruieren und dann entweder mit Archivquellen oder mit sogenannten natürlichen Experimenten auf Kausalität hin untersuchen. Aus statistischer Signifikanz folgt zudem noch nicht automatisch historische Signifikanz, die nur durch Beschäftigung mit relevanten Quellen demonstriert werden kann. Während sich die statistische Signifikanz darauf bezieht, ob ein Effekt existiert, bezieht sich die historische Signifikanz auf das Ausmaß des Effekts. Kein statistischer Test kann eindeutig zeigen, ob der Effekt groß genug ist, um in einem bestimmten historischen Kontext von tatsächlicher Bedeutung zu sein. Dennoch liefert Henrichs Analyse eine spannende und wohl notwendige psychologische Untermauerung der momentan gängigen institutionenökonomischen Interpretation der Großen Divergenz, die hoffentlich auch in der internationalen Politikberatung Gehör finden wird.

■

Caspar Ehlers

Bitte nicht zaubern*

Dass die *self-fulfilling prophecy* ein Einfall der Dämonen sei, die selbst dafür sorgen würden, dass das Vorhergesagte auch einträte, wusste schon Bern von Reichenau († 1048). Dafür stützte er sich auf die Schriften der Kirchenväter, die mantische Praktiken ablehnten, wie es bis heute die katholische und auch weitestgehend die evangelischen Kirchen tun. Dennoch aber, so zeigen Klaus Herbers und Hans-Christian Lehner in ihrer Einleitung (7–21) auf, musste stets gegen Derartiges vorgegangen werden, sei es in der kirchlichen, sei es in der weltlichen Sphäre des Rechts. Der von ihnen herausgegebene Sammelband einer Tagung aus dem Jahr 2018 widmet sich diesem Phänomen und kann sich dabei auf die Datenbank »Mittelalterliche Rechtstexte« stützen sowie auf bereits erschienene oder im Erscheinen begriffene Studien aus dem »Erlanger Internationalen Kolleg für geisteswissenschaftliche Forschung« mit dem Schwerpunkt »Schicksal, Freiheit und Prognose. Bewältigungsstrategien in Ostasien und Europa«.

Auf den wichtigen und nicht immer angemessen herangezogenen Unterschied zwischen Mantik und Divination, der nur vorgeblich pagane von christlichen Handlungsweisen abscheidet, macht Lukas Bothe in seinem Beitrag über »quasidivinatorische Praktiken im Prozessrecht der *Lex Ribuaria*« (23–37) aufmerksam. Gottesurteile – durch Proben oder Zweikämpfe – dienten zur Urteilsfindung im frühfränkischen Recht, das zur Satisfaktion fähige Urteile höher als den Beweisgang geschätzt habe. Im Gegensatz zu diesem Einbezug hellseherischer Prozessbestandteile steht die westgotische Sammlung von Konzilsakten (»La colección canónica Hispana«), die in spätantiker Tradition jedwede mantischen oder divinatorischen Praktiken untersagt (Cornelia Scherer, »Die *Collectio Hispana* als Quelle für mantische Praktiken im Westgotenreich«, 39–54). In dieser Quellengruppe bewegt sich auch die Studie von Roy Flechner (»Divination and Lot-Casting in Early Medieval Canonical Collections«, 55–64). Er kommt bei seinem Vergleich verschiedener Sammlungen zu dem Ergebnis, dass die von ihm edierte »Collectio Hibernensis« und die im westfränkischen Kloster Corbie überarbeitete Fassung der »Vetus Gallica« mehr Augenmerk auf mantische Praktiken wie den Loswurf legen, als andere aus derselben Zeit, ohne aber einen voreiligen Schluss daraus ziehen zu wollen.

Mit großer Kenntnis berichtet Ludger Körntgen über »Mantische Bestimmungen in den frühmittelalterlichen Bußbüchern« vom 7. bis zum 9. Jahrhundert (65–83). Auch hier sind es spätantike

* Klaus Herbers, Hans Christian Lehner (Hg.), Mittelalterliche Rechtstexte und mantische Praktiken (Beihefte zum Archiv für Kulturgeschichte 94), Köln / Wien: Böhlau 2021, 152 S., ISBN 978-3-412-52049-6

Traditionen, die eine von der iro-schottischen Überlieferung abweichende Aufnahme mantischer Praktiken aus dem südwestlichen Raum der Reichskirche erkennen lassen. Dabei spielt etwa die Synode von Ancyra, ca. 314, eine Rolle, deren Kanon durch den aus Syrien nach Canterbury gekommenen Erzbischof Theodor († 690) nach Angelsachsen gelangten (65 f.). Körntgen zeichnet die verschlungenen Pfade der gegenseitigen Beeinflussung in den Bußbüchern bis in die karolingische Reform nach, wo sich immer wieder Übernahmen zur Mantik aus dem Strang der »Iudicia Theodori« aus dem 7. Jahrhundert feststellen lassen.

Den Blick auf Rom öffnet Klaus Herbers (»Mantik und Prognostik in den päpstlichen *Responsa* des frühen Mittelalters«, 85–97), wobei der Charme der von ihm gewählten Quellengruppe darin besteht, dass sie Antworten auf an den Papst gestellte Fragen überliefern und so die Chance bieten, der Realität mantischer Praktiken näher zu kommen. Dazu betrachtet er vier Gruppen solcher Schreiben (87–95), die alle einen Bezug zur frühmittelalterlichen Mission in Europa haben (Angelsachsen, Germanen, Bretonen und Bulgaren). Durch die wiederholte Aufnahme solcher Papstschreiben in andere kanonische Texte erlangte das Wissen um mantische Praktiken stets weitere Verbreitung. Ein im Sammelband des Öfteren erwähntes Beispiel dafür stellt Birgit Kynast vor: »Das Dekret Burchards von Worms (1000–1025) als Quelle mantischer Praktiken« (99–117). Sie greift die Frage nach den Rückschlussmöglichkeiten von inserierten, wesentlich älteren Texten in Bußbüchern auf tatsächliche Gegebenheiten auf und stellt anhand der Interrogationen in Burchards Dekret fest, dass es zumeist darum gehe, herauszufinden, wie affin jemand zu nichtchristlichen Praktiken sei. Bemerkenswert ist, dass drei der Fragen keine älteren Vorbilder zu haben scheinen, und ›echte‹ Hinweise auf Burchard bekannte Handlungen liefern könnten (116 f.).

Einen Ausblick in das 13. Jahrhundert unternimmt Lotte Kéry am Beispiel Bernhards von Pavia († 1213) und der »Glossa Ordinaria« zum »Liber extra« (»Mantische Praktiken und Divination«, 119–143). Bernhard stufte jede Form der Zukunftsvorhersage als strafwürdig ein und bezieht sich dabei, wie die »Glossa«, auf das »Dekretum Gratiani«. Anhand von Textvergleichen zeigt Kéry die Verbindungen auf und stellt sie in den Zusammenhang der kirchlichen Auseinandersetzungen mit mantischen bzw. divinatorischen Praktiken. In ihrem Fazit (142 f.) bemerkt sie das auffällige Fehlen von kommentierenden Verurteilungen mantischer – im Sinne von nichtchristlichen (s. oben) – Praktiken angesichts der aktuellen Auseinandersetzungen der Kirche mit häretischen Bewegungen in dieser Zeit.

Dass der Sammelband kein zusammenfassendes Nachwort bietet, soll ihm nicht angekreidet werden, aber der Rezensent würde doch zwei Bemerkungen machen wollen. Eine unterstreicht die Feststellung von Birgit Kynast als von in gewisser Weise übergeordneter Bedeutung: »Aber letztlich ist auch das Dekret Burchards eine Sammlung, die Normen transportiert; sie wollte nicht das Worms des 11. Jahrhunderts porträtieren« (116 f.). Die andere ist fragender Natur: Warum dienen die mantischen und divinatorischen Handlungen aus den frühchristlichen Synodalbeschlüssen gegen ›östliche‹ Praktiken bis anscheinend in das zweite Mittelalter hinein als Beispiele, auch wenn in den zu missionierenden Bevölkerungen sicherlich auch autochthone Riten der Wahrsagerei angetroffen worden sein dürften? Hinweise auf diese Fragestellung finden sich in dem Sammelband, Antworten weniger.

■

Philipp N. Spahn

Buße als Kommentar*

Dem französischen Rechtshistoriker Paul Fournier (1853–1935) verdankt die kirchenrechtshistorische Forschung die wirkmächtige Leiterzählung von einer Wende im Kirchenrecht, die in der zweiten Hälfte des 11. Jahrhunderts eingesetzt und mit dem Dekret Gratians um 1140 einen vorläufigen Höhepunkt erreicht haben soll. Dementsprechend galt das besondere Interesse der kirchenrechtshistorischen Forschung lange Zeit Gratians Werk, bedingt dessen Entstehungs- und insbesondere dessen Wirkungsgeschichte. Seit einigen Jahren ist diesbezüglich eine Interessenverschiebung zu beobachten. Zusehends finden die vorgratianischen Kirchenrechtssammlungen und speziell die Arbeitsweise ihrer Kompilatoren die Aufmerksamkeit der Kirchenrechtshistoriker, die Fourniers Leiterzählung bisweilen herausfordern und die Bedeutung der vorgratianischen Periode des Kirchenrechts für die Entwicklung desselben aufwerten.

In diesen Zusammenhang stellt Birgit Kynast ihre von Ludger Körntgen betreute, *summa cum laude* bewertete und preisgekrönte Dissertation, deren Gegenstand das Bußbuch des ottonischen Bischofs Burchard von Worms (†1025) aus dem ersten Viertel des 11. Jahrhunderts ist. Burchards Bußbuch steht einerseits in der Tradition frühmittelalterlicher Bußbücher, die mit dem Aufkommen der Tarifbuße Beichtvätern als praxisorientierte Hilfsmittel dazu dienten, einem Vergehen ein rechtes Bußmaß zuzuordnen. Andererseits ist das Bußbuch als fünftes Kapitel des 19. Buchs Teil des 20 Bücher umfassenden Dekrets Burchards, einer Kirchenrechtssammlung, in der thematisch geordnet nicht ausschließlich Fragen der Buße, sondern etwa auch der kirchlichen Hierarchie behandelt sind.

Die Verschränkung zweier Quellengattungen im Dekret Burchards nimmt Kynast zum Anlass, das Bußbuch inhaltlich und redaktionell zu erschließen. Ihr Ziel ist es, einerseits dessen Entstehung auf Grundlage des kirchlichen Rechts nachzuzeichnen sowie die Inhalte der 196 Fragen und Bußen, der Interrogationen, zu erklären, und andererseits die Arbeitsweise Burchards sowie die Ziele, die der Wormser Bischof mit dem Dekret im Allgemeinen und dem Bußbuch im Besonderen verfolgte, herauszustellen.

Wie bewerkstelligt Kynast dieses ambitionierte Unterfangen nun konkret? Bei genauerer Betrachtung weist die Arbeit drei Teile ganz unterschiedlichen Zuschnitts auf. In den ersten fünf Kapiteln sind die Grundlagen für die Untersuchung des Bußbuchs gelegt. Auf eine Einleitung, in der neben allgemeineren Diskussionen über die Genese der kirchlichen Rechtswissenschaft die Entstehungs- und Wirkungsgeschichte von Burchards Dekret sowie der Forschungsstand skizziert sind (I Einleitung, 13–30), folgt eine biographische und werkgeschichtliche Skizze Burchards, von dem nicht nur das Dekret, sondern mit dem Hofrecht auch ein Werk aus dem Bereich des weltlichen Rechts überliefert ist (II Zu Leben und Werk Burchards von Worms, 31–40). Das dritte Kapitel ist der Quellengrundlage Kynasts gewidmet, die in Ermangelung einer kritischen Edition vornehmlich mit drei Handschriften arbeitet, die noch unter Burchard in der Wormser Domschule entstanden sein und daher am ehesten Rückschlüsse auf dessen Arbeitsweise zulassen dürften (III Methodik und Quellengrundlage, 41–54). Gegenstand des vierten Kapitels ist die Quellengrundlage Burchards, der vornehmlich aus Reginos von Prüm Sendhandbuch, darüber hinaus aber auch aus weiteren Rechtssammlungen des Frühmittelalters, etwa der *Collectio Anselmo dedicata*, der *Collectio Hibernensis* und anderen schöpfte (IV Zu den Quellen des Dekrets primär unter Berücksichtigung der Quellen des Frageteils, 55–72). Grundsätzliches zum Bußprozess und -verständnis im

* Birgit Kynast, Tradition und Innovation im kirchlichen Recht. Das Bußbuch im Dekret des Bischofs Burchard von Worms (Quellen und Forschungen zum Recht im Mittelalter 10), Ostfildern: Jan Thorbecke Verlag 2020, 541 S., ISBN 978-3-7995-6090-0

Dekret (V *Corrector siue Medicus*: Buße in Buch XIX des Dekrets, 73–97) beschließt den ersten Teil der Arbeit.

Deren zweiter Teil bildet den Kern der Untersuchung. Zunächst nimmt Kynast das Bußbuch *in toto* in den Blick, erschließt dieses formal und analysiert jede einzelne Interrogatio inhaltlich-kontextuell (VI DB XIX 5: Gestaltung, Aufbau und Inhalte des Frageteils, 99–184). Sodann wendet sich Kynast den Tötungsdelikten im Bußbuch zu, die *pars pro toto* analysiert werden, verbunden mit dem Ziel, die Grundlage zu klären, auf der einem einzelnen Vergehen eine entsprechende Buße zugeordnet ist. Mit großer Akribie erschließt Kynast die betreffenden Interrogationen, stellt jeweils deren Inhalt vor, eruiert die formalen und materiellen Quellen und bündelt die Ergebnisse in instruktiven Zusammenfassungen (VII Analyse der Interrogationes zu den Tötungsdelikten [DB XIX 5 Int. 1–31, 167, 176, 184, 185], 185–366).

Im dritten Teil sind zunächst die Ergebnisse der Bußbuchanalyse in Hinblick auf Burchards Buß- und Rechtsverständnis sowie auf seine Arbeitsweise und auf die Absichten, die der Wormser Bischof mit dem Bußbuch verfolgte, gebündelt (VIII Ergebnisse der Analyse von DB XIX 5, 367–387). Ein knapper Ausblick schlägt den Bogen zurück zur Einleitung und stellt die Ergebnisse in einen allgemeineren Zusammenhang (IX Zusammenfassung und Ausblick, 389–391). Neben einigen Verzeichnissen (1 Abkürzungen, 393; 2 Handschriften, 394 f.; 3 Quellenpublikationen und Hilfsmittel, 396–403; 4 Literatur, 404–431) sind im Anhang Transkriptionen zweier Handschriften des Bußbuchs (5 DB XIX 5 [Transkription von V 586 fol. 161v–182v und F fol. 246r–262r], 432–475), die Kynast im Rahmen ihrer Arbeit heranzieht, eine Konkordanz zu den Quellen des Frageteils (6 Tabellarische Übersicht zu den Quellen des Frageteils [Konkordanz], 476–510) und die Transkription einer Handschrift, die einen Frageteil aus Reginos von Prüm Sendhandbuch enthält und Burchard vorgelegen haben könnte (7 RP I 304 Int. [Transkription von W fol. 70r–71v], 511 f.), zu finden. Verschiedene Register (Verzeichnis der zitierten Handschriften, 513 f.; Stellenregister, 515–525; Personen-, Orts- und Sachregister, 527–541) beschließen den Band.

Durch dieses kleinteilige Vorgehen gelingt es Kynast, die gesteckten Ziele zu erreichen. Für nahezu alle Interrogationen werden die formalen wie materiellen Quellen des Bußbuchs bestimmt, die häufig dieselben waren, die Burchard auch in den übrigen Teilen seines Dekrets verwertete. Grundlage einer Interrogatio konnten nicht nur die formalen Quellen, sondern auch deren bereits erfolgte Bearbeitung in den anderen Teilen des Dekrets sein. Einerseits kann Kynast somit nachweisen, dass Bußtarife von Burchard nicht willkürlich, sondern in der Regel auf Grundlage tradierten kirchlichen Rechts festgesetzt wurden. Und andererseits zeigt Kynast eine wechselseitige Abhängigkeit zwischen dem Bußbuch und dem übrigen Dekretkorpus auf, die gleichzeitig entstanden. Unter anderem aus diesem Grund sei das Bußbuch nicht nur Unterrichtswerk und Praxishilfsmittel gewesen. Es habe auch als Kommentar der kirchenrechtlichen Tradition gedient, die Burchard in den übrigen Büchern des Dekrets kompilierte (383).

Dass das Bußbuch derart gelesen werden kann, steht nach der sorgfältig nachgezeichneten Arbeitsweise Burchards durch Kynast außer Frage. Da dieses oftmals eigenständig überliefert ist (16 f., 21), wird man allerdings fragen dürfen, inwiefern das Bußbuch tatsächlich als Kommentar zu den übrigen Büchern des Dekrets verstanden wurde. Jedenfalls war Burchards Methode eine andere als die der Kommentatoren des kirchlichen Rechts im 12. Jahrhundert. Der Wormser Bischof glich die überlieferten Rechtsbestimmungen den eigenen Bedürfnissen vornehmlich mittels Textbearbeitungen an (vgl. zusammenfassend 372), ein Vorgehen, das gerade aufgrund der wechselseitigen Abhängigkeit von Bußbuch und Dekret das Gesamtwerk Burchards betrifft. Ein »neue[r] Ansatz, Widersprüche nicht durch rhetorische Operationen zu harmonisieren, sondern jeweils begründete Entscheidungen zu treffen«,[1] wurde für den Bereich des Kirchenrechts mit dem Dekret Gratians üblich. Von einem »kanonistischen Werk« (9) des »kano-

1 Ludger Körntgen, Die Kirche im 12. Jahrhundert, in: Thomas Kaufmann, Raymund Kottje (Hg.), Ökumenische Kirchengeschichte, Bd. 2: Vom Hochmittelalter bis zur frühen Neuzeit, Darmstadt 2008, 17–61, 55.

nistisch versierten Bischof[s]« (16; vgl. ferner 14f., 20f.) Burchard zu sprechen, ist vor diesem Hintergrund irreführend.

Die originäre Leistung des Wormser Bischofs schmälert das ebenso wenig wie die Kynasts. Ihre Arbeit schafft Klarheit zu den frühmittelalterlichen Grundlagen, der Entstehung und den Inhalten des Dekrets Burchards, speziell des Bußbuchteils, und veranschaulicht das mitunter mühevolle Ringen des Wormser Bischofs im Umgang mit den kirchenrechtlichen Bestimmungen. Damit hat Kynast eine wichtige Grundlage geschaffen, die für weitere Forschungen zur vorgratianischen Periode des Kirchenrechts wie zum mittelalterlichen Bußwesen unentbehrlich sein dürfte. ■

Albrecht Cordes

Acht und Bann *à la islandaise**

Wie soll man zwischen Geschichte und Geschichten unterscheiden? Aus methodischen Gründen ist das nie einfach, doch die isländischen Sagas erschweren mit ihren spannenden Erzählungen die Differenzierung noch zusätzlich. Gehören die Geschichten aus dem schlanken, seinerseits gut erzählten Buch von Elizabeth Walgenbach zur Literatur- oder zur Geschichtswissenschaft? Die Autorin weist den Leser immer wieder in die richtige Richtung: Wenn einzelne Episoden auch nicht historisch verbürgt sein mögen, steht doch die Geisteshaltung, aus der heraus sie im 13. Jahrhundert erzählt worden sind, als historisches Faktum fest. So fließen in die spannende Geschichte (Fallstudie in Kapitel 4), in der der machtbewusste Bischof dem weltlichen Herrn, der ihm ins Amt verholfen hat, die Stirn bietet, Elemente ein, die dem in Island sofort mehrfach literarisch verarbeiteten *Murder in the Cathedral* von 1170, also der Auseinandersetzung zwischen Thomas Beckett und König Heinrich II., entstammen.

Das begrenzt die Reichweite der zentralen Aussage des Buchs. Mit Präzision und Überzeugungskraft führt die Autorin vor, wie sehr Ächtung und Exkommunikation einander ähneln, wie sie eher Waffen im Kampf zwischen exkommunizierendem Bischof und ächtendem weltlichem Richter bzw. Machthaber sind als echte Sanktionen für individuelles Fehlverhalten, und wie man sich von beidem durch Pilgerfahrten und Herrschergnade wieder befreien kann. Aber ein Saga-Schreiber mit dem Anspruch, eine spannende Geschichte zu erzählen, und mit Sympathie für die Seite des Bischofs ist kein verlässlicher Zeuge dafür, dass ›wirklich‹ das kanonische Recht das weltliche isländische Recht der Ächtung beeinflusst hat, sondern nur dafür, dass das durch seine Brille so aussah. Doch auch dies ist eine wertvolle Aussage über die rechtlichen Vorstellungen einer Person des 13. Jahrhunderts – und zwar einer Person von großem historischem Gewicht. Denn der Autor der *Íslendinga saga*, um die es hier geht, Sturla Þórðarson, hat ebenso wie sein noch berühmterer Onkel Snorri Sturluson nicht nur Sagas, sondern auch Rechtstexte verfasst.

Nach wie vor fasziniert das Island der ›Freistaatszeit‹, also der Epoche vor dem Anschluss der Insel an die norwegische Krone im Jahre 1262; nach wie vor gibt es kaum einen historischen Gegenstand, der sich so gut als Projektionsfläche für altnordische, archaische, heroische, romantische und andere Konzepte eignet. Das Etikett »germanisch« ist nach 1945 allmählich aus der Mode gekommen, aber vieles von dem, was Konrad Maurer und Andreas Heusler im 19. Jahrhundert damit gemeint haben – nämlich die urtümlich-autochthone, von fremden Einflüssen freie und ohne herrschaftlichen Druck entstandene

* Elizabeth Walgenbach, Excommunication and Outlawry in the Legal World of Medieval Iceland (The Northern World 92), Leiden / Boston: Brill 2021, XII + 178 S., ISBN 978-90-04-46091-1

Gesellschafts- und Rechtsordnung – lebt unter dem Titel »altnordisch« und in amerikanischen Büchern mit einprägsamen Titeln wie »Bloodtaking and Peacemaking« oder »Courage« (William Ian Miller, 1997 und 2002) weiter. In jüngerer Zeit schwang das Pendel weit in die andere Richtung, als Hans Henning Hoff in seiner Dissertation (Hafliði Másson und die Einflüsse des römischen Rechts in der Grágás, 2012) in diesem wichtigsten frühen isländischen Gesetz überall römisches Recht entdeckte, was ganz auf der Linie seines Lehrers Hermann Nehlsen lag. Zu dieser die fremden Einflüsse betonenden Richtung gehört auch das Buch von Elizabeth Walgenbach, das wegen der sorgfältigen Quellenarbeit und nicht zuletzt wegen des Lesevergnügens auch denjenigen ans Herz gelegt werden kann, die wie der Rezensent die Originalzitate mangels eigener Sprachkenntnisse überspringen müssen. Ob das Pendel demnächst wieder zurückschwingt und Forscher wieder stärker nach dem spezifisch Isländischen im frühen isländischen Recht suchen, wird sich zeigen.

Es gab nach der Erzähllogik der Sagas aus Exkommunikation und Verbannung immer noch einen Weg zurück zur Versöhnung. Der hartgesottene Feind des oben gemeinten Bischofs Guðmundr, Kolbeinn, mächtigster Fürst im Norden Islands, soll, obwohl exkommuniziert, auf dem Totenbett doch noch seinen Frieden mit Gott gemacht und sogar noch Zeit gefunden haben, die Hymne *heyr himna smiður* – Höre, himmlischer Schmied – zu dichten, die man schön vertont auf YouTube anhören kann.

■

Marietta Auer

Die Kunst des Weglassens*

Das hier zu rezensierende Werk ist große Kunst. Große Kunst vermittelt universelle Einsichten in meisterlich reduzierter Form. Große Kunst ist die Kunst des Weglassens. Bei der Lektüre von Jan Schröders Meisterwerk, das nunmehr in dritter Auflage in vollständiger, zweibändiger Fassung vorliegt, wendet man staunend Seite für Seite und fragt sich, wie so etwas möglich ist: Fünfhundert Jahre Rechtswissenschaftsgeschichte ausschließlich aus den Quellen geschöpft und für jede Periode mit hinreißendem Formulierungsgeschick zum Leben erweckt, wobei die meist ganz einfachen Denkzwänge, unter denen die zeitgenössischen methodischen Richtungsentscheidungen jeweils so und nicht anders getroffen werden konnten, plastisch hervortreten. Dies alles zu einer Gesamterzählung aus einem Guss gefügt, die wiederum einem ganz einfachen Grundgesetz folgt: Methodenfragen sind Rechtsbegriffsfragen. Keine Methodendiskussion ohne Berücksichtigung des jeweiligen zeitgenössischen Rechtsbegriffs und der zugehörigen Rechtsquellenlehre. Eine Methodenlehre, die unter einem bestimmten Rechtsbegriff stilgerecht und wissenschaftlich fruchtbar wirkt, kann unter den Prämissen eines anderen Rechtsbegriffs geradezu abwegig und grundlagenfehlerhaft erscheinen. Die für jegliche künftige Methodendiskussion entscheidende Einsicht lautet: Einen universellen Metastandpunkt, von dem aus man die »Richtigkeit« juristischer Methoden überzeitlich feststellen und Methodenstreitigkeiten ein für alle Mal entscheiden könnte, gibt es nicht.

Das Buch ist über seine 2001, 2012 und 2020 erschienenen drei Auflagen sowie die Zwischenstufe des 2016 separat vorgelegten Bands »Rechtswissenschaft in Diktaturen«[1] hinweg in Schichten gewachsen. Der selbstbewusst gesteckte Anspruch

* Jan Schröder, Recht als Wissenschaft, 2 Bde, 3., überarbeitete und wesentlich erweiterte Aufl., München: C. H. Beck 2020, 858 S., ISBN 978-3-406-73868-5

1 Jan Schröder, Rechtswissenschaft in Diktaturen, München 2016.

einer auf zwei Bände angelegten Gesamtdarstellung der Rechtswissenschaftsgeschichte als Methodengeschichte von der frühen Neuzeit bis zur Gegenwart wurde dabei konsequent immer weiter umgesetzt und ist nunmehr zur Vollendung gelangt. Der Autor ist seinem konzeptionellen Gesamtplan über die ein Vierteljahrhundert währende Entstehungszeit in geradezu stupender Weise treu geblieben. Die Signatur des Werks bildet das Gliederungsschema, das für jede der nun sechs aufeinanderfolgenden Epochen von 1500 bis 1990 dem Aufbau Rechtsbegriff – Rechtsquellenlehre – Juristische Argumentations- und Interpretationslehre – Theorie der wissenschaftlichen Rechtsbearbeitung folgt. Sicherlich ist damit die Prämisse, dass sich aus ebendiesem Aufbau eine sinnvolle Methodenerzählung ergibt, dass sich also der behauptete Zusammenhang zwischen Rechtsbegriff, Rechtsquellenkanon, Methodenlehre und Rechtswissenschaftsverständnis tatsächlich konstruieren lässt, bereits vorausgesetzt. Eindrucksvoll ist allerdings, wie sehr die Schlüssigkeit dieser konstruktiven Hypothese mit jeder Zeitschicht und jeder neuen Auflage des Werks überzeugender hervorgetreten ist und wie sehr gerade das einheitliche Gliederungsschema die epochenübergreifenden langen Linien der Methodenlehre und Rechtswissenschaftsgeschichte beleuchtet.

Ein Beispiel: Zu den langen Linien, die sich wie kunstvolle rote Fäden durch das gesamte Werk ziehen, gehört etwa die beständige Wiederkehr des nie ganz miteinander vermittelbaren Nebeneinanders von juristischer Interpretations- und Argumentationstheorie. Befasst sich erstere mit der Auslegung von Gesetzen, kommt letztere mit Schlussverfahren wie der Analogie im Bereich der Rechtsfortbildung zum Tragen. Doch woher rührt der Bruch zwischen beiden Bereichen, die sich in der gegenwärtigen Methodenlehre durch die unklare Demarkationslinie der Wortsinngrenze kaum verständlich getrennt gegenüberstehen, obwohl Auslegung und Rechtsfortbildung heute doch anerkanntermaßen dem gleichen Ziel dienen sollen, nämlich der Teleologie des Gesetzes durch zweckgerechte Deutung möglichst gerecht zu werden? Die Antwort erschließt sich, wenn man Schröders Meisterwerk ganz durchliest. Dann tritt hinter dem denkzwanghaften Versuch der Nachkriegsmethodenlehre, die Gesamtheit der Methodenlehre als nicht ein-, sondern *zweistufiges* System von Grenzen zulässiger Gesetzesdeutung zu rekonstruieren, der alte Gegensatz von Hermeneutik einerseits und Logik und Topik andererseits zutage und erklärt deren gewissermaßen pfirsichförmige Gestalt, in der ein harter, von einer Bittermandel wahren Sinns ausgefüllter Kern hermeneutischer Auslegung von einer weichen, leicht verletzlichen Frucht logischer Rechtsfortbildung umgeben ist (Bd. 1, 25 ff., 50 ff., 123 ff., 134 ff., 215 ff.; Bd. 2, 177 ff., 200 ff., 237 ff.).

Ein weiteres Beispiel für lange Linien ist der Streit zwischen subjektiver und objektiver Auslegungstheorie (Bd. 1, 16 ff., 349 ff.; Bd. 2, 180 ff., 193, 216 ff.). Was wurde in diesen Streit nicht alles hineingeheimnisst. Philipp Heck überhöhte die subjektive Theorie zur einzig wissenschaftlich haltbaren, da empirisch objektivierbaren Auslegungsmethode. Hermann Kantorowicz schmähte sie als »pseudo-historische« Methode, die auf der Verwechslung des legitimen Zwecks historischer Forschung mit der Begründung normativen Aussagesinns und damit auf einem wissenschaftlichen Kategorienfehler beruhe. Karl Larenz vertrat schon 1933 die objektive Theorie und tat dies erstaunlich unbeeindruckt auch nach 1945, während Bernd Rüthers letztere bekanntlich für das methodische Grundübel der Diktatur schlechthin und die Ursache der angeblichen »unbegrenzten Auslegung« nach 1933 hält.[2] Der Streit ist aber, und das steht nirgendwo so klar wie bei Schröder, durch Argumente nicht entscheidbar, weil in ihm unterschiedliche Rechtsbegriffe kollidieren – ein idealistischer Rechtsbegriff, der objektive Sinndeutungsmethoden bevorzugt, mit einem voluntaristischen Gegenentwurf, der stets für die subjektive Deutung des empirischen Gesetzgeberwillens streitet (Bd. 2, 180). Im Übrigen ist der Prüfhorizont 1933–1945 für die objektive Auslegungstheorie ohnehin zu

2 Zur Auseinandersetzung etwa Marietta Auer, Richterbindung und Richterfreiheit in Regeln und Standards. Ein Klassiker der Methodenlehre *reloaded*, in: Eva Schumann (Hg.), Gesetz und richterliche Macht, Berlin / Boston 2020, 119–154, 128–129.

kurz. Schröder zeigt mit ergreifender Lakonie, dass der methodische Diskurs des Nationalsozialismus keineswegs auf die subjektive Theorie verzichtete, wo sie nützlich war, um dessen je nach Bedarf autoritär oder ideologisch ansetzenden Rechtsbegriff durchzusetzen (Bd. 2, 28 ff.), während die Rechtsprechung in beiden deutschen Diktaturen andererseits gerade nicht zu freiem wertpluralistischem Richterrecht und insoweit auch nicht zu der von Rüthers behaupteten »unbegrenzten Auslegung« ermächtigt war (Bd. 2, 33 ff., 71 f., 95 f.). All dies bietet ein Lehrstück dafür, dass die Methodenlehre nicht der Ort ist, an dem sich der Gerechtigkeitsgehalt einer Rechtsordnung erweist. Das verbreitete Bild der Methodenlehre als »Gerechtigkeitsdidaktik«,[3] die die materielle Richtigkeit der juristischen Entscheidungspraxis einer bestimmten Epoche wesentlich mitbestimmt, ist falsch. Nicht der Methodenschwanz wedelt mit dem Rechtswissenschaftshund, sondern umgekehrt der Rechtswissenschaftshund, fest auf dem Rechtsbegriffsboden stehend, mit dem Methodenschwanz.

Man muss nun, und das ist Schröders meisterliche Einsicht, nur die genannten vier Strukturelemente vom Rechtsbegriff über die Rechtsquellen- und Interpretationslehre bis zur Theorie der wissenschaftlichen Rechtsbearbeitung kennen, um nahezu in jeder Methodenwahl und jedem Methodenstreit das Schwanzwedeln des Rechtswissenschaftshunds zu entdecken. Nicht berücksichtigen muss man dazu: politische Geschichte, Wirtschafts- und Sozialgeschichte;[4] rechtssoziologische Untersuchungen der Institutionen und Praktiken, die die Methodenwirklichkeit einer bestimmten Epoche prägen;[5] rechtsvergleichende Betrachtungen der Frage, ob und unter welchen Prämissen Rechtswissenschaft auch in anderen Rechtssystemen als Wissenschaft betrieben wurde oder wird;[6] methodologische Primärquellen, deren Beitrag nicht über das Debattengrundrauschen der jeweiligen Epoche hinausreicht; *sämtliche* historiographischen Sekundärquellen;[7] weite Teile der Rechtspraxis und schließlich archivalische Quellen, aus denen sich zu alledem sicherlich noch mehr und anderes ergeben mag.[8] All dies könnte man sicher näher erforschen. Schröder tut es nicht. Und der Erfolg seines Werks, dem von Auflage zu Auflage immer seltener entgegengehalten wird, es wäre besser ein anderes Buch geworden, gibt ihm recht.

Eine teils kuriose Lektüre ergeben aus der Rückschauperspektive die zahlreichen Rezensionen, mit denen bereits die beiden Vorauflagen des Werks sowie der separate Diktaturen-Band bedacht wurden. Die erste Auflage von 2001, die nur die ersten drei Teile bis 1850 enthielt und mit der Begründung der positiven Rechtswissenschaft durch die historische Rechtsschule endete, veranlasste einen Rezensenten in dieser Zeitschrift noch zu der Mutmaßung, der Autor wolle »das pandektistische Credo, das Recht sei eine Wissenschaft, auf die gesamte neuere Rechtsgeschichte« extrapolieren.[9] Mit der 2012 erschienenen zweiten Auflage kam kein zweiter Band, wohl aber der den Untersuchungshorizont des ersten Bands bis 1933 ausdehnende vierte Teil hinzu. Vielleicht war das der Punkt, der Schröders Anspruch einer »radikalen Historisierung der Methodengeschichte«[10] endgültig auf der rechtshistorischen Landkarte

3 Treffend Hans-Peter Haferkamp, Rez. 2. Aufl., in: ZRG (GA) 130 (2013) 660–665. Alle im Folgenden zitierten Rezensionen betreffen die jeweils bezeichnete Auflage des hier rezensierten Werks oder den separat veröffentlichten Band »Rechtswissenschaft in Diktaturen« desselben Autors.

4 Kritisch etwa Gerd Roellecke, So hat es doch Methode?, Rez. 1. Aufl., in: FAZ v. 09.10.2001, L 42.

5 Kritisch insbesondere Hubert Rottleuthner, Rez. Diktaturen, in: ARSP 103 (2017) 427–431.

6 Kritisch etwa Tomasz Giaro, Methodenreich (Rez. 1. Aufl.), in: Rg 1 (2002) 241–242; Miloš Vec, Erst das System erzeugt die Lücke (Rez. 3. Aufl.), in: FAZ v. 01.10.2021, 10.

7 Kritisch etwa Hans Erich Troje, Rez. 1. Aufl., in: ZRG (RA) 120 (2003) 306–311; Bernd Rüthers, Rez. Diktaturen, in: JZ 72,14 (2017) 731–732.

8 Kritisch etwa Hans-Peter Haferkamp, Rez. Diktaturen, in: ZRG (GA) 136 (2019) 618–621.

9 Giaro (Fn. 6) 241. Abgesehen von Troje (Fn. 7), Giaro (Fn. 6) und Roellecke (Fn. 4) fallen bereits die Rezensionen zur ersten Auflage durchweg positiv aus, so insbesondere Michael Stolleis, Die juristischen Bücher des Jahres – eine Leseempfehlung, in: NJW 2002,49, 3593–3596, 3594–3595; Stefan Vogenauer, Rez. 1. Aufl., in: ZEuP 12 (2003) 209–211; Clausdieter Schott, Rez. 1. Aufl., in: ZRG (GA) 124 (2007) 567–570; Stephan Buchholz, Rez. 1. Aufl., in: ZNG 27 (2005) 335–336; Gerhard Otte, Rez. 1. Aufl., in: JZ 2002, 708; Arno Buschmann, Rez. 1. Aufl., in: NJW 2002,14, 1029–1030; Miloš Vec, Rez. 1. Aufl., in: Berliner Zeitung, Literaturbeilage v. 09.10.2001, 15.

10 Haferkamp (Fn. 3) 660.

verankerte (und manchen Leser gar voreilig auf den zweiten Band verzichten ließ).[11] Hans-Peter Haferkamp brachte diesen Anspruch in seiner ersten von drei Rezensionen bündig auf den Punkt und fand dabei das oben entlehnte Wort von der »Gerechtigkeitsdidaktik«, von deren »Ballast« Schröders Werk die Methodengeschichte in der Tat befreit hat.[12] Aber was ist mit der von Schröder vorgenommenen Periodisierung? Hier merkt man dem damaligen Rezensenten einen letzten Restzweifel an. Kann man wirklich die gesamte Zeitspanne von 1850 bis 1933 unter die Herrschaft eines einheitlichen »voluntaristischen« Rechtsbegriffs fassen und weder 1900, noch 1918, sondern tatsächlich erst 1933 eine Abschnittsmarke setzen?[13] Ja, man kann, man muss sogar, wenn man den Blick mit Schröder konsequent auf den Rechtsbegriff und nicht auf das Grundrauschen der zeitgenössischen Methodendebatten richtet, die im Kielwasser der kaiserzeitlichen Kodifikationswelle zwischen Zweck- und Interessenjurisprudenz, Positivismus, Idealismus und Freirecht hin- und herschwappten. Auf der von Schröder konsequent durchgehaltenen Flughöhe ebnen sich all diese kleinteiligen Oberflächenwellen ein und geben den Blick auf den Horizont des Rechtsbegriffs des späten 19. und frühen 20. Jahrhunderts frei, der sich in der Tat als »voluntaristisch« beschreiben lässt (Bd. 1, 285 ff. u. ö.).

Der nun hinzugekommene zweite Band, der die »Rechtswissenschaft in Diktaturen« als fünften Teil in das Gesamtwerk eingliedert und dieses durch einen finalen sechsten Teil zur westdeutschen Methodenlehre der Nachkriegszeit von 1945 bis 1990 beschließt, vindiziert den gewagten Satz aus dem Vorwort zur zweiten Auflage, die Methodendiskussion nach 1945 habe »an die Weimarer Republik und nicht an die nationalsozialistische Diktatur« angeknüpft, so dass die Methodengeschichte bis 1933 »unmittelbar an die moderne juristische Methodenlehre« heranführe.[14] Über die solcherart aufgespannte weitere Laufrichtung der roten Linien bis zum Ziel 1990 konnte im Jahr 2012 sogar stolpern, wer sich nicht als Gerechtigkeitsdidaktiker der Methodenlehre verstand. Als 2016 der Diktaturen-Band erschien, lebte die Konjunktur der Ermahnungen, es wäre doch besser ein anderes Buch geschrieben worden, erwartbar noch einmal auf.[15] Die Historiographie der deutschen Diktaturen erwies sich als der eigentliche Prüfstein für Schröders Ansatz, Methodengeschichte wesentlich als Theoriegespräch im Binnenraum der zeitgenössischen Rechtswissenschaft zu rekonstruieren. Hubert Rottleuthner kritisierte, die Funktionsmechanismen einer Diktatur ließen sich »nicht auf ihre Ideologie, und dann noch auf juristische Methodenlehre, reduzieren. Das ›Diktatorische‹ der beiden Regime lässt sich so nicht erkennen.«[16] Haferkamp, der an dem Diktaturen-Band ein zweites Mal als Rezensent tätig war, meinte, dass Schröder das spezifische »Steuerungsdenken« der DDR entgehe, in dem apokryphe politische Vorgaben wichtiger waren als veröffentlichte Theoriequellen: »Die DDR dachte so nicht.«[17] Aber wie »denkt« denn »die Diktatur«? Kommt es darauf überhaupt an? Schröders Kunst des Weglassens bewährt sich gerade hier, nämlich im Weglassen von Kausalitätsartefakten, Relevanzunterstellungen und Wirkhypothesen aller Art. Wer weiß schon, wie die »Steuerung« der Rechtspraxis einer bestimmten Epoche überhaupt jemals funktioniert? Erschließt sich der Charakter der Diktatur nicht gerade an den strukturellen Mustern ihrer Theorie, nämlich an der Perfidie ihres dialektischen Rechtsbegriffs und am Doppeldenk und Doppelsprech ihrer prominentesten Rechtsdenker, dessen Monstrosität sich wiederum erst mit Blick auf die langen Linien des dahinterstehenden humanistischen Erbes vollends enthüllt?

Als wäre die Goldprobe damit nicht längst erbracht, schließt sich daran nunmehr der neue sechste Teil zur westdeutschen Methodengeschich-

11 So tatsächlich Oliver Bach, Rez. 2. Aufl., in: Scientia Poetica 16 (2012) 238–241; ähnlich Peter Kreutz, Rez. 2. Aufl., in: JJZG 11,1 (2017) 36–39; zur 2. Aufl. neben Haferkamp (Fn. 3) zudem Sandro Wiggerich, Rez. 2. Aufl., in: Ber. Wissenschaftsgesch. 36 (2013) 265–266; Christian Baldus, Rez. 2. Aufl., in: GPR 9,5 (2012) 248–249.

12 Haferkamp (Fn. 3) 660.

13 Vgl. Haferkamp (Fn. 3) 662–663.

14 Jan Schröder, Recht als Wissenschaft, 2. Aufl., München 2012, Vorwort; dazu kritisch Haferkamp (Fn. 3) 664.

15 Zur »Rechtswissenschaft in Diktaturen« neben Rottleuthner (Fn. 5), Rüthers (Fn. 7) und Haferkamp (Fn. 8) auch Miloš Vec, Wie man einen Rechtsstaat mit dem Recht beerdigt (Rez. Diktaturen), in: FAZ v. 12.12.2016, 10; Georg Steinberg, Rez. Diktaturen, in: Goltdammer's Archiv 164 (2017) 635–637; Frank Schale, Rez. Diktaturen, in: Jahrbuch Extremismus & Demokratie 29 (2017) 418–419; Wilhelm Tappert, Rez. Diktaturen, in: DRiZ 2016, 429.

16 Rottleuthner (Fn. 5) 428.

17 Haferkamp (Fn. 8) 620.

te bis 1990 an (Bd. 2, 117 ff.). Auch dieser Teil hätte nach Zuschnitt und Umfang ohne weiteres eine eigenständige Monographie gerechtfertigt. Mit der Historisierung der jüngsten Vergangenheit des westdeutschen Methodendiskurses betritt Schröder abermals Neuland und bereitet einen Quellenbestand auf, der bisher allenfalls in Teilausschnitten mit kurzen Blickachsen oder blickverschiebenden Brechungen durch die Refraktionslinse 1933–1945 bearbeitet worden ist. Dabei erweist sich erneut die Leistungsfähigkeit des bewährten Gliederungsschemas. Das beginnt beim Rechtsbegriff: Auf gerade einmal zwei Seiten wird konzise zusammengefasst, wie der vor 1933 vorherrschende, gewissermaßen naiv willensbezogene und zwischen soziologischen, idealistischen und reinen Spielarten hin- und herschwankende voluntaristische Rechtsbegriff des Kaiserreichs und der Weimarer Republik durch die nationalsozialistische Rechtsperversion seine Unschuld verlor und danach nurmehr in deutlich gedämpfter Tonlage wiederaufgenommen werden konnte (117 f.). Nun galt bei vorsichtig wiederhergestelltem Wertpluralismus nur noch als Recht, was verfassungsgemäß war, einem Mindestmaß an Gerechtigkeit und gleichzeitig einem Mindestmaß an sozialer Wirksamkeit genügte – der aus der Diktaturerfahrung geborene moderat positivistisch-voluntaristische Rechtsbegriff Nachkriegswestdeutschlands war geboren. Auf konzisen zwei Seiten ist damit mehr und Treffenderes über das Verhältnis von Kontinuitäten und Diskontinuitäten vor und nach 1933 bis 1945 gesagt als anderswo in langen Abhandlungen und dicken Büchern. Und was auf den darauffolgenden schlanken 176 Seiten folgt, ist erneut eine Reise in ein vergangenes Methodenzeitalter. Meisterlich getroffen ist der Ton der alten BRD mit ihrem vorsichtig zwischen der »materiellen Gerechtigkeit«, »Sittlichkeit« und »Wirksamkeit« positiver Normen hindurchmanövrierenden Vokabular, dem nach der verheerenden Erfahrung der ideologischen Entgleisung des Rechtsbegriffs nur noch »rechtsvernichtende«, keinesfalls aber »rechtsergänzende« oder gar rechtserzeugende Wirkung mehr zukommen konnte (119 ff., 136 f.). Dieser Ton zieht sich weiter durch die Rechtsquellenlehre: Das einst so mächtige Gewohnheitsrecht schrumpft in die Bedeutungslosigkeit, nachdem der Gedanke eines unmittelbar normsetzenden Rechtswillens der Allgemeinheit vor dem Erfahrungshorizont der völkischen Despotie Anathema geworden ist (140 ff.). An die Stelle des Gewohnheitsrechts tritt das Richterrecht als meistdiskutiertes Rechtsquellenproblem der Epoche (149 ff.). Komplettiert wird der aus alledem resultierende Kompromisspositivismus durch vielfältige zählebig vertretene Prinzipientheorien, die in ihrer metaphysisch dünnen Idealität ein Signum der Epoche bilden (161 ff.).

Wie wirkte sich dieses Rechtsbegriffsverständnis auf die Methodenlehre aus? Zunächst in einer existenzphilosophischen Erneuerung der Hermeneutik, die die Interpretationslehre mit einer aktualisierten Genealogie von Martin Heidegger über Hans-Georg Gadamer bis hin zu Josef Esser und dessen Vorverständnis-Lehre versah und zeitgemäß forderte, nicht mehr nur dunkle, sondern alle Stellen des Gesetzes zum Gegenstand der sinndeutenden Auslegung zu machen (177 ff.). Das eröffnete neue Spielräume, ja geradezu einen Drall in die Richtung der objektiven Theorie, die es nunmehr erlaubte, das idealistische Methodenparadigma der zeitgenössischen Wertungsjurisprudenz im geltenden Recht umzusetzen und diesem damit genau die unsichtbare zweite Schicht an wissenschaftlicher Episteme hinzuzufügen, die seit der Wende zur Neuzeit das ununterbrochene Geschäft der Rechtswissenschaft als Wissenschaft gewesen ist. Der damit ausgeleuchtete Tiefenzusammenhang zwischen Wertungsjurisprudenz, residualem Idealismus, epistemologischem Existentialismus und objektiver Theorie zeigt einmal mehr, dass es bei der Auseinandersetzung mit der subjektiven Theorie nicht um Theorien, sondern um Rechtsbegriffe und eigentlich um Weltverständnisse geht (179 ff.). Es folgt eine für jegliche künftige Auseinandersetzung mit der Epoche unentbehrliche Darstellung der Hauptwerke zur Interpretationstheorie von 1945 bis 1990 (183 ff.) als Grundlage für die nachfolgende Kernbohrung in den Pfirsich der zeitgenössischen Methodenlehre von der gesetzesnahen Auslegung (196 ff.) bis hin zur Rechtsfortbildung *praeter* und *contra legem* (232 ff.). Trocken wird die seit ihrer Wiederentdeckung notorische Fehldeutung der Savignyschen Auslegungslehre kommentiert (196); erfrischend die Luft aus dem Ballon der Sprachphilosophie abgelassen (197 f.); köstlich gerät die Beobachtung, dass am Ende der gerichtlichen Verwertungskette philosophischer Großtheorien zur Wortlautauslegung das schlichte Wörterbuch steht (198). Besonderes Augenmerk erfährt die Konstitutionalisierung der Methodenlehre als weiteres Signum der Epoche (212 ff.); einen veritablen Flashback erlebt, wer die ersten Gehversuche der ökonomischen Analyse des Rechts im Deutschland der 1970er und 1980er Jahre nachvollzieht (226). Wünschenswert wäre allenfalls noch eine Mikrogeschichte der Anfänge des heutigen europarechtlichen Methodendschungels gewesen, dessen wegloses Dickicht dem methodologischen Wanderer vielleicht deutlicher als jedes andere juristische Gegenwartsphänomen vorführt, dass die papierene Landkarte der alten BRD heute ein historisches Dokument darstellt (knapp 169 f.).

Zum abschließenden Kapitelabschnitt zur Theorie der wissenschaftlichen Rechtsbearbeitung (258 ff.) hat Haferkamp in seiner dritten und jüngsten Rezension des vollständigen Werks treffend bemerkt, es hätte diesen nach mancher Auffassung nach 1900 gar nicht mehr geben dürfen.[18] Es gibt ihn aber doch. Hier wird eine weitere lange Linie erkennbar, vielleicht die wichtigste des ganzen Werks: Rechtswissenschaftliche Denkstile, die unter einem neuen Rechtsbegriff ihre Anschlussfähigkeit verlieren, verschwinden nicht einfach, sondern tauchen mit gewandelter, epistemologisch aktualisierter Funktion an anderer Stelle des wissenschaftlichen Methodenapparats wieder auf. Jahrhundertelang eingeübte Methodenpraktiken werden nicht einfach verlernt oder vergessen. Man könnte auch sagen: Rechtsbegriffe vergehen, Methoden bestehen. So ist die Zeit des »wissenschaftlichen Rechts« als Rechtsquelle seit dem Ende der Historischen Rechtsschule natürlich passé. Das bedeutet aber keineswegs, dass die Rechtswissenschaft nicht bis heute munter an ihren Systemen, Ordnungen und Begriffsapparaten weiterkonstruieren würde.[19] Ausgangspunkt ist, wie Schröder so bescheiden wie unbeirrbar sperrig festhält, die Dogmatik als Kern der rechtswissenschaftlichen Methode (258 f.). Was macht deren Leistung aus, »begriffliche und systematische Gesichtspunkte« so zu präsentieren, dass sie als »taugliche Argumente im Streit um die richtige praktische Entscheidung« in Betracht kommen (258)? Nun, wie die Frage voraussetzt: Begriff und System. Und so landet auch die deutsche Rechtswissenschaft nach 1945 trotz aller Distanzierung von der vielgeschmähten »Begriffsjurisprudenz« doch wieder bei der Theorie der juristischen Begriffsbildung und vollzieht dabei eine subtile Verschiebung von den in der Nachkriegszeit noch vertretenen Wesens- und Substanzbegriffen hin zu den seit den 1960er Jahren zunehmend dominierenden teleologisch-funktionellen Rechtsbegriffen einer neuen Generation von Nachkriegsjuristen (263 ff.). Auch hier trifft Schröder meisterlich den Sound der sich graduell modernisierenden BRD, in der Karl Engisch seinem Fakultäts- und Generationskollegen Karl Larenz beizeiten höflich mitteilt, dass dessen Ausführungen zum »konkret-allgemeinen Begriff« nicht mehr zeitgemäß seien, woraufhin Larenz diese in seinem Klassikerlehrbuch mit gewohnter Geschmeidigkeit dem neuen Zeitgeist anpasst (266). In den 1960er Jahren übernimmt eine neue Rechtswissenschaftlergeneration das Ruder, die nichts mehr von Wesensbegriffen wissen will, sondern sich stattdessen wie etwa Claus-Wilhelm Canaris um eine teleologische Begriffsbildung unter Verbindung von Induktion und teleologischer Kontrolle bemüht (273) – wie groß der Unterschied zum Stil der unmittelbaren Nachkriegszeit ist, wird hier eindrucksvoll vorgeführt. Auch das Systemdenken der Epoche erhält zwar noch Impulse durch ältere Figuren wie Typus und bewegliches System; auch hier dominiert aber schließlich das teleologische Systemverständnis der jüngeren Wertungsjurisprudenz, das in seiner Verbindung von positivem Recht und teils umstrittenen idealistischen Systembestandteilen wiederum unmittelbar an den zeitgenössischen Rechtsbegriff und dessen Antinomien anschließt (288).

Abschließend bringt Schröder seine große Geschichtserzählung noch einmal auf den Punkt: Auf die verschiedenen Phasen vernunftrechtlicher und idealistisch-frühpositivistischer Rechtsbegriffe bis 1850 folgte im Wesentlichen Voluntarismus bei

18 Hans-Peter Haferkamp, Rez. 3. Aufl., in: ZRG (GA) 139 (2022) 458–461, 461 unter Verweis auf Jannis Lennartz, Dogmatik als Methode, Tübingen 2017, 18. Zur 3. Aufl. zudem Vec (Fn. 6); Cornelia Huber, Rez. 3. Aufl., in: BayVBl. 2021, 723–724; Christian Baldus, Rez. 3. Aufl., in: ZNR 44 (2022) 167–172.

19 Zur zeitgenössischen Debatte etwa Horst Dreier (Hg.), Rechtswissenschaft als Beruf, Tübingen 2018; Eric Hilgendorf, Helmuth Schulze-Fielitz (Hg.), Selbstreflexion der Rechtswissenschaft, Tübingen 2021.

gleichzeitiger Zurückdrängung der verschiedenen Spielarten des Idealismus. Letztendlich dominierte die moderne Deutung des Rechts als pluralistisches Produkt wechselnder gesetzgeberischer Zwecke, durchbrochen nur von den ideologisch-autoritären Entgleisungen des Rechtsbegriffs in den beiden deutschen Diktaturen, in dem der wertpluralistische Grundkonsens der rechtlichen Moderne kurzzeitigen Rückfällen in pervertierte Volks-, Klassen- und Gemeinwohlidealismen geopfert wurde (295). Stimmt das so? Oder erfordert das Bild nicht doch etwas feinere Nachzeichnungen? Ist es beispielsweise sinnvoll, die vor 1933 vertretenen idealistischen, soziologischen und reinen Rechtslehren völlig dem voluntaristischen Grundverständnis des Rechtsbegriffs der Epoche unterzuordnen? Geht dadurch nicht epistemologisches Differenzierungsvermögen verloren, das zum Verständnis der Antinomien des Rechtsbegriffs nach 1945 beitragen könnte, in dem genau dasselbe Spannungsverhältnis zwischen dem Idealismus der Wertungsjurisprudenz, der Hinwendung zur Rechtswirklichkeit und der erneuerten Positivismusdebatte der 1960er Jahre wiederkehrt?[20] In welchem Verhältnis steht Schröders Epochencharakterisierung, die im 20. Jahrhundert nur noch einen dominanten Voluntarismus neben einem immer wieder störend am Bildrand erscheinenden Idealismus erkennen will,[21] zu den zugrundeliegenden rechtswissenschaftlichen Epistemologien, die gerade kein dualistisches, sondern eher ein trialistisches Spannungsverhältnis von idealistischen, empiristischen und analytischen Denkstilen nahelegen?[22] Schröders Kunst des Weglassens gerecht zu werden, heißt jedoch konsequenterweise, ihm neben dem Weglassen allgemeinhistorischer, methodensoziologischer, methodenvergleichender und methodenpraktischer Verzierungen seiner rechtswissenschaftlichen Ideengeschichte nun nicht ausgerechnet den Verzicht auf wissenschaftstheoretische Spekulationen vorzuhalten. Spekulationen mögen den hoffentlich weiterhin zahlreichen Rezensionen dieses Meisterwerks vorbehalten bleiben. Hier sei zum Abschluss noch folgende Spekulation angestellt: Völlig zu Recht wurde Schröders Werk bereits in der Erstauflage unter die »juristischen Bücher des Jahres« gewählt.[23] Nun kommt es bekanntlich nur äußerst selten vor, dass diese Auszeichnung einem Autor in seinem Autorenleben *zweimal* zuteil wird – und wenn, dann, wie sich zu verstehen scheint, nur für zwei *verschiedene* Bücher. Hier liegt nun der singuläre Fall eines Werks vor, das diese Auszeichnung nicht nur einmal, sondern für jede neue Auflage und Textstufe erneut verdient hätte. Kann *dasselbe* Werk *desselben* Autors *zweimal* als »juristisches Buch des Jahres« ausgezeichnet werden? Nun, Kunst des Weglassens: Schröders – übrigens auch formvollendetes[24] – Meisterwerk braucht eigentlich gar keine Auszeichnung mehr. Es ist sich selbst genug.

■

20 Näher Marietta Auer, Selbstreflexion der Privatrechtswissenschaft: Formation, Herausforderungen, Perspektiven, in: Hilgendorf / Schulze-Fielitz (Fn. 19) 301–325, 315–317.

21 Zur Erzählung Voluntarismus versus Idealismus in wiederkehrenden Zyklen seit der Antike klassisch Hans Welzel, Naturrecht und materiale Gerechtigkeit, Göttingen 1962.

22 Zu dieser Erzählung der rechtswissenschaftlichen Moderne Marietta Auer, Politische Theologie als Rechtswissenschaftstheorie, in: RPhZ 7 (2021) 131–140, 133–136.

23 Stolleis (Fn. 9).

24 Einige vernachlässigbare Flüchtigkeitsfehler sollten in der sicherlich bald fälligen 4. Aufl. noch berichtigt werden: In Band 2 jeweils die Jahreszahlen auf S. 183 vor Fn. 326, S. 189 vor Fn. 346, S. 191 vor Fn. 350 sowie doppelte §§-Zeichen auf S. 273 in Zeile 3. Der in Band 1 in der 2. Aufl. noch doppelte § 69 ist bereits korrigiert worden.

Albrecht Cordes

Streit unter Freunden und Verwandten*

Das Buch mit dem sperrigen Titel ist Mechthild Isenmanns von Markus Denzel in Leipzig betreute wirtschaftsgeschichtliche Habilitationsschrift von 2016. Die Autorin führt in Fragestellung, Quellen- und Literaturlage ein und gliedert ihr Werk dann in die drei Hauptteile, nämlich A: eine allgemeine Überlegung zu den Familiengesellschaften vom 14.–17. Jahrhundert (30 Seiten), B: eine Serie von Fallstudien (gut 250 Seiten) und C: eine Analyse (gut 50 Seiten). Ein knappes Resümee und die nötigen, sorgfältig gearbeiteten Verzeichnisse schließen sich an.

Der Schwerpunkt des Buchs liegt also auf den Fallstudien. Sie behandeln Konflikte in und zwischen den bekannten Nürnberger und Augsburger Kaufmannsfamilien Imhoff, Meuting, Paumgartner, Arzt, Behaim, Viatis und Peller und einigen anderen. Dies sind die großen Namen, um die es immer geht, wenn die oberdeutschen Unternehmen jenseits der Fugger und Welser behandelt werden. Die Auswahl überrascht also nicht. Ob kleinere Gesellschaften ihre Konflikte anders lösten, bleibt offen; oft wäre ihnen wohl, wenn sie so hartnäckig gestritten hätten wie manche der großen, das Geld ausgegangen. Die besondere Stärke der Arbeit sind diese Fallstudien: Aus dem überreichen Archivmaterial schält Isenmann einzelne Konflikte heraus. Sie sind es, die aus rechtshistorischer Sicht besondere Aufmerksamkeit verdienen, auch wenn nicht alle, die das Buch zur Hand nehmen, der Autorin in die Details der verästelten Verwandtschaftsverhältnisse usw. folgen werden. Die schiere Menge von spannenden Quellenfunden, die Isenmann in ihren Fußnoten ausbreitet, ist beeindruckend; die reichen Nürnberger und Augsburger Archive erweisen sich wieder einmal als Fundgrube für alle Fragen der spätmittelalterlichen und frühneuzeitlichen Handels- und Wirtschafts(rechts)geschichte.

Teil B besteht aus zwei unterschiedlichen Teilen. Unter B I. geht es auf gut 80 Seiten um einen konkreten Konflikt zwischen Zentrale und Faktorei in der Familie Imhoff. Teil B II. differenziert dann nach vier Typen von Verwandtschaftsbeziehungen, nämlich Vater–Sohn, Onkel–Neffe, Brüder sowie Schwiegervater–Schwiegersohn. Das ist eine spannende Einteilung, denn damit wirft Isenmann die Frage auf, ob es Konfliktverhalten und -verläufe gab, die diesen Konstellationen entsprachen. Stritten Brüder miteinander auf eine Weise, die in generationenübergreifenden Verhältnissen so nicht auftrat? Setzte der reiche Kaufmann X sich mit seinem Sohn anders auseinander als mit seinem Neffen oder seinem Schwiegersohn? Das wäre eine nicht nur psychologisch, sondern auch rechtshistorisch spannende Baustelle, die sofort Folgefragen provoziert. Nur eine sei ausgesprochen: Haben nahe Verwandte größere oder geringere Hemmungen, einander vor Gericht zu ziehen?

Doch diesen Weg verfolgt die Autorin nicht weiter; für allgemeine Aussagen über das Verhalten von bestimmten Typen von Verwandten wären die Fallzahlen wohl auch zu klein und die konkreten Konflikte zu individuell. Aber die nebeneinander gelegten Resultate der Einzelfälle setzen sich zu einem rechtshistorisch wertvollen Bild zusammen: einem Kontext von Konfliktlagen und Lösungsversuchen vor, neben und nach gerichtlichen Auseinandersetzungen. So werden Schichten sichtbar, die man ausblendet (und ausblenden muss), wenn man sich auf Auseinandersetzungen vor Gericht konzentriert.

Auf diese Basis stützt Isenmann ihre »Analyse« (Teil C). Zunächst identifiziert sie fünf Konfliktfelder wie Streit um Abrechnungen, Betrug und Verschwendung, die sicher gut gewählt sind, aber nicht überraschen. Dann folgen fünf heterogene

* Mechthild Isenmann, Strategien, Mittel und Wege der inner- und zwischenfamiliären Konfliktlösung oberdeutscher Handelshäuser im 15. und ›langen‹ 16. Jahrhundert (VSWG-Beiheft 249), Stuttgart: Franz Steiner Verlag 2020, 450 S., ISBN 978-3-515-12574-1

Handlungsfelder (Ausbildung, Heiratspolitik, Gesellschaftsverträge und -versammlungen sowie Testamente), welche die Autorin als Konfliktvermeidungsstrategien verstehen will. In einem Buch, das die »Konfliktlösung« im Titel trägt, ist das vermutlich nötig, aber auf all diesen Feldern waren Konfliktvermeidung und -beilegung sicher nur ein Motiv unter anderen. Die Ausbildung zu einem erfolgreichen Kaufmann hatte bestimmt nicht das primäre Ziel, friedliebenden Nachwuchs heranzuziehen, und die Motive der Testamentserrichtung von Batholomäus Viatis senior (316–319) waren vielfältig, aber eher dazu angetan, Konflikte anzuheizen als sie zu vermeiden. Die Versuchsanordnung »Strategien der kaufmännischen Konfliktlösung« birgt von vornherein die Gefahr, Kaufleute für friedliebender zu halten als sie wirklich waren. In zwei (erst nach Isenmanns Buch erschienenen) Beiträgen haben Philipp Höhn und ich argumentiert, dass Kaufleute Konflikte oft auch köcheln oder sogar eskalieren ließen, wenn das gerade vorteilhaft war.[1]

Diese Überlegungen sind nicht als Kritik am Ansatz des Buchs gemeint, sondern als Einladung, darüber nachzudenken, wie auf Isenmanns Material künftig aufgebaut werden kann. Auch räumlich und zeitlich weist die Arbeit über sich hinaus. Wegen der engen Kontakte über die Alpen, die auch zu Einflüssen in beide Richtungen geführt haben müssen, wüsste man gern mehr über Oberitalien. Nach Nordwesten, Richtung Frankfurt, Köln und in die Niederlande bestanden ebenfalls gute Handelsverbindungen; vor dem Hintergrund der inzwischen zahlreichen wichtigen, aber insgesamt stärker an den Institutionen orientierten Arbeiten von Dave De ruysscher und seinen Schülern liegt ein Vergleich mit Antwerpen nahe, und in den Hanseraum und auch Richtung Prag, Breslau und Krakau hatten die Nürnberger ebenfalls gute Kontakte. Wurden die entsprechenden Konflikte in diesen Wirtschaftsräumen anders ausgetragen? Geht man auf dem Zeitstrahl zurück, so fragt man sich, ob sich im 15. Jahrhundert eine neue Art des Streitens und Verhandelns etabliert hat oder ob wir nur besser informiert sind, weil nach 1400 viel mehr aufgeschrieben wurde als im Jahrhundert davor. Am meisten leuchtet die Grenze in der anderen Richtung des Zeitstrahls ein; durch den Dreißigjährigen Krieg hat sich die Welt völlig verändert. Von 1600 an öffnete sich allmählich die Bühne für einen neuen Typus noch größerer, weltweit agierender Zusammenschlüsse, in denen die Bedeutung der Familien sank und die des Kapitals stieg.[2] Deshalb ist der zeitliche Rahmen mit den 200 Jahren vor dieser Wende gut gewählt. Für alle Fragen, die mit den Nürnberger und Augsburger Handelsgesellschaften in dieser Zeit zusammenhängen, wird das Buch von Mechthild Isenmann mit seinen detailreichen, spannend zu lesenden Fallstudien zur Materialsammlung, zum Wegweiser zu den Archivbeständen und insgesamt zum Referenzwerk werden.

■

1 Albrecht Cordes, Philipp Höhn, Konfliktlösung im Fernhandel, in: David von Mayenburg (Hg.), Konfliktlösung im Mittelalter. Handbuch zur Geschichte der Konfliktlösung in Europa, Bd. 2, Berlin 2021, 283–293, und dies., Fernkaufleute, in: Wim Decock (Hg.), Konfliktlösung in der Frühen Neuzeit. Handbuch zur Geschichte der Konfliktlösung in Europa, Bd. 3, Berlin 2021, 295–303.

2 Ron Harris, Going the Distance. Eurasian Trade and the Rise of the Business Corporation, 1400–1700, Princeton 2020; dazu Albrecht Cordes, Die Organisationsrevolution von 1600/1602, in: Rg 28 (2020) 303–306, http://dx.doi.org/10.12946/rg28/303-306.

Aleksi Ollikainen-Read

The Common Law of the Foreign Past*

Sir John Baker is the (English) lawyer's legal historian, and in his craft he is an unquestionable master. His book, *English Law Under Two Elizabeths*, is an expanded form of his Hamlyn lectures, a series whose explicit purpose is to further the »Common People's« understanding of the »privileges which in law and custom they enjoy« through »comparative jurisprudence«.[1] The lectures are always given by well-established lawyers or scholars, and the list of former lecturers reads like a who's-who of the English legal profession and academia from 1949 onwards.

Given the intended audience, one cannot expect much in the way of overt analysis of historiographical or methodological choices, or other such academic matters. Nor is the author known to be particularly apologetic of his rather internal view of English law, its procedures and practitioners. However, perhaps in an attempt to find an approach more engaging to the general public, the author has chosen to present the lectures and the resulting book as a ›comparative law‹ of English law from the reign of Elizabeth I (r. 1558–1603) and English law from the reign of Elizabeth II (r. 1952 – present). Legal historians familiar with the author's excellent work may be forgiven a degree of amusement about this choice – even Sir John Baker's comparative law scholarship is between English law and English law – but the approach has the potential of making certain historiographical questions comprehensible to a non-expert audience without ever having to mention them. It is difficult to understand the legal normative landscape from 400 years ago without understanding the context in which those norms existed, a methodological assumption that is not too different from the basic idea of comparative law between two modern jurisdictions. However, some questions arise as to how rigorously this approach is followed, to which I shall return below.

As regards its content, the book is classic Baker. It is full of interesting points about the development of the doctrine of precedent and majority judgments (13) and how this relates to archiving practices (154), details on individual cases and their costs (e. g. 21), statistics about the socio-economic status of plaintiffs and defendants (23) and the composition of the legal profession (29). It also includes administrative minutiae of which remedies could be enforced in which court and what modern courts they were consolidated under (e. g. 176–177), difficult logical puzzles of whether common law is extinguished or made dormant by statute that is later repealed (126 onward), and statistics about the number of lawyers in relation to the general population in the 16th century and now (185). It may be doubtful whether members of the general public really perceive the »privileges they enjoy« as a result of these figures or common law logic puzzles, but this approach is very much in keeping with the author's other works.

The book is at its finest as an introductory work of internal legal history, that is, the history of legal thought and the legal profession in England. Its articulation of the basic tenets of the common law as an »immemorial« (e. g. 35) expression of reasoning and logic and its consequent uneasy relation to statute (e. g. 92–94 and 96 onward) are as succinct and accessible as any the reader is likely to find. In particular, the »fiction of legislative intent« (103) and the overall approach – that statutes are intended to cure some mischief within the common law – is an interesting inheritance of the internal logic of the common law that survives in some form to the present day (139) and helps us understand some of the methodological differences between continental and common law systems (though such explanation is not actually attempted in the book).

A minor point of criticism, perhaps inherent in Baker's general approach as the foremost doctrinal

* John Baker, English Law Under Two Elizabeths. The Late Tudor Legal World and the Present, Cambridge: Cambridge University Press 2021, 222 p., ISBN 978-1-108-83796-5

1 Chantal Stebbings, »The Hamlyn Legacy«, in: Claire Palley, The United Kingdom and Human Rights, Hamlyn Lectures Vol. 42, London 1991, xiii–xx.

legal historian of English law in Britain today, is that a general audience (and even trained historians) will not find it easy to navigate the difficult distinctions in 16th-century land law (see, e. g., 113) or highly technical remedies of administrative law (177) without at least the first two years of formal legal education. While some legal sophistication is to be expected from doctrinal legal history, it is perhaps a symptom of a more substantial limitation of this otherwise excellent work.

As noted, the general approach is commendable in that it attempts to teach a general audience not just about the substance of doctrine in the 16th century but also about the methodology of doctrinal legal history in a way that promises to be quite engaging. However, in practice the emphasis of the ›comparative‹ approach seems to be in finding similarities that sometimes feel stretched in order to make pre-Enlightenment English law seem conspicuously modern, without a full explanation of the immense socio-economic differences between the two periods.

This glossing over of the comparative differences in favour of highlighting abstract similarities between the two periods is reflected in the legal analysis as well. Almost entirely absent is any real discussion of the messy multinormativity and legal pluralism of the early modern era. Piepowder courts and the Doctors' Commons are each mentioned only once, without any explanation of the various overlapping jurisdictions and formalistic difficulties that plaintiffs were likely to encounter. Mentioning each type of court only in conjunction with its best feature and without discussing the desperate in-fighting between these jurisdictions in the relevant period[2] makes early modern English law seem like a well-functioning machine of specialist courts and well-defined jurisdictions, and hides the fact that even a term like ›English law‹ might suggest a unity of purpose that is more myth-making for a general audience than scholarship intended to inform.

Similar myth-making appears to apply to the content of law in the 1500s. In an effort to make Elizabethan law seem recognisably modern, Baker argues that it included nascent forms of individual liberty and the ›rule of law‹ that even bound the Queen. However, he then immediately proceeds to show multiple examples that appear to disprove these points. Women, we are told, were free – but could not vote, serve in parliament or on juries, and lost their legal autonomy when they married (40). ›Aliens‹ were protected by the common law – unless they were Jews, Jesuits, Travellers, Irish labourers, black immigrant workers, Hanse merchants, or had previously been expelled or banned from entering the country – and no ›foreigner‹ could buy land (42). Given that these exclusions from the common law's protection amount to most economic or socio-cultural activity (even including travelling »out of ancient custom« or to spread religion), it is difficult to see this as equal protection of foreigners. Similarly, Baker states that Elizabeth I's reign was a »constitutional monarchy« (79), but also notes that she dissolved Parliament at will, declined to summon it at all when it suited her, and locked up MPs if they »overstepped the mark in debates« (80). She imposed martial law in crises, intervened in private suits to preserve her privileges and prerogatives, and proclaimed rigid adherence to formalistic logic to be »absurd« as a reason for not trying Mary, Queen of Scots according to the common law (81–82).

Of course, Baker's claim is only that the roots of our modern legal landscape, with its emphasis on individual liberty and the rule of law, can already be seen during the first Elizabeth's reign, and he does not shy away from pointing out the incongruities mentioned above. However, some of his claims about ›liberty‹ seem so bizarre in their context that I cannot make out whether they are intended as serious academic commentary or as jokes to amuse a lecture hall audience.

Whether inadvertently or intentionally, much of what Baker does to make early modern law reflect the principles of a modern constitutional monarchy seems to line up with the basic myth of the common law as an ancient normative system discovered through reasoned argument that is somehow still recognisably the same, as a system

2 Baker has written about the resolution of some of these tensions in John Baker, The Common Lawyers and the Chancery: 1616, in: idem., The Legal Profession and the Common Law, London 1986, 205–229.

if not in detail, as it was in the days of Sir Edward Coke. Baker is, after all, the common lawyers' legal historian, and the common law survives on its myth of continuity that the Hamlyn lectures exist to highlight. When the book is seen in this light, Baker is only following the expressly stated purpose of the Hamlyn Trust. It is probably not a coincidence that the »common law man« – the personification of the English legal system's central myth of a stubbornly free, responsible, just and reasonable person that English law has as both its fictional maker and subject – was sketched out in early Hamlyn lectures (166). The book is therefore highly commendable and a good introduction to Baker's work, but should be seen within its context as one of a lecture series intended to inform the public about what a magnificent legal system England has.

■

Alejandro García-Sanjuán

Musulmanes entre infieles*

Las interacciones entre cristianos y musulmanes representan un elemento sustancial en las dinámicas políticas, sociales, económicas y culturales del ámbito mediterráneo a partir del siglo VII, cuando se produce el comienzo de la expansión islámica en el Próximo Oriente y el Norte de África, que alcanzó la península ibérica en 711. A partir del siglo XI, sin embargo, el proceso de arabización e islamización de amplias zonas del espacio mediterráneo oriental y meridional fue seguido por una dinámica inversa de expansión cristiana que supuso el retroceso territorial de los musulmanes en distintos escenarios históricos, de forma definitiva, en algunos casos, y temporal, en otros. Un proceso que se extiende más allá de los límites tradicionalmente admitidos del período medieval, con las conquistas portuguesas y españolas en el Norte de África durante el siglo XVI y la posterior dinámica de expansión colonial decimonónica, cuyas consecuencias alcanzan hasta la segunda mitad del siglo XX.

La obra reseñada analiza un capítulo importante de estas cambiantes relaciones entre musulmanes y cristianos en el espacio mediterráneo. Desde una perspectiva histórica amplia, situada entre los siglos XV y XX, *Leaving Iberia* plantea el problema legal y doctrinal asociado a la presencia de comunidades musulmanas que viven bajo el dominio político de autoridades no islámicas. En el contexto expansivo y de superioridad islámica inicial, este asunto no había preocupado a las autoridades musulmanas, más interesadas en definir el estatus legal de las minorías no musulmanas que vivían en el territorio islámico. A partir del siglo XI, en cambio, los ulemas, los hombres de religión que detentan la autoridad religiosa en las sociedades islámicas suníes tradicionales, comienzan a enfrentarse a una realidad hasta entonces inédita o marginal. A lo largo del tiempo, distintos ulemas emitieron fetuas (dictámenes legales) en las que dieron respuestas variadas a este asunto, formulando opiniones contrapuestas sobre la posibilidad de vivir como buen musulmán en un contexto político y social no islámico. En otras palabras, los ulemas debieron enfrentarse al problema de si la doctrina islámica obliga a vivir en la *dār al-islām*, el territorio gobernado por autoridades islámicas, y, por lo tanto, no es legal para el musulmán permanecer en la *dār al-ḥarb*, literalmente, »la casa de la guerra«, es decir, el territorio donde no rigen las normas islámicas.

La estructura de la obra reseñada presenta la siguiente forma. Tras la Introducción (cap. 1), se suceden cuatro partes, en las que la autora aborda el análisis de textos islámicos datados entre los

* Jocelyn Hendrickson, Leaving Iberia. Islamic Law and Christian Conquest in North Africa, Cambridge: Harvard University Press 2021, 417 p., ISBN 978-0-674-24820-5

siglos XV y XX y que se refieren a distintos contextos, aunque bajo el denominador común de haber sido elaborados por ulemas magrebíes adscritos a la tradición legal malikí. La primera se centra en fetuas hasta ahora inéditas de ocho ulemas, fetuas en las que se responde a la ocupación portuguesa en el Norte de África y procedentes del capítulo del yihad de *al-Ǧawāhir al-mujtāra*, obra de ʿAbd al-ʿAzīz al-Zayyātī (m. 1055/1645), de la que al menos 16 copias manuscritas se conservan en bibliotecas y archivos marroquíes.

La segunda parte se refiere a cuestiones que afectan de forma más directa a la historia peninsular, ámbito cuya relevancia resulta central en la evolución del debate sobre el deber de la emigración en la doctrina malikí. Durante más de cuatro siglos, los que transcurren entre la conquista de Toledo en 1085 y el proceso de conversiones forzosas que comienza a finales del siglo XV, los musulmanes vivieron bajo dominio cristiano en la Península en comunidades organizadas y reconocidas legalmente. Desde finales del siglo XV, el problema de los mudéjares peninsulares fue abordado por varios ulemas magrebíes, tal y como acreditan los que la autora llama »tristemente célebres« (*infamous*) textos de al-Wanšarīsī (m. 914/1508) de 1491, conocidos respectivamente como *Asnà-l-matāǧir* y la fetua de Marbella, en los que dicho ulema apela con notoria severidad doctrinal a la obligación de los musulmanes de abandonar el territorio conquistado por los infieles y emigrar a la *dār al-islām*. Tradicionalmente asociados a la situación de los mudéjares peninsulares, a juicio de la autora ambos textos deben asimismo ponerse en relación con el contexto específicamente magrebí, en concreto con el proceso de ocupación portuguesa de puertos norteafricanos que comienza con la conquista de Ceuta en 1415.

La tercera parte se mantiene en el contexto histórico hispano, aunque de nuevo desde la perspectiva de los ulemas magrebíes. En efecto, mientras que los textos de al-Wanšarīsī representan dictámenes que reprueban la permanencia de musulmanes bajo dominio no islámico, en cambio la conocida como fetua de 1504 del ulema magrebí Aḥmad ibn Abī Ǧumʿa al-Wahrānī (m. 917/1511) es célebre precisamente por lo contrario. Remitiéndose a una práctica asociada tradicionalmente con las comunidades chiíes, con frecuencia reprimidas en contextos suníes, el ulema magrebí autoriza a los moriscos, mudéjares peninsulares forzados a la conversión al catolicismo, a mantener sus creencias en secreto. Se basó para ello en la doctrina de la *taqiya*, literalmente »miedo« o »prudencia«, en árabe, que permite a los musulmanes realizar sus prácticas religiosas con disimulo en contextos hostiles.

La cuarta parte se centra en asuntos cronológicamente relativos a la época contemporánea, ya que aborda el problema legal y doctrinal de la obligación de emigrar en el marco de dos contextos norteafricanos específicos, la Argelia del siglo XIX y la Mauritania del XX. Respecto al primero de ambos, la autora analiza nueve textos, seis de los cuales corresponden a ʿAbd al-Qādir al-Ǧazāʾirī (1808–1883), que encabezó un movimiento de yihad contra la ocupación francesa entre 1832 y 1847, en los cuales enfatiza la necesidad de emigrar como forma de reforzar la resistencia contra los ocupantes. En cambio, el texto del muftí de Argel, Muḥammad ibn al-Šāhid al-Ǧazāʾirī (m. 1836–1837), justifica con distintos argumentos la opción de permanecer bajo el dominio infiel, mostrando, una vez más, el carácter controvertido del deber de emigrar en la tradición doctrinal malikí. Por otro lado, como afirma la autora, al menos setenta fetuas, cartas, tratados y poemas que forman parte del debate sobre la sujeción al dominio cristiano en el contexto mauritano han sido publicados hasta ahora, lo que convierte a este dossier en el más robusto del contexto magrebí contemporáneo.

Antes de los apartados finales relativos a cronología, glosario, bibliografía e índices, la última parte de la obra la integra un apartado de Conclusiones, seguido por tres interesantes apéndices. En el primero de ellos, el más importante, dada la naturaleza inédita del material, la autora ofrece la traducción de algunas de las fetuas incluidas en la ya citada compilación titulada *al-Ǧawāhir al-mujtāra*. Los otros dos contienen traducciones de los dos ya comentados dictámenes legales de al-Wanšarīsī (m. 914/1508), *Asnà-l-matāǧir* y la fetua de Marbella, textos mucho más conocidos que cuentan con una tradición historiográfica relativamente amplia, ya que han sido objeto de diversos estudios y traducciones. En efecto, aparte de la versión en castellano de la segunda de ellas publicada en su día por F. Maíllo (»Consideraciones acerca de una fatwà de Al-Wanšarīsī«, *Studia historica. Historia medieval*, 3, 1985, 181–192), el investigador norteamericano A. Verskin publicó una versión inglesa en su obra *Opressed in the Land? Fatwas on Muslims Living under Non-Muslim Rule from the Middle Ages to the Present* (Marcus Wiener

Publishers, 2013, 19–30). El mismo autor incluyó sendas versiones en inglés de ambos textos en otra obra posterior, *Islamic Law and the Crisis of the Reconquista. The Debate on the Status of Muslim Communities in Christendom* (Brill, 2015). La afirmación de la autora en la Introducción (5) de que su obra representa el primer análisis amplio de las respuestas legales islámicas a las conquistas cristianas en la península ibérica y el Norte de África a finales del siglo XV y comienzos del XVI debe, por lo tanto, ser matizada.

Como puede comprobarse, el contenido del libro reseñado se refiere tanto a la Iberia medieval como al ámbito magrebí moderno y contemporáneo. Llama por ello la atención que el título principal haga referencia solo a la Península, pese a que, como la autora propone, algunas de las fetuas más célebres relativas a la inmigración de musulmanes peninsulares deban leerse a la luz de los acontecimientos norteafricanos, y a pesar de que el Magreb fuera el destino de muchas de las comunidades de musulmanes peninsulares que se vieron obligadas a abandonar su territorio.

■

Karoline Noack

A Heroine's Journey to South America*

Liliana Pérez Miguel uses the biography of the *conquistadora* and *encomendera* Inés Muñoz from Seville to present this history of 16th-century female *encomenderos* in the Viceroyalty of Peru, especially in the *audiencia de Lima*. This volume, abundant in sources, is also a contribution to the history of the *encomienda* as such, in which the author explicitly takes up José de la Puente Brunke's work *Encomienda y encomenderos en el Perú* (1991), a text that covers three centuries and has gained the status of a classic. Liliana Pérez builds on, and adds specifics to, Puente Brunke's work to create a database with information on a total of 137 *encomenderas* between 1540 and 1600, which she researched for her prize-winning dissertation defended at the University of Burgos in 2014. With this work, the author fills a gap in the research literature about the history of women and their agency in the Spanish-American colonial system of the 16th century.

The 16th century saw the first encounters between indigenous and European actors during the setting up of a new colonial society; the historical processes in the »contact zone« (Pratt) during this period in particular call for an innovative conceptualisation that includes interdisciplinary approaches and methods. It is well known that the *encomienda* was an important, if not the most significant, intersection between the two populations. Giving an account of these historical encounters from a gender perspective seems highly appropriate.

Pérez Miguel examines the *encomenderas* as a social group in 16th-century Peru by looking at the life of Inés Muñoz, who was – as the author emphasises – the first married Spanish woman to arrive in Peru. Based on Muñoz' biography, which is rich in detail and embedded in historical contexts and their legal, economic and social dimensions, the author develops historical categories that can also be applied to other women in this group.

The book is divided into two parts and five chapters. Part I, which only consists of Chapter 1, provides an overview of the women among the *encomenderos* in Peru in the 16th century. In addition to summarising prior studies on the institution of the *encomienda*, the sections on the different bases for women of diverse origins and population

* Liliana Pérez Miguel, »Mujeres ricas y libres«. Mujer y poder: Inés Muñoz y las encomenderas en el Perú (s. XVI), Sevilla: Consejo Superior de Investigaciones Científicas, Editorial Universidad de Sevilla 2020, 477 p., ISBN 978-84-472-2944-4

categories to become *encomenderas*, together with the new data organised in diagrams, provide valuable information on many previously unknown *encomenderas*. In Chapters 2–5, Part II chronologically maps the biography of Inés Muñoz in her various capacities and functions – as a *pobladora*, i. e. one of the first *vecinos* (a legal category referring to the holders of a town's citizenship), as an *encomendera* and administrator of her *encomiendas*, and as the founder of the Concepción convent in Lima and its first abbess.

It is certainly a complex undertaking for a female researcher and author to write about such a paradigmatic female protagonist of the history of conquest and colonisation, in which women have often remained invisible. The challenge was to do justice to Inés Muñoz in her highly ambivalent role as a very active shaper of relationships, networks and policies during a period when the economic and social foundations of the colonial, expanding and globally embedded exploitation system were laid.

However, unfortunately the author uses the undoubtedly rich source material, often drawn for the first time from a variety of archives, as a mere collection of data or as purely historical facts, largely neglecting to take into account the discursivity and narrativity of the sources and the range of possible interpretations. The attributes extended in these sources towards the female population – such as when poor women are accused of using *trucos y hechizos* (86), or women in general are characterised as *inconstantes y poco calladas* (74), to name just two examples – are not productively explored in their multiple levels of meaning. The terminology documented in the sources is carefully explained in the footnotes, but categories like »race« and »ethnic« are simply used as terms whose meaning is assumed to be definite. Terms such as *mestizas*, *indias*, *negras*, *mulatas*, *criollas*, and *inca* are used as »race« categories and are reflected neither in their relationality with regard to time and space nor in their fluidity, which has been discussed in many historical studies. The reference to the 17th-century jurisconsult Juan de Solórzano Pereira, who defines *mestizo* as *sangre mezclada* (see 56), is anachronistic with regard to the 16th century, but also shows a lack of conceptual separation between the contemporary discourse of the colonial epoch and present-day analysis. It also gives the impression that the author is trying to distil a reality with regard to »race« that goes beyond the reality depicted in the sources, for example when she refers to the summarising term »Spanish women« and the »race« categories that might be covered by this term, including the *españolas de nacimiento además caucásicas* (64). This the author does at her own peril. Works like that of Tamar Herzog, who operates with completely different categories by applying the concept of *vecindad* or the community-building *hacer vecindad* (to make vicinity), in which an important task of the *encomenderas* and *encomenderos* lay, are missing from the present study.

Part II hints at alternative approaches to a biography of Inés Muñoz, showing how her life was interlinked with the developing economic structures of the system of colonial exploitation. However, the author does not actually use these potential approaches, e.g. by including indigenous society in the analysis or by establishing a link between the economic activities taking place in the encomienda and the religious activities of the later abbess. Just one example of this is the so-called »crisis of restitution« (301), which in the 16th century led to numerous *encomenderos* and *encomenderas* attempting to make amends to »their« *indios* by returning, by way of legacies, some of the economic resources that had been expropriated. This rarely studied »crisis of restitution« bundled the socio-economic, legal-political, cultural-historical and religious processes and relationships as if in an optical lens; unfortunately, Liliana Pérez does not seize the opportunity to use this or similar phenomena as a starting point for her biography of Inés Muñoz. This approach would have offered the option of looking at the indigenous population as more than just a passive resource that was being exploited by the *encomienda*, the textile manufacturers, and the cattle herding that was linked to both. Rather, these *indios*, *tributarios*, *mitayos* and *yanaconas*, which here are not further differentiated from one another, could have been shown as active participants in the changing social and economic structures of a colonial situation – this, however, is not covered in this study.

In this »women's history«, which does not apply any gender categories, Inés Muñoz is portrayed rather one-sidedly as a heroine. Her biography appears as a heroine's journey (as is reflected in the title of the book) and as a history of the *encomienda* as a story of successful civilisation, even if there is a woman at its centre.

■

Carolina Jurado

Cacicas en los virreinatos americanos*

A través de la reunión de estudios de caso referidos a diversos ámbitos espaciales americanos y diferentes períodos temporales (siglos XVI al XIX), *Cacicas* constituye una invitación a debatir el abanico de significados y los variados grados de estatus y autoridad que ejercieron las mujeres designadas y/o autodefinidas bajo el término inventado por los españoles tras su conquista de la Hispaniola. Con el propósito de revelar interrogantes en torno a quiénes pudieron ser cacicas coloniales y sus significados, las editoras Margarita Ochoa y Sara Vicuña Guengerich propugnan por una visión de las cacicas como *sujetos históricos significativos* que »construyeron sus conciencias alrededor de su lugar – simbólico o geográfico – y articularon sus identidades desde el interior del dominio colonial« (10), en la senda de los estudios de Rachel O'Toole y Michel-Rolph Troulliot sobre poblaciones silenciadas. Al privilegiar el análisis del »activismo político de las mujeres indígenas« (10) – definido como las acciones que influenciaron movimientos internos visibles para sus comunidades y las intervenciones relativas a su autoridad personal y a los ámbitos familiares, económicos y religiosos –, las editoras contribuyen al estudio de las transformaciones del cacicazgo y del liderazgo indígena en las diferentes regiones americanas durante el dominio castellano.

La propuesta de Ochoa y Vicuña Guengerich pondera la variabilidad e historicidad de las realidades sociales, al apartarse de dicotomías en torno a la continuidad de lideresas indígenas desde el período prehispánico o su invención colonial, y al cuestionar su presencia inequívoca a lo largo de los virreinatos así como la existencia de significados uniformes tras el término cacicas. Sustentando lo anterior, las nueve contribuciones que componen el volumen abordan desde diferentes perspectivas aspectos de las cacicas coloniales, incluyendo la sucesión, el parentesco, el estatus, el control de recursos materiales y humanos, la autoridad y la participación ante la justicia, entre otros, evidenciando el peso de las condiciones locales en la determinación de su presencia y/o ausencia y en su grado de autoridad. Siguiendo criterios geográficos contemporáneos, el libro se divide en dos partes, precedidas por el Prólogo a cargo de Ida Altman, en el cual se analiza la presencia de cacicas y el surgimiento del término en la conquista del Caribe, y la Introducción, en la cual las editoras presentan los objetivos, premisas e inserción del volumen en el campo historiográfico de los estudios de género en los espacios andinos y mesoamericanos y contextualizan la presencia de las cacicas en el mundo genérico del imperio castellano. La primera parte, denominada América del Norte y Central, inicia con el trabajo de Bradley Benton (cap. 1) sobre tres generaciones de cacicas que, desde 1563 y hasta mediados del siglo XVII, ocuparon posiciones de autoridad en Teotihuacán, provocando cambios en los patrones residenciales y étnicos de su comunidad. En el mismo marco temporal, a continuación, Peter Villella (cap. 2) aborda la trayectoria de mujeres pertenecientes a la familia Tapia, vecinas otomíes de Querétaro, y su relación con las posesiones materiales, el estatus noble y la cultura religiosa de la ciudad. En el siguiente capítulo, Margarita Ochoa (cap. 3) traslada la mirada hacia las cacicas urbanas de la ciudad de México durante el período borbónico, evidenciando que, a pesar de no ejercer oficios cacicales, la comunidad reconocía sus estatus y autoridad en la mediación y resolución de conflictos y violencias domésticas a nivel barrial. La sección se cierra con la investigación de Catherine Komisaruk (cap. 4) sobre las élites indígenas del Reino de Guatemala desde el siglo XVIII a mediados del XIX, proponiendo que las instituciones legales coloniales erosionaron los privilegios y el poder de las mujeres de la nobleza indígena »más rápido y más completamente« que aquellos de sus contrapartes masculinos – subsumidos en un proceso de »macehualización« generalizada.

* Margarita R. Ochoa, Sara Vicuña Guengerich (eds.), Cacicas. The Indigenous Women Leaders of Spanish America, 1492–1825, Norman: University of Oklahoma Press 2021, 333 p., ISBN 978-0-8061-6862-3

La segunda parte, titulada Sudamérica, comienza con el estudio de Karen Graubart (cap. 5) sobre la proliferación de reclamos sucesorios y de estatus de cacicas y la creación por parte de mujeres indígenas litigantes de »narrativas de linaje« durante el siglo XVII, sustentadas en la *costumbre* de liderazgos prehispánicos femeninos de »capullanas« en la costa norte del Perú e inspiradas en las batallas legales de las mujeres españolas para suceder en las encomiendas. Manteniendo la mirada en los Andes del norte, a continuación, la investigación de Chantal Caillavet (cap. 6) compara testamentos de autoridades indígenas femeninas y masculinas y, en consonancia con la propuesta de Karen Powers, afirma la existencia de relaciones prehispánicas de género iguales y complementarias, erosionadas posteriormente por la exclusión de las mujeres de los nuevos rituales coloniales de poder, aunque mitigadas por la participación femenina en las cofradías religiosas. En el siguiente capítulo, Liliana Pérez Miguel y Renzo Honores (cap. 7) abordan dos retratos de mujeres indígenas del valle de Chincha que usaron el título de cacicas en la litigación de inicios del siglo XVII para defender sus derechos territoriales y su reputación social, introduciendo sus propias nociones de justicia, experiencias y narrativas prehispánicas, brindando a los y las investigadores/as información sobre sus »dramas sociales« – en términos de Susan Kellogg. A continuación, Sara Vicuña Guengerich (cap. 8) traslada la mirada al altiplano andino bajo las rebeliones indígenas del siglo XVIII, al analizar la trayectoria de la cacica y gobernadora de Azángaro, doña Teresa Choquehuanca, como »sujeto histórico significativo«, en un contexto de conflictividad con sus indios tributarios y líderes indígenas subordinados, que permite visualizar las expectativas indígenas sobre los liderazgos femeninos tanto como las concepciones andinas de género. Por último, a partir de categorías analíticas distintas a las anteriores – como *brokers*, *go-betweens*, *mediators* y *creative misunderstandings* – y en diálogo con la historiografía dedicada a los espacios fronterizos americanos (en particular, Richard White y Juliana Barr), la investigación de Florencia Roulet (cap. 9) retrata la agencia de tres cacicas pertenecientes a »indios bárbaros« que, en la frontera sur de la Gobernación del Río de la Plata, actuaron como embajadoras y mediadoras de paz en la segunda mitad del siglo XVIII, evidenciando la preeminencia de códigos de paz y guerra nativos. El libro cierra con la Conclusión a cargo de Mónica Díaz, que convoca a atender la fluidez identitaria de los actores sociales y la naturaleza retórica de sus discursos de pureza y nobleza en vistas a acercarnos a las complejidades sociopolíticas coloniales; y el Apéndice a cargo de Patrick Werner, que brinda listas de caciques y cacicas en Castilla del Oro (actual Nicaragua) de la primera mitad del siglo XVI, obtenidas de las copias documentales incluidas en la Colección Somoza, de la Fundación Bolaños.

La anterior exposición demuestra que el libro logra ampliamente expandir el rango geográfico y cronológico y el contenido temático de los estudios sobre las cacicas coloniales. Ello se alcanza a partir de investigaciones que manifiestan un profundo conocimiento de la región y del período estudiados y de la lectura interrelacionada de variada documentación inédita – como testamentos, litigios y dotes, entre otros. Si bien, no todos los trabajos utilizan las mismas categorías analíticas y/o presupuestos teórico-metodológicos, la riqueza empírica y la predominancia de detallados estudios de caso permite a los/las lectores/as comprender acabadamente el abanico de significados y la heterogeneidad en el estatus y en la autoridad ejercidos por las mujeres documentadas bajo el mismo término, aspectos enfatizados por las editoras. Por ello, y dado que en la mayoría de los casos estudiados el término »cacica« no implica el ejercicio efectivo del oficio cacical sino diversos aspectos como estatus nobiliario, auto-percepción, intencionalidad judicial, narrativas retóricas, reconocimiento de autoridad, entre otros, el subtítulo *Indigenous Women Leaders* no logra captar la amplitud de su contenido. Asimismo, el libro se hubiera beneficiado de reflexiones de síntesis que permitieran a los lectores reponer las hipótesis transversales o unificar procesos históricos presentes en el imperio castellano que, al tiempo de ponderar la agencia individual de las mujeres – siempre en los marcos corporativos antiguo-regimentales –, permitiera tender puentes en común y recontextualizar las prácticas, los discursos y las trayectorias. Lo anterior, sin embargo, no desmerece el encomiable esfuerzo de las editoras por reunir en un mismo volumen interrogantes y reveladores estudios de caso que brindan a los lectores los elementos necesarios para repensar metodologías, categorías analíticas e históricas, al tiempo que ofrecen una oportunidad para observar – y multiplicar – nuevos estudios sobre los roles políticos de las mujeres indígenas bajo dominio castellano.

■

Armando Guevara Gil

Paisajes de servidumbre y esclavitud en el mundo colonial andino*

Revilla ha escrito una obra muy interesante para comprender la caleidoscópica realidad de las relaciones sociales y laborales en los dos primeros siglos de la colonización española de los Andes. A partir de una vasta pesquisa documental y bibliográfica, la autora nos obsequia un fresco impresionante que contribuirá a superar las tradicionales versiones sobre el rígido carácter estamental y la nítida división entre la República de los Españoles, la República de Indios y la población esclavizada en la sociedad virreinal. A tono con la bibliografía especializada, Revilla disuelve sistemáticamente esas simplificaciones y, a partir de una atenta lectura de sus fuentes, examina la estructuración y reproducción de las diversas formas de subordinación servil en la ciudad de La Plata, Audiencia de Charcas (hoy Sucre, provincia oriental de la República Plurinacional de Bolivia).

Para esta tarea, la autora ha preparado una obra que se compone de una introducción, once capítulos y una sección de conclusiones. El trabajo está respaldado por una bibliografía completa y actualizada, y por una rigurosa investigación documental en archivos de Bolivia, Perú y España. Así, el primer capítulo presenta el mosaico etnopolítico de la provincia de Charcas, originalmente integrado al estado Inca y luego al español. También contiene un apartado sobre el inicio de la convivencia de españoles e indígenas en la ciudad de La Plata, caracterizada por un entretejido de relaciones étnicas y sociales muy complejo debido a la gran diferenciación interna de los grupos en contacto inicial. En el siguiente capítulo, tanto la población esclava de origen africano como los Chiruguanos, un gentilicio que rápidamente se transformó en etnónimo para abarcar a los pueblos ubicados en las cadenas orientales de los Andes, entran en escena. La particularidad en el segundo caso es que lo hacen en condición de esclavos, a pesar de la expresa prohibición legal, teológica y moral impuesta desde la metrópoli.

Esta anomalía es la que genera la discusión sobre los fundamentos jurídicos y teológicos de la esclavitud (capítulo tres). Es muy acertado que Revilla haya resaltado la pluralidad de fuentes (jurídicas, teológicas, morales) que justificaban y regulaban la esclavitud, al punto de la contradicción en relación al matrimonio o el peculio, por ejemplo. Y también que haya enfatizado la localización, en este caso en una Audiencia americana, de las normas y principios dictados en la península ibérica. Esta observación la conduce a una notable exégesis de los debates y regulaciones que se produjeron en la Audiencia de Charcas sobre la esclavitud de personas de origen africano y los Chiriguanos. Queda claro que tanto la reinterpretación de las fuentes metropolitanas como la producción de conocimiento jurídico localizado generaron los códigos semióticos y normativos de la esclavitud y el trabajo servil en esta parte de las Indias.

A continuación (capítulo cuatro) examina los condicionamientos de salud, edad, género y destrezas laborales que influían no solo en el precio que los señores pagaban por los esclavos, incluidos los Chiriguanos, sino en la regulación de las relaciones entre estos. Es interesante observar que cuando las tensiones, violencia y crueldad rebasaban la economía moral de la esclavitud y la servidumbre, tanto indígenas como esclavos afrodescendientes apelaron a las cortes para defender su vida y limitado bienestar, a la fuga o a la resistencia directa. Revilla también estudia las diferentes formas de subordinación laboral y social que padecían los indígenas en el campo y la ciudad. Destacan la mita (traducida como *corvée labor*) y el yanaconaje (trabajadores serviles especializados desarraigados de sus comunidades). Como insiste la autora, estas modalidades eran parte de un *continuum* de rela-

* Paola Revilla Orías, Entangled Coercion. African and Indigenous Labour in Charcas (16th – 17th Centuries), Berlin / Boston: De Gruyter Oldenbourg 2021, 317 p., ISBN 978-3-11-068089-8

ciones serviles en el que la diferencia estaba marcada por la intensidad de la subordinación de los subalternos a otras personas naturales o corporaciones (e. g., conventos, cabildos).

Esa intensidad es analizada en los dos siguientes capítulos en términos de las modalidades físicas (e. g., *carimba* o marca a fuego), simbólicas y rituales que concurrían en la configuración subjetiva y el reconocimiento social de los sujetos subyugados. Bajo una cultura marcadamente patriarcal, caracterizada por la dependencia y la creación de lazos personales asimétricos, esclavos e indígenas, así como libertos sujetos a relaciones serviles, eran incorporados a la esfera de autoridad de sus señores. Esa misma sujeción creaba un manto de tutela que protegía a los subalternos de los abusos de las autoridades y otros señores, españoles o indígenas. El ejercicio de esa tutela contribuía a legitimar a los señores frente a sus dependientes.

Revilla dedica el capítulo ocho a presentar la multifacética configuración de las relaciones sociales presididas por la subordinación. Señores y señoras indígenas dueños de esclavos; afrodescendientes libres y mulatos poseedores de yanaconas y esclavos, inclusive Chiriguanos; yanaconas dueños de esclavos; libertos y mulatos convertidos en yanaconas; e indígenas esclavizados y vendidos por otros indígenas (e. g., Chané) son solo ejemplos de la trama y urdimbre que se tejió en La Plata de los siglos XVI y XVII. Y todo ello ocurrió más allá de los dictados prohibicionistas de la legislación metropolitana y de las barreras étnicas, supuestamente rígidas. La autora hace un gran trabajo al identificar esa variedad de relaciones de dependencia, pero no se dedica a analizar su estructuración jurídica. No fue su objetivo, pero deja magníficas pistas de investigación a los historiadores del derecho.

Ese peculiar tejido social también se expresa en las diversas ocupaciones que desarrollaron los esclavos urbanos (capítulo nueve) para librarse, parcial y temporalmente, del yugo directo de sus señores. Actividades como trabajar por un salario en el campo o la ciudad, especializarse en una rama del comercio o artesanía, o realizar actividades artísticas, les permitieron obtener un salario que compartían con sus señores, pero cuyo ahorro les sirvió para manumitirse, actuar como prestamistas o adquirir bienes. Aquí, nuevamente, se abre un vasto campo de investigación para rastrear puntualmente los *vincula iuris* que canalizaron esas actividades y, de ese modo, mejorar nuestro conocimiento de cómo se configura un derecho local colonial.

Los dos últimos capítulos están dedicados a examinar las diferentes formas jurídicas y económicas conducentes a la manumisión y a la reconstitución del mundo social y personal de los esclavos desarraigados violentamente de sus lugares de origen. Aquí es donde sacramentos y lazos personales como el matrimonio y el bautismo adquirieron trascendencia para generar nuevas redes sociales, identidades grupales y oportunidades de reacomodo en la sociedad colonial. Finalmente, las conclusiones sistematizan los principales hallazgos del trabajo, tan bien sustentados en las fuentes documentales y bibliográficas analizadas. Lo único que lamentar al terminar la lectura de la obra es la cantidad de errores tipográficos. Este lector dejó anotarlos al llegar al medio centenar, un descuido editorial sorprendente que, sin embargo, no desmerece el valor intelectual del aporte de Revilla.

Como todo texto, el de Paola Revilla Orías se puede leer de muchas maneras. No tengo ninguna duda de que la historia colonial, la etnohistoria, la historia de la esclavitud, la historia del trabajo y la historia de Charcas y La Plata tienen entre manos una significativa contribución. La historia del Derecho también. Aunque no está escrito bajo sus cánones y convenciones teóricas y metodológicas, su riqueza radica en que ofrece pistas interesantes y promisorias para los interesados en comprender cómo se forjó un ordenamiento normativo local en el orbe indiano. Los ejemplos casi etnográficos que Revilla brinda nos permiten vislumbrar cómo se forjó el derecho que reguló las relaciones de subordinación laboral en la Audiencia de Charcas y las formas en que este fue articulado por esclavos, indígenas, mestizos y españoles, recreándolo y reproduciéndolo en la cotidianeidad de sus interacciones, en el fragor de sus desencuentros, en los armisticios propios de la *pax* colonial. Por eso estamos ante un libro importante para la historia del derecho.

■

Otto Vervaart

Searching Slavery Laws in British North America*

The presence of enslaved persons in the British parts of North America started long before some of the Founding Fathers owned slaves. Where many scholarly projects only take up the American view emphasising developments just before and during the 19th century, focus on the British side of this history is certainly welcome. Holly Brewer (University of Maryland, College Park) is director and lead editor of the project *Slavery, Law & Power in the British Empire and Early America* (SLP), and her team consists primarily of PhD students.

The SLP website does not have a separate section on law, thus the reader is encouraged to visit all sections where legal documents, laws or statutes are included. Some laws and even legal codes are present in the various chapters, a key section of the website. Legal documents are also present in the section entitled ›NHPRC Sample Documents‹, referring to the National Historical Publications and Records Commission of the United States National Archives. At the moment the number of documents is on the low side. In fact one of the aims of this project is to encourage scholars to submit editions of documents.

The various timelines and maps make the website graphically attractive, and it even includes a game titled ›Age of Empire‹ to raise awareness of the limitations and bias of maps. While the concise selection on literature for the bibliography is well thought out, it is unfortunately limited to just English-language publications. The section containing additional resources offers the reader access to a fine selection of digital projects. The palaeography is not neglected here, and several projects concerning the 19th century are also presented.

I am somewhat mystified, however, by the lack of introductions focusing on the key topics of the the SLP website: slavery, law and power in the early Americas. The three main themes are interconnected in many ways, yet no attempt is made to give due weight to all three. The ›Chapters‹ section is arranged in a rigid chronological order structured according to external political developments. A singular framework to put things into perspec-

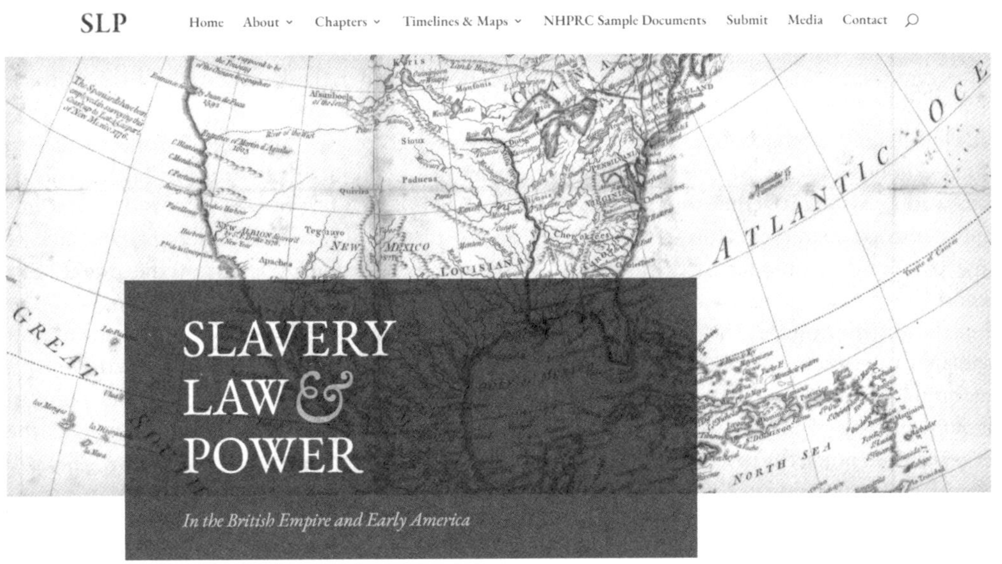

* Slavery, Law & Power in the British Empire and Early America, https://slaverylawpower.org/ (last visited 30 April 2022)

tive is rather meagre. Individual kings, Cromwell, the English parliament and major trading companies rightly so belong to the usual subjects when discussing the threefold core of the SLP project. However, the role of other European countries competing with the British Empire after 1600 is left completely in the dark.

Missing the chance to discuss key themes in greater depth mars the conceptual quality of this project. Not even the Atlantic triangle of trade is deemed worth mentioning. In the section on the Spanish empire from 1350 to 1550, entitled ›Antecedents‹, and duly marked as »under construction«, the Leyes de Burgos and the Leyes de Indias are conspicuously absent.

At the moment the SLP website is more or less an empty shell – one with several partially redeeming features such as the timelines, maps, the map game and the array of additional online resources. I will look here in some detail at a few elements connected with legal matters. The edition of the Barbados Slave Code (1661–1667) is quite useful, including not only the text but also images of the earliest archival record held at The National Archives, Kew, references to original sources and scholarly literature, and also a link to a separate digital library with document images for completed editions. As of right now, only a handful of editions are actually available. Some placeholders are not particularly well chosen: the Haitian declaration of independence (1804) is presented in English.

Having expressed my reservations and critical remarks, it is necessary to look at the exact aims and potential audience of the SLP project. The project team wants to bring together sources from many contexts into an open access format to shed light on the parallel development of democratic structures and the rise of the early modern slave trade within the British Empire. The project aims to help scholars easily access – without paywalls – a range of original sources concerning ongoing debates about law, slavery and power. However, the project team does not seem to be aware of the necessity for a systematic approach to using legal resources. Even in the section with additional resources, subjects such as Parliament, statutes and English legislation do not figure among the resources. How can one proceed to document vital debates without using resources on English parliamentary history? How can one present a solid documentary base without realising the difficulties of obtaining the relevant statutes? Let us mention just one example of a resource directly bearing on slavery, law and power: John Levin's *The Statutes Project*, https://statutes.org.uk/site, which also includes among its online sources legislation for British overseas territories. Of course there should be space for a purely historical approach to matters surrounding slavery and its grim history, but for the SLP project it is counterproductive to omit legal history as an appropriate focus and vital research discipline. To rephrase the title of a recent lecture, law is both a tool and a problem. The absence of questions to be addressed within the context of the SLP project seems to be a sign of inadequate reflection and preparation.

Slavery, Law & Power is a very promising title. It will no doubt be useful to eventually have modern editions of a number of key sources assembled on a website that includes images of the original sources. It appears that the project team aspires to make a contribution to digital public history, yet even this very discipline goes unmentioned. The framework of the SLP project might be technically sound, but at the conceptual level its implications and limits have been given insufficient consideration. Questions and problems are not clearly articulated on the SLP website. Holly Brewer's previous publications and projects have received praise, but the SLP project seems to either still be in its infancy after its official launch on 15 February 2022, or somehow it does not live up to its own aim, which suffers from a lack of concrete steps and goals, and from the absence of a clear conceptual framework. Since many other projects have focused on the actual practice of the slave trade and the lives of enslaved persons, it is surely a good idea to examine the political discourse, developments in government and the uses of legislation. As it stands right now, the SLP project still needs a great deal of work if it intends to fulfil the lofty goals it set out. ■

Gilberto Guerra Pedrosa

Ativos imateriais em processos decisórios do »Brasil holandês«*

O lobby corporativo tem sido visto como um dos fatores mais importantes para a influência das grandes empresas sobre as decisões políticas. A autodeterminação do público no processo democrático estaria em perigo frente ao potencial de captura das instituições políticas, comprometendo a representação política e deixando de lado os interesses coletivos. Esta imagem do domínio do privado sobre o público não correspondia à realidade do início da era moderna. Em seu recente livro sobre a colônia no Brasil da Companhia Holandesa das Índias Ocidentais (WIC) no século XVII, Joris van den Tol apresenta uma lógica inversa: Indivíduos e grupos de pessoas com interesses comuns influenciavam a empresa colonial e organizações políticas através do lobby.

Lobbying in Company conta a história de como atores históricos fundamentalmente diferentes conseguiram combinar seus respectivos objetivos no Brasil colonial e na metrópole holandesa. Este livro explica a partir de vários exemplos como os projetos particulares influenciaram vários órgãos decisórios, chegando até os círculos políticos mais altos da República Holandesa. Esses atores não necessariamente tinham um cargo oficial em Amsterdã ou na breve colônia holandesa no Brasil. Tampouco pertenciam aos estratos privilegiados da sociedade local. Além disso, o livro demonstra que o envolvimento dessas pessoas não se limitava às atividades convencionais correspondentes aos papéis sociais e estatutos jurídicos que desempenhavam. Os numerosos exemplos citados no livro incluem relações desde contatos pessoais e de patrocínio, à publicação e distribuição de folhetos nas grandes cidades da época, ou mesmo através da redação de petições que fogem as formalidades exigidas à época, conforme as próprias exigências dos interessados. Estes atores acoplavam seus projetos individuais por meio das lacunas deixadas pelos procedimentos oficiais da administração colonial, criando assim simultaneamente novas oportunidades e problemas para o projeto oficial da conquista holandesa.

A monografia tem como objetivo complementar os achados de trabalhos anteriores sobre o tema e chamar atenção para a riqueza existente no manancial de manuscritos presentes nos arquivos holandeses (6). Van den Tol não está convencido de que o sucesso das demandas dos atores analisados se deva unicamente a fenômenos fragmentários com base na atuação individual. O lobby, nestes termos, é definido como um processo estruturante de coordenação dos campos de atuação desses indivíduos. As petições figuram como fontes primárias em destaque no livro, de onde se pode compreender de modo mais detalhado a competição entre diversos interesses que mobilizavam acontecimentos já conhecidos pelos historiadores sobre a parte do Atlântico dominada pelos holandeses. Van den Tol agregou à sua pesquisa outras fontes que cobrem o processo decisório das câmaras de comércio regionais nas províncias unidas da Holanda aos conselhos na colônia do Brasil à alta autoridade dos Estados Gerais, ego-documentos – diários de personalidades do »Brasil holandês«, cartas de representantes de empresas, bem como o banco de dados de historiadores especialistas na atividade mercantil do atlântico holandês desenvolvido por Cátia Antunes, professora da Universidade de Leiden. A partir de uma historiografia que continuamente reelabora a governança descentralizada do Atlântico holandês, van den Tol reconstrói a influência desses grupos de interesse, em particular, rastreando o aparecimento de certos nomes nesses documentos. Um dado importante que o autor destaca é a múltipla funcionalidade da estratégia de peticionamento. Eles não apenas serviram como uma ajuda à argumentação através de

* Joris van den Tol, Lobbying in Company: Economic Interests and Political Decision Making in the History of Dutch Brazil, 1621–1656, Leiden / Boston: Brill 2020, 321 p., ISBN 978-90-04-39795-8

uma justificação discursivamente elaborada. Dependendo do contexto, as petições também serviram para obter acesso a certos círculos políticos, para estabelecer relações que antes não eram possíveis devido à situação individual dos atores, ou para acelerar ou atrasar certas decisões (123, 165, 211, 265 ss).

Embora não explicitamente listado, o livro está dividido em quatro partes. Os três primeiros capítulos mostram que o trabalho dos lobbies (grupos de interesse) estão presentes desde a fundação da Companhia Holandesa das Índias Ocidentais (WIC) até o projeto de colonização do Brasil pelos holandeses aprovado pelos Estados Gerais. O primeiro capítulo traz o plano de Willem Usselincx de estabelecer uma West Indies Company já em 1590. No segundo capítulo são abordados os arranjos na então nova colônia, especialmente através da incorporação das câmaras municipais já presentes no Brasil colônia, no segundo capítulo, assim como os debates e disputas entre diferentes grupos de comerciantes e soldados de ambos os lados do Atlântico a respeito do monopólio ou maior abertura comercial para mercadorias vindas do Brasil. Tanto na colônia quanto na metrópole, os habitantes usaram esses eventos como uma oportunidade para realizar seus objetivos pessoais e moldar os projetos originais da companhia no novo mundo. O autor explica o funcionamento da burocracia descentralizada na República Holandesa, especialmente em relação às questões comerciais e militares. A partir das cadeias decisórias que atravessam o Atlântico, Van den Tol detalha a emergência de um quadro mais complexo do domínio holandês no Brasil, que perpassa as limitações das instâncias oficiais europeias e as disputas entre facções no além-mar. Depois de confeccionar uma cartografia de como esses grupos de interesse navegavam pela instável governança holandesa, o autor apresenta seus estudos de caso no terceiro, quarto, quinto e sexto capítulos. Primeiro, estudo de caso como estas atividades cooperativas são mais evidentes nas arenas discursivas dos assuntos atlânticos holandeses. O primeiro caso (quarto capítulo) trata do reino da palavra e do argumento, geralmente, na historiografia sobre os Países Baixos, reservado aos estudos da imprensa e à cultura panfletária na historiografia, é examinado aqui através de manuscritos e petições em que assinavam várias pessoas (141 ss). O segundo caso (quinto capítulo) aborda a importância do capital cultural enquanto ativo imaterial e bem individual dos supostos lobbistas, destinado a alcançar as redes entre os círculos superiores da sociedade holandesa. Evidências dessa sorte são encontradas no diário de Hendrick Haecxs, um antigo comerciante que chegou a membro do alto conselho do governo do Brasil. A abordagem de Van den Tol contrasta com a história econômica que considera os ativos imateriais dos agentes, no caso as relações de mecenato, e apenas enquanto custos de transação para construir relações de confiança moral e reduzir incertezas. O autor aponta para outros papéis. Também pode ser visto como um recurso especial para expandir a margem de manobra da empresa colonial, aumentar sua capacidade de endividamento, comprar favores, resolver conflitos pessoais e controlar informações valiosas (180 ss). No terceiro caso (sexto capítulo), as petições passam a retratar as incapacidades da WIC, complementando as explicações de como portugueses acabaram reconquistando o Brasil apesar da decisão política dos Estados Gerais e do apoio da Câmara de Comércio da Frísia. O autor apresenta petições coletivas de pessoas que viviam na colônia, e como essas delegações brasileiras já teriam acesso às altas instâncias decisórias em Amsterdã, inclusive demonstrando certa familiaridade com os procedimentos formais e as estratégias de litígio à época em vigor. Entretanto, estes esforços para acelerar o processo de aplicação habitual encontraram resistência de algumas câmaras de comércio, como a de Rotterdam. O quarto caso e (sétimo capítulo) trata das petições dos soldados que serviram na Companhia Holandesa das Índias Ocidentais e queriam ser pagos como seus superiores ao retornarem aos seus respectivos países europeus. Em vez de recorrer aos tribunais, eles pediam à empresa que honrasse seus contratos (258). Ao fim, no último capítulo, o autor apresenta um resumo de seus argumentos do que há em comum entre os casos listados: »A atividade de lobby foi uma forma mais cooperativa de interação entre as pessoas e os mandatários políticos do que, por exemplo, o ato de ir ao tribunal. […] Embora a guerra e as revoluções pudessem provocar mudanças nas instituições, nem todas as alterações institucionais ocorreram de forma orgânica ou incremental«[1] (265).

1 *Traduções para o inglês aqui e abaixo por G. G. P.*

A concepção apresentada por van den Tol sobre a atividade de lobby na WIC elucida questões sobre como diferentes interesses individuais encontram ou não espaço para realizarem seus objetivos, quais seriam as possibilidades, limitações, trade-offs que interesses coletivos se harmonizam a situações também distintas. As ações sociais, especialmente as de cunho instrumental explicitas nas fontes pelas partes interessadas tornam-se menos opacas à análise. As observações do autor não caem em lugares comuns, como se, separadamente, empresas, comerciantes, colonos e a população local fossem sujeitos inseridos em uma coletividade que compartilha valores homogêneos comuns apenas entre os seus. O contexto de rápida ascensão e queda do domínio holandês proporciona instabilidade suficiente para observar os limites e possibilidades dessas associações espontâneas e as pressões que elas exerceram sobre os processos decisórios da economia política atlântica holandesa. Os grupos de interesse, entendidos como compromissos cooperativos, mudam com o tempo, assim como as altas cúpulas políticas.

Essencialmente, este livro trata da co-evolução de instituições cruciais para a economia política do Atlântico na prévia modernidade, através do envolvimento de pessoas comuns, o que é raro na historiografia do império holandês. Não obstante, a questão de quando, como, sobre o quê e até que ponto os diferentes tipos de lobbies encontraram um lugar na história econômica do Brasil holandês é certamente um caminho que ainda demanda trabalho para uma melhor compreensão histórica das instituições em mudança. Voltando às primeiras páginas do livro, há um trecho que ainda me faz pensar sobre to como a história do direito observaria as associações espontâneas de diferentes pessoas em grupos de interesse econômico apresentados pelo autor. Van den Tol comenta que a atividade lobbista ainda é pouco explorada pelos historiadores enquanto objeto de estudo e por estes estarem fortemente viculados a um certo paradigma historiográfico que confere ênfase aos conflitos sociais, associado à luta de diferentes grupos por bens escassos e as disputas por na participação política nas instâncias legais do processo decisório ligados à WIC. Em contraste ao paradigma do conflito, a ênfase nas atividades de lobby buscaria, portanto, se referir aos elementos cooperativos dos atores históricos. Seguindo esta linha de argumentação, Joris van den Tol afirma no parágrafo seguinte antes de introduzir uma ideia resumida do livro: »A atividade de lobby poderia (e deveria) ser estudada em relação a qualquer assunto da história e não é de forma alguma exclusivo à experiência colonial holandesa« (2). Apesar das aproximações interdisciplinares propostas pelo autor à sociologia e ao neoinstitucionalismo histórico, a imagem que se tem do direito ainda é marcada pela à aplicação de regras ou à atividade coercitiva do público sobre o privado. Em vários momentos do livro, o componente jurídico se faz presente a partir de uma forma única, de cunho oficial, que determina a atuação dos agentes públicos e condiciona os agentes privados em suas atividades oficiosas, especialmetne a partir da previsão de sanções (17, 20, 30, 50, 52, 53, 63, 66, 229, 262). Entretanto, deve-se notar que o autor mesmo detalha modelos de argumentação, declarações pessoais sobre experiências profissionais nas instâncias judiciais da república holandesa na época, até o uso de subtefúrgios ilícitos que permitiriam uma reflexão menos positivista e mais sociocultural das normas em questão. Curiosamente, porém, a necessidade de afirmação por parte do autor da atividade lobbista acaba por recriar um cenário em que essa ação espontânea de caráter cooperativo estaria sempre um passo à frente da autoridade reguladora oficial (2, 91). Já há muito que a história do direito nos oferece alternativas mais fiáveis a essa pré-compreensão do fenômeno jurídico subtendida nas palavras do autor.

■

Bruno Lima

Private Law and Enslaved Families in Colonial Brazil*

The book *Laços de família: Africanos e crioulos na capitania de São Paulo colonial* delves into the almost entirely erased past of family relationships of enslaved people in late 18th and early 19th century Brazil. Could slaves marry free people? Could they be godparents to free children? How did they structure their families within bondage? Could Africans own slaves? How could they change their legal status, i. e. move from slavery to freedom?

These are some of the legal questions that Fabiana Schleumer, professor of African History at the Federal University of São Paulo, proposes to answer. Defended as a Master's thesis over twenty years ago and only recently published as a book, *Laços de Família* is a representative example of Brazilian historiographic production on social dependency and slavery, both for its limited temporal and spatial scope and for its methodological approach of combining administrative and ecclesiastical sources. In her case study of the village of Cotia, on the outskirts of the city of São Paulo, between the years 1790 and 1810, Schleumer describes a »history of the daily life« (22) of the enslaved people and freedmen in a poor slave-owning society based on smallholder farming. As the author indicates – without actually exploring the comparative perspective – the social structure of the small and peripheral Cotia differed greatly from other regions of the same *capitania* of São Paulo, which were composed of large sugar and coffee plantations. (A *capitania* was the top-tier administrative unit, *vila* and then *freguesia* being the lower levels.)

Schleumer organises her investigation of the local dynamics of family arrangements of Africans and Creoles in Cotia into five chapters. First, she discusses methodology, especially the use of demography in historical research, pointing out the advantages of cross-referencing census data to formulate hypotheses and draw conclusions about the local economy and the everyday life of enslaved and freed people of African origin. In the second chapter, the author reviews and compares the historiography of slave families in Atlantic slave societies, particularly those of the United States of America and Brazil, drawing on a number of anthropological aspects of African family structure, such as the function of betrothal, dowry, marriage, and the role of kinship in African societies. In the third chapter, Schleumer discusses the primary demographic sources of the local *freguesia* of Cotia and examines the structure of slave ownership in that jurisdiction as well as the family and kinship networks arranged within or on the margins of bondage. The author succeeds in proving that there was a predominance of nuclear families over broken or matrifocal ones (172), which denotes a more permanent form of family structure among the enslaved Africans and Creoles. In the fourth chapter, she highlights the participation of women and children in the unequal social relationships in Cotia, taking a close look at both slave-owning women and enslaved or freed African and Creole women. In the fifth and final chapter, Schleumer analyses changes and continuities in social and family relationships of Africans and Creole people in Cotia. Using census data from 1798 and 1808, the author looks in detail at patterns of birth, marriage, death, and social mobility found among the enslaved and freed black population in Cotia.

This book represents analytical gains, especially for understanding the historical relationship between enslaved and freed Africans within a slave society of low population density (60 households) based on smallholder farming. However, it disappoints readers familiar with the social history of slavery in Brazil and the Atlantic world on three fundamental levels: historiography, methodology, and conceptualisation of private law. Historio-

* Fabiana Schleumer, Laços de família: Africanos e crioulos na capitania de São Paulo colonial, São Paulo: Alameda 2020, 320 p., ISBN 978-65-86081-21-0

graphic misconceptions are present in the argument that Cotia's social formation was exceptional. In analysing only that one jurisdiction within the *capitania* of São Paulo, the author argues that slavery in Cotia was singular when compared to the other *freguesias* and *vilas* of the colony. But singular in what respect, if there are no comparisons based on geography – i. e. with neighbouring villages and regions – or along a temporal line? The reader is not informed of Cotia's location on the demographic, economic, ecclesiastical, legal, or administrative map of the *capitania* of São Paulo, nor does the author give any timeframe for the cited historical statistics. The alleged uniqueness of that location leads to assertions that are at best dubious, including the claim that the *freguesia* of Cotia was a »non-polarised society between slave-owners and slaves« (53), something that simply cannot be supported by historical documentation. In fact, slavery played such a crucial role in the organisation of São Paulo's colonial *capitania* that it can be said to have fundamentally shaped society, both at the macro and the micro levels. It is clear, then, that Cotia was, like its neighbouring villages, polarised between slave-owners and slaves – even when such polarisation did not have a direct and vertical impact on the social fringes of the notoriously small free population that did not own slaves.

In turn, the eclectic methodological approach of this book leaves the reader unable to judge the inferences and conclusions that Schleumer takes as evidence throughout the text. Is it accurate to say, for instance, that »[slave-owning] Africans possessed a feeling of brotherhood with their slaves« (83)? There is nothing in the book that leads the reader to believe such a presumption. By resorting excessively and unnecessarily to anthropological clichés from secondary literature, the author departs from the authentic value of the book: the analysis of primary demographic and ecclesiastical sources that illuminate the historical understanding of the family structure of Africans and Creoles in Cotia. Instead, Schleumer goes down a tortuous path of hypothetical connections between African private law and its uncertain reproduction in the family structure of African descendants in Brazil. Finally, the author's superficial understanding of private law in a slaveholding society leaves the reader without explanation or an understanding of what kind of marriages were performed or maintained between freedmen and enslaved people; how enslaved children were registered; or how manumission was accomplished. While the author partially succeeds in describing and cross-referencing demographic and economic data from the sixty households studied, which allows us to see a complex network of relationships mediated by private law, she does not scrutinise the functions that private law played in that society, neither to define a particular form of slave ownership nor to establish a specific model of family that, as the author notes, combined the marriage of »slaves of the same ethnic group« (116) with the marriage of »slaves from the same owner« (117).

Not only does this book employ a precarious historical, methodological, and conceptual perspective, it also contains undeniable stylistic and editorial errors. Over seventeen full pages (220–236) Schleumer quotes the same author exclusively for fifty-eight consecutive times. This type of exhaustive and uncritical citation is repeated many times. However indispensable the work of a particular historian or anthropologist may be, it does not seem reasonable that any expert could rely so heavily on the writings of others and not even promote dialogue among different perspectives over so many pages. Furthermore, the book lacks basic editorial revision. The author indicates maps, graphs and tables that do not actually appear in the text (253, 254, 257, 258, 267), and omits or makes errors in footnotes (e. g. 26, 27, 39, 136, 137, 166, 175, 176, 268).

The book has many faults. But it also has positive features, among them an invitation to the legal historian to dedicate himself or herself to the almost unexplored field of private law in a slave society.

■

Jean-Louis Halpérin

Archipel colonial et justice globale*

Professeure associée d'histoire à la Florida State University, Laurie M. Wood propose, dans ce livre, une étude sur la justice et le droit au sein du »premier empire colonial français« (17e–18e siècles) qui a l'originalité de s'intéresser aux connexions entre les colonies américaines (Nouvelle France au Québec et à l'île Royale, Louisiane et surtout les îles de la Martinique, de la Guadeloupe, de Saint-Domingue et Saint-Christophe, cette dernière jusqu'en 1713) et celles de l'Océan Indien (île Bourbon, aujourd'hui La Réunion; île de France, aujourd'hui Maurice et établissements français de l'Inde comme Pondichéry). Toutes ces colonies ont été dotées par le gouvernement royal d'institutions judiciaires, notamment d'un Conseil supérieur sur le modèle inauguré en métropole par le Conseil provincial d'Artois à Arras (1640), puis imité à Perpignan au Roussillon (1660), à Colmar en Alsace (1667) et plus tard à Bastia en Corse (1768). Non seulement l'institution de dix-sept hautes juridictions de ce type en dehors de la métropole a créé une forme de parenté légale entre les îles des Antilles et des Mascareignes, gouvernées depuis Versailles, directement pour les premières depuis le début du règne personnel de Louis XIV et indirectement pour les secondes avec le relais de la Compagnie des Indes jusque dans les années 1760, mais les échanges d'expériences, de courriers et d'hommes (administrateurs, commerçants, juristes) ont été à l'origine d'un espace socio-économique entre ces diverses colonies recourant à l'esclavage. Par exemple, des expéditions menées depuis l'île Bourbon à Madagascar ont conduit à la capture d'esclaves transportés à la Martinique. Les Antilles et les Mascareignes se sont trouvées associées à la prospérité du commerce des esclaves et du sucre qui permet au royaume de France de s'enrichir dans la seconde moitié du 18e siècle, malgré la perte de territoires en Amérique et en Inde au profit des Britanniques.

À partir des archives des Conseils supérieurs et en analysant un certain nombre de procès ou de conflits administratifs et judiciaires, Laurie M. Wood veut montrer comment a fonctionné une *human ecology of justice* dominée par une *global themistocraty* associant les milieux judiciaires de la métropole (notamment ceux qui ont prêté serment devant le Parlement de Paris) et ceux des colonies. L'étude montre en même temps les difficultés d'établissement et de fonctionnement de ces institutions judiciaires (avec de nombreuses juridictions inférieures en dessous des Conseils supérieurs) et administratives (avec la rivalité entre les gouverneurs militaires et les intendants civils). Dans ces *legal entrepôts* comme l'auteure les désigne, la justice a été, d'abord, rendue en plein air sous un arbre, puis dans des lieux privés comme des cabarets, avant que ne soient bâtis des palais de justice. Le secrétariat d'État à la Marine, auquel sont rattachées les colonies, peine à recruter des magistrats qui ne bénéficient pas, à la différence de leurs collègues de la métropole, de la patrimonialité des offices, ni du système des »épices« (c'est-à-dire du reversement aux juges des frais de procédure payés par les parties). Il faut recourir à des juristes de la métropole tentés par l'aventure ou amenés à quitter les juridictions supprimées par le chancelier Maupeou de 1771 à 1774 et, de plus en plus en avançant dans le temps, à des membres des familles des planteurs. La frontière avec les assesseurs, qui étaient des notables locaux, est d'autant plus ténue que dans certains cas les juges étaient choisis parmi des commerçants. Ces juridictions coloniales étaient, de plus, affectées par les conflits de pouvoirs et d'intérêts entre l'administration et la marine (avec des procès impliquant des soldats, des marins et dans un cas un duel intervenu sur un navire en mer), les négociants et les planteurs, tous associés au commerce des esclaves et souvent tentés de se livrer à la contrebande contre le système de l'exclusif réservant les échanges avec la France. La monarchie ne peut contrôler, à des milliers de kilomètres de Versailles, des crises comme celle dite du *Gaoulé*, à la Martinique en

* Laurie M. Wood, Archipelago of Justice. Law in France's Early Modern Empire, New Haven & London: Yale University Press 2020, XXII + 264 p., ISBN 978-0-300-24400-7

1717, qui vit les notables prendre le contrôle du Conseil supérieur et ordonner le renvoi forcé dans un navire du gouverneur et de l'intendant.

Ces juridictions coloniales devaient appliquer la coutume de Paris aux conflits civils et la législation royale en matière de procédure et d'administration. À ces textes communs avec la métropole, formant ce que l'auteure appelle une *global French legal culture*, s'ajoutaient les édits sur les esclaves, commençant avec celui de 1685 sur la police des îles françaises de l'Amérique jusqu'à ceux appliqués dans les Mascareignes ou en Louisiane et réunis par les éditeurs privés du 18e siècle sous le nom de *Code noir.* L'auteure ne présente pas une étude détaillée des procès qui impliquaient la traite négrière, mais rappelle que, dans quelques cas, les esclaves victimes de traitements cruels pouvaient se plaindre de leurs maîtres devant les juges.

Avec cette dernière mention, qui apparaît limitée sur un sujet aussi essentiel et ignore la littérature française sur cette législation esclavagiste (notamment les travaux de Jean-François Niort sur les »idées reçues« du Code noir), l'on touche les réserves que l'on peut adresser à cet ouvrage, par ailleurs original et stimulant. Les lecteurs non familiers avec l'histoire des institutions françaises auront du mal à comprendre si les règles de l'édit de Saint-Germain de 1679, imposant la possession de la licence en droit aux juges, étaient ou non respectées dans les colonies et quelles différences il y avait entre le secrétariat d'État à la Marine et le Conseil de la Marine (dans le régime de la Polysynodie sous la Régence). Certains des Conseils supérieurs, comme celui de la Nouvelle France étudié par Serge Dauchy (dans la *Revue du Nord* en 2015), ne sont pas pris en compte, alors qu'ils ont rencontré les mêmes problèmes de recrutement des juges (en recourant d'abord à des non-juristes) que ceux des Antilles et des Mascareignes. L'article d'Éric Wenzel (dans la revue *Outre-Mers* en 2018), fondé sur les dossiers de trois cents magistrats des colonies sous l'Ancien Régime, est ignoré, alors qu'il fournit des éléments statistiques et comparés sur les rapports entre juristes et profanes du droit, comme sur la *créolisation* (c'est-à-dire la tendance à choisir les juges parmi des colons nés dans les colonies et parlant créole) de la magistrature, notamment aux Antilles.

On peut s'interroger aussi sur le caractère »global« de cette justice coloniale qui est au centre de la problématique de l'ouvrage: malgré la similitude institutionnelle créée par ces Conseils supérieurs et les circulations entre la métropole et les deux groupes d'îles (et parfois entre les îles à travers deux océans), chaque territoire a vécu sa propre histoire, faite de discontinuités (notamment du fait des guerres avec les Britanniques) et de spécificités dans le recrutement et la créolisation des magistrats. Si c'est le droit de la monarchie française qui s'applique partout, il s'est décliné de manière diverse en matière de régimes des personnes (avec différentes versions du Code noir) et des terres (avec des adaptations de la coutume de Paris au système des plantations, par exemple avec un régime particulier des *habitations* en Guadeloupe). Il nous semble que le droit et la justice dans le premier empire colonial français résultaient davantage d'un bricolage institutionnel et judiciaire (donnant lieu à un contentieux qu'il faudrait connaître plus systématiquement) que de l'extension programmée d'une culture juridique française.

■

Jean-Louis Halpérin

Divya Cherian

Law and Early Modern Empire: The View from Mughal India*

Negotiating Mughal Law is a methodologically innovative book that is a major intervention in the fields of early modern South Asian history, early modern legal history and Islamic law, and the history of the family. The book studies the idea and practice of law in Mughal and post-Mughal South Asia and makes a case for the emergence, in the course of the 17th century, of a »Mughal law«. By tracing the journey of legal forms and practices over three centuries in the region of Malwa in central India, which witnessed the rule of three different empires – the Mughals, the Marathas, and the British – Chatterjee makes a case for law as a vehicle of cosmopolitanism. This is an exciting proposition for a field that so far has largely focused on ›culture‹ – literature, music, dress – as the primary site for the study of early modern cosmopolitanism and the articulation and practice of being Persianate. So, was there a Mughal law and if yes, what was it? First, Chatterjee calls for a move away from imagining an »autonomous body of rules and procedures« and instead articulates a conception of law as a spectrum that extended from state policy to formal academic jurisprudence to more quotidian manuals and ordinary users (20). Chatterjee argues for an approach that does not limit law to institutions, rules, and norms alone. In doing so she builds on approaches to legal history, by now deeply rooted in historical scholarship, that emphasize the interplay between law and society and that see law as an arena of contest.[1] In this conception of law, ordinary folk and ›low-brow‹ specialists could and did shape legal change. The book builds upon Farhat Hasan's study of the Mughal state in the port cities of Surat and Cambay in the 17th century, which highlights the role of local society in shaping the Mughal state and adjudication of legal matters on the ground.[2] Chatterjee's intervention is distinguished by its reflexivity in both method and thought and by the broad and lush canvas that she paints from the vantage point of a single household.

Second, Chatterjee argues, law in Mughal India was not an eclectic mish-mash of different sources of law such as imperial grace, Islamic law, state law, *dharmashastric* (»Hindu«) law, and custom (*dastur, urf*), each with its own authorized experts and conceived of by subjects as distinct. Instead, a Mughal subject operated within an understanding of a systematic body of rules which varied based on regional and social location (39–40, 189). All of these different sources came together into a specific mix for each subject that varied by social and geographic place and over time. Chatterjee presents a picture of Mughal law in which there was no conscious awareness among subjects of multiple sources of law or of multiple legal orders. She notes, »There is no indication that they saw themselves as engaging with an eclectic system – Islamic law in parts and not in others – it appears that they saw it all as ›law‹« (40). This is a strong counterpoint to arguments for early modern legal pluralism – that is, for the coexistence of two or more legal orders in a single territory or community without a coordinating authority or a hierarchical relation between the legal orders. For Chatterjee, a range of sources – »royal and sub-royal orders, administrative conventions and rules, Islamic jurisprudence and local custom« (39–40) – informed the rules that constituted law in Mughal India. And through pre-colonial records this argument counters the persistent colonial representation of a »traditional« gulf between »Islamic law« and *dharmashastric* or »Hindu« law. It is also important for making clear that in the directly administered provinces of the Mughal Empire, as Farhat Hasan has also shown, »Hindu« subjects did not designate ›personal‹ areas such as inheritance and marriage as

* Nandini Chatterjee, Negotiating Mughal Law: A Family of Landlords Across Three Indian Empires, New York: Cambridge University Press 2020, 298 p., ISBN 978-1-108-62339-1

1 For some influential articulations of this approach, see E. P. Thompson, Whigs and Hunters: The Origins of the Black Act, New York 1975, 258–269; and Hendrik Hartog, Pigs and Positivism, in: Wisconsin Law Review (1985) 899–935, here 930.

2 Farhat Hasan, State and Locality in Mughal India: Power Relations in Western India, c. 1572–1730, Cambridge 2004.

subject only to *dharmashastric* law or customary usage and as being beyond the purview of the Mughal state or the *qazi*'s (judge's) office. This adds to the scholarship of Sumit Guha, Indrani Chatterjee, and Ramya Sreenivasan, which has demonstrated the interlinkages between family, household, and state in early modern South Asia.

Chatterjee further elaborates her picture of Mughal law with the contention that ›law‹ in Mughal India derived from a sense of ›right‹ – in both senses of the term (that is, as an entitlement as well as ›what should be‹). This sense of ›right‹ could vary and was derived from protagonists' own perspectives. The term in Mughal discourse that named this concept of rights and rightness, Chatterjee argues, was »*dastur*«, which according to her was »the Mughal name for Islamicate law« (236), though elsewhere in the book she also evokes it as an approximation of »custom«. By going far beyond telling us what Mughal law was not and by making this novel argument about law and legal culture in Mughal India, the book offers an exciting new historiographical intervention on precolonial South Asian law. In doing so, Chatterjee opens up a space for further exploration and debate.

Third, Chatterjee traces a field of legal power playing out between three points, each of which was a source of legal authority: royal grace; locally rooted, land-based power (the *zamindars*); and jurisprudential authority (scholars of Islamic law). *Zamindar* literally means ›landholder‹, and in Mughal administration, the term designated armed households in the countryside whose male members could hold state ranks and offices – such as local revenue collector (*chaudhri*), revenue record keeper (*qanungo*), and tax farmer (*ijaradar*) – in the Mughal administrative hierarchy. The *zamindar* family whose documents form the archive of this book was one of limited and local eminence, based in the town of Dhar in Malwa, a region that today forms part of the Indian state of Madhya Pradesh. They were descendants of a certain Mohan Das and over the centuries held each of the designations in local administration that I listed above. For this reason, documents recording their negotiations and re-negotiations over rights and entitlements with Mughal princes, nobles, and their regional representatives are an important body of sources for exploring the operation and formation of state power on the ground. These documents consist of state functionaries' orders, tax collection contracts, legal deeds, and declarations authorized by the local *qazi*. Through this exploration, Chatterjee shows the power wielded by landlordly operatives like the Das family, which was rooted not only in ›primordial‹ rights in land but also in their active and ongoing participation in revenue collection.

Islamic Law in Hindustan

Chatterjee calls on us to abandon a vision of a Mughal legal archive that derives, she argues, from the Ottoman context, one in which *qazis* copied out their rulings in running registers called *sijills*. Instead, she argues that in most parts of the Islamic world, including Mughal India, *qazis* did not »find it necessary to create and maintain registers, whether recording the adjudication of disputes or the activities of many other branches of government«. She goes on to speculate that the onus may have been on Mughal subjects – the recipients of legal decisions or transfers of rights – to maintain records of entitlements, transactions, and judgments (33). What seems to be at stake here is whether Islamic societies, and the practice of law within them, were marked by a consistent and generalized adherence by *qazis*, with or without state involvement, to a practice of maintaining a running record of their decisions and authorizations. Taken further, what may be at stake here – and what Chatterjee challenges – is the investment in finding recognizably ›Islamic‹ legal orders whose key elements date back to the first few centuries of Islam. The book is then not only about Mughal law but also a study of Islamic law.

The book is original in that it builds a bridge between the study of Islamic law in South Asia and histories of state, society, and politics. Chatterjee asserts that deviations in practice from an idealized Islamic legal practice in ›Islamicate‹ societies need not be explained or justified. Instead, she embraces Chibli Mallat's argument for the recognition of the multilayered nature of the sources of Islamic law and advocates for the scholarly situation of the legal practices of the Mughal Empire squarely within the history of Islamic law. She also sets out to overcome the neglect of sources in Persian and other South Asian languages for the study of Islamic law. By placing her findings in deep conversation with both Mughal and South Asian history on the one hand and the history of Islamic law on the other, Chatterjee has not only covered new historiographical ground, but she has also opened up a whole new field for further exploration and reflection in a way that breaches the ›borders‹ of Islamic law.

Reconstituting Archives

Chatterjee opens up a new way forward by making clear that the absence of a single, codified, top-down body of legal records in the Mughal Empire (and therefore the inability to refer to it) is not a shortcoming that legal historians must overcome. Mughal law can be found in fragments and in scattered collections. The book re-orients Mughal historians' vision to argue that the archives, plural, of the Mughal state were de-centralized and may be found in households of descendants of Mughal-era notables. By turning the gaze from the locality towards the Mughal court through these regional and localized documents (rather than taking the more usual court-to-provinces perspective), it is possible to arrive at a picture of law, legal culture, and legal practice in the Mughal Empire.

Today, the archive that Chatterjee knits together for this book lies scattered across three sites: New Delhi and Dhar (near Mandu in the Malwa region of today's Madhya Pradesh) in India as well as Kuwait. It is an archive of striving, in which the norms of the Mughal state, such as the separation of powers among offices on the ground, are maintained even as they do not impede the acquisition of power, wealth, and status by the landlord family at hand. Chatterjee is attentive to the processes of self-representation and curation that generated the records she studies and the archive she re-assembles: there is a degree of intentionality in the preservation and survival of the documents that are available today and the absence of others. She is mindful of the losses (of language, of authority, of the political orders in which the documents functioned), the dispersal through transactions and donations of many of the documents studied, and the re-organization along new logics in new collections. This aspect of Chatterjee's history can be read in conjunction with Manan Ahmed Asif's reflections on colonial dismemberings, erasures, selections, and reaggregations wrought upon South Asian documentary materials by the creation of colonial archives for the writing of ›modern‹ histories of India.[3] It can also be read alongside Mana Kia's evocation of communities of belonging woven around Persianate ethics, which too were disrupted by colonial and modern allocations of ethnicity and nation.[4] Where Asif and Kia trace the connections drawn within Persian-language histories and literary compendia to represent these pre-modern circuits of belonging, Chatterjee works to draw together all the documents of administration and law she can find pertaining to a single family. Chatterjee's account (in the book's Epilogue) of precisely how she came to remake this archive – through serendipity, training, and vision – is thrilling to read.

On the strength of this book, Chatterjee first makes a case for a turn towards household archives that lie in plain sight across South Asia and for reorienting our imagination of the process of record-keeping in Mughal India away from the center and towards the families that formed the state on the ground. Second, she argues for careful attention to the material, visual, generic, formal, linguistic, and formulaic qualities of archival documents in order to source-critically contextualize and analyze them (an elucidation of this innovative method can be found most fully in Chapter 4 of the book). Third, and most centrally, she makes an argument for the reaggregation of other dispersed archives and for deploying tools of digital history such as statistical analysis to fully discern the patterns and divergences that emerge within them. She concludes the book with an Epilogue that is a manifesto for »reconstructing multiple archives and working towards narrative coherence within each« (43) – a process she terms the »reconstitution of an archive« (226, 235). She suggests that by uniting all the documents, reading them closely, and arranging them chronologically and in relation to each other,

3 Manan Ahmed Asif, The Loss of Hindustan: The Invention of India, Cambridge/MA 2020.
4 Mana Kia, Persianate Selves: Memories of Place and Origin before Nationalism, Stanford/CA 2020.

it is possible to approach an understanding of the legal order as a whole as well as of its parts. This is an exciting proposition and one that raises questions: is it a re-making or a making (anew) of an archive? Does »archival reconstruction« (232) suggest a pre-existing, stable archive whose lost integrity can be restored by today's historians? Chatterjee's methodological call invites further reflection on the category ›archive‹, its meaning in early-modern South Asia / Mughal India, and shifts in the conception, uses, and logics of archiving in the colonial era. It also raises further methodological, affective, and ethical questions about working with families whose ancestors are the subjects of research.

Other Interventions

Chatterjee makes a number of other interlinked interventions in Mughal history and its methods that deserve mention: Chapters 2 and 3 revisit the very foundations of Mughal historiography, explaining genres and types of court and legal documents. *Zamindari*, *mansabdari*, *ijara*, tax collection: Chatterjee adds nuance to our understanding of each of these key institutions of the Mughal Empire to make clear the constant renewal and renegotiation they entailed, which in turn made room for the agency and enterprise of figures like the *kayasth* (scribal-caste) landlords that are her focus. Written documents were of immense significance in holding on to *zamindari* entitlements and to state offices that could be complementary to landholding. The elbowing out of rival claimants – including in this case agnatic kin and a Muslim branch of the Das family – that household memory and later narratives have erased are made visible in Chatterjee's account.

Negotiating Mughal Law is a welcome contribution to the study of law and early modern empire, offering a pre-colonial perspective to a field that is dominated by a focus on European colonial expansion. The book lays out the contours of a history of law for one of the most significant empires in world history, the Mughals. It crosses established fields and opens up new spaces within existing ones while also breaking new ground methodologically. Chatterjee has a clear and ebullient voice, and her writing manages to be both accessible and technical. Given its expansive interpretation of law, it has forged a path forward to bring the legal history of South Asia into conversation with studies of the region's economy, society, politics, and culture. It is an excellent work, one that will fuel new conversations for decades to come and which can enable comparative discussions within and beyond early modern South Asia.

■

Matilde Cazzola

Philanthropy to the Fore*

The global health crisis of the Covid-19 pandemic has recently reminded us of the prominent public role played by philanthropic individuals and foundations in providing emergency assistance and compensating for the shortcomings of the state in the face of complex challenges. However, the history of modern philanthropy in Western Europe, and more specifically Britain, dates back at least two hundred and fifty years and, as shown by the social historian Hugh Cunningham in his latest book *The Reputation of Philanthropy since 1750: Britain and Beyond*, it has been characterised by major transitions. Starting from the observation that philanthropic activities have attracted both

* Hugh Cunningham, The Reputation of Philanthropy since 1750: Britain and Beyond, Manchester: Manchester University Press 2020, VIII + 218 p., ISBN 978-1-5261-4638-0

»praises and abuses« (9), Cunningham investigates how public opinion in Britain from the mid-18th century to the present day, as conveyed by prominent individuals or the press, has responded to acts of giving. As the title of his book suggests, Cunningham retraces the history of British philanthropy through its fame and notoriety. Indeed, he argues that it is precisely because a heated national debate about its merits and faults took shape in Britain during the second half of the 18th century that the actual »birth« of philanthropy can be dated to that time (14).

As Cunningham points out, philanthropy is such an »indeterminate field« (21) of both theoretical investigation and practical activity that it is difficult to assess what was new about the philanthropic movement that emerged in the 1750s and what changed afterwards. This difficulty is not diminished, but rather enhanced, by the author's terminological focus on »philanthropy« as distinct from »charity«, »benevolence« and »voluntary work«, even though the meanings of these terms in primary sources often appear, as Cunningham himself recognises, to overlap. On top of that, philanthropy historically unfolded under extremely different guises, making use of a diverse set of methods, discourses and justifications. Private endowments and subscriptions went hand in hand with social service and public agitation; the progressive, liberal and sometimes even radical stances of philanthropists often overshadowed their conservative social purposes; and religious justifications and dissenting or evangelical criticisms of the Church establishment were used to convey schemes that were mostly secular in their social and political outcomes. Moreover, the reach of philanthropy was both parochial and global, »beginning at home« and then embracing the whole humankind in a »telescopic« stretching (107).

The chapters of the book reconstruct the history of British philanthropy and its reputation in both a thematic and chronological order. Chapter 1 looks at the ways in which historical narratives of philanthropy have been shaped differently by its recent scholarly definitions. Chapters 2 and 3 argue that the »genesis« (34) of philanthropy in Britain can be located in the mid-18th century, when the concept first became prominent in public discourse and the press. Traditionally, charity had existed, in England and elsewhere, as a private act of Christian benevolence expressed by means of donations. Beginning in the later 17th century, it acquired an »associated« dimension (14), with charitable individuals coming together and promoting schemes for the relief and employment of the poor. It was only from the 1750s onwards, however, that charity became explicitly »public and political« (26). This is because its »measure« (13) was no longer exclusively pecuniary, but instead coincided with the extent to which its proponents were able to have an impact on state institutions and policies. Chapters 4 and 5 focus on the prison reformer John Howard – the first Briton generally identified as a philanthropist to be worthy of the name – whose individual yet widely celebrated activism produced a long-standing connection between philanthropy, prison reform and the fight against crime during the 19th century. Chapter 6 examines British views of philanthropy during the French Revolution and the war with France, when the revolutionary connection between philanthropy and universal love for mankind clashed with the national need for loyalty and patriotism in times of war. Chapters 7 and 8 investigate philanthropy and its reputation in the middle decades of the 19th century. Between the 1820s and the 1840s, it became closely linked to the evangelical crusade for the abolition of slavery and concerns for the »protection« of indigenous peoples in settler colonies. However, from the mid-Victorian age, this imperial and global philanthropy was associated with neglect for the poor and the working classes at home, becoming the target of bitter criticism. Finally, chapters 9 and 10 look at how, while at the turn of the 20th century philanthropic activities were understood as different to state intervention, it was the crisis of public social policies in the last decades of the century that ushered in a »new« neoliberal philanthropy (176).

Although since the 20th century charitable initiatives have tended to be seen as an alternative to the welfare state, works such as Cunningham's show that philanthropy, by bringing social issues to the fore of national politics, represented a path towards it. While scholars do not always agree on what the »golden age« of philanthropy was (14–16), one can identify its high point between the later 18th century and the second half of the 19th century. During this period, it no longer aimed at saving the donor's soul, but instead focused on improving the order and well-being of society both at home and in the wider Empire, thereby becoming indistinguishable from social reform in both the domestic and the imperial spheres. After reading Cunningham's book, legal historians might wonder how the reputation of philanthropy historically influenced the breadth of public space it was granted and to what extent it became a partner of the state in developing social policies and prompting pieces of legislation. Between the 1790s and the later 19th century, philanthropists committed to solving the problems of vagrancy and crime offered a helping hand to police reformers (Chapters 4 and 5); as agitators both in and outside Parliament, they worked towards the abolition of the slave trade and slavery, and actively participated in political and economic debates about the reform of the Poor Laws (Chapter 7); meanwhile, as prison reformers and critics of capital punishment, they solicited the establishment of government inspectorates and royal commissions (77–79). Even those philanthropists who criticised state intervention for undermining individual effort and self-help – such as the members of the Charity Organisation Society, established in 1869 – ended up contributing their casework on poverty to state departments as public social workers (173).

More generally, between the 18th and 19th centuries, philanthropy in Britain played a crucial role in promoting »patient research and inductive reasoning«, as well as applying the outcomes to the »solution of problems that straddled the boundaries between the social, the political and the economic« (81). This was bequeathed to the social policymaking of the late 19th and 20th centuries as an enduring legacy. From John Howard onwards, various philanthropists and philanthropic associations adopted the methods of inspection and monitoring; collected statistical information and issued surveys and reports; supported and implemented technological improvements; and built webs of intelligence. This philanthropic approach to social inquiry can be detected behind the letter of epoch-making statutory enactments such as the New Poor Law of 1834. Conversely, a legal-historical focus on philanthropy can show how moral preoccupations and religious apprehensions were intertwined with social, political and economic concerns in the making of the law. This represents a potentially productive challenge to legal historians: how to take seriously the philanthropic and humanitarian motives of historical actors (alongside their criticisms of the state, the Church and colonial establishments) without promoting a »recuperative« analysis of state and imperial policies. From this perspective, the law itself emerges, from time to time, as historically prompted by actors who were neither institutional nor strictly legal, and who could be more aptly described as »concerned citizens« who, while marking the autonomy of civil society from the state through their private and voluntary philanthropic activities, turned civil society into a field in which to develop and publicly promote state policies.

■

Alfons Bora

Unstructured Diversity*

The keyword »diversity« refers to a very broad range of topics. These include, for example, issues of civil status (with implications for labor law); questions of political equality; demands for the implementation of civil and equality rights with regard to race, gender, skin color, ethnic origin, age, disability, or religion; and debates about cultural richness. The latter in turn comprise issues of normative diversity in general and legal plurality in particular, such as are being discussed in the field of

* Christina Brauner, Antje Flüchter (eds.), Recht und Diversität. Lokale Konstellationen und globale Perspektiven von der Frühen Neuzeit bis zur Gegenwart, Bochum: Transcript 2020, 374 p., ISBN 978-3-8376-5417-2

sociology of law under the heading of »legal pluralism« and linked to the concept of »multinormativity« by legal historians.

The volume under review is primarily concerned with questions of normative and legal plurality, although individual contributions also address other topics. It contains eight chapters and a detailed introduction by Christina Brauner, who presents the conceptual and systematic framework of the volume. Before devoting some remarks to this concept, the individual contributions, which follow a predominantly historical orientation, will be introduced very briefly.

Anna Dönecke analyzes processes of law and power formation in French and Dutch trading companies of the 18th century. In this context, legal diversity was more than a mere co-existence of different normative systems; rather, these systems and institutions were put into relation to one another by comparative methods. In the course of these processes, in legal practice the various legal systems became increasingly intertwined.

Andreas Becker uses the example of the Saami in central Sweden in the 17th and 18th centuries to show the importance of law for ordering and categorization the population.

Ninja Bumann describes how, in the 19th century, the Habsburg administration in occupied Bosnia-Herzegovina made use of the local Sharia jurisdiction to incorporate existing legal and power structures into their own system of imperial and colonial authority.

Nina Dethloff shows how the plurality of law plays out in the process of globalization. Using the example of marriage and family law, she examines the hybridization of legal systems that comes about when different legal sources interact. Against this background, she then investigates how, in situations of rich cultural diversity, the rules of both conflict of laws and substantive law ensure coherence, transparency, information, and access to legal institutions, remedies etc.

Fabian Fechner describes the local legal practices of the Jesuit order in India and Peru, pointing out the special role of unwritten law in the face of multi-layered particularisms in the order's provinces. These provinces made use of a reasonably strong local legal culture, which was oral and based more on participatory structures, to evade central regulation by Rome.

Cornelia Aust writes about the legal categorization of the Jewish population in the Polish partition territories under Prussian rule during the late 18th century. She shows the role played by synchronic and diachronic legal comparisons not only in the colonization of non-European territories, but also and very specifically in establishing and stabilizing Prussian central power in the newly acquired territories.

Antje Flüchter examines the significance of comparative practices for the assessment of foreign law by travelers in pre-modern contact zones in Asia. People were aware of the existing cultural diversity, but it was not considered a challenge to rulers or the law; rather, it was compared and interpreted in concrete interactions and then integrated into one's own perspective.

Hanna Sonkajärvi uses insolvency cases and commercial law practices in nineteenth-century Brazil to highlight the relevance of conventions which (in Max Weber's terms) based their legal validity on the rather general – but in practice very palpable – disapproval that ensued if they were broken. The courts in the cases investigated in this chapter followed trade customs, which demonstrated a stronger sense of continuity than laws enacted by the state.

These contributions are consistently very interesting and instructive. They impress by offering a wealth of knowledge, detail, and thoroughness, and provide vivid pictures of the areas of life and the periods studied, thus enabling the kind of experience that makes interdisciplinary contacts so fruitful.

However, in contrast to the strong overall impression given by the individual contributions, the efforts to systematize this rich material – at least from an external disciplinary perspective – fail to convince.

This is mainly due to the very sparse conceptual differentiation at the beginning. The introduction identifies two central questions: first, how society deals with diversity in law, and second, how law responds to diversity in society. Four perspectives of inquiry are linked to these rather obvious questions. The first of these employs a method sometime used in ethnolinguistics: it differentiates between »emic« and »etic«, i. e. between a participatory approach and that of an observer. This is followed by a distinction between two ways of talking about law. The second perspective considers the diversity of law as an expression of differentiated power relations in a society. The third offers a look at the different forms and ways in which the law constructs social differentiations. The fourth perspective examines social practices of comparison.

Two of these four perspectives recognizably map the two central questions addressed above, but no such connection is visible in the first and fourth perspectives. Their conceptual, systematic significance is difficult to discern, especially since – for example in the case of emic / etic – fairly obvious references to familiar methodological differentiations are missing (such as Identity Theory versus Difference Theory, or participation versus observation). Finally, the perspective of comparison is obviously due to the volume's origin in the Bielefeld Collaborative Research Center »Practices of Comparison / Praktiken des Vergleichens« and as such is quite plausible. However, little is gained by the term. Comparison as a method can lead either to the recognition of similarities or to the identification of differences between objects of reality. Accordingly, it fulfills at least two very different functions, which would have to be separated in the analysis and related to the object at hand in order to facilitate understanding.

In general, the reader is irritated not only by a certain conceptual generosity, but also by the structure of both the introduction and the volume as a whole. The presentation of the individual contributions and their assignment to the four thematic complexes do not correspond in any way to the structure of the volume: it begins with the third perspective, followed by the second and fourth, and concludes with the first perspective. If such discontinuity is already disconcerting to the reader, this sensation is only increased by the way the introduction assigns the individual contributions, which deviates significantly from the structure of the volume. These are by no means cosmetic problems. Rather, these multiple inconsistencies render the promised systematics obsolete, prevent the understanding of the context – beyond the very successful individual contributions – and ultimately thwarts any possible gain in knowledge that could be achieved from this compilation.

Finally, given the obvious interdisciplinary nature of the topic, it must come as a surprise that the contact between various scholarly perspectives appears less intensive than it could have been. In other words, the volume would have benefited from more – and, above all, more thorough – interdisciplinarity and an explicit integration of neighboring sciences. It is interesting to note that even specific legal questions and insights are barely given any room; the exception – Dethloff's contribution – and a few sparse words in the introduction only serve to emphasize this observation. This is even more true in relation to the social sciences. Explicit references to sociology of law, for example, are largely absent, with the exception of the contributions by Dethloff and Sonkajärvi. This is all the more surprising, given that sociology of law has addressed the idea of legal plurality since the days of Eugen Ehrlich (1913); has used the term explicitly since it was introduced in John Griffith's 1986 essay; and has incorporated situations outside Europe into its observations from early on, for example in the work of Boaventura de Sousa Santos or, more recently, in extensive studies such as the one on a »global Bukovina« (Gunther Teubner et al.). All this could have provided fertile ground for discussions about the question pursued in this volume.

The overall impression is thus ambivalent. To summarize the above-mentioned findings: this is a volume that is informative in its historical details, and in this respect it is well worth reading. However, it leaves the reader perplexed and wondering what overarching systematic significance these exciting narratives actually have.

■

Karl Härter

Eine Hauptstadt weiblicher Verbrechen? Kriminalität und Geschlecht im frühneuzeitlichen Frankfurt*

Die ausgezeichnete Studie von Jeannette Kamp untersucht den Zusammenhang zwischen weiblicher Kriminalität, Strafjustiz und Stadt für die frühneuzeitliche Reichsstadt Frankfurt am Main. Damit reiht sie sich ein in aktuelle historische Forschungen zu Kriminalität und Geschlecht in Städten, die insbesondere den Anteil von Frauen an der strafgerichtlich verfolgten Kriminalität untersuchen. Zentral ist folglich die Frage, ob aus dem städtischen Kontext eine eher niedrige weibliche Kriminalitätsrate – im frühneuzeitlichen Frankfurt rund 22 Prozent – und typische Muster weiblicher Delinquenz resultierten, die durch unterschiedliche sozioökonomische, rechtliche und institutionelle Bedingungen der vormodernen Stadt geprägt waren. Auf der Basis einer hervorragenden Kenntnis der internationalen Forschungsdiskussion wie der spezifischeren stadtgeschichtlichen Literatur präsentiert Jeannette Kamp ein überzeugendes Forschungsdesign, das etablierte Konzepte und Methoden der historischen Kriminalitäts- und Genderforschung nutzt: Kriminalität wird als Ergebnis sozioökonomischer Faktoren, Normen, Diskurse und konkreter Zuschreibungsprozesse konzipiert und die korrespondierenden *gender patterns* herausgearbeitet. Dies wird mit einem geschlechter- und sozialgeschichtlichen Ansatz verknüpft, der Frauen nicht nur als »Opfer« patriarchalischer Strafjustiz begreift, sondern auch nach der *legal agency* von Frauen und Optionen / Strategien von Justiznutzung fragt. Im Unterschied zu älteren Studien misst die Autorin aber auch den normativen und institutionellen Rahmenbedingungen eine hohe Bedeutung bei, legt einen weiten historischen Begriff von Strafrecht (inklusive der kommunalen Ordnungsgesetze und der juridischen Diskurse) zugrunde und konzipiert Strafjustiz als Teil eines Systems formeller und informeller Sozialkontrolle der vormodernen Stadt. Folgerichtig wertet Jeannette Kamp daher nicht nur die reichhaltig überlieferten Kriminalakten (*Criminalia*) der vom Rat ausgeübten höheren Strafgerichtsbarkeit aus, sondern bezieht auch Quellen der untergeordneten Justizinstitutionen (Sendamt / Konsistorium) und der städtischen Verwaltung mit ein. Die Quellen werden sehr reflektiert und kritisch mit einer quantifizierenden Methodik im Hinblick auf generelle und langfristige Wandlungsprozesse ausgewertet und mit qualitativen Analysen überzeugend ausgewählter Fallbeispiele verknüpft.

Die Fallstudie ist systematisch aufgebaut und stringent durchgeführt: Auf die Forschungsstand, Fragestellungen, Quellen, Methoden und Vorgehen darlegende Einleitung folgt eine kenntnisreiche Darstellung der grundlegenden Strukturen von Strafrecht, Justiz / Verwaltung und des sozioökonomischen Gefüges der frühneuzeitlichen Reichsstadt (Kapitel 2). Daran schließt sich eine erste allgemeine empirische Analyse der Kriminalitätsmuster an (Kapitel 3), die die »gendered patterns of crime« im zeitlichen Verlauf des 17. und 18. Jahrhunderts herausarbeitet. Diese wird in drei weiteren empirischen Kapiteln vertieft, die Formen weiblicher Devianz / Kriminalität für die charakteristischen Bereiche von Eigentumsdelinquenz und »offenem Haus« (Kapitel 4), Ehe und Sexualität (Kapitel 5) und (illegitimer) Mobilität / Migration untersuchen. Jeannette Kamp arbeitet anhand der Sozialprofile der »Täterinnen« den sozioökonomischen Kontext weiblicher Kriminalität im urbanen Raum bestechend heraus und belegt, dass die von unterschiedlichen Institutionen verfolgten und sanktionierten »Verbrechen« aus den prekären Lebensumständen und den Überlebensstrategien von Frauen resultierten. Diese waren jedenfalls im

* Jeannette Kamp, Crime, Gender and Social Control in Early Modern Frankfurt am Main (Crime and City in History 3), Leiden / Boston: Brill 2020, 335 S., ISBN 978-90-04-38844-4

frühneuzeitlichen Frankfurt durch die Zugehörigkeit zu unteren sozialen Schichten, eine hohe Mobilität und ein eher jüngeres Lebensalter unverheirateter Frauen, aber auch durch (begrenzte) Unabhängigkeit und Selbständigkeit im Sinne geringerer Einbindung in soziale-familiäre Netzwerke geprägt: »The social profile of female offenders strengthens the observation that women's crimes in early modern Frankfurt were to a large degree shaped by their precarious socio-economic position« (278). Dabei spielten gerade hinsichtlich Arbeitsmigration und Mobilität Geschlechterstereotypen eine wichtige Rolle. Im Gegensatz zur erwünschten Arbeitsmigration von Gesellen wurde weibliche Mobilität mit sexueller Devianz, Ungehorsam und Streben nach Unabhängigkeit (von Kontrolle) assoziiert und als Bedrohung der patriarchalich-christlichen Ordnung wahrgenommen bzw. verfolgt. Dies gilt ebenso für Eigentumsdelikte im »offenen Haus« bzw. Haushalten der Reichsstadt, die insbesondere Dienstbotinnen zugeschrieben wurden.

Bei den »moral« bzw. »sexual offences« belegt die Autorin ebenfalls, dass über Geschlechterstereotypen und Verfolgung hinaus sowohl auf Seiten der Obrigkeit als auch der betroffenen unverheirateten Frauen (mit illegitimen Kindern) »sozialpolitische« und finanzielle Gründe sowie die Justiznutzungsstrategien und außergerichtliche Konfliktregulierung eine wesentliche Rolle spielten und eine vergleichsweise hohe weibliche Kriminalitätsrate bedingten: »the high number of cases of illegitimacy brought before the *Konsistorium* were the result of both strict control by the authorities, who tried to prevent any type of extrajudicial settlements, and the uses of justice by offenders themselves« (202). Frauen konnten sogar zur Selbstanzeige greifen, um über das Strafverfahren Druck auf Männer auszuüben und dadurch finanzielle Kompensationen für gebrochene Eheversprechen oder Unterhalt für außereheliche Kinder zu erwirken. Abgewogen wertet Jeannette Kamp dies jedoch nicht als »Bündnis«, sondern partielle Interessensidentität von Obrigkeit und Frauen, wobei letztere Justiz im Rahmen ihrer »legal agency« nutzten: »women found ways to accommodate the patriarchal ideologies and adapt them to their own needs, and instrumentally used the interest of the authorities that sought to maintain this order« (283), so das Fazit.

Jeannette Kamp vermeidet folglich dichotomische Deutungen und betont Verschränkung und Zusammenspiel von formeller und informeller Sozialkontrolle bzw. Strafjustiz und außergerichtlichen, infrajustiziellen Praktiken sowie von Strafe und Konfliktregulierung. Als ein wichtiges Ergebnis – das Frankfurt auch von anderen europäischen Städten unterscheidet – hebt die Autorin Pluralität, funktionale Differenzierung und Komplementarität der Institutionen der höheren und niederen Strafgerichtsbarkeit hervor. Sie bildeten nicht nur eine wesentliche Bedingung der »gegenderten« Zuschreibung und Verfolgung devianten bzw. kriminellen Verhaltens, sondern auch der infrajustiziellen Regulierung von Konflikten und der *agency* bzw. Justiznutzung von Frauen (und Männern). Überzeugend erklärt Jeannette Kamp Muster und Wandlungsprozesse von Geschlecht und Kriminalität in Frankfurt nicht allein aus Unterschieden von Stadt und Land, sondern als Produkt einer starken Verschränkung einer funktional differenzierten Justiz mit informeller Kontrolle im Rahmen der patriarchalischen Haushalte, die zutreffend als »integral part in the mechanism of control to maintain public order« (282) charakterisiert werden.

In der abschließenden vergleichenden Einbettung der Ergebnisse und Deutungen (Kapitel 7) kann Jeannette Kamp zahlreiche Übereinstimmungen Frankfurts mit anderen Städten aufzeigen, die charakteristische Geschlechterstereotypen männlicher und weiblicher Devianz / Kriminalität, den prekären, verwundbaren sozialen Status, aber auch Justiznutzung und (limitierte) *legal agency* von Frauen betreffen. Den in Frankfurt vergleichsweise niedrigeren Anteil weiblicher Kriminalität in den meisten (aber keineswegs allen) Deliktbereichen deutet die Autorin im Unterschied zu anderen Städten bzw. Studien nicht nur als Ergebnis der Exklusion von Frauen aus dem öffentlichen Leben und ihrer Beschränkung auf die »private Sphäre« (die das Haus nicht war). Zutreffend sieht sie vielmehr eine wesentliche Differenz in den stärker verdichteten wie differenzierteren Formen strafrechtlicher und informeller Sozialkontrolle: »societies with stronger institutions exercising (informal) social control portray different and lower patterns of female criminality« (277).

Allerdings bleibt der Vergleich teilweise punktuell und auf die jeweiligen empirischen Kapitel beschränkt, in denen auf der Basis der Forschungsliteratur Amsterdam und London sowie gelegentlich einzelne Städte im frühneuzeitlichen Reich als Beispiele herangezogen werden. Im Fazit weist

Jeannette Kamp auch bei den »future pespectives« (284 f.) darauf hin, dass es letztlich an einer Typologie mangelt, die einen systematischeren und allgemeineren Vergleich von Kriminalität, Geschlecht und Sozialkontrolle in der frühneuzeitlichen (europäischen) Stadt erlaubt hätte. Bei den betonten institutionellen Unterschieden der Systeme von Strafjustiz und sozialer Kontrolle hätte zudem die für die Reichsstadt Frankfurt wichtige verfassungsrechtlich-politische Dimension (Rolle des Rates, des Patriziats, Konflikte in der Bürgerschaft) ausführlicher diskutiert werden können. Insgesamt bietet die luzide und klar formulierte Fallstudie jedoch auf einer elaborierten Methodik beruhende, reichhaltige empirische Ergebnisse, die zu überzeugenden Analysen und Deutungen verdichtet werden. Insbesondere die Herausarbeitung der funktionalen Differenzierung des Systems der Strafjustiz und seiner Verschränkung mit informeller Sozialkontrolle, die auch Justiznutzung und *legal agency* von Frauen ermöglichten, bietet für eine an Geschlecht und Justiz interessierte Rechtsgeschichte weiterführende konzeptionelle Anregungen.

■

Peter Collin

Spurensuche in der Handelsjustiz*

Die Geschichte der deutschen Handelsgerichtsbarkeit war bislang ein Stiefkind der justizhistorischen Forschung. Wer sich informieren wollte, musste in der Hauptsache auf mehr als 100 Jahre alte Arbeiten zurückgreifen. An neuerer Forschung ist im Wesentlichen nur ein Abschnitt in Schuberts Geschichte des Gerichtsverfassungsgesetzes[1] zu nennen.[2] Hinzu kommen die, allerdings viel weniger wahrnehmbare und auch wahrgenommene, ungedruckte Dissertation von Dorothea Schön zu den rheinischen Handelsgerichten, welche auf einer Vielzahl archivalischer Quellen fußt[3] und – zeitgleich mit der hier besprochenen Arbeit – die Dissertation von Sebastian Jacob,[4] die sich allerdings, was das hier interessierende 19. Jahrhundert betrifft, auf die gesamtdeutschen Kodifikationsbemühungen konzentriert und das (lange maßgebliche) Recht der Einzelstaaten eher am Rande behandelt.

Für dieses Defizit gibt es gute Gründe. Der erste ist, dass eine eigenständige Handelsgerichtsbarkeit seit 1877 nicht mehr existiert und damit auch kein heute bestehender Gerichtszweig, der Veranlassung gibt, ihn historisch zurückzuverfolgen. Der zweite Grund ist, dass es nie eine einheitliche Handelsgerichtsbarkeit gab, sondern immer nur auf einzelne Territorien und Städte bezogene und zum Teil relativ kurzlebige Regelungen; eine Geschichte »der« deutschen Handelsgerichtsbarkeit zu schreiben, erscheint daher recht mühsam.

Schon allein aus diesen Gründen ist es ein großes Verdienst, dass sich Thomas Vogl in seiner von Phillip Hellwege betreuten Dissertation dem Thema zugewendet hat – wenn auch mit einem spezifischen Fokus. Vogl will den Einfluss des französischen Rechts nachweisen. Genau genommen geht es dabei nicht um das gesamte Recht der Handelsgerichtsbarkeit, sondern um jene Regeln, die Besetzung, Zuständigkeit und bestimmte Verfahrensaspekte regulierten. Die Vorgehensweise stellt sich dann vereinfacht gesehen so dar, dass zuerst das französische Recht dargestellt wird und

* Thomas Vogl, Der Einfluss des französischen Rechts auf die Entwicklung der Handelsgerichtsbarkeit in Deutschland im 19. Jahrhundert, Berlin: Duncker & Humblot 2021, 311 S., ISBN 987-3-428-18128-5

1 Werner Schubert, Die deutsche Gerichtsverfassung (1869–1877), Frankfurt am Main 1981.

2 In einem weiteren Sinne zum Themenfeld gehört noch, allerdings ohne Bezug zur territorialstaatlichen Handelsgerichtsbarkeit, Sabine Winkler, Das Bundes- und spätere Reichsoberhandelsgericht, Paderborn 2001.

3 Dorothea Schön, Die Handelsgerichtsbarkeit im 19. Jahrhundert unter besonderer Berücksichtigung des Rheinlands, Bonn 1999.

4 Sebastian Jacob, Handelsgerichtsbarkeit. Zur Entstehung des Fachrichtertums zwischen Laienexpertise, Verfahrensförmlichkeit und staatlichem Verfahrensmonopol und ihr Einfluss auf die moderne KfH, Baden-Baden 2021.

schließlich einzelne Handelsgerichtsordnungen oder andere Prozessbestimmungen mit den französischen Regeln verglichen werden, oder genauer: Geprüft wird, inwiefern sich in den deutschen Bestimmungen französisches Recht wiederfindet.

Diese Vorgehensweise hat Vor- und Nachteile. Die Vorteile liegen auf der Hand. Die Materialfülle wird derart eingegrenzt und geordnet, dass der Stoff gut portioniert und übersichtlich dargestellt werden kann. Die Konzentration auf bestimmte Regelungselemente erlaubt einen gut nachvollziehbaren Vergleich und relativ klare Aussagen, was Unterschiede und Gemeinsamkeiten betrifft. Allerdings gibt es auch gravierende Nachteile. Wer sich mit derart festgeschraubten Suchscheinwerfern durch die Quellen bewegt, verzichtet von vornherein auf die Untersuchung solcher Problemfelder, die für die Rechtsgeschichte der Handelsgerichtsbarkeit von vitalem Interesse sein könnten – um welche es sich dabei handelt, soll unten näher ausgeführt werden. Zudem ist der Preis der systematischen Abarbeitung der immer gleichen Fragen (im Rahmen einer sehr tiefgestaffelten Gliederung) eine gewisse Eintönigkeit der Darstellung, verstärkt durch den zuweilen durchschimmernden Gutachtenstil.

Dennoch sind die Erkenntnisgewinne erheblich. Dabei ist zu berücksichtigen, dass die vom Autor zugrunde gelegten Untersuchungsachsen – Besetzung, Zuständigkeit und Verfahren – weite und wichtige Teile der rechtlichen Verfassung der Handelsgerichtsbarkeit abdecken. Hinzu kommt, dass die Untersuchung chronologisch umfassend angelegt ist. Denn das erste umfassende Sachkapitel befasst sich mit der Ausgangslage, also dem Rechtszustand vor der Rezeption französischen Rechts. Was hier geboten wird, ist eine teilweise bis ins 16. Jahrhundert zurückgehende systematische Darstellung der Rechtsentwicklung in zehn deutschen Städten. Das hört sich nach wenig an – allerdings nur, wenn man nicht berücksichtigt, dass die Handelsgerichtsbarkeit kein flächendeckend vorhandener Bestandteil der deutschen Gerichtslandschaft war, sondern sich auf die bedeutenden Handelszentren konzentrierte. Was die Charakteristika dieser Handelsgerichtsbarkeit betrifft, ist zunächst das Fehlen einheitlicher Muster zu betonen, vor allem auch im Hinblick auf die Zuständigkeit (oft limitierte Zuständigkeit für bestimmte Wirtschaftsbereiche). Gemeinsam ist den Handelsgerichtsordnungen, dass das Verfahren auf Schnelligkeit ausgerichtet war. Bemerkenswert sind sich in weiten Teilen ähnelnde Besetzungsmodi: Die Handelsgerichte waren niemals autonome Gerichte der Kaufmannschaft, sondern fest in die ständisch-städtischen Machtstrukturen integriert, überall waren neben den Kaufleuten Stadträte vertreten. Als historisches Vorbild für eine nichtstaatliche Selbstregulierung der Wirtschaft, als Referenzfolie justizieller Manifestation von »lex mercatoria« eignen sie sich daher nur eingeschränkt.

Vor diesem Hintergrund treten die Unterschiede zur französischen Gesetzgebung deutlich hervor. Die französischen Handelsgerichte waren nur mit Kaufleuten besetzt. Sie waren umfassend für Handelssachen zuständig und losgelöst von der städtischen Verwaltung. Nur in Orientierung auf ein schnelles Verfahren gibt es Gemeinsamkeiten, aber das dürfte sich auch aus der Natur der Sache ergeben haben.

Die Übernahme (bzw. Berücksichtigung) französischen Rechts begann in den linksrheinischen Departments, dauerhaft mit der Einführung des *Code de commerce* 1809. Dies waren auch die einzigen Gebiete, in welche die französische Handelsgerichtsbarkeit (nahezu) in Reinform eingepflanzt wurde. In allen anderen Territorien kann eigentlich nicht von einer Rezeption des französischen Rechts, sondern nur von einer – zuweilen mittelbaren – Übernahme einzelner französisch-rechtlicher Regelungselemente gesprochen werden. Ein Verdienst von Vogls Arbeit ist es, in akribischer Spurensuche diesen Einflussfaktoren nachgegangen zu sein. Hierzu untersucht er neben den Rheinprovinzen die Gesetzgebung der Modellstaaten (Westfalen, Frankfurt am Main, Berg), Norddeutschlands, Bayerns und Altpreußens. Unabhängig von der Frage nach dem Einfluss des französischen Rechts liegt hiermit erstmals eine umfassende systematische Darstellung der Handelsgerichtsbarkeit vor 1877 vor und damit auch eine solide Grundlage für künftige Forschung.

Als allgemeiner Befund kann für die Zeit bis 1877 ein Trend weg von der einzelstädtischen und hin zur territorialstaatlichen Regelung konstatiert werden (auch wenn dies in Bayern bis 1869 dauerte). Nahezu überall findet sich ein grundlegender Unterschied zum französischen Recht: kein reines Kaufmannsgericht, sondern eine gemischte Besetzung mit Berufsrichtern und Kaufleuten. Hier also setzte sich das französische Vorbild in keiner Weise durch. (Am Rande: Dass das reine Kaufmannsgericht in der rechtspolitischen Diskussion weiterhin stark präsent blieb – was auch unsere heutige Wahrnehmung prägt –, dürfte an der starken Präsenz der rheinischen Juristen gelegen haben.) Ansonsten differierte der französische Einfluss zwischen nahezu Null in Altpreußen und sehr stark z. B. in Hamburg. Als ein wichtiger Impuls des französischen Rechts ist jedoch zu werten, dass das Verfahrensrecht der Handelsgerichte zunehmend als Zivilverfahrensrecht (mit Modifikationen) angesehen wurde und somit separate Verfahrensordnungen mehr und mehr der Vergangenheit angehörten.

Separate Handelsgerichte sollten eigentlich auch zur Justizstruktur des Deutschen Reichs gehören. So war es auch im Entwurf des Gerichtsverfassungsgesetzes vorgesehen. Dass diesem Vorhaben in der Justizkommission des Reichstags energischer Widerstand entgegengesetzt wurde, war daher in gewisser Hinsicht eine Überraschung. Bemerkenswert ist hierbei, dass Einwände grundsätzlicher Art ins Feld gebracht wurden, die in der Arbeit Vogls (die sich weitgehend auf die Darstellung des positiven Rechts und den Abgleich von Normen konzentriert hatte) bisher keine große Rolle gespielt hatten. Zwei tragende Argumente lauteten: Mit der Kodifikation des materiellen Handelsrechts (ADHGB 1869) bedürfe es keines Rückgriffs auf das normative Wissen der Kaufleute mehr. Und es liege nicht im Geist der Zeit, bestimmte Gruppen durch Einrichtung einer Art ständischer Gerichtsbarkeit zu privilegieren. In welchem Maße hier politische oder juristische Vorstellungen eine Rolle spielten, kann nicht mehr ganz nachvollzogen werden. Und in der Tat verlaufen ja auch die politischen Fronten nicht eindeutig. So konnten aus liberaler Sicht Handelsgerichte geboten sein, um der Eigenlogik der Wirtschaft hinreichend Raum zu verschaffen. Ebenso liberaler Natur waren aber auch die Vorbehalte gegen das unzweifelhaft korporative Element dieser Handelsgerichtsbarkeit. Am Ende kam es jedenfalls zu dem noch heute bestehenden Kompromiss in Form der Kammern für Handelssachen bei den Landgerichten. Französischer Einfluss findet sich dabei nur noch in Spurenelementen.

Die Arbeit Vogls zeichnet sich durch eine immense Reichhaltigkeit aus, was die Aufarbeitung des Normenmaterials betrifft. Wer sich in Zukunft mit der Geschichte der Handelsgerichtsbarkeit befasst und wissen will, wo, wann, welches Recht mit welchen Inhalten galt, für den wird das Buch das maßgebliche Referenzwerk sein. Im Hinblick auf die Frage nach den Gründen und Kontexten von Rechtsentwicklungen bleibt die Arbeit etliche Antworten schuldig, die gar nicht so weit über den Rahmen von Vogls Untersuchungsprogramm hinausgehen. Denn auch die Frage nach dem Einfluss des französischen Rechts stellt sich ja als Frage nach dem Warum. Natürlich war Frankreich – aufgrund seiner politischen Dominanz Anfang des 19. Jahrhunderts und aufgrund seines Kodifikationsvorsprungs – das omnipräsente Modell. Die weitere Entwicklung in Deutschland war aber stark beeinflusst durch rechtspolitische Grundstimmungen (auf die Vogl nur auf wenigen Seiten, nämlich in Teil 4. A., eingeht), durch das Verhältnis von Prozessrecht und materiellem (kodifiziertem und Gewohnheits-)Recht und durch das Vorhandensein – jedenfalls ansatzweiser – funktionaler Äquivalente in Form von Handelsschiedsgerichten.[5] Als Fazit kann also festgehalten werden: eine Arbeit, die sich durch Selbstbeschränkung in die Lage versetzt, wichtige Fragen umfassend und seriös zu beantworten, aber noch viel Raum lässt für grundfragenorientierte und kontextbezogene Forschung.

■

5 Siehe dazu Jens Gal, Die Renaissance der (Handels-)Schiedsgerichtsbarkeit im 19. Jahrhundert als Ausdruck regulierter Selbstregulierung?, in: Peter Collin (Hg.), Justice without the State within the State. Judicial Self-Regulation in the Past and Present, Frankfurt am Main 2016, 157–184, 166 f.

Christian Boulanger

Private Law Theory at the Intersection of Legal Scholarship and Sociology*

Although there is certainly no lack of literature on the intellectual history of German legal thinking nor (to a lesser extent) on the history of sociological theory, little research exists that looks at the co-development of these disciplines from the perspective of the history of theory. Doris Schweitzer's habilitation provides a much-needed contribution to this field of research. The main title of her book, »Juridical Sociologies«, expresses the focus of the study on the question »how and in what form the discovery of society in 19th-century German private law has influenced the emerging discipline of sociology« (19). While the author is a sociologist (who also holds a law degree), and the book is written for a sociological audience, it nevertheless has the potential to stimulate productive debates between sociology, legal theory, and legal history.

Schweitzer starts from the observation that contemporary German sociology is not interested in the law. Despite law's enormous significance in social life, the sociology of law plays almost no role in sociological teaching and research, even less than in law schools, where there is a token presence in the curriculum. This is even more surprising given that law plays a central role in the work of scholars who today are considered pivotal in defining both the scope and the content of the emerging discipline. Once established, sociology lost its interest in the law. Why is that? Schweitzer argues that we need to look at the way this relationship was, on the one hand, problematized both in 19th-century private law theory and in the early 20th-century legal-methodological debates, and on the other, in the early sociologies around the turn of the century. She rejects Luhmann's view that the positivization of law was the crucial factor in creating the (semantically based) division between »law« and other subsystems of society. Instead, she opts for a theoretically much more fluid and open heuristic framework that integrates concepts from the history of science and makes use of Foucauldian theory. Using Hans-Jörg Rheinberger's concept of »epistemic thing«, she observes and analyzes the discourses that show how scholars were grappling with a yet undefined subject. This allows her to avoid essentializing concepts such as »law«, »society«, or the disciplines that formed with the express aim to scientifically study them. Schweitzer makes use of Foucault's theorem of »dispositif« as a way to analyze the inseparability of knowledge and power. In her view, Foucauldian analyses, which concentrate on discourses about »truth«, might be of limited value in understanding legal discourses as such. Instead, they are useful when trying to grasp the way disciplines have been grappling with »law« and »society«, and have made truth claims about these epistemic objects (52). The other methodological approach used illustrates the theoretical argument with a close reading of the original scholarly discourses. The author's extensive knowledge of the literature is on display throughout the 662 pages of the book. As she explicitly states, her book does not present new historical sources. Instead, it aims at a sociologically informed analysis of these discourses, with the view to the »sociological rationalities in law«.

The book is divided into two parts. The first part will be very familiar to legal historians of the 19th and early 20th centuries, but less so to sociologists: how Savigny, against the background of extreme legal fragmentation in the various German-speaking territories, successfully created the narrative of law being the emanation of the »Volksgeist« in the form of classic Roman law. According to this narrative, lawyers had the »scientific« methods to recognize the right law by ways of conceptual logic. Though Puchta further refined and formalized this position, it remained contested and its dominance was anything but inevitable. As Schweitzer shows, the question about what the

* Doris Schweitzer, Juridische Soziologien – Recht und Gesellschaft von 1814 bis in die 1920er Jahre, Baden-Baden: Nomos 2021, 664 S., ISBN 978-3-8487-6878-3

law had to do – or should have to do – with society or, in a more abstract and less political way, »life«, became a recurring theme in legal scholarship. For example, Jhering introduced the social via viewing law as a means to an end (*Zweck*). His ideas were successful in the areas of public and criminal law, and early sociologists eventually came to adopt them. However, the dominant private law theorists, such as Winscheid, emphatically rejected Jhering's ideas.

A real turning point in many of the discourses, which reverberated throughout later discussions, was the codification process and eventual adoption of the *Bürgerliche Gesetzbuch* (BGB) in 1900, which ended the idea of law being the exclusive domain of the »legal scientists«. The long-running process provided the occasion for fundamental and critical discussions on the legal theory behind the BGB (among others, Schweitzer presents the contributions made by Gierke, Ehrlich, Menger, and Petrazycki). The debate about the BGB's legal origins, i.e. the influences of Roman and/or German law was intimately connected with the question of whether it was adequate to the task of addressing the social problems of that time – above all given the challenges posed by socialist and social democratic ideas. Particularly interesting is Schweitzer's presentation of the legal-methodological arguments on the question of what influence the emerging social sciences should have. In any case, the forceful critique of self-sufficiency in »legal science« did not have an immediate effect on the outcome; the BGB formalized the abstract-conceptual nature of legal-dogmatic thinking.

A few years later, the status quo was again challenged by the »Free Law Movement« as well as by other groups. In particular, Schweitzer discusses well-known figures such as Kantorowicz, Ehrlich, Heck, Fuchs, Nussbaum, Sinzheimer, and Kelsen, but also lesser-known writers such as Kornfeld and Wurzel. The key was the discovery of the judge as an agent of the voluntaristic creation of law. These discussions began in the 1880s (Bülow, Rümelin, Zitelmann) and continued into the Weimar Republic – Carl Schmitt's writings, for example, have to be read against the background of these discussions. Schweitzer compares the debate to the *Werturteilsstreit* (value-judgment dispute) in the early *Nationalökonomie* (economic sociology), in which the question was whether normative conclusions could be deduced from facts. In legal scholarship, however, the problem was reversed: given the inevitable value judgement inherent in judicial decisions, the question was how empirical evidence could be integrated into legal-dogmatic arguments to ensure the relevance of »life« in the law (365). Schweitzer concludes that while these authors were united in their rejection of the abstract-conceptual logicism of the prevailing method, their positions were too diverse as to be able to bring about a change in doctrinal thinking. As she argues, one major problem was that the attempts to define the role sociology should play for and in legal scholarship depended on how »sociology« was understood (362). The lack of consensus among these writers isn't really so surprising given that no such consensus existed in the young discipline – which meant that there was no clear »other« for legal scholarship to turn to. In the end, the separation of »is« (sociology) and »ought« (law) prevailed, a position that was most forcefully argued by Kelsen. Mainstream legal scholarship perceived sociology as a competitor, a challenge that needed to be handled by an internal legal discussion on how, if at all, specifically defined empirical knowledge could enter the realm of the legal.

The second part of the book differs from the first inasmuch as it concentrates on the relevant sociological writings of Durkheim, Tönnies, and Weber, without embedding the writings in the general sociological discussions of their time analogous to the discussion of the discourse in legal scholarship. Early sociologists were reacting to the same basic situation: the unresolved relationship between the law and the social. They also referred to the same discussions (obviously, as a French scholar, Durkheim to a lesser extent). Contrary to the legal scholars, however, they were interested not in how the social (or »life«) helped to solve legal questions, but rather what the law could empirically teach them about »society« as an epistemic thing. They approached this question from very different perspectives. Durkheim's aim was to reject all philosophical speculation and provide a firm empirical basis for reasoning about »social facts«. For him, law was interesting as a representation of social solidarity. This led him to provide a very narrow reading of the law that ultimately, Schweitzer concludes, was unable to provide a sociological account of law capable of answering questions about legal change or the ordering function of the law. Such an account is of little interest to legal scholars. Tönnies, in contrast, was very much interested in the relationship between law and order, but understood sociology, despite its empirical focus, as a philosophical discipline. He envisioned the discipline as providing a value-free system with concepts and theories that were able to describe and explain social phenomena, very much analogous to the system of German legal scholarship. He explicitly rejected, however, any relevance of sociological concepts for law itself, and was not interested in the social significance of legal theory or method. This proved to be theoretically unattractive for legal theory.

Finally, Schweitzer turns to Weber to locate the missed opportunity for a closer intellectual bond between legal and sociological scholarship. Weber, too, was interested in constructing a system of well-defined concepts as a toolkit for making precise statements about social phenomena and causal relationships that exist between them. As a lawyer, not only did he use the legal terms in his sociological theory, but he also had intimate knowledge of the legal debates discussed in the first part of the book and commented on them in his sociological and comparative account of German legal history. Most importantly, in contrasting the sociological from the legal perspective, he defines the legal as a strictly normative enterprise. This led him to reject the free law movement's demands for greater methodological freedom for judges. To be sure, Weber's objection is not one of principle but is embedded in the particular historical context: due to his comparative research into the nature of the common law, Weber was well aware that it was possible to base a legal system on completely different judicial methodologies. However, he was skeptical – probably rightly so – that the proponents of free law were careful about what they were wishing for. Rather than relying on judges who were recruited and socialized in the German empire's bureaucratic-authoritarian justice system, Weber trusted the democratic process to create the necessary social legislation and hope that doctrine will help to force even conservative judges to implement such legislation.

Be that as it may, Schweitzer's point is that by neatly separating sociology and law along the is-ought axis, Weber was strengthening the separation between sociology and law, or more precisely, »immunizing sociology against the law« (571). His aim was to secure the autonomy of sociology. It also meant that normative questions involving the theory and method of law application were beyond the scope of sociology. This is the point of departure for Schweitzer's criticism of Weber: he places the question of legal normativity outside the reach of sociological analysis and critique. Sociologists, he says, can only observe, whereas the legal-governmental complex with the technologies of power that Foucault focused on stays safely in the hand of the lawyers and outside the challenges of society (580). This is where, for Schweitzer, sociology has taken the wrong turn.

Schweitzer provides a convincing account about the importance of the 19th-century legal discourses for the early sociologists. The detailed presentation of these discourses shows the richness of the debate of that time – almost all the arguments that are still part of today's fundamental legal-theoretical discussions are already present. They could have provided fertile ground for interdisciplinary debates after 1945, and especially in the short-lived blossoming of sociology of law in the 1970. Yet, this did not happen. For Schweitzer, a major reason is internal to the theory – Max Weber assigned the »is« to sociology and the »ought« to law, reaffirming an apolitical view of the law. As I understand Schweitzer here, this created a path-dependent development that ended in a situation where sociology no longer had anything to say about the law (577). I wonder, however, whether Schweitzer's theory-internal explanation might not be too deterministic and too centered on the sociologies of Durkheim, Tönnies, and Weber. For one thing, Marxism-inspired theory never accepted the is-ought dichotomy and provided the motivation for many of the – ultimately unsuccessful – attempts in the 1970s to move legal thought closer to the sociological. The role of the political and intellectual rupture caused by National Socialism would also have to be discussed. Finally, for a more complete picture, we need to look at the external, historically contingent factors in the post-war disciplinary histories to understand the current configuration of sociology and legal scholarship.

Schweitzer ends her book with a call for sociology to reappropriate the law. In order to be able to critique the law and legal power, sociology needs to be able to analyze issues of legal doctrine and method (578). This is only possible if sociologists have the necessary knowledge of these domains and of their histories. On the other hand, legal scholars and legal historians can profit from looking at the intertwined histories of law and sociology. Schweitzer's book provides valuable impulses for these cross-disciplinary perspectives.

■

Manuel Martínez Neira

Revistas jurídicas españolas: 40 años después*

Me hablaba Fernando Liendo del acuse de recibo de Michael Stolleis a su *Avance*. Además de agradecerle el envío, expresión de la amabilidad que caracterizaba al jurista alemán, compartía el interés por la comunicación jurídica, es decir, por los instrumentos a través de los cuales se han formado y difundido las doctrinas jurídicas y que en el siglo XIX tuvieron en la prensa su epicentro. La revista, por lo tanto, como un fenómeno histórico, con unas coordenadas espacio-temporales precisas y concretas, de creación de cultura jurídica, de pensamiento jurídico, y así, para nosotros historiadores, fuente de conocimiento de los mismos.

La historicidad de la revista, a estas alturas del siglo XXI, nos parece algo evidente: los *blogs*, los repositorios, las redes sociales, las *newsletters*, los *papers* … nos permiten seguir los debates científicos que nos interesan adelantándonos a su recepción en una revista, que se produce cuando quizás ya resultan obsoletos. Pero en el siglo liberal esto no sucedía (Petit, 11); al contrario, fue un momento marcado por la novedad de la revista que, de entrada, vino a sustituir al género epistolar como vehículo de comunicación científica.

A pesar de esta palmaria importancia para el conocimiento del derecho del Ochocientos, los estudios sobre revistas españolas (más allá de meros índices acumulativos de algún título precedidos de una breve presentación) vinieron a remolque del ejemplo italiano. En efecto, fue en 1982 cuando Paolo Grossi convocó a un nutrido grupo de especialistas para un encuentro sobre revistas jurídicas, celebrado en abril de 1983 y cuyas actas se publicaron en 1984. A este, siguieron distintas monografías (1897, 1988) y el famoso repertorio de Mansuino (1994). Tomando el relevo, Víctor Tau presidió en septiembre 1994, en Buenos Aires, una reunión sobre revistas jurídicas (los trabajos se publicaron en 1997) que sirvió de catalizador de estudios, proyectos, tesis: dio visibilidad a una actividad ya existente.

A 40 años de distancia de aquel encuentro florentino, aquí nos convocan dos publicaciones nacidas durante la pandemia, de muy distinta factura: el libro de un maestro consagrado y el de su discípulo.

En *Derecho por entregas* de Carlos Petit encontramos una valiosa recopilación de artículos publicados entre 1995 y 2013, ordenados según el momento histórico que ilustran. Los textos originales han sido revisados y alterados »para evitar repeticiones, corregir dislates y uniformar criterios« (Petit, 311). A ellos se antepone un capítulo, a modo de introducción, que ofrece una clave de lectura del volumen: las revistas son »el mejor observatorio de algunas paradojas que condicionan el nacimiento y el desarrollo del derecho liberal« (Petit, 13). De estas paradojas se señalan dos. Por un lado, el enfrentamiento entre legislación y ciencia jurídica. En efecto, por primera vez en la historia, el derecho se concibe como un ordenamiento estatal: lo que significa que está limitado geográfica y socialmente por la soberanía del Estado, que por ello es distinto u opuesto al de los Estados vecinos, particularismo que se enfrenta con el universalismo que postula la ciencia. Por otro lado, este binomio convive en el liberalismo con »ese otro binomio que opuso el *profesor* al *abogado*« (Petit, 16); es decir con »los dos principales modelos de ser y actuar como jurista« (Petit, 14): el profesional *à la Savigny*, que tenía en la cátedra su espacio de trabajo; el modelo forense, cuyos ámbitos naturales fueron el palacio de justicia y la tribuna parlamentaria. Argumento este que ha sido desarrollado por el autor en su *Discurso sobre el discurso. Oralidad y escritura en la cultura jurídica de la España liberal* (Madrid 2020).

Petit no pretende en su libro ofrecer una imagen completa de la cultura jurídica liberal a través de las revistas; más bien, cada capítulo permite indagar en alguno de esos condicionamientos que forzaron una lenta implantación de un derecho

* Carlos Petit, Derecho por entregas. Estudios sobre prensa y revistas en la España liberal, Madrid: Dykinson 2020, 311 p., ISBN 978-84-1377-083-3; Fernando Liendo Tagle, Prensa jurídica española. Avance de un repertorio (1834–1936), Madrid: Dykinson 2020, 235 p., ISBN 978-84-1377-212-7

renovado y así en »la trabajosa construcción de aparatos estatales en una patria que salió destrozada de la crisis del antiguo régimen« (Petit, 27). Encontramos, de este modo, estudios específicos sobre algún título, o causas documentadas a través de los periódicos.

Así, gracias al »Mittermaier-Projekt« pudo consultar las cartas del penalista de Heidelberg Carl Josef Anton Mittermaier (1787–1867) que iluminan algunas circunstancias de un fugaz periódico: *La Escuela del Derecho, revista jurídica dirigida por Don Cayetano de Estér, con la colaboración de eminentes jurisconsultos nacionales y extranjeros*, publicado entre (1863–1865). Una revista que se caracterizó por alejarse de la información positiva más perecedera y ofrecer »una excelente miscelánea de artículos doctrinales« (Petit, 35). En apéndice aparecen las cartas transcritas y un índice de los estudios publicados.

La *Revista de los Tribunales* (1878–1894) le permite rastrear en el giro científico que sufrió la *Revista General de Legislación y Jurisprudencia* en 1883. En efecto, en 1878 con Vicente Romero y Girón como director, la revista asumió la misión de lograr la conclusión de la codificación civil, como obra científica de los jurisconsultos españoles. Por ejemplo, Pisa y Pajares escribió en ella que en los tiempos que alcanzamos »la ciencia precede al legislador, quien recibe las enseñanzas de aquella para traducirla en preceptos« (Petit, 101). Este empeño periodístico se perderá, al asumir nuevos lectores y retos editoriales; pero la *Revista General de Legislación y Jurisprudencia* tomó el relevo. En efecto, en 1878 se incorporó a la *Revista General* Emilio Reus y a partir de entonces (sobre todo al ser nombrado director en 1883) se impuso un proceso de renovación centrado en la dimensión internacional y científica. Esto sucedió en un momento de reforma universitaria, de manera que »las pretensiones científicas de Emilio Reus coincidieron con los intereses de profesores que disputaban ahora el terreno de la prensa periódica« (Petit, 115). Entre los resultados de la nueva orientación, encontramos la alineación con la italianización de la ciencia jurídica española.

También gracias a la prensa, Petit ha podido documentar con esmero los ecos ovetenses de la polémica lección madrileña de Miguel Morayta (1884), con ocasión de la apertura del curso académico. Catedrático de Letras, conocido republicano y masón, hizo una cerrada defensa de la libertad de la ciencia que desencadenó fuerzas ajenas a la universidad, es decir, la reacción de los ultramontanos. Si en Madrid el hecho tuvo sobre todo un matiz político, en Oviedo fue más claramente académico. Allí se vivieron protestas de profesores, huelgas y disturbios serios por parte de los alumnos, cambio de rector, inspección …

Se sirve de la discusión en la prensa del crimen de Fuencarral (1888), pieza del popular género de la causa célebre, para precisar el alcance de las novedades en las ciencias criminales: el de Fuencarral muestra perfectamente las tensiones con las que se abrió paso en España el moderno enjuiciamiento criminal. Un simple robo con homicidio se convirtió en el gran escándalo del siglo por las repercusiones que tuvo en la prensa. Se confrontaron así »los hechos que el público debatía con la comprometida averiguación judicial de circunstancias y culpables, en los términos de unas leyes […] situadas a mitad de camino entre el secreto (del sumario) y la publicidad (del juicio oral)« (Petit, 164).

También desde la atalaya que presentan los periódicos españoles del cambio de siglo observa los comentarios al pensamiento de Cesare Lombroso, cuyos escritos levantaron una viva polémica. El anarquismo, el espiritismo y tantos otros asuntos son debatidos con pasión mencionando al profesor de Turín.

En fin, el análisis de la *Revista de Ciencias Jurídicas y Sociales* (1918–1936) permite identificar un movimiento de reforma que culminó en el proyecto legislativo de Fernando de los Ríos para la universidad. Respondía a un horizonte intelectual de clara tradición krausopositivista que ponía en su centro una complicada historia de la educación jurídica en España.

Pasemos ahora al segundo libro. Fernando Liendo defendió en octubre de 2020 una tesis doctoral titulada »Prensa jurídica y estudios de derecho. España 1836–1883«. Con la experiencia de esa amplia investigación ha publicado el avance de un repertorio de revistas jurídicas que abarca el siglo anterior a la guerra civil española (1834–1936). Ofrece una selección de 137 títulos de revistas redactadas *por* y *para* juristas. Selección que prescinde de aquellas revistas con contenido jurídico pero dedicadas a otras profesiones (médicos, militares, etc.), de las dedicadas a disciplinas no estrictamente jurídicas (criminología), de las publicaciones cuyo objeto son normas o sentencias, de las referidas a la política.

Este *Avance* se inspira en el repertorio de Carlo Mansuino (*Periodici giuridici italiani*, Milano 1994) a la hora de estructurar cada registro: título; subtítulo; otros títulos; fechas de inicio y fin de la publicación; lugar; tipografía; periodicidad; director; colaboradores; descripción del contenido y observaciones aclaratorias; bibliografía sobre el título; biblioteca propietaria del ejemplar consultado para su catalogación; revista predecesora y sucesora; índices acumulados.

Avance en cuanto a provisionalidad, pues el autor es consciente de que faltan títulos y de que la descripción de los mismos debe completarse. Pero la palabra guarda también otro significado semántico que hace referencia al gran salto en el conocimiento que permite esta publicación. Hasta ahora teníamos buenos estudios sobre revistas jurídicas españolas, el aquí reseñado de Carlos Petit, los de Fernando Martínez, Marta Lorente y otros, pero carecíamos de un catálogo como el que ofrece Liendo, con todas las limitaciones que se quieran. Estos 137 títulos dan cuenta de una cronología, lugares de edición, promotores, sectores jurídicos … que permitirán al estudioso ampliar exponencialmente el campo de investigación: algo que siempre agradeceremos a Fernando Liendo.

La publicación viene acompañada de un *database* muy útil pues nos permite ordenar las revistas por fechas, director, lugar de edición, contenido. Por ejemplo, resulta muy ilustrativo que de un golpe de vista podamos observar cómo se repiten entre los directores de revistas los nombres de Agustín María de la Cuadra, Alejo García Moreno, García de Gregorio, Francisco de Cárdenas, Francisco Muñoz, Francisco Pareja, Gumersindo de Azcárate, Pacheco, José María Pantoja, Martínez Alcubilla y otros. De entrada, esto nos ayuda a precisar protagonismos en la construcción de la cultura jurídica liberal española, cuyo conocimiento nos parece tan urgente en la actualidad. ■

Nuno Camarinhas

A Digital Treasure Trove for Portuguese Legal History*

In the past few years, major resources have become available for researchers of Portuguese legal history. In this context, António Manuel Hespanha played a pioneering role; he was responsible for creating the first online digital library on Portuguese and colonial legal texts, hosted by the NOVA School of law (https://novalaw.unl.pt/arquivo-digital-antonio-manuel-hespanha). Here, the user has access to a curated collection of books on doctrinal works, draft legislation, parliamentary debates, legislative pieces, and jurisprudence, mainly covering the constitutional period and the liberal reformations that took place after the 1820 revolution. Inspired by Hespanha's aim to create accessible collections of sources, two other projects focused on legislation from the early modern and modern periods: *Ius Lusitaniae* and, more recently, *O Governo dos Outros*, which integrated the data from the former and extended the chronological scope to the Portuguese colonial experience (http://www.governodosoutros.ics.ul.pt). In the same vein, and building on previous experience with these projects, LEGALPL – Legal Pluralism in the Portuguese Empire (18th–20th centuries) (https://pluralismojuridiconoimperio.fd.unl.pt/), promises to further expand on the digitization of colonial legislation.

What these projects have in common is that they were guided by a questioning of the role of law, jurists, and the legal profession in the shaping of early modern and modern Portugal and its interactions with non-European societies. One

* DIGIGOV – Diário do Governo Digital (1820–1910), https://digigov.cepese.pt/en/homepage (last visited 13 July 2022)

DIGIGOV - DIÁRIO DO GOVERNO DIGITAL 1820-1910

NEWSPAPERS SEARCH STUDIES DIGIGOV/CEPESE CONTACTS

The official newspaper of the Portuguese State, especially during the Constitutional Monarchy (1820-1910), constitutes a basic source for the knowledge of the History of Contemporary Portugal. The official newspaper than published the bulletins of the Royal Court; laws, decrees, regulations and other Royal and Governmental acts; statistical documents; transcripts of the minutes of parliamentary sessions; share prices; customs movement and maritime service bulletins; national and international news; advertisements for goods and services; in short, an important set of official and unofficial information covering multiple sectors of the Portuguese economy, population and society.

Throughout this period, the official journal had its title changed for several times – *Gazeta de Lisboa, Diário da Regência, Crónica Constitucional de Lisboa, Gazeta Oficial do Governo, Diário de Lisboa* and *Diário de Governo* (the title it had for the most time, up to 1976, when it assumed the current title, *Diário da República*), in addition to the titles published at the service of the Liberal Regency, while two Governments coexisted in Portugal (1830-1834), the Chronicles of Terceira and Porto. And yet, the official newspaper would never cease to be published, presenting a remarkable regularity, without parallel in the context of the Portuguese press.

The website **DIGIGOV – Diário do Governo Digital (1820-1910)** features close to 30 000 issues of the Portuguese official newspaper (including supplements, appendices and extraordinary editions) published from September 16, 1820, the date of the first edition of the *Diário do Governo*, inaugurating a new stage in the life of the official newspaper of the Portuguese State, following the Liberal Revolution of August 24, and October 5, 1910, when the final issue of the official newspaper with the arms of the Monarchy was printed, due to establishment of the Republic in Portugal.

Each edition is presented in low resolution pdf (faster access), high resolution pdf (better quality), and jpeg format (non-editable). Any of these versions can be freely downloaded for personal use. The content of the pdf versions is searchable and can be copied in text format directly from the digital pages to a word processor. The studies section presents several articles on the origins of the Portuguese official newspaper, its historical context and evolution in time, the analysis of its main elements (structure, contents, writing, circulation, audience, etc.), and on some of the main foreign official newspapers and other historiographical works carried out based on this source.

DIARIO DO GOVERNO

might say that they were extensions – by way of documentation – of these two research projects, providing source materials to its researchers that simultaneously became available to the whole academic community.

Produced by a different team, from a different school (CEPESE at Universidade do Porto), *DIGIGOV – Diário do Governo Digital (1820–1910)* (https://digigov.cepese.pt/en/homepage) is a different type of project, offering a different type of source. It does not deal directly with the traditional legal texts, and it is not produced by a research team pursuing a given subject or object, but rather is mainly focused on providing access to a large collection of texts: all of the issues of the Portuguese Gazette (*Diário do Governo*) published from the time of the Liberal Revolution of September 1820 until the Republican Revolution of 1910 and encompassing the entire period known as the Constitutional Monarchy. As a project, it is mainly concerned with the community of users it serves, by reconstructing a collection, creating a digital version, and providing the tools needed to search it or simply read it.

DIGIGOV - DIÁRIO DO GOVERNO DIGITAL 1820-1910

NEWSPAPERS SEARCH STUDIES DIGIGOV/CEPESE CONTACTS

Num. 1. An. 1820.

PORTUGAL

DIARIO DO GOVERNO.

SEGUNDA FEIRA 16 DE SETEMBRO.

O homem propenso por natureza, ou educação a deixar-se occultamente seduzir do attractivo das paixões no meio mesmo de huma Sociedade a mais philantrópica, e bem regulada, de cujas leis deva honrar-se infinitamente de ser escravo, sendo assim o mais livre Cidadão, com muita difficuldade se dobra a não seguir os impulsos de seu peito, bem que se convença de que, não se endereçando estes ao proficuo enlace da prospe- rão decahindo paulatinamente de sua representação nacional, e por conseguinte de sua antiga prosperidade.— Accelerando-se porém cada vez mais a progressiva marcha de sua decadencia, devião pela série commum e necessaria dos acontecimentos humanos precipitar-se no pélago dos ultimos horrores, vendo-se (além de exhausto o seu numerario) degradados da consideração, de que havião sido tão legitimamente crédores entre

U.PORTO FCT COMPETE 2020 2020 Porto.

The reconstruction part of the project is considerable, given that there is no complete set of the Portuguese Gazette, and that the surviving and incomplete collections are scattered across the country and often in poor conditions of conservation or even withdrawn from public access. Furthermore, throughout the covered period, the gazette had different titles, and there were even concurring titles in the periods where there were competing governments in Portugal, in a tense situation that evolved into a civil war (1830–34). Hence, one of the merits of the DIGIGOV project is the reconstitution of a complete set of the Gazette in excellent reading conditions.

The website gives the reader a digitized version of the Gazette. It can be read online, through an intuitive interface that allows browsing the different issues, selecting the date of publication, moving from issue to issue, or searching inside a particular issue. It also allows printing or downloading each issue in pdf format, both in low and high resolution, and zooming in and out on every page. Each issue has a basic OCR that makes the text available for searching; however, there are notable shortcomings as far as the quality of the OCR is concerned. Another way of accessing the Gazette is through the advanced search. This tool allows the user to create word or expression queries, using a set of Boolean search operators (AND, OR, AND NOT), proximity operators (NEAR), or similarity operators (SIMILAR) to narrow or widen the search. Technically, these elements are very well developed and efficient. However, the poor quality of some of the electronic text generated by the OCR may result in frustration despite a powerful search engine. On the bright side, its efficiency also helps circumvent the deficiencies of the electronic text.

The website also contains a collection of academic papers on the Portuguese Gazette and the political and cultural environment in which it was produced throughout the period, considering some international ramifications and comparative approaches with British, North American, French, Spanish and Italian as well as Brazilian gazettes.

In its present state – the website was first presented in July 2020 – DIGIGOV is a major contribution to research on 19th century Portugal and the Portuguese empire. More than 30,000 issues of the Portuguese Gazette offer a wealth of information on legal matters (laws, decrees, regulations, and royal and governmental acts), but also on a variety of subjects and forms that range from statistical reports, transcripts of parliamentary sessions, maritime bulletins, prices, national and international news, advertisements. All this gives the researcher of almost any subject a fertile field of all sorts of data. However, a more in-depth analysis reveals a lack of investment in the quality of the electronic text and, most importantly, the absence of curatorship, which would provide the user with the integration of categories of data, or an ontology that would guide the user through the riches of almost a century of a daily gazette. An ontology could enable the categorization of the sections of the different issues; it would aid identification of the government organs producing the decrees and, within each organ, an understanding of their different areas of action and the nature of the texts. All this would greatly improve an online resource of central importance for research. For this period of legal and constitutional reform and of state formation, which included the constitution of a governmental structure around ministries and secretariats, it would be a noticeable improvement if the user could choose from the institutions producing those norms.

As a repository of the information published in *Diário do Governo*, the website meets the requirements expected for this type of project: it is thorough, accessible, easy to use, and provides different resolution levels, assuring the preservation of high-resolution files. However, there is room for improvement, namely at the database level. This would result in a new phase or a whole new project, of course, but with the volume of data that is already collected, it would not be impossible to achieve. The amount of electronic text should be revised – for instance through crowdsourcing and volunteer contribution from members of the community – and, from its wealth of information, a database could be created to give better access to data. Disaggregation of information from the sections of the Gazette would provide a better understanding of what is being published and a way to measure the production volume and rhythms of the different sectors of the new liberal state. A typology of texts would greatly benefit the researcher by allowing a more refined search and providing a better understanding of the institutional activity. When crossed with the temporal dimension, it would become possible to address continuity and change, rhythms and cycles. A third level of action would be the identification of persons and places, aiming at future connectivity with other online databanks.

Despite these shortcomings, DIGIGOV impresses by having compiled, organized and digitized an indispensable source for the study of 19th-century Portugal. Its importance for legal history is self-evident and its utility for historical research in general is, of course, invaluable.

If we consider the work that has been produced by the Portuguese Parliamentary Historical Archives (https://www.parlamento.pt/sites/EN/Parliament/Paginas/Archives.aspx), with its collections and databases on parliamentary debates (https://debates.parlamento.pt) and on Portuguese legislation (https://legislacaoregia.parlamento.pt), the possibilities for research on 19th-century Portugal, and specifically its legal dimensions, have been broadened, and the addition represented by the DIGIGOV project is certainly a major improvement.

■

Miloš Vec

Regionale Konflikte, globales Völkerrecht*

Adamantios Theodor Skordos' Buch verfolgt eine plausible These anhand eines konkreten historischen Beispiels. Die These lautet: Institutionen des modernen, globalen Völkerrechts haben regionale Ursprünge. Sie sind aus spezifischen Konfliktkonstellationen entstanden, in denen begünstigende Faktoren normerzeugende Wirkung entfaltet haben, und Südosteuropa hat dabei eine wichtige Rolle gespielt. Das Buch von Skordos ist eine Leipziger Habilitation, die am Leibniz-Institut für Geschichte und Kultur des östlichen Europa (GWZO) entstand. Die südosteuropäische Prägung des modernen Völkerrechts führt Skordos anhand von fünf Beispielen aus den vergangenen 200 Jahren vor Augen. Sie verteilen sich relativ gleichmäßig über die Zeit und werden in ähnlich umfangreichen Kapiteln behandelt, was eine darstellerische Ausgewogenheit verleiht. Keines der Beispiele ist für sich völlig neu oder der Forschung unbekannt, aber Skordos verknüpft sie auf interessante und methodisch transparente Weise zu einem überzeugenden Gesamtbild. Schon Marie-Janine Calic hatte 2016 den Balkan »als Laboratorium [für] neue Instrumente der Diplomatie und des Völkerrechts sowie der Krisenbewältigung« bezeichnet (Skordos, 478), und das belegt Skordos jetzt exemplarisch in seiner Habilitation.

Er verzichtet klugerweise auf Komparative und Superlative, wo er die Bedeutung des südosteuropäischen Konfliktgeschehens für das Völkerrecht behauptet. Damit spricht er anderen Geschichtsregionen weder ab, dass sie auch einen Beitrag geleistet haben, noch insinuiert er, dass deren Beitrag geringer gewesen sein könnte. Jedenfalls im Moment fehlen noch entsprechend angelegte Studien zu anderen Weltregionen, die solche Vergleiche überhaupt erst ermöglichen würden. Dass Südosteuropa eine »große Bedeutung« (18) gehabt hat, tritt umso klarer und überzeugender in allen fünf Beispielen hervor. Ausgangspunkt und zugrundeliegende These ist, dass diese Region ein besonderes Konfliktpotenzial birgt. Skordos benennt im Rückgriff und in der Zusammenfassung von anderen Studien gewaltbegünstigende Faktoren (24). Denn Staatsgründungen, Nationswerdungen und Formen des sozialen Wandels seien hier in spezifischer Weise erfolgt, nämlich durch Abspaltung von Großreichen. Daher habe sich »eine neue Logik von Massengewalt erstmals in den ›imperialen Bruchzonen‹ [...] Südosteuropas durchgesetzt« (25). Im Buch wird immer wieder auf die ethnonationale Gewalt unter Beteiligung irregulärer Krieger verwiesen (34, 465, 468, 479). Revolutionäre Nationalbewegungen – ursprünglich von sehr kleinen Eliten getragen – hätten immer wieder Expansionspläne formuliert, die sich auf Gebiete richteten, die eigentlich ethnisch vielfältig besiedelt waren. Dieser »irredentistische Expansionsnationalismus« ist ein Schlüssel zum Verständnis der Aggressionspolitik (365).

Seine fünf Fallbeispiele beginnen historisch mit der Reaktion der europäischen Staaten auf die »Orientalische Frage« im frühen 19. Jahrhundert. Dort erfolgte militärisches Eingreifen im Namen der Humanität, erstmals kurz nach dem Wiener Kongress, und die Völkerrechtswissenschaftler der Zeit verliehen diesem Vorgehen juristische Legitimität. Leider berücksichtigt Skordos nicht die wichtige, 2019 erschienene Studie von Fabian Klose, die sich mit der Geschichte humanitärer Interventionen im 19. Jahrhundert eingehend auseinandersetzte und dabei auch auf die imperialistischen Motive der Großmächte hinwies.[1] Ein Einwand gegen die Darstellung aus Sicht der Wissenschaftsgeschichte des Völkerrechts wäre, dass Skordos in diesem Teil ältere, aus Sicht des Rezensenten klischeehafte Annahmen über die Verdrängung des Naturrechts durch Rechtspositivismus im Völkerrecht fortschreibt (137, 481). Sie sind gerade im Feld der humanitären Intervention fragwürdig,

* Adamantios Theodor Skordos, Südosteuropa und das moderne Völkerrecht: Eine transregionale und globale Geschichte im 19. und 20. Jahrhundert (Moderne europäische Geschichte 19), Göttingen: Wallstein 2021, 528 S., ISBN 978-3-8353-3003-3

1 Fabian Klose, »In the Cause of Humanity«. Eine Geschichte der humanitären Intervention im langen 19. Jahrhundert, Göttingen 2019.

weil diese Interventionen eben nicht auf Verträge und geltendes Gewohnheitsrecht gestützt wurden. Stattdessen argumentierten die Völkerrechtler des späten 19. Jahrhunderts gerade auf diesem Gebiet mit Topoi wie »Natur der Sache«, »Naturrecht«, »allgemeinen Vernunftgründen« oder Ähnlichem. Gerade darin zeigt sich, dass das Völkerrecht hier noch im Werden begriffen war und (verkleidete) Zweckmäßigkeitserwägungen Lücken schlossen.

In jedem Fall aber ist Skordos zuzustimmen, dass das 1815 auf dem Wiener Kongress von den Großmächten eigentlich zugunsten des monarchischen Prinzips verabredete Interventionsrecht im Verlauf des Jahrhunderts zunehmend eine neue humanitäre Stoßrichtung bekommt, und der griechische Aufstand von 1822 bildete den Auftakt dazu. Ein wichtiger Baustein dafür war die Wahrnehmung der dort stattfindenden Kriegsgewalt insbesondere der Osmanen als ausgesprochen grausam, geradezu »barbarisch« und regulierungsbedürftig (60). Dem schließen sich weitere Ausführungen von Skordos zu Fortbildungen des Völkerrechts (Seerecht, Neutralitätsrecht, Erweiterung der christlich-europäischen Völkerrechtsgemeinschaft) im Kontext des Pariser Friedensvertrags von 1856 an, die gleichfalls im Zeichen der Orientalischen Frage stehen. Schließlich geht es vor allem ab dem vierten und letzten russisch-türkischen Krieg des 19. Jahrhunderts noch ein weiteres Mal um Einschränkungen der Souveränität durch Rechte der internationalen Staatengemeinschaft. Mit diesen sollten Minderheitenrechte geschützt werden, indem nämlich Auflagen für die Anerkennung von neuen Staaten gemacht wurden und erneut ein Interventionsrecht begründet wurde (123).

Im zweiten, dritten und vierten Kapitel steht die Zwischenkriegszeit im Mittelpunkt; statt Völkerrechtswissenschaft analysiert Skordos im zweiten Kapitel zunächst Rechtsprechung, nämlich die Stellungnahmen des Ständigen Internationalen Gerichtshofs in Den Haag (PCIJ). Drei südosteuropäische Streitfälle wurden den Richtern vom Völkerbundrat zur Begutachtung vorgelegt und sie werden den internationalen Minderheitenschutz weiterentwickeln. Auch dieser Minderheitenschutz, der in allen Pariser Verträgen verankert war, hatte einen »markanten ostmittel- und südosteuropäischen Stempel« (168). Danach widmet sich Skordos im dritten Kapitel der Konvention von Lausanne. Sie wird 1923 zwischen Griechenland und der Türkei geschlossen und legitimiert im Nachhinein einen umfassenden gegenseitigen Bevölkerungsaustausch. Das Völkerrecht, das hier zwar nicht originär entsteht (es gab Vorgänger-Vereinbarungen), ist gleichwohl politisch besonders wirkmächtig. Spätere Legitimationen von Bevölkerungstransfer, Zwangsumsiedlung und Vertreibung finden in dem Vertrag von Lausanne ihr Vorbild (289). Interessanterweise sind diese späteren politisch-historischen Bezugnahmen ebenso selektiv wie inhaltlich falsch: Die gewaltvollen Aspekte dieser griechisch-türkischen Zwangsmigration werden entweder ausgeblendet oder mit einem höheren Gut gerechtfertigt, nämlich Frieden und Stabilität in der Region durch »Entmischung«. Schließlich behandelt das vierte Kapitel die Versuche der 1930er Jahre, einen internationalen Tatbestand des Terrorismus zu verankern, nationale Strafrechte zu vereinheitlichen und einen neuen Strafgerichtshof zu gründen. Anlass ist das Attentat auf den jugoslawischen König Aleksandar I. Karađorđević und den französischen Außenminister Louis Barthou in Marseille 1934. Zwar gelingt es nicht, hier eine völkerrechtliche Strafgerichtsbarkeit einzuführen, aber erneut ist das Wirken des Völkerrechts damit keineswegs vergeblich gewesen. Die erarbeiteten Konventionen zur Bekämpfung des Terrorismus und zur Schaffung eines internationalen Strafgerichtshofs von 1937 treten zwar nicht in Kraft. Der in ihnen verankerte Komplementaritätsgrundsatz bleibt aber Referenzpunkt künftiger Debatten des Völkerstrafrechts in der Zeit nach dem Zweiten Weltkrieg (333), und auch die Anti-Terrorismus-Konvention von 1937 wird in den 1990er Jahren wieder aufgegriffen (349). Das fünfte Kapitel analysiert ausgewählte Innovationen, die die postjugoslawischen Kriege seit den 1990er Jahren auslösen. Dazu gehört insbesondere die Einrichtung des ICTY (International Criminal Tribunal for the former Yugoslavia), seine Rechtsprechung sowie der Streit über die Anerkennung des Kosovo. Auch hier wird das humanitäre Völkerrecht und das Völkerstrafrecht maßgeblich fortgebildet – und übrigens ein Paradigmenwechsel vom Bevölkerungstransfer zugunsten eines Vertreibungsverbots vollzogen (462).

Skordos kann sich bei seiner Darstellung auf Einzelstudien aus verschiedenen Feldern und Disziplinen stützen, die er zusammenführt. Die kulturhistorische Studie ist lesbar und argumentiert ausgewogen, bezüglich der Völkerrechtsgeschichte lautet ein Leitnarrativ »Verrechtlichung« (482). Primärquellen wie Sekundärliteratur werden viel-fach herangezogen, wobei aus Sicht des Rezensenten in der konkreten Wortlaut-Analyse die Stimme des Verfassers durchaus deutlicher herausgehoben hätte werden können. So aber findet man auf zahlreichen Seiten lange Passagen zitiert, die nicht wirklich interpretiert werden. Auch die zeitgenössische Völkerrechtswissenschaft wird umfassend herangezogen und auch dabei gilt das Argument des Verfassers: Gerade Völkerrechtler aus der Region haben insbesondere in den Fallstudien 2 bis 4 eminent zur Normentstehung beigetragen, und die Liste der Namen ist lang und umfasst sowohl bekanntere als auch unbekanntere Gelehrte. An einer Stelle des Buches lautet die Aufzählung Dimitrij Ivanovič Kačenovski, Vladimir Bezobrazov, André N. Mandelstam und Fëdor Fëdorović Martens, Vaspasian Pella, Ludwik Ehrlich, Raphael Lemkin und Nikolaos Politis (57). Angemessenerweise zieht Skordos Primärquellen jenseits der sonst in der Völkerrechtsgeschichte dominierenden westeuropäischen Sprachen heran. Hier sind es beispielsweise auch Serben, Rumänen oder Griechen, die in den Fußnoten auftauchen. Ob sie wirklich und ausschließlich Mitglieder einer »transnationalen Gelehrtengesellschaft« (57) waren, scheint jedenfalls einseitig. Hat doch die Studie von Anthea Roberts gerade die nationalen Prägungen der Völkerrechtswissenschaft herausgearbeitet.[2] – Übrigens fehlen von der Monarchie bis zur Republik viele wichtige zeitgenössische österreichische Völkerrechtler.

■

Raquel R. Sirotti

The Workings of Private Colonization in Mozambique*

Control over land lies at the center of colonial history, not only because access to land is usually considered the quintessential symbol of territorial domination, but also due to its relevance in colonial enterprises. Through land policies, borders were formed, native populations were relocated or even exterminated, labor exploitation was regulated, and taxes were imposed and charged. Put differently, land was (and still is) a synonym for power. In Africa, disputes over land were also a geopolitical affair. In the late 19th century, the so-called »Scramble for Africa« determined the effective occupation of African territories by European colonial powers. Land policies therefore became an instrument for guaranteeing the maintenance of sovereignty over overseas territories.

Apart from shedding light on these and other issues, Barbara Direito's book brings another layer of complexity to the topic. It covers the land policies applied in the territory formerly governed by one of the most powerful and long-lasting charter companies in African history, the Mozambican Company (*Companhia de Moçambique*).

A common practice since the beginning of European colonial expansion, the resort to charter companies went into decay from the mid-19th century onwards due to the spread of liberal ideas that argued for commercial monopolies to be replaced by increased state investment in colonization projects. However, the principle of effective occupation, determined by the Berlin Conference of 1884–1885, provoked a resurgence of charter companies in Africa as part of a strategy of »cheap imperialism«, that is, of the control of colonial possessions at low cost to the colonial powers.

2 Anthea Roberts, Is International Law International?, Oxford 2017.

* Bárbara Direito, Terra e Colonialismo em Moçambique. A região de Manica e Sofala sob a Companhia de Moçambique, 1892–1942, Lisboa: Imprensa de Ciências Sociais 2020, 306 p., ISBN 978-972-671-622-8

In the Portuguese case, the conflict with the British over the Zambezi valley made the charter model especially attractive. As Direito explains, the granting of a large part of Mozambican territory to private colonizers was related, amongst other things, to the threat posed by the British magnate Cecil Rhodes, head of the British South African Company, who intended to extend British domination towards the Manica region. In an attempt to guarantee an active and profitable presence in the area, the Portuguese government granted state-like powers to the *Companhia de Moçambique* in early 1891. From then on, the Company acquired, among other rights and privileges, the power to lease, explore, and colonize all the territories under its concession.

But *Terra e Colonialismo em Moçambique* is not only about charter companies and land policies in Portuguese Africa. Direito's research provides a detailed analysis of how access to land was essential for social control, and therefore for the implementation of a broader colonial project involving public and private initiatives. For this reason, she argues that land policies can only be understood in connection with the regulation of agricultural activity and labor exploitation. This core argument guides the book's structure, which is divided into three parts and seven chapters.

Part one deals with the origins of Company rule. Its two chapters alternate descriptions of social, cultural and economic elements of the regions colonized by the *Companhia de Moçambique* with information on the reasons why the Portuguese government gave over the colonization of a great share of current-day Mozambican territory to two private companies (the *Companhia de Moçambique* and the *Companhia do Niassa*, which was active in the northern part of the colony). The chapters provide an overall picture of how company institutions worked on the ground and how officials navigated their operation. Although the *Companhia de Moçambique* was strongly criticized by Portuguese officials since its very creation, Direito shows how it managed to build a structured and pervasive governance regime in its territories.

Part two discusses the three pillars sustaining the power over land exerted by the *Companhia de Moçambique*: land grant policies, labor policies, and agricultural policies. Tensions and conflicts between the Company and multiple sub-concessionaries as well as between African populations, European settlers and Company officials are presented as the connecting thread between the ways in which the Company regulated land, labor, and agriculture. Direito also demonstrates the great power that company officials and other agents on the ground – such as surveying directors – had in processes of normative production, e. g. in land demarcation and distribution.

Part three covers the effects and repercussions of these policies. Its two chapters are especially enlightening, as they try to bring African voices into the equation. The topic of indigenous reservations (in what context and for what reasons they were created, how long they lasted, and what functions they served) stands out as a crucial element in the relationship between land ownership and indigenous populations. Yet, more information on how Africans actually disputed access to land would have been interesting. Direito does not use court cases or other sources which could contain further traces of African voices. Requests by Africans for land possession and acquisition are only mentioned in passing, and usually used as a reference for showing which elements were considered by county chiefs in the process of awarding land titles.

Despite demonstrating that the Mozambican Company regulated access to land in a fairly autonomous manner, Direito's study implies that these regulations were very much in line with the land policies applied in the territories ruled directly by the Portuguese government. Furthermore, the comparison with other African colonial states such as South Africa, Kenya and Southern Rhodesia leads to the conclusion that Company land regulations were also embedded in a broader African landscape. But still, was there anything special or unique about the charter companies' rule and the way land access was granted and regulated in their territories? These questions remain unanswered. While offering a sizeable, compelling, and original case study on land policies in the regions colonized by the *Companhia de Moçambique*, the emphasis on regulations and practices performed by a private institution might also interest the reader in potential correlations with other charter companies active in Mozambique (such as the Nyassa Company) and elsewhere in Africa.

■

Maysa Espíndola Souza

The Aftermath of Slavery in São Tomé and Príncipe*

The *curadorias dos serviçais e colonos* were important institutions during Portuguese colonialism in the 19th and 20th centuries. With minor differences in their design, these institutions existed throughout Portuguese domains in Africa, namely Angola, Cape Verde, Portuguese Guinea, Mozambique, and São Tomé and Príncipe. The main function of the *curadorias* was to manage African labour; after the abolition of slavery the colonial administration had to conclude labour contracts with the local population in the territories under its rule. Thus, the history of the *curadorias* is intertwined with attempts to create a hired labour force in Africa. It is important to highlight that an awareness of the entanglements between law and labour facilitates a better understanding of the complexities surrounding the legal status and experiences of hired *serviçais* (servants).

Maria Nazaré de Ceita's book, *A curadoria geral dos serviçais e colonos (S. Tomé e Príncipe 1875/1926)*, uses a case study of the São Tomé archipelago to demonstrate how central the *curadorias* were to colonialism. The book, published in April 2021, results from the author's master's dissertation, *Para uma história da Curadoria Geral dos Serviçais e Colonos de S. Tomé e Príncipe (1875–1926)*, defended in 2006 at the School of Arts and Humanities, University of Lisbon.

Ceita's study is the first time an author proposes to discuss the relevance of *curadorias* in the colonial experience of the Portuguese Empire. Ceita's book tackles the challenge of connecting scattered discussions in the bibliography and analysing often unpublished historical sources about *curadorias*. These sources comprise documentation from the *curadorias* themselves such as reports, correspondence, notices, and lists of labourers. The author also analyses reports from governors, denouncements of working conditions, bulletins, newspapers, legislation, and interviews with former employees and labourers. The diversity of sources underscores the importance of consulting not only Portuguese archives, but also local records. At the Historical Archive of São Tomé and Príncipe, Ceita was able to consult unique sources that helped answer her research questions. This bibliography is wide-ranging and fulfils the objective of demonstrating the archipelago's place in the Portuguese Empire; unfortunately, though, it does not include the bibliographical production produced from 2006 onwards.

Besides the introduction and conclusion, the book is divided into three parts, each with two chapters. In the first part, *A criação da curadoria geral dos serviçais e colonos no cenário colonial do arquipélago*, Chapter 1, *Génese e institucionalização da curadoria geral dos serviçais e colonos*, Ceita sets the context of how the *curadorias* were established in the archipelago. At the same time, tensions between former slaves and masters intensified, and the gradual process of abolishing slavery subjected the captive population to private and public tutelage. With the abolition, the former slaves refused to perform contract labour and abandoned their employers, who in many cases had been their masters. The creation of the *curadoria* and the new duties of the *curadores* were primarily aimed at mediating the difficult labour relations on the islands. The author then dedicates Chapter 2, *A curadoria geral dos serviçais e colonos: legislação, demografia e poder colonial*, to discussing the centrality of legislation in labour policies. Another important aspect of the chapter is a brief presentation of the *curadorias*' relations with the county administration, the police, the provincial governor, the local labour board, the secretary general of the government, the employers, and the indigenous population. A section describing the relations of the *serviçais* to the curator, which unfortunately the author did not include, could give us some clues to

* Maria Nazaré de Ceita, A curadoria geral dos serviçais e colonos (S. Tomé e Príncipe 1875/1926), Lisboa: Novembro 2021, 226 p., ISBN 978-989-54984-4-4

understand whether the *serviçais* understood the curator as a mediator of labour relations.

In the second part of the book, *Inventário e estudo das funções da curadoria geral dos serviçais e colonos e das suas repercussões sociais*, Chapter 3, *A curadoria: funções legais e formas de funcionamento*, Ceita analyses the legal and administrative functions of the *curadorias*. She points out that even though it was carried out by free labourers, contract labour involved some level of coercion, whether in recruitment, transportation, daily work, or in re-hiring. Police surveillance and violence were constant in the lives of the workers. In Chapter 4, *A curadoria, população autóctone e os contratados*, Ceita then discusses the process of land concentration on the islands. The local population struggled to maintain their properties in the face of the advancing European landowners. The author points out that the expropriations were frequently unduly assisted by the local authorities. In addition to land control, the archipelago of São Tomé and Príncipe also practiced a tight control over vagrancy. The hired serviçais who ran away from their employers were considered to be vagrants, but equally so was the local population of the islands.

The third and last part, *A companhia Ilha do Príncipe / Roça Água Izé: Estudo de caso*, contains an analysis of life on the plantations, taking as an example Roça Água Izé, an important property whose first owner was directly involved in discussions about the abolition of the Atlantic slave trade and the emancipation of slaves. João Maria de Sousa e Almeida was one of the driving forces of cocoa production in the archipelago. In Chapter 5, *Água Izé: criação, organização e expansão de uma unidade de produção centrada no cacau*, Ceita shows that the Sousa e Almeida estate, which at certain times was the largest cocoa exporter in the archipelago, had almost 3,000 hired workers. The data on wages and high mortality of workers, for example, allow conclusions about the process of wealth generation on the islands. This makes the theme of the exploitation of *serviçais* stand out even more. The last chapter, *O quotidiano da roça: »o tocar do sino«: do acordar ao adormecer – o quotidiano da roça através dos depoimentos orais*, draws attention to a type of sources little explored in the history of law: oral sources. The analysis of both oral and written sources allows the discussion of specific aspects of the relations between *serviçais* and *curadorias*. From the testimonies of former employees, the historian presents information about the tasks of the *curadorias*, the supervision of working conditions, corporal punishment, and the relations between European and African employees within the *curadoria*, for example. From the testimonies of the *serviçais*, the historian discusses aspects of recruitment, working conditions, and contacts with the *curadorias*. It is interesting how Ceita shows that one of the former *serviçais* was sent to São Tomé to pay off his family's debts in Angola.

This study is a significant contribution to legal history and, equally, to labour history. It demonstrates how *curadorias* were fundamental to the contract labour system in the Portuguese Empire. One dimension little explored by Ceita concerns the importance of the *curadoria* as a court. The curators had the power to adjudicate on labour issues through summary lawsuits. These lawsuits enable the scholar to understand what the expectations of employers and *serviçais* were regarding labour contracts, and it emerges that the *serviçais* fought to maintain their conditions as free labourers despite the employers' attempts. The book *Alma Negra: Depoimento sobre a questão dos Serviçais de S. Tomé*, attributed to a curator of the Island of Príncipe, presents accounts of what appear to be the *serviçais* themselves about their living and working conditions, but the author does not analyse these statements. Undeniably, the *curadorias* were often on the side of the employers; however, as it is possible to observe in many lawsuits, the *curadorias* also investigated complaints and enforced labour regulations that were contrary to the interests of the employers and colonial authorities. The lawsuits of the *curadorias* allow us to explore even the contradictions that surrounded the institution and the pressure that the workers themselves exerted.

Maria Nazaré de Ceita's book is much more than mere presentation of information about the history of the archipelago of São Tomé and Príncipe. It presents an analysis of labour relations, the hired labour system, legal statutes, and colonialism as an aftermath of slavery in the Atlantic world.

■

Tom Ginsburg

An Archeology of Law in Thailand*

From the perspective of comparative law, Thailand is anomalous – a distinct case that is difficult to categorize, with many apparently paradoxical features. Like Japan, the country retained its political independence, navigating the storms of Western colonialism to modernize on its own terms after concluding a treaty with the British in 1855. To manage this process, it borrowed law and legal institutions on a massive scale, primarily from France, Germany and Japan, giving us a complex and layered set of legal institutions. The depth of penetration of the formal law, however, is sometimes quite shallow.

The political system, too, is *sui generis*. Notoriously unstable when it comes to formal constitutions, the basic political structure is organized around a conservative monarchy that has provided continuity for several centuries. Formally subject to constitutional limitations, this monarchy has drawn on Buddhist idiom to deploy a good deal of informal power. The overall picture is one of formal legality whose operation is underpinned by informal structures that are difficult to grasp.

Until now, Thailand's legal history has not been the subject of much scholarly attention in foreign languages. This book, jointly edited by Professors Andrew Harding and Munin Pongsapan, is an important corrective. With a set of fresh and diverse essays, contributed by a mix of established foreign scholars and younger scholars based in Thailand, the volume provides an essential reference for this important jurisdiction and marks a major development in Southeast Asian legal studies generally.

The book is organized roughly chronologically, beginning with the legal history of Siam before the country's intensive encounter with colonialism. Evidence for this period is scarce. Since the writing of Robert Lingat in the 1930s, it has always been assumed that Buddhist ideas of universal moral law, embodied in the *Thammasat*, have provided the major source of law, with royally promulgated rules providing only interstitial norms. The *Thammasat* derived from the *dharmasastras*, Sanskrit texts of religious origin that were influential in Southeast Asia. Lingat's characterizations placed natural law ideas at the center. In an important revisionist essay that begins Part I, Professors Chris Baker and Pasuk Phongpaichit take issue with this standard story, focusing on the famous Three Seals Code of 1805. They demonstrate that this document was a kind of assemblage of texts, borrowing material from neighboring jurisdictions, but also reflecting an older tradition of royal lawmaking in Siam. Law, in the Austinian sense of a sovereign command backed by force, clearly had a role to play from early on, even if European analysts tended to minimize its presence. Kongsatja Suwanapech follows with a history of the initial Royal Commands, statements given by Thai monarchs upon their ascension to the throne. The chapter illustrates how these have evolved over time to fit the political and idiomatic needs of particular kings. King Chulalongkorn (reign 1868–1910) drew on a Buddhist theory of the *Mahasommutiraj*, or Great Elected, which resonated with contemporary European ideas, while also providing a basis for absolutism. This theory proved useful in 1932 after the People's Party revolution ended the absolute monarchy in favor of a constitutional monarchy. Although that revolution formally placed the people in the position of being the source of power, the precise locus of sovereignty remains distinctly ambiguous today. In the design of Royal Commands, we observe the active construction of political legitimation by monarchs and their elite allies, seeking to limit popular sovereignty.

The remainder of Part I shows the continuing relevance of the early period for Thai legal culture today. Buddhist idiom retains a good deal of force, as shown by Khemthong Tonsakulrungruang in his chapter, an example of a growing scholarly project to call attention to the important but understudied category of Buddhist law. Eugénie Mérieau traces

* Andrew Harding, Munin Pongsapan (eds.), Thai Legal History: From Traditional to Modern Law, Cambridge: Cambridge University Press 2021, 293 p., ISBN 978-1-108-83087-4

the history of Thailand's *lèse majesté* law, which has been a tool of repression deployed by a long series of military dictators. David Engel shows how the distinct legal consciousness of Northern Thailand survives and has been deployed in mass political demonstrations involving a »blood curse« ritual. The persistence of »traditional« ideas in Thai law is not only a story of society resisting modern legal norms of foreign origin, but of the active deployment of traditional idiom by elites seeking to preserve hierarchies. It is also a story of the public retaining ideas about karma, power and authority. Clearly, as William Faulkner famously said, »The past is never dead. It's not even past.«

Part II of the book focuses on foreign law influence during the period of high reform, after the signing of the Bowring Treaty with Great Britain in 1855. Individual chapters examine the laws of contract, trust, administration, family law, criminal law, and the treatment of Thailand under international legal standards of »civilization«. This section of the book illustrates the *bricolage* character of reforms. A particularly interesting example here is the chapter by Surutchada and Adam Reekie on the role of British judges in the Supreme Court of Siam in the early 20th century. Despite no formal treaty requirement to do so, Siam's legal system brought in numerous foreign advisers, who had a profound influence on the country's legal development. That British judges would be included is somewhat surprising, given that most of the original legal borrowings were from civil law jurisdictions such as France and Japan. British judges sitting on the Supreme Court decided many cases, despite the fact that they »had no more experience of interpreting and applying a civil law code than the Siamese judges with whom they were sitting« (115). The judges left their mark through precedential types of reasoning and their application of the common law institution of the trust. The encounter is somewhat paradigmatic of Thailand's strategy for retaining independence through law: the country played one foreign power off against another and drew influences from a variety of sources without a strict orthodoxy.

Part III brings the story to the contemporary period, the unstable cycles of constitutional change that have persisted since the 1932 revolution. As Rawin Leelapatana writes, this period has been one of a quest for a »nirvana« of a stable constitutional order, something that has not materialized. The political cycles of coups followed by weak democratic governments have persisted, and yet one also sees conceptual and institutional evolution. As Duncan McCargo notes in his chapter, beginning in the early 1990s judges were increasingly called in to resolve political disputes, a phenomenon which continued into this century. Political violence and coups have also been normalized in a legal sense, as Tyrell Haberkorn's chapter on amnesties shows.

Why should a non-specialist be interested in the legal history of this midsize country in Southeast Asia? The successful deployment of Western law by elites to retain freedom of maneuver in an era of colonialism is illuminating for understanding societies which were not so successful. The creative work of political and legal elites to create hybrid concepts suggests much more agency for non-Western subjects than the focus on colonialism might indicate. As in many other countries, we observe a lingering disjuncture between formal law and lived experience, but Thailand offers a distinctly Buddhist context to view these interactions. This might contribute to a richer understanding of how religion and law interact than the literature on majority Muslim and Christian societies has presented us with.

Andrew Harding, in other work quoted by Peter Leyland in his chapter on administrative justice, has characterized law in Southeast Asia using a geologic metaphor, with layers put on top of each other without actually replacing what is below (195–196). Sometimes, the lower layers are still visible, even if not easy to distinguish from each other. The archeology of these layers in Thailand is a project now coming to fruition, for which we can be grateful.

■

Adolfo Giuliani

Rethinking Emilio Betti, the anti-Gadamer*

Emilio Betti staked out an original theory that made interpretation (anciently named ›hermeneutics‹) the key to explaining the legal phenomenon. In his mature work, *General Theory of Interpretation* (*Teoria generale dell'interpretazione*, I–II, 1955, hereinafter GTI), he expanded this idea into a wide-ranging theory that made hermeneutics a general method that not only blurred the line between individual legal disciplines but also between law and other human sciences. Law, in this view, is a spiritual creation encoded in perceptible and objective forms that are transmitted over time. It follows that its complex architecture can be known and explained, as it is in the nature of the legal phenomenon to be written in the language of hermeneutics. Despite the theory's philosophical significance and the subsequent debates that involved, among others, Hans-Georg Gadamer and Franz Wieacker, it failed to be accepted by mainstream scholarship and Betti came to be remembered as an outsider, a solitary figure, isolated and misunderstood, a dreamer, even the last Romantic. To put it bluntly, why?

This issue, traditionally addressed by Betti studies, is also dealt with in this book, but with such forthright clarity and original results as to make the volume a substantial advance and a fundamental rethinking of Betti. Edited by Antonio Banfi, Massimo Brutti and Emanuele Stolfi, this book collects thirteen essays delivered at a conference marking the 50th anniversary of Betti's death in 1968. While the contributions address a wide variety of interdisciplinary concerns implied by Betti's wide-ranging theory, sometimes with considerable attention to detail, to this reviewer the book's major thrust lies in three arguments.

The first relates to Betti's relationship to Fascism. Massimo Brutti's contribution takes us to the years from the fall of Fascism (1943) to the publication of the *General Theory of Interpretation* (1955). Betti's personal story was woven into that political context. He was not a bystander but an enthusiastic supporter of the Fascist regime, initially removed from teaching in 1945 but reinstated to a university position the year after. This experience left perceptible marks on his work. One is a clear principle of objectivity that gave life to his theory of interpretation. What Betti proposed seemingly arose from his revulsion of political discord: he responded to the corrosive power of war propaganda with truth-seeking and a concern for how to achieve a correct understanding of human communication (Brutti 59, GTI 87). Betti's interpretive theory also implies an appeal to tolerance, as understanding goes hand in hand with dialogue and a sensitivity to circumstances. Another mark is apparent in Betti's references to a distinctive European consciousness. He believed in a European spiritual core based on a common cultural stock (Cervati) that was now threatened by both Anglo-American utilitarism and Soviet materialism. By shifting the emphasis from an author in isolation to his historical context, Betti appears as part of a larger experience in which his personal story is interwoven with the story of a generation that lived through the tragic decades of the rise of totalitarianisms and World War II.

The volume's second main thrust relates to Betti's theory of interpretation. When Betti presented his theory in embryonic form in 1927, he started from a question that could be phrased as »how we can hope to understand the legal past in the present time?« He proposed to reconcile the two opposite ends of juristic experience: historical tradition and the legal system, or in his parlance, »Roman law and present-day dogmatics«. However, he added an important proviso. He spoke of dogmatics without paying attention to the work of the post-Pandectists of his day. While the latter studied legal systems *per se*, Betti postulated the

* Antonio Banfi, Emanuele Stolfi, Massimo Brutti (eds.), Dall'esegesi giuridica alla teoria dell'interpretazione: Emilio Betti (1890–1968), Rome: Roma TrE-Press 2020, 329 p., ISBN 979-12-80060-21-1

historical dimension of the conceptual framework (dogmatics) by which legal systems work (Zaccaria, Nitsch, Petrillo). According to him, historical (legal) experience, encoded in historical texts, would remain silent without a conceptual framework that makes unfamiliar factual experience intelligible according to familiar categories, which Betti called representative forms (Nitsch). By fitting facts into pre-existing patterns of interpretation and explanation, these representative forms give meaning to historical data that would otherwise be lost. An important corollary is that knowledge is not a passive reception but an active process of the production of meaning, which operates with the assistance of forms and concepts. Moreover, such a conceptual framework (following G. B. Vico's ›maker's knowledge‹ principle) is »made«, hence postulating the historicity of both subject and object.

If we turn to the core of Betti's idea of interpretation, we see that its main feature was a resolute concern with objectivity. To understand the legal past, the purely historical cannot be separated from the formal (dogmatics). And because the process of knowing is filtered through forms of representation, such an approach dismisses the primacy of facts affirmed by positivism, but without falling into subjectivism. The purpose of Betti's theory was to restore the autonomy of law in its historical dimension.

This appeal to objectivity divided Betti from Gadamer (Zaccaria, Petrillo, Vargiu). Starting from different premises, Gadamer broadened the province of interpretation to embrace the whole human condition. To Gadamer, humans are situated in a flow of memories and experiences continuously re-appropriated: living is interpreting. However, objectivity is missing in this picture, and it is precisely to its disappearance that Betti (and Wieacker) reacted, protesting that historical knowledge should not be tainted by implicit or subconscious assumptions. Betti believed that an objective reality existed and was knowable through forms of representation. In private law, for example, according to one of his well-known formulations, interpretation addressed not *voluntas* but the *declaratio voluntatis* (Banfi). To Betti, interpretation is a process to grasp meaning, not a mode of being.

If we turn to the sources that support Betti's methodological project, it should be noted that, though he did use authors clearly steeped in romantic idealism (e. g. Hartmann, Schleiermacher and Humboldt), Betti worked out his position from a broader background. His ideas of representative forms and of a triadic cognitive process was drawn from Charles Peirce (GTI 27, 79), and other sources point in the direction of Ernst Cassirer's *Philosophy of symbolic forms* (1923). This observation would be of little importance without at the same time noting that those sources had been used by Hermann Kantorowicz for his ground-breaking *Definition of law* (1939). This observation (and others that could be easily drawn from Betti's sources) strongly suggest that Betti should be seen not as an epigone of 19th-century romanticism, but as the proponent of an intellectual project that was in touch with contemporary and forward-looking debates on a dialogue between law, linguistic philosophy, semiotics and science.

Thirdly, in his introductory essay, Italo Birocchi raises the question whether there is »a place for a new hermeneutics for the open normative regimes of the globalisation age«. Three features of Betti's hermeneutics to be gleaned from the present book point to a positive answer:

i) Interdisciplinarity: it seems that one of the traits of the 21st century has been to refute one of the fundamental claims voiced during the 20th century, namely, to separate law and its autonomous rational foundation from politics and morality. Authors as diverse as Kantorowicz, Kelsen and Hart reacted to the clash of ideologies of their time with their determination to place the law on a rational islet to keep it separate from a sea of moral or political relativism. Today, however, we are more open to accepting that law's normativity cannot be established without first confronting a broader normativity that encompasses plural statements of various sorts: legal, moral, political and aesthetic, to name but a few. Betti believed in an interdisciplinary perspective: in his mind, knowing the law is a cognitive pursuit that transcends the purely legal.

ii) Objectivity: today, having dismissed postmodern scepticism about the truth-content of language, we are more inclined to reconsider the forms by which the legal phenomenon can be objectively known. It is precisely Betti's denial of Gadamer's hermeneutical philosophy that makes his position attractive.

iii) Conceptual pragmatism: there is a growing awareness that the legal conceptual framework has a historical or pragmatic nature, which in turn demands an appropriate epistemology. Betti's reference to the ›maker's knowledge‹ tradition, currently revived by the philosophy of information, indicates a fertile path of research that begins from the question originally asked by Betti in 1927: how can we hope to understand the legal past in the present time?

If those premises are correct, Betti certainly has something interesting to tell us.

■

Christoph Schönberger

Weimarer Grenzüberschreitungen*

Der hundertste Geburtstag der Weimarer Reichsverfassung hat eine Fülle wissenschaftlicher Bilanzliteratur hervorgebracht. In diesen Zusammenhang gehört auch der vorliegende Sammelband, dessen Beiträge auf eine von den Herausgebern veranstaltete Tagung in Weimar im April 2019 zurückgehen. Für die deutschen Beiträger wird dabei zumeist das Konzept verfolgt, die Hauptbeiträge jüngeren Autorinnen und Autoren zu übertragen, die dann von älteren Wissenschaftlern kommentiert werden.

Mit »Weimar international« widmet sich der Band einer thematischen Nische, die in der Jubiläumsliteratur ansonsten nur vereinzelt eine Rolle gespielt hat.[1] Ausweislich der Einleitung der Herausgeber verstehen diese die »internationale« Dimension der Weimarer Reichsverfassung in erster Linie als Analyse von Rezeptionsprozessen in zwei Richtungen: der Rezeption ausländischer Vorbilder in der Weimarer Reichsverfassung einerseits, der Rezeption der Weimarer Reichsverfassung im Ausland andererseits (3 f.). Diesen Rezeptionsprozessen sind denn auch die meisten Beiträge des Bandes gewidmet.

Mit dieser Fokussierung auf Rezeptionsprozesse ist allerdings eine gewisse Beschränkung des Themenfelds verbunden. Vieles, was zur »internationalen« Dimension der Weimarer Reichsverfassung gehört, gerät auf diese Weise nur am Rande oder gar nicht in den Blick. Augenfällig ist das zunächst für den völkerrechtlichen Kontext der Weimarer Verfassungsschöpfung. Die Herausgeber heben zwar die Bedeutung des Versailler Vertrags für die Arbeit der Nationalversammlung hervor (6), diese wird im Band aber nicht näher behandelt. Ebenso wenig geht es dem Band in der großen Mehrheit seiner Beiträge darum, das Weimarer Verfassungswerk durch die vergleichende Analyse der zeitgenössischen Verfassungen und Verfassungsentwicklungen anderer europäischer Staaten besser zu verstehen.[2] Denn die Analyse von Rezeptionsprozessen ist selbstverständlich nicht gleichbedeutend mit einer umfassenden vergleichenden Einordnung der deutschen Verfassungsgebung des Jahres 1919.

Glücklicherweise wird die Konzentration auf Rezeptionsvorgänge jedoch am Anfang des Bandes gleich zweimal durchbrochen. Dies geschieht zunächst durch den hervorragenden Überblicksbeitrag von Jana Osterkamp, der das Weimarer Verfassungswerk als Teil einer europäischen »Verfassungswelle« nach dem Ersten Weltkrieg versteht und durch den Kommentar von Rainer Wahl anregend ergänzt wird. Aus der Konkursmasse der zusammengebrochenen multinationalen Imperien Österreich-Ungarn, Osmanisches Reich und Russ-

* Thomas Kleinlein, Christoph Ohler (Hg.), Weimar international. Kontext und Rezeption der Verfassung von 1919, Tübingen: Mohr Siebeck 2020, VIII + 269 S., ISBN 978-3-16-158877-8

1 Siehe aber: Ewald Wiederin, Die Weimarer Reichsverfassung im internationalen Kontext, in: Horst Dreier, Christian Waldhoff (Hg.), Das Wagnis der Demokratie: Eine Anatomie der Weimarer Reichsverfassung, München 2018, 45–64; Christoph Schönberger, Zwischen Versailler Vertrag und europäischer Verfassungswelle: Die Weimarer Verfassung im internationalen Kontext, in: Horst Dreier, Christian Waldhoff (Hg.), Weimars Verfassung. Eine Bilanz nach 100 Jahren, Göttingen 2020, 75–86, sowie die Beiträge zu »Translating Weimar« in: Rg 27 (2019) 175–230.

2 Dazu aber bereits Christoph Gusy (Hg.), Demokratie in der Krise. Europa in der Zwischenkriegszeit, Baden-Baden 2008.

land entstanden damals neue, unsichere Nationalstaaten mit heterogener Bevölkerung, die sich fortschrittliche demokratische Verfassungen gaben (etwa Polen, die Tschechoslowakei, Rumänien, Finnland und die baltischen Staaten), deren Verfassungsentwicklung in der Zwischenkriegszeit aber nicht selten durch ein Schwanken zwischen den neu demokratisierten Parlamenten und einer Präsidialherrschaft mit autoritärer Entwicklungsmöglichkeit gekennzeichnet war. So sehr die Weimarer Republik insoweit eine Sonderstellung einnimmt, weil hier kein Staat neu gegründet wurde und die Nationalitätenkonflikte durch die Gebietsverluste nach dem Ersten Weltkrieg in Deutschland an Bedeutung verloren, so aufschlussreich ist es doch, ihren Weg gerade auch als Teil dieses mitteleuropäischen Krisenpanoramas in den Blick zu nehmen.

Ebenso aufschlussreich ist der vergleichende Blick auf die französische Dritte Republik, mit dem Mattias Wendel die Beiträge zu »Weimar im internationalen Kontext« eröffnet. Wendel behandelt allerdings nicht eigentlich die Rezeption französischer Verfassungsvorbilder durch Hugo Preuß und die Nationalversammlung. Er begnügt sich insoweit lediglich mit dem Hinweis, neben anderen ausländischen Traditionen fänden sich in der Weimarer Institutionenarchitektur »gleich mehrere Bausteine, die dem französischen Verfassungsrecht der damaligen Zeit entstammen« (64). Hier wäre es sinnvoll gewesen, etwas genauer auf diese – zeitgenössisch weitgehend uneingestandene – Rezeption einzugehen und dabei etwa näher herauszuarbeiten, dass Frankreich damals in Europa das einzige große republikanische Vorbild bildete, worauf Michael Stolleis in seinem Kommentar hinweist (78). Wendel bietet aber eine vergleichende Analyse der Grundstrukturen der französischen Dritten Republik im Kontrast zu denjenigen der Republik von Weimar. Er arbeitet dabei heraus, dass beide Systeme aus unterschiedlichen Gründen große Probleme mit der Regierungsstabilität hatten, und sich jeweils anders entwickelten, als im ursprünglichen Verfassungsgefüge angelegt: in Frankreich hin zur Schwächung des Staatspräsidenten und einer Vorherrschaft des Parlaments, in Deutschland umgekehrt hin zu einer Präsidialdiktatur in den letzten Jahren Weimars. Zutreffend arbeitet Wendel dabei heraus, dass die französische Verfassung in der Gründungsphase Weimars zumeist als abschreckendes Gegenbild fungierte, weil Hugo Preuß und die Nationalversammlung einen »Parlamentsabsolutismus« fürchteten. Eine bedeutsame Rolle spielte insoweit der elsässische Staatsrechtler Robert Redslob, der in einem 1918 erschienenen Buch über »Die parlamentarische Regierung in ihrer wahren und unechten Form« die Kritik der französischen Staatsrechtslehre der Dritten Republik am französischen »Parlamentsabsolutismus« in deutscher Sprache zusammenfasste und damit die deutsche Tendenz bestärkte, im Reichspräsidenten als »Ersatzkaiser« ein Gegengewicht gegen das Parlament zu suchen. Zu Recht weisen Wendel und Stolleis dabei darauf hin, dass das französische Gegenbild 1918/19 deshalb in dieser Weise wirksam werden konnte, weil es erlaubte, ältere deutsche Traditionslinien des Ideals einer überparteilich gedachten Exekutive und des Misstrauens gegen die Parlamente unter demokratischen Bedingungen zu erneuern (72, 78 f., 81 ff.).

In der Folge enthält der Band Einzelbeiträge zum Weimarer Bundesstaat (Almut Neumann mit Kommentar von Stefan Oeter), zu Gleichheitsrechten und sozialen Grundrechten (Anna Katharina Mangold mit Kommentar von Gerhard Lingelbach) und schließlich zum Weimarer Religionsverfassungsrecht (Ansgar Hense mit Kommentar von Wolfgang Huber). Die Beiträge zum Weimarer Bundesstaat arbeiten zutreffend die starken Kontinuitätslinien zum Bundesstaat des Kaiserreichs heraus, die trotz der grundlegenden Umstellung von einem monarchischen auf einen demokratischen Föderalismus erhalten blieben (Exekutivföderalismus, Reichsrat in der Nachfolge des Bundesrats, Problem eines hegemonialen Föderalismus durch die Größe Preußens). Einwirkungen ausländischer Vorbilder und insbesondere der traditionellen demokratischen Bundesstaaten USA und Schweiz gab es hingegen kaum. Neumann führt als einziges Beispiel die Homogenitätsklausel in Art. 17 WRV an, für die es Vorbilder im schweizerischen und US-amerikanischen Verfassungsrecht gab (89 f.). Angesichts der Fortführung grundlegender Strukturen des deutschen Bundesstaates aus dem Kaiserreich und des gleichzeitigen massiven Unitarisierungsschubs nicht zuletzt in der Finanzverfassung lässt sich allerdings kaum Neumanns Aussage rechtfertigen, die Weimarer Neuregelungen hätten sich »in wichtigen Bereichen an internationalen Vorbildern, allen voran dem US-amerikanischen und dem schweizerischen Bundesstaat« orientiert (93). Die weitgehend ausgebliebene Rezeption verweist vielmehr umgekehrt darauf, dass dem Weimarer Bundesstaat eine spezifisch föderative Legitimität gerade fehlte und Weimar insofern nicht nur, wie Stefan Oeter treffend-überspitzt formuliert, eine »Demokratie ohne Demokraten«, sondern erst recht ein Bundesstaat ohne Föderalisten war (118). In ihrem Beitrag über Gleichheitsrechte und soziale Grundrechte hebt Anna Katharina Mangold mit Recht hervor, dass die Einführung des Frauenwahlrechts in Weimar auf eine transnationale Frauenbewegung zurückging und die Einführung sozialer Grundrechte auch eine Reaktion auf die Herausforderung durch die bolschewistische Revolution in Rußland darstellte (119 ff.). Der Kommentar von Gerhard Lingelbach geht dabei genauer auf die Debattenbeiträge von Frauen in der Nationalversammlung ein (137 ff.). Ansgar Hense bietet einen souveränen Überblick über das Religionsverfassungsrecht der Weimarer Verfassung (147 ff.). Er geht dabei auch auf rechtsvergleichende Aspekte ein und betont, dass in der Nationalversammlung immer wieder fragmentarisch Wissen über ausländische Regelungsmodelle Erwähnung fand und besonders die französische Trennungsgesetzgebung von 1905 nicht selten als Kontrastmodell fungierte.

Der letzte Teil des Bandes bietet Beiträge über die Rezeption des Weimarer Verfassungsrechts im Ausland. Carlos Miguel Herrera berichtet über die Bedeutung Weimars im französischen Rechtsdenken der Zwischenkriegszeit und zeigt dabei ein Maß der Auseinandersetzung, wie es sich zeitgenössisch wohl in keinem anderen Land fand (177 ff.). Die französische Diskussion war dabei hin- und hergerissen zwischen dem tiefen Misstrauen gegenüber der jungen deutschen Demokratie, das in der außenpolitischen Rivalität wurzelte, und der Faszination für den verfassungstechnischen Modernisierungsschub, den die Weimarer Reichsverfassung im Vergleich mit dem traditionellen Verfassungsrecht der Dritten Republik bedeutete (Direktwahl des Staatsoberhaupts, Formen der direkten Demokratie, Frauenwahlrecht, Verhältniswahlrecht, soziale Grundrechte). Es sei angemerkt, dass diese Intensität der Auseinandersetzung an eine lange Tradition in der Staatsrechtslehre der Dritten Republik anknüpfen konnte, die sich nach der Kriegsniederlage 1870 in der Auseinandersetzung mit dem Staatsrecht des deutschen Kaiserreichs entwickelt hatte. Bedauerlicherweise weist Herrera nur nebenbei darauf hin, dass dieser deutsch-französische Diskursraum noch bis hinein in die Vorgeschichte der Vierten und Fünften Republik reicht (198), und geht diesen Nachwirkungen der Weimarer Verfassung in Frankreich nach dem Zweiten Weltkrieg nicht näher nach.

Der Beitrag von Jens Meierhenrich zur Bedeutung der Weimarer Verfassung in der angloamerikanischen Welt beschäftigt sich nicht eigentlich mit der Rezeption der Weimarer Verfassung, sondern mit dem historischen Bild der Weimarer Republik in der angloamerikanischen Welt (199 ff.). Er zeigt insoweit – in verspäteter Parallele zur Entwicklung in der Geschichts- und Rechtswissenschaft der Bundesrepublik – eine Entwicklung auf, in der das frühe Bild einer missglückten Verfassung zunehmend abgelöst wurde durch das Bild einer in vielerlei Hinsicht innovativen Verfassung in ungünstiger Zeit.

Der Beitrag von Piotr Czarny über die Rezeption Weimars in Polen (221 ff.) stellt am polnischen Beispiel einen Aspekt der Rezeption der Weimarer Reichsverfassung im Ausland heraus, der in Deutschland heute nur ungern gesehen und behandelt wird: nämlich das Vorbild der Stellung des Reichspräsidenten für Länder, die in der Zwischenkriegszeit zu einer Stärkung der Exekutive gegenüber dem Parlament oder sogar autoritären Verfassungen übergehen wollten, wie es etwa auch in Österreich Ende der 1920er Jahre der Fall war. Für Polen zeigt Czarny dabei, dass dort zunächst das Vorbild der französischen Dritten Republik prägend war, man aber im Verlauf der 1920er Jahre zunehmend auf eine Stärkung der Rolle des Staatspräsidenten setzte und sich dabei von der Weimarer Verfassung inspirieren ließ. Der Beitrag weist so auf ein unbequemes Desiderat der Forschung zur Rezeption Weimars hin: die Vorbildfunktion Weimars für Verfassungsreformen mit dem Ziel, die Exekutive gegenüber dem Parlament zu stärken. In diesen Zusammenhang würde auch die nähere Untersuchung der Bedeutung Weimars für die Verfassung der französischen Fünften Republik gehören.

Etwas quer zu den sonstigen Beiträgen des Bandes liegt der faszinierende Beitrag von Eli M. Salzberger über die Bedeutung der Weimarer Rechtskultur in Israel (232 ff.). Offenkundig geht es insoweit nicht um eine Rezeption Weimars durch den Verfassungsgeber, fehlt es doch in Israel bis heute an einem zusammenfassenden Verfassungstext. Man arbeitet vielmehr mit einer Vielzahl von sogenannten *basic laws*, die seit 1958 schrittweise verabschiedet wurden. Salzberger geht es vielmehr um die Analyse des Einflusses, den in Deutschland geborene und in der Weimarer Zeit ausgebildete Juristen auf die israelische Rechtsentwicklung der ersten Jahrzehnte ausübten, insbesondere als Richter des israelischen *Supreme Court*. Salzberger konstatiert dabei eine aufgeklärt-rechtsstaatliche und gemäßigt positivistische Grundhaltung dieser Juristen, die sie in die Rechtsprechung hineintrugen. Prägend war dabei nach seiner Rekonstruktion allerdings weniger die Weimarer Verfassung als die deutsche juristische Sozialisation der entsprechenden Personen in der Weimarer Republik, die wache Auseinandersetzung mit den Gründen für den Untergang Weimars und die Offenheit dafür, die in Auseinandersetzung mit Weimar entstandene Konzeption der »streitbaren Demokratie« für die israelische Situation zu aktivieren.

Insgesamt bereichert der vorliegende Band die gelegentlich etwas sehr deutsch-introvertierte Diskussion über die Weimarer Reichsverfassung durch vielfältige Beiträge zu deren internationalem Kontext. Auf vielstimmige Weise erweitert sich so das Bild der Weimarer Verfassung, was weitere Forschungen zu deren internationaler Dimension anregen kann. Gerade die Verortung im internationalen Umfeld lässt die Weimarer Verfassung als eine wesentliche Etappe auf dem Weg zur Etablierung demokratischer Verfassungsstaaten hervortreten. Diese vergleichende Einordnung macht in besonderer Weise deutlich, dass der demokratische Verfassungsstaat nie zum selbstverständlichen Besitz werden kann, sondern in jedem Gemeinwesen und in jeder Epoche immer neu gewonnen werden muss.

■

Reinhard Zimmermann

Hero auf dem Felsenturme …*

I. Fritz Schulz, Fritz Pringsheim, Paul Koschaker, Franz Wieacker und Helmut Coing gehören zu den großen Rechtshistorikern des 20. Jahrhunderts. Sie stehen im Mittelpunkt des hier zu besprechenden Buches. Wer, wie der Verfasser dieser Besprechung, von den meisten von ihnen in seiner Arbeit nachhaltig inspiriert worden ist,[1] wird das Buch mit gespannter Aufmerksamkeit zur Hand nehmen, zumal es sich um den Schlussstein eines jahrelangen, durch einen ERC Grant geförderten Forschungsprojekts handelt (»the final end point of a long and happy journey«, wie der Autor etwas tautologisch schreibt, xii), das seinerseits die Keimzelle eines Academy of Finland Centre of Excellence war.[2] Im Untertitel des Buches werden zudem eine Reihe von Themen aufgerufen, die von erheblichem zeitgeschichtlichen Interesse sind, aber auch bereits die ersten Fragen aufwerfen: Koschaker, Wieacker und Coing als »Exile Scholars«? Schulz und Pringsheim als Protagonisten eines Kampfes um die Zukunft Europas? Rätselhaft auch der Haupttitel des Buches (Wie passt er zu den verschiedenen Elementen des Untertitels? Welches »Reich des Rechts« ist gemeint?), und

* Kaius Tuori, Empire of Law. Nazi Germany, Exile Scholars and the Battle for the Future of Europe, Cambridge: Cambridge University Press 2020, XVI + 313 S., ISBN 978-1-108-48363-6

1 Zu Fritz Schulz (Classical Roman Law und Prinzipien des römischen Rechts) vgl. Reinhard Zimmermann, The Law of Obligations: Roman Foundations of the Civilian Tradition, Oxford 1996, xv; zu Franz Wieacker (Privatrechtsgeschichte der Neuzeit) vgl. Reinhard Zimmermann, Foreword, in: Franz Wieacker, A History of Private Law in Europe, Oxford 1995, v–xiii, xii; zu Paul Koschaker (Europa und das römische Recht) vgl. Reinhard Zimmermann, Europa und das römische Recht, in: AcP 202 (2002) 243–316 (244–249).

2 Als »Kulmination« desselben Forschungsprojekts bezeichnen die Herausgeber Kaius Tuori und Heta Björklund den Sammelband Roman Law and the Idea of Europe, 2019; dazu Reinhard Zimmermann, Rez., in: ZEuP 30 (2022) 227–229. Dem Projekt verdanken wir auch Monographien über Koschaker (von Paolo Beggio), Wieacker (von Ville Erkillä; dazu Reinhard Zimmermann, Ville Erkillä, The Conceptual Change of Conscience: Franz Wieacker and German Legal Historiography 1933–1968, in: ZRG (RA) 137 (2020) 543–548) und Schulz (von Jacob Giltaji).

ebenso rätselhaft das Titelbild »Hero« des viktorianischen Historienmalers (Sir) Lawrence Alma-Tadema (über den es im Art History Archive heißt, seine Bilder seien »without deep-meaning or significance, essentially his work was decorative«): »Hero« hier übrigens nicht im Sinne des Wortes »Held«, sondern als Priesterin der Aphrodite, die am westlichen Ufer des Hellespont auf ihren den Fluten entsteigenden Liebhaber Leander wartet.

II. Gegliedert ist das Buch in sieben Abschnitte; außer einer Einführung und den Schlussfolgerungen sind dies fünf Abschnitte, in deren Mittelpunkt jeweils einer der eingangs erwähnten Rechtshistoriker steht.

In Abschnitt 2 ist dies Fritz Schulz (1879–1957). Freilich geht es nicht um das Oeuvre von Schulz insgesamt, sondern um eine Vortragsreihe aus dem Sommersemester 1933 (also fast unmittelbar nach der nationalsozialistischen Machtübernahme), die im darauffolgenden Jahr unter dem Titel »Prinzipien des römischen Rechts« als Buch erschien. Dabei handelte es sich um »a counter-attack against the move of the Nazi party to cut back the study of Roman law, which was considered an ›un-German‹ subject«.[3] Tuori befasst sich zunächst mit ein paar anderen der politisch relevanten Prinzipien (Isolierung, Tradition, Nation, Humanität, Treue und Sicherheit), bevor er dann schwerpunktmäßig auf das Freiheitsprinzip zu sprechen kommt. Dieses sieht er in engem Zusammenhang mit, ja in Abhängigkeit von, dem Autoritätsprinzip. In merkwürdiger Weise, so Tuori, biete Schulz hier eine konservative Verteidigung der liberalen Tradition. Schulz habe sich einerseits auf den klassischen Liberalismus des 19. Jahrhunderts gestützt und andererseits auf Jherings »Geist des römischen Rechts«. Tuori berichtet dann die Geschichte von Schulz' Emigration nach England und von der Übersetzung seiner »Prinzipien« ins Englische (»Principles of Roman Law«, 1936), bevor er unter der Überschrift »Exiles and Scholarly Change« auf die »transformative« Wirkung der Erfahrung des Exils auf die vertriebenen Gelehrten zu sprechen kommt. Im Falle von Schulz konstatiert er einen Wandel »from purely technical or discipline-internal debates to political argumentation« (83) (an anderer Stelle ist von »both covert and open political themes« die Rede, 75). Zum Vergleich zieht Tuori die Wirkung des Exils auf das Werk anderer Gelehrter heran, darunter Hannah Arendt, Franz Neumann, Ernst Levy und Arnaldo Momigliano.

Im dritten Abschnitt wird der Blick auf Fritz Pringsheim (1882–1967) gerichtet, wiederum aber vor allem auf eine Arbeit, den Aufsatz »Legal Policy and the Reforms of Hadrian« (JRS 24 (1934) 141–153); er beruht auf einem Vortrag in Cambridge vom Oktober 1933. Tuori schildert die akademische Marginalisierung von Pringsheim in Freiburg und seinen Weg ins Oxforder Exil, macht seine Leser dann mit dem Inhalt des erwähnten Aufsatzes vertraut (einer »Idealisierung« von Kaiser Hadrian (88) und seiner kosmopolitischen Reichsidee als – unausgesprochenem – »counterpoint to the emerging totalitarian state«, 103), und kontextualisiert diesen Aufsatz dann biographisch und ideengeschichtlich. Auch in Pringsheim sieht Tuori einen Römischrechtler, der sich zunächst hauptsächlich mit technisch-juristischen Fragen beschäftigt habe, der nun aber, unter der Erfahrung der Entfremdung, die historische Tradition in den Dienst gegenwärtiger Zwecke stellte. Von zentraler Bedeutung seien dabei für Pringsheim, wie für Kaiser Hadrian, die Ideen der Gleichheit und der Rechtsstaatlichkeit gewesen. Wiederum vergleicht Tuori die Erfahrungen von Pringsheim mit denen anderer emigrierter Gelehrter, darunter F. A. Hayek, Leo Strauss, Ernst Kantorowicz, Ernst Fraenkel und nochmals Franz Neumann.

Abschnitt 4 behandelt die von vielen Zeitgenossen empfundene Krise des römischen Rechts in

3 Wolfgang Ernst, Fritz Schulz (1879–1957), in: Jack Beatson, Reinhard Zimmermann (Hg.), Jurists Uprooted: German-speaking Émigré Lawyers in Twentieth-century Britain, Oxford 2004, 105–203 (124). Ernst zitiert auch F.A. Mann mit der Aussage, »in truth and substance« sei diese Vorlesungsreihe »nothing but a veiled attack on Nazi despotism and lawlessness« gewesen.

den 1930er Jahren und die einflussreichste Antwort darauf. Diese stammte von dem Keilschriftrechtler Paul Koschaker (1879–1951), und sie habe, so Tuori, die Diskussion auf ein europäisches Narrativ orientiert. Im Zentrum dieses Abschnitts steht damit zum einen die während der Nazizeit publizierte Schrift »Die Krise des römischen Rechts und der romanistischen Rechtswissenschaft« (erschienen 1938 in den Schriften der Akademie für Deutsches Recht) und zum anderen das bald nach deren Ende publizierte Buch »Europa und das römische Recht« (1947, 4. Aufl. 1966). Tuori sieht Koschakers »main claim to fame« (126) in seinem außerordentlich wachen Gespür für den jeweils richtigen Zeitpunkt für zwei Publikationen, mit denen er das Problem des Selbstverständnisses seiner Disziplin vor dem Hintergrund sich wandelnder Verhältnisse behandelte. Dabei habe sich seine Vision von der Bedeutung des römischen Rechts und dessen europäischer Tradition von 1938 bis 1947 im Grunde kaum geändert. Zur Kontextualisierung dienen, was die Krisenschrift betrifft, vor allem die Ideen von Koschakers italienischem Freund Salvatore Riccobono sowie seinem faschistischen Kollegen (und zeitweiligem Justizminister Mussolinis) Pietro de Francisci. Interessant ist die »Obsession« des faschistischen Italien mit dem antiken Rom, die in einem gewissen Gegensatz zur Animosität der Nationalsozialisten zu der bedeutendsten Emanation des antiken Rom, dem römischen Recht, stand. Als wichtigstes Vermächtnis von Koschaker bezeichnet Tuori dessen »cultural theory of European legal tradition« (167). Auch die Nationalsozialisten hätten aber mit der Eroberung weiter Teile Europas im Zweiten Weltkrieg ein neues Verhältnis zur Tradition des Heiligen Römischen Reichs und zur europäischen Dimension einer (nunmehr allerdings germanisch oder nordisch geprägten) Reichsidee gewonnen. (Tuori spricht von einem »Nazi enthusiasm for Europe« (155), dessen Wurzeln in der SS gelegen hätten.)

Nach dem Ende des Krieges galt es die europäische Rechtstradition »neu zu gestalten« (»reconfiguring European legal tradition«), wie es in der Überschrift zum fünften Abschnitt heißt. Der hauptsächliche Neugestalter in den Augen von Tuori (vielleicht ließe sich aber auch von einem »Gründer und Bewahrer«[4] sprechen) war Franz Wieacker (1908–1994) und zwar mit seiner »Privatrechtsgeschichte der Neuzeit« (1952, 2. und bis heute maßgebliche Aufl. 1967). Diese Meistererzählung, die den geistigen Horizont von Generationen historisch interessierter Jurastudenten geprägt hat, steht im Mittelpunkt dieses fünften Abschnitts. Zu den Fragen, die Tuori besonders interessieren, gehört, inwieweit Wieacker Koschakers Europabild popularisiert hat und inwiefern er sich von diesem abgesetzt habe (das sei insbesondere im Hinblick auf die Interpretation der Zeit von 1880–1930 der Fall gewesen). Vor allem aber fragt Tuori nach Kontinuitäten im Denken Wieackers vor und nach 1945. Dazu schildert er dessen Karriere als eines »young lion of Nazi legal academia« (173) und weist auf Wurzeln des europäischen Narrativs in der Nazizeit hin. Es geht dabei zum einen um das bei der Reform des Studienplans von 1935 neu geschaffene Fach der Privatrechtsgeschichte der Neuzeit, für das Wieacker das einflussreichste Lehrbuch schuf, und zum anderen wiederum um den schon im Koschaker-Abschnitt erwähnten »strong push towards Europeanism« (217) der Nationalsozialisten. Andere Themen, die zur Sprache kommen, sind die Entnazifizierung nach dem Krieg (von Wieacker und von »Mitläufern« allgemein), die Idee deutscher Dominanz in der geistigen Entwicklung Europas, die in Wieackers Buch zum Ausdruck komme, Verwissenschaftlichung und Rationalisierung als prägende Elemente der Privatrechtsgeschichte, die Vorstellung einer organischen Entwicklung, und die intellektuelle Verbindung von Wieacker mit Emilio Betti und Hans-Georg Gadamer.

Fortgeführt wurde das europäische Narrativ dann, das ist Gegenstand des sechsten Abschnitts, durch Helmut Coing (1912–2000). Leitmotive sind hier die Naturrechtsrenaissance der unmittelbaren Nachkriegszeit (zu der Coing vor allem durch sein Buch »Die obersten Grundsätze des Rechts: ein Versuch zur Neugründung des Naturrechts«, 1947, beitrug), die Ideen der Freiheit und des subjektiven Rechts, die in der europäischen Tradition angelegt gewesen seien, und die Vorstellung eines Rückgriffs auf die Tradition als zen-

4 Franz Wieacker, Gründer und Bewahrer: Rechtslehrer der neueren deutschen Privatrechtsgeschichte, Göttingen 1958.

tralen Bestandteils einer europäischen Zukunft. Kontextualisierend wird auf den europäischen und globalen Menschenrechtsdiskurs hingewiesen sowie wiederum auf das Werk von Franz Neumann und Leo Strauss. Gewirkt habe Coing durch die Gründung des Frankfurter Max-Planck-Instituts für europäische Rechtsgeschichte vor allem als Administrator. Ein natürlicher Champion für eine auf Rechten gegründete europäische Tradition sei Coing angesichts seiner Herkunft und seiner Aktivitäten vor 1945 nicht gewesen. »His career«, schreibt Tuori gegen Ende der Einleitung des sechsten Abschnitts etwas enigmatisch, »may be defined as one of an opportunist but behind the façade it is evident that the Nazi years had taken their toll«.[5]

III. Insgesamt werden damit über die fünf Abschnitte hinweg fesselnde Themen angesprochen, einflussreiche Akteure vorgestellt, und auch vielfältige Werturteile abgegeben, über die sich streiten lässt. Doch lässt sich all das unter eine übergreifende Themenstellung fassen? Die europäische Rechtsvereinheitlichung, so die dem Buch vorangestellte Kurzzusammenfassung, werde häufig mit Bezug auf die inhärente Einheitlichkeit der europäischen Rechtstradition gerechtfertigt, die auf das antike Rom zurückreiche. Untersucht werden solle die »Erfindung dieser Tradition«, die auf eine Reihe von Gelehrten zurückgeführt werden könne, die durch den Terror und Totalitarismus des Naziregimes »getrennt« waren. Als nach England und in die USA Vertriebene hätten sie versucht, Brücken zwischen der kontinentalen und der anglo-amerikanischen Tradition zu bauen und dabei Ideen wie die Rechtsstaatlichkeit, Freiheit und Gleichheit in das europäische Erbe zu integrieren. Andere hätten sich der Nazi-Revolution angeschlossen, die ihre eigene Vision europäischer Einheit propagiert habe. Nach dem Ende des Zweiten Weltkrieges seien das Naturrecht und die Menschenrechte in das europäische Projekt eingefügt worden. Das sich daraus ergebende Narrativ sei in der Folge ein vereinheitlichender Faktor im Kalten Krieg gewesen: als Selbstdefinition gegen die Herausforderung des Kommunismus.

Im ersten Abschnitt des Buches (»Introduction«) wird das auf knapp 40 Seiten näher ausgeführt. Dabei tritt eine Reihe von Widersprüchen zutage. Zu der ersten dieser beiden Gruppen von Gelehrten (also den Vertriebenen und Ausgestoßenen – »exiles and outcasts«) werden zunächst (4) Schulz, Pringsheim und Koschaker gerechnet, zur zweiten (also den Kollaborateuren und Mitläufern – »collaborators and bystanders«) Wieacker und Coing. Kaum zwei Seiten weiter (5) wird Koschaker aber mit Wieacker und Coing als »active participant in the Nazi regime in academia« bezeichnet. Dieser Widerspruch hängt zusammen mit einem unklaren Begriff des Exils. Er wird auch in den Abschnitten des Buches über Schulz und Pringsheim deutlich. Einerseits wird mehrfach auf die »transformative« Macht des Exils verwiesen und darauf, dass die Protagonisten der Idee einer europäischen Rechtstradition sich in einer fremden Kultur zurechtfinden mussten (»it was crucial for the development of the idea of a European legal heritage that the main figures were exiles who were immersed in a foreign culture«, 5; vgl. auch etwa 72 oder das Adorno-Zitat auf 263). In der Tat schreibt Fritz Schulz selbst in seinem berührenden »Meine liebe Helga«-Brief vom 27.08.1946,[6] dass er »in Deutschland niemals zu dieser Reife gediehen [wäre] wie hier im freien England«. Doch zum einen war Fritz Schulz kein Protagonist der Idee einer europäischen Rechtstradition, und Fritz Pringsheim war es ebenfalls nicht. Zum anderen stammen die im Zentrum der Aufmerksamkeit von Tuori stehenden Texte von Schulz und Pringsheim aus dem Jahre 1933; sie wurden also verfasst viele Jahre bevor beide nach England gingen (1939); Pringsheim war damals noch in Freiburg in Amt und Würden. Exil könnte insofern also nur »inneres Exil« bedeuten, eine Abkehr von den nunmehr herrschenden politischen Verhältnissen (vgl. etwa 23, 31), und allenfalls in diesem Sinne könnte also auch Koschaker zu den »exiles und

5 Seine Haltung während der Nazizeit reflektiert Coing selbst in seinem »Lebensbericht«: Helmut Coing, Für Wissenschaft und Künste: Lebensbericht eines europäischen Rechtsgelehrten, hg. von Michael F. Feldkamp, Berlin 2014. Den Begriff der inneren Emigration hält er für unzutreffend und spricht stattdessen etwas gewunden von »innerer Fernhaltung«, vgl. Reinhard Zimmermann, Rez., in: RabelsZ 79 (2015) 219–229 (225 f.).

6 Abgedruckt als Anhang der Schulz-Biographie von Ernst (Fn. 3) 198–200 (198).

outcasts« gerechnet werden – auch wenn die Verwendung dieser Bezeichnung für ein Mitglied der Akademie für Deutsches Recht[7] nicht ganz leicht fällt. (Auf einer Karte der »migration routes of some emigré scholars 1933–1960«, die dem ersten Abschnitt des Buches beigegeben ist (21), wird sogar die zeitweise Übersiedlung von Koschaker als hochverehrter Gastprofessor nach Ankara drei Jahre nach Ende des Zweiten Weltkriegs aufgeführt.) Nicht nur sind Schulz und Pringsheim also keine Beispiele für die These, dass die Entwicklung der Europa-Idee durch die Immersion in eine fremde Kultur zu erklären sei, die führenden Vertreter dieser Idee (Koschaker, Wieacker, Coing) widerlegen sie geradezu.

Doch nicht nur die Einführung, auch die anderen Abschnitte des Buches sind von steilen Thesen und Ungenauigkeiten durchzogen, die gerade auch den interessierten und positiv disponierten Leser immer wieder irritiert zurücklassen. Das beginnt bereits damit, dass Tuori das Bild der europäischen Rechtstradition, das Koschaker, Wieacker und Coing entworfen haben, als eine »Erfindung« betrachtet (»an invented tradition«, 19): als eine politische Botschaft mehr als alles andere. Es bestehe heute Konsens darüber, dass es eine derartige einheitliche Tradition nicht gegeben habe (221).[8] Wirklich? Alles nur Einbildung oder Fiktion, was Coing in seinen beiden Bänden eines Europäischen Privatrechts unter dem Begriff des »Gemeinen Rechts« darstellt?[9] Dieses Werk, das sich mit den Rechtsinstitutionen statt lediglich mit dem (äußeren) Ablauf der Rechtsgeschichte befasst, ist ein besonders wichtiger Beitrag zur Vergegenwärtigung der Tradition, die Tuori kritisch analysiert, wird von ihm aber überhaupt nicht erwähnt. Übrigens schreibt Tuori an einer Stelle ausdrücklich, es gehe ihm nicht um den Nachweis, die »common past theory« sei falsch (7), bezeichnet es dann aber nur ein paar Seiten weiter als Ziel seiner Untersuchung, »to question the utility and accuracy of the common past theory« (13).

Was die transformative Kraft des Exils betrifft, so diagnostiziert Tuori, wie erwähnt, bei Schulz einen Wandel von einem rechtstechnisch orientierten zu einem an politischen Themen interessierten Autor. »Classical Roman Law« (1951), die Studien über Bracton (1943–1946), auch die »History of Roman Legal Science« (1946) politische Bücher? Tuori erwähnt nur das zuletzt genannte Werk und sieht hinter der historischen Fassade »a message and an agenda« (70). Die Freiheit der Rechtswissenschaft und die Trennung von Recht und Politik nennt Tuori in diesem Zusammenhang, fügt aber selbst hinzu, dass das Themen sind, die Schulz mit der Tradition des 19. Jahrhunderts verbinden. Wenn die »History of Roman Legal Science« ein politisches Buch mit einer für die Gegenwart relevanten Botschaft sein soll, dann trifft dies auf alle Bücher zu, die sich mit der Geschichte der Rechtwissenschaft im gesellschaftlichen und kulturellen Kontext ihrer Zeit befassen.[10] Und wie lag es bei Pringsheim? Sein von Tuori herausgestellter »turn« von 1933/34 (88) war allenfalls ephemer; er bestand in einem oder allenfalls zwei Aufsätzen.[11] Danach kam z. B. die Beschäftigung mit den Basiliken, und es kam vor allem »The Greek Law of Sale« (1950). Das sieht auch Tuori, der es einigermaßen unerwartet findet, dass Pringsheim während seiner Zeit in Oxford »conspicuously free« war von allen zeitgenössischen Implikationen (117). Was sagt uns das also über die Erfahrung des Exils auf die Produktion von Rechtshistorikern?

Tuori hält es für eine unbequeme Wahrheit, dass Gelehrte, wenn sie einmal irgendwo Wurzeln geschlagen haben, jahrzehntelang an denselben Themen zu arbeiten fortfahren, mit denen sie ihre Karriere begonnen haben (173). Das ist eine von

7 Tommaso Beggio, Paul Koschaker (1879–1951): Rediscovering the Roman Foundations of European Legal Tradition, Heidelberg 2018, 79–83.

8 Immerhin fügt er hinzu, gegeben habe es, wie sich sogar mit einiger Sicherheit sagen lasse, »legal traditions that may or may not be reduced to a central principle«: das ist wiederum eine der ausgesprochen sibyllinischen Feststellungen des Buches.

9 Helmut Coing, Europäisches Privatrecht, Band I: Älteres Gemeines Recht, München 1985; Helmut Coing, Europäisches Privatrecht, Band II: 19. Jahrhundert, München 1989.

10 »The emergence of the science of law, […] and its development in the Roman society and culture of its time, is the subject of the History of Roman Legal Science«: Ernst (Fn. 3) 175.

11 Der eine, von Tuori behandelte Aufsatz ist der oben zitierte aus dem Journal for Roman Studies. Der andere greift dasselbe Thema auf und erschien 1933 in Deutschland. Dazu bemerkt Tuori, dass »the conclusions drawn and the explicitness with which they are presented are markedly different, the German text being much more technical and understated« (94 f., Fn. 16).

vielen allgemeinen Aussagen, mit denen der Leser wenig anfangen kann. Schulz hat sich am Anfang seiner Karriere mit klassischem römischen Recht und mit deutscher Rechtsdogmatik befasst; am Ende schrieb er, unter anderem, eine Wissenschaftsgeschichte des römischen Rechts und arbeitete über Bracton. Er wechselte im Übrigen bemerkenswert häufig die Universitäten (Innsbruck, Kiel, Göttingen, Bonn, Berlin, dann Vertreibung aus Deutschland). Paul Koschaker, dessen Karriere unmittelbar vor der erwähnten Aussage über die Stabilität der typischen deutschen Karrieren behandelt wird, lebte und unterrichtete in Prag, Frankfurt, Leipzig, Berlin und Tübingen. Er war ein bedeutender Keilschriftrechtler, publizierte aber vier Jahre vor seinem Tod sein berühmtes Europa-Buch. Nur Coings Karriere war durch eine stabilitas loci geprägt; doch auch er beschäftigte sich in seiner Karriere nicht nur mit der Rezeption des römischen Rechts in Frankfurt und Europa, sondern mit einer Vielzahl weiterer Themen; so schrieb er eine Monographie über die Treuhand, überarbeitete ein Lehrbuch zum Erbrecht und verfasste ein Buch mit dem Titel »Grundzüge der Rechtsphilosophie«. In seinem Lebensbericht legt er selbst einen Schwerpunkt auf sein zivilrechtliches Werk.[12] Was soll also die erwähnte allgemeine Aussage und wie wird sie plausibilisiert? – Zu den besonders unglaubwürdigen Thesen des Buches gehört auch die, dass Wieacker von der im Zweiten Weltkrieg plötzlich ausbrechenden Europabegeisterung der SS beeinflusst worden sei. Auch dass der Fokus einer Reihe von Kapiteln der »Privatrechtsgeschichte der Neuzeit« auf Deutschland liegt, ist weder erstaunlich noch kritikwürdig bei einem Buch, das schon im Untertitel den Vermerk trägt »unter besonderer Berücksichtigung der deutschen Entwicklung«. Insbesondere folgt daraus nicht, dass Wieackers Geschichtsbild von einer Teleologie des deutschen Rechtserbes (208) geprägt gewesen sei. Zudem: Was ist überhaupt das deutsche Rechtserbe (»German legal heritage«), und worin bestünde dessen »Teleologie«?

Auch im Detail ist manches schief oder geradezu falsch. Ernst Rabel ist nicht nach Großbritannien emigriert und Franz Haymann war alles andere als »influential [...] in Britain« (beide Feststellungen auf 4). Mario Bretone würde sich vermutlich wundern, sich in eine Reihe von Autoren gestellt zu sehen (19), die das hohe Lied der gemeinsamen europäischen Rechtstradition singen.[13] Wolfgang Kunkel kommt in dem Buch an genau einer Stelle vor. Es heißt dort, er sei in die SS eingetreten, habe aber immer treu zu seinem Lehrer Ernst Levy gehalten (79). Für die SS-Mitgliedschaft von Kunkel bringt Tuori, wie für viele seiner Aussagen, keinen Beleg. Auch wenn sie belegt sein sollte,[14] bietet sie, um es zurückhaltend auszudrücken, eine etwas unterkomplexe Charakterisierung Kunkels.[15] Max Kaser stand den Nationalsozialisten nicht näher als Wieacker (vgl. aber 185). Tuori betont sehr stark die Verbindung von Freiheit und Autorität bei Fritz Schulz (»freedom was paired with the concept of authority«, 86), spricht dann aber wieder davon, er habe, wie Arnaldo Momigliano, Freiheit und Frieden nebeneinandergestellt (61). Wenig weiterführend, angesichts ihres Selbstverständnisses als Fachgelehrte des römischen Rechts, ist der Vergleich von Schulz und Pringsheim mit emigrierten Vertretern der Sozialphilosophie, der politischen Philosophie, der Politikwis-

12 Dazu Zimmermann (Fn. 5) 220 f.

13 Die von ihm 1996 in dem Gipfeltreffen auf dem Monte Verità angestimmte Melodie klingt jedenfalls ganz anders. Er kritisiert gerade ein Studium des römischen Rechts, das nicht so sehr »la comprensione storica di un passato anche remoto« verfolge, sondern »la custodia o la ripresa di una tradizione, il riconoscimento della sua continuità millenaria, reale o fittizia che sia«: Mario Bretone, La »coscienza ironica« della romanistica, in: Pio Caroni, Gerhard Dilcher (Hg.), Norm und Tradition: Welche Geschichtlichkeit für die Rechtsgeschichte?, Köln 1998, 35–57 (57).

14 In den Nachrufen von Helmut Coing (ZRG [RA] 98 [1981] iii–xvi) und Dieter Nörr (Gedächtnisschrift für Wolfgang Kunkel, Frankfurt am Main 1984, 9–24) ist sie nicht erwähnt, auch nicht in dem Beitrag von Dieter Nörr mit dem Titel »Aus dem Nachlass von Wolfgang Kunkel«, in der Gedächtnisschrift, 293–316. Demgegenüber erwähnt Dorothee Mussgnug in ihrer Einleitung zu Ernst Levy und Wolfgang Kunkel: Briefwechsel 1922–1968, Heidelberg 2005, 9 f., dass Kunkel 1933 »förderndes Mitglied der SS« geworden sei. Auch für diese Angabe fehlt ein Nachweis; möglicherweise entstammt sie Kunkels Heidelberger Personalakte.

15 Kunkel stand der nationalsozialistischen Ideologie vollkommen fern und hat, in seinen eigenen Worten (zitiert nach dem Nachruf von Coing [Fn. 14] v), »der Parteidoktrin niemals irgendwelche Zugeständnisse gemacht«. Das bestätigen alle, die ihn gekannt haben; vgl. nur etwa Nörr (Fn. 14) 312–315 und zuletzt Uwe Wesel, Wozu Latein, wenn man gesund ist?, München 2022, 59 (»völlig weiße Weste«).

senschaften und der politischen Publizistik. Geradezu herabgewürdigt werden die fünf Protagonisten des Buches, wenn sie eingangs als »legal scholars with some background in Roman law and legal history« vorgestellt werden (1 f.). Ebenso unangemessen ist die Formulierung, »Levy would constantly pester Kunkel about different jobs he should apply for« (79).

Leider enthält das Buch auch eine Vielzahl von Flüchtigkeiten formaler wie inhaltlicher Art. Tuori spricht von einem »overly critical approach to interpolationism« (147), wenn er den »overly critical approach of interpolationism« meint; Pringsheim habe im Ersten Weltkrieg fünf Jahre an der Front gekämpft (89); manche Fußnoten stehen an der falschen Stelle (z. B. 199, Fn. 75); Riccobonos faschistische Idealisierung des römischen Rechts wird im Abstract zu Abschnitt 3 angekündigt, aber erst in Abschnitt 4 behandelt; und manches mehr.

IV. Das Buch schließt in einem 7. Abschnitt mit Schlussfolgerungen (»Conclusions«). Hier wird dies und das noch einmal angesprochen, ohne dass so recht ein roter Faden erkennbar wäre. Auch neue Themen werden angetippt: Frankreich unter der Vichy-Regierung zum Beispiel (270 f.) oder dass den aus Deutschland vertriebenen Romanisten eine veritable Renaissance des römischen Rechts in Großbritannien zu verdanken sei (263). Zu letzterem Punkt liest man bei Peter Birks, was die Lehre betrifft, anderes: »The […] story […] is a miserable one«.[16] Natürlich ist auch von »Konstruktivismus« die Rede (272). Im Übrigen hätten, so der vorletzte Gedanke des Buches, die in ihm behandelten Gelehrten eine Debatte beflügelt, der eine »policy of othering« und eine weiße, konservative und nationalistische Perspektive zugrunde lagen. Umso überraschender dann ganz am Ende der Aufruf zur Rückbesinnung auf die von Fritz Schulz propagierten Prinzipien des römischen Rechts, oder doch einige von ihnen. »Just an idea«, wie Tuori keck hinzufügt (272). Eine Rückbesinnung also auf eine Vision, die zuvor als zutiefst konservativ charakterisiert worden war und als Schwanengesang auf eine Tradition, die auf dem römischen Recht beruht und die europäische Rechtswissenschaft vereint hat (85). Nun also doch: Inspiration aus der Vergangenheit für die Zukunft?

Das Buch von Kaius Tuori leidet im Grunde darunter, dass es zu ambitioniert ist. Es behandelt zu viele mehr oder weniger miteinander zusammenhängende Themen, die jedes für sich eine monographische Behandlung verdienten; und es tut dies anhand von fünf Gelehrten, die nicht mehr eint, als dass sie deutschsprachige Rechtshistoriker romanistischer Provenienz waren und, wie übrigens alle ihre Zeitgenossen, auf die eine oder andere Weise von der »Nazirevolution« (1, 13) betroffen waren. Die Exilerfahrung im eigentlichen Sinne des Wortes und die »common past theory«, die zwei zentralen Leitmotive des Buches, bilden jedenfalls kein einendes Band. So schaut man zum Schluss noch einmal auf das Titelblatt. »Empire of Law«? Rom und vielleicht auch das zweite Rom? Hero auf dem Felsenturme / vor dem ewgen Wogensturme / dort in Sestos, einsam grauend / nach Abydos' Küste schauend …? Dekorativ, aber sinnfrei, wie das Gemälde von Lawrence Alma-Tadema? Oder ein Symbol für Humanität, Gleichheit oder Freiheit? »The basic premise of constructivism is that the text and thus the past have no innate meanings« (272). So liegt wohl auch hier die Bedeutung im Auge des Betrachters …

■

16 Peter Birks, Roman Law in Twentieth-century Britain, in: Jack Beatson, Reinhard Zimmermann (Hg.), Jurists Uprooted: German-speaking Émigré Lawyers in Twentieth-century Britain, Oxford 2004, 249–268 (260). Anders der Beitrag zur Forschung: »That the uprooted Romanists enlarged and invigorated the community of scholars working in this country is indisputable. Had they not come, this field of research would have been unimaginably impoverished.« Aber: »They bear some responsibility for undermining the very subject that fascinated them. They did not look up from their books« (beide Zitate auf 250).

Alessandro Somma

Democrazia o capitalismo. Sulla inevitabile matrice autoritaria del neoliberalismo*

Il neoliberalismo sorge sul finire degli anni Trenta del Novecento per impedire che dal fallimento del laissez faire derivi il superamento del capitalismo. Non ha certo condiviso l'idea secondo cui l'ordine politico deve immischiarsi nelle vicende dell'ordine economico, ma neppure ha sostenuto l'opposto: per i neoliberali i mercati sono istituzioni incapaci di affermarsi e di prosperare autonomamente. E se lo Stato non promuove attivamente il loro funzionamento, questi sono inesorabilmente condannati all'autofagia: non sono storicamente possibili.

Questa conclusione viene contestata soprattutto nel discorso pubblico, dove sono ancora ricorrenti coloro i quali reputano che il neoliberalismo si basi sulla credenza nella capacità dei mercati di autoregolarsi. Nella letteratura scientifica un simile assunto è invece da tempo efficacemente contestato,[1] sicché non è questa la principale acquisizione dello studio di Thomas Biebricher. Lo stesso possiamo dire dell'individuazione delle coordinate politiche e culturali del neoliberalismo, a cui lo studio dedica ampio spazio, che evidentemente non rileva per il solo ordine economico: la ricerca in questo ambito è oramai consolidata.[2]

Il merito della ricerca di Biebricher è aver contestato la rappresentazione del neoliberalismo come fenomeno attraversato da profonde divisioni, tanto da mettere in forse la legittimità della categoria. Questa rappresentazione è invero diffusa, in particolare nella letteratura che esalta le differenze tra ordoliberalismo e Scuola austriaca, ovvero tra personalità come Friedrich Böhm, Walter Eucken e Alexander Rüstow da una parte, e Ludwig von Mises e Friedrich von Hayek dall'altra.[3] La considerazione per lo sfondo politico e culturale del neoliberalismo aiuta però a comprendere come le differenze tra questi pensatori, a tratti rilevanti, riguardino a ben vedere gli aspetti quantitativi ma non anche qualitativi del fenomeno. Quelle differenze attengono invero all'individuazione delle misure che lo Stato deve di volta in volta adottare al fine di rendere il capitalismo storicamente possibile. Rispecchiano cioè il livello di ingerenza nell'ordine economico, che evidentemente dipende dal contesto in cui operano i pubblici poteri: non è definibile a priori attraverso un catalogo insensibile al trascorrere del tempo o alla collocazione spaziale dell'esperienza di volta in volta presa in considerazione. Tanto che von Hayek può commentare nel modo seguente l'uso di »economia sociale di mercato«, ovvero del nome scelto in Germania per indicare l'ordoliberalismo alla conclusione del secondo conflitto mondiale: »non mi piace questo uso, anche se grazie a esso alcuni amici tedeschi sembrano riusciti a rendere appetibile a circoli più ampi il tipo di ordine sociale che difendo«.[4]

Biebricher documenta la comune matrice delle diverse espressioni del neoliberalismo a partire dalle modalità scelte per mettere il mercato al riparo dalla democrazia: per spoliticizzarlo, ovvero per impedire che il conflitto redistributivo promuova forme di allocazione delle risorse alternative a quelle derivanti dal libero incontro di domanda e offerta. Di qui una definizione particolarmente felice di neoliberalismo come teoria e pratica concernete »la costrizione del mercato capitalista entro forme politiche autoritarie«.

A ben vedere il neoliberalismo non è ostile alla democrazia, bensì indifferente alle sue sorti. Quest'ultima ben può essere sacrificata se la sua compressione o al limite la sua cancellazione è funzionale a rendere il capitalismo storicamente

* Thomas Biebricher, Die politische Theorie des Neoliberalismus, Berlin: Suhrkamp 2021, 346 p., ISBN 978-3-518-29926-5

1 Per tutti Quinn Slobodian, Globalists. The End of Empire and the Birth of Neoliberalism, Cambridge (MA) / London 2018.

2 Ad es. Raimondo Cubeddu, Atlante del liberalismo, Roma 1997.

3 Ad es. Philip Plickert, Wandlungen des Neoliberalismus. Eine Studie zu Entwicklung und Ausstrahlung der Mont Pèlerin Society, Stuttgart 2008.

4 Friedrich A. Hayek, Law Legislation and Liberty, vol. 2, Chicago / London 1976, 79, n. 26.

possibile. Questo si verifica però puntualmente, se non altro perché il presidio della concorrenza richiede di polverizzare le concentrazioni di potere economico cui si deve il conflitto redistributivo: è l'unico modo per condannare l'individuo a tenere i soli comportamenti descrivibili in termini di reazioni automatiche agli stimoli del mercato. Anche per questo l'equilibrio tra capitalismo e democrazia appare sommamente instabile, e in qualche modo relativo a una fase transitoria: verso la compressione dell'uno o dell'altra.

Insomma, se il neoliberalismo è intimamente incompatibile con la democrazia è perché mira a presidiare il capitalismo, o se si preferisce a liberare la forza attrattiva della normalità capitalistica. È cioè votato a tutelare il mercato come principale strumento di redistribuzione della ricchezza, e a neutralizzare qualsiasi deviazione da un simile schema in quanto inesorabilmente destinata a introdurre il superamento del capitalismo. Così facendo, si pone però come teoria e pratica votata al superamento della democrazia.

Queste precisazioni ci portano a valorizzare quanto Karl Polanyi aveva indicato essere l'essenza del fascismo: la soppressione delle libertà politiche realizzata al fine di riformare le libertà economiche.[5] E in ultima analisi conducono a stabilire un nesso tra fascismo e neoliberalismo, peraltro evidente considerando le vicende che hanno accompagnato la nascita dell'ordoliberalismo sul finire degli anni Trenta del Novecento. Il tutto documentato da ricerche in cui si mette in luce la convergenza tra fascismo e volontà neoliberale di mettere il mercato al riparo dalla dittatura dei numeri alimentata dalla democrazia,[6] così come l'attiva partecipazione di ordoliberali all'amministrazione dell'economia nazista.[7]

Biebricher menziona il nesso tra fascismo e neoliberalismo nel momento in cui allude al ruolo di primo piano rivestito in particolare da Friedman e dai cosiddetti Chicago boys nel regime instaurato in Cile da Augusto Pinochet. Nulla dice però a proposito dell'ordoliberalismo tedesco, che anzi viene rappresentato come ostile alla dittatura nazista.[8] Perde così una buona occasione per stigmatizzare un costume diffuso nella letteratura tedesca, indisponibile a mettere in cattiva luce un mito fondativo della Repubblica federale come l'economia sociale di mercato. Anche se questa è stata concepita per riproporre sotto mentite spoglie l'ordoliberalismo compromesso con il nazismo, ovvero per far credere che la formula indichi la volontà di edificare una sorta di capitalismo dal volto umano, mentre intende semplicemente alludere alla circostanza per cui il mercato è un'istituzione sociale in quanto tale. Il tutto architettato da una personalità come Alfred Müller-Armack,[9] un iscritto della prima ora al Partito nazista poi riciclatosi come stretto collaboratore di Ludwig Erhard.

Se non altro Biebricher evidenzia come il neoliberalismo in quanto fondamento dell'Unione europea abbia connotazioni autoritarie, evidenti nelle vicende che da alcuni anni caratterizzano i Paesi dell'Est e da ultimo nelle misure adottate per fronteggiare l'emergenza pandemica. Di qui la conferma di come l'autoritarismo non sia un elemento estraneo al neoliberalismo, e soprattutto di come non sia certo idoneo a introdurre un suo superamento, sebbene le voci di una fine imminente si succedano con regolare frequenza: tanto da autorizzare Biebricher a ironizzare sulla loro valenza di mero auspicio destinato a restare tale.

Certo i segnali di una crisi del neoliberalismo, o meglio dalla sua essenza di pratica bisognosa di nutrirsi di crisi e per questo inesorabilmente votata a provocarle, sono oramai innumerevoli e destinati o introdurre una sua parabola discendente. Il sospetto è però che questo avverrà nel lungo periodo, ovvero »quando saremo tutti morti«: come amava replicare Keynes a chi sosteneva che la mano invisibile avrebbe primo o poi messo ordine nel mercato.

■

5 Karl Polanyi, The Great Transformation. The Political and Economic Origins of Our Time (1944), Boston Ma. 2001.

6 Alessandro Somma, La dittatura dello spread. Germania, Europa e crisi del debito, Roma 2014, 56 ss.

7 Ralf Ptak, Vom Ordoliberalismus zur Sozialen Marktwirtschaft. Stationen des Neoliberalismus in Deutschland, Opladen 2004, 62 ss.

8 Sulla scia di Michel Foucault, Nascita della biopolitica. Corso al Collège de France (1978–1979), Milano 2004, 93 ss.

9 Lo rivendica lui stesso: Alfred Müller-Armack, Voce »Soziale Marktwirtschaft«, in: Handwörterbuch der Sozialwissenschaften, vol. 9, Stuttgart 1956, 392.

Joachim Rückert

Jongleur im Rechts(wissenschafts)zirkus*

Eine originelle Arbeit, höchst anspruchsvoll angelegt, zugleich doch ziemlich schlank, literarisch recht gelehrt, im großzügigen Gespräch mit Philosophie und Soziologie, im Hintergrund im »kritischen« Fahrwasser (Marx, Benjamin, Foucault, Derrida, Latour, Althusser, Freud), freilich mit Kautelen (vgl. 83, 104 zu marxistischen Rechtstheorien) und angereichert mit eindrucksvoll originellen, neu erklärenden Abbildungen (z. B. 52 f.).

Der Titel allein sagt nicht viel. Zwar ist »Projekt« klar, »Rechtsgeltung« einigermaßen klar, »institutionell« aber schon ziemlich unklar, zumal wenn es in »offener Textur« (188) endet, und »kulturelle Verortung« sagt alles bzw. nichts (vgl. 175). Recht gilt, »indem es angewendet« wird (93). Institution ist etwas, das »institutionalisiert und d. h. materialisiert sein muss« (74) … Das klingt zunächst einfach, aber der Autor macht daraus anspruchsvolle, nicht selten überfordernde Gedankengänge. Zum Ausgleich formuliert er immer wieder sprachlich elegant und prägnant.

Sein Projekt stemmt er in fünf lapidaren Paragraphen, einmal Institutionen, viermal Recht: Rechtsdogmatik, Rechtsfetisch, Rechtsglaube, Rechtsinterpretation. Die Rechtsdogmatik sieht er »auf der Suche nach einem Gegenstand« (21 ff.), der Rechtsfetisch ist natürlich die Rechtsform (77 ff.), der Rechtsglaube ist trügerisch (118 ff.), die Institutionen gehen in Kultur auf (139 ff.), die Rechtsinterpretation ist »Kampf um Bedeutung« unter bestimmten institutionellen Bedingungen (193), die Arbeit am Recht sei am Ende nicht Grund, sondern Moment, nicht Anfang, sondern Resultat (215). So weit so gut. Von der Dogmatik her richtet er nun den Blick anders, von der »Normpyramide« auf die »hängenden Dächer des Rechts« – ein schönes, kunstreiches »Gegenbild« (50). Die Funktionsweise des Rechts will er so eher horizontal und flach denken, gewissermaßen in der Luft hängend statt pyramidal fix, wie man es vor allem Puchta und der Pandektenwissenschaft lange unzutreffend polemisch zuschrieb in den lange bestimmenden Erzählungen von Wieacker und Larenz,[1] während vielmehr an eine organische »Genealogie«, ein »Abstammungsverhältnis«, und nie an bloß formale Logik gedacht war.[2] Mit seinem Bild will Engelmann stillschweigend der wirkmächtigen internen Alternative Pyramide / Genealogie entkommen – jedenfalls erscheinen weder Wieacker noch Larenz in seinem Literaturverzeichnis. An sein neues Bild knüpft er in diesem Sinne das weitere wichtige Bild, »hinreichende Stabilität« müsse aus einer »instituierten kulturell eingespielten Praxis« geliefert werden (51). Also heißt die Devise etwa: rein ins Recht, aber doch raus aus dem Recht. Vielleicht lässt sich so sogar die Botschaft des Buches fassen. Sie wird am Ende als »Umstellung« umschrieben: »Die Umstellung von einer am Ende substanzbasierten oder seinslogi-

* Andreas Engelmann, Rechtsgeltung als institutionelles Projekt. Zur kulturellen Verortung eines rechtswissenschaftlichen Begriffs, Weilerswist: Velbrück Wissenschaft 2020, 230 S., ISBN 978-3-95832-209-7

1 Franz Wieacker, Privatrechtsgeschichte der Neuzeit, Göttingen 1952, 239: »Begriffsjurisprudenz … deduktive Methode … wie bei Christian Wolff«; schärfer noch 2. Aufl. 1967, 399: »strenger Begriffsformalismus«, »verhängnisvoll« (401); Karl Larenz, Methodenlehre der Rechtswissenschaft, Berlin 1960, 16–22, Begriffspyramide, formale, logische, deduktive Begriffsjurisprudenz (mit Franz Jerusalem, Kritik der Rechtswissenschaft, Frankfurt am Main 1948, und Walter Wilhelm, Zur juristischen Methodenlehre im 19. Jahrhundert, Frankfurt am Main 1958, 86); in der Sache ebenso 5. Aufl. 1983, 20–24.

2 Georg F. Puchta, Cursus der Institutionen (1841), 3. Aufl., Leipzig 1850, Buch 1: Enzyklopädie, §§ 21–27: System der Rechtsverhältnisse und §§ 28–30: System der Rechte, sowie § 33 zur systematischen Erkenntnis. »ist die Erkenntnis des inneren Zusammenhangs … das Einzelne als Glied des Ganzen … [daraus] Genealogie der Begriffe, darin liegt, daß man diese Leiter nicht als bloßes Schema von Definitionen betrachten darf« (100 f.); und ders., Lehrbuch der Pandekten, 1. Aufl., Leipzig 1838, Vorrede VI gegen Stahl: »organisches Verhältnis … [nicht] bloß logisch und rationalistisch«. Klärend jetzt bes. Hans-Peter Haferkamp, Die Historische Rechtsschule, Frankfurt am Main 2018, 189 ff.: Strukturbildung im Organismus. Logik wurde im 19. Jahrhundert meist weit material gedacht, s. Joachim Rückert, Logik, Berechenbarkeit, Rechtssoziologie – Anmerkungen zu Max Weber und Hubert Treiber, in: ZRG (GA) 135 (2018) 408–428.

schen Vorstellung von Recht auf einen performativen Rechtsbegriff müsste so vor allem auch darin gesehen werden, dass man nicht mehr davon ausgehen kann, dass es ›das Recht‹ gibt und man mit dieser Tatsache ›umgehen‹ muss, sondern dass es das Recht nur *in* einer bestimmten Umgangsweise *gibt*.« (217); das war auch schon unterwegs erwogen worden (69). Die Aussage ist an sich schlicht: Metaphysik ade, Performanz und ständiges Umgehen mit Recht als Gegenwart, peripatetisches Umherwandeln statt Pyramide und Anwendung. Das hat man oft gehört. Der erste Satzteil ist einfach anerkannt zeitgemäß, der zweite Satzteil eine doch etwas einseitig verallgemeinerte und wiederkehrende Mode. Neue Kleider für das Recht?! Schön anzusehen, auch bisweilen elegant zu tragen, gut zu leben, aber sowohl empirisch als auch normativ nur bei sehr konzentriertem Zugriff auf bestimmte Probleme wirklich ergiebig. Es gäbe auch konzentrierte juristische Beispiele, etwa die Frankfurter Untersuchung »Die juristische Willenserklärung – eine sprechakttheoretische Analyse«[3] oder die ›Rechtskraft‹ von Sprachwandel.[4] Aber das ist natürlich viel zu kleinräumig und konkret, viel zu wenig geistreich und groß gedacht. Zwei Distanzierungen durch Anführungszeichen und zwei Betonungen durch Kursivdruck in diesem einen Satz zur Umstellung indizieren zugleich Engelmanns stetes Bemühen um bedeutsames Sprechen. Er steigert seinen Zugriff auch relativ häufig durch All- und Nur- und Jedes- und Immer-Sätze (vgl. 70, 83, 100, 105, 107, 134, 135, 136, 141, 189, 191, 196, 205, 215, 220 f. usw.). Sie gehen freilich empirisch wie normativ durchweg zu weit.

In jedem seiner Kapitel kreist er nun über dem Phänomen Recht, aber es bleibt beim Kreisen. Hätte uns der Autor ein Personenregister gegönnt, so könnte man leichter seine Mitflieger beim Kreisen erkennen. Es ist jedenfalls eine bestimmte und recht illustre Gesellschaft, von Santner und Derrida über Benveniste, Certeau, Zizek und Menke, Wittgenstein, MacIntyre, Brandom, M. Douglas, R. Cover, L. Rosen bis zu S. Freud, und dazwischen viel gegen und für H. L. A. Hart, zu S. Buckel, und, und … – ersichtlich ein Füllhorn von leidenschaftlicher Lektüre und Denkarbeit. Respekt. Diese Fluggesellschaft hält er dauernd im Gespräch, in aktualisierter, immer wieder auch politisierender Weise, Empirisches und Normatives in schwebender Vermischung, historisch recht sorglos um die jeweilige Zeitlichkeit. Er kann wirklich souverän die Bälle jonglieren.

Bleiben wir bei diesem Bild: Die herkömmlichen, recht klaren Felder Dogmatik, Rechtsfetisch für Rechtsform, Rechtsglaube, Institutionen und Rechtsinterpretation, die Engelmann aufruft, bilden die Stationen seiner souveränen Jongleurskunst. Man kann sich daran freuen, mitfreuen und mitängstigen, wenn es riskant wird. Man kann den Glanz und die Fülle des Spiels genießen. Man sollte das aber nicht so ganz nüchtern zerlegen und zerfallen lassen, wie es mir nahe läge. Die Arbeit bereichert und regt an in vielen wenig bedachten Perspektiven. Genießen Sie, liebe Leser, also den großen Jongleur im kleinen Rechts(wissenschafts)-zirkus.

■

3 Kyriaki Archavlis, Die juristische Willenserklärung – eine sprechakttheoretische Analyse, Tübingen 2015.

4 Stark gemacht von Nicola Rowe, Recht und sprachlicher Wandel. Entwicklung einer institutionellen Auslegungstheorie, Baden-Baden 2003.

Michael Grünberger

Ein Plädoyer für eine normativ gewendete Rechtsdogmatik*

I. Die deutschsprachige Rechtswissenschaft beschäftigt sich seit geraumer Zeit besonders intensiv mit dem, was nach Auffassung vieler ihr »Markenkern« ist: der Rechtsdogmatik. Zu den vielen Büchern, Sammelbänden und Aufsätzen[1] scheint mit der im Sommer 2019 an der Rechtswissenschaftlichen Fakultät der Universität Hamburg angenommenen, von Ivo Appel betreuten Dissertation von Alexander Stark ein weiteres Buch dazuzukommen. Dieser Eindruck stimmt – teilweise. Seine Hauptforschungsfrage lautet nämlich, ob die Rechtsdogmatik ein Potential für Interdisziplinarität hat oder ob es der *strictly legal point of view*[2] unmöglich macht, interdisziplinär gewonnenes Wissen in genuin rechtsdogmatischen Operationen fruchtbar zu machen (vgl. 17). Starks These ist, »dass rechtsdogmatisches Arbeiten zwar durch (perspektivenbedingte) Engführungen gekennzeichnet ist, auch auf dieser Grundlage jedoch erhebliche Interdisziplinaritätspotentiale identifiziert werden können« (V). Stark entwickelt und entfaltet diese These in drei Schritten – die zugleich auch die drei Teile der Arbeit bilden:

Der erste Teil (»Rechtsdogmatik«, 19–170) unternimmt »eine möglichst differenzierte Analyse dessen, was ›Rechtsdogmatik‹ ist und was darunter verstanden werden kann« (V). Stark entwickelt hier die These, dass (lediglich) zwei Bedingungen vorliegen müssen, damit man Aussagen über Recht als »Rechtsdogmatik« einordnen kann (29–66): Sie müssen (a) einen »Rechtssatzbezug« haben. Dafür genüge es, dass die Aussagen »eine Sinnbeziehung zu dem (potentiell) geltenden Recht eines Rechtssystems herstellen« (45). Die Aussagen müssen (b) eine Teilnehmerperspektive einnehmen (60). Teilnehmerperspektive bedeutet, dass rechtsdogmatisch argumentierende Akteure »Aussagen über das Recht so aufstellen, als ob sie Rechtsakteure wären« (64). Dafür muss man wissen, dass Stark strikt zwischen den Rechtsakteuren der Rechtspraxis (144 ff.) und rechtsdogmatischen Akteuren, insbesondere der dogmatischen Rechtswissenschaft (142) trennt. Im Gegensatz zu vielen[3] zählt Stark den Systembezug zwar zu einer charakteristischen, aber nicht notwendigen Voraussetzung für Rechtsdogmatik (66 ff.).

Im zweiten Teil (»Interdisziplinarität«, 171–230) konzipiert Verf. im ersten Schritt den Begriff der Interdisziplinarität und grenzt ihn von »Disziplinarität«, »Multi-, Intra- und Transdisziplinarität« ab (173–201). Im zweiten Schritt skizziert er, wie eine »Interdisziplinarität zu den Bedingungen der Rechtsdogmatik« abstrakt aussehen könnte (213–227).

Im dritten Teil (»Interdisziplinarität von Rechtsdogmatik«, 231–366) demonstriert Stark, dass auch eine »nur« deskriptive Rechtsdogmatik über zahlreiche interdisziplinäre Andockstellen verfügt (233–265). Weil das an den auf außerrechtliche Wissensbestände verweisenden Begriffen in Rechtssätzen und rechtsdogmatischen Sätzen (zur Unterscheidung, s. 31 ff.) liegt, ist das eine in der Sache unbestrittene, aber auch sehr bescheidene Form von Interdisziplinarität. Deshalb geht Verf. darüber hinaus und wirbt für eine normative Rechtsdogmatik (265–312): »Sie ermittelt, ob für die Ausübung rechtlich nicht angeleiteter Handlungsspielräume [der Rechtsakteure] nicht-rechtliche, normative Gründe bestehen« und treffe Aussagen darüber, »für welche Option die besseren

* Alexander Stark, Interdisziplinarität der Rechtsdogmatik (Grundlagen der Rechtswissenschaft 37), Tübingen: Mohr Siebeck 2020, 423 S., ISBN 978-3-16-158962-1

1 Nachweise bei Nils Jansen, Rechtsdogmatik, Rechtswissenschaft und juristische Praxis, in: AöR 143 (2018) 623–658.

2 Zum Begriff s. affirmativ Wolfgang Ernst, Gelehrtes Recht – Die Jurisprudenz aus der Sicht des Zivilrechtslehrers, in: Christoph Engel, Wolfgang Schön (Hg.), Das Proprium der Rechtswissenschaft, Tübingen 2007, 3–49, und kritisch Thilo Kuntz, Auf der Suche nach einem Proprium der Rechtswissenschaft, in: AcP 219 (2019) 254–299, 259 ff.

3 Zuletzt etwa Philipp Sahm, Elemente der Dogmatik, Weilerswist 2019, 59 ff.

Gründe sprechen« (215). Die Rechtsdogmatik als rationale Disziplin (vgl. 274) solle (vgl. 289) auf das in außerrechtlichen Zusammenhängen gewonnene Wissen zurückgreifen, wenn, erstens, die vorrangig zu beachtenden rechtlichen Gründe Handlungsspielräume gewähren und wenn, zweitens, den Akteuren dieses Wissen epistemisch zugänglich ist (274 f.). Konkurrieren mehrere nicht-rechtliche Gründe, habe die Auswahl der maßgeblichen normativen Gründe (zum Begriff s. 268 f.) »auch unter Beachtung der rechtlichen Gründe zu erfolgen« (276 f.). Im letzten Abschnitt geht Stark auf eine Reihe von möglichen Einwänden gegen die normative Rechtsdogmatik ein, darunter auf die kelsenianischen Argumente eines Methodensynkretismus und der rechtspolitischen Betätigung im Gewand der Wissenschaft (323–331).

II. Ein Anliegen des Buchs ist es, einen modernen Begriff von Rechtsdogmatik zu prägen. Damit ist Stark nicht allein. In jüngster Zeit sind dazu eine Reihe von Monographien erschienen.[4] Bei mir hat der von Stark vorgeschlagene Begriff einige Fragen aufgeworfen. Rechtsdogmatik sei neben der Methode, den Produkten dieser Methode auch eine Disziplin (77); genauer: »eine wissenschaftliche Disziplin und nicht der Rechtspraxis zugehörig« (62). Die Rechtsdogmatik als Teil des wissenschaftlichen Systems (vgl. 141) betrachte das Recht zwar von einer Beobachterposition aus, habe dabei aber eine (hypothetische) Teilnehmerperspektive einzunehmen (62), während die Rechtsakteure aus der Rechtspraxis geltendes Recht setzen und in dieser Funktion keine Rechtsdogmatik betreiben und auch nicht dem Wissenschaftssystem angehörten (144). Diese Unterscheidung kann ich nicht ganz nachvollziehen: Einerseits entwickelten die Rechtsakteure »als Rechtserzeugungsinstanzen […] keine rechtsdogmatischen Systeme und gehören nicht dem Wissenschaftssystem an« (144). Andererseits seien sie »nur bei Gelegenheit, *en passant* rechtsdogmatische Akteure« (142). Aber bei welcher Gelegenheit? Wann genau ist eine Aussage des BGH oder des BVerwG ein Rechtssatz und wann ein rechtsdogmatischer Satz? Das bleibt unklar. Und wie kann eine Rechtsakteur*in zugleich (!) Teilnehmer*in des Rechtssystems und *en passant* als rechtsdogmatische Akteur*in in der Beobachterposition sein (vgl. 62)? Ich bezweifle auch, dass die Arbeit damit das in Deutschland praktizierte Verständnis, wonach Rechtsdogmatik »einen gemeinsamen Kommunikationsraum für Wissenschaft und Praxis [schafft]«,[5] begrifflich adäquat erfasst. Ist es mit Blick darauf nicht »überzeugender, die Rechtsdogmatik als eine eigenständige Denkform zwischen den Polen von Theorie und Praxis zu verstehen«?[6]

Stark unterscheidet innerhalb der Rechtsdogmatik als (wissenschaftlicher) Disziplin zwischen einer praktischen und einer theoretischen Rechtsdogmatik (82 ff.). Die praktische Rechtsdogmatik sei »auf die unmittelbare Hilfestellung zur praktischen Falllösung gerichtet« (82), während die theoretische Rechtsdogmatik »in größerer Distanz zur (hypothetischen) Anwendungssituation [steht] und den Einschränkungen der praktischen Rechtsdogmatik in geringerer Intensität [unterliegt]«. Letztere erinnert mich sehr an das Postulat einer praxisentlasteten, wissenschaftlichen Rechtsdogmatik, der es »um die juristische Analyse und Strukturierung normativer Zusammenhänge: um Panoramen von Konstruktionsmöglichkeiten und Entscheidungsoptionen« geht.[7] Unterscheidungskriterium sei die Art der nicht-rechtlichen handlungsleitenden Gründe: Bei der praktischen Rechtsdogmatik seien es autoritative Gründe, während bei der theoretischen Dogmatik inhaltliche Gründe maßgeblich seien. Diese Begründung hat aber ein enormes Problem mit dem wissenschaftlichen Wahrheitsbegriff: Kann man noch von einer wissenschaftlichen Operation sprechen, wenn nicht-rechtliche Autoritätsargumente (u. a. Vereinbarkeit mit der herrschenden Meinung, 83) handlungsleitend sein sollen? Hier zeigt sich, dass die einheitliche Verortung von Rechtsdogmatik als wissenschaftliche Disziplin ganz erhebliche Folgeprobleme aufwirft. Versteht man Rechtsdogmatik dagegen als eine rationale Reflexionsebene spezifischer gesellschaftlicher (konkret: rechtlicher) Praktiken,[8] kann man unterhalb dieser Ebene an der hilfreichen Differenzierung zwischen praktischer

4 Christian Bumke, Rechtsdogmatik, Tübingen 2017; Jannis Lennartz, Dogmatik als Methode, Tübingen 2017; Sahm (Fn. 3).

5 Wissenschaftsrat, Perspektiven der Rechtswissenschaft in Deutschland, 2012, 31.

6 Sahm (Fn. 3) 71.

7 Nils Jansen, Rechtswissenschaft und Rechtssystem, Baden-Baden 2018, 58, 63.

8 Vgl. Sahm (Fn. 3) 70 ff. im Anschluss an Gunther Teubner, Rechtswissenschaft und -praxis im Kontext der Sozialtheorie, in: Stefan Grundmann, Jan Thiessen (Hg.), Recht und Sozialtheorie im Rechtsvergleich, Tübingen 2015, 145–168, 164.

(dem Rechtssystem zugehöriger) und theoretischer (dem Wissenschaftssystem zugehöriger) Dogmatik festhalten.

Eine wichtige Rolle kommt der Unterscheidung von deskriptiver und normativer Rechtsdogmatik zu (89 ff.; 265 ff.): Erstere beschränke sich auf den Aspekt der Rechtserkenntnis (92 ff.), während letztere »auf die Rechtserzeugungsanteile bei Rechtsanwendungsvorgängen gerichtet ist und bei [der] die dogmatischen Akteure ein normatives Erkenntnisinteresse verfolgen« (95). Stark sieht in der deskriptiven Rechtsdogmatik mit Recht das klassische Selbstverständnis von Rechtsdogmatik (92). Ich halte dieses Leitbild für einen Mythos.[9] Stark dagegen glaubt, dass das zumindest als Ausgangspunkt dogmatischer Argumentation valide ist. Ich meine, dass auch dieser eingeschränkten Bedeutung zwingende Gründe entgegenstehen. Es gibt mit der Rechtsgeschichte, der Rechtsoziologie oder der Rechtsvergleichung zwar eine Reihe von Bindestrich-Wissenschaften, die strikt deskriptive Aussagen über Rechtssätze treffen können; eine Rechtsdogmatik, die sich fragt, welchen Inhalt das geltende Recht hat und die dabei die Teilnehmerperspektive der Rechtsakteure einzunehmen hat (vgl. 63), operiert insoweit *per definitionem* normativ.

Das Erkenntnisinteresse der von ihm präferierten normativen Rechtsdogmatik sieht Stark darin, »Antworten auf die Frage zu erarbeiten, wie die Rechtsakteure in bestimmten Konstellationen handeln sollen« (265). Konkret bedeutet das Programm, dass der rechtsdogmatische Diskurs, erstens, Rechtssätze evaluieren und, zweitens, »Antworten auf die Frage, welche von mehreren jeweils rechtlich zulässigen Interpretationsvarianten gewählt werden sollte«, finden soll (278). Drittens sollte er die Rechtsakteure auch anleiten zu entscheiden, »welche normativen Gründe für die Ausübung der rechtlich nicht angeleiteten Handlungsspielräume bestehen (können) und welches Gewicht diese Gründe für spezifische rechtliche Konstellationen haben« (278). Das interdisziplinäre Potential der normativen Rechtsdogmatik sieht Stark daher »in der Wahl zwischen zwei [rechtlich] zulässigen Interpretationsvarianten« (283) und dafür »können« [m. E. müsste auch hier »sollen« stehen, weil er diese Berücksichtigung als Rationalitätsgebot formuliert] »außerrechtliche normative Gründe vorgebracht werden und entscheidend sein« (283). Die normative Rechtsdogmatik ermögliche insbesondere die Berücksichtigung folgenorientierter interdisziplinärer Perspektiven (vgl. 292 ff.). Mich hat er damit überzeugt. Aber eine Frage bleibt unbeantwortet: Was genau unterscheidet diesen von einem ganz »normalen« teleologischen Zugang? Auch eine klassische Konzeption von Rechtsdogmatik hat diese Andockstellen. Ich meine, dass es entscheidend darauf ankommt, wie man die normativen Entscheidungsparameter im interdisziplinären Durchgang erweitert und ob man diesen Vorgang transparent macht. Dass Verhaltenssteuerung und Folgenberücksichtigung maßgebliche Elemente normativer rechtsdogmatischer Operationen sind,[10] wissen wir mittlerweile. Am Beispiel der Diskussion über die regulatorische Rechtsdogmatik[11] sieht man aber, wie konfliktträchtig es nach wie vor ist, diese Vorgänge transparent zu machen und beim (normativen) Namen zu nennen.

III. Als »rechtstheoretisches Buch«, dessen Gegenstand »die ›Andockstellen‹ im Rahmen der Rechtsdogmatik für die Einbeziehung von Erkenntnissen anderer Disziplinen« sind (6), plädiert es für eine interdisziplinär angereicherte Rechtsdogmatik. Für ihr Gelingen kommt es ganz entscheidend auf das »Wie« an. Stark ist skeptisch, ob eine allgemeine Rezeptionstheorie für die interdisziplinäre Wissenserschließung möglich ist (vgl. 15 ff.). Deshalb stünden »die Art und Weise der Einbeziehung und Verarbeitung nachbardisziplinärer Wissensbestände [...] nicht im Zentrum des Erkenntnisinteresses« (15). Ich teile seine Auffassung, dass es nicht darum gehen könne, »welche konkreten Wissensbestände welcher Disziplinen in welchen Kontexten einpassungstauglich sind« (7). Das kann eine Arbeit nicht leisten. Aber: Auch Stark muss Wege skizzieren, wie man unter Berücksichtigung der disziplinären Eigenrationalität der Rechtsdogmatik Interdisziplinarität ermög-

9 Michael Grünberger, Responsive Rechtsdogmatik – Eine Skizze, in: AcP 219 (2019) 924–942.

10 Dazu Gerhard Wagner, Zivilrechtswissenschaft heute. Zwischen Orakeldeutung und Maschinenraum, in: Horst Dreier (Hg.), Rechtswissenschaft als Beruf, Tübingen 2019, 67–182.

11 Alexander Hellgardt, Regulierung und Privatrecht, Tübingen 2016.

licht (211 ff.). Daher beschreibt die Arbeit einen zweistufigen »Transformationsvorgang«: Zunächst wird »eine Theorie aus dem jeweiligen interdisziplinären Verwendungskontext« dekontextualisiert, um sie im Anschluss »auf der Grundlage der eigendisziplinären Perspektive« der Rechtsdogmatik »zu rekontextualisieren« (216 f.). Dafür benötigt die interdisziplinäre Rechtsdogmatik zumindest eine »Wissenstransformationsregel« (215) und eine Methode zur »Selektion von Wissen und Disziplinen« (220). Beides sind ambitionierte Anforderungen für rechtsdogmatisch arbeitende Rechtswissenschaftler*innen. Auf die praktischen Gefahren, die dabei lauern, weist etwa W. Ernst als Vertreter eines *strictly legal point of view* mit guten Gründen hin. Ich zweifle deshalb, ob es genügt, zu zeigen, dass aus rechtstheoretischer Sicht die Rechtsdogmatik in der Lage ist, rechtsexternes Wissen zu verarbeiten, wenn man das entscheidende »Wie« aus dem Zentrum des Erkenntnisinteresses ausschließt. Ich meine, dass eine Arbeit über die Interdisziplinarität der Rechtsdogmatik diesen berechtigten Einwand der Traditionalisten nicht nur kursorisch aufgreifen müsste. Das sieht auch Stark so, weil er dem Problem immerhin einen Abschnitt widmet (211–227). Dieser zählt aber nicht zu den wichtigsten Teilen der Arbeit. Ich meine, dass Stark hier tiefer hätte bohren müssen.

In der Sache gibt es eine Reihe von Mitstreiter*-innen, die das zentrale Argument für eine sich abschottende Rechtsdogmatik entkräften: »Es ist für gelingende Interdisziplinarität weder möglich noch auch nur nötig, den außerjuristischen Fachwissenschaften, die als Theorieexporteure in der Rechtswissenschaft fungieren, vollständig nach deren jeweils eigenem methodischen Selbstverständnis gerecht zu werden.«[12] Damit die Rechtsdogmatik aber an dieses Wissen anknüpfen kann, bedarf es eines rechtlichen Bezugsrahmens. Den liefert die Rechtstheorie, weil sie Selektionsfilter – systemtheoretisch gesprochen: Möglichkeiten der strukturellen Kopplung – entwickeln kann, wie man das Wissen dieser Disziplinen im Recht und nach Maßgabe der Eigenrationalität des Rechts rekonstruieren und fruchtbar machen kann.[13] Notwendig ist also »eine multidisziplinär anreichernde Rechtstheorie im methodischen und wissenschaftstheoretischen Niemandsland zwischen Rechtsdogmatik und dogmatiknahem Grundlagenverständnis einerseits und völlig fachfremden, außerjuristischen Methoden und Fachkulturen andererseits«.[14] Das trifft sich mit dem Ziel von Stark, »die Distanz zwischen den theoretischen Grundlagen- und den gebrauchsorientierten rechtsdogmatischen Subdisziplinen zu verringern« (366). Wie aber sollen Rechtstheorie und/oder Rechtsdogmatik die aus »bunter Theorie und Bastelei« (M. Auer) gewonnene Fluidität fruchtbar machen, ohne sich dabei als eigene Disziplin zu verlieren? Stark besteht mit Recht darauf, dass »die Einbeziehung nachbarwissenschaftlicher Wissensbestände [...] nach den Bedingungen des Rechts zu erfolgen habe« (13). Für dieses Problem hat G. Teubner[15] eine mich überzeugende Lösung vorgeschlagen: Wir müssen, erstens, im Recht tatsächlich das von allen (!) Sozialtheorien gelieferte Wissen berücksichtigen (»Transversalität«). Das ist ein hoher Anspruch. Stark will daher nur die Wissensbestände berücksichtigen, »die den Akteuren epistemisch zugänglich sind« (275). Das trifft dann zu, wenn man von einer ausreichenden personalen und methodischen Diversität ausgeht. Dann kann sich die normative Rechtsdogmatik für die Wissenserschließung auf Arbeitsteilung stützen: Nicht jede muss alles machen; es genügt, wenn die theoretische Rechtsdogmatik als kollektives Unternehmen die entsprechenden Erkenntnisse bereitstellt. Zweitens ist dafür ein Übersetzungsvorgang notwendig, der die von den Nachbardisziplinen gelieferten Wissensbestände innerhalb des autonomen Rechts und seiner Wissenschaft mit systeminternen Begriffen umweltsensibel so re-konstruiert, dass sie für die Rechtsdogmatik anschlussfähig sind (»Responsivität«). Darin sehe ich den entscheidenden Schritt für eine normativ operierende Rechtswissenschaft.[16]

IV. Das Buch tritt mit dem Anspruch an, dass seine »Überlegungen zu dem Interdisziplinaritäts-

12 Marietta Auer, Zum Erkenntnisziel der Rechtstheorie, Baden-Baden 2018, 36.

13 Ausführlich Michael Grünberger, Rechtstheorie statt Methodenlehre?!, in: Susanne Hähnchen (Hg.), Eine Methodenlehre oder viele Methoden?, Tübingen 2020, 79–110, 98 ff.

14 Auer (Fn. 12) 37.

15 Teubner (Fn. 8) 145.

16 Grünberger (Fn. 9) 928 ff.

potential der Rechtsdogmatik für alle drei Rechtsgebiete Anwendung« finden (9). Das ist bei einem rechtstheoretischen Zugang auch zu erwarten. In der Sache kann das Buch dieses Versprechen auch halten. Ich habe es daher nicht nur aus rechtstheoretischer, sondern auch aus zivilrechtsdogmatischer Perspektive mit Gewinn gelesen. Aber gerade weil es den expliziten Anspruch erhebt, Aussagen für alle drei Fachsäulen zu treffen, hat mich an dem Buch ein deutlicher *bias* in der Auswahl der rezipierten Literatur etwas irritiert. Die zentralen (deutschen) Gesprächspartner*innen des Autors sind alle im Öffentlichen Recht zu Hause. Das Buch zitiert zwar eine Reihe zivilrechtlicher Kolleg*innen; wenn man genau hinschaut, spielen deren Texte aber keine tragende Rolle in der Argumentation. Es gibt eine ganze Reihe von Aussagen, die mit vielen Nachweisen belegt werden – und dort sucht man Texte von Autor*innen, die den anderen Fachsäulen zugeschrieben werden, häufig vergeblich. Um das sichtbar zu machen, habe ich mich in meiner Besprechung entschieden, ausschließlich solche Beiträge zu zitieren, die ich – mit Ausnahme des Aufsatzes von W. Ernst und der sporadisch zitierten Arbeit von P. Sahm – in der Arbeit nicht wiedergefunden habe. Für die 2019/2020 erschienenen Beiträge erkläre ich mir das damit, dass die Dissertation vor dem Sommersemester 2019 abgeschlossen war und Anfang 2020 zum Druck vorbereitet wurde. Aber dass die Texte von Auer, Hellgardt, Jansen (u. a. im AöR!), Teubner oder Wagner nicht ausgewertet wurden, hat mich doch etwas überrascht. Es ist nicht ohne Ironie, dass gerade ein Buch, welches für das Interdisziplinaritätspotential der Rechtsdogmatik wirbt, sich hinsichtlich der Möglichkeiten einer tatsächlich gelebten »Intradisziplinarität« (vgl. 201) etwas abschottet.

Dieses Defizit ist – und diese Klarstellung ist mir wichtig – nicht dem Autor anzulasten. Ich sehe in dieser selektiven Rezeption strukturelle Ursachen, die im deutschen Rechtswissenschaftssystem liegen. Die Dogmatikkompetenz ist für Berufungskommissionen an deutschen Fakultäten weiterhin ein zentrales Merkmal wissenschaftlicher Qualifikation.[17] Stark geht mit einem dezidiert rechtstheoretischen Buch bereits ein Risiko ein; für nicht wenige Fakultäten ist er damit schon zu »theorielastig« und nicht anwendungsbezogen genug. Dieses Risiko muss man als Nachwuchswissenschaftler*in minimieren! Dafür ist es naheliegend, sich mit den Texten der Personen auseinanderzusetzen, die in der eigenen Disziplin verortet sind und die auch den nicht rechtstheoretisch arbeitenden Vertreter*innen des eigenen Fachs in den Berufungskommissionen bekannt sind. Hier führt die, spätestens nach dem ersten Examen einsetzende, wissenschaftliche Sozialisation in einer der drei rechtsdogmatischen Säulen zu problematischen Pfadabhängigkeiten. Diese schlagen sich auch in der Rezeption rechtswissenschaftlicher Literatur nieder – jedenfalls dann, wenn der Untersuchungsgegenstand mit Rechtsdogmatik zu tun hat. Ich bedauere diesen Zustand: Wenn es uns – und ich meine damit die etablierten Wissenschaftler*innen, die über Karrieren (mit-)entscheiden – nicht nachhaltig gelingt, in unseren Texten diese Pfadabhängigkeiten aufzubrechen und zu zeigen, wie man erfolgreich intra-, inter- oder vielleicht (entgegen der Skepsis von Stark auf 196ff.) auch transdisziplinär innerhalb der (dogmatisch sowie nicht-dogmatisch arbeitenden) Rechtswissenschaft operieren kann, dürfen wir nicht erwarten und schon gar nicht verlangen, dass es die prekär beschäftigten Nachwuchswissenschaftler*innen anders machen. Wir sollten es uns manchmal etwas weniger gemütlich machen und neben der IntERdisziplinarität auch die IntRAdisziplinarität innerhalb der Rechtsdogmatiken stärken.

V. Alexander Stark hat ein Buch geschrieben, das im Kern eine gelungene Verteidigung der Rechtsdogmatik gegenüber ihren Kritiker*innen, zugleich aber auch eine Inschutznahme vor den Traditionalisten und Kelsenianern unter ihren Befürworter*innen ist. Das Buch hat zwei Ziele: Es will, erstens, eine Konzeption von »Rechtsdogmatik als gründeresponsive Deliberation«, vorlegen, um »das Verständnis von und für Rechtsdogmatik zu verbessern« (366). Damit reiht es sich ein in eine Kette von jüngeren Beiträgen, die auf jeweils unterschiedlichen Wegen zeigen, dass ein Nachdenken über Rechtsdogmatik produktive Irritationen aufwirft und dass es sich auch als moderne Rechtswissenschaftler*in lohnt, (vorzugsweise) »theoretische Rechtsdogmatik« zu betreiben. Zweitens will es zeigen, dass die – je nach Standpunkt – bemängelte oder positiv konnotierte fehlende Anschlussfähigkeit der Rechtsdogmatik für interdisziplinäre

17 Kuntz (Fn. 2) 279ff.

Erkenntnisse (vgl. Nachweise auf 2, Fn. 3) aus rechtstheoretischer Perspektive (vgl. 6 f.) nicht zutrifft. Dass er diese These auch für die »deskriptive Rechtsdogmatik« entfaltet, lese ich als Reverenz gegenüber einer immer noch einflussreichen Meinung; ich persönlich halte sein Plädoyer für eine normative Rechtsdogmatik für wichtiger und zukunftsträchtiger. Damit entwirft er ein rechtstheoretisches Gerüst, das auch die Traditionalisten unter den Rechtsdogmatiker*innen überzeugen könnte, ihre normativen Prämissen nicht mehr in der teleologischen Argumentation zu verstecken und Rechtswissenschaft wieder vermehrt als Rechtssetzungswissenschaft zu betreiben. Dass er dabei die alles entscheidende Frage nach dem »Wie« etwas stiefmütterlich behandelt, finde ich schade – aber das ist letztlich eine Konsequenz der selbst gesetzten Forschungsfrage, die ich als Leser zu akzeptieren habe. Das Buch verdeutlicht, dass Rechtsdogmatik als solche nicht abgeschottet betrieben werden muss. Wenn wir von den rechtlich und dogmatisch eröffneten »Interdisziplinaritätspotentialen« keinen Gebrach machen, ist das eine bewusste Entscheidung – und als solche im wissenschaftlichen Diskurs rechtfertigungsbedürftig. Das ist vielleicht die wichtigste Leistung dieser Arbeit. Den zukünftigen Forschungsbedarf sehe ich darin, Methoden und Zugänge zu entwickeln, die die damit verbundenen Übersetzungsvorgänge anleiten können. Auch wenn dazu – wie oben (III.) gezeigt – schon einiges skizziert wurde: Es bleibt noch viel zu tun!

■

Ralf Seinecke

Endlich!*

I. »Legal Pluralism Explained« ist erst einmal eine Ansage. Seit Jahrzehnten nimmt der Rechtspluralismus-Talk immer weiter zu. Nachdem der Begriff sich zunächst in der Rechtsanthropologie der 1970er und 80er Jahre etabliert hatte, wanderte er von dort in die politische und Rechtstheorie der 1990er Jahre, um dann spätestens seit den 2000er Jahren auch im Völker-, Europa- und transnationalen Recht und sogar in der nationalen Dogmatik anzukommen.[1] Inzwischen ist er recht konsolidiert.[2] Rechtspluralismus, Diversität und Multinormativität sind Teil unseres multipluralen Zeitgeistes: Vielfalt ist gut, Einfalt hingegen doof. Dabei ist Rechtspluralismus ein recht dunkler Begriff. Oft wird er unscharf und vage gebraucht. Das liegt weniger an den mit ihm befassten Rechtswissenschaften. Rechtspluralismus entstand als Kampfbegriff und ist heute eben auch Modebegriff. Gegen ein bisschen Rechtspluralismus kann doch niemand etwas haben. Der sympathische Klang der Vielfalt überspielt die meisten Zweifel.

Umso wichtiger ist das Buch Tamanahas: Endlich wird »Rechtspluralismus erklärt«. Schon seit den 1990er Jahren beteiligt sich Tamanaha an den Debatten um Rechtspluralismus. Zwar gehört er nicht zu den Rechtspluralist*innen der ersten Stunde. Doch bereits seit seiner Dissertation »Understanding Law in Micronesia« von 1993 begleitet er die Studien zum Rechtspluralismus kritisch.[3] Was aber erklärt nun Tamanaha? Wie klärt er über Rechtspluralismus auf? Seine Geschichte geht so:

* Brian Z. Tamanaha, Legal Pluralism Explained. History, Theory, Consequences, New York: Oxford University Press 2021, x + 217 S., ISBN 978-0-19-086155-1

1 Dazu den Überblick bei Ralf Seinecke, Das Recht des Rechtspluralismus, Tübingen 2015, 58–65.

2 Etwa in den Handbüchern aus der jüngeren Zeit Paul Schiff Berman (Hg.), The Oxford Handbook of Global Legal Pluralism, Oxford 2020; Davies Gareth, Matej Avbelj (Hg.), Reasearch Handbook on Legal Pluralism and EU Law, Cheltenham / Northampton 2018.

3 Brian Z. Tamanaha, Understanding Law in Micronesia. An Interpretive Approach to Transplanted Law, Leiden 1993; ders., The Folly of the ›Social Scientific‹ Concept of Legal Pluralism, in: Journal of Law and Society 20 (1993) 192–217; ders., A Non-Essentialist Version of Legal Pluralism, in: Journal of Law and Society 27 (2000) 296–321; ders., Understanding Legal Pluralism: Past to Present. Local to Global, in: Sydney Law Review 30 (2008) 375–411.

»Rechtspluralismus erklärt« bedeutet zunächst »Rechtspluralismus ist überall« (1).[4] In der Tradition des frühen anthropologischen Rechtspluralismus richtet er sich gegen den »Rechtsmonismus« (*legal monism*). Dieser »monistische Gesetzesstaat« (monist law state) beherrsche das (westliche) Rechtsdenken seit mehr als drei Jahrhunderten (213) und trage »totalitäre« Züge (210). Dagegen biete Rechtspluralismus deskriptiv ein realistischeres Bild des Rechts und normativ einen angemesseneren und lebensnäheren Rechtsbegriff. Rechtspluralismus dürfe dabei aber nicht abstrakt begriffen werden (*abstract legal pluralism*). Vielmehr werde nur ein »volkstümlicher« Begriff des Rechtspluralismus (*folk legal pluralism*) seinen vielfältigen Phänomenen gerecht. Für deren Untersuchung empfiehlt Tamanaha die Unterscheidung von Gemeinschaftsrecht (*community law*), politischem bzw. Herrschaftsrecht (*regime law*) und schließlich Zwischengemeinwesenrecht (*cross-polity law*).

II. Das Buch bietet eine gewaltige Tour d'Horizon in vier Etappen: den »Rechtspluralismus im historischen Kontext« (19–54), den »postkolonialen Rechtspluralismus« (55–96), den »Rechtspluralismus des Westens« (97–127) sowie den »nationalen und transnationalen Rechtspluralismus« (129–168). Das ist viel Rechtspluralismus – vielleicht zu viel für ein schlankes Buch von 213 Seiten. Tamanaha schöpft nicht aus eigenen Quellen und nur selten aus eigenen Forschungen, sondern meist aus zweiter Hand. Anders ließe sich das enorme Programm auch kaum stemmen. Für Tamanaha ist Rechtspluralismus eben überall.

Epistemisch ist das alles hochproblematisch: Die emphatische Behauptung eines ubiquitären Rechtspluralismus geht weit und schürt bereits Misstrauen. Die Rückgriffe auf historische und anthropologische Studien erfolgen höchst selektiv. Die pointillistische Darstellung alternativer Rechtsordnungen neben dem nationalstaatlichen Recht des Westens wirkt eher anekdotisch. Die weltanschaulichen Präferenzen der zahlreichen Agitatoren des Rechtspluralismus werden ausgeblendet. Schließlich wird die subjektive Perspektive in der Wahl des Begriffs des Rechtspluralismus nicht reflektiert. Denn letztlich ließen sich alle Phänomene des Rechtspluralismus aus der Rechtsgeschichte, der (postkolonialen) Rechtsanthropologie, dem nationalstaatlichen, internationalen und transnationalen Recht auch ohne das Wort »Rechtspluralismus« gut beschreiben.

Das wird in der Präsentation von »Rechtspluralismus im historischen Kontext« besonders deutlich. Schon die Auswahl der historischen Topoi ist kontingent. Zwar will Tamanaha lediglich die »historische Normalität des Rechtspluralismus« (19) zeigen. Eine Begründung seiner Auswahl hätte dieses Anliegen freilich nicht desavouiert. Stattdessen folgt er der üblichen Chronologie: Antike, Mittelalter, Neuzeit. Immerhin. Im Römischen Reich habe vor allem das Personalitätsprinzip den Rechtspluralismus erzeugt (21–24). In der zweiten Hälfte des Mittelalters (24–26) seien das dann verschiedene »Arten von Recht« (25) gewesen: »kaiserliche und königliche Edikte und Gesetze, kanonisches Recht, ungeschriebene Gewohnheitsrechte von Stämmen und Orten, geschriebenes germanisches Recht, verbleibendes römisches Recht, städtische Statuten, das Recht der Kaufleute und Zünfte, und in England das *common law*, auf dem Kontinent das römische Recht der Juristen« (25). Dass das etwa für den deutschsprachigen Raum noch bis weit ins 19. Jahrhundert galt, hat Tamanaha offenbar niemand gesagt.[5] Den längsten Abschnitt widmet er dabei der »Herausbildung des Gesetzesstaates« (*law state*) (26–36). Hier gibt er Chronologie und jede klare Darstellung auf. Stattdessen bietet er eine rechtshistorische, historiographische und ideengeschichtliche Melange. Irgendwie geht es um »rivalisierende Rechtskräfte« (27) wie Imperien, Kirche, Adel und Städte (27–31), erste Schritte zur »Vereinheitlichung des Rechts« in Frankreich im 13. Jahrhundert (31), den Westfälischen Frieden (29), die neuen Juristenfakultäten des 12. Jahrhunderts (32), schließlich Machiavelli (33), Bodin (33–36) und Hobbes (34–35). Für Neuzeit und Moderne wählt er dann das Osmanische Reich als Beispiel (36–39). Dort hätten Millets verschiedenen religiösen Gruppen »rechtliche Autonomie« gewährt (37). Weiter schreibt Tamanaha über andere »Exterritorialitäten auf der Welt« (39–44) sowie den »vielfältigen Rechtspluralismus im osmanischen Reich« (44–46). Einen letzten Ab-

4 So schon Tamanaha (2008) (Fn. 3) 375: »Legal pluralism is everywhere«. *Übersetzungen aus dem Englischen hier und im Folgenden von R.S.*

5 Dazu Ralf Seinecke, Die deutschsprachige Rechtswissenschaft seit 1800 und der Rechtspluralismus, in: ZRG (GA) 137 (2020) 272–363.

schnitt widmet er dem »Gesetzesstaat« der »British East India Company« (46–52).

Aber was soll das alles? Die Antwort gibt Tamanaha in einem letzten kurzen Abschnitt zu »Gebrauch und Missbrauch des Bildes vom monistischen Gesetzesstaat« (52–54). Tamanaha beschreibt das Bild vom einheitlichen Recht als gefährliche Ideologie. Denn es habe einen Beitrag zur Kolonialisierung der Welt durch die Europäer geleistet: »Länder, die nicht den Standards des monistischen Gesetzesstaates entsprechen, seien, in dieser Sicht, defizitär, und riefen nach Übernahme« (53). Dagegen schreibt Tamanaha seine Geschichte des pluralen Rechts. Er interessiert sich nicht genuin historisch. Eine ernstzunehmende Rechtsgeschichte des Rechtspluralismus müsste vielmehr wichtige Vorfragen klären: Welchen Gewinn verspricht die Verwendung des Begriffs des Rechtspluralismus in der Untersuchung von historischen Epochen, in denen Recht aus unterschiedlichen Quellen geschöpft, ohne klare Jurisdiktionen gesprochen oder ohne offiziellen Rechtsstab durchgesetzt wurde? Wie und wozu hilft Rechtspluralismus, wenn Recht eng in andere normative Ordnungen verstrickt war, Gerichte fehlten oder soziale Ordnungen sich autark gegenüber einem herrschaftlichen Recht behaupteten? Auf diese Fragen gibt es gute Antworten. Eine Geschichte des Rechtspluralismus sollte nicht schweigend an ihnen vorbeischreiten.

Ähnliche methodische Probleme werfen die drei Kapitel zum postkolonialen, westlichen, nationalen und transnationalen Rechtspluralismus auf. Tamanahas Schlussfolgerungen sind dennoch deutlich: In postkolonialen Gesellschaften unterstütze Rechtspluralismus (normativ) den »Rechtsstaat« (*rule of law*) durch die Anerkennung von Rechtsordnungen in Gemeinschaften, für die staatliches Recht »keine tragfähige Alternative« sei (96). In westlichen Gesellschaften weise der »etatistische Monismus«, also »die Annahme eines exklusiven, einheitlichen, höchsten Rechts des Staates«, sogar »eine potentielle Affinität zum Totalitarismus« auf (127). Überraschenderweise meldet Tamanaha dann gegenüber dem globalen Rechtspluralismus erhebliche »Zweifel« an (157–161). Die Erkenntnisse des systemtheoretischen Rechtspluralismus Gunther Teubners ließen sich etwa auch ohne dessen »dichten theoretischen Unterbau« (162) gewinnen. Allgemeiner hätten die globalen Rechtspluralismen »wenig zu sagen, abgesehen von der Beachtung der Komplexität und Interaktion« in globalen Rechtsprozessen und der »Befürwortung von flexiblen, verhandelbaren« Lösungen (168). Der Begriff des »globalen Rechtspluralismus« könne deshalb ruhig aufgegeben werden (168). Er interessiert Tamanaha einfach nicht.

III. Im fünften Kapitel »abstrakter versus volkstümlicher Rechtspluralismus« widmet sich Tamanaha schließlich der Theorie. Er stellt die Gretchenfrage des Rechtspluralismus: Nun sag, wie hast Du's mit dem Recht? Oder einfacher: »Was ist Recht?« (169) Tamanaha antwortet wieder meinungsstark: Die Suche nach dem Recht des Rechtspluralismus leide unter abstrakten Definitionen. Alle bisherigen Definitionen von Eugen Ehrlich (178–182) über John Griffiths (170–173) bis zum postmodernen Rechtspluralismus (200–201) erfassten entweder zu viele oder zu wenige normative Phänomene als Recht oder scheiterten gänzlich daran, Rechtspluralismus allgemeiner zu charakterisieren (202). Sie litten unter einem letztlich essentiellen Rechtsbegriff (174). Dagegen entwickelt er sein »volkstümliches Recht« (*folk law*):[6] »Der volkstümliche Rechtspluralismus identifiziert Recht, indem er fragt, was die Menschen in einem bestimmten sozialen Umfeld kollektiv anerkennen und durch ihre sozialen Praktiken als Recht behandeln« (176). Zentral für Tamanaha sind hier Sprache und Praxis der jeweiligen Rechtsgemeinschaft. Deshalb übersetzt er Recht in seiner Definition gleich noch in fünf (europäische) Sprachen. Nicht, dass ihm jemand entgegnet, die Französin kenne kein »Recht« und auch kein »law«, sondern nur »droit«. Und hoffentlich fragt sie Tamanaha nicht nach dem Rechtsstatus der »coutumes«.

Mit dem volkstümlichen Rechtsbegriff will Tamanaha Recht nicht auf ein »singuläres Phänomen« reduzieren (175). Vielmehr sei Recht, »was immer Menschen gemeinsam als Recht in sozialen Gemeinschaften betrachten« (175). Dadurch könnten »verschiedene Arten von Recht« – »Gewohnheitsrecht, religiöses Recht, internationales Recht, transnationales Recht etc.« – aus und in ihrer eigenen Rechtsart untersucht werden (175). Dass dieser Rechtsbegriff offensichtlich »mysteriös« oder mindestens tautologisch sei, hat Tamanaha immerhin John Gardner verraten – auch wenn

6 Dazu schon der Aufsatz Tamanaha (2000) (Fn. 3).

Tamanaha dessen Argument einfach negiert (207). Schon Eugen Ehrlich hatte 1913 einen ähnlichen Weg versucht und deutlich bekannt, dass zwischen Recht und den »außerrechtlichen Normen zweifellos ein unverkennbarer Gegensatz« bestehe, »so schwer er bei dem heutigen Stande der Wissenschaft zu bestimmen sei«.[7] Immerhin gab sich Ehrlich damit nicht zufrieden und setzte auf die *opinio necessitatis* als das entscheidende Gefühl zur Abgrenzung von Recht und Nicht-Recht.[8]

Brian Tamanaha ist wohl auch das noch zu abstrakt. Er erkennt Recht intuitiv an Worten und in sozialen Praktiken. Das kann man so machen, ist aber letztlich eine seltsame wissenschaftliche Haltung. Sie durchzieht das ganze Buch: Historische und postkoloniale Rechtspluralismen sind gut. Globale und abstrakte Rechtspluralismen sind überflüssig. Staatliche Rechtsvorstellungen sind ideologisch, gar totalitär. Die weltanschauliche Agenda und epistemische Signatur des Rechtspluralismus selbst aber interessiert nicht. Alles erklärt? Endlich!

■

Louis Pahlow

Keynes und das Bonner Grundgesetz*

In der Rechtsgeschichte der Bundesrepublik sind wirtschaftliche Konzeptionen und Theorien als Bausteine für die Rechtsentwicklung häufig ausgemacht worden. Zu einem der Gründungsnarrative des neuen Staates wird nicht ganz zu Unrecht der sog. Ordoliberalismus gezählt, der aber von einigen sogar zum Fahrplan für »soziale Marktwirtschaft« mit Leistungswettbewerb und GWB überzeichnet wurde. Die Rechtsgeschichte und auch die Wirtschaftsgeschichte haben diese Beschreibungen in den letzten Jahren deutlich relativiert. Auch in Bezug auf die Chicago School sind die Ideen von Allokationseffizienz und Transaktionskosten bislang nur in ausgewählten Bereichen der Gesetzgebung nachgewiesen worden. Und wie steht es mit John Maynard Keynes? Er gilt als der bedeutendste Nationalökonom der Zwischenkriegszeit. Seine »Allgemeine Theorie der Beschäftigung, des Zinses und des Geldes« (»The General Theory of Employment, Interest and Money«) aus dem Jahre 1936 markiert eine Bruchstelle in der Ökonomik des 20. Jahrhunderts. Keynes forderte darin – vereinfacht ausgedrückt – angesichts der zuvor erlebten Weltwirtschaftskrise eine Abkehr von der liberalen Praxis des sog. »Laissez-faire«, welche bis zum Ausbruch des Ersten Weltkrieges das wirtschaftspolitische Leitbild der meisten großen Wirtschaftsnationen der westlichen Welt gewesen war. Stattdessen wollte Keynes im Falle einer wirtschaftlichen Depression die staatliche Wirtschafts- und Finanzpolitik durch konjunkturgerechte Maßnahmen zur Stabilisierung der Gesamtwirtschaft verpflichten. In diesem Zusammenhang hat die nach Keynes angeregte und massiv einsetzende Politik des sog. »Deficit Spending« besondere Bekanntheit erlangt.

Alexander Kustermann geht der Rezeption von Keynes im Haushaltsverfassungsrecht der Bundesrepublik nach. Im Zeitalter von Schuldenbremse und Investitionsstau hat das Thema ohne Frage aktuelle Relevanz. Die Arbeit zielt – wohl auch wegen dieser Gegenwartsbezüge – auf die recht-

7 Eugen Ehrlich, Grundlegung der Soziologie des Rechts, 1. Aufl., München/Leipzig 1913, 131, 5. Aufl., hg. v. Manfred Rehbinder, Berlin 2022, 196.

8 Dazu statt vieler Ralf Seinecke, Ehrlichbilder: Freirecht, Rechtssoziologie und Rechtspluralismus – zum 100. Todestag von Eugen Ehrlich, in: ZEuP 30 (2022) 302–336.

* Alexander Kustermann, Konjunktursteuerung durch »Deficit Spending«? Eine rechtshistorische Untersuchung zu den ideengeschichtlichen Ursprüngen des Stabilitätsgesetzes und der Haushaltsreform 1967–1969, Tübingen: Mohr Siebeck 2020, 252 S., ISBN 978-3-16-157645-4

lichen Ursachen überbordender Staatsverschuldung, die in den letzten Jahrzehnten einen Wandel durchlebt habe. Eine kritische Haltung in Bezug auf kreditfinanziertes Wachstum bis etwa zur Mitte des 20. Jahrhunderts sei von einer wohlfahrtsstaatlichen Orientierung der Staatsausgaben abgelöst worden. Seit den späten 1960er Jahren sei von einer »Enttabuisierung der öffentlichen Verschuldung« die Rede. Bis heute, wie Kustermann feststellt, werde dieser Wandel auf Keynes zurückgeführt. Damit ist die zentrale Fragestellung der Arbeit, nämlich ob und inwieweit die Haushaltsreformen in den 1960er Jahren auf Keynes basieren, skizziert. Kustermann geht ihr ausgewogen und umsichtig unter Berücksichtigung der einschlägigen juristischen, aber auch wirtschaftshistorischen und politikgeschichtlichen Literatur nach. Schon deshalb verdient die Arbeit Lob, weil viele der rechtshistorischen Analysen, zumal wenn sie sich auf die Gesetzgebungsgeschichte konzentrieren, diese Perspektiven nach wie vor ausblenden.

Das Werk folgt einem chronologischen Aufbau, der zum einen die ideengeschichtlichen Grundlagen berücksichtigt und zum anderen akteursorientiert den unterschiedlichen finanzpolitischen Denkmustern nachgeht. Ein Vorteil der Arbeit liegt in der klaren Sprache und Struktur, die sich auf drei zentrale Thesen konzentriert, die anhand der genannten Methoden herausgearbeitet und weitgehend stichhaltig belegt werden. Kustermann überzeugt durch eine präzise Rekonstruktion der ideengeschichtlichen Wurzeln und Verästelungen einer kreditfinanzierten Haushaltspolitik des Staates für Anschubinvestitionen und zur Krisenbewältigung, die er bis in die Zwischenkriegszeit zurückverfolgt. Anhand einer Analyse der involvierten Akteure, die sich weitgehend auf Haushaltspolitiker, Finanzwissenschaftler und Nationalökonomen konzentriert, zeigt die Arbeit, dass noch vor der Publikation der »General Theory« von 1936 kreditfinanzierte Ausgabenprogramme des Staates zur Bekämpfung der Deflation in Deutschland vorgeschlagen und diskutiert wurden. Das ist für den versierten Wirtschaftshistoriker, der sich mit der Weltwirtschaftskrise ausführlich beschäftigt hat, zwar keine neue Erkenntnis; aber für die rechtswissenschaftliche Grundlagenforschung allemal wert, in Erinnerung gerufen zu werden.

Mit seiner akteursorientierten Methode kann Kustermann auch die zweite These erklären, nach der das Stabilitätsgesetz nur den vorläufigen Endpunkt eines »jahrzehntelangen Suchprozesses« dargestellt habe. Zunächst wird eine Erklärung dafür geliefert, warum das Bonner Grundgesetz von 1949 konjunkturpolitische Mechanismen zumindest nicht ausdrücklich berücksichtigt hatte. Kustermann macht dafür vor allem die personelle Besetzung der Ausschüsse des Parlamentarischen Rates verantwortlich: Mit der Ausarbeitung der haushaltsverfassungsrechtlichen Vorschriften waren überwiegend Praktiker aus der Weimarer Zeit und dem »Dritten Reich« betraut worden. Dagegen fanden sich keine hauptamtlichen Hochschullehrer aus dem Bereich der Nationalökonomie. Auch wurden solche zumindest in Bezug auf das Haushaltsverfassungsrecht nicht als Sachverständige angehört. Damit war es vor allem der ehemalige preußische Finanzminister Hermann Höpker-Aschoff, der sich als mehrheitlich respektierter Experte für Finanzfragen in vielen wesentlichen Punkten bei der Erarbeitung der entsprechenden Vorschriften durchsetzen konnte. Zugleich zeigt sich aber auch, dass einflussreiche Akteure wie Höpker-Aschoff profunde Kenner der Schriften Keynes' waren. Allerdings konnte sich der Parlamentarische Rat bezüglich der Kreditbegrenzungsregeln nicht auf eine ausdrückliche Ausnahmevorschrift zur Überwindung einer Wirtschaftskrise einigen. Dadurch, dass die Kreditaufnahme gemäß Art. 115 GG »in der Regel nur für Ausgaben zu werbenden Zwecken« erfolgen durfte, ging Höpker-Aschoff davon aus, dass der Bund ggf. kurzfristig und unter Einhaltung der parlamentarischen Mitwirkungsrechte Konjunkturpolitik betreiben könne.

Die fehlenden Hinweise im Grundgesetz sind also kein hinreichender Beleg dafür, so Kustermann, dass es nicht auch vor 1965 bereits zu konjunktursteuernden Maßnahmen kommen konnte bzw. kam. Anhand der Diskussion nach Inkrafttreten des Grundgesetzes zeigt Kustermann, dass bereits unter dem ersten Kabinett Adenauer eine breite Diskussion über den konjunkturpolitischen Aufgabenbereich der öffentlichen Haushalte begann. Während geplante Defizithaushalte im Hinblick auf den Wortlaut des ursprünglichen Art. 110 GG für verfassungswidrig gehalten wurden, diskutierten andere längst entsprechende Steuerungsmöglichkeiten durch eine antizyklische Finanzpolitik. Ökonomen und Finanzwissenschaftler befürworteten seit den frühen 1950er Jahren eine Überwindung der als veraltet angesehenen Vorschriften des Haushaltsrechts, warnten vereinzelt aber auch vor Verabsolutierungen der

»neuen Lehren«. Der Ordoliberalismus, so Kustermann, konnte weder in den wissenschaftlichen Beiräten noch in den Positionspapieren wichtiger Forschungsinstitute einen vergleichbaren Einfluss ausüben. Auch die entsprechenden Empfehlungen der wissenschaftlichen Beiräte von BMWi und BMF, die Kustermann heranzieht, zeigten Elemente einer »Globalsteuerung«. Das deckt sich mit bisherigen wirtschaftshistorischen Analysen, die bereits vor dem Regierungswechsel zur Großen Koalition hinter den Kulissen des politischen Tagesgeschäfts entsprechende Vorarbeiten für eine »globalgesteuerte« Wirtschaftspolitik ausfindig gemacht haben.

Für seine dritte These, nach der die Große Koalition ein Wegbereiter des Kompromisses in der Krise gewesen sei, trägt Kustermann allerdings kaum neue Erkenntnisse zusammen. Die Arbeit konnte sich hier ohnehin auf wichtige Vorarbeiten der Wirtschaftsgeschichte stützen. Die Große Koalition entwickelte mit dem Stabilitätsgesetz letztlich einen Instrumentenkasten, der ganz unterschiedliche wirtschaftswissenschaftliche Ideen miteinander verband. Insgesamt liegt uns mit der vorliegenden Bonner Dissertation eine profunde Rezeptionsgeschichte nicht nur zu Keynes, sondern auch zu den Legitimationsstrategien kreditfinanzierter Haushaltspolitik vor. Kustermann relativiert die bisherige juristische Literatur, die häufig John Maynard Keynes bzw. »den« Keynesianismus für die Haushaltspolitik der 1960er Jahre, ja für »Deficit Spending« generell verantwortlich gemacht hat. Stattdessen erhalten wir einen erfrischend fundierten und differenzierten Blick auf die verschiedenen Ideenstränge kreditfinanzierter Haushaltspolitik. Die Arbeit geht damit weit über eine reine Gesetzgebungsgeschichte der entsprechenden Haushaltsbestimmungen des Grundgesetzes hinaus. Insgesamt eine empfehlenswerte Lektüre für jeden wirtschafts- und haushaltsgeschichtlich Interessierten, die sich ganz nebenbei hervorragend liest und durch zahlreiche, bislang unbekannte Quellen ergänzt wird.

■

Valeria Vegh Weis

Kriminalisierung des Bösen*

Mark S. Berlin, Assistenzprofessor für Politikwissenschaft an der Marquette University, legt mit der hier besprochenen Arbeit eine ambitionierte Studie über die innerstaatliche Gesetzgebung zu Gräueltaten vor, zu denen Völkermord, Kriegsverbrechen und Verbrechen gegen die Menschlichkeit gehören.[1] Seine Untersuchung verwendet verschiedene Methoden: Auf der quantitativen Ebene präsentiert Berlin einen eigens erstellten globalen Datensatz über nationale Gesetze zu Gräueltaten. Dieser enthält das Jahr, in dem jedes Land diese Art von Gesetzen verabschiedet hat, sowie Daten darüber, wann und ob dies durch die Verabschiedung eines neuen Strafgesetzbuchs geschah, was die Grundlage für weitere Studien zu diesem Thema bildet. In qualitativer Hinsicht befasst sich der Autor mit der Analyse spezifischer Fallstudien und legt dabei einen Schwerpunkt auf Guatemala, wo ein 36-jähriger Bürgerkrieg (1960–1996) mehr als 75.000 zivile Todesopfer forderte.

Berlin argumentiert, dass »der Schlüssel zum Verständnis, *warum* Staaten Gräueltaten kriminalisieren, darin liegt, *wie* sie dies tun« (3), obwohl der Autor auch auf das *Wer* und das *Wann* achtet. In Bezug auf die Akteure (*wer*) argumentiert er, dass dies kein besonders relevanter Faktor sein sollte. In der Tat ist es so, dass »demokratischere Staaten mit größerer Wahrscheinlichkeit als weni-

* Mark S. Berlin, Criminalizing Atrocity: The Global Spread of Criminal Laws against International Crimes, Oxford: Oxford University Press 2020, 250 S., ISBN 978-0-19-885044-1

1 David Scheffer, Genocide and Atrocity Crimes, in: Genocide Studies and Prevention 1,3 (2006) 229–250. *Übersetzungen aus dem Englischen hier und im Folgenden von V. V. W.*

ger demokratische Staaten gezielt Gesetze gegen Gräueltaten erlassen«, aber »wenn sie sich für eine Neugestaltung ihrer Strafgesetzbücher entscheiden, ist es nicht wahrscheinlicher oder unwahrscheinlicher, dass demokratischere Staaten Gräueltaten kriminalisieren« (21). Darüber hinaus erklärt der Autor, dass sowohl demokratische als auch totalitäre »Staaten eher dazu neigen, Gesetze über Gräueltaten in neue Gesetzbücher aufzunehmen, wenn erstens eine größere Anzahl ihrer regionalen juristischen Amtskollegen dies bereits getan hat und zweitens Strafrechtsspezialisten dort mit professionellen Netzwerken verbunden sind, die anfällig für den Einfluss der AIDP [International Association of Penal Law] sind« (21). In Zahlen ausgedrückt, informiert Berlins aufschlussreiche Datenbank darüber, dass 2018 »drei Viertel aller unabhängigen Staaten ein nationales Strafrecht gegen Völkermord, Kriegsverbrechen oder Verbrechen gegen die Menschlichkeit hatten« und dass »zum Zeitpunkt ihrer Kriminalisierung etwa die Hälfte dieser Staaten Autokratien waren« (25).

In Bezug auf das *Wann* widerspricht Berlin der allgemeinen Auffassung, dass sich in der Zeit vom Ende des Zweiten Weltkriegs über die Ausweitung eines globalen Verständnisses von Menschenrechten bis hin zur Schaffung internationaler Gerichtshöfe in den 1990er Jahren (Internationaler Strafgerichtshof für das ehemalige Jugoslawien und Internationaler Strafgerichtshof für Ruanda) nicht viel in Sachen Kriminalisierung von Gräueltaten getan hat. Entgegen dieser Auffassung weist der Autor quantitativ nach, wie viele Länder in diesem Zeitraum Grausamkeitsverbrechen in ihrer Gesetzgebung berücksichtigt haben.

In Bezug auf das »*Wie*«, den Hauptbeitrag des Buches, erklärt Berlin, dass es hauptsächlich zwei Möglichkeiten gebe, dies zu tun: entweder gezielt durch Gesetze über Gräueltaten, die bestehende Gesetze ändern oder als eigenständiges Gesetz verabschiedet werden (z. B. ein Gesetzentwurf, der speziell der Umsetzung der Konvention über die Verhütung und Bestrafung des Völkermordes in nationales Recht gewidmet ist) oder als Teil einer breiteren, groß angelegten Reform des nationalen Strafrechts (z. B. ein völlig neues Strafgesetzbuch, das einen ganzen Abschnitt über Gräueltaten enthält). Berlin geht davon aus, dass der zweite Weg der wahrscheinlichste ist. Dafür gibt er drei Hauptgründe an: 1. Das für die Ausarbeitung eines neuen Strafgesetzbuchs erforderliche Fachwissen macht es wahrscheinlicher, dass die Regierungen die Aufgaben an technokratische Fachleute delegieren, die keine bestimmte politische Ideologie im Sinn haben. 2. Ein neues Strafgesetzbuch kann dazu beitragen, das Image des Landes als eines solchen zu stärken, das sich Modernisierung auf die Fahnen geschrieben hat, was in einer globalisierten Nachkriegswelt auch die Menschenrechte und die Verhütung von Gräueltaten einschließt. 3. Das Ausmaß dieser Art von Reform, das die Intensität der Prüfung von einzelnen Projektteilen verringert, erleichtert die Verabschiedung ansonsten polemisch betrachteter Bestimmungen.

Ein Problem von Berlins Argumentation besteht jedoch in der Annahme, dass Technokraten ohne Rücksicht auf ihre ideologischen oder politischen Vorstellungen ausgewählt werden bzw. dass sie solche Vorstellungen gar nicht besitzen. In diesem Zusammenhang stellt er fest: »Während Aktivisten in erster Linie durch moralische Überzeugungen motiviert sind, sind technokratische Experten durch ihr Engagement für ihre berufliche Praxis und den Fortschritt des technischen Wissens motiviert« (40). Man könnte jedoch dagegenhalten, dass diese »Unparteilichkeit« selten vorkommt. Technokraten haben Ideen, Positionen, Laufbahnen, politische Neigungen und manchmal gar Verpflichtungen gegenüber Auftraggebern. Wenn wir uns auf die Ursprünge des Völkermords als Verbrechen selbst konzentrieren, können wir feststellen, dass Raphael Lemkin der wichtigste »Technokrat« war, der sich für die Gesetzgebung und die Aufnahme dieser Verbrechen bei den Nürnberger Prozessen einsetzte.[2] Als Überlebender des Naziregimes war er keineswegs ideologie-

2 Philippe Sands, East West Street: On the Origins of Genocide and Crimes Against Humanity, New York 2016; Valeria Vegh Weis, The Role of the Jewish Victims in the Post-Holocaust Transitional Justice Process in Germany, Institut für Kriminologische Forschung, Universität Hamburg, 2020 [Vortrag].

frei, sondern engagierte sich stark für den Prozess, mit dem Angeklagte zur Rechenschaft gezogen werden können; dieser wiederum führte zur UN-Konvention über die Verhütung und Bestrafung des Völkermordes von 1948 sowie zur anschließenden Aufnahme dieses Vertrags in die nationale Gesetzgebung.

Eine weitere heikle Dimension lässt sich in Berlins drittem Argument erkennen, da es davon ausgeht, dass die politischen Entscheidungsträger das »Paket« eines neuen Strafgesetzbuchs akzeptieren werden, ohne jeden einzelnen Bestandteil darin sorgfältig zu studieren. Diese Annahme ist aber unwahrscheinlich; vielmehr dürften insbesondere diejenigen Teile des Strafgesetzbuchs, die sich mit Straftaten befassen, für welche die Entscheidungsträger selbst verfolgt werden können, auf deren Interesse stoßen. Ein weiteres Argument, das Berlin in diesem Zusammenhang nicht in Erwägung zieht, ist die Tatsache, dass viele Regierungen – auch diejenigen, die in Gräueltaten verwickelt sind – an der Verabschiedung von Gesetzen gegen Gräueltaten interessiert sein könnten, um der Welt zu zeigen, dass sie sich der Rechtsstaatlichkeit und den Menschenrechten verpflichtet fühlen. Die Notwendigkeit, neben der Rolle der Technokraten nach weiteren Erklärungsvariablen zu suchen, wird auch dadurch deutlich, dass Berlin negative Fälle aufzeigt, in denen Technokraten zwar eine Gesetzgebung zu Gräueltaten einbrachten, diese aber von der politischen Macht wieder abgeschafft wurde, was Zweifel an der Fähigkeit von Technokraten aufkommen lässt, rechtliche Änderungen dieser Art durchzusetzen.

Schließlich enthält das Buch aus der Perspektive des Globalen Südens einige problematische Passagen, die entweder aus mangelndem Wissen über Lateinamerika herrühren oder sogar als paternalisierende bzw. koloniale Sichtweise gelesen werden können. So beginnt das Buch mit drei Beispielen von Ländern, die die Verabschiedung von Gesetzen gegen Gräueltaten im eigenen Land bewertet haben: Guatemala, Uruguay und Norwegen. Berlin fährt dann fort: »Intuitiv dürfte von den drei Staaten der wahrscheinlichste Kandidat für die Verabschiedung einer innerstaatlichen Gesetzgebung gegen Gräueltaten Norwegen sein, das sich einer langen Tradition der Förderung der Menschenrechte im In- und Ausland rühmen kann« (2). Diese Aussage vernachlässigt die Tatsache, dass Lateinamerika zum Zeitpunkt dieser Entscheidungen – in den 2000er Jahren – bereits weltweit als Vorreiter in Sachen Menschenrechte anerkannt war.[3] Darüber hinaus argumentiert Berlin, dass die Einbeziehung der Kriminalisierung von Gräueltaten ein Prozess von »oben nach unten« ist, der eher von Technokraten durchgeführt wird. In Lateinamerika ging der große Impuls zur Kriminalisierung von Gräueltaten jedoch von Menschenrechtsaktivisten, also von unten nach oben aus.[4] Schließlich könnte es auch interessant sein zu fragen, ob die Kriminalisierung von Gräueltaten auch in den Verfassungsreformen stattfinden könnte, wie es in Argentinien der Fall war.

Freilich stellt keiner dieser Kritikpunkte die Relevanz von Berlins Arbeit in Frage. Die Bemerkungen regen lediglich die Einbeziehung inländischer und internationaler Aktivisten als wichtigen Faktor an und hinterfragen die vermeintliche Neutralität von Technokraten sowie die angebliche Nachlässigkeit der Regierungen, wenn diese umfassendere Strafrechtsreformen verabschieden, ohne auf die Einbeziehung von Gräueltaten zu achten.

In einer Zeit, in der sich internationale Verbrechen ausbreiten (Afghanistan, Myanmar, Ukraine) und in der die breitere Übernahme internationaler Verträge, die sich mit Grausamkeitsverbrechen befassen (insbesondere das Römische Statut), in nationales Recht immer noch eine ausstehende Aufgabe ist, ist dieses Buch ein willkommener und zum Nachdenken anregender Beitrag.

3 Alison Brysk, The Political Impact of Argentina's Human Rights Movement: Social Movements, Transition and Democratization, Ph.D. thesis, Stanford 1990, verfügbar unter: https://www.proquest.com/openview/a33ee07/89dbe4a13c3dce6ac0c19c996/1?pq-origsite=gscholar&cbl=18750&diss=y; Kathryn Sikkink, From Pariah State to Global Protagonist: Argentina and the Struggle for International Human Rights, in: Latin American Politics and Society 50,1 (2008) 1–29; Kathryn Sikkink, The Justice Cascade. How Human Rights Prosecutions Are Changing World Politics, New York 2011; Kathryn Sikkink, Carrie Booth Walling, The Impact of Human Rights Trials in Latin America, in: Journal of Peace Research 44,4 (2007) 427–445.

4 Valeria Vegh Weis, The Relevance of Victims' Organizations in the Transitional Justice Process: The Case of the Grandmothers of Plaza de Mayo in Argentina, in: Intercultural Human Rights Law Review 60 (2017) 1–70.

Auf der Grundlage eines soliden methodischen Konzepts eröffnet Berlin neue Dimensionen für ein zentrales Problem unserer Zeit. Wissenschaftler/innen und Studierende aus verschiedenen Forschungsbereichen (Völkerrecht, internationales Strafrecht, Politikwissenschaft, internationale Beziehungen, Rechtsgeschichte und Kriminologie), aber auch das allgemeine Publikum und politische Entscheidungsträger werden von den bahnbrechenden Erkenntnissen seiner Arbeit profitieren.

■

Karla L. Escobar H.

Beyond Drugs, State and Legality*

Estefanía Ciro's book »Levantados de la Selva: Vidas y legitimidades en los territorios cocaleros del Caquetá« is based on her doctoral research in sociology, which in 2017 won the UNESCO/Juan Bosch Prize for the Promotion of Social Science Research in Latin America and the Caribbean.

This volume is the product of interdisciplinary work moving between the fields of economics, history, and sociology, and, therefore, draws on different kinds of historiographies: those dedicated to the sociology of exclusion, the effects of anti-drug policies in Latin America, and the historiography of rurality. This detailed review of the academic literature is accompanied by what I consider the most valuable part of the book: a rigorous ethnographic work about the men and women dedicated to coca leaf cultivation and the processing of coca paste in the region. The arguments put forward by Ciro are underpinned throughout the book by numerous interviews transcribed in extensive quotations that offer the reader a multifaceted picture of the coca issue.

Ciro divides her work into seven chapters plus an introduction and conclusions. Each chapter first offers a description of the lives of the *cocaleros* and *cocaleras* and the different problems that cut across their life experiences. These narratives are then tied together by diverse cross-cutting analyses. The book's narrative begins with a reflection on the role that moralizing discourses have played in thinking about public policy concerning coca cultivation and the problems that this approach has entailed. It then discusses the role of violence, particularly that perpetrated by the state in the region, the role of paramilitarism, the guerrilla and international anti-drug policies, the historical migratory processes in the territory that characterize the life trajectories of its interviewees, and the analysis of the economic practices that characterize rural production in the Amazon region from a historical perspective.

This analysis is carried out at different scales, starting with the most immediate presentation of the lives of the interviewees: their life trajectories, their visions of themselves and their families, their expectations for the future, and their fears, dreams, and claims. These life experiences are complemented by other elements: accounts of settlement dynamics, forms of property ownership, local, regional and national economic practices, national and local legal discourses, and global political projects. This multi-scalar and contextual view considers both long-term and short-term events through which the author manages to foster a fruitful discussion on the various dichotomies that have characterized the narratives on the coca economy and the Amazon region. The author closes her study with a diagnosis of the »coca problem« in the region after the peace accords with the FARC guerrilla and makes important recommendations for the development of public policy in the region based on her findings.

* Estefanía Ciro Rodríguez, Levantados de la selva: Vidas y legitimidades en los territorios cocaleros del Caquetá, Bogotá: Ediciones Uniandes 2020, 308 p., ISBN 978-958-774-883-3

Ciro's book is the product of rigorous and thoughtful research, and her arguments are thought-provoking and invite debate as well as being proactive: something we do not find very often in contemporary academic scholarship. Although it is not a work of legal history, it shares several concerns that many historians of law have today and traces a methodological path for thinking about solutions to contemporary issues based on historical analysis, aspects I consider to be of key importance for our discipline today. The author also participates in contemporary scholarship discussions related to how to understand illegality and marginalization in given normative orders.

Ciro keeps questioning the alleged dichotomy between what is considered legal and illegal in the contexts she studies and, by acknowledging that this dichotomy is actually a fiction, presents a rich grayscale between the two points. In that sense, the author facilitates a visualization of how the act of calling something »illegal« translates into everyday life. Who benefits from making something illegal, and what's the net of power relations woven from such an act? What are the particular differences between participating in an illegal or a legal global market? Ciro's text accounts for many of these nuances on multiple levels: from the idea of »la mata que mata« (the plant which kills) – a word-playing slogan reproduced by the Colombian National Narcotics Directorate in 2008 that many Colombians like myself grew up with due to its wide dissemination in different media – to the affirmation of the complete opposite, »amor por la mata« (the love for the plant), claimed by one of Ciro's interviewees. The author analyses the multiple dynamics in which the paths of the illegal and the legal intersect. These intersections are located in diverse spaces: in types of land ownership, in the collective and individual desires for »social improvement«, in the practices of economizing and consumption behavior, in the forms of family structures, in individual and collective strategies for »making a life for oneself« and »surviving«, in the generational migration practices, in the strategies made up by hundreds of people who live amid the war between the state forces, the guerrillas and the paramilitaries, and many more. All these different practices are constructed following disputed notions of law and justice that cross the everyday lives of the interviewed *campesinos*.

These reflections on the legal and the illegal and their blurred borders lead to another of Ciro's central debates: the critique of the supposed »absence of the state« as the leading cause of illegal economies and the »mythological discourse« constructed across Colombian territory about the Amazonian region as a »no man's land« or as a »lawless region«. Ciro demonstrates in detail how, on the contrary, the state has a strong presence, not as a provider of services or a guardian of fundamental rights, but rather in its militaristic and warlike dimension, a situation that spawns a profound sense of discontent with and distrust of the state and its representatives. This feeling, shared by many of the interviewees, underlies an argument that has been heard in other spheres that see the state as one of the many actors violating the law in frontier regions. This discussion is not a minor issue in Colombian historiography. The thesis of the »weakness of the state« and the »wildness« of the Amazonian people was a commonplace justification for the use of violence in Colombia for a long time and, as Ciro points out, that view has produced weak public policies centered on creating a so-called »culture of legality« in the region without solving the structural issues linked to the rural crisis in the country and the militarized presence of the state.

Another essential aspect of Ciro's work is the in-depth characterization of the peasant population related to coca crops and coca paste production. Her work manages to show a very diverse and complex peasantry that goes beyond the stereotypes some literature has put forward, painting the peasants as a homogeneous and »isolated« group, usually opposed to the »modern« world. Quite the contrary is true: Ciro shows how the coca economy is deeply rooted in capitalist practices that peasants quickly learned to adopt and that, actually, follow patterns typical of other types of agro-export economies. This is another relevant contribution to economic history and specifically to the history of the rural world including in the literature about Campesino and *indígena* people in the Amazon.

This type of account of local history is highly relevant and should be widely read in the so-called global north. It not only brings new dimensions to the urgent discussion about drug penalization but also serves to evaluate, from a historic perspective, the terrible consequences that people have paid in the name of the euphemistic process called »the war on drugs«.

■

Luisa Stella de Oliveira Coutinho Silva

»Gênero: uma categoria útil« para a História do Direito Global?*

Nesta resenha, analiso duas publicações sobre a histórias das mulheres, questões de gênero, perspectivas globais e a história do império português. Colocando esses campos em perspectiva e explorando as ferramentas proporcionadas pelas publicações, exploro novas possibilidades abertas pelos livros e proponho o desenvolvimento de um novo campo – uma história do direito das mulheres a partir de uma perspectiva global, usando como ponto de partida a história do império português. Como historiadora do direito, as razões que me motivam a aproximar as obras que vou analisar partiram do questionamento sobre como a história do direito pode nos ajudar a desenvolver uma história das mulheres e de gênero a partir também da influência da história global.

O primeiro livro em análise é um compêndio sobre a história de gênero global, a segunda edição de um compêndio de 2004 (*A Companion to Gender History*). A edição mais recente, entretanto, insere a palavra »global« no seu título; assim como também atualizações dos artigos já existentes; sete novos artigos e uma introdução sensível a questões políticas, que inclui uma reflexão acerca dos impactos da pandemia de Covid-19 na vida diária de pesquisadores, a produção acadêmica das mulheres, as desigualdades e os desequilíbrios produzidos. O livro possui 36 artigos escritos por 37 autores. Dois deles homens, e apenas oito estão afiliados a instituições fora dos Estados Unidos.

O resultado é um livro organizado em duas partes. A primeira reúne temas e conceitos relevantes para os estudos de gênero sexualidade, trabalho, família, mitos e rituais, raça e diferenças, cultura material, arte visual, revolução e anti-imperialismo e movimentos feministas. A segunda parte está organizada por ordem cronológica-geográfica, que inclui estudos desde as mais antigas sociedades (100,000 BCE) até o período posterior à segunda guerra mundial em diversos locais do mundo.

Os artigos, de um modo geral, e a inserção da expressão global na nova edição, refletem a mudança nos estudos de gênero e na história das mulheres dos últimos 30 anos: a tendência a se »fazer« essas disciplinas considerando os processos globais, acentuando uma crítica às interpretações eurocêntricas e anglofônicas, às experiências »ocidentais« e colonialistas. Os artigos reforçam a ideia de que não há generalização possível de ser feita em relação ao gênero e que esse deve ser estudado e considerado sempre em uma situação relacional que envolva questões de classe, sexualidades e orientação sexual, etnia, religião, raça e outras categorias de diferença e dá ênfase às questões de colonização e influências imperiais à da agência e opressão das mulheres. Ressalta-se sempre, implícita ou explicitamente, que cada aspecto da existência humana é tocado pelo gênero; no âmbito social está refletido na família, no trabalho e no lazer, nos padrões de casamento e nas diferenças de classe. Deu-se que, ao longo do tempo / história, as experiências humanas foram moldadas por »princípios« de gênero, seja através da história política, militar e jurídica, da antropologia, dos estudos culturais seja nos usos simbólicos e metafóricos de categorias.

Mas, se esses conceitos e ideias são identificados de maneira fácil, pontualmente, em uma linha do tempo ou em locais (geográficos) específicos no livro, as interconexões que caracterizam o global e

* Teresa A. Meade, Merry E. Wiesner-Hanks (eds.), A Companion to Global Gender History. 2nd edition, Hoboken (NJ): Wiley-Blackwell, 654 p., ISBN 978-1-119-53580-5; Francisco Bethencourt, Gendering the Portuguese-speaking World, from the Middle Ages to the Present, Leiden: Brill 2021, 288 p., ISBN 978-90-04-45672-3

seu intenso debate teórico em busca de definições e características não são exatamente estabelecidas. Ou seja, os artigos não estão conectados, cumprindo sua função de compendiar a informação em coleção, de forma séria e com uso amplo de fontes, mas que não dialogam diretamente com a mais recente discussão sobre história global.[1] Entretanto, trazem, de modo tangencial, à obra inteira, a expressa crítica, tão cara aos estudos globais, ao eurocentrismo e ao colonialismo. Os artigos esboçam, de modo geral, um *puzzle* da história global que não se encaixa, deixando à dúvida a sua pertinência contextual teórica, mas mostram, ao mesmo tempo, a relevância das peças avulsas de qualidade e sua importância historiográfica através do uso das mais diversas fontes: tradições textuais (religiosas, médicas, normativas, leis), cultura material (terracota, vestidos, bicicletas, tecidos), mitos e rituais, imagens, restos do corpo humano, sepultamentos, vestígios químicos, objetos em geral, leis, normas, ideias, entre muitos outros.

Eu vejo a aproximação dos ramos em questão, a história global, a história das mulheres e os estudos de gênero, a partir de duas possibilidades, ou de dois caminhos a serem considerados para se justificarem, que são: a aproximação teórica dos campos para a construção de uma disciplina que tem sido denominada de várias formas[2] – esforço que surgiu a partir do trabalho de pesquisadores como Peter Stearns, Sarah Hughes, Bonnie Smith, Judith Zinsser, Margaret Strobel e a própria Merry Wiesner-Hanks, que edita o compêndio –, em segundo lugar, mas não por ordem de importância, os encontros e as reivindicações internacionais feministas, particularmente acentuados no século XX.

Nesse último século, a agenda feminista passou a incluir mais mulheres das Américas Central e do Sul, África e Ásia, trazendo mais diversidade e novos problemas ao movimento feminista que crescia a um exponente mundial. Novos termos passaram a ser considerados, incluindo não apenas uma luta pelos direitos internacionais das mulheres, mas a criação de redes transnacionais e de uma história internacional das mulheres. Essa »consciência internacional« sobre as reivindicações das mulheres e as questões de gênero podem ser destacadas em encontros como o Congresso Internacional das Mulheres de 1915, passando pela Declaração das Nações Unidas da década das mulheres (1976–1985) e a Convenção pela Eliminação de todas as Formas de Discriminação (CEDAW), e até nos movimentos mais recentes como o MeToo e a marcha feminista contra a eleição de Trump.

A agenda feminista e os estudos de gênero convergiram com a história global, abrindo espaço para um novo campo. Assim como temos ainda hoje um constante debate acerca da sua própria caracterização, a inclusão das mulheres e das questões de gênero na história mundial ou, em uma perspectiva global, tem crescido e proliferado. As justificativas e conexões envolvem questões inerentes às próprias críticas ao eurocentrismo, do foco no »Ocidente«, e de uma necessidade de perspectivas transnacionais (como o feminismo transnacional e a presença das mulheres de terceiro mundo, por exemplo) na escrita da história. Esse novo campo tem tidos vários focos: examinar e integrar a história de todos os países ou locais do mundo, enfatizando e relativizando os Estados Unidos e a Europa, e usar algumas áreas menos favorecidas pela historiografia, passando pela comparação das experiências das mulheres de vários locais diferentes até a discussão de certos tópicos ou conhecimentos específicos do campo. Juntando perspectivas, esse novo ramo tenta dar sentido a conceitos da história global a partir da experiência das mulheres, das sexualidades e das questões de gênero em torno de vários eixos: encontros, fronteiras, migração, transnacionalismo, pós-colonialismo, identidades regionais e nacionalismos. A partir da novidade trazida pela abordagem, pergunta-se, também, como as questões de gênero moldaram os impérios e

1 Nesta resenha não vou entrar nos pormenores da diferenciação teórica entre história mundial e história global, incluindo o intenso debate sobre sua constituição, características e metodologias, não por desmerecer sua importância, nem confundi-las pelo mesmo, mas para utilizar o limite de palavras para direcionar o argumento da proposta.

2 *Gender in World History*; *Women in World History*; *A History of Women in the World*; *Envisioning Women in World History*; *Gender Systems in World History*; *Engendering World History*; *Gender at the Base of World History*; *World History and the History of Women*; *Gender and Sexuality*; *Global Gender History*.

influenciaram opressões tendo em considerações particularidades globais e locais.

O novo campo, entre todas essas possibilidades, está longe de uma delimitação estática, o que deve ser visto positivamente pelo debate que gera. Mas, haveria ainda algo inovador a acrescentar diante de tantas divergências? Existe uma inovação que continue a sustentar a importância da condução da narrativa histórica para o campo das experiências críticas, distante de processos históricos sem agentes e abstratos, que repetem cotidianamente tópicos acríticos comuns de séculos atrás? Quais caminhos podem continuar sendo abertos sem cairmos nas armadilhas que criticamos?

Para introduzir minha proposta de inovação, passo agora a analisar o segundo livro anunciado.

Gendering the Portuguese-Speaking World é uma coletânea de artigos sobre gênero no mundo português falante em um longo espaço temporal, desde a Idade Média até o presente. O volume é editado pelo Professor Francisco Bethencourt, um dos historiadores mais influentes da história da expansão ultramarina portuguesa e de outras questões sensíveis à história dos impérios, como racismo, gênero e cidadania.

O volume é uma preciosidade: a introdução e a conclusão, escritas pelo Professor Bethencourt, endereçam com precisão as discussões mais atuais das teorias de gênero e colocam em perspectiva artigos sobre história das mulheres, homens, masculinidades e gênero. O livro possui 12 capítulos divididos em duas partes: uma sobre Portugal e o Império; a segunda sobre a modernidade e o período pós-colonial. A obra coloca inteligentemente, como corte de sistematização, a colonização portuguesa, sendo que as teorias pós-coloniais são exploradas em ambas as partes.

A primeira parte traz artigos sobre Portugal continental, os quais exploram a construção da masculinidade através do estudo do cavalheirismo e da feminilidade nas cortes; uma análise do patriarcado português em relação a outros patriarcados da Europa e sua conexão com o cotidiano das mulheres e com a luta contra um patriarcado que não pode ser considerado fixo. No campo das religiosidades, um artigo trata da vida conventual de mulheres em Lisboa, sob o argumento de que a reclusão feminina conventual não foi literalmente seguida em Lisboa. As fontes revelam casos quase como imagens de uma vida muito mais personalizada e livre nessas instituições, através das visitas recebidas, das festas, além dos contatos das freiras com o mundo exterior para manter seus direitos e proteger suas economias, na escrita de cartas e poesias.

Para além do continente, há artigos que analisam as diferenças de gênero em várias partes do Império, como Brasil, Goa, a bacia do Zambeze, Angola, Malabar, Etiópia, outros locais no oceano Índico, mostrando, por exemplo, que estruturas jurídicas encontradas em Portugal não podem ser generalizadas pelo Império porque esses espaços não eram meros depositórios de instituições de Portugal (embora, por vezes, os exemplos escolhidos concentrem-se apenas em direitos garantidos, como o direito de testemunhar, de ser testemunha e de serem dotadas ou não, ou, então, analisa e generaliza leis, como as Ordenações Manuelinas). A questão central e de grande valor diante das fontes é saber como os portugueses lidaram com as relações de gênero nessas localidades e, como bem menciona um artigo sobre o Império, a necessidade de uma definição de mulher em contexto, comparada aos papéis sociais atribuídos a homens e mulheres. Também há casos de práticas de casamento, adultério, diferentes tipos de constituições familiares, agência econômica e militar das mulheres nos locais antes da chegada dos portugueses, mostrando que elas estavam ativamente envolvidas no comércio e na guerra (mas esses casos foram encontrados mais na literatura da época e menos em situações práticas). Outros textos exploram questões de linguagem e a importância das bibliotecas de mulheres.

A segunda parte retrata questões de pós-colonialismo na construção do serviço público de saúde de Angola e Moçambique; experiências transgênero em Moçambique contemporânea, através da análise do discurso; conexões literárias de obras clássicas em Portugal e no Brasil, para explicar questões queer e a homofobia no Brasil e em Angola do século XIX; a análise literária de obras angolanas no fim do século XIX e no início do século XX e a resistência feminina na elite luso-africana em momentos determinantes da colonização e, por fim, um artigo sobre as experiências reprodutivas de mulheres que não correspondem às categorias normativas mais aceitas em Portugal, no século XXI, como os pais transgênero e as mães lésbicas.

Assim, no todo, essa obra tem uma importância significativa no desenvolvimento da história das mulheres, masculinidades, sexualidades e gênero em Portugal e em outros países relacionados a

Portugal, por causa da colonização e da expansão ultramarina, por questionar a construção da história sob uma perspectiva de gênero e de interpretações e uso de fontes que refletem questões de gênero na atualidade.[3] O livro representa uma perspectiva de longo termo, sem necessariamente ter a ambição de representar todas as partes do mundo, de forma conectada e crítica em relação ao imperialismo e às consequências do colonialismo.

Ademais, o livro coloca em diálogo várias linhas historiográficas dentro do estudo de gênero e das sexualidades em Portugal, Brasil, Angola, Moçambique e outros locais que tiveram contato com esses países em decorrência da colonização e construção (plural) do império, principalmente, em relação à homossexualidade, às pessoas transgênero e às identidades queer. A obra atualiza a discussão teórica sobre os países envolvidos incluindo, de fato e como é mencionado, tópicos pouco estudados nesses lugares.

Sendo esses locais colocados em perspectiva, Portugal não aparece no centro, mas como conexão. Refletindo décadas de discussões historiográficas acerca da centralidade do Império (as discussões acerca da relação centro-periferia, por exemplo), o livro faz, com muita sutileza, a conexão entre o global e o local, enquanto os artigos transitam em relatar experiências de pessoas reais no passado e a caracterizações de fontes mais gerais sobre o império.

Mas, afinal, e o que isso tudo tem a ver com o direito?

Se eu iniciei por dizer que sou uma historiadora do direito e como tal iria analisar os livros escolhidos, vou, então, complicar esse entrelaçamento de campos e perspectivas para perguntar: e o direito? Como o direito é representado e qual o seu papel na construção das disciplinas da história global das mulheres e de gênero e da história das mulheres, sexualidades e gênero no império português?

Vou usar, como ponto de partida, a identificação do tratamento do direito nas obras em questão. No compêndio, há várias maneiras de identificar as menções ao direito nos diferentes artigos. Muitas vezes, os autores recorrem ao uso de generalizações a partir de leis emblemáticas, específicas e simbólicas (código de Hamurábi, leis de Justiniano, código napoleônico, código islâmico de família, código Tang, código legal de 1858 do império otomano, código civil germânico, código soviético da família de 1919, constituição mexicana de 1917, constituição da Índia de 1950, lei de Allah, constituição Japonesa de 1889, lei sálica, lei revolucionária de 1994, entre outros). Por outro lado, o uso do termo *legal* se dá em diversas conotações: instrumentos, barreiras, existência, exclusão, direitos, restrições, preocupações, registro, status, estruturas, processos, regimes, código, administração, matérias, estudiosos, textos, instituições, termos, pano de fundo, espaço. Já o termo *law* refere tanto ao direito de alguns locais, países ou grupos (direito islâmico), como a sistemas específicos (direito canônico, direito comum, direito natural, direito romano, direito de família, direito costumeiro).

Portanto, o uso e a compreensão do direito variam entre os artigos. Mas, no geral, o direito não é expressamente mencionado ou objeto de atenção primeiro do estudo, aparecendo paralelamente. O único capítulo que trata especificamente do direito e da política (cap. 4) condiciona a conceptualização do direito e da política às relações familiares, sexuais e de gênero. Entretanto, o direito aparece sempre associado, resumido e atrelado à política e aos ditames do patriarcado. Há uma instrumentalização do direito pela ordem política e uma manipulação dos casamentos, dos dotes, do comportamento das esposas e do legado das viúvas, por exemplo, por homens poderosos. Grande parte do artigo, nesse sentido, está dedicado às descrições das mulheres de um ponto de vista da filosofia política (Machiavel e Locke), ou da atuação delas na Revolução Industrial. Há leis mencionadas em várias partes da Europa, mostradas descritivamente, mas, ademais, a sua conexão é feita por um destaque dos direitos das mulheres, que foram excepcionalmente conquistados por mulheres da elite ou das classes que governavam.

Outra maneira de retratar e abordar o direito (cap. 3) é mostrando a imprecisão da utilização de

3 Novamente, aqui, por uma questão de espaço e pertinência não vou me concentrar em mostrar como a história das mulheres e de gênero tem sido desenvolvida no contexto da história de Portugal e de sua colonização.

códigos legais para entender a sociedade, acentuando a necessidade de se virar para a prática. Assim, existe uma simplificação entre direito e lei, estando o campo das práticas fora do entendimento do direito.

O comportamento das mulheres é colocado em perspectiva em relação à letra da lei, quando destoam, e não como condicionante que precisa ser analisada diante de vários outros eixos de análise – aqueles mesmos levantados em várias outras partes da obra pela interseccionalidade. Portanto, um outro problema que surge é a generalização dos agentes, do direito e da elite, como se o poder só fosse desafiado pelas mulheres dessa condição (cap. 5).

O capítulo 17, que menciona em um subcapítulo as estruturas legais da Europa medieval, tem uma introdução resumida sobre sistemas legais e direciona o seu foco para a análise do dote e do preço da noiva. Explica como várias tradições jurídicas (germânica, romana, judia e os costumes locais) foram manipuladas para regular os casamentos e a transferência de propriedade, direcionando sua análise para direitos específicos como garantias que podiam ser conquistadas (divórcio, poder realizar transações comerciais, ter bens e posses).

O capítulo 22, afinal, o único capítulo que explora a história e influência do império português, refere-se à capacidade de adaptação das mulheres aos sistemas legais estrangeiros nos contextos coloniais. O argumento defendido é que as mulheres se acomodaram ao imperialismo europeu, ao usar sistemas legais para protegerem a si mesmas e as suas famílias e propriedades. Apesar desta posição indicar uma interpretação que privilegia a ação das mulheres, sem ser apenas aquelas das elites, o direito manipulado é compreendido como um sistema estrangeiro, fixo, que é trazido de fora para uma nova sociedade.

Outra possibilidade explorada é o papel do chamado direito costumeiro (*customary law*), mencionado no capítulo 23 (em contraposição ao direito europeu, que é só »direito«). Embora o imperialismo em várias partes de África, tenha favorecido a continuação do que chamaram de direito costumeiro sob o poder dos chefes locais, ao mesmo tempo, aproveitou para congelar alguns desses direitos que eram mais convenientes à política colonial como tradição. O mesmo argumento é utilizado no capítulo 26 para mostrar como os britânicos escolhiam o direito costumeiro da Índia que lhes favorecia para argumentar que a criação de suas leis melhorava a condição da mulher indiana.

Já nos sistemas legais muçulmanos (cap. 24), as mulheres aparecem exercendo papéis ativos em tribunais islâmicos, exigindo direitos demonstrados por processos dos séculos XVIII e XIX do Cairo, Alepo, Damasco e Istambul. O texto reconhece que a vida jurídica nos tribunais é apenas uma parte por onde a relação entre as mulheres e o direito pode ser analisada, com destaque para a atividade econômica das mulheres.

No segundo livro, o termo *legal* (em inglês) aparece relacionado com: mecanismos, estrutura, sistema, adoção, posse, responsabilidade do menor, aborto, direitos, reconhecimento, modelos, guardiões, testamento, supervisão de homens, esposo, transformações, guarda, separação, documento, status, práticas, reconhecimento, documento, espaço, transações. Enquanto que *law* está associado ao direito costumeiro, à lei mental, lei racial, códigos legais, lei (no geral), lei portuguesa, leis sobre herança e propriedade, direitos garantidos pela lei (nas Ordenações), direito português, direito canônico, lei da natureza, direito civil, lei tridentina, leis do indigenato, leis trabalhistas, lei de aborto, leis sobre reprodução.

Perpassam aí várias compreensões do direito: a de que institutos jurídicos não eram simplesmente transplantados às várias partes do império, até os direitos específicos das mulheres (*legal rights*), que podem ser conquistados.

Professor Bethencourt finaliza ao dizer que a sexualidade, a diversidade relacional e a definição de gênero são importantes e impactam, entre outros, o quadro legal (*legal framework*). Mas, aponta para uma diferenciação entre quadros europeus legais e religiosos (5); estruturas legais e sociais (9); a ideia do direito costumeiro em espaços coloniais (9) e, finalmente, que os direitos das mulheres estavam estabelecidos desde a Idade Média (267).

Nas duas obras, portanto, embora não sejam obras da história do direito ou que proponham a análise do direito, servem como ricos pontos de partida e de apoio para repensar possíveis caminhos que aproximem a história global das mulheres e de gênero, a história de Portugal, do império português e da colonização portuguesa e à história do direito.

Mas, qual direito? Um direito que não seja apenas ditado pela política e pelo patriarcado, que não seja manipulado apenas por mulheres da elite; ou, sendo de outras condições, não apareçam como manipuláveis por serem estrangeiros; e caso sejam estrangeiros, não se resuma ao costumeiro nem ao isolamento. Por fim, um direito que não se separe do social, das práticas, da religião, do costumeiro, nem seja caracterizado por direito fixos pelos quais se luta – ideia muitas vezes anacrônica, porque atribui uma ideia de direito à conquista de direitos específicos que só surgem nesse formato, após as revoluções liberais.

É preciso um movimento que compreenda o direito de forma dissociada de uma concepção moderna e legalista. Se os estudos de gênero e a história global avançaram em criticar as construções nacionalistas e as perspectivas eurocêntricas, se a junção dos campos prosperou, isso foi possível apenas através de um entendimento e uso diferente do que significa lei, normas e direito.

Por isso, eu proponho como ponto de partida repensar o direito no início do período moderno. Um direito que não passou ainda pelos nacionalismos, não está atrelado ao estado-nação e não tem uma única fonte ou é produzido por um único ente. O direito, assim, tem várias jurisdições a que se pode recorrer e aplicar, não depende unicamente, nem de perto, de leis escritas, tem na sua caracterização forte influência da religião e é igualmente produzido e discutido nesse âmbito.

O direito precisa, assim, superar a separação entre o que estava escrito em documentos e as práticas das mulheres (prática e teoria) e negar-se a explicar o comportamento e as atitudes das pessoas através de uma excepcionalidade diante desses documentos escritos (o que era a regra no início da modernidade). Descumprir a lei não é sempre exceção, ato de rebeldia ou excepcionalismo, mas parte da ordem de um mundo que entendia o direito para além de leis escritas – leis que podiam ser descumpridas com o aval do rei e sua graça, por exemplo, ou que consistiam em traduzir normas religiosas na sua prática. Mas, acima de tudo, esse direito era vivo e estava constantemente em mudança, seja pela ação das mulheres, seja pelas discussões de juristas letrados, ou da aplicação de juízes pouco letrados ou de um bispo em um constante processo de tradução cultural que reflete reproduções sociais. Tal direito não garantia direitos específicos, mas era flexível segundo o status, ou o estado das pessoas no mundo, seu gênero, seu ofício, sua liberdade, sua posição na família e suas condições financeiras ou de nobiliarquia.

Portanto, o que esta proposta leva em consideração e acredita ser primordial na construção do novo inclui seis passos ou componentes. Primeiro: tem sido comum retratar a história global das mulheres e de gênero como a história de pessoas ficando mais conectadas, como um processo linear de globalização proporcionado pela Europa. Essa perspectiva reforça problemas antigos de generalização de uma mulher, ou de que as mulheres são iguais e facilmente identificáveis, ou que dialogam de forma idêntica e compartilham os mesmos desafios. Uma nova perspectiva global pode ser uma alternativa para supcrar a criticada ideia de uma mulher só, representativa: a mulher indiana, a mulher do Brasil colonial, a mulher na América Latina, etc. Pode-se, assim, evitar a essencialização das mulheres e das categorias de gênero em geral. Ao mesmo tempo que resolve o problema da generalização, também pode apresentar alternativas aos problemas da regionalização extrema. Isso quer dizer que se deve levar em conta o local e suas próprias construções de gênero e sua inserção em uma escala transnacional.

Segundo: uma história global das mulheres e de gênero pode retirar o foco da história das mulheres das questões reducionistas da família e da vida privada; ao mesmo tempo, pode resolver o problema das visões equivocadas da redução da história global aos estudos de área.

Terceiro: é preciso proporcionar novas organizações temporais que não se assemelhem àquela tradicional europeia de periodização da historiografia. Esse ponto reforçaria a luta contra o eurocentrismo, porque é sempre a organização europeia de períodos históricos que se utiliza. Visa-se, assim, mudar finalmente o foco das grandes narrativas da história, que muitas vezes são descritas sem agentes ou estão profundamente focadas na história de grandes atores homens.

Quarto: compreender o direito da maneira proposta pode também revolucionar o uso de temas analíticos mais amplos. Tem sido repetitivo como o uso de lugares tópicos como religião, economia, direito e política, império, colonialismo, resistência, revolução, patriarcado, trabalho, cultura (material, visual) são sempre utilizados. Pensar o direito, suas jurisdições e suas normatividades – que incluam princípios, discursos, práticas, instituições e regras – cria oportunidades para análises tópicas mais complexas e inovadoras.

Quinto: é necessário compreender o direito sem fazer comparações anacrônicas, sem reduzir a história global e o direito a meras relações de um direito independente e desenvolvido de certo lugar em comparação aos costumes dos outros; sem confundir o direito como um mecanismo político; e sem associar o direito apenas a leis icônicas, mas, principalmente, afastar a insistência na busca dos direitos das mulheres ou como elas foram excepcionais no passado.

Sexto: Usar, como ponto de partida, outras configurações geográficas, que sugiro, inicialmente, ser a história do direito no Império Português. Se continuarmos a colocar o maior número possível de lugares enquanto fazemos a história das mulheres e de gênero a partir de uma perspectiva global, continuaremos mantendo a falta de conexão e a comparação – assim, serão sempre lugares aleatórios. Mas, escolhendo tal caso, poderíamos mostrar situações locais dentro de uma estrutura global. Processos globais poderão ser rastreados em diferentes partes do mundo, mas serão sempre diferentes nos cantos do Império. No entanto, o movimento contrário é essencial para quebrar também as correntes do eurocentrismo e das historiografias nacionalistas. Trabalhar em detalhes com esses locais, seus arquivos (locais) e uma variedade ampla de fontes pode ajudar a decifrar o silêncio dos arquivos sobre gênero e sexualidades, criar leituras sofisticadas e mais precisas da história do direito para além dos enfoques reducionistas nas leis ou no reclame de direitos (numa acepção moderna); e até mesmo renovar as necessidades pós-coloniais, descoloniais e decoloniais por sua proximidade com os espaços locais e com a voz das mulheres (sem que haja alguém »que fala pelo subalterno«).

Mas essa é apenas UMA das possibilidades, ou um dos direitos. Faz-se urgente abrir espaços para outras narrativas normativas que expliquem como outros sistemas de gênero foram construídos diante de outros direitos. O »outro« não pode fazer parte do costumeiro; e o direito não pode focar apenas nas descrições de leis ou nos sistemas europeus.

Retomando a relação entre gênero e história desenvolvida pela revolução feita pelo artigo de Joan Scott, eu defendo que o gênero não é apenas uma categoria de análise histórica que reflete as relações de poder, mas um vetor de análise essencial da história global, que pode revelar as construções e conexões de sistemas de construção de gênero. Nela, a história do direito pode desenvolver-se como uma desafiadora maneira de explicar, de forma inteligível, as particularidades da relação entre o local e global. E, nestse olhar, próprio para o passado, o caso do Império Português pode servir como o elo de conexão e comparação (em opção a escrever sobre todas as partes do mundo), de modo a respeitar a asserção de que o gênero enquanto sistema é uma criação, de que o biológico é dado e pertence a um conhecimento que foi também em si construído e sistematizado.

■

Andreas Fahrmeir

Historiographiegeschichte an den Schnittstellen*

Das Völkerrecht stützt sich nicht nur auf explizite Normen, sondern auch auf die Beobachtung vergangener Praktiken, aus denen Regeln mit verbindlichem Charakter abgeleitet werden können. Daraus ergeben sich auch für die Praxis Schnittstellen zu anderen Disziplinen: Geschichte des internationalen öffentlichen Rechts, Rechtsgeschichte, historisch informierte Politikwissenschaft und Geschichtswissenschaft sind Fächer, in denen dieselben Texte (vorwiegend) als historische Quel-

* Ignacio de la Rasilla, International Law and History. Modern Interfaces (Cambridge Studies in International and Comparative Law 152), Cambridge: Cambridge University Press 2021, XII + 443 S., ISBN 978-3-1-108-47340-8

len gelesen werden. Das führt dazu, dass das Feld durch eine gewisse Unübersichtlichkeit gekennzeichnet sein kann, denn verschiedene Disziplinen verfolgen unterschiedliche Erkenntnisinteressen, gehen gemäß eigener Traditionen vor und sind in Debatten eingebunden, die über den Bezug zum Völkerrecht hinausgehen, aber auf dessen Grundlagen zurückwirken können. Ihre Ergebnisse für die Praxis nutzbar zu machen, erfordert daher eine Kenntnis dieser spezifischen Perspektiven. Ziel dieses Buches ist es, eine solche Orientierung zu bieten.

Dies geschieht in insgesamt elf analog aufgebauten Kapiteln. Das erste widmet sich dem »turn to the history of international law« im Allgemeinen. Es verweist auf die zunehmende Institutionalisierung einer historischen Perspektive innerhalb der Disziplin des Völkerrechts. Diese Beobachtung verbindet es mit einem Überblick der Debatten über die Genealogie des Völkerrechts, die darum kreisen, inwieweit diese vor Klassiker wie Grotius zurückreicht und etwa auch die Schule von Salamanca einbezieht (wie es etwa im jüngsten Werk Marti Koskenniemis, To the Uttermost Parts of the Earth: Legal Imagination and International Power 1300–1870, Cambridge 2021, geschieht), und welche Konsequenzen ein solcher Blick auf Herrschaftsordnungen vor dem westfälischen System impliziert.

Die folgenden zehn Kapitel behandeln unterschiedliche Ausprägungen der Historiographie zum Völkerrecht: Kontextualisierung (man könnte auch sagen: Historisierung), kritische und postmoderne Ansätze, »Third World Approaches to International Law« (»TWAIL«), globale Zugänge, feministische Zugänge bzw. Frauen und Völkerrecht, normative Zugänge, sozialwissenschaftlich inspirierte Zugänge, institutionalistische Zugänge und biographische Zugänge. Das letzte Kapitel ist Multiperspektivität und Periodisierungsfragen gewidmet. Am Anfang der Kapitel steht jeweils eine einführende Bemerkung zur Charakterisierung, es folgt eine Vorstellung der Tendenz(en) der Forschung, eine Bewertung des Beitrags der jeweiligen Strömung zur »Wissensproduktion« sowie ein Hinweis auf Debatten und Kritik. Am Schluss steht eine abschließende Würdigung.

Das TWAIL-Kapitel illustriert, wie das funktioniert. Es beschreibt zunächst das Anliegen, nach den Kontinuitäten des kolonialen Völkerrechts in der postkolonialen Welt zu fragen und deren Bedeutung durch eine ›Dezentrierung‹ der bislang dominanten Traditionen zu verringern. In einem nächsten Schritt werden zwei Generationen von TWAIL vorgestellt: Die erste schrieb parallel zur Dekolonisation, die zweite seit den 1990er Jahren. Mit Blick auf die »Wissensproduktion« hätten beide eine kritische Lektüre der Klassiker vorangetrieben, allerdings vornehmlich mittels binärer Gegensätze wie dem zwischen Zentrum und Peripherie operiert. Die Kritik konzentriert sich insbesondere auf drei Punkte: die mögliche politische Annäherung vor allem der zweiten Generation an illiberale Regime, da der Ansatz dazu dienen könne, das geltende Völkerrecht zu delegitimieren; die Spannung zwischen dem Bezug auf den globalen Süden und der Anbindung zahlreicher Autorinnen und Autoren an führende nordamerikanische Universitäten; schließlich die inhaltliche Neigung, bei der Bewertung historischer Texte deren Entstehungszusammenhang nicht besonders stark in Betracht zu ziehen. Zusammenfassend wird der Bewegung das Potential attestiert, zu einer aufgeklärteren Zukunft des Völkerrechts beizutragen; zugleich wird deutlich, dass die Sympathien des Autors stärker den im nächsten Kapitel vorgestellten, sich durch ähnliche Gegenstände, aber einen neutraleren Zugang auszeichnenden, globalen Perspektiven gelten.

Die Kapitel ermöglichen einen raschen Überblick und verweisen Lesende auf die einschlägigen Monografien und Handbücher. Dabei gelingt es dem Verfasser, den Forschungsstand im Kernfach der Geschichte des Völkerrechts ebenso wie in den benachbarten Disziplinen in die Darstellung zu integrieren. Das unter schwierigen Bedingungen verfasste Buch – die Niederschrift wurde im Frühjahr 2020 in Wuhan abgeschlossen, und das Werk ist »the white angels of Wuhan and elsewhere« gewidmet – erfüllt seinen Zweck somit hervorragend.

Natürlich gibt es auch Rückfragen, etwa zu Auswahl und Anordnung der behandelten Themen. Die Auswahl ist nicht frei von Überschneidungen: So ließen sich Biografien von weiblichen Akteuren im Bereich des Völkerrechts sowohl im Kapitel Biografien als auch im Kapitel zu Frauen im Völkerrecht behandeln; ebenso bestehen Ähnlichkeiten zwischen »TWAIL«-, globalen und multiperspektivischen Ansätzen. Das ist schwer zu vermeiden, da sich die Darstellung an Debattenkontexten orientiert, die – zumindest teilweise – Selbstbeschreibungen von ›epistemic communities‹ spiegeln. In der Tat geht es vor allem darum, diese in dem Buch auffindbar zu machen.

Das hat freilich zur Folge, dass die Charakterisierung des Beitrags der Strömungen zur Forschung, der ohnehin auf einer eher abstrakten Ebene referiert werden muss, die Entwicklung des empirischen Forschungsstands und der im Laufe der Zeit vorrangig diskutierten Probleme weniger klar hervortreten lässt. Insofern ist nicht ganz evident, warum die Kapitel – vom ersten und letzten abgesehen – in dieser Reihenfolge angeordnet sind. Man hätte sich den (gewiss schwierigen) Versuch vorstellen können, eine chronologische Anordnung zu wagen, die versucht hätte, nachzuverfolgen, warum sich methodische und perspektivische Zugänge ablösten. Dabei hätten sich sicher unterschiedliche Möglichkeiten ergeben, je nachdem, welche der behandelten Disziplinen man in den Mittelpunkt gestellt hätte – etwa wären aus einer geschichtswissenschaftlichen Perspektive Historisierung und Biographie weiter vorne (und eng aufeinander bezogen) platziert worden. Ein solcher Zugang hätte den Vorteil haben können, sichtbar zu machen, welche neuen Strömungen auf welche Schwächen der älteren reagierten und welche Folgefragen sich daraus ergaben.

Gewichtiger ist der Einwand, dass der Zuschnitt der Kapitel mal methodische, mal thematische und mal genre-bezogene Differenzierungen ins Zentrum stellt: Biographien können nicht nur Männer oder Frauen behandeln, sondern auch methodisch eher kontextualisierend-heuristischen, postmodernen oder sozialhistorischen Zugängen verpflichtet sein. Zwar wird bei der Lektüre der Kapitel deutlich gemacht, dass die Zugriffe in diesem Sinne auf unterschiedlichen Ebenen angesiedelt sind, aber zumal für eine breitere Lesendenschaft wäre eine einführende oder abschließende Notiz hierzu hilfreich gewesen. Anders gewendet: Dass jede Betrachtung von Schnittstellen auch eine Entscheidung darüber voraussetzt, wo Schnitte gesetzt werden sollen, hätte noch expliziter gemacht werden können. Allerdings können die Zäsuren in einer komplexen Forschungslandschaft nie unumstritten sein, und der Vorschlag zu einer Gliederung des Felds, den de la Rasilla vorlegt, ist auch dann anregend, wenn man ihn nicht in jedem Detail übernehmen würde.

■

Inge Van Hulle

Museums Also Lie*

The question of restitution has become a hot topic both in academic circles and amongst the broader public. Although legal historians have been notably absent from these debates, for several years now historians, legal experts, sociologists and political scientists have delved into the question of whether, how and when the restitution of cultural goods by Western museums to the Global South will take place. Despite this academic attention, the debate concerning restitution suffers from historical amnesia: the overall impression reigns that the demand for restitution of cultural goods is a fairly recent one. As Bénédicte Savoy illustrates in her latest book »Afrikas Kampf um seine Kunst. Geschichte einer postkolonialen Niederlage«, this could not be further from the truth. Through a meticulous, year-by-year reconstruction, Savoy recounts the history of missed opportunities for restitution by uncovering the deliberations and failed initiatives that took place in the period from 1965 to 1985, primarily between West German museums and African countries, with a few detours to the United Kingdom, France and Belgium. For the reconstruction of this hidden history, Savoy employs a treasure trove of untapped archival material, media coverage, films and documenta-

* Bénédicte Savoy, Afrikas Kampf um seine Kunst. Geschichte einer postkolonialen Niederlage, München: C.H. Beck 2021, 256 p., ISBN 978-3-406-76696-1

ries. In doing so, Savoy employs a sociological approach and manages to reconstruct who the main actors were; which camps and alliances existed both for and against restitution; and – perhaps most importantly – which arguments they employed.

Savoy's more sociological history of restitution highlights the unrelenting force of a number of key actors that have remained under the radar in more traditional, institutional accounts. These include first and foremost the African protagonists. The book starts in 1965 when the first call for restitution was raised in an article published by Dahomeyan journalist Paulin Joachim in *Bingo*, a Francophone African journal (12). However, the first real public debates on restitution were initiated in the 1970s by African artists and filmmakers, for example, through the iconic film »You hide me« (22). African artists and states continued to use artistic expressions and exhibitions to illustrate the intimate connection between restitution and the enhancement of African cultural independence, awareness and self-confidence. This culminated – as Savoy illustrates – in the Festac '77, the Second World Black and African Festival of Arts and Culture, in Nigeria, which used a replica of a famous ivory mask of Queen Idia – in possession of the British Museum (86) – as its logo. The masks were looted by the British during the ransack of the palace of the Oba of Benin in 1897 and are still today symbolic of restitution debates, particularly in the United Kingdom.

Moreover, in the diplomatic sphere, African actors proved instrumental in the creation of an institutional and legal framework for restitution. The Nigerian archaeologist Ekpo Eyo, for example, as one of the four vice-directors of ICOM (International Council of Museums) and Nigerian director of antiquities, in September 1971, aided Nigerian demands for a permanent loan of a number of cultural goods from the German Foreign Ministry (27). By the mid-1970s, restitution had reached the international stage, in large part also thanks to Mobutu Sese Seko's scathing speech before the UN General Assembly in which he scorned the pillaging of the African continent and the usurpation and destruction of its natural resources. This led to the adoption of resolution 3187, which called for the restitution of works of art to countries that were victims of appropriation. To this must also be added the humanist appeal in 1978 by the Director-General of UNESCO, Ahmadou-Mahtar M'Bow, to »at least give back those representative treasures of art that are the most important and dear (...) and whose absence is the most difficult to bear« (103).

While pressure was mounting on Western museums to heed the call for restitution, Western museum representatives dug their heels firmly into the sand. Once again, Savoy unearths the background of the museum protagonists who opposed restitution: an older generation of West-German, mostly ex-NSDAP, white male museum directors, more often than not with a legal background (135). They had no qualms about warding off African demands using any means necessary: delay tactics, racism and paternalism, the spread of false information, or the exclusion of their pro-restitution colleagues, such as Herbert Ganslmayer, the director of the Übersee-Museum in Bremen, who remained undeterred in his resolve to aid the African cause.

When reading Savoy's book, one cannot help but experience profound feelings of exasperation, anger and vicarious shame. This is because Savoy's masterful, yet factual account brilliantly uncovers how »museums also lie« (83). One such example is a letter dated July 1976 from Friedrich Kußmaul, President of the Stiftung Preußischer Kulturbesitz and director of the Linden-Museum in Stuttgart, to the Minister of Culture of Baden-Württemberg (77–79). In the letter Kußmaul told a tall and fabricated tale of how he had been approached by a Swiss art broker who had offered him a »significant« Benin mask that had in fact already been restituted to Nigeria, only to then be sold again by the Nigerian government »for a millions-worth value«. The news of the letter subsequently reached Ekpo Eyo, who set the record straight. This is just one of many, at times, shocking anecdotes.

Apart from outright lies, the arguments that museum officials put forward to deflect restitution are all too familiar, as Savoy shows. These included exaggeration of restitution demands, scare-mongering about the disappearance of Western museum collections, deflection through calls for a »concerted European« approach, politicisation of the discussion, accusations of emotionality on the part of African claimants and, of course, juridical obfuscation.

Savoy's book indeed also opens avenues for legal historians. It hints at the importance of legal professionals and of legal discourse in shaping arguments pro and contra restitution: from conceptual obfuscation concerning »property«, »possession«, »restitution« or »return« by museum directors to the debate around the naming of a UNESCO Intergovernmental Committee, which had to be changed from the »Intergovernmental Committee Concerning Restitution or Return of Cultural Property« to the less contentious »Intergovernmental Committee for Promoting the Return of Cultural Property to its Countries of Origin or its Restitution in Case of Illicit Appropriation« (ICPRCP). This book is a must-read for anyone interested in restitution debates, and certainly for those legal historians among them. The first comprehensive legal history of African-European restitution debates remains to be written.

■

Jasper Kunstreich

Turmbauten*

Die europäische Bankenunion ist noch jung; sie beinhaltet eine weitreichende Übertragung nationaler Kompetenzen auf neugeschaffene, zentrale europäische Einrichtungen, ein einheitliches europäisches Regelwerk und eine gemeinsame Aufsicht des europäischen Finanzmarktes. Sie ist zugleich Europas Antwort auf die Finanzkrise von 2008, die in der Folgezeit die gemeinsame Währung an den Rand des Auseinanderbrechens brachte und die Europäische Union in eine tiefe Existenzkrise stürzte. Sie ist Produkt einer Dekade, in der das Projekt der Europäischen Union in nie gekannter Form im Fokus politischer Krisen und Kämpfe stand. All das wird noch von künftigen Generationen aufzuarbeiten sein.

Pedro Gustavo Teixeira legt hier eine erste Historisierung der europäischen Bankenunion vor. Es soll ausdrücklich »die Rechtsgeschichte der Bankenunion« sein und sie beginnt am Anfang, was ein bisschen an die Zivilrechtshistoriker erinnert, bei denen alles in Rom begann. Diesen Anfang datiert er auf Ostern 1956 in Südfrankreich, von wo aus er dann in chronologischer Abfolge die Integrationsbemühungen durch Recht und Regulierung auf dem Gebiet des Finanzmarktes abschreitet. In seiner Bewertung ist die Bankenunion die bislang am weitesten fortgeschrittene Integrationsleistung des Binnenmarktes und zugleich doch unvollständig: Denn die zwar weitgehende Übertragung von Kompetenzen auf die supranationale Ebene wird nur unzureichend durch die korrespondierende Übertragung von Haftung flankiert. Es gibt noch kein europäisches *Risk-sharing*, das den Namen verdient (273). Das Regelwerk privatisiere stattdessen die Risiken. Die ursprünglich mit Einrichtung des ESM verknüpfte Intention, in Schieflage geratene Banken durch unterliegende gemeinsame Verbindlichkeiten aller Euro-Staaten direkt rekapitalisieren zu können, wurde nämlich in der Folgezeit wieder zurückgenommen durch *Bail-in* Vorgaben für Aktionäre, Gläubiger und Sparer. Für Teixeira ein Taschenspieler-Trick: Anstatt den Rückgriff auf den Steuerzahler auf europäischer Ebene möglich zu machen, um Bankenkrisen – wie 2008 – wirksam meistern zu können, habe man den Steuerzahler lieber gänzlich aus der Gleichung genommen (252). Damit aber setze man sich weiter der Gefahr aus, dass Finanz- und Wirtschaftskrisen unversehens zu heftigen Verteilungskonflikten führen. Folglich ist

* Pedro Gustavo Teixeira, The Legal History of the European Banking Union: How European Law Led to the Supranational Integration of the Single Financial Market, Oxford: Hart 2020, XXV + 337 S., ISBN 978-1-50994-062-2

die Bankenunion selbst noch kein Schlussstrich, sondern verlangt zur Dauerhaftigkeit nach weiteren Stabilisierungsmechanismen.

Wenn Teixeira die Bankenunion gleichwohl als das am weitesten fortgeschrittene Integrationsprojekt bezeichnet, dann macht er das vor allem an ihrer Bauweise fest. Denn die Bankenunion vereinheitliche für ein bestimmtes Rechtsgebiet sowohl Regelwerk, als auch Rechtssetzungsautorität und gerichtliche Kontrolle; es sei weitgehende Supranationalisierung allein mit den Mitteln des Sekundärrechts erreicht worden. Es ist diese Fokussierung auf die Bauweise, die bereits im schön gestalteten Cover angedeutet wird – Griogio de Chiricos *Nostalgia of the Infinite* von 1911 mit seinem neuzeitlichen Turmbau zu Babel. Teixeira geht es um die rechtliche Bauweise, was ihm Begrenzung seines Untersuchungsgegenstandes und Vorgabe seiner Herangehensweise ist.

Der Autor periodisiert seinen Untersuchungszeitraum, indem er wie bei einer architektonischen Betrachtung die Bauweisen eines in mehreren Abschnitten errichteten Turmes beschreibt. Die einzelnen Phasen heißen dann Integration durch Harmonisierung (1973–1984), Integration durch Wettbewerb (1985–1997), Integration durch Steuerung (1998–2007), (Dis-)Integration durch Krise (2008–2012) und Integration durch Zentralisierung (2013 bis heute). Man sagt, Periodisierung sei bei aller damit einhergehender Problematik eines der Kerngeschäfte von Historikerinnen und Historikern. Auch hier erweist sie sich als überaus hilfreich, führt sie doch die Leser durch das Geschehen, durch eine schier unübersichtliche Abfolge von Ausschüssen und *Policy-proposals* und kondensiert die einzelnen Abschnitte auf ein Charakteristikum.

Das Quellenmaterial, das hier ausgewertet wird, besteht aus einer Reihe von offiziellen Studien und Berichten, vorgelegt von Zentralbanken, EZB und anderen internationalen und supranationalen Organisationen, Memoranden und Communiqués von Kommission und Rat sowie den zahlreichen, die Namen ihrer Vorsitzenden verewigenden Ausschussberichten. Die Auswertung neueren Archivmaterials sucht man indes fast vergeblich, was sicher der Wahl eines noch von Schutzfristen betroffenen, so rezenten Themas geschuldet ist.

Inhaltlich gibt es ein Seitenmotiv, dass immer wieder angestimmt wird: Das Trilemma der Währungsunion, drei Politikziele, die nicht gemeinsam verwirklicht werden können, so dass stets eines der drei »geopfert« werden muss: (1) Integration der Finanzmärkte, (2) Stabilität der integrierten Märkte und (3) nationale Souveränität in der Finanzpolitik (vgl. 153). Es taucht zum ersten Mal im sog. Spaak-Bericht (14) auf und zieht sich dann als wiederkehrende Problemstellung durch alle beschriebenen Phasen. Es handelt sich um die Ableitung eines Problems, das bereits seit Bretton-Woods bekannt war, nämlich die Unmöglichkeit, stabile Wechselkurse, freien Kapitalverkehr und autonome Geldpolitik gleichzeitig zu verwirklichen, bekannt geworden als das Mundell-Fleming-Modell.[1] Die im Verlauf des Buches vorgestellten Bauweisen, die Wahl der Instrumente (Mindestharmonisierung oder Vollharmonisierung) und die verwendeten Materialien (der Europäische Pass für Finanzprodukte oder das *Single Rulebook*) lesen sich dann als Versuche, die Quadratur des Kreises zu erreichen. Teixeira kann am Ende des Buches die Unvollständigkeit der Bankenunion als Aufgabe für die Zukunft formulieren, weil sie denklogisch bereits von Beginn an angelegt war.

Auf diese Weise – und das dürfte der Hauptkritikpunkt an diesem Buch sein – tappt die Erzählung in die Teleologie-Falle. Die historischen Ereignisse fügen sich in ihrer Periodisierung in eine fast lineare Entwicklung bis hin zum heutigen Zustand. Es hätte gar nicht anders kommen können. Wir leben in der besten aller möglichen Bankenunionen, die aber noch unvollständig ist, weshalb auch bereits die Zukunft vorgegeben ist.

1 Barry Eichengreen, Rui Pedro Esteves, International Finance, in: Stephen Broadberry, Kyoji Fukao (eds.), Cambridge Economic History of the Modern World, Vol. 2, Cambridge 2021, 501–525; Maurice Obstfeld, Kenneth Rogoff, The Mirage of Fixed Exchange Rates, in: Journal of Economic Perspectives 9 (1995) 73–96.

Das mag eine Folge davon sein, dass sich das Buch bewusst auf die »Komitologie« der Europäischen Union fokussiert, also die Praxis, in großem Umfang Verwaltungs- und Expertenausschüsse zu bilden. Die in kompliziertem EU-Jargon gefassten Berichte dieser Ausschüsse bilden das Haupt-Quellenmaterial. Diesen Jargon macht sich der Autor häufig selbst zu eigen. Dadurch entstehen viel zu lange, nicht lesbare Sätze.

Hier ist ein erster Versuch der Historisierung vorgelegt worden, der in der Fülle der zusammengetragenen Ausschussberichte, institutionellen Beschreibungen und Gesetzgebungsmaterialien nachfolgenden Arbeiten Referenzpunkt sein wird. Das Buch ist eine institutionelle Chronik. Ereignisse und Abläufe werden in ihrer zeitlichen Reihenfolge so angeordnet, dass das Hier und Jetzt nur folgerichtig erscheint. Jede Zeit und Ordnung braucht ihre Chronisten. Die historische Aufarbeitung der Europäischen Bankenunion ist, wie es Teixeira ja auch über seinen Untersuchungsgegenstand selbst sagt, allerdings damit noch nicht abgeschlossen.

■

IMAGINE

Marginalien marginalia

Abb. 1: Anonym (Maître d'Amiens), »Au juste poids véritable balance«, 1518/19, Öl auf Holz, 173 × 95 cm, mit Rahmen 224 × 135 cm; Gesamtansicht nach Huchard et al. (eds.) (1995) 69

Erk Volkmar Heyen

Gruppenbild mit Dame: »Au juste poids véritable balance« (Amiens, 1518/19), Gerechtigkeitsfiguration im Licht politischer Marienfrömmigkeit

Unter dem Titel »Gruppenbild mit Dame« wurde in der vorliegenden Zeitschrift schon einmal ein rechtshistorisch bemerkenswertes Gemälde besprochen: das Porträt eines in Antwerpen residierenden, für das Herzogtum Brabant zuständigen Gildengerichts, gemalt 1594 von Maarten de Vos.[1] Im Blick standen dabei weniger die Porträtierten als vielmehr eine allegorische Frauenfigur, anhand von Waage und Schwert leicht und sicher als Justitia zu erkennen, und vier ihr zur Seite gestellte Repräsentanten antiker Gesetzgebungsgeschichte, nämlich Moses und Justinian, Numa Pompilius und Lykurg.[2]

Während die Figur der Justitia dort bereits eine Ausgestaltung erfahren hat, wie sie uns auch heutzutage vertraut ist, scheint sie in dem hier vorzustellenden, nur wenige Jahrzehnte älteren Gemälde aus der Brabant benachbarten Picardie auf den ersten Blick zu fehlen. Die genauere Betrachtung führt in die Vorgeschichte der Justitia-Figuration, in eine Zeit, in der das Gerichtsverständnis noch stärker von Religion durchdrungen war und das, was wir Staat nennen, im Gewirr vielfältiger, familien- und erbrechtlich begründeter Herrschaftsansprüche erst am Anfang seines Werdens stand. Sich nicht nur als Abbild, sondern auch als Vorbild begreifend, wirkt das Gemälde darauf hin, in einem umstrittenen politischen Raum Recht zu stiften, nicht auf dieselbe Weise wie ein ausdrücklicher Text, aber eindrücklich, durch Mahnung und Einstimmung, fordernd und fördernd zugleich. Freilich – dies wird noch kritisch zu würdigen sein – zielt die herrschende Interpretation des Gemäldes in eine andere Richtung.[3]

I. Erste Annäherung

Das Gemälde präsentiert sich in einem aufwändig geschnitzten Rahmen, der stilistisch überwiegend der Spätgotik, teils aber schon der Frührenaissance zuzuordnen ist und ursprünglich bemalt war (Abb. 1). Wegen seiner ausgeprägt manieristischen Art wird es keinem französischen, sondern einem aus dem Raum von Antwerpen und Leiden oder den noch nördlicheren Niederlanden stammenden Künstler zugeschrieben. Dieser ließ sich jedoch bislang nicht sicher identifizieren und wird darum nach wie vor behelfsmäßig als »Maître d'Amiens« bezeichnet.[4]

Im unteren Register findet sich der Auftraggeber im Kreise seiner Familie und Freunde abgebildet:[5] Antoine Picquet, ein in Amiens für den König tätiger und dabei auch mit Rechtsfragen

1 Heyen (2009). Wesentliche Ergebnisse dieses Aufsatzes sind übernommen in ders. (2013) 65 ff. (mit Farbabbildung). Das wissenschaftliche Interesse an der Visualisierung des Rechts hat in den letzten Jahren erheblich zugenommen, gerade auch in historischer Hinsicht. Einen Überblick zu den vielfältigen Perspektiven und Methoden der Forschung gibt Behrmann (2020), leider unter Beschränkung auf anglophone Literatur.

2 Wolters van der Wey (2015) nennt 198 f. nur Moses, Justinian, Numa Pompilius, schweigt jedoch zur vierten Person, deren Kennzeichnung durch ein allegorisches, in seiner Deutung lange Zeit umstrittenes Bild erfolgt; siehe dazu ausführlich Heyen (2009) 66 ff. Bedauerlicherweise wiederholt die Verfasserin neuerdings ohne Begründung das Ergebnis von Mutmaßungen älterer Literatur (Plutarch); siehe Wolters van der Wey (2018) 170.

3 Siehe dazu jüngst die ausführlichen Bildkommentare von Séguin (2021c) und Scaillíérez (2017c), jeweils mit umfassenden Literaturhinweisen und mehreren Farbabbildungen.

4 Zu den weiteren ihm zugeschriebenen Werken siehe Scaillíérez (dir.) (2017a) 60 ff., zu seiner Gesamtwürdigung dies. (2017b) 35 f. und dies. (2017e).

5 Eine besonders große Farbabbildung dieses personenreichen Registers bietet Scaillíérez (dir.) (2017a) 30 f.

Abb 2: Verfeinerte Ansicht des Gemäldes »Au juste poids véritable balance«, © C2RMF / Thomas Clot

befasster Beamter, der als »conseiller« und »procureur du roi« bezeichnet wird.[6] Das mittlere Register bestimmen Repräsentanten eines der Stadt übergeordneten politischen Lebens, darunter namentlich der französische König François I. (rechts), Papst Leo X. und Kaiser Karl V. (beide links). Aus ihrem Kreis erhebt sich – ins obere Register überleitend und dabei einen Horizont eigener Art bildend, eine Schwelle zwischen säkularem und sakralem Raum – eine zwischen den Schalen einer großen Waage thronende Maria mit dem Jesuskind. Hoch oben wird die Waage von Gottvater gehalten und dabei von einer den Heiligen Geist verkörpernden bekrönten Taube etwas aus dem Lot gebracht. Die eigentliche Ursache für die Neigung des Waagebalkens ist jedoch, dass das Jesuskind die ihm erreichbare Schale zu sich heran und dabei nach unten zieht.

Seinen Titel hat das Gemälde von der Devise erhalten, die vor dem Porträt seines Stifters in Form einer Banderole aufsteigt und wie folgt lautet: »Au juste pois veritable balance« (Abb. 3; heute würde man »poids« statt »pois« schreiben und auf das erste »e« in »veritable« auch einen *accent aigu* setzen). Die Übertragung ins Deutsche ist nicht ganz leicht. Das Wort »balance« bezeichnet ursprünglich – entsprechend seiner italienischen Wurzel – eine anhand von zwei Schalen wiegende Waage. Davon abgeleitet kann es aber auch das Gleichgewicht zwischen diesen beiden Schalen oder überhaupt Gleichgewicht bedeuten.

Geht man von der zweiten Bedeutung aus, ließe sich als Übersetzung »Bei rechtem Gewicht wahres Gleichgewicht« denken. Sie widerspräche freilich dem Verständnis des Malers, zeigt doch sein Gemälde eine Waage, die aus dem Gleichgewicht gebracht worden ist. Legt man die erste Bedeutung zugrunde, könnte die Übersetzung »Bei rechtem Gewicht wirkliche Waage« lauten. »Wirklich / véritable« meint dann in aufrichtiger, treuer Weise zur unparteilichen Feststellung der Wahrheit bestimmt, während »recht / juste« nicht auf eine bloß technisch genaue Bestimmung des Gewichts zielt, sondern auf eine Bestimmung, die beim Wiegen den Umständen auf billige, angemessene Weise Rechnung trägt und insofern einen gewissen Beurteilungsspielraum beansprucht.[7]

In einem tieferen, sich nicht auf den technischen Aspekt von Waage und Wägung beschränkenden Verständnis könnte hier zudem die Beziehung von Wahrheit (*vérité*) und Gerechtigkeit (*justice*) angesprochen sein, und dies in zugleich religiöser und politischer Hinsicht. Es handelt sich anscheinend um eine auch inhaltlich nicht

Abb. 3: Stifter Antoine Picquet (aus Abb. 2)

6 Séguin (2021c) 87 präzisiert »procureur et conseiller au bailliage d'Amiens«. Laut Anm. 8 stieg Picquet wenige Jahre später zum *bailli* auf, einem für die gesamte königliche Verwaltung eines größeren Bezirks zuständigen und üblicherweise auch mit militärischen Befugnissen ausgestatteten Beamten, dem auf dem Gebiet der Rechtsprechung erstinstanzlich mehrere *prévôts* zuarbeiteten.

7 In seiner Übersetzung der Devise stellt der englischsprachige Museumsführer Gewicht und Waage einfach nebeneinander und verwendet dabei für »juste« und »véritable« dasselbe Wort: »True weight, true scales«; siehe Huchard et al. (eds.) (1995) 68. Die Reihenfolge legt es gleichwohl nahe, das Gewicht als die das Wägungsergebnis und damit die Richtigkeit der Waage bestimmende Größe anzusehen. Dass falsches Wiegen nicht nur am Gewicht, sondern auch an der Waage selbst, ihrem Mechanismus liegen kann, veranschaulicht das Eingreifen der Taube.

ganz einfache, vielmehr zum Einfühlen und Nachdenken auffordernde Devise. Steht sie möglicherweise in Zusammenhang mit Psalm 85, der in seinen Schlussversen 11 und 12 Gott darum bittet – so die auf Luther zurückgehende deutsche Übersetzung – »dass Güte [*misericordia* in der tradierten lateinischen Fassung] und Treue [*veritas*] einander begegnen, Gerechtigkeit [*iustitia*] und Friede [*pax*] sich küssen; dass Treue auf der Erde wachse und Gerechtigkeit vom Himmel schaue«? Auf die für das Gemälde maßgebliche Interpretation wird noch zurückzukommen sein.

Die Gründe für den komplexen Charakter der Devise ergeben sich aus besonderen sozialen und politischen Umständen. Insofern bedeutsam ist zunächst, dass das Gemälde aus einer regionalen Tradition heraus entstand: der in Amiens schon 1389 begründeten und fortan jährlich erneuerten Tradition einer Bildstiftung, für die eine ortsansässige, der Marienverehrung gewidmete literarische Vereinigung die Verantwortung trug, eine Bruderschaft angesehener Bürger namens »Confrérie Notre-Dame du Puy d'Amiens«. »Puy« – heutzutage nur noch ein aus der Geographie der Auvergne geläufiger Ausdruck für einen sockelförmigen Berg – bedeutet hier ein der Kathedrale der Stadt zugeordnetes Podium, von dem aus Gedichte zum Lobpreis Marias vorgetragen wurden. Mit »Puy d'Amiens« kann aber auch die örtliche Bruderschaft selbst bezeichnet sein.

Die Marienverehrung prägte das spätmittelalterliche Christentum. Dies gilt auch und insbesondere für Frankreich, wo sie eng verbunden war mit dem hier seit dem 13. Jahrhundert landesweit einsetzenden und dabei europaweit ausstrahlenden Bau gotischer, ebenso leicht wie mächtig himmelwärts strebender Kathedralen. Zu deren frühen Beispielen gehören die Kathedrale von Reims, die Krönungskirche der französischen Könige, aber auch die – 1981 zum »Weltkulturerbe« der UNESCO erklärte – Kathedrale von Amiens, deren zu Beginn des 16. Jahrhunderts geschnitztes Chorgestühl in kunstvoller Ausführlichkeit Marias Leben vor Augen stellt.[8]

Die der Marienverehrung dienenden Bildstiftungen des Puy d'Amiens beruhten auf dem Gewinn eines poetischen Wettbewerbs, den durchzuführen dem für ein Jahr gewählten Vorsteher der Bruderschaft oblag, ihrem *maître* (in anderen Orten der Picardie und Normandie »prince« genannt).[9] Grundlage dafür war eine von ihm Anfang Januar, dem Beginn seiner Amtszeit, auszugebende Devise ganz eigener Art und Absicht, nämlich eine Maria auf allegorische Weise ehrende kurze Verszeile, die von den Teilnehmern des Wettbewerbs als Thema oder Refrain ihrer Poesie aufzugreifen war und zugleich dem Gemälde als Inspirationsquelle diente.[10] Da in jener Zeit das neue Jahr mit dem Osterfest einsetzte, wurde der nach heutiger Rechnung im Januar 1519 festgelegten Devise die Jahreszahl 1518 zugeordnet, ein Verfahren, das sich auch auf die Bezeichnung des auf der Devise beruhenden Gemäldes auswirkte, obwohl es erst gegen Ende des Jahres 1519 vollendet wurde.

Die Devise und die Ausgestaltung des Gemäldes von 1518/19 standen unter dem Eindruck des königlichen Besuchs, den Amiens im Juni 1517 empfangen hatte, vollzogen in der aufwändigen Form einer *entrée solennelle*, also einer Form, die dazu diente, die Legitimität des Königs (Schutz und freigiebige Milde) und die Loyalität der Stadt (Rat und Hilfe) vor Augen zu führen und sich ihrer beidseitig zu vergewissern. Begleitet wurde François I. dabei von seiner Ehefrau Claude de France, die ihm im folgenden Jahr den ersehnten Thronfolger schenken sollte, seiner Mutter Louise de Savoie und seiner Schwester Marguerite. Das Gemälde nimmt darauf insofern Bezug, als es im Hintergrund des Königs – umringt von einer zum Ausritt versammelten, dabei vornehm gekleideten und von Standarten begleiteten Gesellschaft – eine Dame mit Krone und Herrschaftsstab, also die Königin zeigt, während im Vordergrund zwei Pagen das Schwert und den Falken des Königs

8 Siehe Lemé-Hébuterne (2007), insbes. 97 ff.

9 Einen Überblick zu den kulturellen Interessen und Strukturen solcher vornehmlich nordfranzösischen Bruderschaften gibt Reid (2019).

10 Siehe Gros (1992) 56 ff. (»Le Puy et l'art pictural«), 70 ff. (»Le chant royal du Puy d'Amiens«), sowie ders. (1996) 134 ff., 189 f. und – das Verhältnis von Gemälde und Poesie anhand eines Beispiels von 1471 beleuchtend – 201 ff., 236 ff. Poesie mit Bezug auf das Gemälde von 1518/19 scheint sich nicht erhalten zu haben.

tragen.[11] Anlässlich dieses Besuchs fand auch die Gemäldesammlung des Puy d'Amiens königliche Aufmerksamkeit, insbesondere bei Louise, der daraufhin 1518 ein bis heute erhaltenes Buch geschenkt wurde, in dem sich die seit 1460 überlieferten Gemälde und Dichtungen widerspiegeln.

Die offene Einbeziehung von Papst und Kaiser verleiht dem Gemälde aber noch eine über diesen Besuch hinausweisende politische Dimension, die für seine angemessene Interpretation von Belang ist. Sie gilt es nunmehr zu erschließen.

II. Betrachtung der politischen und religiösen Lage

François I., geboren 1494 als François d'Angoulême, hatte Anfang 1515, nachdem sein Vorgänger und Schwiegervater Louis XII. ohne männliche Erben gestorben war, aufgrund günstiger Verwandtschaftsverhältnisse den Thron Frankreichs besteigen können. Befeuert von jugendlichem Ehrgeiz und Draufgängertum war er noch im September desselben Jahres nach Italien gezogen und hatte – durch einen bei Marignano erfochtenen und seitdem berühmt gebliebenen Sieg über Schweizer Söldner – das 1512 von Louis XII. verlorene Herzogtum Mailand zurückerobert, unter Berufung auf Erbrechte und in der Hoffnung, damit seine politische Stellung im Heiligen Römischen Reich, zu dem das Herzogtum gehörte, zu verbessern und so möglicherweise die Nachfolge des bereits kränkelnden Kaisers Maximilian I. antreten zu können. Nachdem es ihm trotz Einsatz außergewöhnlich hoher Geldsummen nicht gelungen war, in Frankfurt zum Kaiser gewählt zu werden (der glücklichere Karl V. vermochte den Kurfürsten mit Hilfe eines Darlehens des Augsburgers Jakob Fugger mehr zu bieten), nahm er die kriegerische Auseinandersetzung mit dem Hause Habsburg wieder auf. Außenpolitisch sollte sie seine gesamte Regierungszeit bestimmen.

Das Gemälde von 1518/19 präsentiert ihn im königlichen Ornat, mit Krone, Szepter und einem

Abb. 4: König François I. (aus Abb. 2)

lilienverzierten sowie hermelinbesetzten Brokatmantel (Abb. 4). Darüber hinaus trägt er eine goldene Halskette, die man dem – Mitte des 15. Jahrhunderts von Louis XI. für einige Auserwählte gestifteten – *Ordre de Saint Michel* zuordnen darf, also dem Orden des Erzengels Michael, des Drachentöters, wie ihn die sogenannte Apokalypse, die Offenbarung des Johannes in Kapitel 12, Vers 7 ins Bild setzt. Anders als beim Ordensstifter, kommt eine besondere religiöse Devotion dadurch nicht mehr zum Ausdruck, sie lag François I. eher fern. Sein ausgeprägter Geltungsdrang, der ihn 1519 in Chambord den Bau eines höchst anspruchsvollen Schlosses beginnen ließ, hinderte

11 Zu weiteren, im Folgenden aber nicht erwähnten Einzelheiten des Gemäldes siehe die ausführliche Bildbeschreibung von Séguin (2021c).

ihn jedoch nicht, sich zur Stärkung seiner Legitimität christlicher Referenzen zu bedienen und sein Königtum nach dem Vorbild seiner Vorgänger als »très chrétien« anzusehen und entsprechend darstellen zu lassen.[12] Auch widersprach er nicht literarischen Versuchen, seine königliche Gewalt ethisch zu konturieren, also die Tradition eines durch Regentenspiegel gemäßigten Königtums aufzugreifen und maßvoll fortzuentwickeln. Zu nennen sind hier, ebenfalls in dieser Zeit erschienen, »La Grande Monarchie de France« von Claude de Seyssel und »L'Institution du Prince« von Guillaume Budé.[13]

Dass das politische Denken in einer Phase des Umbruchs sich befand und neue Horizonte sich öffneten, wird auch an zwei zeitgenössischen Werken höchst unterschiedlichen Charakters deutlich: »Il Principe« von Niccolò Machiavelli, verfasst 1513 in Florenz, wenn auch erst posthum (1532) veröffentlicht, und »De optima rei publicae statu deque nova insula Utopia« von Thomas Morus, erschienen 1516 in Leiden. Während Morus hier aus seinem christlichen, dabei aber auch kirchenkritischen Humanismus heraus die politische Wirklichkeit seiner Zeit durch ein gleichheitsorientiertes gesellschaftliches Gegenbild ethisch in Frage stellt und so das Mögliche in den Blick rückt, widmet sich Machiavelli – politisch-administrativ erfahren und eigentlich Anhänger einer auf Freiheit und Gemeinwohl zielenden republikanischen Verfassung – in seiner Schrift den ungeschönten Machtaspekten einer Alleinherrschaft, den Ungleichheiten in ihrer politischen Wirklichkeit und den Techniken, die zu ihrer Aufrechterhaltung eingesetzt werden.

Im Vergleich zu François I. wirkt Papst Leo X. – aus der in Florenz herrschenden Familie der Medici und im Amt seit 1513 – trotz Insignien weniger vorteilhaft präsentiert (Abb. 5). Obwohl 1519 erst 44 Jahre alt, tritt er im Gemälde als ein schon recht alter Mann in Erscheinung, so dass man sich unwillkürlich fragt, ob Würde und Tatkraft hier einander noch entsprechen (Raffael hat ihn 1518 ganz anders vor Augen geführt). Diese zweifelhafte Darstellung überrascht insofern, als sich Leo X. doch bei den Kurfürsten dafür eingesetzt hatte, François I. zum Kaiser zu wählen, und der Maler dies hätte positiv berücksichtigen können. Andererseits gibt sie ihm aber Gelegenheit, den hinter den Papst gesetzten Bischof von Amiens[14] nicht nur deutlich jünger, sondern auch in stattlicher Selbstsicherheit auftreten zu lassen. Dazu trägt bei, dass dieser mit einem sogenannten Lothringer

Abb. 5: Papst Leo X. und Kaiser Karl V. (aus Abb. 2)

12 So entstand um 1520 ein Gemälde, das ihn sogar als Johannes den Täufer zeigt, mit einem Lamm auf den Schultern. Zu den Verständnisschwierigkeiten, die ein solches Werk bereitet hat, siehe Walbe (1974) 37 ff., und zum heutigen Stand der Interpretation und Zuschreibung Scailliérez (2017d). Zu weiteren allegorischen Darstellungen von François I. siehe Sauvion (2006), zu seiner Verherrlichung darüber hinaus auch Gaehtgens / Hochner (dir.) (2006) und Burke (2015).

13 Siehe Knecht (2002), besonders 90 ff.; der Einfluss dieser Schriften auf das tatsächliche Regierungshandeln von François I. wird als sehr gering eingeschätzt.

14 So die Identifizierung von Séguin (2021c) 86.

Kreuz ausgestattet ist, Ausdruck der sich schon ab dem 14. Jahrhundert entwickelnden Eigenständigkeit der Gallikanischen Kirche gegenüber dem Papst, die François I. durch das 1516 mit Leo X. geschlossene Konkordat von Bologna hatte erneuern und vor allem hinsichtlich der Bischofsernennungen noch weiter ausbauen können.[15] Letztendlich – nach Beendigung der Hugenottenkriege in der zweiten Hälfte des 16. Jahrhunderts und der Aufhebung des Edikts von Nantes 1598 – wird der gallikanische Katholizismus, verkörpert namentlich durch die Kardinäle Richelieu und Mazarin, ein tragendes Element des französischen Königtums bleiben und den Aufstieg Frankreichs im europäischen Machtgefüge sichern.

Leo X. steht in besonderem Maße für eine Verweltlichung der Kirche. Die Kritik daran war nicht neu. Jan Hus in Prag hatte Reformen schon zu Beginn des 15. Jahrhunderts gefordert, Girolamo Savonarola in Florenz gegen dessen Ende sie nicht nur gefordert, sondern auch durchzusetzen und in eine politische Form zu übertragen versucht, doch endete beider Leben durch Hinrichtung. Leo X. hingegen sah sich nicht als strengen Kirchenreformer, sondern als großzügigen Kunstförderer, übertrieb es aber mit dem Neubau des Doms St. Peter in Rom, dessen außergewöhnlich hohe Kosten er mit einem maßlosen Ablasshandel zu bewältigen suchte. Als Martin Luther, ein aufmerksamer Leser der Schriften Savonarolas, Rom besuchte, geriet er darüber in solche Empörung, dass er dazu äußerst kritische, theologisch pointierte Thesen formulierte, sie 1517 an der Schlosskirche in Wittenberg veröffentlichte und zu ihrer Diskussion aufrief. Vom großen Widerhall im Reich war 1519 in der Picardie freilich noch kaum etwas zu spüren, ganz anders als in der Zeit darauf, als die Reformation hier ebenfalls Boden fasste.

Wie Leo X., wirkt auch Karl V. im Gemälde weniger günstig dargestellt als François I. und dies nicht nur, weil ihn der Maler ganz an den Rand gerückt hat (Abb. 5). 1500 geboren, tritt er hier übertrieben kindlich in Erscheinung, ausgestattet zwar mit den Insignien seiner kaiserlichen Stellung, in die er Ende Juni 1519 auf dem Reichstag in Frankfurt gewählt worden war, aber kaum kräftig genug, ihr gerecht werden zu können.[16] Im Norden war er dem französischen König schon etwas früher zum unmittelbaren Nachbarn geworden. Als Enkel von Kaiser Maximilian I. und Maria von Burgund in Gent geboren, erhielt er 1515 die Würde eines Herzogs von Burgund, die Brabant einschloss. Erasmus hat ihm 1516 seine Schrift »Institutio principis christiani« gewidmet, ein Werk, das auf das politische Denken Platons, Ciceros, Senecas und Plutarchs zurückgreift und seinerseits u. a. Seyssel und Budé beeinflusst hat.

Die politische Dimension des Gemäldes zeigt sich aber nicht nur auf dieser länderübergreifenden Ebene von König, Papst und Kaiser. Sie rückt hier auch lokal, im Zusammenhang mit Amiens, in den Blick und erhält dadurch eine eigene Färbung. Denn die Stadt lag schon seit alten Zeiten in einem Grenzraum, umstritten zunächst zwischen Galliern und Römern, dann Franken und Normannen, Franzosen und Engländern, schließlich Franzosen und Burgundern sowie habsburgischen Flamen. 1471 freilich war Amiens mitsamt der Picardie durch Louis XI. dem letzten Herzog der Burgunder, Charles le Témeraire, entrissen und seitdem von der französischen Krone erfolgreich behauptet worden. Dessen ungeachtet fühlte man sich hier weiterhin zunächst als Picarde, weniger als Franzose, denn mit der Bevölkerung jenseits der Grenze gab es von familiären Bindungen getragene sprachliche und kulturelle Gemeinsamkeiten, zu denen auch die Pflege einer poetisch gestimmten Marienfrömmigkeit gehörte.[17]

Wirtschaftlich bedeutend und vergleichsweise wohlhabend aufgrund ihres grenzüberschreitenden Tuchhandels, wurde die Stadt von einem Bürgermeister (*mayeur*), zwölf Ratsherren (*échevins*) und einem Vertreter des Königs (*prévôt*) verwaltet. Mangels Gewaltenteilung oblagen ihnen dabei auch Rechtsprechungsaufgaben, an deren Erfüllung teilweise zudem noch der örtliche Bischof und das Domkapitel beteiligt waren.[18] Die könig-

15 Ausführlich zu diesem Konkordat Knecht (1994) 90 ff. Grundlegend zur Verbindung von Politik und Religion im französischen Königtum Schramm (1960).

16 Siehe zum Vergleich das 1516 entstandene Porträt des damals sogar noch drei Jahre jüngeren und doch überzeugender wirkenden Karl, wie es die Abbildung in Séguin (dir.) (2021a) 90 zeigt.

17 Siehe mit Bezug auf Gent, Antwerpen und Brüssel Devaux (2003) 382 ff., u. a. mit dem Hinweis, 1519 sei auch dort die Wahl des Habsburgers Karl zum Kaiser bejubelt worden.

18 Siehe Paresys (1998) 139 ff.

liche Herrschaft hatte Mühe sich durchzusetzen und sann auf Verwaltungsreformen. Männer pflegten auf die eine oder andere Weise bewaffnet zu sein. Gewalttätige Streitereien, zumal solche aufgrund angeblicher Ehrverletzungen, waren alltäglich und verlangten nach einer Neuordnung des Strafrechts.[19]

In dieser komplexen Konstellation von rivalisierenden politischen Mächten und ökonomischen Interessen wurde der christlichen Religion anscheinend eine Aufgabe und Wirkkraft eigener Art zugesprochen: die der Mäßigung der Konflikte durch Stiftung eines für alle zu beachtenden und insoweit dem Frieden förderlichen normativen Rahmens. Die Wirklichkeit freilich widerstrebte solchen Hoffnungen sehr deutlich. Ungeachtet dessen stellte sich die in Malerei und Poesie gefasste Marienfrömmigkeit des Puy d'Amiens auf die Seite dieser Hoffnungen, beklagte also nicht das Misslingende, sondern setzte auf Ermunterung zum Besseren. In dem Gemälde von 1518/19 geschieht dies freilich nicht leichthin, sondern verbunden mit einer äußerst ernsthaften Erinnerung und Mahnung, wie jetzt zu zeigen sein wird.

III. Genauere Betrachtung von Waage und Wägung

Für den heutigen Betrachter sind diese Erinnerung und Mahnung nicht ohne weiteres augenfällig. Lässt man den Blick über das Gemälde wandern, so hält er sich leichter an die Hinweise auf Wohlstand in Stadt und Land: wohl bestellte Felder, ansehnliche Häuser, seetüchtige Schiffe, festliche Kleidung, darüber hinaus auch noch an die Hinweise auf eine freigebige Mildtätigkeit, die anscheinend aus christlichem Geist geschieht, nehmen doch die beiden allegorischen Figuren die Goldmünzen, die sie verteilen, von dem vor Maria aufgestellten großen Tisch.

Wer die Bildbetrachtung damit beschließen wollte, übersähe jedoch einen für die Bildinterpretation zentralen Aspekt, nämlich dass die über dem Tisch hängenden Waagschalen nicht leer sind und sich auch nicht in einem ruhigen Gleichgewicht befinden, wie es der uns vertrauten Justitia-Figuration entspräche. Vielmehr hockt in der linken, vom Jesuskind leicht nach unten gezogenen Waagschale eine einzelne kleine menschliche Figur, während die aufsteigende rechte Waagschale mit etwas unkenntlich Bleibendem so stark gefüllt zu sein scheint, dass sie nach hinten kippt (Abb. 6).

Es handelt sich um die Darstellung einer sogenannten Seelenwägung, eine Veranschaulichung dessen, was im Jüngsten Gericht geschehen wird. Der Mensch, über dessen Leben zu richten ist, »Seelenkind« genannt, sitzt in einer Waagschale und wartet auf das Wägungsergebnis. Dieses wird hier aber durch das Eingreifen des Jesuskindes zu seinen Gunsten entscheidend verändert: Seine Waagschale senkt sich, und zwar so stark, dass der Teufel, der – so darf man das Bild der Tradition entsprechend ergänzen – die andere Waagschale mit schwerem Gewicht beladen hat, um die Wägung zu eigenen Gunsten zu beeinflussen, damit keinen Erfolg hat.

Der bildhafte Gedanke der Seelenwägung ist einer Religiosität verpflichtet, die von Gabe und Gegengabe und insofern von Vergeltung – sanfter ausgedrückt: von Ausgleich – geprägt ist. Es überrascht daher nicht, dass sie bereits in vorchristlichen Religionen Ausdruck gefunden hat.[20] Eigentlich bricht das Christentum mit solchen Traditionen, versteht es doch die Liebe Gottes zu den Menschen als ein Gnadengeschenk, auf das diese mit Nächstenliebe zu antworten eingeladen werden (Matthäus-Evangelium, Kap. 10, Vers 86: »Umsonst habt ihr empfangen, umsonst sollt ihr geben.«). Gleichwohl haben sich daraus im Laufe des Mittelalters erschreckend harte, bedrückende Weltgerichts-Vorstellungen entwickeln können.

19 Dabei wurde der im Falle einer nur fahrlässigen Tötung mögliche Straferlass mittels *lettre de rémission* zu einem Instrument, die Bevölkerung für die königliche Herrschaft zu gewinnen; siehe Paresys (1998) 133 ff. Das Verhältnis von Stadt und König bedurfte noch vielfältiger Justierungen, nicht zuletzt auf dem Gebiet der Rechtssetzung; siehe zu dieser Entwicklung Gauvard (2003).

20 Grundlegend Kretzenbacher (1958), insbes. 65 ff. für die Zeit des christlichen Mittelalters. Siehe auch Pleister (1988) 33 ff. (»Seelenwägung und gerechtes Gericht«).

Abb. 6: Maria mit dem Jesuskind zwischen den Waagschalen einer Seelenwägung (aus Abb. 2)

Die zentrale Figur in der christlichen Darstellung der Seelenwägung ist der Erzengel Michael, der sonst eher durch ein Schwert als durch eine Waage gekennzeichnet wird.[21]

Aus der Malerei lassen sich dafür viele Beispiele anführen, darunter in der norditalienischen Stadt Bergamo eine Weltgerichtsdarstellung aus dem frühen 13. Jahrhundert, die zudem auch rechtshistorisch bemerkenswert ist, da sie einen Gerichtssaal, nämlich die »Aula della Curia« des Bischofspalastes schmückt.[22] Das wohl berühmteste Beispiel entstand um 1450 aus der Hand von Rogier van der Weyden. Es gehört zu einem Altar, den der burgundische Kanzler Nicholas Rolin für das von ihm gestiftete Armenhospital in Beaune in Auftrag gegeben hat. Im geschlossenen Zustand zeigt er den Stifter,[23] im geöffneten eine Darstellung des Jüngsten Gerichts, in deren Mitte – unterhalb des Weltenrichters Christus, aber dort von beeindruckender Statur – der Erzengel Michael mit seiner Waage steht. Das Motiv der Seelenwägung ist hier insofern etwas abgewandelt, als in der einen Waagschale die Tugenden (»virtutes«) versammelt sind, in der anderen die Sünden (»peccata«).[24]

Was davon dem Schöpfer des Gemäldes von 1518/19 bekannt war, ist nicht überliefert. Er hatte aber in Amiens ein ebenfalls höchst eindrucksvolles Beispiel aus der Bildhauerei vor Augen, und zwar an der Westfassade der Kathedrale, im Tympanon des Hauptportals.[25] Dort findet sich inmitten einer ebenfalls berühmt gewordenen Darstellung des Weltgerichts, unterhalb von Christi Thron, eine Seelenwägung durch den Erzengel Michael abgebildet.[26] Er trägt eine Waage, in deren sinkender Schale als Verkörperung des in die Wägung eingreifenden Christus ein sanftes Lamm (*Agnus Dei*) liegt, während in der trotz Gewichtsbeschwerung steigenden Schale eine Teufelsfratze herausschaut.

Dass die uns heutzutage vertraute Justitia-Figuration auf die Ausgestaltung des Erzengels Michael mit Schwert und Waage zurückgeht, ist an sich bekannt.[27] Man sollte daher meinen, dass die bisherige Interpretation des Gemäldes von 1518/19 wesentlich durch seinen Bezug zum Erzengel bestimmt worden ist. Dies ist aber nicht der Fall. Im Gegenteil, die herrschende Interpretation weist an dieser Stelle in eine ganz andere Richtung. Maßgeblich dafür ist ein Aufsatz von Anne-Marie Lecoq aus dem Jahre 1977, dem sich die seitdem dazu erschienene kunsthistorische Literatur angeschlossen hat.[28] Die folgende Auseinandersetzung kann sich daher auf die einschlägigen Passagen dieses Aufsatzes konzentrieren.

21 Zu unterscheiden von seiner Rolle bei der Seelenwägung anlässlich des Jüngsten Gerichts ist seine ebenfalls stark rechtlich konturierte Rolle bei der ab dem 12. Jahrhundert verstärkt einsetzenden Imagination der Zeit zwischen dem Tod, durch den sich Körper und Seele trennen, und dem Jüngstem Gericht, zu dessen Vollzug sie sich wieder vereinigen; siehe dazu ausführlich Baschet (1995). Besonders anschaulich wird die Zeit nach dem Tod durch ein im 14. Jahrhundert entstandenes und bis ins 16. hinein weit verbreitetes literarisches Werk: die durch Buchmalerei veranschaulichte »Pilgerfahrt der Seele« (»Pèlerinage de l'âme«) des Zisterziensermönchs Guillaume de Diguleville; siehe Duval / Pomel (dir.) (2008). Darin tritt der Erzengel Michael als ein Wächter des Paradieses auf, der die Zugangsberechtigung des Pilgers mit Hilfe seiner »balance de justice« prüft. »Raison«, »Vérité« und »Justice« wirken als Richter und Zeugen, während der Teufel die Anklage vertritt und »Miséricorde« die Verteidigung übernimmt. Letztlich bewirkt aber Christus selbst einen dem Pilger günstigen Ausschlag der Waage. Siehe auch Kretzenbacher (1958) 156 ff., wo verbunden mit einer zusammenfassenden Übersetzung ins Deutsche aus dem sprachlichen Original jene Stellen zitiert werden, die sich auf die vom Erzengel gehaltene Waage der Gerechtigkeit beziehen (158 und 160 f.).

22 Siehe dazu Wartenberg (2015) 12 ff.

23 Ihm verdankt sich noch ein weiteres kunstgeschichtlich bedeutsames Werk, nämlich »Die Madonna des Kanzlers Nicholas Rolin« von Jan van Eyck, gemalt 1435–37; siehe dazu ausführlich Heyen (2013) 43 ff.

24 Siehe dazu Kemperdick (1999) 65 ff., mit großer farbiger Detailabbildung (70). Ein ebenfalls frühes und berühmtes Beispiel aus der deutschen Bildhauerei findet sich im Bamberger Dom, und zwar an dem von Tilman Riemenschneider gefertigten Hochgrab für Kaiser Heinrich II. und seine Gemahlin Kunigunde.

25 Sehr gute Farbabbildungen vom Zustand nach der Restaurierung, welche die ursprüngliche Farbigkeit wieder hervortreten ließ, in Kasarska (2012) 175 (Seelenwägung im Tympanon), 184 f. (Hauptportal der Westfassade insgesamt).

26 Eine Darstellung, die bereits von Kretzenbacher (1958) 150 ff. (Abb. 42 und 43), hervorgehoben worden ist. Zu einer ausführlichen Beschreibung und Würdigung des Hauptportals, insbes. des Tympanons siehe Schlink (1991) 58 ff. (Seelenwägung Abb. 13), 134 ff., und Murray (2021) 128 ff. (Seelenwägung Abb. 2.35).

27 Siehe die Abbildungen in Kissel (1997) 26, 33 f., 43, 55, 75.

28 Siehe Lecoq (1977), insbes. 67 ff., auch – ihren Standpunkt wiederholend – dies. (1987) 326 ff. und 333, sowie Scaillièrez (2017c) und Séguin (2021c), jeweils mit weiteren Nachweisen.

Lecoq fragt sich zwar durchaus, ob in dem Gemälde eine Seelenwägung dargestellt wird, spricht sich aber – auf die Gründe wird noch zurückzukommen sein – entschieden gegen eine solche Sichtweise aus. Von der Devise heißt es, sie bleibe rätselhaft und werfe kaum Licht auf das gezeigte Geschehen.[29] So wundert es nicht, dass auch für die Deutung des Gemäldes Waage und Wägung nicht den Ausgangspunkt bilden und keine bestimmende Kraft zugesprochen erhalten. Stattdessen begibt sich Lecoq auf die Suche nach einer anderen interpretatorischen Perspektive[30] und gewinnt sie aus jener Szene, die der Waage und Wägung vorgelagert ist und hier noch näherer Betrachtung bedarf: der Austeilung der Goldmünzen, die auf dem vor Maria aufgestellten Tisch liegen.

Deren Deutung als »allégorie de l'Eucharistie« überrascht, zumal sie von Lecoq ungewöhnlich rigide vorgetragen wird. Der Tisch erscheint als Altar und die Goldmünze als Hostie. Das Weihwasserbecken samt Wedel, Kerzen, Kreuze u. a. werden zu Hinweisen auf eine Messfeier erklärt und die üppig ausgeformten Frauengestalten, welche die Goldmünzen austeilen, zu Messgehilfinnen (»acolytes«[31]). Sogar der im Hintergrund des Gemäldes sichtbare Anbau von Getreide und Wein wird in diesen Zusammenhang eingeordnet und folglich zu einem Hinweis auf Brot und Wein des Abendmahls.

Diese Deutung überzeugt mich nicht.[32] In der Eucharistie repräsentiert eine Hostie den Leib Christi. Weihung und Spende sind an einen Priester gebunden, zeremoniell festgelegt und von ernster Achtung getragen. Eine Hostie in der bis dahin völlig unüblichen Form einer Goldmünze – gemeinhin Ausdruck einer höchst weltlichen Wertschätzung – ins Bild zu setzen, hätte daher den Anschein einer anstößigen Verweltlichung ihres Charakters geweckt. Die Anstößigkeit wäre noch dadurch gesteigert, dass im Gemälde auch der Umgang mit den Münzen auf höchst weltliche Weise erfolgt: Sie werden von einem Tisch genommen, auf dem drei Fürstenkronen ruhen (darunter ganz rechts eine, deren Verzierung mit einer Lilie auf das französische Königtum weist); manche Münzen fallen vom Tisch; ein Bettler sammelt eine davon auf, um sie in seine Bettelschale zu den bereits empfangenen zu legen (Abb. 7).

Abb. 7: Bettler mit Goldmünzen (aus Abb. 2)

Ein solcher Anschein der Verweltlichung hätte zudem gerade in Amiens provokant wirken müssen, weil er dort – worauf Lecoq überhaupt nicht eingeht – in einen augenfälligen Widerspruch geraten wäre zum Ernst der Weltgerichtsdarstellung am Hauptportal der Kathedrale, für deren Ausschmückung das Gemälde letztlich bestimmt war. Denn am Hauptportal traf ja jeden Besucher vor dem Eintreten der durchdringende Blick des seine Wundmale zeigenden Christus, also eines

29 Lecoq (1977) 67: »Il faut le reconnaître, le refrain palinodial, formulé comme un proverbe, demeure sibyllin et n'éclaire guère le sens de la scène.«

30 Lecoq (1977) 69: »Tout porte donc à croire que le peintre a réutilisé les grandes lignes d'un schéma connu en les adaptant à l'illustration d'un autre sujet.«

31 So die Wortwahl von Lecoq (1987) 326.

32 Knecht (1994) 281 hingegen hat sie offenbar so überzeugt, dass er im Rahmen einer knappen Erläuterung der Abbildung des französischen Königs lapidar feststellt: »Francis I. and his suite receive communion. [...] The king holds out a hand to receive a gold coin symbolizing the Eucharist.« Begründet wird diese Sicht nicht. Lecoq (1977) wird auch nicht zitiert, doch findet Lecoq (1987) Aufnahme ins Literaturverzeichnis.

Christus, der »im Sakrament des Altars leibhaftig anwesend ist«.[33]

Einer Gleichsetzung oder Anverwandlung von Goldmünze und Hostie steht schließlich auch entgegen, dass die Austeilung zwei weiblichen Figurationen anvertraut ist, deren extravagante Kleidung – anders als es Lecoqs Einordnung als »acolytes« nahelegt – keinerlei liturgischen Bezug erkennen lässt[34] und stattdessen auf einen allegorischen Gehalt deutet.[35]

Die nähere Bestimmung dieses allegorischen Gehalts setzt allerdings ein zutreffendes Verständnis von Waage und Wägung voraus und damit die richtige Beantwortung der Frage, ob hier eine Seelenwägung anzunehmen ist. Lecoqs Verneinung beruht auf zwei nicht überzeugenden Behauptungen.[36]

Der ersten zufolge soll die Annahme einer Seelenwägung nur dann gerechtfertigt sein, wenn sie einer bestimmten Form genügt, nämlich einerseits die zu wiegende Seele zeigt und andererseits einen Kampf zwischen Engel und Teufel um den gewünschten Ausschlag der Waage. Diese Behauptung ist nicht nur unzutreffend, sondern auch erstaunlich. Denn schon die Seelenwägung im Tympanon der Kathedrale von Amiens zeigt ja, dass das Seelenkind durch ein *Agnus Dei* ersetzt sein kann, und in der berühmten Weltgerichtsdarstellung van der Weydens in Beaune sind die Waagschalen, wie ebenfalls schon erwähnt, noch einmal ganz anders gefüllt. Es besteht also insoweit eine erhebliche Variationsbreite.

Der zweiten Behauptung zufolge sind die Waagschalen leer. In der linken finde sich nur der Widerschein der daneben gestellten Frauengestalt und die rechte Schale sei wohl gerade vom Wind erfasst. Auch diese Behauptung lässt erstaunen, ja sie erweckt den Eindruck der Voreingenommenheit. Zwar kann man zugeben, dass die malerische Gestaltung der Seelenwägung ungewöhnlich ist. Aber kann dies ein ausreichender Einwand sein, wenn doch Lecoq selbst allenthalben die Außergewöhnlichkeit dieses manieristischen Werks betont, seine malerische Virtuosität, ja sogar seinem Schöpfer eine »turbulente personnalité«[37] zuerkennt?

Abb 8: Waagschale mit Seelenkind (aus Abb. 2)

Selbst wenn Lecoqs Behauptung hinsichtlich der bisher anzutreffenden bildnerischen Form einer Seelenwägung zutreffend wäre, dürfte man sich doch nicht mit dieser Feststellung begnügen, sondern müsste weitere Fragen stellen: Warum

33 So Schlink (1991) 106.

34 Solche weiblichen Figurationen sind keine Eigentümlichkeit des Gemäldes von 1518/19, der Maler verwendet sie ebenfalls in seinem Gemälde von 1519/20, und zwar wiederum ohne liturgischen Bezug; siehe die Farbabbildung in Scailliérez (2017b) 59.

35 Auch Séguin (2021c) 84 spricht von »allégories féminines«, verzichtet dabei aber auf eine nähere Bestimmung. Implizit erfolgt sie durch Übernahme von Lecoqs Deutung als Messgehilfinnen. Diesbezüglich vorsichtiger formulierte noch Lecoq (1977) 69: »Rien ne nous autorise à donner un nom aux deux jeunes femmes chargées de la distribution. Leur riche parure de fantaisie montre quelles appartiennent au monde de l'allégorie, mais aucun attribut spécial ne permet de les caractériser. Il faut donc simplement y voir deux émanations de Marie, donnant forme à son rôle d'auxiliaire et d'intermédiaire de la Rédemption.«

36 Im Original – Lecoq (1977) 68 – lautet die entscheidende Textpassage: »La représentation du Jugement Dernier, même réduite […] au moment de la pesée des âmes, exige pour être intelligible deux conditions: que l'âme soit figurée sur un des plateaux, et qu'il y ait quelque part combat de l'ange et du démon pour faire pencher la balance d'un côté ou de l'autre. Ces deux motifs sont constants depuis des origines du thème en Occident, ils traversent tout le moyen âge et on le retrouve en plein XVIe siècle. Rien de tel n'apparaît ici: les bassins sont vides, celui de droite se balance au gré du vent, celui de gauche ne contient que le reflet de la dame au riche vêtement qui se trouve à [69] proximité, et l'on a l'impression que le *bambino* est occupé plutôt à jouer avec un des cordons qu'à intervenir dans le destin d'une âme.«

37 Lecoq (1977) 72.

erwecken die Lichtreflexe in der linken Schale den Eindruck einer kleinen menschlichen Gestalt, und was könnte der Maler sich dabei gedacht haben? Warum hätte er bei der Ausgestaltung der rechten Schale einen so kräftigen Windstoß darstellen sollen oder wollen, dass die Schale umschlägt? Schließlich, warum zeigt er eine von Gottvater gehaltene Waage und lässt die Taube des Heiligen Geistes den Ausschlag der Waage beeinflussen, wenn er keine Seelenwägung andeuten wollte? Dass Lecoq sich solchen, doch eigentlich naheliegenden Fragen nicht einmal stellt, lässt sie auf die beschriebenen Abwege geraten.

Ist im Ergebnis also nachdrücklich daran festzuhalten, dass das Gemälde eine Form der Seelenwägung präsentiert, so kann man doch von Lecoq etwas Wichtiges für das Verständnis der Devisen des Puy d'Amiens lernen und daraus auch einen angemessenen Standpunkt für die Deutung des Gemäldes gewinnen. Sie hat nämlich überzeugend nachgewiesen, dass die vorausgegangenen Devisen gemeinhin nach einem bestimmten Muster – von ihr »loi du genre« genannt – gebaut sind.[38] Demnach beziehen sie sich auf Maria in ihrem Verhältnis zu Jesus Christus und weisen ihr dabei hinsichtlich des mit ihm verbundenen Heilsgeschehens eine dienende, helfende Rolle zu.

Auf die Devise des Gemäldes von 1518/19 übertragen heißt dies, dass sie Maria als Waage und Jesus als Gewicht anspricht. Diese Sicht erlaubt es, die eingangs noch vorsichtig entwickelte deutsche Übersetzung »Bei rechtem Gewicht wirkliche Waage« in eine leicht verbesserte, weil geschärfte Fassung zu überführen, nämlich: »Rechtem Gewicht wirkliche Waage«.[39] Für uneingeweihte Ohren klingt sie zwar etwas seltsam und rätselhaft, doch gehört solche metaphorische Dichte ja zum Wesen der Devisen des Puy d'Amiens. Will man sie dennoch zur leichteren Verständlichkeit etwas auflockern, könnte man wohl auch sagen »Wirkliche Waage dem rechten Gewicht« oder – in Einvernehmen mit Lecoq, die das anfängliche, auf Jesus bezogene »à / au« als »pour« verstehen möchte[40] – »Für rechtes Gewicht wirkliche Waage«.

Wichtiger freilich ist die Feststellung, dass sich dieses Verständnis der Devise – anders als Lecoq in Vernachlässigung der *loi du genre* meint – auch im Gemälde widerspiegelt. Wie in den früheren Werken des Puy d'Amiens, erhält Maria einen zentralen und damit prominenten Platz. Doch diesmal wird er, inspiriert von der Devise, auf einzigartige Weise gestaltet: Maria thront zwischen den Schalen einer großen Waage, so dass die devisengemäße Gleichsetzung von Maria und Waage anschaulich wird. Als Waage wird Maria eine zwar bedeutsame, aber doch nur dienende Rolle zugewiesen. Wie auch Gottvater, der die Waage hält, greift sie in die Seelenwägung nicht selbst ein. Der Eingriff erfolgt zum einen und nur leicht durch die Taube des Heiligen Geistes, zum anderen und vor allem aber – in einem emphatischen Sinne wirklich heilsam – durch das Jesuskind auf Marias Schoß. Christus also ist es, der den entscheidenden Impuls für die Seelenwägung setzt und so für das »rechte Gewicht« sorgt.

Diese Klarstellung ermöglicht es nun, die Austeilung der Goldmünzen auf eine zwanglose Weise allegorisch zu deuten. Ausgangspunkt dafür ist, dass im Gemälde dem Geben der Goldmünzen eine Bereitschaft zum Empfangen entspricht, und zwar, wie angesichts sich streckender und öffnender Hände unstrittig ist, auf Seiten sowohl der Armen als auch der Mächtigen, hier vor allem Kaiser, Papst und König.[41] Die Gleichstellung ungeachtet großer Unterschiede in der gesellschaftlichen und politischen Stellung weist auf grundsätzlich gleiche Bedürftigkeit im Verhältnis zu Gott. Es bedarf insoweit keiner Unterscheidung in der allegorischen Charakterisierung der weiblichen Figurationen, denen die Austeilung übertragen ist:[42] Beide repräsentieren in ihrem Handeln die durch Jesus Christus vermittelte

38 Lecoq (1977) 68 f.

39 Insofern ist die englische Übersetzung des Museumsführers – Huchard et al. (eds.) (1995) 68: »True weight, true scales« – unbefriedigend. Sie wird der Kernstruktur der Devise nicht ganz gerecht.

40 Lecoq (1977) 68.

41 Diese Sicht würde erklären können, warum unter den üblichen Herrschaftszeichen, mit denen der Maler die königliche Stellung von François I. verdeutlicht, eines fehlt: die *main de justice*, eine goldene Hand als Zeichen seiner Jurisdiktionsgewalt. Da diese im Jüngsten Gericht nicht zählt, hätte es nämlich irritieren können, sie in dem vorliegenden Zusammenhang gleichwohl zu zeigen. Laut Knecht (1994) 545 wurde François I. zusammen mit seiner *main de justice* bestattet, so wichtig war sie ihm.

42 So noch Foucart (1965) 145 und Anm. 6, mit seiner Frage, ob sie Tugenden darstellen, nämlich »Miséricorde« und »Justice«.

Barmherzigkeit Gottes. Sie als einen großen Schatz anzusehen, ist verständlich und lässt sich gut anhand von Goldmünzen veranschaulichen.[43] Verstehen lässt sich jetzt auch die auf den ersten Blick befremdliche Szene, dass bei der Austeilung der Goldmünzen die Hand des Hofnarren Triboulet zugunsten der Hand seines Königs beiseite geschoben wird (Abb. 4): Sie bringt zum Ausdruck, dass nicht zuletzt – vielleicht sogar in besonderem Maße? – ein Herrscher der Barmherzigkeit Gottes bedarf. Diese beschwichtigt gewissermaßen die göttliche Gerechtigkeit, deren durchgreifender Anspruch in der Seelenwägung zum Ausdruck kommt.

Barmherzigkeit wird hier aber nicht nur thematisiert als die Barmherzigkeit Gottes gegenüber den Menschen, sondern darüber hinaus als die nach christlichem Verständnis damit eng verbundene Barmherzigkeit der Menschen untereinander, nicht zuletzt gegenüber den Armen. Auch diese mitmenschliche Barmherzigkeit betrifft – insoweit eine politische Dimension gewinnend – die Herrscher selbst, wie das Gemälde wohl auch dadurch zum Ausdruck bringt, dass die Goldmünzen von dem Tisch genommen werden, auf dem ihre Kronen liegen, insbesondere die des französischen Königs.

Wenngleich Maria im Vergleich zu Christus nur eine dienende Aufgabe erfüllt, so bleibt diese doch für die Menschen wichtig, da Maria die in ihrem Sohn ruhende göttliche Barmherzigkeit zu vermitteln hilft. Insoweit ist es auch verständlich, dass sie es ist, die im Gemälde von 1518/19 entsprechend der Tradition des Puy d'Amiens den zentralen Platz einnimmt.

Dennoch ist sie, für sich genommen, noch nicht die »Dame«, auf die der Titel dieses Aufsatzes zielt. Denn Marias Platz im Gemälde ist zugleich ein Platz zwischen zwei Waagschalen und damit ein Platz, der in der uns heutzutage vertrauten Justitia-Figuration von einer allegorischen Frauengestalt mit Schwert und Waage eingenommen wird. Wenngleich nur eine Waage und kein Schwert zu sehen ist, darf das Schwert doch mitgedacht werden, und zwar aufgrund der mit der gezeigten Seelenwägung typischerweise verbundenen Assoziation des Erzengels Michael, den das Schwert kennzeichnet. Insofern überlagern sich hier auf subtile Weise Maria, Erzengel Michael und Justitia, oder anders und pointierter ausgedrückt: kann man hier von einer bemerkenswerten Vorformung der uns vertrauten Justitia-Figuration sprechen.

IV. Schlussbemerkung

Religion für politische Zwecke und Politik für religiöse Zwecke zu nutzen, hat eine lange und vielfältige Tradition. Ihre Überzeugungen und Interessen beeinflussen sich wechselseitig. Religion vermag politischen Strukturen und Handlungen Legitimation und Kohärenz zu geben, Politik den Wirkungskreis und die Durchsetzungskraft von Religion zu stärken oder zu schwächen. Auch das Gemälde des Puy d'Amiens von 1518/19 zeugt davon.

Angeregt von der Devise »Au juste poids véritable balance« veranschaulicht es das politische Problem des Ausgleichs zwischen weltlichen Mächten als religiöses Problem des Ausgleichs von Gerechtigkeit (*iustitia*) und Barmherzigkeit (*misericordia*). Das religiöse Gerichts- und Gnadenbild überformt so das Herrschaftsbild. Die Großen der Welt sollen ihre Macht nicht leichtsinnig auf der Seite des Rechts wähnen und sie daher auch nicht rücksichtslos durchzusetzen versuchen. Denn auch ihre Seelen werden einst im Jüngsten Gericht gewogen werden. Zur Selbstüberhebung besteht mithin kein Anlass.

Amiens hatte gleichwohl Grund, besorgt zu sein. Die Stadt befand sich in einem ökonomisch-politischen Spannungsfeld zwischen dem Landesherrn der Picardie, also dem König Frankreichs, und dem Landesherrn des benachbarten Brabant, auf den ersten Blick zwar nur ein Herzog, aber inzwischen einer aus dem Hause Habsburg, der als

43 Wenn Lecoq (1977) die Goldmünzen als »trésor« bezeichnet, so ist dies also für sich genommen noch nicht zu beanstanden. Irrig wird es erst, wenn sie sich aufgrund ihrer Verneinung einer Seelenwägung zu Umdeutungen gezwungen sieht, nämlich zum einen das Wort »juste« aus der Devise statt auf das Gewicht auf die Verteilung dieses Schatzes zu beziehen und zu behaupten, als »homme de justice« habe Picquet dafür Sorge getragen, dass der Maler den Akzent seines Gemäldes auf die »juste distribution du trésor« lege, und zum anderen »juste poids« als »juste prix« zu lesen, den Christus zu bezahlen habe »pour racheter l'humanité captive de la faute« (alle Zitate 69).

Karl V. gerade zum Kaiser des Heiligen Römischen Reichs aufgestiegen war. Sie hatte also ein besonders lebhaftes Friedensinteresse.

Davon zeugt auch ihre Festkultur, die sich jährlich auf rituelle Weise bestätigte – in Schrift und Bild, Schauspiel und Musik – und dabei erneuerte. Sie diente der Gewinnung eines kommunalen Ethos, das den inneren Zusammenhalt förderte und nach außen als Zeichen berechtigter Selbstbehauptung verstanden werden konnte.

In seiner Mischung von Huldigung und Mahnung diente auch das Gemälde von 1518/19 dieser Selbstbehauptung, nicht im Rahmen einer klar formulierten, zu scharfen Konsequenzen bereiten Argumentation, sondern mit Hilfe einer weicheren, symbolischen Kommunikation, die Deutungsspielräume eröffnete. Das Machtgefälle zwischen König und Stadt sollte durch ästhetische Gestaltung moderiert werden. Dabei half die emblematische Seite des Gemäldes, die Verbindung zwischen dem knappen Text der Devise und dem sie zwar nicht ausformulierenden, wohl aber veranschaulichenden und dabei affektiv aufladenden Bild.

Dass im Mittelpunkt eine Waage steht, ist mithin auf doppelte Weise treffend: zum einen als Erinnerung an das Jüngste Gericht, dem sich im Rahmen eines Abwägungsprozesses eigener Art alle Christen werden stellen müssen, mächtige wie machtlose; zum anderen als Erinnerung daran, dass es für das Wohlergehen der Stadt Amiens einer Abwägung ihrer Interessen mit den Interessen von König, Kaiser, Papst und Bischöfen bedurfte, der die gemeinsame Marienfrömmigkeit den förderlichen Boden bereiten sollte.

Damit wird zugleich anschaulich, wie und warum die Gestalt des Erzengels Michael, des Seelenwägers, mit der uns vertrauten allegorischen Figuration der Justitia in Verbindung steht: Sie ruft in Erinnerung, dass dem normativen Anspruch von Recht und Gerechtigkeit in letzter Hinsicht ein religiöses Gründungselement eigen ist.

■

Bibliographie

- Baschet, Jérôme (1995), Jugement de l'âme, jugement dernier: contradiction, complémentarité, chevauchement?, in: Revue Mabillon. Revue internationale d'histoire et de littératures religieuses 67 (6 n. s.), 159–203
- Behrmann, Carolin (2020), Law, Visual Studies, and Image History, in: Stern, Simon et al. (eds.), The Oxford Handbook of Law and Humanities, Oxford, 39–64
- Burke, Peter (2015), Images de trois rois. François Ier entre Charles Quint et Henri VIII, in: Petey-Girard, Bruno, Magali Vène (dir.), François Ier. Pouvoir et image [Ausstellungskatalog], Paris, 24–43
- Devaux, Jean (2003), Littérature et politique au cœur de la cité: des puys marials aux chambres de rhétorique, in: Arnould, Jean-Claude, Thierry Mantovani (dir.), Première poésie française de la Renaissance. Autour des Puys poétiques normands, Paris, 373–393
- Duval, Frédéric, Fabienne Pomel (dir.) (2008), Guillaume de Digulleville. Les Pèlerinages allégoriques, Rennes
- Foucart, Jacques (1965), Maître d'Amiens, in: Ministère des Affaires Culturelles (dir.), Le XVIe Siècle Européen. Peintures et Dessins dans les Collections Publiques Françaises [Ausstellungskatalog], Paris, 144–149
- Gaehtgens, Thomas W., Nicole Hochner (dir.) (2006), L'image du roi de François Ier à Louis XIV, Paris
- Gauvard, Claude (2003), Théorie, rédaction et usage du droit dans les villes du royaume de France du XIIe au XVe siècle, in: Monnet, Pierre, Otto Gerhard Oexle (Hg.), Stadt und Recht im Mittelalter. La ville et le droit au Moyen Âge, Göttingen, 25–71
- Gros, Gérard (1992), Le Poète, la Vierge et le Prince du Puy. Étude sur les Puys marials de la France du Nord du XIVe siècle à la Renaissance, Paris
- Gros, Gérard (1996), Le Poème du Puy marial. Étude sur le serventois et le chant royal du XIVe siècle à la Renaissance, Paris
- Heyen, Erk Volkmar (2009), Gruppenbild mit Dame: »Das Gericht der Brabanter Münzergilde« von Maarten de Vos (1594), in: Rechtsgeschichte. Zeitschrift des Max-Planck-Instituts für europäische Rechtsgeschichte 15, 62–76, online: http://dx.doi.org/10.12946/rg15/062-076
- Heyen, Erk Volkmar (2013), Verwaltete Welten – Mensch, Gemeinwesen und Amt in der europäischen Malerei, Berlin
- Huchard, Viviane et al. (eds.) (1995), The Museum of Picardy, Amiens, Paris
- Kasarska, Iliana (2012), La sculpture des portails, in: Bouilleret, Jean-Luc et al. (dir.), Amiens. La grâce d'une cathédrale, Strasbourg, 175–212
- Kemperdick, Stephan (1999), Rogier van der Weyden. 1399/1400–1464, Köln
- Kissel, Otto Rudolf (1997), Die Justitia. Reflexionen über ein Symbol und seine Darstellung in der bildenden Kunst, 2. Aufl., München
- Knecht, Robert J. (1994), Renaissance Warrior and Patron. The Reign of Francis I., Cambridge

- Knecht, Robert J. (2002), François Ier et le ›miroir des princes‹, in: Halévi, Ran (dir.), Le Savoir du Prince. Du moyen âge aux lumières, Paris, 81–110
- Kretzenbacher, Leopold (1958), Die Seelenwaage. Zur religiösen Idee vom Jenseitsgericht auf der Schicksalswaage in Hochreligion, Bildkunst und Volksglaube, Klagenfurt 1958
- Lecoq, Anne-Marie (1977), Le Puy d'Amiens de 1518, la loi du genre et l'art du peintre, in: Revue de l'Art 38, 63–74
- Lecoq, Anne-Marie (1987), François Ier imaginaire. Symbolique et politique à l'aube de la Renaissance française, Paris
- Lemé-Hébuterne, Kristiane (2007), Les stalles de la cathédrale Notre-Dame d'Amiens. Histoire, iconographie, Paris
- Murray, Stephen (2021), Notre-Dame of Amiens. Life of the Gothic Cathedral, New York
- Paresys, Isabelle (1998), Aux marges du royaume. Violence, justice et société en Picardie sous François Ier, Paris
- Pleister, Wolfgang (1988), Der Mythos des Rechts, in: ders., Wolfgang Schild (Hg.), Recht und Gerechtigkeit im Spiegel der europäischen Kunst, Köln, 8–43
- Reid, Dylan (2019), Confraternities and Poetry: The Francophone Puys, in: Eisenbichler, Konrad (ed.), A Companion to Medieval and Early Modern Confraternities, Leiden, 385–405
- Sauvion, Valérie (2006), Les portraits allégoriques de François Ier au XVIe siècle, in: Girault, Pierre-Gilles, François Ier, images d'un roi, de l'histoire à la légende [Ausstellungskatalog], Blois, 22–29
- Scailliérez, Cécile (dir.) (2017a), François Ier et l'art des Pays-bas [Ausstellungskatalog], Paris
- Scailliérez, Cécile (2017b), Un courant maniériste venu du Nord. Le rayonnement de Jan de Beer et de la culture leydo-anversoise, in: dies. (dir.) (2017a), 32–48
- Scailliérez, Cécile (2017c), Maître d'Amiens, »Au juste pois [*sic*] véritable balance«, allégorie mystique en l'honneur de la Vierge, in: dies. (dir.) (2017a), 54–59
- Scailliérez, Cécile (2017d), Jean Clouet, »Saint Jean Baptiste sous les traits de François Ier«, in: dies. (dir.) (2017a), 245–246
- Scailliérez, Cécile (2017e), Le Maître d'Amiens (Toonen Ariaenssone?), in: dies. (dir.) (2017a), 434
- Schild, Wolfgang (1995), Bilder von Recht und Gerechtigkeit, Köln
- Schlink, Wilhelm (1991), Der Beau-Dieu von Amiens. Das Christusbild der gotischen Kathedrale, Frankfurt am Main / Leipzig
- Schramm, Percy Ernst (1960), Der König von Frankreich. Das Wesen der Monarchie vom 9. zum 16. Jahrhundert. Ein Kapitel aus der Geschichte des abendländischen Staates, Bd. 1: Text, Bd. 2: Anhänge, Anmerkungen, Register, 2. Aufl., Darmstadt
- Séguin, François (dir.) (2021a), Les Puys d'Amiens. Chefs-d'œuvre de la cathédrale Notre-Dame [Ausstellungskatalog], Dijon
- Séguin, François (2021b), Histoire et institutions de la confrérie du Puy d'Amiens, in: ders. (dir.) (2021a), 16–27
- Séguin, François (2021c), Maître d'Amiens, »Au juste pois véritable balance«, in: ders. (dir.) (2021a), 84–87
- Walbe, Brigitte (1974), Studien zur Entwicklung des allegorischen Porträts in Frankreich von seinen Anfängen bis zur Regierungszeit König Heinrichs II., Diss. phil. Frankfurt am Main
- Wartenberg, Imke (2015), Bilder der Rechtsprechung. Spätmittelalterliche Wandmalereien in Regierungsräumen italienischer Kommunen, Berlin / Boston
- Wolters van der Wey, Beatrijs (2015), Corporate Splendour. Civic Group Portraits in Brabant 1585–1800. A Social, Typological and Iconographic Approach, Turnhout (niederländisch 2012)
- Wolters van der Wey, Beatrijs (2018), Civic Bodies and their Identification with Justice and Law in Early Modern Flemish Portraiture, in: Huygebaert, Stefan et al. (eds.), The Art of Law. Artistic Representation and Iconography of Law and Justice in Context, from the Middle Ages to the First World War, Cham, 169–179

Daniel Damler

Capital of Doom: Eighty Years under Emergency Rule. Nevertheless, Gotham City Persists*

Those who feel they have reached the end of their tether after two years of pandemic-induced emergency rule may find consolation in the thought that things are far more uncomfortable elsewhere. In Gotham City, for example. In Batman's home town, chaos is a daily occurrence. And the world watches; the world in an almost literal sense. Gotham first appears in the fourth issue of »Batman«, published in the winter of 1940/41, and ever since then, people across all continents have been taking an interest in the fate of the fictitious metropolis, home to millions. Even more so since its move to the silver screen: the last two films of Christopher Nolan's »Dark Knight« trilogy alone raked in over a billion dollars each at the box office.

Gotham represents a permanent state of emergency, the rule of crime, and a mind-boggling level of failure on the part of the state. Yet it also stands for the triumph of a heroic form of republicanism as practised by its most prominent citizen, Bruce Wayne a.k.a. Batman. Which prompts the question: what is the special flavour of this society, what are the collective phobias that yield such a rich harvest?

In antiquity, the destruction, depredation or desecration of cultural sites frequently signified the utmost threat to the stability of state and society. This could justify almost any measure, even if from an objective military or police perspective the deed did not carry the relevance that was accorded to it, purely because of the symbolic value of the threatened object.

The world of the 20th and 21st centuries is located in a symbolic power field, just as it was in antiquity. This is manifested by two iconic Gotham landmarks, which criminals and terrorists love to get their hands on: Blackgate Prison, the infamous jail, and Arkham Asylum, the even more infamous psychiatric ward introduced to the comic book series in 1974, where villains such as the Joker and Two-Face are locked up.

Those buildings have an unsettling effect. They represent the latent fear, stoked by rumours and conjecture, of inmates who have cut all ties to society. They also embody the guilt trip of a citizenry that has no trust in the integrity of its justice system. They are toxic places in the heart of an unstable republic. Any failure of the protective barriers that separate those in power from those exiled here leads to the ultimate catastrophe. The psychological effect triggered by a sudden loss of control has left its mark on world history more than once – just consider the storming of the Bastille on 14th July 1789, or the seizing of the Kresty prison in St Petersburg during the February Revolution of 1917.

One could call it a trademark for Batman and his opponents that the common symbolism of good and evil is rejected and reversed. Batman is the virtuous knight performing good deeds, but his armour is black, while the Joker carries out his vile crimes in a clown's white make-up. Perhaps even more noticeable and influential than costumes and camouflage is the systematic symbolic inversion of the city's architecture and event locations. The supervillains make a point of selecting public spaces for their attacks, spaces that serve as inner-city oases and refuges for Gotham's citizens who, plagued by violence and social misery, hope to enjoy a few carefree hours, a time-out from the stress and strain of their daily lives: the zoo, a circus, a stadium, museums, botanical gardens.

* Translation by Vera Mark. A slightly different German version of this article appeared in the *Frankfurter Allgemeine Sonntagszeitung* on 20 June 2021, p. 41, under the title »Wer den Ausnahmezustand beherrscht«. For a more in-depth analysis see DANIEL DAMLER, Gotham City. Architekturen des Ausnahmezustands, Frankfurt am Main / New York 2022.

Terror is brought precisely to the innermost sanctuary of innocence, to the inviolable, taboo core, the holy shrine of cultured society. Frequently the reason for this is that the perpetrators, for example the Joker, were deprived of such spaces during a childhood filled with violence. Those that pursue this course are assured of eternal enmity. Not a single step further, one wants to shout at them. It's bad enough that you pick barracks, bars, petrol stations, public toilets or factory floors to stage your crimes, but stay away from humanity's heartland! There are limits even for you, you must respect the tacit, minimal consensus of civilised peoples!

Thus one wants to appeal to them, but they lack any scruples; all they have is a highly developed sense for the logic of escalation. And so they storm the sacred temples, they deface invaluable artworks as if those were rusty dustbins, and at Christmas they toss hand grenades into toyshop windows. Their deeds carry one message only: forget the petty crimes on your streets, this, only this, is the state of emergency!

And as if all that wasn't enough, Gotham is threatened to be utterly annihilated by the nuclear bombs of Ra's al Ghul's League of Assassins, the ice canon of Mr Freeze or similarly hellish contraptions. The myths and legends of Western civilisation are a treasure trove for tales about the violent demise of great urban centres. The devastation of Sodom and Gomorrah, the downfall of Babylon and Troy, the destruction of Carthage and Jerusalem, and the struggle for Rome in late antiquity: looking at these events one finds that those who suffer these terrible fates are most often portrayed as perpetrators rather than victims. They are used by God – or the Gods, fate, history, or the *Weltgeist* – to serve as an example for disobedience, depravity, iniquity. The catastrophe is intended as a beacon, a warning for future generations.

The topic of decadence is such an essential element of any tale of downfall or decline that in the case of a metropolis faced with attacks on its physical substance, its most important edifices, infinitely more is at stake than merely its continued existence. A city fighting against its destruction is always also fighting for its place in history, for its legitimation, its right to exist, in the past as in the present, for the right to survive as a memory of a place where life was good. A city that succumbs to destruction inflicts retroactive injustice on itself and anyone who ever lived there. This raises the stakes infinitely.

So the citizens of Gotham need to tough it out – and they need institutions that protect them from the worst, for they cannot count on help from the outside. Granted, the general take is that the city is legally part of the United States, and its streets are filled with people from all corners of the world. But national or international solidarity when the going gets tough? Negative. Moreover, in borrowing from New York, the map of Gotham designed by Eliot R. Brown in 1998 shows the city as a group of isles, an island just like Plato's Atlantis and More's Utopia, implying a self-centred orientation, a typically insular focus on oneself. If necessary, the tunnels and bridges connecting Gotham to the mainland can be blown up to really drive home the point that this is a city state of classic design.

So in this self-reliant republic, who can, who should take the lead in an emergency? Not Gotham's regular institutions, that's for sure; they offer a pitiful picture. The police can't even handle run-of-the-mill crimes, let alone supervillains with superior intellect and equipment. The political and administrative institutions, to the degree that they're not entirely paralysed by internal squabbling, have to jump through complicated hoops to reach consensus and, as a consequence, their reactions to any kind of threat usually comes way too late.

In brief: this is more or less the situation described by Machiavelli with a view to the republics of antiquity and the Renaissance. The ordinary course of business was too slow, he complained, which posed enormous risks should they have to deal with a situation that suffered no delays. Therefore, so the recommendation by the political philosopher from Florence, the constitution should allow the establishment of a dictatorship for such situations of urgency. He referred to the eponymous institution under Roman law, not to the construct we nowadays associate with the term, not *tyrannis*, not despotism, not Caesarism. In ancient Rome, the dictator was a high-level magistrate; this was not a permanent position, and a dictator could be appointed only in specific circumstances, in particular in the event of war or internal unrest. The period of office was limited to six months.

And would you know it, Gotham does exactly what Machiavelli recommends: it adopts the ›Roman‹ solution. The magistrate appoints a trustworthy, capable citizen to save the fatherland, someone who in times of need takes the measures necessary to overcome the crisis. To bring this about, a representative of the citizenry climbs up to the roof of the police headquarters, switches on a spotlight, and delivers Gotham's appeal for help and the task at hand to the bat thus attracted. Once the job is done, the saviour quickly withdraws, sheds his armour and all burden, and Bruce Wayne, independently wealthy, lives his quiet life in a grand mansion at the edge of the city.

This interpretation is supported by one of the key scenes in the »Dark Knight« trilogy: the argument between District Attorney Harvey Dent and his girlfriend Rachel, who questions Batman's democratic legitimacy. Dent, on the other hand, does not hesitate to take the Dark Knight's side and expressly places him in the tradition of ancient Roman dictatorship.

From a US-American perspective, this avowal is not nearly as surprising as it may seem. After the end of the Civil War, George Washington immediately relinquished his position as commander-in-chief of the Continental Army and withdrew to his country estate Mount Vermont. Washington was seen as something of a reincarnation of the legendary Cincinnatus, a shining example who lived in the 5th century BCE. Called to the position of dictator from his farm across the Tiber, he wrapped up what he'd been tasked with in a record-breaking

sixteen days and did not remain in office for a moment beyond that. The Washington-Cincinnatus lore has enjoyed widespread popularity in the United States until the present day.

This take on republicanism focuses on the individuals' duties rather than their rights. Its role model is the engaged citizen who gets involved in matters of state whenever it counts; it sees corruption, greed and abuse of power as the greatest vices and a sense of responsibility, incorruptibility and self-restraint as the greatest virtues. In general, everything revolves around virtue and personal proficiency – the Greek *arete*, the Roman *virtus*, the Florentine *virtù*. This does not mean that republicanism stands in direct contrast to liberalism, but it does place different emphases.

To therefore condemn it as reactionary, or ignore it entirely, would be a mistake. The US-American philosopher Robert Pippin made a valid point when he wondered whether the current tendency to question the legitimacy of everything and everyone wasn't going a bit too far and in doing so neglected the actual business of political psychology. The question what type of psychological constitution is required for which political regime or form of government is one that we should still treat as relevant today.

And yet, we must not lose sight of the Achilles heel of republican heroism. The voluntary withdrawal after completion of the task is a tricky issue. Not only does it require the victorious heroes to admit that they are superfluous as of now. When the citizenry acquires a taste for its own powerlessness and feels quite at home therein, it is likely to simply let things run their own course. But that is not an option. Seeing oneself as at the mercy of Gods and superheroes is questioning one of the most important achievements of Greek and Roman antiquity: the discovery of politics as self-determined action.

Let us hope, then, that Batman's fellow citizens will continue to find a way out of this labyrinth of self-inflicted disempowerment and that we can spend another 80 years admiring Gotham City's glorious demise.

■

S. 45
Big Apple, NYC, 1992

S. 64
View from ›Top of the Rock‹ (Rockefeller Center), NYC, 2019

S. 81
Chelsea Hotel, NYC, 2019

S. 95
Skyline with super-slender skyscrapers, NYC, 2019
Joggers in Central Park, NYC, 2017

S. 117
Artificial palm tree on Coney Island Beach, NYC, 2019

S. 130
Snake lady, Fourth of July, NYC, 1992
Reflection in a puddle, NYC, 2019

S. 145
Truth, NYC, 2017

S. 146
William Copley, »Think« (1961), Whitney Museum of American Art, NYC, 2019
Toy Soldier, NYC, 1992

S. 147
Statue of Liberty, NYC, 2017
»America«, Whitney Museum of American Art, NYC, 2019

S. 160
Radio City Hall, NYC, 2019

S. 172
Chrysler Building, NYC, 2017
View of the Lower East Side from Brooklyn, NYC, 2017

S. 183
Young tree in November, NYC, 2019

S. 197
Brooklyn Bridge, NYC, 2017
Grand Central Station, NYC, 2017

S. 198
Wall Street, NYC, 2017
National Debt, NYC, 1992

S. 333
Imagine, Strawberry Fields (Central Park West), NYC, 2017
In front of Jackson Pollock's »One: Number 31, 1950«, MoMA, NYC, 2019

S. 353
Hudson River Talk, NYC, 1992
Twilight, Hudson River and New Jersey, NYC, 2019

S. 354
Dusk, Hudson River and New Jersey, NYC, 2019

S. 355
Shadows, Coney Island Station, NYC, 2019

S. 356
Times Square, NYC, 2017

S. 357
Cop, NYC, 1992

S. 358
Lincoln Center at night, NYC, 2019

S. 367
Fire escape ladders, Chelsea, NYC, 2019

S. 368
JoJo's Philosophy, Greenwich Village, NYC, 2019

S. 380
A second view from ›Top of the Rock‹ (Rockefeller Center), NYC, 2019

Elizabeth Papp Kamali

The Horrible Sepulture of Mannes Resoun: Intoxication and Medieval English Felony Law

The modern Anglo-American common law tends toward a hardline stance on intoxication, typically not treating it as an excuse to a criminal charge but offering a few well-guarded exceptions, most notably the idea in some jurisdictions that intoxication may be invoked to negate specific intent given its deleterious effect on cognitive capacity. A similar ambivalence toward the intersection of intoxication and criminal responsibility may be found in early English felony law, which offered no formal, intoxication-based exceptions to liability, but nevertheless countenanced jurors exercising their prudential judgment to treat intoxication as either an inculpatory or exculpatory factor in particular cases. Medieval English felony law treated drunkenness similarly to anger, recognizing that both conditions – which could be intertwined – often traced their roots to condemnable character formation and long-cultivated habit, and yet could result in a person's detachment from their capacity to reason and exercise self-control while under the influence. In the legal context, drunkenness was not equated with insanity, which was presumptively exculpatory, despite the fact that the two conditions could result in similar effects on a defendant's observable behavior. Evidence from non-legal texts, including vernacular literature and guides for confessors, helps explain the concerns medieval English judges and jurors brought with them to the task of felony adjudication when faced with alcohol-laced facts, revealing a world in which tavern culture ensured alcohol's omnipresence, but in which drunkenness was nevertheless not generally available as an excuse, partial or otherwise, for allegedly felonious behavior.

Keywords: intoxication, felony, medieval England

■

Jan Schröder

Zur Bedeutung der Wörter in der Rechts- und Sprachtheorie der frühen Neuzeit

In the middle of the 20th century, Ludwig Wittgenstein developed the thought that the meaning of a word is its »use in language«. In fact, in the late 17th century, this idea was absolutely dominant and undisputed. In contrast to older theories, the first conferral of meaning (imposition) and etymology were no longer considered decisive. The reason for the transition to the usage theory was the awareness of the historicity, i. e. the changeability, of language. Furthermore, the authority of a linguistic creator was now considered relevant only in technical languages, but not in colloquial language. This was possibly due to the rise of the vernacular languages.

Keywords: word meaning, usage theory of meaning, philosophy of language, historicity of language, early modern period

■

Peter Collin, Wim Decock, Nadine Grotkamp, David von Mayenburg, Anna Seelentag

History of Conflict Resolution in Europe – A Project Report

The four-volume *Handbuch zur Geschichte der Konfliktlösung in Europa* (Handbook on the history of conflict resolution in Europe) deals with the history of institutionalised and rule-based conflict resolution in judicial and extra-judicial forms. It covers the period from antiquity up to the recent past, and the articles take up central problems of conflict resolution or describe the development in specific European regions and states. This contribution provides information on the handbook project, the origins of which reach back to 2012 and came to a conclusion with the publication of the handbook in 2021. The article describes the debates on conflict resolution within the juridical field and offers information about both the central concepts and content of the handbook.

Keywords: conflict resolution, justice, extra-judicial, Europe

■

Karl Härter, Valeria Vegh Weis

Transnational Criminal Law in Transatlantic Perspective (1870–1945): Introductory Notes, Initial Results and Concepts

The article outlines the scope and concepts of the research project »Transnational Criminal Law in Transatlantic Perspective (1870–1945)« and introduces the respective case studies of the Focus. Although research has studied the history of crime, criminal justice, policing and punishment in Latin America, the transatlantic dimension of transnational criminal law has still to be explored by legal history. This could be achieved by applying the concepts of »historical regimes of normativity« and »global legal history« integrating as well approaches of »critical criminology« and »criminal selectivity«. This conceptional framework allows to study the transatlantic dimension of transnational crime, norms, discourses and practices as the formation of a transnational regime. In this regime not only states but also non-governmental actors from the Global North and the Global South played a vital role, exchanged and created legal knowledge and normativity as well as narratives of »international crime« which also had an impact on the respective domestic levels of criminal law, criminalisation, policing and criminal justice. In this regard, research on the formation of transnational-transatlantic criminal law regimes could gain new insights in the legal history of criminal law as well as to current issues of the global governance of crime.

Keywords: transatlantic history, transnational criminal law, international crime, regimes of normativity, critical criminology

■

Elizabeth Gómez Alcorta

Congresos criminológicos internacionales y su impacto en los códigos penales de América Latina (1870–1945)

Departing from the analysis of different international congresses concerning criminal issues carried out between 1870 and 1945 mostly in Europe, the article traces the expansion of the category of »dangerousness« (*estado de peligrosidad*) in Latin America at discursive and normative levels. It focuses on the particular role that these congresses played as tools for the universalization of norms and in the production of modes of subjectivity based on a racist social classification, which was widely accepted by Latin-American elites. Thus, the presence of the Latin American delegations in these congresses gave rise to theoretical frameworks for social control and transnational criminal law regimes. The article shows how the construction of »dangerousness« as a transnational criminal legal-political concept could become an instrument of control and consolidation of a new world order.

Keywords: Latin America, International Criminology Conferences, 1870–1945, social control, dangerousness

■

Nicolás Duffau

Italian Immigration, Crime, and Police Actions in Uruguay: The Volpi-Patroni Case (1882)

In March 1882, the Kingdom of Italy suspended diplomatic relations with the Republic of Uruguay because two Italian immigrants accused of murder, Raffaele Volpi and Vicenzo Patroni, had been tortured by the Uruguayan police. At that time, criminals and marginalized people were commonly stigmatized and persecuted by the authorities, who considered them to be blocking the political and cultural development of »modern« Uruguay. This context framed the episode. Through historical analysis of the Volpi-Patroni case, its broad press coverage and transnational impact, this article examines the complex process of social identity formation at the time of the massive arrival and inclusion of foreigners into Uruguay society in the last two decades of the 19th century.

Keywords: Italy, Uruguay, immigration, transnational law, crime, modernization

■

Paul Knepper

The League of Nations, Traffic in Women and the Transnationalization of Criminal Law

During the 1920s, the Advisory Committee on the Traffic in Women, of the League of Nations operated as a legal regime in the transnationalization of criminal law. This can be seen in its management of the first ›worldwide‹ investigation into the traffic in women which sent undercover investigators to more than a 100 countries across Europe, the Americas, and the Mediterranean. The Advisory Committee initiated ›trafficking‹ as a transnational crime and advanced the understanding of transnational criminal law beyond concepts of professional criminality.

Keywords: traffic in women, transnational crime, white slave trade, international crime, sociological jurisprudence

■

Gerd Bender

Duale Autonomie. Zur Rechtsgeschichte des Arbeitsmarktregimes

The article deals with the legal history of the so-called dual system of industrial relations. In this constellation, which is typical for the German version of the labour market regime, the institutions of sectoral collective bargaining autonomy, based on the principle of association, and company autonomy, based on micro-corporatism, are linked. Coordination takes place through state law as well as the norm-generating practice of the actors involved. The article reconstructs the history of this dual autonomy, whose beginnings go back to the end of the 19th century. Particular emphasis is placed on norm-setting in the early Weimar Republic, which culminated in the Works Council Act of 1920. In its wake, the association model of collective bargaining autonomy became the centre of the labour market regime, and workplace autonomy was relegated to a secondary role. Macro-corporatist considerations, which also existed in the context of the constitutional discussion, took a back seat. The article does not provide a history of stability. At the end of the Weimar Republic, the dual system was the focus of a crisis of confidence and of institutions that heralded the end of the Weimar social model. The discourse at the time was heavily influenced by vehement demands that the need of companies for more flexibility be met by favouring company agreements over collective ones, but the decline of the republic put an end to these debates. Finally, the article looks at parallels that emerged later in the West German debate on the functional deficits of collective bargaining autonomy.

Keywords: labour market regime, dual system of interest representation, history of normativity

■

Rebecca Zahn

Industrial Democracy in the UK: Precursors to the Bullock Report

Many of the debates in the British labour movement on how to ensure and implement »industrial democracy« through worker representatives on company boards reached their peak in 1977, when the Report of the Committee of Inquiry on Industrial Democracy (»the Bullock Report«) recommended the appointment of worker representatives to the boards of companies for which they work. No consensus could be found on the Report's implementation and the political and industrial turbulence that followed in the late 1970s and throughout the 1980s resulted in the abandonment of the recommendations. However, debates over how much »say« workers should have in the running of their employers' business and what form this »voice« should take have not subsided. This article uses the Bullock Report as an entry point to reconsider the feasibility of worker representation on company boards in the UK from a labour law perspective. In doing so, the article compares the Bullock Report with debates which took place between the two World Wars – an intellectually rich but often neglected period when the British trade union movement was at a critical point in its development. By using insights from labour law history and comparative law, the article reveals the points at which historical factors led to certain choices. An awareness of these historical factors and choices facilitates a reassessment of traditional narratives.

Keywords: Industrial Democracy, worker representation, collective bargaining, UK, trade unions

■

Thorsten Keiser

Angestellte zwischen Rechts- und Sozialgeschichte: Forschungsfragen zur Entstehung einer Arbeitnehmerkategorie

The article deals with the development of the law of employees (*Angestellte*) in Germany. At the beginning of the 20th century, the new category of white-collar workers increasingly became the focus of the legal, economic and social sciences. The article discusses what legal-historical research questions result from this. Central problems of the employment relationship of that time are outlined using source examples from both case law and the contemporary legal literature. It becomes clear that the white-collar workers' self-image played a major role in the development of the law of employees. In many respects, the latter was characterised by the attempt to demarcate it from that of labourers (*Arbeiter*), though there were also convergences. Overall, the history of the law of employees is still a blind spot in comparison to the already well-researched history of the law of industrial workers.

Keywords: employees, white-collar workers, law, social history

■

Martin Otto

Auch eine Gewerkschaft? Der Deutschnationale Handlungsgehilfenverband und die Angestellten

During the Weimar Republic, German white-collar workers (*Angestellte*) preferred non-socialist trade unions. Socialist ›free unions‹ (*freie Gewerkschaften*) only played a minor role among middle-class employees. The biggest union by far was the »German National Union of Commercial Employees« (*Deutschnationaler Handlungsgehilfenverband*, DHV) with 400.000 exclusively male and mostly protestant members. Founded in Hamburg in 1893, with roots in Adolf Stoecker's nationalist Christian social movement, it defined itself explicitly as a Christian union with anti-socialist and also antisemitic tendencies. The number of commercial employees rose during the German Empire, and most clerks obviously lacked any chance of becoming independent. The new category of employees, who saw themselves as strongly distinct from manual workers, was neglected by the political Left. The right-wing DHV offered its members a vast number of social activities as well as housing and insurance, and even owned a number of publishing companies. However, it acted like any union in terms of providing advice to its members and negotiating wage agreements, nor did it hesitate to initiate strike action. Already before the First World War, the DHV moved towards a more pragmatic position. In labour law, it favoured special corporatism with proposals partly similar to those of socialist and liberal unions. In 1928, the DHV leadership broke with Hugenberg's DNVP and began supporting the democratic conservatives. Although many of its members turned into ardent National Socialists, other members and officials became part of the German resistance. After 1945, the difficult heritage of the DHV led to the creation of the *Deutsche Angestelltengewerkschaft* (›German Employees Union‹), which took on the role of an independent union for white-collar workers outside the ›unitarian‹ DGB.

Keywords: employees, antisemitism, trade union, Weimar Republic, labour law

■

Johanna Wolf, Tim-Niklas Vesper, Benjamin Spendrin, Matthias Ebbertz

Neue Ansätze in der Arbeitsrechtsgeschichte. Ein digitales Quelleneditionsprojekt am Max-Planck-Institut für Rechtsgeschichte und Rechtstheorie

The article is a working paper from the project ›Non-state law of the economy. The normative order of industrial relations in the metal industry from the Empire to the early years of the Federal Republic of Germany‹, undertaken at the Max Planck Institute for Legal History and Legal Theory in Frankfurt am Main (mpilhlt). A key part of the project is the creation of a digital edition of primary sources that reflects the diversity of norms and regulations in factories of the metal industry in the 19th and 20th centuries. The article illustrates the multiplicity of these normative arrangements by looking at work regulations (*Arbeitsordnungen*) and explains their importance for the history of labour law as well as the theoretical links to the research of the mpilhlt. Using the regulation of working hours as an example and selecting specific keywords – including the regulation of work breaks, of smoking and of child labour, and the introduction of measures to monitor individual working time – the article demonstrates the possibilities of analysis offered by a digital source edition and discusses preliminary methodological considerations and challenges of the digital editing of legal sources.

Keywords: labour law history, digital edition, multinormativity, work regulations (*Arbeitsordnungen*), working time regulations

■

Erk Volkmar Heyen

Gruppenbild mit Dame: »Au juste poids véritable balance« (Amiens, 1518/19), Gerechtigkeitsfiguration im Licht politischer Marienfrömmigkeit

The article explores a religious aspect of the genesis of the figure of ›Lady Justice‹ (with sword and scales), describing and interpreting a painting that owes its existence to a local literary association dedicated to the veneration of the Virgin Mary. The work, which shows a very large number of figures, reflects not only the religious but also the socio-economic and political interests of a town in the tense Franco-Dutch border region in the early 16th century. In its centre, Mary with infant Jesus sits enthroned between two scales. She is surrounded by, among others, King François I, Pope Leo X and Emperor Charles V. Contrary to the prevailing interpretation of the painting but in accordance with its titular motto, this article assigns the work to the European pictorial tradition of a ›weighing of souls‹, which – together with the archangel Michael – underlies the figural representation of ›Lady Justice‹. This also affects our interpretation of other aspects of the painting, so that, viewed as a whole, it expresses a connection between justice and mercy.

Keywords: ›Lady Justice‹, Last Judgment, weighing of souls, Virgin Mary, François I.

■

JoJo's Philosophy
BAR & GRILL
Sullivan St
Bleecke
AUX P.O. Nicholas Pekearo
ONE WAY
ON WAY
MÖGE T

Marietta Auer
p. 232–238
Max-Planck-Institut für Rechtsgeschichte und Rechtstheorie, Frankfurt am Main, auer@lhlt.mpg.de
Die Kunst des Weglassens
[The Art of Omission]

Ulrike Babusiaux
p. 218–220
Universität Zürich, Rechtswissenschaftliches Institut, Lehrstuhl für Römisches Recht, Privatrecht und Rechtsvergleichung, ulrike.babusiaux@uzh.ch
Häresie(n) zum und im spätantiken Recht
[Heresy (or Heresies) on and in Late Antique Law]

Gerd Bender
p. 148–159
Max-Planck-Institut für Rechtsgeschichte und Rechtstheorie, Frankfurt am Main, bender@lhlt.mpg.de
Duale Autonomie. Zur Rechtsgeschichte des Arbeitsmarktregimes
[Dual Autonomy. On the Legal History of the Labor Market Regime]

Alfons Bora
p. 265–267
Universität Bielefeld, alfons.bora@uni-bielefeld.de
Unstructured Diversity

Christian Boulanger
p. 273–275
Max Planck Institute for Legal History and Legal Theory, Frankfurt am Main, boulanger@lhlt.mpg.de
Private Law Theory at the Intersection of Legal Scholarship and Sociology

Nuno Camarinhas
p. 278–280
CEDIS, NOVA School of Law, Universidade NOVA de Lisboa, nuno.camarinhas@novalaw.unl.pt
A Digital Treasure Trove for Portuguese Legal History

Matilde Cazzola
p. 263–265
Max Planck Institute for Legal History and Legal Theory, Frankfurt am Main, cazzola@lhlt.mpg.de
Philanthropy to the Fore

Divya Cherian
p. 260–263
Princeton University, dcherian@princeton.edu
Law and Early Modern Empire: The View from Mughal India

Peter Collin
p. 65–80
Max-Planck-Institut für Rechtsgeschichte und Rechtstheorie, Frankfurt am Main, collin@lhlt.mpg.de
History of Conflict Resolution in Europe – A Project Report

Peter Collin
p. 270–272

Max-Planck-Institut für Rechtsgeschichte und Rechtstheorie, Frankfurt am Main, collin@lhlt.mpg.de
Spurensuche in der Handelsjustiz
[Searching for Elements in Commercial Judiciary]

Albrecht Cordes
p. 231–232

Goethe-Universität Frankfurt am Main, cordes@jur.uni-frankfurt.de
Acht und Bann à *la islandaise*
[Excommunication and Outlawry à *la islandaise*]

Albrecht Cordes
p. 239–240

Goethe-Universität Frankfurt am Main, cordes@jur.uni-frankfurt.de
Streit unter Freunden und Verwandten
[Quarrel Among Friends and Relatives]

Luisa Stella de Oliveira Coutinho Silva
p. 320–326

Max Planck Institute for Legal History and Legal Theory, Frankfurt am Main, coutinho@lhlt.mpg.de
»Gênero: uma categoria útil« para a História do Direito Global?
[»Gender: a Useful Category« for Global Legal History?]

Daniel Damler
p. 355–358

Max-Planck-Institut für Rechtsgeschichte und Rechtstheorie, Frankfurt am Main, damler@lhlt.mpg.de
Capital of Doom: Eighty Years under Emergency Rule. Nevertheless, Gotham City Persists

Wim Decock
p. 65–80

CULouvain, wim.decock@uclouvain.be
History of Conflict Resolution in Europe – A Project Report

Nicolás Duffau
p. 118–129

Facultad de Humanidades y Ciencias de la Educación, Universidad de la República, Montevideo, Uruguay, nicolas.duffau@fhuce.edu.uy
Italian Immigration, Crime, and Police Actions in Uruguay: The Volpi-Patroni Case (1882)

Thomas Duve
p. 5–7

Max-Planck-Institut für Rechtsgeschichte und Rechtstheorie, Frankfurt am Main, sekduve@lhlt.mpg.de
Editorial

Matthias Ebbertz
p. 199–213
Max-Planck-Institut für Rechtsgeschichte und Rechtstheorie, Frankfurt am Main, ebbertz@lhlt.mpg.de
Neue Ansätze in der Arbeitsrechtsgeschichte. Ein digitales Quelleneditionsprojekt am Max-Planck-Institut für Rechtsgeschichte und Rechtstheorie [New Approaches in Labor Law History. A Digital Source Edition Project at the Max Planck Institute for Legal History and Legal Theory]

Caspar Ehlers
p. 227–228
Max-Planck-Institut für Rechtsgeschichte und Rechtstheorie, Frankfurt am Main, ehlers@lhlt.mpg.de
Bitte nicht zaubern
[Please Do Not Use Magic]

Karla L. Escobar H.
p. 318–319
Max Planck Institute for Legal History and Legal Theory, Frankfurt am Main, escobar@lhlt.mpg.de
Beyond Drugs, State and Legality

Maysa Espíndola Souza
p. 285–286
Max Planck Institute for Legal History and Legal Theory, Frankfurt am Main / Federal University of Santa Catarina, espindola@lhlt.mpg.de
The Aftermath of Slavery in São Tomé and Príncipe

Andreas Fahrmeir
p. 326–328
Goethe-Universität Frankfurt am Main, fahrmeir@em.uni-frankfurt.de
Historiographiegeschichte an den Schnittstellen
[At the Intersection of the History of Historiography]

Alejandro García-Sanjuán
p. 243–245
Universidad de Huelva, sanjuan@uhu.es
Musulmanes entre infieles
[Muslims Among Infidels]

Tom Ginsburg
p. 287–288
University of Chicago Law School, tginsburg@uchicago.edu
An Archeology of Law in Thailand

Adolfo Giuliani
p. 289–291
Max Planck Institute for Legal History and Legal Theory, Frankfurt am Main, a.giuliani@pm.me
Rethinking Emilio Betti, the anti-Gadamer

Elizabeth Gómez Alcorta
p. 96–116

Universidad de Buenos Aires, evga_72@yahoo.com.ar
Congresos criminológicos internacionales y su impacto en los códigos penales de América Latina (1870–1945)
[International Criminological Congresses and Their Impact on Penal Codes in Latin America (1870–1945)]

Nadine Grotkamp
p. 65–80

Goethe-Universität Frankfurt am Main, grotkamp@jur.uni-frankfurt.de
History of Conflict Resolution in Europe – A Project Report

Michael Grünberger
p. 305–310

Universität Bayreuth, Lehrstuhl für Bürgerliches Recht, Wirtschafts- und Technikrecht, gruenberger@uni-bayreuth.de
Ein Plädoyer für eine normativ gewendete Rechtsdogmatik
[A Plea for a Normative Legal Doctrine]

Gilberto Guerra Pedrosa
p. 253–255

Max-Planck-Institut für Rechtsgeschichte und Rechtstheorie, Frankfurt am Main, guerra@lhlt.mpg.de
Ativos imateriais em processos decisórios do »Brasil holandês«
[Immaterial Assets in Decision-making Processes in »Dutch Brazil«]

Armando Guevara Gil
p. 249–250

Universidad para el Desarrollo Andino, jguevara@udea.edu.pe
Paisajes de servidumbre y esclavitud en el mundo colonial andino
[Landscapes of Servitude and Enslavement in the Colonial Andean World]

Jean-Louis Halpérin
p. 258–259

Ecole normale supérieure – PSL, jean-louis.halperin@ens.fr
Archipel colonial et justice globale
[Colonial Archipelago and Global Justice]

Karl Härter
p. 84–94

Max-Planck-Institut für Rechtsgeschichte und Rechtstheorie, Frankfurt am Main, haerter@lhlt.mpg.de
Transnational Criminal Law in Transatlantic Perspective (1870–1945): Introductory Notes, Initial Results and Concepts

Karl Härter
p. 268–270
Max-Planck-Institut für Rechtsgeschichte und Rechtstheorie, Frankfurt am Main, haerter@lhlt.mpg.de
Eine Hauptstadt weiblicher Verbrechen? Kriminalität und Geschlecht im frühneuzeitlichen Frankfurt [A Capital of Female Crime? Crime and Gender in Early Modern Frankfurt]

Erk Volkmar Heyen
p. 336–352
Universität Greifswald, Rechts- und Staatswissenschaftliche Fakultät, lsheyen@uni-greifswald.de
Gruppenbild mit Dame: »Au juste poids véritable balance« (Amiens, 1518/19), Gerechtigkeitsfiguration im Licht politischer Marienfrömmigkeit [Group Portrait With a Lady: *Au juste poids véritable balance* (Amiens, 1518/19), a Figuration of Justice in the Light of the Political Veneration of the Virgin Mary]

Steffen M. Jauß
p. 216–218
Goethe-Universität Frankfurt am Main, jauss@jur.uni-frankfurt.de
Institutiones Hammurapi? [Institutes of Hammurabi?]

Carolina Jurado
p. 247–248
Consejo Nacional de Investigaciones Científicas y Tecnológicas (CONICET) / Universidad de Buenos Aires, carolinajurado@conicet.gov.ar
Cacicas en los virreinatos americanos [*Cacicas* in Spanish American Viceroyalties]

Elizabeth Papp Kamali
p. 20–44
Harvard Law School, ekamali@law.harvard.edu
The Horrible Sepulture of Mannes Resoun: Intoxication and Medieval English Felony Law

Thorsten Keiser
p. 173–182
Justus-Liebig-Universität-Gießen, thorsten.keiser@recht.uni-giessen.de
Angestellte zwischen Rechts- und Sozialgeschichte: Forschungsfragen zur Entstehung einer Arbeitnehmerkategorie [Employees between Legal and Social History: Research Questions on the Emergence of a New Category of Workforce]

Marie Seong-Hak Kim
p. 220–222
St. Cloud State University, mskim@stcloudstate.edu
The Legal Past of Asia When It Was the World

Paul Knepper
p. 131–144
Department of Justice Studies, San José State University, paul.knepper@sjsu.edu
The League of Nations, Traffic in Women and the Transnationalization of Criminal Law

Jasper Kunstreich
p. 330–332
Max-Planck-Institut für Rechtsgeschichte und Rechtstheorie, Frankfurt am Main, kunstreich@lhlt.mpg.de
Turmbauten
[A Proud Tower]

Anselm Küsters
p. 225–227
Max-Planck-Institut für Rechtsgeschichte und Rechtstheorie, Frankfurt am Main, kuesters@lhlt.mpg.de
Eine allumfassende Geschichtstheorie ohne Geschichte
[An All-Encompassing Theory of History Without History]

Bruno Lima
p. 256–257
Max Planck Institute for Legal History and Legal Theory, Frankfurt am Main, lima@lhlt.mpg.de
Private Law and Enslaved Families in Colonial Brazil

Manuel Martínez Neira
p. 276–278
Universidad Carlos III de Madrid, manuel.martinez@uc3m.es
Revistas jurídicas españolas: 40 años después
[Spanish Legal Journals: 40 Years Later]

David von Mayenburg
p. 65–80
Goethe-Universität Frankfurt am Main, lehrstuhl.mayenburg@jura.uni-frankfurt.de
History of Conflict Resolution in Europe – A Project Report

Karoline Noack
p. 245–246
Universität Bonn, Abteilung Altamerikanistik und Ethnologie, knoack@uni-bonn.de
A Heroine's Journey to South America

Aleksi Ollikainen-Read
p. 241–243
Max Planck Institute for Legal History and Legal Theory, Frankfurt am Main, ollikainen-read@lhlt.mpg.de
The Common Law of the Foreign Past

Martin Otto
p. 184–196
Fernuniversität Hagen,
martin.otto@fernuni-hagen.de
Auch eine Gewerkschaft? Der Deutschnationale Handlungsgehilfenverband und die Angestellten [Another Kind of Trade Union? The German National Union of Commercial Employees (*Deutschnationaler Handlungsgehilfenverband*) and Clerks]

Louis Pahlow
p. 313–315
Institut für Rechtsgeschichte, Goethe-Universität Frankfurt am Main, pahlow@jur.uni-frankfurt.de
Keynes und das Bonner Grundgesetz
[Keynes and the Constitution of the Federal Republic]

Joachim Rückert
p. 303–304
Goethe-Universität Frankfurt am Main,
rueckert@jur.uni-frankfurt.de
Jongleur im Rechts(wissenschafts)zirkus
[Juggler in the Legal (Scientific) Circus]

Helwig Schmidt-Glintzer
p. 222–224
Universität Göttingen / Universität Tübingen,
Helwig.Schmidt-Glintzer@zentr.uni-goettingen.de
Das Recht der Mitte
[Chinese Legal Civilization]

Christoph Schönberger
p. 291–294
Universität zu Köln,
Christoph.Schoenberger@uni-koeln.de
Weimarer Grenzüberschreitungen
[Weimar Across Borders]

Jan Schröder
p. 46–63
Juristische Fakultät der Universität Tübingen,
jan.schroeder@uni-tuebingen.de
Zur Bedeutung der Wörter in der Rechts- und Sprachtheorie der frühen Neuzeit
On the Meaning of Words in Early Modern Legal Theory and Theory of Language

Anna Seelentag
p. 65–80
Generalzolldirektion Bonn,
AnnaMargarete.Seelentag@zoll.bund.de
History of Conflict Resolution in Europe – A Project Report

Ralf Seinecke
p. 310–313
Max-Planck-Institut für Rechtsgeschichte und Rechtstheorie, Frankfurt am Main, seinecke@lhlt.mpg.de
Endlich!
[Finally!]

Raquel R. Sirotti
p. 283–284
Max Planck Institute for Legal History and Legal Theory, Frankfurt am Main, sirotti@lhlt.mpg.de
The Workings of Private Colonization in Mozambique

Alessandro Somma
p. 301–302
Sapienza Università di Roma, alessandro.somma@uniroma1.it
Democrazia o capitalismo. Sulla inevitabile matrice autoritaria del neoliberalismo
[Democracy or Capitalism. On the Inescapable Authoritarian Essence of Neoliberalism]

Philipp N. Spahn
p. 229–231
Unabhängiger Wissenschaftler, rg@lhlt.mpg.de
Buße als Kommentar
[Penance as Commentary]

Benjamin Spendrin
p. 199–213
Max-Planck-Institut für Rechtsgeschichte und Rechtstheorie, Frankfurt am Main, spendrin@lhlt.mpg.de
Neue Ansätze in der Arbeitsrechtsgeschichte. Ein digitales Quelleneditionsprojekt am Max-Planck-Institut für Rechtsgeschichte und Rechtstheorie
[New Approaches in Labor Law History. A Digital Source Edition Project at the Max Planck Institute for Legal History and Legal Theory]

Inge Van Hulle
p. 328–330
Max Planck Institute for Legal History and Legal Theory, Frankfurt am Main, vanhulle@lhlt.mpg.de
Museums Also Lie

Miloš Vec
p. 281–283
Institut für Rechts- und Verfassungsgeschichte, Universität Wien, milos.vec@univie.ac.at
Regionale Konflikte, globales Völkerrecht
[Regional Conflicts, Global International Law]

Valeria Vegh Weis
p. 84–94
Universität Konstanz / Universidad de Buenos Aires, valeriaveghw@gmail.com
Transnational Criminal Law in Transatlantic Perspective (1870–1945): Introductory Notes, Initial Results and Concepts

Valeria Vegh Weis
p. 315–318

Universität Konstanz / Universidad de Buenos Aires, valeriaveghw@gmail.com
Kriminalisierung des Bösen
[Criminalization of Evil]

Otto Vervaart
p. 251–252

Independent scholar, otto.vervaart@ziggo.nl
Searching Slavery Laws in British North America

Tim-Niklas Vesper
p. 199–213

Max-Planck-Institut für Rechtsgeschichte und Rechtstheorie, Frankfurt am Main, vesper@lhlt.mpg.de
Neue Ansätze in der Arbeitsrechtsgeschichte. Ein digitales Quelleneditionsprojekt am Max-Planck-Institut für Rechtsgeschichte und Rechtstheorie
[New Approaches in Labor Law History. A Digital Source Edition Project at the Max Planck Institute for Legal History and Legal Theory]

Johanna Wolf
p. 199–213

Max-Planck-Institut für Rechtsgeschichte und Rechtstheorie, Frankfurt am Main, wolf@lhlt.mpg.de
Neue Ansätze in der Arbeitsrechtsgeschichte. Ein digitales Quelleneditionsprojekt am Max-Planck-Institut für Rechtsgeschichte und Rechtstheorie
[New Approaches in Labor Law History. A Digital Source Edition Project at the Max Planck Institute for Legal History and Legal Theory]

Rebecca Zahn
p. 161–171

University of Strathclyde, Glasgow, UK, rebecca.zahn@strath.ac.uk
Industrial Democracy in the UK: Precursors to the Bullock Report

Reinhard Zimmermann
p. 294–300

Max-Planck-Institut für ausländisches und internationales Privatrecht, Hamburg, r.zimmermann@mpipriv.de
Hero auf dem Felsenturme …
[Hero on the Rocky Towers …]

Marietta Auer	Frankfurt am Main
Ulrike Babusiaux	Zürich
Gerd Bender	Frankfurt am Main
Alfons Bora	Bielefeld
Christian Boulanger	Frankfurt am Main
Nuno Camarinhas	Lissabon
Matilde Cazzola	Frankfurt am Main
Divya Cherian	Princeton, NJ
Peter Collin	Frankfurt am Main
Albrecht Cordes	Frankfurt am Main
Luisa Stella de Oliveira Coutinho Silva	Frankfurt am Main
Daniel Damler	Frankfurt am Main
Wim Decock	Louvain-la-Neuve
Nicolás Duffau	Montevideo
Thomas Duve	Frankfurt am Main
Matthias Ebbertz	Frankfurt am Main
Caspar Ehlers	Frankfurt am Main
Karla L. Escobar H.	Frankfurt am Main
Maysa Espíndola Souza	Frankfurt am Main / Florianópolis
Andreas Fahrmeir	Frankfurt am Main
Alejandro García-Sanjuán	Huelva
Tom Ginsburg	Chicago
Adolfo Giuliani	Frankfurt am Main
Elizabeth Gómez Alcorta	Buenos Aires
Nadine Grotkamp	Frankfurt am Main
Michael Grünberger	Bayreuth
Gilberto Guerra Pedrosa	Frankfurt am Main
Armando Guevara Gil	Lima
Jean-Louis Halpérin	Paris
Karl Härter	Frankfurt am Main
Erk Volkmar Heyen	Greifswald
Steffen M. Jauß	Frankfurt am Main
Carolina Jurado	Buenos Aires
Elizabeth Papp Kamali	Cambridge, MA
Thorsten Keiser	Gießen
Marie Seong-Hak Kim	St. Cloud, MN
Paul Knepper	San José, CA
Jasper Kunstreich	Frankfurt am Main
Anselm Küsters	Frankfurt am Main
Bruno Lima	Frankfurt am Main
Manuel Martínez Neira	Madrid
David von Mayenburg	Frankfurt am Main
Karoline Noack	Bonn
Aleksi Ollikainen-Read	Frankfurt am Main
Martin Otto	Hagen

Louis Pahlow	Frankfurt am Main
Joachim Rückert	Frankfurt am Main
Helwig Schmidt-Glintzer	Göttingen / Tübingen
Christoph Schönberger	Köln
Jan Schröder	Tübingen
Anna Seelentag	Bonn
Ralf Seinecke	Frankfurt am Main
Raquel R. Sirotti	Frankfurt am Main
Alessandro Somma	Rom
Philipp N. Spahn	Gelnhausen
Benjamin Spendrin	Frankfurt am Main
Inge Van Hulle	Frankfurt am Main
Miloš Vec	Wien
Valeria Vegh Weis	Konstanz / Buenos Aires
Otto Vervaart	Utrecht
Tim-Niklas Vesper	Frankfurt am Main
Johanna Wolf	Frankfurt am Main
Rebecca Zahn	Glasgow
Reinhard Zimmermann	Hamburg

POLITISCHE PHILOSOPHIE UND RECHTSTHEORIE DES MITTELALTERS UND DER NEUZEIT

Texte und Untersuchungen. Herausgegeben von Thomas Duve, Alexander Fidora, Heinz-Gerhard Justenhoven, Matthias Lutz-Bachmann und Andreas Niederberger. Beirat: Francisco Bertelloni, Armin von Bogdandy, Norbert Brieskorn, Juan Cruz Cruz, Otfried Höffe, Ruedi Imbach, Bernhard Jussen, Jürgen Miethke, Martha Nussbaum, Ken Pennington und Michael Stolleis. GLIEDERUNG: Abt. I: Texte; Abt. II: Untersuchungen. *2010 ff. Leinen. ISBN 978 3 7728 2500 2.* *21 Bände auch als eBook lieferbar*

LEONARDUS LESSIUS

De iustitia et iure caeterisque virtutibus cardinalibus.
Über die Gerechtigkeit und das Recht und die übrigen Kardinaltugenden

Lat./dt. Herausgegeben von Nils Jansen. Ins Deutsche übersetzt von Klaus Wille. Unter Mitarbeit von Konstantin Liebrand. – *PPR I,15.1-10. Ca. 10 Bände. 2020ff. Leinen. ISBN 978 3 7728 2900 0.*

TEIL I: De prudentia. Über die Klugheit. De iustitia in genere eqs. Grundbegriffe. – *PPR I,15.1. 2020. LXII, 564 S., 2 Abb. Ln. € 268,-; bei Gesamtabnahme € 248,-. ISBN 978 3 7728 2901 7. eBook € 268,-.* *Lfb.*

TEIL II: De restitutione. Über die Restitution. Mit einer Einleitung von Tilman Repgen. – *PPR I,15.2,1-2. 2022. 2 Bände. Zus. CVI, 898 S. Ln. € 468,-; bei Gesamtabnahme € 448,-. ISBN 978 3 7728 2902 4. eBook € 468,-.* *Lfb.*

Im zweiten Teil der Ausgabe von ›De iustitia et iure caeterisque virtutibus cardinalibus‹ aus dem Jahr 1605 bietet Leonardus Lessius eine konzentrierte Darstellung der spätscholastischen Lehre von der Restitution: der Lehre von der Verpflichtung zum Schadensersatz und zum Bereicherungsausgleich. Nach römisch-katholischer Lehre durfte eine Sünde nur vergeben werden, wenn der Schädiger den Schaden wiedergutgemacht bzw. fremdes Gut zurückgegeben hatte (Restitution). Damit wurde die Restitution zum Angelpunkt, der das theologische Naturrecht in eine genuine Rechtsordnung transformierte, die das tägliche Leben der Gläubigen bestimmte. Lessius erläutert hier kasuistisch ein breites Panorama einzelner Rechtsverletzungen (etwa am Leben, Körper, Eigentum oder der Ehre) und der darauf bezogenen Delikte. Insgesamt bietet dieser Teil des Werks ein buntes Bild der frühneuzeitlichen katholischen Alltagsmoral.

Joachim Rückert
Idealismus, Jurisprudenz
und Politik bei
Friedrich Carl von Savigny
Savignyana 15